T0178256

Lecture Notes in Computer Science 14497

Founding Editors

Gerhard Goos
Juris Hartmanis

Editorial Board Members

The series Lecture Notes in Computer Science (LNCS), including its subseries Lecture Notes in Artificial Intelligence (LNAI) and Lecture Notes in Bioinformatics (LNBI), has established itself as a medium for the publication of new developments in computer science and information technology research, teaching, and education.

LNCS enjoys close cooperation with the computer science R & D community, the series counts many renowned academics among its volume editors and paper authors, and collaborates with prestigious societies. Its mission is to serve this international community by providing an invaluable service, mainly focused on the publication of conference and workshop proceedings and postproceedings. LNCS commenced publication in 1973.

Bin Sheng · Lei Bi · Jinman Kim ·
Nadia Magnenat-Thalmann · Daniel Thalmann
Editors

Advances in Computer Graphics

40th Computer Graphics International Conference, CGI 2023
Shanghai, China, August 28 – September 1, 2023
Proceedings, Part III

Springer

Editors
Bin Sheng 🆔
Shanghai Jiao Tong University
Shanghai, China

Jinman Kim 🆔
University of Sydney
Sydney, NSW, Australia

Daniel Thalmann
Swiss Federal Institute of Technology
Lausanne, Switzerland

Lei Bi 🆔
Shanghai Jiao Tong University
Shanghai, China

Nadia Magnenat-Thalmann 🆔
MIRALab-CUI
University of Geneva
Carouge, Geneve, Switzerland

ISSN 0302-9743   ISSN 1611-3349 (electronic)
Lecture Notes in Computer Science
ISBN 978-3-031-50074-9   ISBN 978-3-031-50075-6 (eBook)
https://doi.org/10.1007/978-3-031-50075-6

This Springer imprint is published by the registered company Springer Nature Switzerland AG
The registered company address is: Gewerbestrasse 11, 6330 Cham, Switzerland

Paper in this product is recyclable.

Preface Lecture Notes in Computer Science (14497)

CGI is one of the oldest annual international conferences on Computer Graphics in the world. Researchers are invited to share their experiences and novel achievements in various fields of Computer Graphics and Virtual Reality. Previous recent CGI conferences have been held in Sydney, Australia (2014), Strasbourg, France (2015), Heraklion, Greece (2016), Yokohama, Japan (2017), Bintan, Indonesia (2018), and Calgary in Canada (2019). CGI was virtual between 2020 and 2022 due to the COVID pandemic. This year, CGI 2023 was organized by the Shanghai Jiao Tong University, with the assistance of the University of Sydney and Wuhan Textile University, and supported by the Computer Graphics Society (CGS). The conference was held during August 28 to September 1, 2023.

These CGI 2023 LNCS proceedings are composed of 149 papers from a total of 385 submissions. This includes 51 papers that were reviewed highly and were recommended to be published in the CGI Visual Computer Journal track. To ensure the high quality of the publications, each paper was reviewed by at least two experts in the field and authors of accepted papers were asked to revise their paper according to the review comments prior to publication.

The CGI 2023 LNCS proceedings also include papers from the ENGAGE (Empowering Novel Geometric Algebra for Graphics & Engineering) 2023 Workshop (11 full papers), focused specifically on important aspects of geometric algebra including surface construction, robotics, encryption, qubits and expression optimization. The workshop has been part of the CGI conferences since 2016.

We would like to express our deepest gratitude to all the PC members and external reviewers who provided timely high-quality reviews. We would also like to thank all the authors for contributing to the conference by submitting their work.

September 2023

Bin Sheng
Lei Bi
Jinman Kim
Nadia Magnenat-Thalmann
Daniel Thalmann

Organization

Honorary Conference Chairs

Enhua Wu   Chinese Academy of Sciences/University of Macau, China

Dagan Feng   University of Sydney, Australia

Conference Chairs

Nadia Magnenat Thalmann   University of Geneva, Switzerland

Bin Sheng   Shanghai Jiao Tong University, China

Jinman Kim   University of Sydney, Australia

Program Chairs

Daniel Thalmann   École Polytechnique Fédérale de Lausanne, Switzerland

Stephen Lin   Microsoft Research Asia, China

Lizhuang Ma   Shanghai Jiao Tong University, China

Ping Li   Hong Kong Polytechnic University, China

Contents – Part III

Visual Analytics and Modeling

Graphics and AR/VR

Medical Imaging and Robotics

Detection and Recognition

AMDNet: Adaptive Fall Detection Based on Multi-scale Deformable Convolution Network

Minghua Jiang, Keyi Zhang, Yongkang Ma, Li Liu, Tao Peng, Xinrong Hu, and Feng Yu[✉]

School of Computer Science and Artificial Intelligence,
Wuhan Textile University, Wuhan 430200, China
yufeng@wtu.edu.cn

Abstract. Recent studies by the World Health Organization have shown that human falls have become the leading cause of injury and death worldwide. Therefore, human fall detection is becoming an increasingly important research topic. Deep learning models have potential for fall detection, but they face challenges such as limited utilization of global contextual information, insufficient feature extraction, and high computational requirements. These issues constrain the performance of deep learning on human fall detection in terms of low accuracy, poor generalization, and slow inference. To overcome these challenges, this study proposes an Adaptive Multi-scale Detection Network (AMDNet) based on multi-scale deformable convolutions. The main idea of this method is as follows: 1) Introducing an improved multi-scale fusion module, enhances the network's ability to learn object details and semantic features, thereby reducing the likelihood of false negatives and false positives during the detection process, especially for small objects. 2) Using the Wise-IoU v3 with two layers of attention mechanisms and a dynamic non-monotonic FM mechanism as the boundary box loss function of the AMDNet, improves the model's robustness to low-quality samples and enhances the performance of the object detection. This work also proposes a diversified fall dataset that covers as many real-world fall scenarios as possible. Experimental results show that the proposed method outperforms the current state-of-the-art methods on a self-made dataset.

Keywords: Fall detection · Fall dataset · Multi-scale deformable convolution · Loss function · Multi-scale feature fusion

1 Introduction

Falls are a leading cause of injury and death worldwide [19], especially among older adults. Falling accidents, such as escalator failures, are becoming increasingly frequent. Fall detection is a popular research topic in the field of public safety, and vision-based methods are considered the most promising. However, in practice, accurate fall recognition faces several challenges, as described below:

B. Sheng et al. (Eds.): CGI 2023, LNCS 14497, pp. 3–14, 2024.
https://doi.org/10.1007/978-3-031-50075-6_1

1) Current public fall datasets have several limitations, such as being limited to a single scene, a high degree of sample repetition, and a lack of samples from occluded objects.
2) There are various postures associated with human falls, and existing object detection algorithms often fail to extract meaningful features from these postures due to insufficient utilization of global context information, suboptimal feature extraction, and high computational requirements. These limitations result in low detection accuracy, poor generalization ability, and slow inference speeds.
3) False detection and missed detection can be common issues when attempting to accurately detect falls due to factors such as environmental conditions and occlusion.

To address these limitations, we propose AMDNet, an adaptive fall detection Network based on multi-scale deformable convolutions to improve the accuracy of fall detection. The main contributions of this work are as follows:

1) We construct a diversified falls dataset, which differs from existing publicly available datasets. The images in this dataset are collected from various real-world scenarios, including indoor and outdoor environments, different lighting conditions, varied body types, and different fall poses.
2) We propose a multi-scale deformable convolution network to achieve more accurate and robust fall detection by optimizing the network architecture and convolution operation.
3) We adopt the Wise-IoU regression loss function in the multi-scale deformable convolution network to improve the model's robustness to low-quality samples and enhance the performance of object detection.

2 Related Works

The current mainstream fall detection methods can be roughly divided into two categories: methods based on wearable devices and methods based on computer vision [1,10,18]. Wearable approaches typically use sensors attached to the body, such as accelerometers, gyroscopes, and pressure sensors, to detect falls [6,7,9,16,21]. For example, Montanini et al. [13] used pressure sensors and accelerometers embedded in shoes to detect and identify falling events. Antwi-Afari et al. [2] utilized a wearable insole pressure system to assess the fall risk of construction workers by analyzing their plantar pressure patterns and biomechanical gait stability parameters. Pandya et al. [14] achieved real-time fall detection by integrating accelerometer and gyroscope sensors. Wearable fall detection methods usually require complex devices that need to be charged frequently and are inconvenient to wear. In contrast, computer vision-based fall detection methods only require fixed equipment, such as cameras, and offer the advantages of simplicity, efficiency, and low cost. As a result, computer vision-based methods have received increasing attention in recent years. With the widespread use of IoT and cameras, computer vision-based methods have become ideal for fall detection applications.

The effectiveness of deep learning in various computer vision applications has been proven, with convolutional neural networks (CNNs) receiving much attention in recent years. Chen et al. [5] proposed a robust fall detection method using Mask-CNN and attention-guided Bi-directional LSTM in complex backgrounds, achieving accurate results. Zhang et al. [20] devised a fall detection algorithm based on temporal and spatial body posture changes. Determining the occurrence of falls by creating an evolutionary map of human behavior. Zhu et al. [23] developed an algorithm utilizing a deep vision sensor and a convolutional neural network to train on extracted three-dimensional posture data of the human body and create a fall detection model. However, the algorithm's timeliness is relatively limite is relatively limited. Cao et al. [4] proposed a fall detection algorithm that integrates motion features and deep learning, leveraging YOLOv3 for human target detection and fusing motion features with deep CNN-extracted features to precisely detect falls. Li et al. [11] proposed an optimized YOLOv5s-based fall detection method that uses MobileNetV3 as the backbone network for feature extraction and applies a lightweight attention mechanism to enhance the detection accuracy of the model. Although these fall detection methods have achieved high accuracy in controlled environments, they still face challenges in practical applications. One of the main challenges is the limited generalization ability of the model, which reduce performance when tested on data from different environments or populations. This is mainly due to limited diversity and quantity of training data, which cannot fully represent real-world scenarios. Another challenge is the slow speed of model inference, which makes it difficult to meet the real-time requirements of some applications. The main reason for this is that deep learning models usually require a lot of computation, which is time-consuming and resource-intensive. To address these challenges, we propose an adaptive fall detection method based on multi-scale deformable convolution network, which aims to enhance the model's robustness and reduce its computational complexity without sacrificing performance.

3   AMDNet Framework

This paper proposes a fall detection algorithm based on an Adaptive Multi-scale Detection Network (AMDNet) that can rapidly and accurately recognize human fall events. The algorithm architecture is inspired by the YOLO object detection network [15] and incorporates multi-scale deformable convolutions to achieve adaptive fall detection.

AMDNet is a deep learning-based algorithm designed for fall detection. The framework of AMDNet is as shown in Fig. 1. Its backbone network is based on the CSPDarknet53 architecture [3] and consists of CBL and C2f modules. The CBL module encapsulates three main functions: convolutional layer, batch normalization [8], and a LeakyReLU activation function. This lightweight design allows the CBL module to be easily embedded into deep learning models for feature extraction. The C2f module is used to enhance the network's receptive field and representation capability. It is a lightweight convolutional block that performs

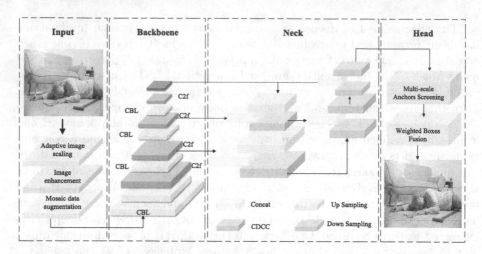

Fig. 1. AMDNet Framework.

feature extraction and integration in both the channel and contextual directions. By splitting and integrating input feature maps, the C2f module can enhance the network's representation capability and adaptability, reduce the network's computational complexity and parameter count, and improve the network's computational efficiency. The combination of CBL and C2f modules achieves higher accuracy and detection speed. By using an efficient backbone network model, computational speed can be greatly increased and training parameters can be reduced, while still ensuring detection accuracy. This results in more efficient fall detection.

The feature fusion layer of the AMDNet adopts the core idea of PANet [12], which aims to improve the network's perception and expression abilities for features of different scales and levels. Specifically, the layer first constructs a feature pyramid by obtaining feature maps of different scales from the backbone network. Then, the top-down path upsamples the low-resolution feature maps to match the size of high-resolution feature maps for feature fusion at different levels. The fused feature maps are then extracted by CDCC blocks, which consist of a series of deformable convolution blocks for feature extraction and enhancement. Meanwhile, the bottom-up path downsamples the high-resolution feature maps to reduce their resolution and extracts higher-level semantic information through CDCC blocks for prediction. The CDCC blocks effectively combine deep and shallow information, preserving image information on the original feature map layers, and possess strong receptive fields and expression abilities for detecting objects of different sizes. The feature fusion layer plays a role in feature fusion and integration in the object detection task, enabling the detector to better handle feature information of different scales and semantic levels. This improves the accuracy and robustness of object detection.

3.1 CDCC Block

To better adapt to the diverse range of human body posture changes involved in the fall detection task, we propose the CDCC block. This module mainly uses multi-scale deformable convolution [22] to improve the network's ability to focus on the target area and better adapt to changes in human body posture during falls. This enhances the network's ability to extract fall target features. Additionally, the CDCC block can effectively extract features and achieve multi-scale feature fusion, which improves the accuracy of fall detection. Overall, the CDCC block improves the network's adaptability and robustness in fall detection tasks, enabling the network to better handle the diversity of human body posture changes. The CDCC block structure is shown in Fig. 2.

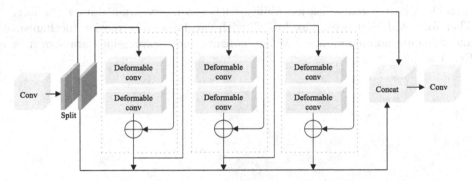

Fig. 2. The strucutre of CDCC blocks. CDCC feature enhancement module consists of a residual structure composed of multi-scale deformable convolutions.

After performing a convolution operation on the input feature map, the CDCC block splits the output feature map into two parts based on channel numbers. One part is used for subsequent feature fusion, while the other part is used for feature extraction. This avoids operating on all channels during extraction, reducing computational complexity to make the model more lightweight. Moreover, splitting the feature map into two parts enables different operations to be applied to different parts, further improving the feature representation ability. Specifically, the feature extraction part of the CDCC module uses a residual structure composed of deformable convolutions. Deformable convolution adaptively extracts local features, which can extract more abundant and accurate feature information, thereby enhancing the model's receptive field and detection ability of small targets. The residual connection is used to prevent information loss and gradient vanishing by directly transferring the previous feature information to the following layers. This is achieved by adding the input feature map to the output feature map processed by the deformable convolutional layer. The feature fusion part uses the channel concatenation operation to merge the feature information of the branch part and the extraction part, resulting in a more comprehensive feature representation. Therefore, the CDCC module helps to improve feature representation capabilities and computational efficiency, and can also improve the performance of object detection.

3.2 Loss Function

The performance of object detection depends on the design of the loss function. The bounding box loss function is an important part of the object detection loss function, and an appropriate loss function can significantly improve the performance of the object detection model. In this paper, we employ the Wise-IoU loss function [17] as the bounding box regression loss, which combines a dynamic nonmonotonic focusing mechanism and the use of "outliers" to evaluate the quality of anchor frames. This avoids excessive punishment of geometric factors such as distance and aspect ratio, and improves the performance of the model in cases where the quality of the training data annotations is low. Additionally, when the predicted box overlaps significantly with the target box, the loss function weakens the punishment of geometric factors, enabling the model to achieve better generalization ability with less intervention during training. Therefore, AMDNet uses Wise-IoU v3 with two layers of attention mechanism and dynamic non-monotonic FM mechanism, whose expressions are shown in Eqs. 1 and 2.

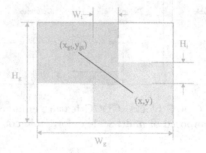

Fig. 3. The smallest enclosing box (purple) and the central points' connection (red), where the area of the union is $S_u = wh + w_{gt}h_{gt} - W_iH_i$. (Color figure online)

$$L = \left(1 - \frac{W_iH_i}{S_u}\right)\exp\left(\frac{(x_p - x_{gt})^2 + (y_p - y_{gt})^2}{(W_g^2 + H_g^2)^*}\right)\gamma \tag{1}$$

$$\gamma = \beta/\delta\alpha^{\beta-\delta} \tag{2}$$

where β is used to measure the abnormality of the predicted box, where a smaller abnormality value indicates a higher quality of the anchor box. Therefore, β is used to construct a non-monotonic focus number, which assigns smaller gradient gains to predicted boxes with larger abnormality values. In the formula, α and δ are hyperparameters, while the meanings of other parameters are shown in Fig. 3.

4 Dataset

Currently, there are several publicly available datasets for vision-based fall detection, including UR Fall Detection (URFD) Dataset, Multicam (Multiple

Cameras Fall Dataset), Fall Detection Dataset (FDD), and Le2i Fall Detection Dataset. The URFD dataset contains 30 simulated fall videos and 40 non-fall videos. The Multicam dataset contains 24 performances, each captured by 8 synchronized cameras from different angles. The FDD dataset contains 22,636 images, while the Le2i dataset contains 191 videos, covering varying numbers of falls and non-falls videos. These datasets share the following common characteristics:

1) High degree of sample repetition.
2) Unbalanced number of positive and negative samples.
3) Usually only contain indoor scenes.
4) All falling events are simulated situations.
5) Lack of small and occluded object samples.

To address the limitations of existing fall datasets, we create a Diversified Fall dataset (DFD), which contains 9,696 samples from two classes: 'fall' and 'non-fall'. Figure 4 shows some examples from DFD. The images in DFD include indoor and outdoor environments, various lighting conditions, different body types, and different fall postures to cover as many realistic fall situations as possible. This dataset is of great significance for studying human fall detection in real-world scenarios. To increase the diversity of samples in our limited dataset, we apply several data augmentation methods to some of the images. For example, we add random noise to the original images, apply blurring, and perform color transformations by changing the order of color channels.

5   Experimental Results and Discussion

The experimental environment consists of a Windows 10 operating system, a NVIDIA RTX 3050 graphics processor, and the PyTorch deep learning framework. The development environment is PyCharm and the Python 3.9.16 programming language, along with torchvision 0.14.1, numpy 1.23.0, PyTorch

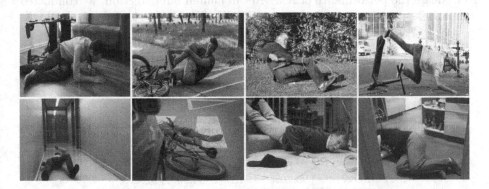

Fig. 4. Sample examples from the proposed dataset. The proposed dataset includes different fall cases from different scenarios, different perspectives, and different individuals.

1.13.1, and OpenCV 4.7.0. During model training, the initial learning rate is set to 0.01, with a total of 300 epochs, and the learning rate momentum is set to 0.937.

5.1 Evaluation Metrics

The fall detection problem is treated as a binary classification problem, where each input has two possible outcomes: True (T) and False (F). In the fall detection problem, T means that a fall has occurred, while F means that no fall has occurred. To compare and evaluate the performance of experiments carried out by different researchers, various evaluation metrics have been devised. Some widely used key indicators are listed below.

$$\text{Recall} = \frac{TP}{TP+FN} \tag{3}$$

$$\text{Precision} = \frac{TP}{TP+FP} \tag{4}$$

$$F1 - Score = 2 \times \frac{\text{precision} \times \text{recall}}{\text{precision} + \text{recall}} \tag{5}$$

The important indicators mentioned above can be defined by True Positive (TP), True Negative (TN), False Positive (FP), and False Negative (FN). Among them, TP indicates that a fall event is correctly detected, FP indicates that a non-fall event is falsely detected as a fall event, and FN is the opposite, indicating that a real fall event is incorrectly detected as a non-fall event. TN means correctly identifying non-fall events as non-fall events. These metrics are commonly used definitions in binary classification problems and are crucial for evaluating the performance of fall detection systems.

5.2 Comparative Experiment

To evaluate the performance of AMDNet in human fall detection, we conducted comparison experiments with Faster-RCNN, YOLOV4, YOLOV5, YOLOX,

Table 1. The result of comparative experiment.

Model	Precision	Recall	mAP	F1-Score
Faster-RCNN	45.13%	92.59%	85.53%	59.50%
YOLOv4	88.15%	49.94%	72.05%	61%
YOLOv5	89.20%	91.90%	93.60%	90.52%
YOLOX	93.28%	86.59%	90.33%	89.50%
YOLOv7	90.70%	94.20%	94.90%	92.41%
YOLOv8	92.60%	94.50%	96.80%	93.54%
AMDNet	96.50%	95.90%	98.20%	96.19%

YOLOV7, and YOLOV8. To ensure a fair comparison, all models are trained on the same platform. Currently, YOLOV8 is one of the best-performing versions of the YOLO series object detection algorithms [15]. Table 2 shows the model experimental results of six classic networks and AMDNet on our self-collected human fall dataset DFD. The experimental results demonstrate that AMDNet achieves excellent detection performance and high accuracy on the self-made DFD dataset. Compared with traditional human detection algorithms and other object detection algorithms, AMDNet recognizes fall events more accurately with better robustness and generalization (Table 1).

5.3   Ablation Experiment

To comprehensively evaluate the proposed network framework and understand the performance of each proposed module, we conducted ablation experiments. These experiments gradually dissected each part to determine its impact on the overall performance of the model, in order to fully evaluate the contribution of each module to the speed and accuracy of the network.

From Table 2, it can be seen that the introduction of the CDCC block in the network increases the evaluation metrics Precision, Recall, and F1-Score by 2.6%, 1.2%, and 1.9%, respectively. This indicates that the CDCC block can enhance the ability to extract human fall features, thereby making fall detection more accurate. The effectiveness of the Wise-IoU loss function has been demonstrated in the fall detection task, as shown in the first and third rows of the table.

From the fourth and fifth rows, it can be seen that when different improvement methods are combined, the performance of the model is further slightly improved on the basis of certain improvements, rather than simply adding up. In summary, the combination of different methods can enhance the detection performance of the model, indicating that the proposed method is feasible and necessary.

Table 2. The result of ablation experiment.

AMDNet	CDCC	WIou	Precision	Recall	F1-Score
✓	–	–	92.60%	94.50%	93.54%
✓	✓	–	95.20%	95.70%	95.44%
✓	–	✓	95.30%	96.10%	95.69%
✓	✓	✓	96.50%	95.90%	96.19%

5.4   Detection Results

After testing in real falling scenarios, the algorithm's detection results are shown in Fig. 5. The figure presents several common types of falls, where group (a) indicates that the algorithm can accurately detect human falls in good outdoor ambient lighting conditions; group (b) shows scenes with relatively dark lighting that are prone to falling, but the algorithm can still accurately detect human falls; and group (c) shows some relatively complex and occluded human falls, but the algorithm can still accurately detect them. Therefore, in most cases, the algorithm is less affected by environmental disturbances and can accurately detect human falls, providing protection for personal safety.

Fig. 5. Group (a) demonstrates the effectiveness of fall detection in a conventional scene, while group (b) shows the algorithm's ability to detect falls in challenging environments such as elevators and stairs. Group (c) presents the algorithm's performance in complex and occluded scenes, where it is still able to detect falls accurately. These results demonstrate the robustness of the AMDNet in various real-world scenarios and its potential for improving personal safety.

6   Conclusion and Outlook

The proposed deformable convolution-based fall detection network and diverse fall dataset have effectively improved the accuracy of human fall detection and have practical value for real-time detection and early warning of human falls. Our proposed method achieved an F1-Score of 96.19%, outperforming six classical object detection networks. However, there is still room for improvement, especially in complex scenes and objects with more occlusions. To address this issue, in future work, we plan to expand the dataset by adding more postures of falling in complex scenes and continue exploring ways to reduce the number of network model parameters while improving the detection rate. Additionally, we will investigate the use of other advanced techniques to further enhance the detection performance. We believe that these improvements will help make the proposed fall detection system more robust and effective in real-world scenarios.

Acknowledgment. This work was supported by national natural science foundation of China (No. 62202346), Hubei key research and development program (No. 2021BAA042), open project of engineering research center of Hubei province for clothing information (No. 2022HBCI01), Wuhan applied basic frontier research project (No. 2022013988065212), MIIT's AI Industry Innovation Task unveils flagship projects (Key technologies, equipment, and systems for flexible customized and intelligent manufacturing in the clothing industry), and Hubei science and technology project of safe production special fund (Scene control platform based on proprioception information computing of artificial intelligence).

References

1. Ali, S.G., et al.: Experimental protocol designed to employ Nd: YAG laser surgery for anterior chamber glaucoma detection via UBM. IET Image Process. **16**(8), 2171–2179 (2022)
2. Antwi-Afari, M.F., Li, H.: Fall risk assessment of construction workers based on biomechanical gait stability parameters using wearable insole pressure system. Adv. Eng. Inform. **38**, 683–694 (2018)
3. Bochkovskiy, A., Wang, C.Y., Liao, H.Y.M.: YOLOv4: optimal speed and accuracy of object detection. arXiv preprint arXiv:2004.10934 (2020)
4. Cao, J., Lyu, J., Wu, X., Zhang, X., Yang, H.: Fall detection algorithm integrating motion features and deep learning. J. Comput. Appl. **41**(2), 583 (2021)
5. Chen, Y., Li, W., Wang, L., Hu, J., Ye, M.: Vision-based fall event detection in complex background using attention guided bi-directional LSTM. IEEE Access **8**, 161337–161348 (2020)
6. Fanez, M., Villar, J.R., de la Cal, E., Gonzalez, V.M., Sedano, J., Khojasteh, S.B.: Mixing user-centered and generalized models for fall detection. Neurocomputing **452**, 473–486 (2021)
7. Hussain, F., Hussain, F., Ehatisham-ul Haq, M., Azam, M.A.: Activity-aware fall detection and recognition based on wearable sensors. IEEE Sens. J. **19**(12), 4528–4536 (2019)
8. Ioffe, S., Szegedy, C.: Batch normalization: accelerating deep network training by reducing internal covariate shift. In: International Conference on Machine Learning, pp. 448–456. PMLR (2015)
9. Lee, J.S., Tseng, H.H.: Development of an enhanced threshold-based fall detection system using smartphones with built-in accelerometers. IEEE Sens. J. **19**(18), 8293–8302 (2019)
10. Li, J., et al.: Automatic detection and classification system of domestic waste via multimodel cascaded convolutional neural network. IEEE Trans. Industr. Inf. **18**(1), 163–173 (2021)
11. Li-zhan, W., Xia-li, W., Qian, Z., Wei-hao, W., Chao, L.: An object detection method of falling person based on optimized yolov5s. J. Graph. **43**(5), 791 (2022)
12. Liu, S., Qi, L., Qin, H., Shi, J., Jia, J.: Path aggregation network for instance segmentation. In: Proceedings of the IEEE Conference on Computer Vision and Pattern Recognition, pp. 8759–8768 (2018)
13. Montanini, L., Del Campo, A., Perla, D., Spinsante, S., Gambi, E.: A footwear-based methodology for fall detection. IEEE Sens. J. **18**(3), 1233–1242 (2017)
14. Pandya, B., Pourabdollah, A., Lotfi, A.: Fuzzy logic web services for real-time fall detection using wearable accelerometer and gyroscope sensors. In: Proceedings

of the 13th ACM International Conference on PErvasive Technologies Related to Assistive Environments, pp. 1–7 (2020)

15. Redmon, J., Divvala, S., Girshick, R., Farhadi, A.: You only look once: unified, real-time object detection. In: Proceedings of the IEEE Conference on Computer Vision and Pattern Recognition, pp. 779–788 (2016)

16. de Sousa, F.A.S.F., Escriba, C., Bravo, E.G.A., Brossa, V., Fourniols, J.Y., Rossi, C.: Wearable pre-impact fall detection system based on 3D accelerometer and subject's height. IEEE Sens. J. **22**(2), 1738–1745 (2021)

17. Tong, Z., Chen, Y., Xu, Z., Yu, R.: Wise-IoU: bounding box regression loss with dynamic focusing mechanism. arXiv preprint arXiv:2301.10051 (2023)

18. Wei, H., Zhang, Q., Qin, Y., Li, X., Qian, Y.: YOLOF-F: you only look one-level feature fusion for traffic sign detection. Vis. Comput. 1–14 (2023)

19. World Health Organization: Falls (2022). https://www.who.int/news-room/fact-sheets/detail/falls

20. Zhang, J., Wu, C., Wang, Y.: Human fall detection based on body posture spatio-temporal evolution. Sensors **20**(3), 946 (2020)

21. Zhao, S., Li, W., Niu, W., Gravina, R., Fortino, G.: Recognition of human fall events based on single tri-axial gyroscope. In: 2018 IEEE 15th International conference on networking, sensing and control (ICNSC), pp. 1–6. IEEE (2018)

22. Zhu, X., Hu, H., Lin, S., Dai, J.: Deformable convnets V2: more deformable, better results. In: Proceedings of the IEEE/CVF Conference on Computer Vision and Pattern Recognition, pp. 9308–9316 (2019)

23. Zhu, Y., Zhang, Y., Li, S.: Fall detection algorithm based on deep vision sensor and convolutional neural network. Opt. Tech. **47**(1), 56–61 (2021)

A HRNet-Transformer Network Combining Recurrent-Tokens for Remote Sensing Image Change Detection

Tao Peng[1,2], Lingjie Hu[1], Junjie Huang[1,2(✉)], Junping Liu[1,2], Ping Zhu[1,2], Xingrong Hu[1,2], and Ruhan He[1,2]

[1] Wuhan Textile University, Wuhan 430200, Hubei, China
jjhuang@wtu.edu.cn
[2] Engineering Research Center of Hubei Province for Clothing Information, Wuhan 430200, Hubei, China

Abstract. Deep learning is developing rapidly and has achieved significant results in the field of remote sensing image change detection. Manual inspection is time-consuming and labor-intensive compared to deep learning, which makes it an inevitable trend to replace manual labor. In this paper, we introduce HTRNet (A HRNet-Transformer Network Combining Recurrent-tokens). Our approach addresses the following challenges: We use HRNet to retain spatial and channel information in image features, avoiding the loss of spatial information that occurs with convolution-based methods. To mitigate the model's bias caused by non-uniformly distributed bitemporal semantic information, we propose a Recurrent-tokens module to enrich contextual information. Our model generates a binary mask map considering both pixel classification and position. We use the Cosine-embedding loss to measure similarity between the generated mask and ground truth. Experimental results on LEVIR-CD & DSIFN-CD datasets demonstrate that HTRNet outperforms SOAT methods in various metrics. Additionally, our model exhibits smoother edges and robustness in predictions. In summary, HTRNet effectively addresses key challenges in change detection, achieving superior performance compared to existing methods.

Keywords: Change Detection · Transformer · Siamese Network · Remote Sensing · Attention Mechanism · Multilayer Perceptron

1 Introduction

Change detection (CD) is a common task in the processing and analysis of remotely sensed images. Its goal is to compare images of the same area in different temporal states and identify relevant changes in typical elements. Some common types of changes include building changes, forest changes, land changes, water changes, and so on. In practical application scenarios, detecting these

B. Sheng et al. (Eds.): CGI 2023, LNCS 14497, pp. 15–26, 2024.
https://doi.org/10.1007/978-3-031-50075-6_2

changes provides valuable information for urban planning, disaster assessment, environmental monitoring, and other purposes.

In CD, the changes in typical elements are often affected by various confounding factors. For instance, differences in lighting conditions during image acquisition can result in variations in brightness and shadows, while changes in shooting seasons can lead to differences in the main backgrounds of the images. These confounders increase the difficulty of the task. In recent years, there has been a shift from manual detection to computer-based detection in the analysis of remote sensing images, resulting in improved efficiency and cost reduction. Researchers have made significant progress in applying neural networks to CD, demonstrating the excellent performance of deep learning in this field. Recently, CNN and DNN based methods have been employed in CD, enabling the extraction of advanced semantic features from remote sensing images at different times. These approaches have focused on stacking more convolutional layers, utilizing dilated convolutions and attention mechanisms, and increasing the reception field (RF) of models through resolution compression and feature dimensionality doubling operations [1].

However, most existing methods struggle to effectively capture long-distance spatial-temporal relationships and often exhibit poor performance in modeling global information [3,4,6,9]. An effective deep learning model is needed to extract features of typical elements. Sun et al. [17] proposed a high-resolution network (HRNet) to address these limitations. Their model incorporates a high-resolution network branch and gradually adds parallel network branches with varying resolutions, allowing for the fusion of features from different layers. Through this approach, HRNet learns high-resolution semantic information that contains rich details and maintains high-resolution representations throughout the network training process. In this paper, our goal is to overcome the issue of spatial information loss in feature extraction of typical elements in CD [7,18,19]. We employ HRNet to preserve richer spatial and channel information by fusing multiresolution and multi-scale features of images. This approach reduces missed detection of large typical elements and false detection of small atypical elements.

Recently, the self-attentive module has gained significant attention in the task [10,12,20]. Chen et al. [1] developed a Transformer-based model for the task. They transformed the underlying features of the images into a set of semantic tokens, representing different tenses of the semantic tokens S_A and S_B. These tokens were then concatenated to obtain $Concat(S_A, S_B)$. The spliced token set was inputted into the transformer encode module, which modeled the bitemporal feature map context to generate a compact set of semantic tokens $Concat(S_A', S_B')$, containing rich contextual information. The output of the transformer encoder was divided into encoded tokens S_A' and tokens S_B' based on the stitching order. Finally, the output of the transformer decoder was separately outputted to obtain the enhanced feature map of the bitemporal image. However, in our experiments, we observed that samples with a non-uniform distribution of bitemporal semantic information caused the model to be influenced by confounding factors. The simple concatenation of tokens led the model to learn knowledge that deviated from true semantics during training, resulting in false correlations. To address this issue, we propose a Recurrent-tokens module to enrich the contextual information, thereby reducing the bias introduced by the model.

Furthermore, we address the challenge of imbalanced positive and negative samples in the task. Negative samples represent typical elements that remain unchanged, while positive samples represent elements that undergo changes. The significant imbalance ratio between positive and negative samples can affect the learning process of the model, as a large number of negative samples dominate the loss function and cause the model to focus excessively on the majority category, ignoring the minority category [8,11,14,16]. In our approach, we introduce a mixed loss based on the Cross-entropy function. By incorporating the Cosineembedding loss, we measure the similarity between the generated mask and the ground truth at a large scale, enabling pixel-level and global-level optimization. This helps embed the initial input into a more informative representation.

Building upon their work, we have developed the HTRNet network with the following main contributions:

(1) Most feature extraction backbones do not fully capture the spatial information of images. In the task, we leverage HRNet to preserve rich spatial and channel semantic information in the feature maps of bitemporal images.
(2) Token sets with a non-uniform distribution of bitemporal semantic information can lead to the model learning spurious statistical associations, impacting its robustness. To address this, we introduce a Recurrent-tokens module to enhance the token set of the input transformer encoder, capturing full contextual information. The output of the transformer decoder is then split into new tokens with weighted contextual information, effectively balancing the bitemporal semantic information in the token sets.
(3) We consider both pixel classification results and locations, leading us to design a set of mixed loss functions based on Cross-entropy loss and Cosineembedding loss. This enables optimization of the model at both the pixel-level and global-level, resulting in output results with improved discriminability between the two distributions.

The results on the LEVIR-CD & DSIFN-CD demonstrate that HTRNet achieves improvements compared to the previous SOAT performance. Intuitively, on the binary mask image generated by the prediction head, compared with other schemes, our prediction object will be smoother on the edge of the graph.

2   Methods

The HTRNet network consists of three main modules and the structure is shown in Fig. 1:

(1) Basic feature extraction module. Preserving the channel semantic information and spatial semantic information in bitemporal images as much as possible through a Siamese architecture based on HRNet as the backbone of the network;

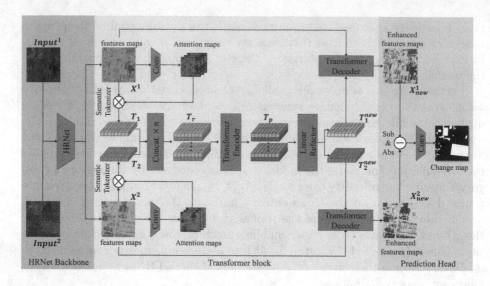

Fig. 1. Illustration of our HTRNet model.

(2) Transformer module. The image basic features X^1 and X^2 extracted from the backbone are separated into a series of visual words, and the two sets of tokens T_1 and T_2 are obtained by the semantic tokenizer module, these tokens are fed into the Recurrent-tokens module to obtain T_r, so that the non-uniform bitemporal information in the original tokens is balanced and the inevitable bias generated by the model is mitigated. Then the context information in tokens is fully modeled by the operation of $transformer\_encoder(T_r)$, and then subsequently split to get a set of $chunk(T_p)$, these split tokens are weighted and summed to get T_1^{new} and T_2^{new}, two sets of context-rich tokens. After these initial tokens are processed in a series, the operation of $transformer\_decoder(T_i^{new})$ is continued to map the tokens rich in context information back to the image feature space to obtain the pixel-level features of the image;

(3) Feature Difference Module. The original image feature map is processed to get $X_{new}^i, i \in (1,2)$ of size $HW \times C$,and they are convolved to get two binary masks of size $HW \times 2$ and the final binary mask map is predicted by fusing these differences features through Prediction head module.

We take advantage of the Siamese architecture based on HRNet to incorporate HTRNet into a typical image change detection pipeline to get the basic feature map of the input levels and scales. The main effect of the transformer is the image and obtain feature fusion and feedback at different self-attention mechanism. The transformer module can make the image features fully enriched with contextual information to model the image in long time span. Finally, we use a set of mixed loss optimization models for pixel classification results and classification locations.

2.1 Feature Extraction of Bitemporal Images

In the task, not only the classification results of accurate pixels are needed, but also the classification locations of accurate pixels. Nevertheless, going to predict the change locations of high-resolution original image samples in a low-resolution feature map can be difficult. The task requires a model that can retain excellent spatial location information while also retaining rich high-latitude semantic information. We use an HRNet-based Siamese architecture as a basic feature extraction network for input bitemporal images $input^1$ and $input^2$, which can extract high-level semantic information in the image channels along with low-level semantic information in the spatial information.

HRNet consists of sub-networks that branch into images of multiple spatial resolutions in parallel, and builds feature maps by reusing modules to fuse the outputs of the sub-networks. HRNet adds batch normalization and residual concatenation to the parallel stream to enhance feature extraction. And HRNet consists of four stages and a Prediction-head during the training process. After the original image is extracted as the feature map input, multiple resolution branch streams in each stage are run in parallel, and the branches of each stage are convolved four times, followed by branch expansion into the next stage. The feature map of the input image is branch and fused at each stage of the feature map can be represented formally as:

$$\begin{cases} (T_{11}, T_{12}) = S_1 \left(Input^i \right) \\ (T_{21}, T_{22}, T_{23}) = S_2 \left(T_{11}, T_{12} \right) \\ (T_{31}, T_{32}, T_{33}, T_{34}) = S_2 \left(T_{21}, T_{22}, T_{23} \right) \\ (T_{41}, T_{42}, T_{43}, T_{44}) = S_4 \left(T_{31}, T_{32}, T_{33}, T_{34} \right) \end{cases} \tag{1}$$

where S_i represents the processing operations of each stage on the resolution streams in other branches.

The four sub-networks of the HRNet backbone output feature maps at different resolutions, and then we choose to upsample these feature maps across resolutions and stitch them along the channel direction to finally output high-resolution feature maps that fuse features at different scales. Formally, this can be expressed as:

$$Predicted\_head = \mathop{||}_{i=1}^{4} \text{Upsample}(T_{4i}) \tag{2}$$

where "$||$" represents the concatenation operation on a series of different tensors.

Finally, through HRNet, the input of the bitemporal image is transformed into a set of basic feature maps rich in channel semantic information and spatial semantic information.

2.2 Transformer Blocks

We continue to use the basic feature maps of bitemporal images obtained by HRNet, and input the two feature maps extracted from $input^1$ and $input^2$ into two semantic tokenizer modules respectively. Semantic tokenizer can extract compact semantic tokens from each temporal feature map, and the information between these semantic concepts can be transferred to each other in the bitemporal image. The bitemporal image is divided by the semantic tokenizer into a number of visual units, each of which corresponds to a token vector. Semantic tokenizer learns a set of spatial attention feature maps, and expresses them as a set of tokens. It can be defined formally as:

$$
\begin{aligned}
T^i &= \left(A^i\right)^T X^i, & i &\in (1,2) \\
&= \left(\text{Softmax}\left(\phi\left(X^i; W\right)\right)\right)^T X^i, & i &\in (1,2)
\end{aligned}
\tag{3}
$$

where T^i is two groups of tokens with a size of $L \times C$, and L is the size of the vocabulary set of tokens. X^i represents a bitemporal feature map with a size of $HW \times L$, $\phi(*)$ represents the point-wise convolution of the learnable kernel with a size of $C \times L$.

Since T^1 and T^2 generated by samples with non-uniform bitemporal information will contain a large number of confounding factors, we design a Recurrent-tokens module to mitigate the inevitable bias generated by the model. The recurrent tokens (T_r) are obtained by concatenating T^1 and T^2 with N times, which can be expressed formally as:

$$
T_r = \mathbin{\big\|}_{i=1}^{n} (T_1, T_2)
\tag{4}
$$

The resulting T_r is used to model the context between these tokens by the transformer. The self-attention module is the main component of the transformer encoder. Subsequently, the transformer can take full advantage of long-range concepts in space-time based on tokens in tokens to obtain Processed-Tokens (T_p) after the Multiple Self-Attention (MSA) and MultiLayer Perceptron (MLP) modules in the transformer. Next, this set of T_p is linearly spilt into a set of $Chunk(T_p)$, which can be represented formally as:

$$
Chunk(T_p) = \mathbin{\big\|}_{i=1}^{n} (T_{1_i}, T_{2_i})
\tag{5}
$$

where T_{1_i} denotes tokens T_1 of group i, T_{2_i} denotes tokens T_2 of group i.

Then, $chunk(T_p)$ is weighted and summed to obtain two sets of context-rich tokens T_1^{new} and T_2^{new}, which can be represented formally as:

$$
\begin{cases}
T_1^{new} = \sum_{i=1}^{n} w_i T_{1_i} \\
T_2^{new} = \sum_{i=1}^{n} w_i' T_{2i}
\end{cases}
\tag{6}
$$

Finally, these context-rich tokens continue to be fed into the transformer decoder module, through which these context-rich tokens can concept back into the image feature space to obtain image pixel-level features.

2.3   Prediction Head and Loss

Up to now, the original bitemporal image will be processed through a series of complex modules, and the network finally outputs two enhanced feature maps X_{new}^i, $i \in (1, 2)$ with a size of $HW \times C$, then X_{new}^i will continue to be changed by convolution to obtain two binary images X_{new*}^i, $i \in (1, 2)$ with a size of $HW \times 2$, and input them into HTRNet Prediction head to obtain the final binary mask map, which can be expressed formally as:

$$\begin{cases} P = \text{Softmax}\left(\left|X_{new\,*}^1 - X_{new\,*}^2\right|\right) \\ predicted\_head = \text{Argmax}(P) \end{cases} \tag{7}$$

where P represents the final prediction score, and the *Argmax* operation is performed on each pixel of P to obtain the final predicted image.

Moreover, in the task, we should focus on the changes of typical elements. However, in actual scenarios, there is a serious imbalance problem in the classification of samples, where unchanged pixels account for most of the bitemporal samples and changed pixels account for only a small fraction. These confounding factors badly increase the difficulty of the task, so we also need to consider both the classification results and positions of pixels. We design a mixed loss based on Cross-Entropy Loss and Cosine-embedding Loss, then we use the weighted summation of them.

We compound Cross-Entropy Loss and Cosine-embedding Loss as a set of mixed loss functions, represented formally as:

$$L_{mix} = \alpha\text{CELoss} + \beta\text{CosEmbLoss} \tag{8}$$

where α & β are the parameters that balance *CELoss* and *CosEmbLoss*.

By using mixed loss functions, multiple metrics can be considered comprehensively, and more flexible goal control can be achieved during training.

3   Experiments and Analysis

3.1   Dataset

We conducted experiments using two publicly available CD datasets, namely LEVIR-CD and DSIFNCD.

The image preprocessing operations and dataset splitting strategy are the same as the baseline [1]: For the LEVIRCD dataset, it is divided into training, validation, and test sets with a ratio of 7:2:1, respectively. As for the DSIFN dataset, the division ratio is 90:8:2 for training, validation, and test sets.

3.2   Implementation Details and Performance Metrics

We implement our model via PaddlePaddle. During the training process, the batch size is set to 16 and the number of training epochs to 300. The model is trained with AdanW optimizer, and the learning rate we take is the dynamic

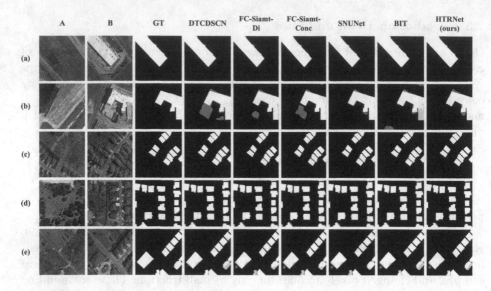

Fig. 2. We show some examples of our predictions on the LEVIR-CD, as well as comparisons with some other methods. Different colors can make the results more intuitive, where red indicates misidentified pixels and green indicates missing pixels. (Color figure online)

warming-up learning rate NoamDecay [15] with an initial value of 0.001 for the learning rate. Our framework is an FCN-based model that allows end-to-end training of the input. We compare the performance with the SOTA methods in several metrics, these evaluation metrics include Precision (P), Recall (R), F1, Intersection over Union (IoU), overall accuracy (OA), etc.

3.3   Results and Evaluation

Some existing SOTA methods are listed for their performance in the task. FC-EF [3], FC-Siam-Conc [3] and FC-Siam-Di [3] are purely convolutional based methods, DTCDSCN [13], STANet [2], IFNet [21] and SNUNet [5] are attention-based methods. We compare the performance of HTRNet with them.

Table 1 show the results of change detection on two different datasets (LEVIR-CD & DSIFN-CD). Quantitative results show that HTRNet exceeds the performance of SOTA on multiple indicators and has significant advantages. Figure 2 & Fig. 3 show some prediction mask maps of HTRNet on LEVIR-CD & DSIFN-CD. The visual intuitive representation shows that our model can significantly reduce the false detection of large typical elements and the missed detection of small atypical elements. And the model mitigates the creation of voids in the interior of the typical elements in the area of change, and it can be seen that the typical elements generate smoother edges in the changing area.

Qualitative and quantitative analysis shows that HTRNet can successfully output image feature maps in multi-scale fusion through HRNet, accurately cap-

Table 1. The comparison results of various schemes are shown, where P stands for precision and R stands for recall. All data in all tables are reported in percentage (%).

Method	LEVIR-CD					DSIFN-CD				
	P	R	F1	IoU	OA	P	R	F1	IoU	OA
FC-EF	86.91	80.17	83.40	71.53	98.39	72.61	52.73	61.09	43.98	88.59
FC-Siam-Di	89.53	83.31	86.31	75.92	98.67	59.67	65.71	62.54	45.50	86.63
FC-Siam-Conc	91.99	76.77	83.69	71.96	98.49	66.45	54.21	59.71	42.56	87.57
DTCDSCN	88.53	86.83	87.67	78.05	98.77	53.87	77.99	63.72	46.76	84.91
STANet	83.81	**91.00**	87.26	77.40	98.66	67.71	61.68	64.56	47.66	88.49
IFNet	**94.02**	82.93	88.13	78.77	98.87	67.86	53.94	60.10	42.96	87.83
SNUNet	89.18	87.17	88.16	78.83	98.82	60.60	72.89	66.18	49.45	87.34
BIT	89.24	89.37	89.31	80.68	98.92	68.36	70.18	69.26	52.97	89.41
HTRNet (ours)	91.83	87.31	**90.51**	**82.78**	**99.08**	**85.68**	**80.13**	**88.02**	**79.88**	**92.83**

Table 2. Ablation experiment results.

Methods	HN	RL	ML	LEVIR-CD		DSIFN-CD	
				F1	IoU	F1	IoU
Base	✗	✗	✗	89.31	80.68	69.26	52.97
Proposal1	✓	✗	✗	89.89 (0.58)	80.98 (0.30)	77.63 (8.37)	65.48 (12.51)
Proposal2	✗	✓	✗	89.96 (0.65)	81.62 (0.94)	74.85 (5.59)	69.64 (16.67)
Proposal3	✓	✓	✗	90.22 (0.91)	82.43 (1.75)	86.42 (17.16)	74.58 (21.61)
Proposal4	✓	✓	✓	90.51 (1.20)	82.78 (2.10)	88.02 (18.76)	79.88 (26.91)

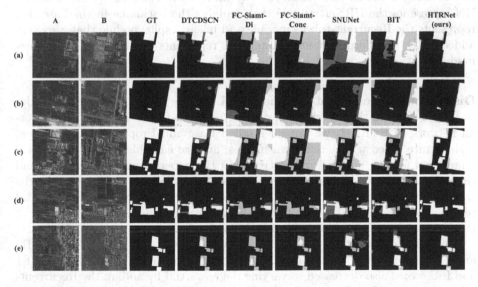

Fig. 3. We show some examples of our predictions on the DSIFN-CD, as well as comparisons with some other methods.

ture the channel information and spatial information of images. The Recurrent-tokens module and transformer can be used to fully model the bitemporal images at the global-level, and to fully exploit the long-range concepts in space-time of the images to enhance the pixel-space feature representation. Finally, in the back-propagation link of the model, a set of mixed loss functions is used to provide additional guidance to the model learning process, fully considering the classification results and classification positions of pixels, and embedding the initial input into a more informative representation.

3.4   Ablation Experiment

Effect of the Proposed Modules. HTRNet integrates the Siamese backbone based on HRNet, the transformer block based on Recurrenttokens module, and the mixed loss. To accurately evaluate the contribution of each module to the overall network structure of HTRNet, we designed the following ablation experiments in Table 2.

Base: Siamese network with ResNet18 backbone, using transformer codec module and a single loss function for training. Proposal1: Siamese network with HRNet backbone, transformer codec module, and a single cross-entropy loss for training. Proposal2: Siamese network with ResNet18 backbone, Recurrent-tokens module, linearly split operation in transformer codec, and a single cross-entropy loss for training. Proposal3: Siamese network with HRNet backbone, Recurrent-tokens module, linearly split operation in transformer codec, and a single cross-entropy loss for training. Proposal4: Siamese network with HRNet backbone, Recurrent-tokens module, linearly split operation in transformer codec, using a mixed loss (cross-entropy and cosine embedding) for training. HN represents the HRNet module that replaces the backbone in the base, RL represents the Recurrent-tokens module and linearly split module that are extra added to the transformer structure, and ML represents the improved mixed loss module.

Discussion of Recurrent-Tokens and Linearly Split Module. In order to further confirm the contribution of the Recurrent-tokens module to the overall network of HTRNet, we further studied Base and Proposal2. The Siamese architecture is fed with bitemporal images, and we call this pair of bitemporal image sets as "A" and "B" respectively. In the experiment of Base, we found that replacing the "A" and "B" entered into the Siamese architecture in the training set with "B" and "A" has a nonnegligible impact on the experimental results. This demonstrates that the model is subject to unavoidable bias due to the input order of the bitemporal images in the dataset.

Table 3 shows that after replacing the training set "A" and "B" with "B" and "A", F1 and IoU in LEVIR-CD decreased respectively. In DSIFN-CD, F1 and IoU scores also decreased to varying degrees. And by adding the Recurrent-tokens and linearly split module, the changes in F1 and IoU in LEVIR-CD are very small. In DSIFN-CD, the changes of F1 and IoU are also slight.

Table 3. Ablation experiments with swapped bitemporal image order.

	Methods	LEVIR-CD		DSIFN-CD	
		F1	IoU	F1	IoU
Baseline	Base_AB	89.31	80.68	69.26	52.97
	Base_BA	82.74 (−6.57)	72.67 (−8.01)	61.43 (−7.83)	43.45 (−9.52)
Ours	Proposal2_AB	89.96	81.62	74.85	69.64
	Proposal2_BA	90.37 (0.41)	81.28 (−0.34)	73.83 (−1.02)	73.83 (−1.02)

4 Conclusion

The proposed model, called HTRNet, combines the HRNet and Transformer architectures to improve the accuracy of change detection. The model consists of several key components and utilizes mixed losses for effective training. The HRNet-based Siamese architecture is employed as the backbone of the model. This helps to retain important channel and spatial details throughout the network. To address the bias issue in the original tokens, a Recurrent-tokens module is introduced. This module corrects the bias and provides improved tokens that capture more accurate contextual information. To guide the training process, a set of mixed losses is used. These losses are carefully selected and combined to optimize the model's performance. The specific choice and combination of loss functions depend on the requirements of the change detection task. Experimental results demonstrate the effectiveness of HTRNet compared to SOAT approaches. The model shows improved performance on various evaluation metrics such as F1 score, IoU, and OA. It excels in identifying changes of interest and minimizing the influence of confounding factors in the bitemporal remote sensing images.

References

1. Chen, H., Qi, Z., Shi, Z.: Remote sensing image change detection with transformers. IEEE Trans. Geosci. Remote Sens. **60**, 1–14 (2021)
2. Chen, H., Shi, Z.: A spatial-temporal attention-based method and a new dataset for remote sensing image change detection. Remote Sens. **12**(10), 1662 (2020)
3. Daudt, R.C., Le Saux, B., Boulch, A.: Fully convolutional Siamese networks for change detection. In: 2018 25th IEEE International Conference on Image Processing (ICIP), pp. 4063–4067. IEEE (2018)
4. Daudt, R.C., Le Saux, B., Boulch, A., Gousseau, Y.: Urban change detection for multispectral earth observation using convolutional neural networks. In: IGARSS 2018-2018 IEEE International Geoscience and Remote Sensing Symposium, pp. 2115–2118. IEEE (2018)
5. Fang, S., Li, K., Shao, J., Li, Z.: SNUNet-CD: a densely connected Siamese network for change detection of VHR images. IEEE Geosci. Remote Sens. Lett. **19**, 1–5 (2021)
6. Gao, Y., Dai, M., Zhang, Q.: Cross-modal and multi-level feature refinement network for RGB-D salient object detection. Vis. Comput. 1–16 (2022)

7. Guo, Z., Shuai, H., Liu, G., Zhu, Y., Wang, W.: Multi-level feature fusion pyramid network for object detection. Vis. Comput. 1–11 (2022)
8. Han, M., Li, R., Zhang, C.: LWCDNet: a lightweight fully convolution network for change detection in optical remote sensing imagery. IEEE Geosci. Remote Sens. Lett. **19**, 1–5 (2022)
9. Jégou, S., Drozdzal, M., Vazquez, D., Romero, A., Bengio, Y.: The one hundred layers tiramisu: fully convolutional DenseNets for semantic segmentation. In: Proceedings of the IEEE Conference on Computer Vision and Pattern Recognition Workshops, pp. 11–19 (2017)
10. Jiang, N., Sheng, B., Li, P., Lee, T.Y.: PhotoHelper: portrait photographing guidance via deep feature retrieval and fusion. IEEE Trans. Multimed. (2022)
11. Li, X., He, M., Li, H., Shen, H.: A combined loss-based multiscale fully convolutional network for high-resolution remote sensing image change detection. IEEE Geosci. Remote Sens. Lett. **19**, 1–5 (2021)
12. Lian, Y., Shi, X., Shen, S., Hua, J.: Multitask learning for image translation and salient object detection from multimodal remote sensing images. Vis. Comput. 1–20 (2023)
13. Liu, Y., Pang, C., Zhan, Z., Zhang, X., Yang, X.: Building change detection for remote sensing images using a dual-task constrained deep Siamese convolutional network model. IEEE Geosci. Remote Sens. Lett. **18**(5), 811–815 (2020)
14. Pan, F., Wu, Z., Liu, Q., Xu, Y., Wei, Z.: DCFF-Net: a densely connected feature fusion network for change detection in high-resolution remote sensing images. IEEE J. Sel. Top. Appl. Earth Observ. Remote Sens. **14**, 11974–11985 (2021)
15. Popel, M., Bojar, O.: Training tips for the transformer model. arXiv preprint arXiv:1804.00247 (2018)
16. Shrivastava, A., Gupta, A., Girshick, R.: Training region-based object detectors with online hard example mining. In: Proceedings of the IEEE Conference on Computer Vision and Pattern Recognition, pp. 761–769 (2016)
17. Sun, K., Xiao, B., Liu, D., Wang, J.: Deep high-resolution representation learning for human pose estimation. In: Proceedings of the IEEE/CVF Conference on Computer Vision and Pattern Recognition, pp. 5693–5703 (2019)
18. Sun, Y., Zheng, W.: HRNet-and PSPNet-based multiband semantic segmentation of remote sensing images. Neural Comput. Appl. **35**(12), 8667–8675 (2023)
19. Yang, X., Fan, X., Peng, M., Guan, Q., Tang, L.: Semantic segmentation for remote sensing images based on an AD-HRNet model. Int. J. Digit. Earth **15**(1), 2376–2399 (2022)
20. Yuan, Y., Lin, L.: Self-supervised pretraining of transformers for satellite image time series classification. IEEE J. Sel. Top. Appl. Earth Observ. Remote Sens. **14**, 474–487 (2020)
21. Zhang, C., et al.: A deeply supervised image fusion network for change detection in high resolution bi-temporal remote sensing images. ISPRS J. Photogramm. Remote. Sens. **166**, 183–200 (2020)

UPDN: Pedestrian Detection Network for Unmanned Aerial Vehicle Perspective

Minghua Jiang[1,2], Yulin Wang[1], Mengsi Guo[1], Li Liu[1], and Feng Yu[1,2]([⊠])

[1] School of Computer Science and Artificial Intelligence,
Wuhan Textile University, Wuhan 430200, China
[2] Engineering Research Center of Hubei Province for Clothing Information,
Wuhan 430200, China
yufeng@wtu.edu.cn

Abstract. Pedestrian detection for Unmanned Aerial Vehicle (UAV) perspective has significant potential in the fields of computer vision and intelligent systems. However, current methods have some limitations in terms of accuracy and real-time detection of small targets, which severely affects their practical application. To address these challenges, we propose UPDN, a novel network designed to improve detection comprehensive performance while maintaining high speed as much as possible. To achieve this objective, UPDN incorporates two key modules: the Spatial Pyramid Convolution and Pooling Module (SPCPM) and the Efficient Attention Module (EAM). The SPCPM effectively captures multi-scale features from pedestrian regions, enabling better detection of small targets. The EAM optimizes network operations by selectively focusing on informative regions, enhancing the overall efficiency of the detection process. Experimental results on the constructed dataset demonstrate that UPDN outperforms other classic detection methods. It achieves state-of-the-art results in terms of both Average Precision (AP) and F1 score, achieving a detection speed of 107.37 frames per second (FPS). In summary, UPDN provides an efficient and reliable solution for pedestrian detection from a UAV perspective, offering a feasible approach for real-world applications.

Keywords: Pedestrian detection · UAV · Small target

1 Introduction

Unmanned aerial vehicle (UAV) target detection technology has been widely applied in various practical scenarios, such as plant protection [14], wildlife conservation [7], personnel search and rescue [17], and urban monitoring [1]. Compared to common fixed cameras on the streets, UAVs have stronger mobility and can perform detection tasks in a wider range of scenarios.

Among them, pedestrian detection technology is a key part used in personnel search and rescue, and it also plays a crucial role in fields such as video monitoring [23], and autonomous driving [2]. Although there are some related

B. Sheng et al. (Eds.): CGI 2023, LNCS 14497, pp. 27–39, 2024.
https://doi.org/10.1007/978-3-031-50075-6_3

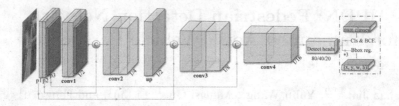

Fig. 1. The overall framework of UPDN is a pedestrian detection algorithm that utilizes a unique perspective from an UAV. The algorithm consists of several key components, including the SPCPM, the EAM, and the SIOU loss function. This diagram is intended to describe the main flow, where up represents the upsample operation and conv is not limited to conv2d operations, *3 because there are three detection heads.

studies on pedestrian detection [5,6,9,16], existing methods still have limitations and room for improvement in terms of terminal deployment, robustness in complex scenarios, and real-time performance. From the high-altitude perspective of UAVs, there may be relatively less occlusions in crowds, but this brings problems such as complex backgrounds, small targets, lost key information, or excessively large algorithm models, which hinder the deployment and application of pedestrian detection systems in real-world scenarios. To address these limitations, this paper proposes UPDN (Pedestrian Detection for Unmanned Aerial Vehicle Perspective), see Fig. 1, a novel network designed specifically for efficient and accurate pedestrian detection for the UAV perspective. The goal of UPDN is to improve detection speed while maintaining high accuracy, achieving real-time pedestrian detection in UAV images.

UPDN's crucial component, the Spatial Pyramid Convolution and Pooling Module (SPCPM), is designed to improve the representation of small targets by capturing multi-scale information and effectively integrating it into feature maps. Another important component of UPDN is the Enhanced Attention Module (EAM), which enhances the model's representation and discriminative capabilities by introducing spatial attention. The SIOU can help the model to carry out target detection more accurately through four loss constraints.

In the experimental session, we evaluated the multidimensional performance of UPDN on a constructed dataset using 9 metrics and compared it with seven classical algorithms. The results demonstrate that UPDN outperforms several classical algorithms, achieving state-of-the-art performance in terms of average accuracy (AP), F1 score, and recall. Furthermore, UPDN achieves a remarkable detection speed of 107.37 frames per second (FPS), making it suitable for real-time applications. UPDN addresses the unique challenges of detecting pedestrians from the UAV perspective, and the potential for various applications in surveillance, security, and autonomous systems. In summary, the four contributions of this study are:

- UPDN algorithm shows excellent comprehensive performance in pedestrian detection, especially in the UAV scenario.

- The SPCPM boost the representation and detection of small targets. The EAM enhance the model's representation and discriminative capabilities.
- The combination of SPCPM, EAM, and SIOU helps to the aggregate performance and efficiency of the UPDN algorithm, enhancing the capability of feature representation, small target detection, complex background detection, and target location.
- The dataset we built provides a broad benchmark for pedestrian detection and provides strong support for the evaluation of algorithms, while also providing a useful resource for future research.

The rest of this paper is organized as follows. Section 2 introduces related work on pedestrian detection for UAV images. Section 3 outlines the proposed UPDN framework. Section 4 discusses the experimental settings, dataset description, evaluation metrics, and effect analysis. Finally, Sect. 5 summarizes the entire paper and proposes future research directions.

2 Related Works

2.1 Pedestrian Detection Algorithms

Pedestrian detection is a crucial task in the field of computer vision. Traditional pedestrian detection methods relied on handcrafted features and machine learning classifiers [20,24], such as Haar features and Adaboost algorithm. However, these methods have limited performance when dealing with complex scenes.

Nevertheless, pedestrian detection algorithms based on Convolutional Neural Networks (CNNs) have made significant progress. Classic CNN-based pedestrian detection algorithms, such as Faster R-CNN, SSD, and YOLO [3,8,13,25], have achieved more accurate and efficient detection. However, these algorithms still face many challenges.

2.2 UAV Perspective Pedestrian Detection

In UAV perspective pedestrian detection, traditional methods struggle to meet the practical requirements due to the varying camera viewpoints and reduced target sizes. Consequently, researchers have proposed a range of pedestrian detection methods [11,18] specifically tailored for the UAV perspective.

One common approach is to enhance pedestrian detection performance through multi-scale feature fusion. These methods leverage feature pyramid networks or multi-scale convolution and pooling operations to capture target information at different scales [19,22], thereby improving the model's perception capabilities. Another approach is the incorporation of attention mechanisms to enhance the focus on pedestrians [10,21]. By introducing attention modules within the network, models can automatically learn which features are crucial for pedestrian detection, thereby boosting detection performance.

Additionally, researchers have explored techniques such as data augmentation [15], and model optimization [12] to enhance the performance and generalization capabilities. However, despite the progress made, UAV vision pedestrian detection still faces challenges in accurately detecting small-scale pedestrians, handling complex scenarios and lost target key information with cluttered backgrounds and occlusions.

3   Approach Overview

3.1   SPCPM

The SPCPM enhances the representation of small targets in UAV-based pedestrian detection scenarios, as shown in Fig. 2. It leverages spatial pyramid convolution and pooling operations to effectively capture multi-scale information. SPCPM improves the network's ability to handle objects of different sizes and provides comprehensive feature information. Experimental results demonstrate its effectiveness, with improvements observed in evaluation metrics such as AP, F1 score, precision, and recall.

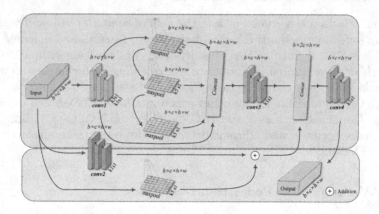

Fig. 2. The SPCPM is a crucial component of the pedestrian detection algorithm, particularly challenging UAV-based scenarios with small targets. It is designed to enhance the representation and detection of small targets by effectively capturing multi-scale information through spatial pyramid convolution and pooling operations. The SPCPM effectively captures multi-scale information and emphasizes important features in the input feature maps, enhancing the performance of the pedestrian detection algorithm. Its purpose is to enhance the extracted features from the input image and improve the model's performance in detecting pedestrians in UAV-based images.

The operations performed by SPCPM preserve the feature information while increasing the receptive field of the network. By capturing multi-scale information through spatial pyramid convolution and pooling processing, SPCPM enhances the network's ability to handle objects of different sizes. The module effectively provides more comprehensive feature information, particularly for small targets, thereby improving the network's detection capabilities in UAV-based pedestrian detection scenarios.

Experimental results demonstrate the usefulness and effectiveness of the SPCPM. The performance evaluation indicates a significant improvement in some evaluation metrics. The AP shows a notable rise of 3.81%, while the F1 score boosts from 0.19 to 0.22 and recall increases from 10.37% to 12.78%. These improvements validate the module's effectiveness in enhancing the model's detection performance. The module maintains operational efficiency, with a slight decrease in FPS and reasonable increases in parameter count and computational complexity. The benefits in detection performance justify the module's inclusion in the pedestrian detection methodology. Furthermore, the SPCPM contributes to the operational efficiency of the network. The FPS measure shows a slight decrease from 119.17 to 117.50, indicating that the module does not significantly affect the network's processing speed. Although the module introduces additional parameters and computational complexity, with the parameter count growing from 7.022M to 13.450M and the GLOPS from 15.946G to 21.093G, the resulting boost in model size and computational load is reasonable considering the notable improvements in detection performance.

3.2 EAM

In the field of object detection, the attention mechanism is often introduced into the deep learning network structure. The EAM as shown in Fig. 3 introduced in this study builds upon the foundation of channel attention mechanisms while incorporating spatial features to enhance the performance of the network.

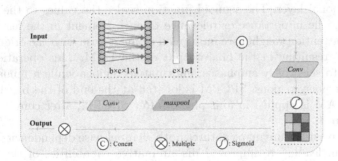

Fig. 3. The EAM is another key component of the pedestrian detection algorithm proposed in the research paper. The module introduces additional spatial attention, which is emphasizing important features and suppressing irrelevant ones, the EAM improves the comprehensive performance of the model in detecting pedestrians from UAV-based images.

The EAM is designed to selectively capture both channel-wise dependencies and spatial information to improve the overall representation and discriminative

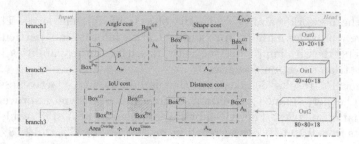

Fig. 4. The SIOU consists of four key aspects: center coordinate loss, width and height loss, confidence loss, and class loss.

power of the network. The EAM begins with a 1D convolutional layer that operates on the input feature map. This operation enables the module to capture channel-wise dependencies by modeling interactions between different channels. The resulting intermediate feature representations provide an initial understanding of the input data. To further enhance the module's understanding of spatial information, we introduce an additional pathway that involves a convolutional layer followed by max pooling. This parallel spatial pathway focuses on extracting relevant spatial features and provides valuable spatial context to the module.

To combine the channel and spatial information effectively, the outputs of the channel-wise and spatial pathways are concatenated along the channel dimension. This fusion step allows the learned channel-wise dependencies to be integrated with the captured spatial features. The concatenated feature map is then passed through a subsequent convolutional layer, enabling the module to adaptively transform its dimensionality back to the original input size. To generate attention weights, we apply a sigmoid activation function to the output of the convolutional layer. The sigmoid function scales the values to the range [0, 1], indicating the importance or relevance of each element in the feature map. Finally, the attention weights are multiplied element-wise with the original input feature map, resulting in the final output of the EAM. This operation allows the module to selectively emphasize informative regions while attenuating less important or noisy regions. SPCPM is located at the end of the backbone network, and EAM is applied in four places, after SPCPM, after conv1, after up, and after conv4.

The enhanced feature map captures both channel-wise dependencies and spatial attention, leading to improved discriminative capabilities of the network. Experimental results on the constructed data demonstrate the effectiveness of the EAM in pedestrian detection tasks. AP is increased by 1.15%, and F1 value is increased from 0.19 to 0.21. Although the accuracy index has decreased, the two core comprehensive indicators have been significantly improved, so EAM is recognized as effective.

3.3   Loss Function

The loss function used in UPDN is the standard Single Intersection over Union (SIOU) loss, as shown in Fig. 4. It is defined as the negative logarithm of the

Table 1. The outcome of the pedestrian detection comparison experiment.

Model	Shape	AP (%)	Precision (%)	Recall (%)	F1	FPS	Params (M)	GLOPS(G)	Param size (MB)	Total size (MB)
Retinanet	600 × 600	3.54	92.05	1.34	0.03	41.29	36.330	145.339	\	\
SSD	300 × 300	4.33	52.95	1.65	0.03	89.40	23.612	60.597	90.07	503.67
Faster RCNN	600 × 600	4.35	39.11	5.68	0.10	17.08	136.689	369.719	521.43	2096.31
Yolov3	416 × 416	11.23	45.99	12.05	0.19	106.02	615.238	65.597	234.59	12228.39
Centernet	512 × 512	16.40	67.78	10.96	0.19	103.84	32.665	70.217	124.61	1686.61
Yolov5s	640 × 640	21.69	90.77	10.37	0.19	119.17	7.022	15.946	26.79	830.29
Yolov7tiny	640 × 640	21.05	82.35	11.97	0.21	118.47	6.014	13.181	\	\
Ours	640 × 640	**26.85**	88.41	13.88	**0.24**	107.37	14.239	21.306	54.32	905.51

IOU between the predicted bounding box (bbox) and the ground truth bbox. Although we did not make changes to the SIOU loss function, we included it in our paper to give readers an understanding of the fundamental components of our object detection model.

4 Experiments and Results

4.1 Experimental Setup

The experimental platform is configured as follows: The system version used is Windows 10 Pro 64-bit, the processor is an Intel Core i9-12900KF 12th Gen running at 3.2 GHz, and the graphics processing unit is an NVIDIA GeForce RTX 3090 Ti 24 GB. The system utilizes Python 3.8.15 along with the following libraries: numpy 1.24.1, opencv-python 4.6.0.66, torchvision 0.13.0+cu116 and torch 1.12.0+cu116.

4.2 Experimental Data

In this chapter, we conduct experiments on a pedestrian detection dataset that we have constructed. The data comprises 16,953 samples gathered from various sources, including subsets of pedestrian samples from the VisDrone dataset [4], subsets of pedestrian samples from the Tinyperson dataset, and pedestrian samples collected by us. The data we collect is obtained using the DJI Magic3. These samples are incorporated to enhance the quality of the dataset and support the robustness of the subsequent algorithm model. By including a diverse range of perspectives, our data better reflects real-world scenarios and contributes to the improved performance and generalizability of the algorithm.

Table 2. The outcome of the pedestrian detection ablation experiment.

Model	Shape	AP (%)	Precision (%)	Recall (%)	F1	FPS	Params (M)	GLOPS (G)	Param size (MB)	Total size (MB)
Base	640 × 640	21.69	90.77	10.37	0.19	119.17	7.022	15.946	26.79	830.29
EAM+SIOU	640 × 640	22.84	85.53	12.07	0.21	100.86	7.451	15.795	28.42	851.52
SPCPM+SIOU	640 × 640	25.50	89.62	12.78	0.22	117.50	13.450	21.093	51.31	893.09
E+S+SIOU (Ours)	640 × 640	**26.85**	88.41	13.88	**0.24**	107.37	14.239	21.306	54.32	905.51

4.3 Evaluation Metrics

To comprehensively assess the detection performance of the proposed model, we chose AP and F1 as the primary evaluation metrics for our models. In addition, there are several other metrics commonly used for evaluating the performance and efficiency of deep learning models, including Precision, Recall, FPS, Params, GFLOPS, Params size, and Total Size.

4.4 Experimental Analysis

In this section, we provide a detailed analysis of our experimental results. We conducted experiments on our constructed dataset and report the results in terms of AP, F1, FPS, Precision, Recall, Params, GLOPS, Param size, and Total size. Instead of pursuing high accuracy through stacking a large number of modules, we aim to strike a balance between comprehensive performance (AP and F1) and speed on a concise structure, in order to prepare for possible terminal deployment, reduce reliance on high-cost hardware, and save costs while ensuring property.

In Fig. 5, it showcasing the network's ability to accurately detect pedestrians in challenging conditions. The images are annotated with the predicted pedestrian bounding boxes, corresponding class labels, and confidence scores. The visual evidence demonstrates the effectiveness and robustness of the UPDN network in handling diverse real-world scenarios, validating its suitability for pedestrian detection tasks across different conditions in UAV vision applications.

Therefore, we compare the performance of UPDN with different algorithms of their small version in our experiments. The results show that UPDN achieves excellent performance, with the best AP and F1 scores of 26.85% and 0.24, respectively. The FPS also meets real-time requirements, exceeding 25 with a value of 107.37. Other parameters, including Precision at 88.41%, Recall at 13.88%, Params at 14.239M, GFLOPS at 21.306G, Param size at 54.32 MB, and Total size at 905.51 MB, are also reported.

More specifically, we compare the performance of our proposed algorithm with seven other classic algorithms, including Retinanet, SSD, Faster RCNN, Yolov3, Centernet, Yolov5s, and Yolov7tiny in Table 1. In terms of AP and F1, our proposed algorithm has at least improved by 5.16% and 0.03 compared with other algorithms. Although our model may not reach the highest in other indicators, it demonstrated strong comprehensive performance in balancing Precision and Recall, as evidenced by the AP and F1 scores.

Next, we conduct ablation experiments on the UPDN algorithm to evaluate the impact of each component on the overall performance in Table 2. Specifically, when SPCPM is used, the AP and F1 scores of UPDN improve by 3.81% and 0.03, respectively, while when EAM is used, the AP and F1 scores contribute by 1.15% and 0.02, respectively. This effectively demonstrates the effectiveness of the SPCPM and EAM. The results show that each component contributes significantly to the overall performance, with the SPCPM contributing the most.

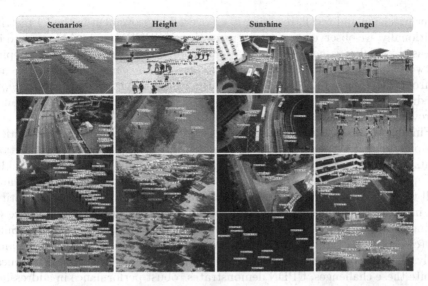

Fig. 5. It illustrates the pedestrian detection performance of the UPDN network in various scenarios, including different scenes, altitudes, lighting conditions, and camera angles. The figure is divided into four sections, each displaying four representative images.

We also test the case of applying both the SPCPM and EAM to UPDN. The results show that when these two modules work together, they achieve a synergistic effect greater than the sum of their individual effects, which is very exciting. Meanwhile, when removing the SPCPM from UPDN, the AP and F1 scores decrease by 4.01% and 0.02, respectively, while when removing the SPCPM from the model, the AP and F1 scores dropped by 1.35% and 0.03, respectively. This indicates the higher potential and synergistic effect of the SPCPM and EAM.

Combining the analysis of other evaluation indicators, the parallel design of the SPCPM enables the network to maintain a high feature processing speed even with increased processing steps and parameters. This parallelism allows the model to efficiently handle input features and enhance the overall algorithm performance. By utilizing multi-scale spatial pyramid convolution and pooling operations, the SPCPM captures multi-scale information, thereby improving the model's receptive field and feature representation capability. This further enhances the network's ability to detect small targets, which is particularly crucial in pedestrian detection scenarios based on UAVs.

Furthermore, the incorporation of multiple EAM in the model, despite increasing the model's size, leads to performance improvements for UPDN. This is evidenced by the observed increase in the GLOPS metric, indicating improved computational speed. The EAM introduce additional attention mechanisms, enabling the model to focus on important features and enhance its representation and discriminative capabilities. This attention mechanism contributes to higher precision and recall, resulting in an overall improvement in the F1 metric. Additionally, we observed that the introduction of SPCPM and EAM resulted in increased model parameters, computational complexity, and model size. Despite the two-fold increase in the largest of these parameters, such as Params increasing from 7.022M to 14.239M, the magnitude of this increase remains acceptable due to the model's initial small parameter size. Moreover, the performance improvements are evident, particularly the Recall metric.

Finally we select some representative and convincing pedestrian detection examples in real scenes, and use 4×4 image grid to visualize the prediction results of the algorithm, as shown in Fig. 6. (a) represents various sports fields, (b) depicts outdoor scenes, (c) showcases scenes with crowded environments and small targets, and (d) displays other miscellaneous scenarios. It is worth noting that in subplot (a), there are instances of motion blur due to the presence of moving drones. In subplot (b), the first column exhibits target occlusion. Subplot (c) contains a significant amount of occlusion caused by dense pedestrians. Lastly, the last column of subplot (d) includes interference from complex scenes. Despite these challenges, UPDN demonstrates robust performance in addressing these issues, underscoring its superior capabilities.

In conclusion, the introduction of the SPCPM and EAM demonstrates considerable performance gains while maintaining efficiency. The optimization of feature processing speed, enhancement of the model's receptive field and feature representation capabilities, and improved handling of small targets and complex scenes collectively contribute to the significant improvements in our algorithm's performance and efficiency. Adopting the strategy of trading minor overheads for substantial performance gains proves meaningful and impactful in the context of pedestrian detection tasks.

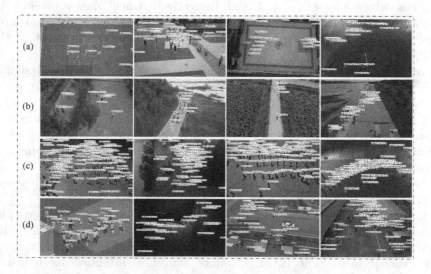

Fig. 6. (a) various sports fields, (b) outdoor scenes, (c) crowded scenes with small targets, and (d) other scenes.

5 Conclusion

In this study, we propose UPDN, a novel pedestrian detection algorithm from UAV perspective, incorporating the SPCPM, EAM, and SIOU. Through extensive experiments and evaluations, we demonstrate the superior performance of our algorithm in terms of AP, F1, Recall, and other evaluation metrics. The SPCPM effectively handles input features and enhances the algorithm's overall performance by capturing multi-scale information. The EAM introduce additional spatial attention, improving the model's characterization and discriminative capabilities. The SIOU loss function improves the algorithm's ability to handle small object detection and complex scenes. Moreover, extensive experiments on the constructed dataset, illustrated that the UPDN outperformed seven classical algorithms, reached the state-of-the-art performance in AP, F1 and Recall, achieving detection speeds of 107.37 FPS. Our research contributes to advancing the field of pedestrian detection and holds great potential for various applications in surveillance, security, and autonomous systems.

Acknowledgement. This work was supported by national natural science foundation of China (No. 62202346), Hubei key research and development program (No. 2021BAA042), open project of engineering research center of Hubei province for clothing information (No. 2022HBCI01), Wuhan applied basic frontier research project (No. 2022 013988065212), MIIT's AI Industry Innovation Task unveils flagship projects (Key technologies, equipment, and systems for flexible customized and intelligent manufacturing in the clothing industry), and Hubei science and technology project of safe production special fund (Scene control platform based on proprioception information computing of artificial intelligence).

References

1. Audebert, N., Le Saux, B., Lefèvre, S.: Beyond RGB: very high resolution urban remote sensing with multimodal deep networks. ISPRS J. Photogramm. Remote. Sens. **140**, 20–32 (2018)
2. Chen, J., Du, C., Zhang, Y., Han, P., Wei, W.: A clustering-based coverage path planning method for autonomous heterogeneous UAVs. IEEE Trans. Intell. Transp. Syst. **23**(12), 25546 25556 (2021)
3. Chen, Z., Qiu, J., Sheng, B., Li, P., Wu, E.: GPSD: generative parking spot detection using multi-clue recovery model. Vis. Comput. **37**(9–11), 2657–2669 (2021)
4. Du, D., et al.: VisDrone-DET2019: the vision meets drone object detection in image challenge results. In: Proceedings of the IEEE/CVF International Conference on Computer Vision Workshops (2019)
5. Guo, G., Chen, P., Yu, X., Han, Z., Ye, Q., Gao, S.: Save the tiny, save the all: hierarchical activation network for tiny object detection. IEEE Trans. Circuits Syst. Video Technol. (2023)
6. Hong, M., Li, S., Yang, Y., Zhu, F., Zhao, Q., Lu, L.: SSPNet: scale selection pyramid network for tiny person detection from UAV images. IEEE Geosci. Remote Sens. Lett. **19**, 1–5 (2021)

7. Kellenberger, B., Marcos, D., Tuia, D.: Detecting mammals in UAV images: best practices to address a substantially imbalanced dataset with deep learning. Remote Sens. Environ. **216**, 139–153 (2018)
8. Li, J., et al.: Automatic detection and classification system of domestic waste via multimodel cascaded convolutional neural network. IEEE Trans. Industr. Inf. **18**(1), 163–173 (2021)
9. Liu, W., Liao, S., Ren, W., Hu, W., Yu, Y.: High-level semantic feature detection: a new perspective for pedestrian detection. In: Proceedings of the IEEE/CVF Conference on Computer Vision and Pattern Recognition, pp. 5187–5196 (2019)
10. Luo, Q., Shao, J., Dang, W., Geng, L., Zheng, H., Liu, C.: An efficient multi-scale channel attention network for person re-identification. Vis. Comput. 1–13 (2023)
11. Ma, X., Zhang, Y., Zhang, W., Zhou, H., Yu, H.: SDWBF algorithm: a novel pedestrian detection algorithm in the aerial scene. Drones **6**(3), 76 (2022)
12. Murthy, C.B., Hashmi, M.F., Keskar, A.G.: Optimized MobileNet+ SSD: a real-time pedestrian detection on a low-end edge device. Int. J. Multimed. Inf. Retrieval **10**, 171–184 (2021)
13. Redmon, J., Farhadi, A.: YOLO9000: better, faster, stronger. In: Proceedings of the IEEE Conference on Computer Vision and Pattern Recognition, pp. 7263–7271 (2017)
14. Shao, Z., Li, C., Li, D., Altan, O., Zhang, L., Ding, L.: An accurate matching method for projecting vector data into surveillance video to monitor and protect cultivated land. ISPRS Int. J. Geo Inf. **9**(7), 448 (2020)
15. Tang, Y., Li, B., Liu, M., Chen, B., Wang, Y., Ouyang, W.: AutoPedestrian: an automatic data augmentation and loss function search scheme for pedestrian detection. IEEE Trans. Image Process. **30**, 8483–8496 (2021)
16. Wang, X., He, N., Hong, C., Wang, Q., Chen, M.: Improved YOLOX-X based UAV aerial photography object detection algorithm. Image Vis. Comput. 104697 (2023)
17. Wang, Y., Liu, W., Liu, J., Sun, C.: Cooperative USV–UAV marine search and rescue with visual navigation and reinforcement learning-based control. ISA Trans. (2023)
18. Xie, H., Shin, H.: Two-stream small-scale pedestrian detection network with feature aggregation for drone-view videos. Multidimension. Syst. Signal Process. **32**, 897–913 (2021)
19. Yang, P., Zhang, G., Wang, L., Xu, L., Deng, Q., Yang, M.H.: A part-aware multi-scale fully convolutional network for pedestrian detection. IEEE Trans. Intell. Transp. Syst. **22**(2), 1125–1137 (2020)
20. Zhang, S., Bauckhage, C., Cremers, A.B.: Informed Haar-like features improve pedestrian detection. In: Proceedings of the IEEE Conference on Computer Vision and Pattern Recognition, pp. 947–954 (2014)
21. Zhang, S., Yang, J., Schiele, B.: Occluded pedestrian detection through guided attention in CNNs. In: Proceedings of the IEEE Conference on Computer Vision and Pattern Recognition, pp. 6995–7003 (2018)
22. Zhang, T., Cao, Y., Zhang, L., Li, X.: Efficient feature fusion network based on center and scale prediction for pedestrian detection. Vis. Comput. **39**(9), 3865–3872 (2023)
23. Zhang, Y., Xu, C., Hemadeh, I.A., El-Hajjar, M., Hanzo, L.: Near-instantaneously adaptive multi-set space-time shift keying for UAV-aided video surveillance. IEEE Trans. Veh. Technol. **69**(11), 12843–12856 (2020)

24. Zhou, H., Yu, G.: Research on fast pedestrian detection algorithm based on autoencoding neural network and AdaBoost. Complexity **2021**, 1–17 (2021)
25. Zhu, X., Lyu, S., Wang, X., Zhao, Q.: TPH-YOLOv5: improved YOLOv5 based on transformer prediction head for object detection on drone-captured scenarios. In: Proceedings of the IEEE/CVF International Conference on Computer Vision, pp. 2778–2788 (2021)

Learning Local Features of Motion Chain for Human Motion Prediction

Zhuoran Liu[1], Lianggangxu Chen[1], Chen Li[1], Changbo Wang[1],
and Gaoqi He[1,2(✉)]

[1] School of Computer Science and Technology,
East China Normal University, Shanghai, China
`51255901106@stu.ecnu.edu.cn`
[2] Chongqing Key Laboratory of Precision Optics,
Chongqing Institute of East China Normal University, Chongqing, China
`gqhe@cs.ecnu.edu.cn`

Abstract. Extracting local features is a key technique in the field of human motion prediction. However, Due to incorrect partitioning of strongly correlated joint sets, existing methods ignore parts of strongly correlated joint pairs during local feature extraction, leading to prediction errors in end joints. In this paper, a Motion Chain Learning Framework is proposed to address the problem of prediction errors in end joints, such as hands and feet. The key idea is to mine and build strong correlations for joints belonging to the same motion chain. To be specific, all human joints are first divided into five parts according to the human motion chains. Then, the local interaction relationship between joints on each motion chain is learned by GCN. Finally, a novel Weights-Added Mean Per Joint Position Error loss function is proposed to assign different weights to each joint based on the importance in human biomechanics. Extensive evaluations demonstrate that our approach significantly outperforms state-of-the-art methods on the datasets such as H3.6M, CMU-Mocap, and 3DPW. Furthermore, the visual result confirms that our Motion Chain Learning Framework can reduce errors in end joints while working well for the other joints.

Keywords: Human motion prediction · Joint motion chain · Local feature learning · MCLF

1 Introduction

Human motion prediction (HMP) aims to forecast future body poses based on the historical body poses during motion [10]. It is an important topic in the fields of computer graphics and vision because it benefits numerous other applications such as autonomous driving [4], pedestrian tracking [8,27], and more [21,22].

Supplementary Information The online version contains supplementary material available at https://doi.org/10.1007/978-3-031-50075-6_4.

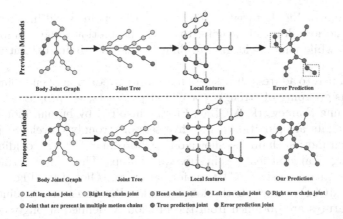

Fig. 1. Prediction of shot put motion. Top: The previous work, Liu et al. [15] only involved a simple partitioning of the human body joints. For a single joint, its divided set does not cover all joints that have strong correlations with that single joint (such as the pink waist joint and purple hand joint). **Bottom:** Our method was inspired by the principles of human biomechanics. To capture local features, we divided all the joints of the human body into five sets based on joint motion chains. Each set in the joint tree represents a complete path from a leaf node to the root node.

Predicting human posture requires extracting global and local features of joints [7]. There exist both strong and weak correlations between the joints. Global features of the joints capture the relationships among all the joints [5]. Local features of the joints primarily focus on the relationships between strongly correlated joints [26]. To extract the local features, There are two methods proposed for partitioning strongly correlated joint sets. Liu et al. divided all human joints into five limbs as shown on the top of Fig. 1 and placed the joints belonging to the same limb in adjacent positions in the model's input [15]. Then, they used CNN to extract local features. Li et al. divided the body into upper and lower parts to extract local features [14].

However, Due to incorrect partitioning of strongly correlated joint sets, existing methods ignore parts of strongly correlated joint pairs. For example, when considering the shot put motion, it is the pink waist joint shown on the top of Fig. 1 that drives the motion of the purple hand joint to throw the shot put. It can be observed that the pink waist joint and the purple hand joint exhibit a strong correlation during the motion. As shown on the top of Fig. 1, Liu et al. did not group the pink waist joint and purple hand joint together when extracting local features [15]. Incorrect grouping of strongly correlated joint sets led to inaccurate predictions, especially evident in the prediction errors of the end joints such as hands and feet, as indicated by the red box in Fig. 1.

Fortunately, we investigated the underlying reasons behind the prediction errors of the end joints from human biomechanics [2]. Human biomechanics argues that the waist is considered the core of human motion [17]. The force generated by the waist is transmitted through the joint motion chain, as shown on the bottom of Fig. 1, to every joint along the chain, resulting in the over-all human motion. Joints belonging to the same motion chain exhibit strong correlations, while joints belonging to different motion chains exhibit weak correlations [1].

In this paper, to address the issue of inaccurate prediction of end joints caused by erroneous grouping of strongly correlated joint sets, we propose the Motion Chain Learning Framework (MCLF). Firstly, inspired by human biomechanics, All human joints are partitioned into five sets of strongly correlated joint sets based on their motion chains, as shown on the bottom of Fig. 1, providing a basis for extracting local joint features in subsequent steps. Then, after extracting the temporal information using DCT transformation, the Global-local Feature block (GLCB) in MCLF extracts both global and local features of the joints, where the local features are obtained from the previously defined strongly correlated joint sets. The weakly correlated joint pairs also play a role in motion prediction, Therefore, global features are still extracted to capture the overall interactions of each joint with the entire set of human joints, including both strong and weak correlations. Finally, a novel loss function called Weights-Added Mean Per Joint Position Error (WA-MPJPE) is proposed, which assigns different weights to each joint based on its importance in human biomechanics. The weight of each joint is closely related to its floor in the human joint tree, where joints closer to the root node have higher importance and larger weights.

Our contributions are as follows: (1) A novel method for grouping strongly correlated joints is proposed to extract more effective local features of joints. The joints are divided into different sets based on their motion chains. (2) A novel motion prediction model named MCLF is proposed to solve the problem of inaccurate prediction in end joints caused by erroneous grouping of strongly correlated joint sets. (3) A novel loss function named WA-MPJPE is proposed to assign different weights to each joint. Extensive evaluations demonstrate that our approach significantly outperforms state-of-the-art methods on the datasets. Furthermore, the visualization confirms that our MCLF can reduce errors in end joints while working well for the other joints.

2   Related Works

Human Motion Prediction. HMP is an important topic in the fields of computer graphics and computer vision because it benefits numerous other applications such as autonomous driving, human-computer interaction, and more. Recently, many deep learning-based methods have been proposed and achieved significant results. Early approaches in HMP employed recurrent neural networks [9,12,16] However, RNNs suffer from the issue of error accumulation as the predictions progress. To address this, other works applied CNNs to address HMP by treating pose sequences as images and using 2D convolutions for processing [15,20,24] More recently, there has been an increasing use of GCNs for HMP, where the human body joints are treated as a graph structure [6,19].

Extracting Local Features in HMP. In previous works, researchers have already recognized the importance of extracting local features from joints. Wang

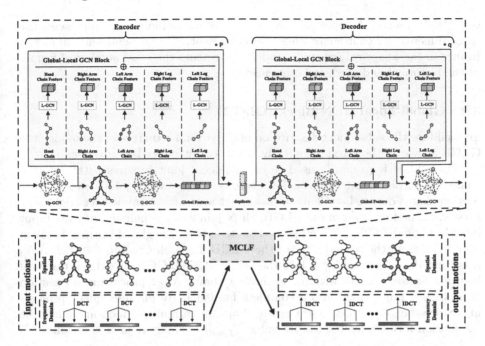

Fig. 2. Network architecture. The network employs DCT and IDCT for frequency and spatial domain transformations, respectively. Motion prediction is performed using MCLF, which addresses the issue of inaccurate prediction of end joints.

et al. [25] divided the human body into five trunks and used fully connected networks for feature encoding. They extracted local joint relationship features, aggregated and combined them into upper and lower body regions, and continued to extract more comprehensive local joint relationship features. Liu et al. [15] arranged the joints belonging to the same trunk in adjacent positions in the model's input. This arrangement allows CNN to capture local interaction relationships initially during convolution. Li et al. [14] utilized their proposed graph scattering technique to construct adaptive graph scatterings on different body parts. They fused the decomposed features based on the inferred spectral importance and the interaction among body parts. However, the above-mentioned methods did not consider all strongly correlated joint pairs. In this paper, we extract local features by using strong-correlation joint sets obtained through motion chain partitioning.

3   Methodology

3.1   Problem Formulation

The problem of human motion prediction can be described as predicting future sequence $X_{T_p+1:T_f}$ based on a given historical sequence $X_{1:T_p} = [x_1, x_2, \cdots, x_{T_p}]$

$\in \mathbb{R}^{N*D_p*T_p}$, where N represents the number of human joints, D_p represents the three-dimensional coordinate values for each joint, T_p represents the number of frames in the historical sequence, and T_f represents the total number of frames in the historical and predicted sequences.

3.2 Global-Local GCN Block (GLGB)

To facilitate the subsequent description of the overall structure of the model, the GLGB shown in the green area of Fig. 2 will be introduced in advance.

The GLGB is primarily used to extract local joint features within motion chains and global joint features. Let there be a total of N joint nodes, with 5 motion chains denoted as Chain = [head, left arm, right arm, left leg, right leg]. Firstly, in the first layer of the GLGB, all N joints of the human body are input into the Global-GCN (G-GCN) as a whole to extract the global features between joints. Then, in the second layer of the GLGB, for each Chain[i], $i \in [1, 2, ..., 5]$, it is treated as a set and input into the Local-GCN (L-GCN) to extract the local features between joints within the motion chain. After processing all motion chains, they are merged into a complete human body for subsequent processing. Since the gray joints shown in Fig. 2 appear in multiple motion chains, the calculation formula for the feature value F_{finall} of the gray joint is as follows:

$$F_{finall} = \frac{\sum_{i=1}^{M} S_i * F_i}{\sum_{i=1}^{M} S_i}, \tag{1}$$

where M represents the number of motion chains, in this paper, M is set to 5. F_i represents the feature value of the gray joint in the i-th motion chain, and S_i is calculated as follows:

$$S_i = \begin{cases} 1 & \text{if the gray joint is in the i-th motion chain} \\ 0 & \text{else} . \end{cases} \tag{2}$$

3.3 Model Architecture

As shown in Fig. 2, First, the Discrete Cosine Transform (DCT) is used to encode the temporal features of the input and transform the input from the spatial domain to the frequency domain. Then, MCLF is used to perform motion prediction in the frequency domain. Finally, the inverse Discrete Cosine Transform (IDCT) is applied to obtain the predicted human body pose represented in coordinate form. The details of our full method are described as follows:

Step 1: Discrete Cosine Transform. Our model also utilizes the DCT transform to encode temporal information [19]. To utilize the DCT, the original motion prediction problem is transformed from predicting future sequence $X^{pre}_{T_p+1:T_f}$ based on a historical sequence $X^{his}_{1:T_p}$ to predicting the DCT coefficients of the future sequence based on the DCT coefficients of the observed sequence. To achieve this, we replicate the last frame X_{T_p} of the historical sequence $T_f - T_P$ times, resulting in a sequence $X^{his}_{1:T_f}$ of length T_f. Then, we compute its DCT coefficients to predict the real sequence $X_{1:T_f}^{pre}$. We represent the trajectory of the K-th joint along T_f frames of the input sequence as $X_{k,1:T_f}^{his} = (x_{k,1}, x_{k,2}, \ldots, x_{k,T_f})$. After the DCT, our input pose sequence $X_{1:T_f}^{his}$ is transformed into $C_{1:T_f}^{his} = [c_1, \ldots, c_{T_f}] \in \mathbb{R}^{N \times D_p \times T_f}$. After the DCT transformation, MCLF is utilized to perform motion prediction in the frequency domain. From a macro perspective, MCLF can be seen as an encoder-decoder network.

Step 2: Encoder. The encoder consists of an Up-GCN and multiple GLGBs. The Up-GCN is primarily used for feature dimensionality expansion, mapping from history pose space $C_{1:T_f}^{his} \in \mathbb{R}^{N*D_p*T_f}$ to feature space $C_{1:T_f}^{En} \in \mathbb{R}^{N*F_p*T_f}$. The GLGB employs residual connections and does not perform dimensionality reduction or expansion on the joint features. After encoding the feature information with the encoder, the feature space has a dimension of $C_{1:T_f}^{En} \in \mathbb{R}^{N*F_p*T_f}$.

Step 3: Decoder. We also use the duplicate operator to replicate the input tensor along the time dimension, mapping the feature space from $C_{1:T_f}^{En} \in \mathbb{R}^{N*F_p*T_f}$ to $C_{1:T_f}^{De} \in \mathbb{R}^{N*F_p*2T_f}$, which serves as the input to the decoder [18]. This increases the model parameters of the decoder and improves the prediction accuracy. Subsequently, multiple GLGBs are used to decode the feature space, and finally, the Down-GCN is applied to reduce the dimensionality of the data, mapping from the feature space $C_{1:T_f}^{De} \in \mathbb{R}^{N*F_p*2T_f}$ to predicted pose space $C_{1:T_f}^{pre} \in \mathbb{R}^{N*D_p*2T_f}$. Due to the usage of the duplicate operator, we take the data from the last T_f frames as the result. After decoding, The predicted pose space $C_{1:T_f}^{pre}$ has a dimension of $\mathbb{R}^{N*D_p*T_f}$.

Step 4: Inverse Discrete Cosine Transform. The predicted results obtained from MCLF in the frequency domain, denoted as $C_{1:T_f}^{pre}$, need to be transformed back to the spatial domain using the inverse discrete cosine transform (IDCT). For $C_{1:T_f}^{pre}$, we represent the trajectory of the k-th joint along T_f frames of the predicted pose space as $C_{k,1:T_f}^{pre} = (c_{k,1}, c_{k,2}, \ldots, c_{k,T_f})$. After the IDCT, the predicted pose space $C_{1:T_f}^{pre}$ in the frequency domain is transformed into the final predicted pose space $X_{1:T_f}^{pre}$ in the spatial domain.

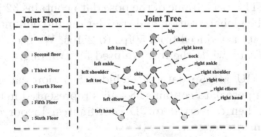

Fig. 3. On the left side, different colors are assigned to joint nodes at different floors in the joint tree. On the right side, the positions of different joint nodes in the human body joint tree are shown.

3.4   Loss Function

Previously, the commonly used method employed Mean Per Joint Position Error (MPJPE) as the loss function for the model:

$$\ell_{MPJPE} = \frac{\sum_{t=1}^{T_f} \sum_{n=1}^{N} \|\hat{\mathbf{p}}_{n,t} - \mathbf{p}_{n,t}\|^2}{N * T_f}, \tag{3}$$

where N represents the number of joints, T_f represents the total number of frames, $\hat{\mathbf{p}}_{n,t} \in \mathbb{R}^3$ represents the predicted position of the n-th joint in frame t, and $\mathbf{p}_{n,t}$ represents the corresponding ground truth.

However, this approach does not align with the biomechanical principles of human motion, as the importance of each joint in motion varies. As shown in Fig. 3, the joints closer to the root joint (i.e., the joints closer to the starting point of the kinematic chain) play a more significant role in transmitting forces, indicating their higher importance. Inspired by human biomechanics, we propose a new loss function named Weights-Added Mean Per Joint Position Error (WA-MPJPE) that considers the varying importance of different joints in motion:

$$\ell_{WA-MPJPE} = \frac{\sum_{t=1}^{T_f} \sum_{n=1}^{N} (F + 1 - floor(\hat{\mathbf{p}}_{n,t})) * \|\hat{\mathbf{p}}_{n,t} - \mathbf{p}_{n,t}\|^2}{(\sum_{f=1}^{F} sum(f) * (F + 1 - f)) * N * T_f}, \tag{4}$$

where F represents the maximum floor of the joint tree, as depicted in Fig. 3. The function $floor()$ retrieves the floor of a joint, and $sum()$ retrieves the number of nodes corresponding to different floors. $(F + 1 - floor(\hat{\mathbf{p}}_{n,t}))$ is a weighting term we introduce to quantify the importance of a joint node $\hat{\mathbf{p}}_{n,t}$ in human motion.

4   Experiments

4.1   Datasets and Implementation Details

Human3.6M [11]. Human3.6M consists of 15 action categories performed by 7 actors (S1, S5-S9, S11). Each frame of the pose data contains 32 joints. Similar to [6,19], we remove the global rotation and translation and eliminate 10 redundant joints. The frame rate is reduced from 50fps to 25fps. We use S5 and S11 as the test and validation sets, while the rest are used for training.

CMU Mocap. CMU Mocap dataset includes 8 action categories, and each frame of the human pose data contains 38 joints represented in exponential map format, which are then converted to 3D coordinates. In our experiments, we retain 25 joints from the dataset.

3DPW [23]. 3DPW dataset captures human poses from indoor and outdoor scenes. Each pose consists of 26 joints, and we use 23 joints from the dataset.

Implementation Details. To maintain consistency with other methods such as [6,15,19], we use MPJPE as the evaluation metric in our experiments. When

Table 1. Comparisons of short-term prediction on Human3.6M. Results at 80 ms, 160 ms, 320 ms, and 400 ms in the future are shown. The best results are highlighted in bold

scenarios	walking				discussion				directions				phoning				average			
millisecond	80	160	320	400	80	160	320	400	80	160	320	400	80	160	320	400	80	160	320	400
LTD [19]	8.9	15.7	29.2	33.4	9.8	22.1	39.6	44.1	12.6	24.4	48.2	58.4	11.5	20.2	37.9	43.2	12.1	25.0	51.0	61.3
LPJP [3]	7.9	14.5	29.1	34.5	8.3	21.7	43.9	48.0	11.1	22.7	48.0	58.4	10.8	19.6	37.6	46.8	10.7	23.8	50.0	60.2
TraCNN [15]	8.2	14.9	30.0	35.4	7.5	20.0	41.3	47.8	9.7	22.3	50.2	61.7	10.7	18.8	37.0	43.1	10.2	23.2	49.3	59.7
MSR [6]	8.7	15.5	28.4	32.4	9.3	22.1	40.5	45.5	11.4	21.9	**45.8**	56.1	11.8	20.6	37.5	41.7	11.3	24.3	49.9	60.1
Ours	**7.1**	**14.3**	**23.7**	**27.6**	**7.1**	**19.2**	**37.1**	**45.5**	**9.6**	**21.8**	47.6	**55.8**	**10.2**	**18.5**	**33.5**	**39.4**	**9.7**	**22.4**	**47.3**	**58.4**

Table 2. Comparisons of long-term prediction on Human3.6M. The best results are highlighted in bold.

scenarios	walking		eating		smoking		discussion		greeting		phoning		posing		average	
millisecond	560	1000	560	1000	560	1000	560	1000	560	1000	560	1000	560	1000	560	1000
convS2S [13]	59.2	71.3	66.5	85.4	42.0	67.9	84.1	116.9	–	–	–	–	–	–	–	–
LTD [19]	42.2	51.6	57.1	69.5	32.5	60.7	70.5	99.6	95.8	89.9	62.6	113.8	107.2	211.8	78.9	112.6
TraCNN [15]	37.9	46.4	59.2	71.5	32.7	58.7	75.4	103	91.4	**84.3**	62.3	**113.5**	111.6	210.9	77.7	110.6
MSR [6]	42.1	43.5	57.0	71.5	35.2	62.5	75.4	113.5	100.1	95.1	63.7	113.9	103.0	219.9	78.7	115.7
Ours	**35.5**	**43.3**	**55.9**	**69.4**	**32.3**	**58.1**	**69.3**	**99.1**	**90.4**	86.7	**61.8**	115.1	**102.9**	**209.7**	**75.5**	**110.4**

using Human3.6M and CMU Mocap datasets, the input length is 10 frames, and the output length is 25 frames. For the 3DPW dataset, the input length is 10 frames, and the output length is 30 frames. Due to the utilization of 35 frames and 40 frames respectively, the DCT coefficients were set accordingly to 35 and 40 for lossless reconstruction. The model is trained for a total of 60 epochs with a batch size of 32. The learning rate is set to 0.0005 with a decay of 0.96 per epoch. The encoder comprises 4 GLGBs, while the decoder consists of 8 GLGBs. The training is conducted on an Intel i9-10900K CPU and NVIDIA RTX 3090 GPU.

Table 3. prediction on CMU-Mocap

millisecond	80	160	320	400	1000
LTD [19]	9.3	17.1	33.0	40.9	86.2
TraCNN [15]	8.3	15.6	33.4	43.1	92.8
MSR [6]	8.1	15.2	30.6	38.6	**83.0**
Ours	**7.5**	**14.1**	**27.8**	**36.0**	83.6

Table 4. prediction on 3DPW

millisecond	200	400	600	800	1000
LTD [19]	35.6	67.8	90.6	106.9	117.8
TraCNN [15]	30.0	59.7	85.3	**99.0**	107.7
MSR [6]	37.8	71.3	93.9	110.8	121.5
Ours	**27.8**	**57.7**	**84.9**	99.5	**103.7**

4.2 Results

We compare our method with convS2S [13], LTD [19], LPJP [3], TraCNN [15], and MSR [6] methods. We present the comparison results of our method and these methods on three datasets for short-term predictions (less than 400 ms) and long-term predictions (400 ms to 1000 ms).

Result on H3.6M. Table 1 shows the quantitative comparison of our method with state-of-the-art methods on the Human 3.6M dataset for short-term prediction. Table 2 shows the quantitative comparison of our method with state-

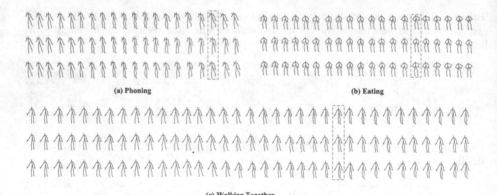

(a) Phoning   (b) Eating

(c) Walking Together

Fig. 4. Visualization on the Human3.6M dataset. From top to bottom, we show the ground truth, the predictions of TraCNN [15], and our method.

of-the-art methods on the Human 3.6M dataset for long-term prediction. Scenario "average" refers to the average error across all 15 actions. Due to space constraints, we only present experimental results for a subset of actions in the paper. The complete experimental results for all actions are provided in the supplementary materials. It can be observed that our method outperforms previous state-of-the-art methods in most cases in terms of the total of 15 motions, 6-time steps, and average motion error. This demonstrates the effectiveness and feasibility of incorporating knowledge from human biomechanics, such as motion force generation and joint motion chains, in motion prediction.

Figure 4 illustrates the visual results of our method compared to SOTA methods for motion prediction. From top to bottom, the images show the ground truth, TraCNN [15], and our method. Figure 4 represents both short-term (i.e., 10 frames) and long-term prediction (i.e., 25 frames). In Fig. 4(a), as indicated by the red circle, our method successfully predicts the action of bending the leg in the "phoning" motion, which is not predicted by TraCNN. Similarly, in Fig. 4(b), as indicated by the red circle, the ground truth shows only one hand near the waist, while the other method predicts both hands near the waist, whereas our method successfully predicts the presence of only one hand near the waist. This demonstrates that our approach can reduce errors in end joints while working well for the other joints. The reason why our method achieves more accurate predictions compared to other approaches is that our approach for extracting local joint features aligns with biomechanics. Partitioning strongly correlated joint sets based on human body joint motion chains allows us to consider all strongly correlated joint pairs, enabling the extraction of powerful local features. The visualizations of the results in Fig. 4 shows that our method produces pose predictions that are closer to the ground truth.

Results on CMU Mocap and 3DPW. Table 3 and Table 4 show the average prediction errors of our method and other methods for short-term and long-term predictions, respectively. It can be observed that our method achieves better results compared to other methods.

Table 5. Ablation experiments were conducted on the Human3.6m dataset, and the average values were taken as the comparison results.

exp	80 ms	160 ms	320 ms	400 ms	560 ms	1000 ms	average
1	10.89	23.67	48.74	59.15	77.27	112.98	55.45
2	10.20	23.15	47.97	58.93	77.17	111.16	54.76
3	9.89	22.78	47.53	58.61	76.21	110.93	54.33
4	9.81	22.98	47.41	58.75	76.23	110.69	54.31
5	9.85	22.99	47.49	58.81	76.25	111.01	54.40
6	**9.74**	**22.38**	**47.28**	**58.43**	**75.53**	**110.42**	**53.96**

4.3 Ablation Study

Through ablation experiments, we investigated the impact of several key components of our proposed method on the H3.6M dataset, aiming to gain a deeper understanding of our approach.

Specifically, as shown in Table 5. To demonstrate the effectiveness of our method, we conducted five new designs: exp 1: one G-GCN layer + one G-GCN layer GLGB, exp 2: one L-GCN layer + one L-GCN layer GLGB, exp 3: one G-GCN layer + one TraCNN [15]-style L-GCN layer GLGB, exp 4: using MPJPE as the loss function instead of our WA-MPJPE, and exp 5: using WA-MPLPE but higher-floor nodes are assigned higher weights.

Effectiveness of Global-Local GCN Block. As shown in Table 5, exp 6 represents our complete method. We designed three ablation experiments to demonstrate the effectiveness of the GLGB. **1) exp 1:** We replaced the original structure of the GLGB, which consists of one layer for extracting global features and one layer for extracting local features, with two layers dedicated to extracting global features. The average prediction error increased from 53.96 to 55.45. This significant performance drop indicates the importance of local features for motion prediction. **2) exp 2:** We replaced the original structure of the GLGB with two layers solely focused on extracting local features. The average prediction error increased to 54.76, demonstrating that solely considering local features is also unreasonable and that global features need to be taken into account. Moreover, the performance drop in exp 2 was lower compared to exp 1, further supporting the notion that local features are more crucial for motion prediction than global features. **3) exp 3:** We replaced our proposed method of dividing the strong correlation joints into sets based on motion chains with the traditional partitioning method shown on the top of Fig. 1. The average prediction error increased to 54.33, confirming the advancement of our partitioning approach, which considers all strongly correlated joint pairs.

Through these three ablation experiments, we can first demonstrate the rationality of partitioning joints based on human body joint motion chains. It helps the model learn better local features, leading to more accurate motion predictions. Secondly, it validates the rationality of our model structure, where both local and global features are useful for human motion prediction, with local features being more crucial.

Effectiveness of WA-MPJPE. We designed two ablation experiments to demonstrate the effectiveness of WA-MPJPE. **1) exp 4:** We replaced our proposed WA-MPJPE with the traditional MPJPE loss. The average prediction error increased to 54.31, demonstrating the effectiveness of assigning weights to joints based on their importance when calculating the loss function. **2) exp 5:** In WA-MPJPE, higher weights are assigned to more important joints, which correspond to lower floor levels in the joint tree. We modified the weight assignment to prioritize joints with higher floor levels. The average prediction error increased to 54.40, even surpassing the performance degradation observed in exp 4 with the MPJPE (assigning equal weights to each joint). This confirms the rationality of our weight assignment approach.

Through these two ablation experiments, we demonstrated the effectiveness of our designed WA-MPJPE. On one hand, joints that are more critical for human motion should be assigned larger weights. On the other hand, joints closer to the root node play a more significant role in the overall transmission of forces during human motion and should be assigned larger weights.

5   Conclusion and Future Work

In this work, a motion chain learning framework is proposed to address the issue of inaccurate prediction of end joints caused by incorrect partitioning of strongly correlated joint sets. Inspired by human biomechanics, all human joints are partitioned into five sets of strongly correlated joint sets based on their motion chains. Then, GCN is utilized to extract local features for each joint within these sets. The extracted local features, along with the global features, are used together for motion prediction. Experimental results on multiple datasets demonstrate the effectiveness of our proposed method.

It can be observed that our model performs well in short-term predictions but has some limitations in long-term predictions. Long-term predictions rely more on distant observation frames. Therefore, in future work, we can increase the computational weight of distant observation frames to enhance the accuracy of long-term predictions.

Acknowledgements. This work was supported in part by Natural Science Foundation Project of CQ (No. CSTC2021JCYJ-MAXMX0062), National Natural Science Foundation of China (No. 62002121 and 62072183), Shanghai Science and Technology Commission (No. 21511100700, 22511104600), the Open Project Program of the State Key Lab of CAD&CG (No. A2203), Zhejiang University.

References

1. Arus, E.: Biomechanics of Human Motion: Applications in the Martial Arts. CRC Press, Boca Raton (2012)
2. Bartlett, R.: Introduction to Sports Biomechanics: Analysing Human Movement Patterns. Routledge (2014)

3. Cai, Y., et al.: Learning progressive joint propagation for human motion prediction. In: Vedaldi, A., Bischof, H., Brox, T., Frahm, J.-M. (eds.) ECCV 2020, Part VII. LNCS, vol. 12352, pp. 226–242. Springer, Cham (2020). https://doi.org/10.1007/978-3-030-58571-6_14

4. Chen, S., Liu, B., Feng, C., Vallespi-Gonzalez, C., Wellington, C.: 3D point cloud processing and learning for autonomous driving: impacting map creation, localization, and perception. IEEE Signal Process. Mag. **38**(1), 68–86 (2020)

5. Cui, Q., Sun, H., Yang, F.: Learning dynamic relationships for 3D human motion prediction. In: Proceedings of the IEEE/CVF Conference on Computer Vision and Pattern Recognition, pp. 6519–6527 (2020)

6. Dang, L., Nie, Y., Long, C., Zhang, Q., Li, G.: MSR-GCN: multi-scale residual graph convolution networks for human motion prediction. In: Proceedings of the IEEE/CVF International Conference on Computer Vision, pp. 11467–11476 (2021)

7. Ding, P., Yin, J.: Towards more realistic human motion prediction with attention to motion coordination. IEEE Trans. Circuits Syst. Video Technol. **32**(9), 5846–5858 (2022)

8. Fan, C., Zhang, R., Ming, Y.: MP-LN: motion state prediction and localization network for visual object tracking. Vis. Comput. 1–16 (2021)

9. Fragkiadaki, K., Levine, S., Felsen, P., Malik, J.: Recurrent network models for human dynamics. In: Proceedings of the IEEE International Conference on Computer Vision, pp. 4346–4354 (2015)

10. Gui, L.Y., Wang, Y.X., Ramanan, D., Moura, J.M.: Few-shot human motion prediction via meta-learning. In: Proceedings of the European Conference on Computer Vision (ECCV), pp. 432–450 (2018)

11. Ionescu, C., Papava, D., Olaru, V., Sminchisescu, C.: Human3. 6M: large scale datasets and predictive methods for 3D human sensing in natural environments. IEEE Trans. Pattern Anal. Mach. Intell. **36**(7), 1325–1339 (2013)

12. Jain, A., Zamir, A.R., Savarese, S., Saxena, A.: Structural-RNN: deep learning on spatio-temporal graphs. In: Proceedings of the IEEE Conference on Computer Vision and Pattern Recognition, pp. 5308–5317 (2016)

13. Li, C., Zhang, Z., Lee, W.S., Lee, G.H.: Convolutional sequence to sequence model for human dynamics. In: Proceedings of the IEEE Conference on Computer Vision and Pattern Recognition, pp. 5226–5234 (2018)

14. Li, M., Chen, S., Zhang, Z., Xie, L., Tian, Q., Zhang, Y.: Skeleton-parted graph scattering networks for 3D human motion prediction. In: Avidan, S., Brostow, G., Cissé, M., Farinella, G.M., Hassner, T. (eds.) ECCV 2022, Part VI. LNCS, vol. 13666, pp. 18–36. Springer, Cham (2022). https://doi.org/10.1007/978-3-031-20068-7_2

15. Liu, X., Yin, J., Liu, J., Ding, P., Liu, J., Liu, H.: TrajectoryCNN: a new spatio-temporal feature learning network for human motion prediction. IEEE Trans. Circuits Syst. Video Technol. **31**(6), 2133–2146 (2020)

16. Liu, Z., et al.: Towards natural and accurate future motion prediction of humans and animals. In: Proceedings of the IEEE/CVF Conference on Computer Vision and Pattern Recognition, pp. 10004–10012 (2019)

17. Lu, T.W., Chang, C.F.: Biomechanics of human movement and its clinical applications. Kaohsiung J. Med. Sci. **28**, S13–S25 (2012)

18. Ma, T., Nie, Y., Long, C., Zhang, Q., Li, G.: Progressively generating better initial guesses towards next stages for high-quality human motion prediction. In: Proceedings of the IEEE/CVF Conference on Computer Vision and Pattern Recognition, pp. 6437–6446 (2022)

19. Mao, W., Liu, M., Salzmann, M., Li, H.: Learning trajectory dependencies for human motion prediction. In: Proceedings of the IEEE/CVF International Conference on Computer Vision, pp. 9489–9497 (2019)
20. Pavllo, D., Feichtenhofer, C., Auli, M., Grangier, D.: Modeling human motion with quaternion-based neural networks. Int. J. Comput. Vision **128**, 855–872 (2020)
21. Qin, Y., Chi, X., Sheng, B., Lau, R.W.: GuideRender: large-scale scene navigation based on multi-modal view frustum movement prediction. Vis. Comput. 1–11 (2023)
22. Song, S., Chau, L.P., Lin, Z.: Portrait matting using an attention-based memory network. Vis. Comput. 1–14 (2023)
23. Von Marcard, T., Henschel, R., Black, M.J., Rosenhahn, B., Pons-Moll, G.: Recovering accurate 3D human pose in the wild using IMUs and a moving camera. In: Proceedings of the European Conference on Computer Vision (ECCV), pp. 601–617 (2018)
24. Vukotić, V., Pintea, S.-L., Raymond, C., Gravier, G., van Gemert, J.C.: One-step time-dependent future video frame prediction with a convolutional encoder-decoder neural network. In: Battiato, S., Gallo, G., Schettini, R., Stanco, F. (eds.) ICIAP 2017, Part I. LNCS, vol. 10484, pp. 140–151. Springer, Cham (2017). https://doi.org/10.1007/978-3-319-68560-1_13
25. Wang, H., Ho, E.S., Shum, H.P., Zhu, Z.: Spatio-temporal manifold learning for human motions via long-horizon modeling. IEEE Trans. Visual Comput. Graphics **27**(1), 216–227 (2019)
26. Yan, S., Xiong, Y., Lin, D.: Spatial temporal graph convolutional networks for skeleton-based action recognition. In: Proceedings of the AAAI Conference on Artificial Intelligence, vol. 32 (2018)
27. Zhang, T., Cao, Y., Zhang, L., Li, X.: Efficient feature fusion network based on center and scale prediction for pedestrian detection. Vis. Comput. **39**(9), 3865–3872 (2023)

Hand Movement Recognition and Analysis Based on Deep Learning in Classical Hand Dance Videos

Xingquan Cai, Qingtao Lu, Fajian Li, Shike Liu, and Yan Hu$^{(\boxtimes)}$

North China University of Technology, Beijing 100144, China
huyan0413@126.com

Abstract. Hand movement recognition is one of hot research topics in the field of computer vision, which has received extensive research interests. However, current classical hand dance movement recognition has high computational complexity and low accuracy. To address these problems, we present a classical hand dance movement recognition and analysis method based on deep learning. Firstly, our method extracts the key frames from the input classical hand dance video by using an inter frame difference method. Secondly, we use a method based on stacked hourglass network to estimate the 2D hand poses of key frames. Thirdly, a network named HandLinearNet with spatial and channel attention mechanisms is constructed for 3D hand pose estimation. Finally, our method uses ConvLSTM for classical hand dance movement recognition, and outputs corresponding classical hand dance movements. The method can recognize 12 basic classical hand dance movements, where users can better analyze and study classical hand dance.

Keywords: Classical hand dance · Hand movement recognition · Stacked hourglass network · Attention mechanisms

1 Introduction

The basic movements in Chinese classical dances are charming and elegant. In classical dance performances, actors often use various hand movements to express emotions or move the plot forward [1]. Hence, many researchers have been studying the movements in classical hand dance in the recent past.

The main contributions of this paper are as follows:

(1) We propose a classical hand dance movement recognition and analysis method based on deep learning to solve the problem of high computational complexity and low accuracy.
(2) We design and develop an easy-to-use classical hand dance movement recognition and analysis system, so that users can recognize, analyze and study classical hand dance movements through videos.

(3) The method we proposed will help users strengthen their cognition and research of Chinese classical hand dance, and also contribute to the popularization and dissemination of Chinese traditional culture, which can enhance the cultural confidence.

The rest of the paper is organized as follows. The related works are introduced in Sect. 2. Section 3 presents the classical hand dance movement recognition and analysis method. The experimental results are introduced in Sect. 4. Finally, Sect. 5 concludes this paper.

2 Related Work

With the development of deep learning, more and more researchers have investigated how to leverage deep learning in the acquisition of 3D hand pose [2,3]. For instance, Zimmermann et al. [4] proposed a three-stage network to estimate hand pose from a single color image. However, this method only uses 2D joint point position to estimate 3D pose, ignoring the color texture features in the color image. Zhang et al. [5] proposed an end-to-end hand pose estimation method to avoid the loss of information in the image. However, it was difficult to directly return the internal parameters, and it was not quite effective. Ge et al. [6] proposed a method for estimating hand pose and generating hand masks using a single RGB image, which used an hourglass network model and linear regression to generate a hand model with better robustness. According to human retina properties, attention mechanisms have been proposed and widely used to improve the performance of models by enhancing key information [7]. Woo et al. [8] proposed convolutional block attention module (CBAM), which injects attention maps along two independent dimensions of channel and spatial of feature maps, improving the representational ability of CNNs [9]. Traditional gesture recognition methods have low classification accuracy, slow speed and poor stability [10]. Koller et al. [11] combined 2DCNN with traditional gesture recognition methods and achieved good results, but this method ignored temporal and spatial information. Pigou et al. [12] proposed a dynamic gesture recognition model using CNN to extract spatial features of dynamic gestures and then uses bidirectional LSTM to extract global spatio-temporal features after dimensionality reduction. As a variant of LSTM, ConvLSTM has better spatio-temporal feature extraction ability than LSTM, which can preserve spatial features while extracting temporal features of image sequences [13]. Peng et al. proposed a new gesture recognition method based on feature fusion network and ConvLSTM [14] with high recognition accuracy.

Based on the above analysis, we first extract the key frames of classical hand dance video by inter frame difference method, then use the 2D hand pose estimation algorithm based on hourglass network to detect 2D joint points, and then integrate attention mechanism to construct HandLinearNet network model to estimate 3D hand pose, and finally use ConvLSTM to realize classical hand dance movement recognition and analysis.

3   Method

We first input classical hand dance video and extract key frame images using an inter-frame difference method. Then our method uses an hourglass network to estimate 2D pose of the key frame images. After that, our method constructs a HandLinearNet network which is fused with attention mechanism for 3D pose estimation. Finally, our method uses a ConvLSTM network to recognize and analyze the estimated hand pose for classical hand dance movements, which allows users to better understand Chinese classical hand dance.

3.1   Key Frame Extraction

Our method adopts the inter frame difference method to extract key frames in classical hand dance videos. Specifically, our method first reads the video, then calculates the difference between each pixel in the current frame and the previous frame. Afterwards, our method adds up the difference of each pixel to get the difference intensity of the two frames, and gets the average inter frame difference intensity based on the total number of pixels. Then, the average inter frame difference intensity time series are smoothed to remove the noise. The frames corresponding to the extreme values after smoothing are the key frames of the video.

3.2   2D Hand Pose Estimation

In this paper, we study the 2D hand pose estimation algorithm based on distribution perception and hourglass network to estimate 2D pose on the key frames of classical hand dance movements.

Heat Map Encoding. Currently, continuous heat map encoding based on two-dimensional Gaussian distribution is commonly used. The two-dimensional Gaussian distribution is shown in Eq. (1):

$$G(x; \mu, \Sigma) = \frac{1}{(2\pi|\Sigma|^{\frac{1}{2}})} \exp\left(-\frac{1}{2}(x - \mu)^T \Sigma^{-1}(x - \mu)\right) \tag{1}$$

where x is the pixel position in the heat map, μ is the mean of the Gaussian kernel corresponding to the key point coordinates, and Σ is the covariance matrix. However, two-dimensional Gaussian distributed heat map encoding does not handle the errors introduced during the image resolution reduction, so we use a heat map encoding method centered on subpixel position to generate an unbiased heat map. Specifically, we use the key point coordinates g = (u, v) in the original image to calculate the key point coordinates g' in the image after the resolution reduction, which is calculated as shown in Eq. (2):

$$g' = \lambda g = (\lambda u, \lambda v) \tag{2}$$

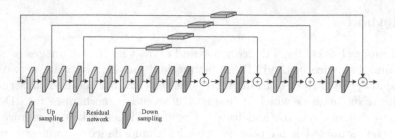

Fig. 1. Hourglass network structure.

where λ is the scaling factor, that is the resolution reduction or enlargement ratio. However, errors can be introduced in the process of quantizing the key point coordinates in the images with reduced resolution, which may lead to errors in the heat map obtained by encoding. In addition, this can have an impact on the training of the subsequent network model, which in turn affects the generated predicted heat map.

To solve this problem, our method places the center of the heat map at the non-quantized position g', where g' is the exact true key point coordinate, and then encodes the heat map by a two-dimensional Gaussian distribution centered on the true key point coordinate g', as shown in Eq. (3):

$$G(x, y; g') = \frac{1}{2\pi\sigma^2} \exp\left(-\frac{(x - u')^2 + (y - v')^2}{2\sigma^2}\right) \quad (3)$$

where (x, y) is the coordinate of the pixel in the heat map and σ is the standard deviation.

Stacked Hourglass Network Construction. A stacked hourglass network model can capture and fuse the information of all scales of the image to obtain the interrelationship between multiple hand skeletal joint points, which can achieve good results in understanding the consistency of each joint point of the hand. We construct the stacked hourglass network model by cascading two hourglass networks, and the structure of the hourglass network is shown in Fig. 1.

Heat Map Decoding. We use a Taylor expansion-based distribution-aware method to relocate the maximum points in the heat map. We first use a two-dimensional Gaussian filter to smooth the heat map and adjust the heat map distribution. Then, we use a second-order Taylor expansion to relocate the maximum points in the heat map to obtain the joint point coordinates. Finally, we map the coordinates to the original resolution image space to obtain the predicted joint point coordinates of the original image.

3.3   3D Hand Pose Estimation

The goal of this section is to construct a 3D hand pose estimation network HandLinearNet. The HandLinearNet network model for 3D pose estimation can be divided into three steps. First, a hand region image and a 2D joint heat map are convolved and cascaded to obtain the feature map. Then, the attention mechanism is introduced for constraint. Finally, the 3D pose in the world coordinate system can be obtained from the estimated translation and rotation in the camera coordinate system.

Fusing RGB Images and Joint Heat Maps. In this section, we use a two-dimensional joint heat map H as the input to the neural network C_{1j}, and a hand region image P is used as the input to the neural network C_{2j} After inputting the data into C, the corresponding data F is obtained. We cascade the output F_{11} of C_{11} and the output F_{21} of C_{21} to obtain F_1, which can estimate the 3D hand joint position in the camera coordinate system. We also cascade the output F_{12} of C_{12} and the output F_{22} of C_{22} to obtain F_2, which can estimate the rotation angle of the camera. The process is shown in the following equations:

$$F_{1j} = H * C_{1j} \tag{4}$$

$$F_{2j} = P * C_{2j} \tag{5}$$

$$F_k = F_{1j} \oplus F_{2j}, k = 1, 2 \tag{6}$$

where F_{ij} is the result of the output of the convolution operation; C_{ij} is the convolution module. $*$ is the convolution operation performed by C_{ij} on the two-dimensional joint heat map H and the hand region image P. $\oplus$ is the cascade operation. This method maximizes the use of spatial and texture information implied in the hand image, which can solve the problem of insufficient context in the process of 3D gesture estimation.

Adding Attention Module. We use an attention mechanism to optimize the 3D hand pose estimation network. When estimating 3D pose based on 2D information, the occlusion of the hand can lead to the loss of information, so we add an attention module of channel and spatial dimensions after the convolutional layer to enhance partial information and suppress the background information to improve the network detection performance.

(1) We construct a channel attention module, as shown in Fig. 2. First, average pooling and maximum pooling are performed on the image features to obtain two $1 \times 1 \times C$ feature descriptions. Then, these descriptions are input to two fully connected layers $FC1$ with shared parameters to reduce the channels to C/r, where r is the channel reduction rate. Then the number of channels is increased to the initial C by the second fully connected layer $FC2$ after the activation using ReLU function. Finally, the output results of the two features are summed and activated using the Sigmoid function to obtain Fc.

(2) Spatial attention module. As shown in Fig. 3, the flow chart of spatial attention module is shown. First, the image features are pooled by maximum pooling and average pooling respectively, and two features with spatial size

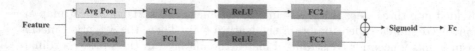

Fig. 2. Channel attention module.

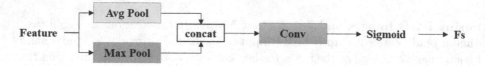

Fig. 3. Spatial attention module.

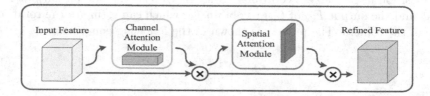

Fig. 4. Structure of attention module.

of $W \times H \times 1$ are generated. Then, the two features are stitched according to channels and passed through a convolution layer. Finally, we use the Sigmoid function for activation to obtain the spatial attention mechanism weight coefficient F_s.

(3) By connecting two attention modules sequentially, a feature map with more hand semantic information and spatial background information can be obtained, which makes the network model more stable and robust, as shown in Fig. 4.

3.4   Classical Hand Dance Movement Recognition

This section describes the process of identifying classical hand dance movements from skeletal sequences. Hand dance movement recognition from skeletal sequence data is challenging, since the same hand movement may vary in speed, shape, duration, and wholeness due to spatial and temporal variation.

Constructing ConvLSTM Model. To fully analyze the skeletal sequence data, we use a convolutional long and short-term memory (ConvLSTM) network to extract the spatio-temporal features of the skeletal sequences. ConvLSTM can process both spatial and temporal data in one network. The internal structure of the ConvLSTM network memory unit is shown in Fig. 5.

The overall framework of classical hand dance movement recognition based on skeletal sequence data is shown in Fig. 6, and the specific steps are as follows.

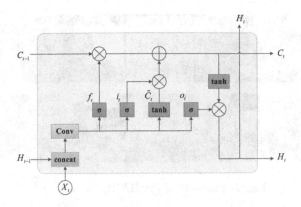

Fig. 5. Schematic diagram of the internal structure of the ConvLSTM network memory unit.

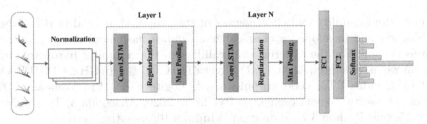

Fig. 6. ConvLSTM model framework diagram.

Step 1. Inputting 3D hand skeletal sequence data. In the proposed framework, the hand dance movement skeletal sequence data obtained from Sect. 3.3 consists of K sets of 3D right-angle coordinate sequences of hand joints, where K is the number of frames of each hand dance movement. In the kth frame, the 3D right-angle coordinates of joint j among the N joints representing the hand is $j_k^n = (x, y, z)$, and N is set to 21. Then, the hand skeletal sequence data are normalized to fit the specific input form of the ConvLSTM network.

Step 2. Extracting spatio-temporal features. After inputting the hand dance movement skeletal sequence, the spatio-temporal features of the hand dance movement skeletal sequence are extracted by several ConvLSTM-based modules. Each module includes a ConvLSTM layer, a regularization layer and a pooling layer.

Step 3. Outputting the classification results. The extracted spatio-temporal features are processed by two fully connected layers and then fed into a softmax classifier to predict the probability distribution of hand dance movement categories.

Fig. 7. Example of FreiHAND dataset.

4   Experimental Results

To verify the feasibility and effectiveness of the proposed method in this paper, we designed and developed a classical hand dance movement recognition and analysis system. For the experimental validation, the computer hardware environment we used is Intel(R) Xeon(R) Silver 4110 CPU @ 2.10 GHz, 64 GB RAM, NVIDIA Quadro RTX 6000 graphics card, Logitech HD Pro Webcam C920 camera. The software environment is PyCharm 2020, Anaconda 3, TensorFlow-GPU1.15, and Python 3.7 running on Windows 10 operating system.

4.1   Dataset Construction

In this paper, we first pre-trained the constructed network using the FreiHAND dataset, and then retrained and fine-tuned the trained network with the classical hand dance movement dataset.

FreiHAND Dataset. FreiHAND is a realistic dataset containing various hand pose joint points and shapes proposed by Zimmermann et al. The current version of the FreiHAND dataset contains 32560 unique training samples and 3960 unique evaluation samples. The training samples contain original RGB images and corresponding labels. To expand the size of the training set, Zimmermann et al. performed background replacement and post-processing on all the original images in the green cloth background to obtain synthetic images with complex backgrounds, resulting in a total training set containing 130240 samples, which is shown in Fig. 7.

Classical Hand Dance Video Dataset. Since there is no open-source classical hand dance dataset, we construct a small classical hand dance movement dataset. The dataset is constructed based on 10 people (5 males and 5 females), and each person shoots 100 video sequences. For these video sequences, each video sequence contains from 3 to 5 randomly different classical hand dance

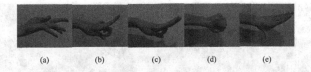

Fig. 8. Some samples of basic hand forms in classical hand dance. (a) Orchid Finger, (b) Single Finger, (c) Sword Finger, (d) Fist, (e) Tiger Palm.

movements. In this paper, we used 12 movements from the basic hand forms of classical hand dance, namely: Orchid Palm, Orchid Finger, Single Finger, Sword Finger, Tiger Palm, Flat Palm, Fist, Flower Finger, Buddha Hand, Open Three Fingers, Bent Three Fingers, and Antler Style. Some samples of basic hand forms in classical hand dance are shown in Fig. 8.

4.2   Experimental Results Visualization

To enable users clearly observe skeleton joint positions, directions, angles and other information in classical hand dance movements, we visualize the obtained 2D poses, 3D poses, and the recognized classical hand dance movements.

Hand Pose Estimation Results. To highlight the positions of key joints in classical hand dance movements, we perform 2D joint point detection on key frame images of classical hand dance based on distribution perception and hourglass network model.

The visualization results of hand pose estimation are shown in Fig. 9 and Fig. 10. The first rows in Fig. 9 and Fig. 10 show the key frame images of split classical hand dance movement. In the second rows, 2D skeletal joint point sequence visualization of classical hand dance movement frame images are displayed. And in the third rows, 3D skeletal joint point sequence visualization of classical hand dance movement frame images are demonstrated.

Classical Hand Dance Movement Recognition and Analysis Results. The sample experimental results are shown in Fig. 11. The first column shows the key frame images of classical hand dance movements, and the second column shows the results of the recognition and analysis of classical hand dance movements. From Fig. 11, it can be seen that the video contains four classical hand dance movements, which are Orchid Finger, Tiger Palm, Sword Finger and Fist. Their types are also analyzed along with the recognition of the classical hand dance movements.

4.3   Evaluation Metrics

In this paper, we use Mean End Point Error (Mean EPE) and Median End Point Error (Median EPE) as the evaluation metrics in the experiment to assess the

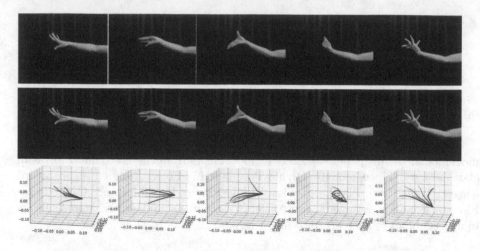

Fig. 9. Visualization of hand pose estimation of user A.

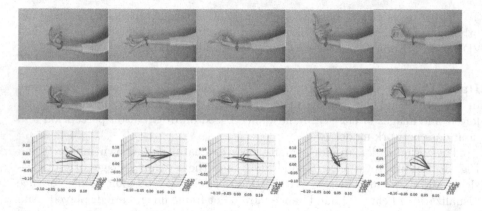

Fig. 10. Visualization of hand pose estimation of user B.

performance of the hand pose estimation method proposed in this paper. The End Point Error (EPE) represents the estimated Euclidean distance between the estimated key point coordinates and the actual value of the coordinates. Mean EPE first calculates the mean value of the end point error of all test samples at each key point, and then calculates the average for all key points. Median EPE first calculates the median of the end point error of all test samples at each key point, and then calculates the average of all key points. The error results before and after retraining and fine-tuning the trained network for the classical hand dance movement dataset are shown in Table 1 and Table 2.

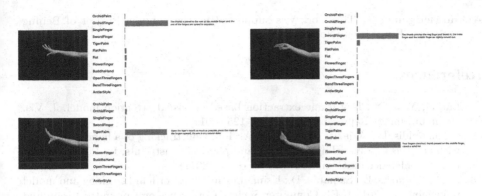

Fig. 11. Visualization of classical hand dance movement recognition and analysis.

Table 1. 2D joint point error results on the classical hand dance dataset.

	Before fine-tuning	After fine-tuning
Mean EPE (pixel)	4.32	3.16
Median EPE (pixel)	3.57	2.33

Table 2. 3D joint point error results on the classical hand dance dataset.

	Before fine-tuning	After fine-tuning
Mean EPE (mm)	16.76	13.84
Median EPE (mm)	14.85	12.74

5   Conclusions

To address the issues of high computational complexity and low accuracy in classical hand dance movement recognition, we propose a deep learning-based classical hand dance movement recognition and analysis method. Firstly, the method reads the input classical hand dance video frame by frame, performs the difference operation between two adjacent frames to extract the key frames of the video by finding the local maximum. Afterwards, the method uses a network model based on distribution perception and stacked hourglass to extract the features of key frame images at different scales. The method inputs the obtained resolution feature maps to the convolutional layer to predict the probability of skeletal joint point to exist on each pixel, and outputs the joint point heat map to get the 2D joint point coordinates. Then, the method fuses the attention mechanisms of both spatial and channel dimensions to construct the HandLinearNet network and estimate the 3D hand pose on the input joint heat map and RGB images to obtain the 3D joint point coordinates. Finally, the method uses the obtained 3D skeletal joint point sequences to perform the recognition and the corresponding analysis of classical hand dance movements using a ConvLSTM network.

Acknowledgements. This work was supported by the Funding Project of Beijing Social Science Foundation (No. 19YTC043).

References

1. Lai, J., Yang, Y.: Key frame extraction based on visual attention model. J. Vis. Commun. Image Represent. **23**(1), 114–125 (2012)
2. Oikonomidis, I., Kyriazis, N., Argyros, A.: Full DoF tracking of a hand interacting with an object by modeling occlusions and physical constraints. In: IEEE International Conference on Computer Vision. IEEE (2011)
3. Lu, S., Metaxas, D., Samaras, D.: Using multiple cues for hand tracking and model refinement. In: 2013 IEEE Computer Society Conference on Computer Vision and Pattern Recognition. IEEE (2013)
4. Zimmermann, C., Brox, T.: Learning to estimate 3D hand pose from single RGB images. In: IEEE International Conference on Computer Vision. IEEE (2017)
5. Zhang, X., Li, Q., Mo, H., Zhang, W.: End-to-end hand mesh recovery from a monocular RGB image. In: 2019 IEEE/CVF International Conference on Computer Vision. IEEE (2019)
6. Ge, L., Ren, Z., Li, Y., Xue, Z.:3D hand shape and pose estimation from a single RGB image. In: IEEE Conference on Computer Vision and Pattern Recognition. IEEE (2019)
7. Cao, Y., Liu, C., Sheng, Y., Huang, Z., Deng, X.: Action recognition model based on 3D graph convolution and attention enhanced. J. Electron. Inf. Technol. **43**(7), 2071–2078 (2021)
8. Woo, S., Park, J., Lee, J.-Y., Kweon, I.S.: CBAM: convolutional block attention module. In: Ferrari, V., Hebert, M., Sminchisescu, C., Weiss, Y. (eds.) ECCV 2018. LNCS, vol. 11211, pp. 3–19. Springer, Cham (2018). https://doi.org/10.1007/978-3-030-01234-2_1
9. Burger, I., Lerasle, F., Infantes, G.: Two-handed gesture recognition and fusion with speech to command a robot. Auton. Robot. **32**(2), 129–147 (2012)
10. Kuremoto, T., Kinoshita, Y., Feng, L., Watanabe, S., Kobayashi, K.: A gesture recognition system with retina-V1 model and one-pass dynamic programming. Neurocomputing **116**(2), 291–300 (2013)
11. Raj, R., Dharan, S., Thomas, S.: Optimal feature selection and classification of Indian classical dance hand gesture dataset. Vis. Comput. **39**(9), 4049–4064 (2023)
12. Ma, J., Lv, Q., Yan, H., Ye, T., Shen, Y., Sun, H.: Color-saliency-aware correlation filters with approximate affine transform for visual tracking. Vis. Comput. **39**(9), 4065–4086 (2023)
13. Bayoudh, K., Knani, R., Hamdaoui, F., Mtibaa, A.: A survey on deep multimodal learning for computer vision: advances, trends, applications, and datasets. Vis. Comput. **38**(8), 2939–2970 (2022)
14. Zeghoud, S., et al.: Real-time spatial normalization for dynamic gesture classification. Vis. Comput. **38**(4), 1345–1357 (2022)

4RATFNet: Four-Dimensional Residual-Attention Improved-Transfer Few-Shot Semantic Segmentation Network for Landslide Detection

Shiya Huang[1], Qiang Li[1(✉)], Jiajun Li[2], and Jinzheng Lu[1]

[1] School of Information Engineering, Southwest University of Science and Technology, Mianyang 621010, Sichuan, China
liqiangsir@swust.edu.cn
[2] School of Environment and Resource, Southwest University of Science and Technology, Mianyang 621010, Sichuan, China

Abstract. Landslides are hazardous and in many cases can cause enormous economic losses and human casualties. The suddenness of landslides makes it difficult to detect landslides quickly and effectively. Therefore, to address the problem of intelligent analysis of geological landslides, we propose a 4RATFNet network for few-shot semantic segmentation detection in the case of insufficient number of labeled landslide images. First, a residual-attention module is designed to fuse channel features and spatial features for residual fusion. Second, improved transfer learning is used to optimize the parameters of the pre-trained network. Third, the network downscales the four-dimensional convolutional kernel into a pair of two-dimensional convolutional kernels. Finally, the few-shot semantic segmentation network is used to extract support image features and complete the landslide detection for the same features in the query image. The experimental results show that the method performs better when tested on Resnet50 backbone and Resnet101 backbone when the sample size of labeled landslide images is insufficient. Compared with traditional semantic segmentation methods, it can obtain better segmentation results and achieve higher mean intersection over union, indicating that our network has obvious advantages and wider applicability.

Keywords: Four-dimensional convolution kernel · Residual-attention mechanism · Improved transfer learning · Few-shot semantic segmentation · Landslide detection

1 Introduction

Landslide is a highly destructive natural disaster and a derivative of many other natural hazards [1]. Broadly speaking, landslides encompass debris flow and rockfalls, which can be very hazardous [2]. Because of the great danger of landslides

B. Sheng et al. (Eds.): CGI 2023, LNCS 14497, pp. 65–77, 2024.
https://doi.org/10.1007/978-3-031-50075-6_6

and the obvious characteristics of landslides, it is of great significance to detect landslides. It allows ground personnel to promptly respond based on the information obtained.

In recent years, scholars have studied landslide detection methods. Traditional approaches involve field investigations using manual surveys and tools. However, such investigations cover a wide range, and considering the significant hazards of landslides, they can lead to personnel losses and wastage of resources. With the continuous development of computer science, various intelligent technologies have been applied to landslide detection. These include methods based on knowledge prior [3] and machine learning [4]. Tian et al. [5] improve the Transformer model using the temporal convolutional network. This model is sensitive to rapid landslide deformations and has high accuracy. Ding et al. [6] establish a landslide probability model to make effective judgments for landslide detection in specific areas and avoid overfitting issues.

Given that the neural networks currently used for landslide detection require landslide datasets of a certain sample size for training, and that there are few publicly available landslide datasets with annotations. Landslide detection is limited by insufficient training samples and long processing time.

Therefore, we use semantic segmentation [7,8] and attention mechanism [9,10] to achieve landslide detection. We design a few-shot semantic segmentation network based on improved residual attention and optimized transfer learning for landslide detection, as shown in Fig. 1. The residual attention module is designed to focus on both the original images and the key regions of the landslide to capture their feature information. An optimized transfer learning is designed to enhance the underlying feature extraction from few-shot datasets. The mean intersection over union (mIoU) [11] and the foreground-background intersection over union (FB-IoU) [12] are used as performance metrics to evaluate the effectiveness of landslide segmentation detection. The two proposed modules further improve the network response speed and landslide segmentation accuracy.

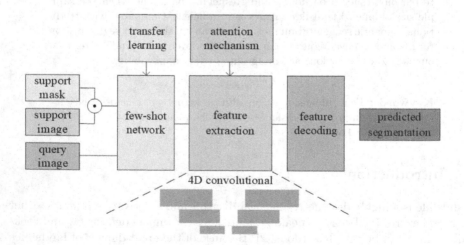

Fig. 1. Structure of 4RATFNet network

2   Related Works

2.1   Few-Shot Semantic Segmentation Network

Few-shot semantic segmentation was first proposed by Shaban et al. [13]. Compared with semantic segmentation based on traditional neural networks, the required datasets are greatly reduced. In the few-shot semantic segmentation network, the support image, support mask image and query image are input in the network that has been trained. And by learning the features of the support image and support mask image, we determine whether there are the same features in the query image and make prediction by mask annotation in the query image. After the few-shot semantic segmentation network was proposed, there have been many more advanced studies for few shots. Zhao et al. [14] achieve the improvement of the performance of the unknown class segmentation by introducing the object module to reduce the interference of the background and to mitigate the overfitting of the network. Min et al. [15] squeeze the network by four-dimensional hyper-correlation and fuse the features at different levels to obtain accurate segmentation results for unknown classes. Fan et al. [16] propose a self-support segmentation network based on the fact that pixels of different objects of the same class are more similar. However, the currently proposed few-shot semantic segmentation networks have not been specifically designed for landslide detection. Landslides have different image features compared to the images in the network training dataset. They occur over large areas and can be easily obscured by forests. When directly using existing networks for landslide detection, the segmentation accuracy is low.

2.2   HSNet Network

The public datasets required for landslide detection are few, and the number of labeled samples is insufficient. The hyper-correlation squeeze few-shot semantic segmentation network (HSNet) [15] achieves high-dimensional feature extraction through multi-level features and 4D convolutions, and segments the same features in the query image. The network structure of HSNet is shown in Fig. 2. First, the support image and support mask image undergo a Hadamard product and are then fed into the hyper-correlation construction module along with the query image. Different hierarchical features are constructed using cosine similarity, forming a hyper-correlation pyramid. Second, the pyramid is input into the 4D convolutional pyramid encoder module, achieving feature downsampling and upsampling and acquiring multi-level features. Finally, the upsampled recovered features are fed back to the 2D convolutional context decoder module to determine the class of each pixel point and get the predicted output of the query mask. The HSNet network can achieve segmentation on the query image when the number of support images is limited. We use this network as the original model and adapt the network in a scenario specific to landslide detection. The network is eventually made capable of segmenting landslide images with high accuracy without relying on a large number of datasets.

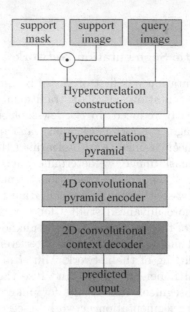

Fig. 2. HSNet network structure

3   Proposed Method

3.1   4D Convolutional

The 4D convolution module in the network is chosen to replace one 4D convolutional kernel with a pair of 2D convolutional kernels [15]. This reduces the number of 4D convolutional kernels used and reduces the loss of network resources. Due to too many parameters, some weight parameters in the neural network are chosen to be sparsely discarded. Focusing only on the parts that have a greater impact on certain weight positions in the network reduces the scale of the network and makes the computation faster.

In the four-dimensional space, let $(x, x') \in R^4$, $\mathbf{x}$ and $\mathbf{x}'$ respectively represent the positions of two 2D spaces, that is, the surrounding parts of a point on the 2D plane. In the encoder module, 4D convolution is used to obtain the relevant features of the image. The cosine similarity tensor is $c \in R^{H \times W \times H \times W}$, and the 4D convolution kernel is $k \in R^{k' \times k' \times k' \times k'}$. Four-dimensional convolution at position $(x, x') \in R^4$:

$$(c * k)(x, x') = \sum_{(p,p') \in \Psi(x,x')} c(p, p') \times k(p - x, p' - x') \tag{1}$$

where $\Psi(x, x')$ represents a group of neighborhood areas centered on the 4D position (x, x'), which means in the 4D area (x, x'), there is $\Psi(x, x') = \Psi(x) \times \Psi(x')$. 4D convolution operations consume a lot of computing power and occupy a large amount of storage resources.

In order to reduce the application limit of the network to 4D convolution, the method of weight sparseness is used to discard the network weight parameters. The weight sparse process is shown in Fig. 3. In the 2D space represented by $\mathbf{x}$ and $\mathbf{x}'$, relative to each other, the pixels around the center of the two pixels are regarded as having no influence or less influence points. During 4D convolution operation, two pixel centers only have weight values with the other center and the pixel points around the other center. These two centers ignore unimportant weight values for pixels surrounding their own centers, thus accomplishing weight sparsity.

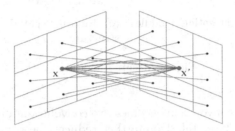

Fig. 3. Weight sparse process

After weight sparsity in the network, when the 4D position (x, x') is adjacent to each other in the corresponding 2D subspaces, the corresponding region set is collected, which is defined as:

$$\Psi_C(x, x') = \{(p, p') \in \Psi(x, x') : p = x\} \tag{2}$$

$$\Psi_{C'}(x, x') = \{(p, p') \in \Psi(x, x') : p' = x'\} \tag{3}$$

The region set of the two centers as a whole is defined as:

$$\Psi_{CA}(x, x') = \Psi_C(x, x') \cup \Psi_{C'}(x, x') \tag{4}$$

A 4D convolution in the center can be formulated as the sum of two separate 4D convolutions:

$$(c * k_{CA})(x, x') = (c * k_C)(x, x') + (c * k_{C'})(x, x') \tag{5}$$

where k_C and $k_{C'}$ are the 4D convolution kernels in the respective central region sets respectively. When computing results for a single center:

$$(c * k_C)(x, x') = \sum_{p' \in \Psi(x')} c(x, p') k_C^{2D}(p' - x') \tag{6}$$

$$(c * k_{C'})(x, x') = \sum_{p \in \Psi(x)} c(p, x') k_{C'}^{2D}(p - x) \tag{7}$$

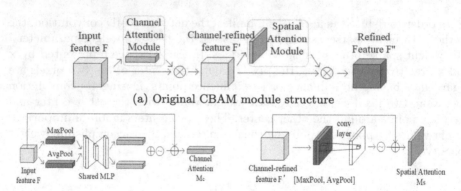

(a) Original CBAM module structure

(b) Residual-channel attention module structure

(c) Residual-spatial attention module structure

Fig. 4. Attention module

Therefore, the 4D convolution becomes two convolutions on 2D slices through the convolution operation [15]. This further reduces the computational load of convolution and speeds up the operation, which is formulated by Eq. (8):

$$(c * k_{CA})(x, x') = \sum_{p' \in \Psi(x')} c(x, p') k_C^{2D}(p' - x') + \sum_{p \in \Psi(x)} c(p, x') k_{C'}^{2D}(p - x) \quad (8)$$

3.2   Residual-Attention Module

In order to better focus on important areas in the image, human vision is simulated to focus on key content. In the residual module of the HSNet backbone, the CBAM attention module [17] is introduced and improved into the first and last layers of the network. As shown in Fig. 4(a), the preliminary feature **F** obtained after processing is used as input, and the channel attention and the spatial attention are performed in sequence. Finally the improved feature after processing is obtained. The processing is denoted by Eq. 9 and Eq. 10 as:

$$F' = M_c(F) \otimes F \quad (9)$$

$$F'' = M_s(F') \otimes F' \quad (10)$$

where $\otimes$ represents element-wise multiplication, $M_c \in R^{C \times 1 \times 1}$ is the 1D channel attention map obtained after processing by the channel attention module, and $M_s \in R^{1 \times H \times W}$ is the 2D spatial attention map obtained after processing by the spatial attention module.

The residual-channel attention module structure is shown in Fig. 4(b). Firstly, max-pooling and average-pooling are performed on the input feature **F** to aggregate the spatial information of image features. Secondly, the obtained spatial context descriptor is passed into the shared network for processing, and the channel attention feature vector is obtained by first reducing and then increasing the number of channels. Thirdly, the channel attention feature vectors of max-pooling and average-pooling are summed element-wise. Fourthly, use the sigmoid function for normalization. Finally, the input and output are connected with residuals to obtain a one-dimensional channel attention map M_c.

The residual-spatial attention module structure is shown in Fig. 4(c). Firstly, the channel information of the image is aggregated by max-pooling and average-pooling in the channel direction on the feature $\mathbf{F}'$ improved by the channel. Secondly, dimensionality splicing and merging are performed on the two-layer features. Thirdly, the result is processed by a convolutional layer with a channel number of 1 to adjust the number of channels. Fourthly, use the sigmoid function for normalization. Finally, the input and output are connected with residuals to obtain the two-dimensional spatial attention map M_s.

3.3   Improved-Transfer Learning

Due to the introduction of the residual attention mechanism, the backbone model of the network has changed. If training is performed directly without using a pretrained model, the network may have slow convergence speed and low segmentation accuracy. Therefore, an improved transfer learning approach is adopted to optimize the network model parameters. It can enhance the learning capability of the network to extract the underlying image features.

The HSNet network after adding the residual attention mechanism selects Resnet50 and Resnet101 as the backbone of the model. After adding channel attention and spatial attention, the network structure changes and the model parameters increase. Therefore, the parameters of the pre-trained model obtained on the ImageNet dataset [18] are used to optimize the network parameters. The ImageNet dataset is a large-scale dataset with more than 14 million images and more than 20,000 categories. Compared with the FSS dataset [19] used in this paper, it has more images and image categories. The FSS dataset contains 1000 categories, each category has 10 images, which is suitable for landslide recognition and segmentation in the case of few samples. When using the pre-trained model of the ImageNet dataset to optimize parameters, the network has more training samples and has stronger generalization.

Improved transfer learning improves the performance of the model on the target domain based on the source domain model. Its structure is shown in Fig. 5. The source dataset is the ImageNet dataset, which is trained on the Resnet50 and Resnet101 backbone to obtain a network model to complete the task. The target dataset is the FSS dataset, which is also trained on the Resnet50 and Resnet101 backbone after adding the residual attention module. The transfer of the network is completed by comparing and adding new weights to the new weight file. The new pre-trained models of Resnet50 and Resnet101 networks after adding the residual attention module on the ImageNet dataset network are obtained through improved transfer learning. And they are used to complete new tasks in the target domain.

4   Experiments

4.1   Datasets

The dataset in this paper uses the FSS dataset [19] for training, and the high-precision aerial imagery and interpretation dataset [20] for testing. We choose the FSS dataset when training the neural network. Compared with the commonly used few-shot datasets PASCAL-5i [13] and COCO-20i [21], the FSS dataset is more effective for model training and have more types. We group the FSS dataset, set 520 of them as the training set, and set 240 of them as the validation set. The types are selected randomly and are not repeated. There is no intersection between the types of the training set and the validation set. To test the segmentation performance of this network in landslide detection, the public dataset of landslides [20] is selected. There are a total of 59 landslide images with pixel-level annotations.

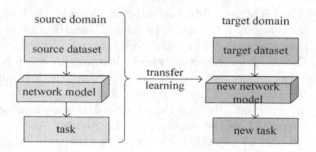

Fig. 5. Improved transfer learning structure

4.2   Evaluation Metrics

In order to verify the performance of the model, we use mIoU [11] and FB-IoU [12] as evaluation metrics to evaluate the error between the predicted segmentation results of the network and the ground truth. The mIoU is to calculate the mean intersection over union of all different types of objects that need to be segmented. The intersection of the pixel points of the predicted segmentation and the ground truth is divided by the pixel point union to obtain the ratios. Then, they are added and divided by the number of types to obtain the mIoU, as shown in Eq. 11:

$$mIoU = \frac{1}{C}\sum_{i=1}^{C} IoU_i = \frac{1}{C}\sum_{i=1}^{C} \frac{pre_i \cap truth_i}{pre_i \cup truth_i} \quad (11)$$

where C is the number of different types that need to be segmented, pre is the prediction result, and truth is the ground truth. FB-IoU calculates the foreground IoU and background IoU respectively, and takes their average value to obtain the FB-IoU, as shown in Eq. 12:

$$FB - IoU = \frac{1}{2}(IoU_F + IoU_B) \tag{12}$$

where IoU_F is the foreground IoU of the image, and IoU_B is the background IoU of the image.

4.3 Comparative Experiments

Table 1 presents the performance of the currently relevant neural network-based landslide detection methods. Our network is compared with mask region-based convolution neural network(Mask R-CNN) [22] and susceptibility-guided fully convolutional neural network(SG-FCNN) [23]. Mask R-CNN [22] conducts experiments on the Resnet50 and Resnet101 backbones and builds its own landslide dataset. The mIoU values for segmentation of newly formed landslides are listed in Table 1. On the two backbone networks, the mIoU values are 64.95% and 77.94%, respectively. SG-FCNN [23] uses landslide sensitivity as a prior knowledge. Based on the fully convolutional neural network, a boundary and morphological optimization (BMO) module and a mean changing magnitude of objects (MCMO) module are added to effectively improve the accuracy of landslide detection. In Table 1, the value of mIoU for landslide detection using this method in two regions is recorded. The mIoU value is 84.65% on region A and 76.03% on region B. Therefore, the mIoU value of this method is 80.34%.

Table 1. Comparison of the results of the relevant methods

	mIoU	FB-IoU
Resnet50+Mask R-CNN [22]	64.95	–
Resnet101+Mask R-CNN [22]	77.94	–
SG-FCNN+BMO+MCMO [23]	80.34	–
Ours with Resnet50	**82.85**	**89.69**
Ours with Resnet101	**84.19**	**90.63**

The comparison of the data in Table 1 shows that the network in this paper improves 17.9% in mIoU over network [22] and 2.51% over network [23] with ResNet50 as the backbone. In the case of ResNet101 as the backbone, it improves 6.25% over network [22] in mIoU and 3.85% over network [23]. Among these networks, the proposed network in this paper has the highest mIoU, the best effect of segmenting landslides, and requires the least number of landslide datasets, which proves the superiority of the proposed model.

4.4 Ablation Study

In order to verify the effectiveness of the residual-attention module and improved-transfer learning, these two components are studied qualitatively through the ablation study. Eight comparative experiments are carried out, four experiments each with Resnet50 and Resnet101 as the backbone. They are a network without the residual-attention module and not using improved-transfer learning, a network with the residual-attention module but not using improved-transfer learning, a network without the residual-attention module but using improved-transfer learning, and a network with both the residual-attention module and improved-transfer learning. The mIoU and FB-IoU are used as evaluation metrics for the ablation experiments. Since training the network is time-consuming, 160 iteration rounds are set for each ablation experiment to compare their evaluation metrics.

The results of the ablation experiments are shown in Table 2, where the mIoU is the main observation. It can be found that the performance of the network improves substantially after adding improved-transfer learning, and improves marginally after adding the residual-attention module. The Resnet50 backbone improves mIoU by 0.7% with the addition of the residual-attention module, by 28.24% with the addition of improved-transfer learning, and by 28.39% when both modules are added. The Resnet101 backbone improves mIoU by 1.03% with the addition of the residual-attention module, by 30.56% with the addition of the improved-transfer learning, and by 30.91% with the addition of both modules.

Table 2. Results of ablation experiments

	mIoU	FB-IoU
Resnet50	54.46	70.71
Resnet50+CBAM	55.16	71.07
Resnet50+transfer learning	82.70	**89.69**
Ours with Resnet50	**82.85**	**89.69**
Resnet101	53.28	69.90
Resnet101+CBAM	54.31	70.26
Resnet101+transfer learning	83.84	90.26
Ours with Resnet101	**84.19**	**90.63**

The results of the ablation experiments show that the model obtained from the original backbone network is not ideal when the number of landslide samples is small. The use of improved-transfer learning can fully exploit the underlying features of the image, so that it can be applied to the detection of landslide features to obtain the underlying features more accurately. Using the residual-attention module can focus the attention of the network on the foreground portion of the image, thus focusing on a relatively small area of landslides occurring in most of the background.

Figure 6 and Fig. 7 respectively show the visualized results of the ablation experiments using ResNet50 and ResNet101 as the backbones. It can be observed that the best segmentation performance, closest to the ground truth, is achieved when both backbones use the improved transfer learning and residual attention modules simultaneously.

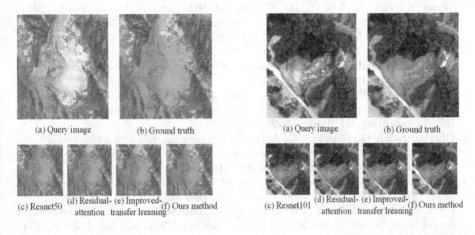

| (a) Query image | (b) Ground truth |
| (c) Resnet50 | (d) Residual-attention | (e) Improved-transfer lreaning | (f) Ours method |

| (a) Query image | (b) Ground truth |
| (c) Resnet101 | (d) Residual-attention | (e) Improved-transfer lreaning | (f) Ours method |

Fig. 6. Visualization results of Resnet50

Fig. 7. Visualization results of Resnet101

5 Conclusion and Future Work

In this paper, we propose a few-shot landslide detection method based on residual attention and improved transfer learning. For the problem of few public labeled datasets of landslide, a 4RATFNet network is used to complete the landslide detection. The residual attention mechanism is introduced to focus on the foreground landslide regions in the image from both channel and space aspects, which effectively suppresses the interference of cluttered background. The introduction of improved transfer learning effectively optimizes the pre-trained parameters of the network under the change of the network structure. Our proposed method outperforms existing newer landslide detection methods on the evaluation metric mIoU. And the effectiveness of the two modules is demonstrated by metrics mIoU and FB-IoU. However, our network needs to manually label landslide images in the initial stage, and the more types of landslides are labeled in this stage, the higher the accuracy of final detection will be. In future work, we will preprocess the few-shot datasets to reduce the differences between them and the public large sample datasets, so as to achieve an increase in the similarity between the two datasets and improve the accuracy of landslide detection.

Acknowledgements. This work was supported by the Sichuan Science and Technology Program under Grant No. 2022YFG0148 and the Heilongjiang Science and Technology Program under Grant No. 2022ZX01A16.

References

1. Wang, X., Fan, X., Xu, Q., Du, P.: Change detection-based co-seismic landslide mapping through extended morphological profiles and ensemble strategy. ISPRS J. Photogramm. Remote. Sens. **187**, 225–239 (2022)
2. Ghorbanzadeh, O., Shahabi, H., Crivellari, A., Homayouni, S., Blaschke, T., Ghamisi, P.: Landslide detection using deep learning and object-based image analysis. Landslides **19**(4), 929–939 (2022)
3. Feizizadeh, B., Ghorbanzadeh, O.: GIS-based interval pairwise comparison matrices as a novel approach for optimizing an analytical hierarchy process and multiple criteria weighting. GI_Forum **1**, 27–35 (2017)
4. Ghorbanzadeh, O., Blaschke, T., Aryal, J., Gholaminia, K.: A new GIS-based technique using an adaptive neuro-fuzzy inference system for land subsidence susceptibility mapping. J. Spat. Sci. **65**(3), 401–418 (2020)
5. Tian, Y., et al.: A transformer-based model for short-term landslide displacement prediction. Acta Sci. Naturalium Univ. Pekinensis **59**(2), 197–210 (2023)
6. Ding, X., Zhao, X., Wu, X., Zhang, T., Xu, Z.: Landslide susceptibility assessment model based on multi-class SVM with RBF kernel. China Saf. Sci. J. **32**(3), 194–200 (2022)
7. Huang, Y., Shi, P., He, H., He, H., Zhao, B.: Senet: spatial information enhancement for semantic segmentation neural networks. Vis. Comput. 1–14 (2023)
8. Ma, Z., Yuan, M., Gu, J., Meng, W., Xu, S., Zhang, X.: Triple-strip attention mechanism-based natural disaster images classification and segmentation. Vis. Comput. **38**(9–10), 3163–3173 (2022)
9. Qin, Y., Chi, X., Sheng, B., Lau, R.W.: GuideRender: large-scale scene navigation based on multi-modal view frustum movement prediction. Vis. Comput. 1–11 (2023)
10. Yang, P., Wang, M., Yuan, H., He, C., Cong, L.: Using contour loss constraining residual attention U-net on optical remote sensing interpretation. Vis. Comput. 1–13 (2022)
11. Chen, Q., Yang, Y., Huang, T., Feng, Y.: A survey on few-shot image semantic segmentation. Front. Data Comput. **3**(6), 17–34 (2021)
12. Rakelly, K., Shelhamer, E., Darrell, T., Efros, A., Levine, S.: Conditional networks for few-shot semantic segmentation. In: International Conference on Learning Representations (2018)
13. Shaban, A., Bansal, S., Liu, Z., Essa, I., Boots, B.: One-shot learning for semantic segmentation. In: British Machine Vision Conference 2017, pp. 167.1–167.13 (2017)
14. Zhao, Y., Price, B., Cohen, S., Gurari, D.: Objectness-aware few-shot semantic segmentation. arXiv preprint arXiv:2004.02945 (2020)
15. Min, J., Kang, D., Cho, M.: Hypercorrelation squeeze for few-shot segmentation. In: Proceedings of the IEEE/CVF International Conference on Computer Vision, pp. 6941–6952 (2021)
16. Fan, Q., Pei, W., Tai, Y.W., Tang, C.K.: Self-support few-shot semantic segmentation. In: Avidan, S., Brostow, G., Cissé, M., Farinella, G.M., Hassner, T. (eds.) ECCV 2022, Part XIX. LNCS, vol. 13679, pp. 701–719. Springer, Cham (2022). https://doi.org/10.1007/978-3-031-19800-7_41

17. Woo, S., Park, J., Lee, J.Y., Kweon, I.S.: CBAM: convolutional block attention module. In: Ferrari, V., Hebert, M., Sminchisescu, C., Weiss, Y. (eds.) ECCV 2018. LNCS, vol. 11211, pp. 3–19. Springer, Cham (2018). https://doi.org/10.1007/978-3-030-01234-2_1

18. Deng, J., Dong, W., Socher, R., Li, L.J., Li, K., Fei-Fei, L.: ImageNet: a large-scale hierarchical image database. In: 2009 IEEE Conference on Computer Vision and Pattern Recognition, pp. 248–255. IEEE (2009)

19. Li, X., Wei, T., Chen, Y.P., Tai, Y.W., Tang, C.K.: FSS-1000: a 1000-class dataset for few-shot segmentation. In: Proceedings of the IEEE/CVF Conference on Computer Vision and Pattern Recognition, pp. 2869–2878 (2020)

20. Zeng, C., Cao, Z., Su, F., Zeng, Z., Yu, C.: High-precision aerial imagery and interpretation dataset of landslide and debris flow disaster in Sichuan and surrounding areas. China Sci. Data 7(2), 195–205 (2022)

21. Nguyen, K., Todorovic, S.: Feature weighting and boosting for few-shot segmentation. In: Proceedings of the IEEE/CVF International Conference on Computer Vision, pp. 622–631 (2019)

22. Jiang, W., et al.: Deep learning for landslide detection and segmentation in high-resolution optical images along the Sichuan-Tibet transportation corridor. Remote Sens. 14(21), 5490 (2022)

23. Chen, Y., et al.: Susceptibility-guided landslide detection using fully convolutional neural network. IEEE J. Sel. Top. Appl. Earth Observ. Remote Sens. 16, 998–1018 (2022)

Reinforce Model Tracklet for Multi-Object Tracking

Jianhong Ouyang[1,2]([✉]), Shuai Wang[1,2], Yang Zhang[3], Yubin Wu[1,2],
Jiahao Shen[1,2], and Hao Sheng[1,2]

[1] State Key Laboratory of Virtual Reality Technology and Systems,
School of Computer Science and Engineering, Beihang University,
Beijing 100191, People's Republic of China
oy_jh@buaa.edu.cn
[2] Zhongfa Aviation Institute, Beihang University, Hangzhou 311115, China
[3] College of Information Science and Technology, Beijing University of Chemical
Technology, Beijing 100029, People's Republic of China

Abstract. Recently, most multi-object tracking algorithms adopt the
idea of tracking-by-detection. Related studies have shown that significant improvements with the development of detectors. However, missed
detection and false detection are more serious in occlusion situations.
Therefore, the tracker uses tracklet (short trajectories) to generate more
perfect trajectories. There are many tracklet generation algorithms, but
the fragmentation problem is still prevalent in crowded scenes. Fixed
window tracklet generation strategies are not suitable for dynamic environments with occlusions. To solve this problem, we propose a reinforcement learning-based framework for tracklet generation, where we regard
tracklet generation as a Markov decision process and then utilize reinforcement learning to dynamically predict the window size for generating
tracklet. Additionally, we introduce a novel scheme that incorporates the
temporal order of tracklet for association. Experiments of our method on
the MOT17 dataset demonstrate its effectiveness, achieving competitive
results compared to the most advanced methods.

Keywords: Tracklet · Reinforce · Policy Gradient · Tracklet
association · Multiple Object Tracking

1 Introduction

In recent years, with the rapid development of artificial intelligence technology,
the demand in the field of safety supervision is gradually increasing. As the basis
of behavior analysis and anomaly detection, multiple object tracking (MOT) is
one of the most researched topics. Tracking multiple objects [1] refers to obtaining the complete trajectory of each object in a sequence of images.

Detection-based tracking methods have become popular in the field of multi-
object tracking as they leverage object detection to initialize and maintain object

B. Sheng et al. (Eds.): CGI 2023, LNCS 14497, pp. 78–89, 2024.
https://doi.org/10.1007/978-3-031-50075-6_7

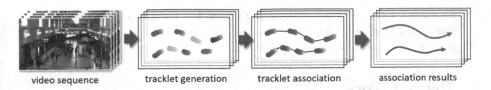

video sequence   tracklet generation   tracklet association   association results

Fig. 1. Tracklet-based Multi-Object Tracking

tracks. However, the accuracy of object detection is often compromised by various challenges, including occlusion, scale variations, and cluttered backgrounds.

Both detection missing and false alarm can lead to track drift, identity switches, and even complete track lost. To improve the robustness of tracking algorithms in the face of detection inaccuracies, researchers have proposed the use of tracklet. As shown in Fig. 1, Tracklet-based tracking is different from detection-based tracking. Instead of directly calculating the tracking results, the approach involves generating tracklets first and then performing short trajectory association to obtain the final tracking results. Tracklet, known as trajectory fragments, provide a local context for object association and help mitigate the impact of detection errors. By relying on shorter temporal intervals, trackers are less sensitive to error detector responses and individual missing detections. However, there are some problems with tracklets.

Currently, the majority of tracklet algorithms use fixed window sizes to generate tracklets, without considering environmental factors. This leads to poor quality of generated tracklets and suboptimal tracking results. To address this issue, the process of generating tracklets is modeled as a Markov process. A reinforcement learning approach is then employed to perceive the current scene and predict the optimal dynamic window size for tracklets.

Tracklets are often treated as detections for association, where the mean of all detection features and positions in the tracklet is typically used to represent it. However, the temporal characteristics of tracklets are not taken into account, which is crucial for tracklet association. To address this issue, we leverage smoothed features to represent the tracklet features. For each segment of the tracklet, we assign forward temporal smoothed features and backward temporal smoothed features, corresponding to forward temporal detection positions and backward temporal detection positions, respectively, for using in tracklet association.

In summary, our main contributions include:

(1) We propose a reinforcement learning-based method for generating tracklets that effectively adapts to the dynamic environment, enabling adaptive generation of high-quality tracklets.
(2) Design a time-based representation method for tracklets that captures the temporal information of the tracklets, enabling extraction of sequential patterns in tracklets.

(3) Develop a dynamic tracklet tracking method that adaptively generates and associates tracklets, achieving competitive results on the MOT17 dataset compared to most advanced methods.

2   Related Work

Multi-Object Tracking: In recent years, MOT research has been further developed, most of which are based on detection and tracking methods [1]. There are numerous tracking methods that focus on spatio-temporal features. Wojke et al. [22] proposed DeepSORT, a multi-object tracking algorithm that combines deep learning and sorting techniques. It utilizes convolutional neural networks (CNNs) to extract appearance features and a motion model for target association. Sheng et al. [14] proposed a hypothesis testing-based tracking method with spatio-temporal joint interaction modeling, which is an improvement over previous methods that only consider spatial or temporal interactions. Yang et al. [21] proposed ST3D, a single-shot multi-object tracker that leverages multi-feature fusion to capture spatial and temporal information. Our contribution mainly lies in the generation of tracklet and the utilization of spatio-temporal features.

Tracklet Based Tracking: To address challenges such as missed detections in crowded scenes, the concept of tracklets has been proposed as a solution. Tracklets offer advantages in avoiding identity exchange and recovering missed detections. Wang et al. [16] proposed an online learning method to characterize the motion and appearance of trajectory segments. Wang et al. [18] proposed to generate track segments using epipolar geometry and constructed a multi-scale TrackletNet to cluster track segments into groups considering their appearance and temporal features. Chen et al. [19] proposed a multi-task CNN for appearance modeling of trajectory segments, including spatial and temporal features. Sheng et al. [11] proposed an iterative multiple hypothesis tracking approach that incorporates tracklet-level association. Our approach primarily focuses on dynamically adjusting the window size of tracklet.

Deep Reinforcement Learning: In recent years, deep reinforcement learning has achieved remarkable success in various vision applications, including object detection, face recognition, and image super-resolution. Current deep reinforcement learning methods can be categorized into two main classes: deep Q-learning [25, 27] and policy gradient [26]. In the first class, Q-values are used to capture the expected return for actions in specific states. For example, Cao et al. [28] proposed an attention-aware face hallucination framework using deep reinforcement learning. It sequentially discovers attended patches and enhances facial parts by leveraging the global interdependency of the image. In the second class, policies are explicitly represented as probability distributions, and their parameters are updated using gradient-based methods to enhance the policy. Liu et al. [29] utilized a policy gradient method to optimize a range of captioning metrics. Several recent studies have focused on enhancing multi-object tracking through reinforcement learning techniques. Yun et al. [17] proposed an action-decision network for locating and sizing objects, while Supancic et al. [13] developed a decision policy tracker using reinforcement learning for attention control and appearance model updates. Our approach applies reinforcement learning to multi-object tracking in diverse scenes, with a particular focus on the length of dynamic tracklet.

3 Proposed Method

3.1 Markov Decision Process for Tracklet Generation

In our framework, the lifetime of tracklet generation is modeled with a Markov Decision Process (MDP).

The MDP consists of the tuple $(S, A, T(\cdot), R(\cdot), \gamma)$:

- The state $s \in S$ encodes the frame.
- The action $a \in A$ which can be performed to the agent.
- The state transition function T defines the probability distribution of transitioning from one state to another given an action: $T(s, a, s')$.
- The real-valued reward function R: $S \times A \rightarrow R$ defines the immediate reward received after executing action a to state s.
- The symbol γ represents the discounted factor, which indicates the degree of discounting future rewards. It takes values in the range $\gamma \in [0, 1]$.

States. We consider each frame of the video sequence as a state in the tracklet generation process. Assuming a video sequence has n frames, the corresponding states are represented as $S = s_1, s_2, ..., s_n$. Figure 2 illustrates the transitions between the frames in the video. In the tracklet generation process, we treat the first frame as the initial state. Then, we select the size of the tracklet window and generate the tracklet. The state transitions to the initial frame of the next tracklet window, and this process continues until the last frame is reached. For example, starting from the initial state $frame_1$, we select a tracklet window size of m. Then, within the window from $frame_1$ to $frame_m$, we generate the tracklet. After completion, the state transitions to $frame_{m+1}$.

Actions and Transition Function. The action space corresponds to the range of tracklet window lengths. Let's define m as the maximum length of the tracklet window. The action space can be represented as $A = a_1, a_2, ..., a_m$, where each action corresponds to a specific length of the tracklet window. For example, a_m corresponds to a tracklet window of length m. Figure 2 illustrates these transitions and actions. In our MDP, the function $T(s, a, s')$ is not deterministic and needs to be learned, which will be addressed in the next section.

Tracklet Generation. We treat the generation of tracklets within the window as an optimization problem. We define $e_{ij} \in \{0, 1\}$, where 0 indicates that detection i and detection j are not associated, and vice versa. Similarly, w_{ij} represents the similarity between detection i and detection j. Equation 1 computes the maximum sum of all edge weights. Equation 2 states that for any three

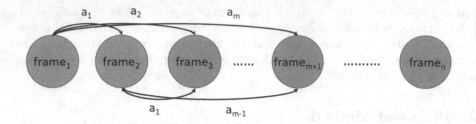

Fig. 2. Markov Decision Process for Tracklet Generation

detections i, j, and k, if i is connected to j and j is connected to k, then i and k must also be connected.

$$\max_{e_{ij}} \sum_{e_{ij}} w_{ij} e_{ij} \qquad (1)$$

$$e_{ij} + e_{jk} <= e_{ik} + 1 \qquad (2)$$

Reward Function. In our Markov decision process (MDP), the reward is defined based on the quality of tracklet generation. We draw inspiration from the evaluation metrics [31] used in multi-object tracking to formulate the reward function.

$$R(s_t, a_t, s_{t+1}) = GT \times MOTA = GT - FN - FP - IDSW \qquad (3)$$

The reward for transitioning from state s_t to state s_{t+1} via action a_t in Eq. 3 is determined by evaluating the tracklet generated between the two states. This evaluation is represented by the product of $GT \times MOTA$, which allows the accuracy of $MOTA$ to be quantified numerically. Here, $MOTA$ refers to Multiple Object Tracking Accuracy, GT represents the number of detections between state s_t and state s_{t+1}, FN denotes the number of False Negatives, FP corresponds to the number of False Positives, and $IDSW$ represents the number of ID Switches.

3.2 Policy Gradient for the MDP Model

In MDP, a policy π is a mapping from the state space S to the action space A, i.e., $\pi : S \to A$. Given the current state of the agent, a policy determines which action to take. Equivalently, the decision making in MDP is performed by following a policy. In this section, we employ a classification network to implement the policy, which corresponds to the previously mentioned $T(s, a, s')$ function.

In Fig. 3, We propose a Tracklet Window Decision Net which empoys ResNet50 as the backbone and takes the image as input. The ResNet50 model consists of 4 ResNet blocks, each comprising multiple convolutional layers and residual connections. The final output layer is a fully connected layer that generates an m-dimensional probability distribution. To ensure the probabilities sum

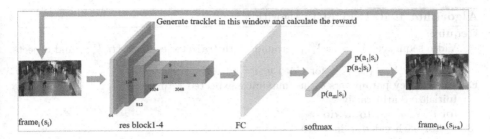

Generate tracklet in this window and calculate the reward

$p(a_1|s_i)$
$p(a_2|s_i)$

$p(a_m|s_i)$

frame$_i$ (s_i)   res block1-4   FC   softmax   frame$_{i+a}$ (s_{i+a})

Fig. 3. Tracklet Window Decision Net

up to 1, we apply the softmax function for normalization. The m-dimensional output represents the probabilities of m actions, denoted as $p(a_1|s_i)$, $p(a_2|s_i)$, ..., $p(a_m|s_i)$. The action is selected based on these probabilities. Furthermore, based on the selected action, we determine the length of the tracklet window, generate the tracklet, and calculate the corresponding reward. This process continues to predict future frames until the last frame is reached.

We employ the classical policy gradient algorithm, REINFORCE [15], to train our proposed action probability prediction neural network. Let $V = \{v_i\}_{i=1}^{N}$ denote a set of video sequences for training, where N is the number of sequences. Suppose there are N_i ground truth targets $T_i = \{t_{ij}\}_{j=1}^{N_i}$ in video v_i. Our goal is to train an action prediction network to improve the quality of tracklet generation.As shown in Algorithm 1, we train the designed policy network parameters using ground truth. For each episode, we train on all videos. For each video, we initialize the agent at the first frame and initialize an empty reward list. Then, based on the policy network, we select an action and determine the size of the tracklet window. In particular, if the window range exceeds the last frame, we truncate it to the last frame. We generate a tracklet within the window and calculate the reward using Eq. (3), which is then added to the reward list. We update the state to the next window's starting frame and repeat this process until the last frame. Finally, we use the recorded reward list and the REINFORCE algorithm to update the network parameters.

3.3 Flexible Association Based on Dynamic Tracklet

In the previous sections, we obtained more reliable tracklet using reinforcement learning methods. In this section, we focus on the feature representation of tracklet, specifically considering their temporal characteristics, in order to achieve improved association performance.

Figure 4 illustrates the association between adjacent tracklet, where it is evident that the features and positions of the tracklet should align closely at the association points. Therefore, we have designed a method to capture the temporal smoothness of tracklet and their corresponding position representation.

We define T as a tracklet and d_i as a detection. For each detection, we assume p_i represents its spatial position and f_i represents its feature. Let T_i denote a tracklet consisting of k detections.

Algorithm 1. REINFORCE Algorithm

Require:

Video sequences $V = \{v_i\}_{i=1}^{N}$, ground truth trajectories $T_i = \{t_{ij}\}_{j=1}^{N_i}$ and object

detection $D_i = \{d_{ij}\}_{j=1}^{N'_i}$ for video $v_i, i = 1, ..., N$

Ensure: Policy parameters θ that maximize expected return

1: Initialize θ arbitrarily
2: **for** $episode = 1$ to M **do**
3:    **for** each video v_i in V **do**
4:        Initialize the state at first frame
5:        $state \leftarrow 1$
6:        $r \leftarrow$ reward empty list
7:        $last\_frame \leftarrow$ last frame of v_i
8:        **while** $state \leq last\_frame$ **do**
9:            Follow the current policy and choose an action a.
10:           Determine the length of the frame window, len_window.
11:           **if** $state + len\_window > last\_frame$ **then**
12:               $len\_window \leftarrow last\_frame + 1 - state$
13:           **end if**
14:           Compute the tracklet in the window $[state, state + len\_window - 1]$
15:           Compute the reward r' according to Eq. (3)
16:           r.append(r')
17:           $state \leftarrow state + len\_window$
18:       **end while**
19:       $T \leftarrow r.length$
20:       **for** $t = 1$ to T **do**
21:           Compute the return $G_t = \sum_{k=t}^{T} \gamma^{k-t} r_k$
22:           Update $\theta \leftarrow \theta + \alpha \gamma^t G_t \nabla_\theta \ln \pi_\theta(a_t|s_t)$
23:       **end for**
24:   **end for**
25: **end for**
26: **return** θ

We define the begining position and ending position of a tracklet as follows:

$$\begin{cases} P_{i,begin} = p_1 \\ P_{i,end} = p_k \end{cases} \tag{4}$$

Equation (6) performs forward feature smoothing, while Eq. (5) performs backward feature smoothing.

$$G_i = \begin{cases} f_k & i = k \\ \lambda f_i + (1 - \lambda)G_{i+1} & i < k \end{cases} \tag{5}$$

$$H_i = \begin{cases} f_1 & i = 1 \\ \lambda f_i + (1 - \lambda)H_{i-1} & i > 1 \end{cases} \tag{6}$$

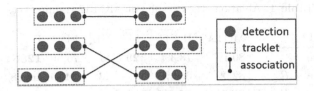

Fig. 4. Tracklet-level Association

Equation (7) defines the begining feature and ending feature of a tracklet.

$$\begin{cases} F_{i,begin} = G_1 \\ F_{i,end} = H_k \end{cases} \tag{7}$$

As shown in Eq. 8, we calculate the cost by considering the ending feature position of the previous tracklet and the begining feature position of the subsequent tracklet. For spatial position, we use the Euclidean distance to calculate the spatial distance. For feature comparison, we employ the cosine distance. In Eq. 9, we combine the feature and distance costs by assigning different weights to calculate the overall distance. Finally, we utilize the resulting cost to perform the association of tracklet.

$$\begin{cases} cost_{pos} = Euclid(P_{i,end}, P_{i+1,begin}) \\ cost_{fea} = cos(F_{i,end}, F_{i+1,begin}) \end{cases} \tag{8}$$

$$cost = \mu cost_{fea} + (1 - \mu) cost_{pos} \tag{9}$$

4   Experiments

4.1   Dataset and Metrics

We assess the performance of our tracker using the MOT 2017 dataset [30], which is a widely recognized public benchmark for multiple object tracking. The dataset includes 42 sequences, comprising of 21 training and 21 testing sequences, with a total of 33,705 frames. The dataset is similar to MOT 2016, but with different sets of detections for each video obtained using three detectors. As the performance of the detector greatly influences the tracker, we choose to use MOT 2017 instead of MOT 2016 for comparison experiments. This allows for better evaluation of the performance of our tracking algorithm under varying detector conditions. To ensure fair comparison and to test the actual performance of our method, we refrain from using any private detectors to gain additional detections.

For quantitative evaluation, we use the commonly adopted CLEAR MOT metrics [31]. These metrics include basic items such as false positives (FP↓), false negatives (FN↓), identity switches (IDS↓), mostly tracked targets (MT↑, >80%), mostly lost targets (ML↓, <20%), and track fragmentations (FM↓). The

Table 1. Ablation study results on MOT17 training set.

Method	MOTA↑	IDF1↑	MT↑	ML↓	FP↓	FN↓	IDs↓
Baseline	80.1%	73.3%	**329**	43	7529	**12864**	824
Baseline + R	82.0%	66.2%	301	**43**	**2440**	16468	1242
Baseline + R + F	**83.1%**	**79.7%**	314	52	5168	13069	**760**

multiple object tracking accuracy (MOTA↑) is the main overall indicator that combines FP, FN, and IDS. Another overall evaluation metric is the IDF1↑ [32], which is the ratio of correctly identified detections over the average number of ground truth and computed detections. While MOTA mainly focuses on whether targets are tracked or not, IDF1 evaluates whether a target is labeled with a unique ID. The ↑ symbol indicates that higher values are better, while the ↓ symbol indicates that lower values are better.

4.2 Ablation Study

Table 1 shows the ablation study results of the baseline method and our proposed method. We use TLMHT [11] as the baseline method, which is a tracklet-based multi-hypothesis tracking algorithm. As shown in Table 1, R represents our proposed reinforcement learning-based tracklet generation, and F represents the association of tracklet using temporal features and spatial positions. For the second row in Table 1, the increase of MOTA indicates the effectiveness of our proposed reinforcement learning-based tracklet generation. This proves that by predicting the size of the tracklet window using reinforcement learning, the environment changes can be well perceived, and the window size can be adjusted to control the length of the tracklet, thus improving the quality of the tracklet and the tracking accuracy. For the third row, by using the positions and feature distances of our designed tracklet, MOTA and IDF1 are increased and IDS is decreased. This proves that the position and feature of the tracklet designed by us can enhance the representation capability of the target feature, thus improving the adaptability of our tracking model to complex and changing scenes and enhancing the robustness and accuracy of the tracker.

4.3 Benchmark Evaluation

In this section, we test our tracking method on MOT2017 test dataset and compare with other competitors method. In Table 2, we list the results of some classic tracking methods. Our method is denoted Ours in the table, the best result in bold. The whole result can be found on MOT challenge site.

Compared with the classic detection-based tracking algorithms Fair [24], RobinTracker [7], our method significantly outperforms them in terms of MOTA, IDF1 and ID. It can be seen that tracklet have advantages in trajectory association. Compared with data-generated GRTU [10], our method performs better

Table 2. Comparison on MOT17 benchmark.

Method	MOTA↑	IDF1↑	MT↑	ML↓	FP↓	FN↓	IDs↓
TransCenter [9]	73.2%	62.2%	960	435	23112	123738	4614
Fair [24]	73.7%	72.3%	1017	408	27507	117477	3303
RobinTracker [7]	74.1%	70.9%	969	456	26910	115551	3786
GRTU [10]	74.9%	75.0%	1170	444	32007	107616	**824**
TrTrack [8]	75.2%	63.5%	1320	240	50157	86442	3603
FCG [6]	76.7%	**77.7%**	1005	414	**13284**	116205	1737
Ours	**77.9%**	73.0%	**1293**	**228**	39323	**82440**	2973

on MOTA, MT, ML, metrics. Compared with the transformer-based tracking methods TransCenter [9], TrTracker [8], our method has higher MOTA, IDF1. Compared with tracklet based FCG [6], although its IDF1 is higher than ours, our method has higher MOTA, MT, ML metrics than it is significantly better. Our method has lower FN and FN+FP, reflecting the advantage of our reinforcement learning algorithm in optimizing trajectory segments.

In addition, compared to all methods in the list, we get the lowest FN and get the best MOTA has a performance of 77.9. We get the highest MT of 1293 and the lowest ML of 228. The results demonstrate the competitiveness of our tracking algorithm

5 Conclusion

This paper proposes a reinforcement learning-based tracklet generation framework, which regards tracklet generation as a Markov decision process, and trains a neural network using policy gradient to predict the frame window size of tracklet. The framework adapts to tracklet features for association and the ability of reinforcement learning to adapt to the environment is used to improve the quality of tracklet generation. Using tracklet for association can reduce the impact of false detections and missed detections, making the framework more robust. The experiments show that reinforcement learning can bring improvements in predicting the window size of tracklet, and future work will apply reinforcement learning to other modules of multi-object tracking to further improve the accuracy of the tracker.

Acknowledgement. This study is partially supported by the National Key R&D Program of China (No. 2022YFB3306500), the National Natural Science Foundation of China (No. 61872025). Thank you for the support from HAWKEYE Group.

References

1. Luo, W., et al.: Multiple object tracking: a literature review (2014). arXiv:1409.7618. http://arxiv.org/abs/1409.7618
2. Wang, S., Sheng, H., Yang, D., Zhang, Y., Wu, Y., Wang, S.: Extendable multiple nodes recurrent tracking framework with RTU++. IEEE Trans. Image Process. **31**, 5257–5271 (2022)
3. Sheng, H., et al.: High confident evaluation for smart city services. Front. Environ. Sci. **10**, 950055 (2022)
4. Wu, Y., Sheng, H., Zhang, Y., Wang, S., Xiong, Z., Ke, W.: Hybrid motion model for multiple object tracking in mobile devices. IEEE Internet Things J. **10**, 1–14 (2022)
5. Wang, S., Sheng, H., Zhang, Y., Yang, D., Shen, J., Chen, R.: Blockchain-empowered distributed multi-camera multi-target tracking in edge computing. IEEE Trans. Ind. Inform. 1–14 (2023)
6. Girbau, A., Marques, F., Satoh, S.: Multiple object tracking from appearance by hierarchically clustering tracklets. In: 33rd British Machine Vision Conference 2022, BMVC 2022, London, UK, 21–24 November 2022 (2022)
7. Cao, J., Zhang, J., Li, B., Gao, L., Zhang, J.: RetinaMOT: rethinking anchor-free YOLOv5 for online multiple object tracking. Complex Intell. Syst. (2023)
8. Sun, P., et al.: TransTrack: Multiple Object Tracking with Transformer, arXiv:2012.15460 (2020)
9. Xu, Y., Ban, Y., Delorme, G., Gan, C., Rus, D., Alameda-Pineda, X.: TransCenter: Transformers with Dense Queries for Multiple-Object Tracking, arXiv (2021)
10. Wang, S., Sheng, H., Zhang, Y., Wu, Y., Xiong, Z.: A general recurrent tracking framework without real data. In: Proceedings of the IEEE/CVF International Conference on Computer Vision (2021)
11. Sheng, H., Chen, J., Zhang, Y., Ke, W., Xiong, Z., Yu, J.: Iterative multiple hypothesis tracking with tracklet-level association. IEEE Trans. Circuits Syst. Video Technol. **29**(12), 3660–3672 (2019)
12. Dollar, P., Appel, R., Belongie, S., Perona, P.: Fast feature pyramids for object detection. Pattern Anal. Mach. Intell. **36**, 1532–1545 (2014)
13. Supancic III, J., Ramanan, D.: Tracking as online decision-making: learning a policy from streaming videos with reinforcement learning. In: ICCV, pp. 322–331 (2017)
14. Sheng, H., et al.: Hypothesis testing based tracking with spatio-temporal joint interaction modeling. IEEE Trans. Circuits Syst. Video Technol. **30**(9), 2971–2983 (2020)
15. Williams, R.J.: Simple statistical gradient-following algorithms for connectionist reinforcement learning. Mach. Learn. **8**(3–4), 229–256 (1992)
16. Wang, B., Wang, G., Chan, K.L., Wang, L.: Tracklet association by online target-specific metric learning and coherent dynamics estimation. IEEE Trans. Pattern Anal. Mach. Intell. **39**(3), 589–602 (2017)
17. Yun, S., Choi, J., Yoo, Y., Yun, K., Choi, J.Y.: Action-decision networks for visual tracking with deep reinforcement learning. In: CVPR, pp. 2711–2720 (2017)
18. Wang, G., Wang, Y., Zhang, H., Gu, R., Hwang, J.-N.: Exploit the connectivity: multi-object tracking with TrackletNet (2018). arXiv:1811.07258. http://arxiv.org/abs/1811.07258
19. Chen, L., Ai, H., Chen, R., Zhuang, Z.: Aggregate tracklet appearance features for multi-object tracking. IEEE Signal Process. Lett. **26**(11), 1613–1617 (2019)

20. Bernardin, K., Stiefelhagen, R.: Evaluating multiple object tracking performance: the CLEAR MOT metrics. Image Video Process. (2008)
21. Yang, B., et al.: ST3D: A Simple and Efficient Single Shot Multi-Object Tracker with Multi-Feature Fusion, arXiv preprint arXiv:2002.01604 (2020)
22. Wojke, N., Bewley, A., Paulus, D.: Simple online and realtime tracking with a deep association metric. IEEE Trans. Pattern Anal. Mach. Intell. (2017)
23. Xiang, Y., Alahi, A., Savarese, S.: Learning to track: online multi-object tracking by decision making. In: ICCV, pp. 4705–4713 (2015)
24. Zhang, Y., Wang, C., Wang, X., Zeng, W., Liu, W.: FairMOT: on the fairness of detection and re-identification in multiple object tracking. In: Proceedings of the IEEE Conference on Computer Vision and Pattern Recognition (2020)
25. Gu, S., Lillicrap, T., Sutskever, I., Levine, S.: Continuous deep Q-learning with model-based acceleration. In: ICML, pp. 2829–2838 (2016)
26. Silver, D., Lever, G., Heess, N., Degris, T., Wierstra, D., Riedmiller, M.: Deterministic policy gradient algorithms. In: ICML, pp. 387–395 (2014)
27. Watkins, C.J.C.H., Dayan, P.: Q-learning. Mach. Learn. 8(3–4), 279–292 (1992)
28. Cao, Q., Lin, L., Shi, Y., Liang, X., Li, G.: Attention-aware face hallucination via deep reinforcement learning. In: CVPR, pp. 690–698 (2017)
29. Liu, S., Zhu, Z., Ye, N., Guadarrama, S., Murphy, K.: Optimization of image description metrics using policy gradient methods. arXiv preprint arXiv:1612.00370 (2016)
30. MOTChallenge: MOT17: a benchmark for multi-object tracking. http://motchallenge.net/data/MOT17/. Accessed 25 April 2023
31. Bernardin, K., Stiefelhagen, R.: Evaluating multiple object tracking performance: the CLEAR MOT metrics. EURASIP J. Image Video Process. 2008(1), 1–10 (2008)
32. Ristani, E., Solera, F., Zou, R., Cucchiara, R., Tomasi, C.: Performance measures and a data set for multi-target, multi-camera tracking. In: Hua, G., Jégou, H. (eds.) ECCV 2016. LNCS, vol. 9914, pp. 17–35. Springer, Cham (2016). https://doi.org/10.1007/978-3-319-48881-3_2
33. Sheng, H., et al.: Near-online tracking with co-occurrence constraints in blockchain-based edge computing. IEEE Internet Things J. 8(4), 2193–2207 (2021)
34. Luo, Q., Shao, J., Dang, W., et al.: An efficient multi-scale channel attention network for person re-identification. Vis. Comput. (2023)
35. Li, Y., et al.: A lightweight scheme of deep appearance extraction for robust online multi-object tracking. Vis. Comput. 1–17 (2023)
36. Zhang, X., Wang, X., Chunhua, G.: Online multi-object tracking with pedestrian re-identification and occlusion processing. Vis. Comput. 37, 1089–1099 (2021)
37. Zhang, Y., Yang, Z., Ma, B., et al.: Structural-appearance information fusion for visual tracking. Vis Comput (2023). https://doi.org/10.1007/s00371-023-03013-7

Analysis of Corporate Community of Interest Relationships in Combination with Multiple Network

Yipan Liu (iD), Song Wang$^{(\boxtimes)}$ (iD), Hao Hu (iD), and Shijie Chen (iD)

School of Computer Science and Technology, Southwest University of Science and Technology, Mianyang 621010, Sichuan, China
wangsong@swust.edu.cn

Abstract. Visualizing the complex relationship among enterprises is ponderable to help enterprises and institutions to find potential risks. Small and medium-size enterprises' (SMEs) loans have higher risk and non-performing rates than other types of enterprises, which are prone to form the complex relationship. Nowadays, the analysis of enterprises' relationships networks mainly focus on the guaranteed relationships among enterprises, but it lacks the holistic analysis of the enterprise community of interest. To address these issues, the concepts of the enterprise community of interest and the investment model withing enterprise community of interest are proposed; The centrality, density, and network diameter algorithms in graph theory are used to evaluate the network of enterprise community of interest; The problem of graph isomorphism are used to query the network of users interested enterprises' relationships; The portrait of enterprise is used to evaluate the enterprise community of interest; In the end, we study the impact of debt relationship among enterprise community of interest. Based on these ideas, to verify the effectiveness of the method, an enterprise relationship network analysis system which included 6745 enterprise nodes and 7435 enterprise relationship data of Shanghai is developed.

Keywords: Enterprise relationship network · Enterprise relationship analysis · Community of interests · Mortgage relations · Enterprise portrait

1 Introduction

According to the data of the fourth Economic Census, the number of people working in SMEs has accounted for 80 percent of the total number of employees. Due to insufficient mortgage guarantees and asymmetric information [1], it is particularly important to analyze the mortgage relationship and enterprise investment. Also, network analysis is widely used in social, Internet [23, 24], transportation, life science [2], and other fields. So it is necessary to study the enterprises' relationships by using network relationships. The phenomenon of enterprises' guarantee networks exists in most countries, which are worth analysising the guarantee relationship to study the influence of risk diffusion [3]. Most SMEs often need "fast, diversified, and flexible" funding and need mortgages to obtain funds [4]. The short establishment, small size, and lack of detail information of SMEs result in fewer loan opportunities, higher risks, and capital shortfalls [5]. Thus, the SMEs are easy to form a complex enterprise mortgage relationship and enterprise equity pledge relationship. In terms of enterprise risk assessment, research mainly analysis the characteristics of the enterprise, such as the judicial litigation risk of the government, enterprise credit risk [6], and enterprise social news risk reported by some social media. In terms of enterprise relationships, a part of the research only focus on enterprise relationship, such as the guarantee and mortgage relationship [7]. But it ignores the basic attributes of the enterprise, such as the size of assets. The study of enterprise is divided into the study of their own characteristics and the impact of single-enterprise relationships. To better analyze the relationship among enterprises, there are some issues need to be addressed here: firstly, combined with the enterprise characteristics and relationships, the enterprise community of interest characteristics should be analyzed; Secondly, analysis of the influence of debt enterprise to the community of interest is carried out.

2 Related Work

2.1 Enterprise Risk Assessment

In terms of credit, there were many data-driven credit scoring schemes, such as visualization in credit scoring methods based on neural networks [8]. The XGBoost credit rating model were constructed to evaluate the enterprise based on SMOTE series algorithm [9]. Nils [10] used the structural model after Merton (1974) to explore the relationship between a company's stock return and credit risk. Finally he found that the enterprie's stock return increased with the credit default risk premium. Combined with the financial data of bank, Hui [11] conducted regression analysis and Hosmer Lemeshow randomness test to build a logistics risk assessment model. Kang believed that enterprise bond yields reflect the concern about debt deflation and when debt is nominal, unexpectedly low inflation would increase real debt and default risk. Dawei proposed an unbalanced network risk diffusion model to predict the short-term default risk of enterprises and proposed [12] a positive weighted K-nearest neighbor algorithm for the independent case without default contagion to improved prediction accuracy. In the case of credit, commercial banks assess the risk of companies in order to maximize profits [13]. For funds that are likely to default, the impact in the credit business is measured quantitatively to reduce losses [14].

2.2 Enterprise Relationship Network

By mining the financial characteristic data among enterprises, the network topology layout could be used to represent the mutual relationship between each unit, which was widely used in the financial field [15, 16]. In terms of enterprise relationship, the enterprise loan guarantee relationship was introduced into the network topology layout structure to show the multi-level default risk visualization [17]. Sassa [18] proposed a structure-based suggestion exploration method, which suggested appropriate structures according to user's requests to support the effective exploration of large-scale networks.

Junrui [19] used a knowledge graph construction method for graph neural networks to quantify the correlation among enterprise. In the field of financial relationship data, the relationship among banks was represented through network [25] visualization. For example, text data was collected from financial forums to generate and visualize a jointly mentioned bank network [20]. It also effectively reveals financial crimes such as money laundering and fraud in the financial activity network through up-down interaction [21]. Therefore, the 2-dimensional network [26] topology layout was suitable for discussing specific cases and detailed analysis, but the relationship would be relatively disordered under large-scale data.

The analysis of companies is divided into enterprise characteristic analysis and enterprise relationship analysis. However, the analysis of enterprises characteristics lacks the analysis of the impact among enterprise; In contrast, enterprises relationship analysis is missing enterprise characteristics.

3 Exploration of Enterprise Relationships

The main analysis tasks of this paper are to study enterprise stakeholder networks and enterprise collateral relationships:

TASK1: Exploring different communities of interest extracted from enterprise relationship network [22], and evaluating enterprise investment relationship networks.
TASK2: Researching the impact of changes in debt enterprises on the community of interest in combination with enterprise portraits.
TASK3: Combined with enterprise portrait and enterprise relationship network, we can conduct a custom network similarity search (Fig. 1).

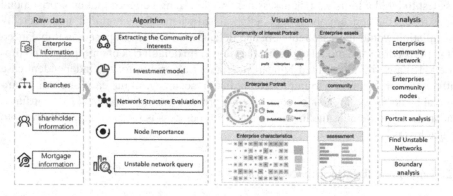

Fig. 1. Overview of the approach

3.1 Analysis the Enterprise Community of Interest

a) Basic concept

Community of interest: The community of interest is a connected graph $G = (V, E)$, the G represents the network topology formed, the V represents set of enterprise nodes, and the E represents the investment relationship of enterprises.

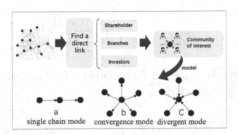

Fig. 2. Mining process of community of interest

Investment model: the investment made by enterprise 'A' only to enterprise 'B' is called the single chain mode (Fig. 2(a)); Enterprise 'A' accepting investment from multiple enterprises is called convergence mode (Fig. 2(b)). Enterprise 'A' investment in multiple enterprises is called divergent mode (Fig. 2(c)).

b) Community of interest network characteristics

Network density: As shown in Formula (1), $Density(G)$ means the ratio of already linked vertex pairs to the theoretically possible vertex pairs, $\dfrac{\sum\limits_{1}^{n} Degree(v_i)}{2}$ represents the number of edges and 'n' represents the number of nodes in the graph.

$$Density(G) = \frac{\sum\limits_{1}^{n} Degree(v_i)}{n(n-1)} \tag{1}$$

Average degree: As shown in Formula (2), $\sum\limits_{j=1, j\neq i}^{n} f(v_i, v_j)$ represents the degree of a node.

$$Average\ Degree(G) = \frac{\sum\limits_{i=1}^{n} \sum\limits_{j=1, j\neq i}^{n} f(v_i, v_j)}{n} \tag{2}$$

Diameter of the community of interest network: As shown in Formula (3), $MaxP(v_i, v_j)$ represents the maximum distance between two nodes.

$$Diameter(G) = \frac{2Max(MaxP(v_i, v_j)), i \neq j}{n(n-1)} \tag{3}$$

Average path length: As shown in Formula (4), $ShortesP(v_i, v_j)$ represents the shortest distance between two points.

$$AverageP(G) = \frac{2 \sum\limits_{i \geq j} ShortesP(v_i, v_j)}{n(n-1)} \tag{4}$$

Degree centrality: As shown in formula (5), d_{ij} represents the edge among two points.

$$Degree(v_i) = \frac{\sum\limits_{j=1}^{n} d_{ij}(i \neq j)}{n} \tag{5}$$

Closeness centrality: As shown in Formula (6). The $ShortesP(v_i, v_j)$ indicates the shortest distance among two nodes.

$$CloseCen(v_i) = \frac{1}{\sum\limits_{j=1}^{n} ShortesP(v_i, v_j)} \tag{6}$$

Between centrality: As shown in formula (7), $sd(j, i, k)$ represents the shortest path that passes through node 'i' from node 'k' to node 'j', and $\sum\limits_{j,k=1}^{n} s(j, k)$ represents the number of all paths between nodes j and k.

$$BetweenCen(v_i) = \frac{\sum\limits_{j,k=1}^{n} sd(j, i, k)}{\sum\limits_{j,k=1}^{n} s(j, k)}, (j \neq k) \tag{7}$$

c) Construction of enterprise interest community and portrait construction

We use the maximum connectivity subgraph algorithm (Eq. (8)) to find the community of interest in the network topology. The G_c represents community of interest; The E_i represents the set of edges in the connected graph network; The f_n represents the set of points in the connected graph; The $GetE$ extract points from edge set.

$$G_c = set \left(\sum_{i=1}^{m} \sum_{\substack{E_i = e_i \\ E_n = E - E_i}}^{f_n(E_n) \cap f_n(E_i) = \emptyset} E_i = GetE(f_n(E_n) \cap f_n(E_i)) \right) \tag{8}$$

As shown in Fig. 3, the portrait is mainly divided into three layers from inside to outside. The inner word cloud represents the business scope. The outer nodes' position represents the time when the enterprise joined and the colors represent the different states of the enterprise. The outermost layer is the average profit of the real community of interests.

$$Abnorma(G) = \frac{\sum_{i}^{n} f_{abn}(v_i)}{n \times \lambda} \tag{9}$$

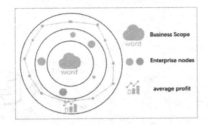

Fig. 3. Portrait of enterprise community of interest

3.2 Analysis of Mortgage Relationship of Enterprise Community of Interest

The Fig. 5 shows the explore the process of enterprise benefit community boundaries. There exists a debtor firm linking the community of interest A and community of interest B. Combined with the analysis of enterprise portrait, the debtor enterprise has great instability and becomes part of community B. Combining the analysis of the community analysis in 3.1, we compare the state of community A and community B. By analyzing the characteristics of the community of interest, we determine whether the original community of interest will change due to debtor.

For the analysis of debt nodes, we analyze them in three aspects. Firstly, we calculate the importance of the evaluation of nodes in the enterprise community of interest (see Sect. 3.1) and obtain the influence of debt nodes on the enterprise community of interest. Combined with enterprise characteristics, we design the enterprise portrait to quickly understand the debt enterprise. We select the indicators that are closely related to enterprise operation and credit, such as profit, credit history, and assets (Fig. 4b). The portraits are introduced to check the operating conditions of debt enterprises over a while (Fig. 4a). The center of the enterprise portrait indicates the industry type to which the enterprise belongs; the outward circular icons represent the enterprise characteristics acquired by the enterprise at different times. In addition, the circular icon represents the proportion of corporate debt and profit. The operating quota of the outermost term is used to check the operating status of the enterprise over a period of time.

3.3 Explore the Similar Relationship to Avoid Risk in Time

Combined with the topology structure and abnormal characteristics of the enterprise's community of interests, the enterprise's community of interests is evaluated and

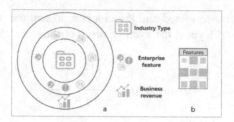

Fig. 4. The portrait of enterprise

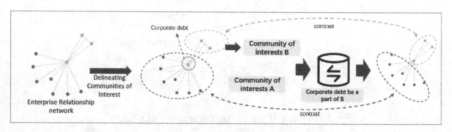

Fig. 5. Research on mortgage boundary

described from the aspects of the overall network structure, node importance, and comprehensive portrait. If the important nodes or an important paths section are the abnormal enterprises, they will have a significant impact on the enterprise relationship network and easily cause changes in the enterprise relationship network.

To discover the hidden risk in time, it is necessary to analyze the enterprise relationship and search for similar relationship, which can provide early warning and avoid risks in time.

We use the isomorphism problem in graph theory to solve similar network problems. For two enterprise communities of interest $G(V, E)$ and $G'(V', E')$. If there is a bijection $f : V \rightarrow V'$, such that for any two points u, v in V, the edges $f(u)f(v) \in E'$ and $uv \in E$, we say that $G(V, E)$ and $G'(V', E')$ are isomorphic.

Firstly, the user choose the model network which has the abnormal enterprise node. The next step we choose a part of network to explore. Then we extract the subnetwork from the target network which has the same number of nodes of model network. Finally, we use the isomorphism algorithm to determine whether the structure is the same.

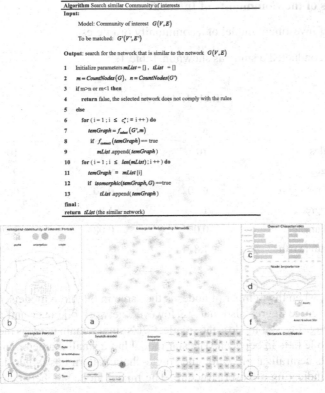

```
Algorithm Search similar Community of interests
Input:
        Model: Community of interest  G(V,E)

        To be matched:  G'(V',E')

Output: search for the network that is similar to the network  G(V,E)

1    Initialize parameters mList = [] ,  tList  = []
2    m = CountNodes (G),   n = CountNodes(G')
3    if m>n or m<1 then
4        return false, the selected network does not comply with the rules
5    else
6        for ( i = 1 ; i ≤ c*_n ; = i ++ ) do
7            temGraph = f_select (G',m)
8            if f_connect (temGraph) == true
9                mList .append( temGraph )
10       for ( i = 1 ; i ≤ len(mList) ; i ++ ) do
11           temGraph  =  mList [i]
12           if isomorphic(temGraph, G) ==true
13               tList .append( temGraph )
final :
return tList (the similar network)
```

Fig. 6. System interface of enterprise relationship

4   The Influence of Debt Enterprises on Interest Communities

4.1   Explore the Similar Relationship to Avoid Risk in Time

We developed an enterprise relationship analysis system using real data from Shanghai (Fig. 6). Large spherical nodes in Fig. 6a represent the community of interest. Figure 6b shows the enterprise community, 6c presents its basic characteristics, 6d illustrates node importance, and 6e displays the evaluation network. Figure 6f details enterprise assets, 6g depicts custom matching, 6h shows enterprise portraits, and 6i outlines basic enterprise characteristics.

4.2   Analysis of the Community of Interest

a) Analysis of investment model of a community of interest

In Fig. 7. We conducted a study as shown in Table 1.

Table 1. Overall index

project	a	b	c
Number of nodes	10	10	10
Number of edges	9	9	9
The density of the figure	0.20	0.20	0.20
The average degree	1.8	1.8	1.8
The network diameter	0.067	0.089	0.20
The average path length	1.8	3.11	3.64

In Table 1, when the number of nodes is the same in the three models, edges, graph density, and average degree also match. However, network diameter and average path length differ: Fig. 7a's star mode is the smallest, 7c's single-chain mode is the largest, and 7b's hybrid mode falls in between. The star model has a small diameter and segmented paths due to its centralization, while the single-chain pattern has larger diameters and longer paths, indicating a looser structure. The mixed mode sits between the star and single modes.

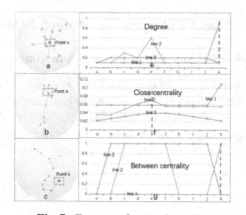

Fig. 7. Features of enterprise nodes

Then we analyze the node centrality of the enterprise community of interest and obtain the results shown in Fig. 7. Figure 7 e represent the degree centrality of each enterprise node in the enterprise interest community. Figure 7 f represent the closeness centrality of each enterprise node. Figure 7 g represent the between centrality of the enterprise node. Line 1 represent the star-shaped community of interest in Fig. 7 e. Line 2 represents the mixed community of interest in Fig. 7 f. Line 3 represent the single-chain community of interest in Fig. 7 g.

In Fig. 7, Line 1 remains straight until point k, which acts as a central hub connecting multiple enterprises in a star-like pattern. Line segment 2, particularly node e, maintains high centrality within a mixed-mode community. Line 3 is symmetric across all modes. Higher closeness centrality of a middle enterprise node in Fig. 7b significantly impacts the entire enterprise community. The star model consistently shows high degree and betweenness centrality, indicating close interconnections among enterprises. In contrast, the single-chain model's high closeness centrality highlights the community's vulnerability to disruptions from individual path interruptions.

b) Community of interest portrait and matching query

We created a community portrait in Fig. 8c, with dots representing different companies. In Fig. 8b, the horizontal axis denotes mean path, and the vertical axis represents anomaly index. Figure 8f reveals an enterprise with low profit but high debt. When we identify an anomalous community in the network, users can define a matching corporate community (Fig. 8d) and search for similar structures across all enterprises (Fig. 8e), with results highlighted in red.

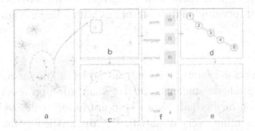

Fig. 8. Enterprise node characteristics

Degree and closeness centrality measure community structure, while betweenness centrality identifies key bridge nodes. Key nodes are vital in complex interest communities, as abnormalities in non-endpoint enterprises can harm the entire community. Simplified network topology reduces disruptions, benefiting the enterprise network. In diverse interest communities, decompose into basic models, like star and betweenness centrality, to prevent disruptions and fragmentation, which investors dislike.

4.3   Analysis of the Mortgage Community of Interest Relationship

In Fig. 9f, enterprise has substantial land resources. Despite past abnormal information, its centrality in Fig. 9b (9g, 9h, 9i) suggests a non-critical position within the community. The profile shows profitable performance surpassing debt, making it less critical for the entire community in case of collateral risks.

But in Fig. 9b community of interest, firm node d has this severe business operating condition. In Fig. 9b community of interest, enterprise node 'd' (Fig. 9e) has a serious business operating condition; Observing and analyzing the centrality of each node of the enterprise community of interest b, we learn that the enterprise node 'd' is at a high index of degree centrality, closeness centrality and between central.

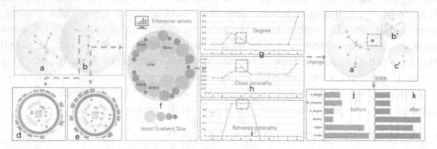

Fig. 9. Boundary analysis

This means that the enterprise node is in a key position and at the center of the entire community of interest; Suppose a collateral event occurs at this node, causing a split in the enterprise com-munity of interest (Fig. 9a', b', c'), which could easily lead to a series of incalculable reactions; Analyzing the community of interest before and after the change b (Fig. 9j, k), it is found that the graph density possesses a large change. Therefore, we suggest focusing on the enterprises with a larger degree.

5 Evaluation

We invited 15 volunteers to evaluate the analysis model of this paper, including 5 under-graduate students, 9 graduate students, and 1 visualization professional in the field of finance. The evaluation method adopts a five-point rating scale, which is divided into 1 and 5 points, representing "very dissatisfied", "dissatisfied", "fair", "satisfied", and "very satisfied" respectively (Table 2).

Table 2. Questionnaire evaluation.

Question	description
Q1	Whether the structure of the whole community of interest can be observed
Q2	Be able to effectively present and analyze large-scale corporate relationships
Q3	Whether it can effectively evaluate the network structure and node importance of the enterprise community of interests
Q4	Whether network matching can be done effectively
Q5	Be able to effectively demonstrate that the mortgage relationship arises
Q6	Whether it is easy to analyze the impact of debt on enterprises

Figure 10 displays user evaluation results. The paper excels in large-scale data pre-sentation analysis (Q2). It effectively observes community structure (Q1) and analyzes network nodes' importance (Q3). The method enables efficient querying of unstable investment networks (Q4), enhances the display of collateral relationships between companies (Q5), and effectively analyzes the impact of mortgage relationships on interest communities (Q6).

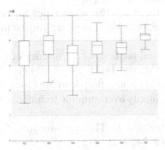

Fig. 10. Evaluation results

6 Conclusion

This paper introduces the concept of interest communities, analyzes enterprise relationships, and evaluates them through network analysis. It also examines the impact of collateral relationships among these communities. User evaluations validate the model, revealing that diverse perspectives enhance stability assessment within and among enterprise communities. Areas for improvement include considering additional characteristics for individual enterprise evaluation and exploring the impact of debt firms on critical path propagation.

Acknowledgement. This work was supported by Natural Science Foundation of Sichuan Province (Grant No. 2022NSFSC0961) the Ph.D. Research Foundation of Southwest University of Science and Technology (Grant No. 19zx7144) the Special Research Foundation of China (Mianyang) Science and Technology City Network Emergency Management Research Center (Grant No. WLYJGL2023ZD04).

References

1. Stroebel, J.: Asymmetric information about collateral values. J. Financ. **71**(3), 1071–1112 (2016)
2. Silva, J.S., Saraiva, A.M.: A methodology for applying social network analysis metrics to biological interaction networks. In: Proceedings of the 2015 IEEE/ACM International Conference on Advances in Social Networks Analysis and Mining, pp. 1300–1307 (2015)
3. Niu, Z., Li, R., Wu, J., et al.: iconviz: Interactive visual exploration of the default contagion risk of net-worked-guarantee loans. In: 2020 IEEE Conference on Visual Analytics Science and Technology (VAST). IEEE, pp. 84–94 (2020). Author, F.: Contribution title. In: 9th International Proceedings on Proceedings, pp. 1–2. Publisher, Location (2010)

4. Deyoung, R., Gron, A., Torna, G., et al.: Risk overhang and loan portfolio decisions: small business loan supply before and during the financial crisis. J. Financ. **70**(6), 2451–2488 (2015)
5. Garvin, W.J.: The small business capital gap: the special case of minority enterprise. J. Financ. **26**(2), 445–457 (1971)
6. Ng, C.K., Smith, J.K., Smith, R.L.: Evidence on the determinants of credit terms used in interfirm trade. J. Financ. **54**(3), 1109–1129 (1999)
7. Niu, Z., Cheng, D., Zhang, L., et al.: Visual analytics for networked-guarantee loans risk management. In: 2018 IEEE Pacific Visualization Symposium (PacificVis). IEEE, pp. 160–169 (2018)
8. Sarlin, P., Marghescu, D.: Visual predictions of currency crises using self-organizing maps. Intell. Syst. Account. Financ. Manag. **18**(1), 15–38 (2011)
9. Shen, F., Zhao, X., Kou, G., et al.: A new deep learning ensemble credit risk evaluation model with an improved synthetic minority oversampling technique. Appl. Soft Comput. **98**, 106852 (2021)
10. Friewald, N., Wagner, C., Zechner, J.: The cross-section of credit risk premia and equity returns. J. Financ. **69**(6), 2419–2469 (2014)
11. Sun, H., Guo, M.: Credit risk assessment model of small and medium-sized enterprise based on logistic regression. In: 2015 IEEE International Conference on Industrial Engineering and Engineering Management (IEEM). IEEE (2015)
12. Cheng, D., Niu, Z., Zhang, L.: Risk research of large-scale unbalanced guarantee network loan. Chin. J. Comput. **43**(04), 668–682 (2020)
13. Bian, W.-L.: Research on credit risk management of commercial banks in China. New Econ. **2**(2), 50–51 (2016)
14. Nijskens, R., Wagner, W.: Credit risk transfer activities and systemic risk: how banks became less risky individually but posed greater risks to the financial system at the same time. J. Bank Fiannc. **35**(6), 1391–1398 (2011)
15. Flood, M.D., Lemieux, V.L., Varga, M., Wong, B.W.: The application of visual analytics to financial stability monitoring. J. Financ. Stab. **27**, 180–197 (2016)
16. Sarlin, P.: Macroprudential oversight, risk communication and visualization. J. Financ. Stab. **27**, 160–179 (2016)
17. Cheng, D., Niu, Z., Liu, X., Zhang, L.: Risk assessment of contagion paths in complex guaran-tee networks. Sci. China: Inform. Sci. **51**(07), 1068–1083 (2021)
18. Chen, W., Guo, F., Han, D., et al.: Structure-based suggestive exploration: a new approach for effective exploration of large networks. IEEE Trans. Visual Comput. Graphics **25**(1), 555–565 (2018)
19. Zhang, J., Song, Z.: Research on knowledge graph for quantification of relationship between enterprises and recognition. In: 2019 4th IEEE International Conference on Cybernetics (Cybconf). IEEE (2019)
20. Rönnqvist, S., Sarlin, P.: Bank networks from text: interrelations, centrality and determinants. Quant. Financ. **15**(10), 1619–1635 (2015)
21. Didimo, W., Liotta, G., Montecchiani, F., Palladino, P.: An advanced network visualization system for financial crime detection. In: Visualization Symposium (PacificVis), 2011 IEEE Pacific, pp. 203–210. IEEE (2011)
22. Suh, A., Hajij, M., Wang, B., et al.: Persistent homology guided force-directed graph layouts. IEEE Trans. Visual Comput. Graphics **26**(1), 697–707 (2019)
23. Goswami, S.: Enhancement of the effective bandwidth available to a client host in a network by using multiple network devices concurrently. In: International Conference on Information and Communication Technology for Competitive Strategies. Springer Nature, Singapore (2022). https://doi.org/10.1007/978-981-19-9638-2_13
24. Yadav, S., Raj, R.: Power efficient network selector placement in control plane of multiple networks-on-chip. J. Supercomput. **78**(5), 6664–6695 (2022)

25. Bharatula, S., Murthy, B.S.: A novel spectrum sensing technique for multiple network scenario. In: Proceedings of International Conference on Communication and Artificial Intelligence: ICCAI 2021. Springer Nature, Singapore (2022). https://doi.org/10.1007/978-981-19-0976-4_9
26. Xing, G., et al.: Improving UWB ranging accuracy via multiple network model with second order motion prediction. Cluster Comput. 1–12 (2023)

MS-GTR: Multi-stream Graph Transformer for Skeleton-Based Action Recognition

Weichao Zhao[1,2], Jingliang Peng[1,2], and Na Lv[1,2(✉)]

[1] Shandong Provincial Key Laboratory of Network Based Intelligent Computing, University of Jinan, Jinan 250022, China
[2] School of Information Science and Engineering, University of Jinan, Jinan 250022, China
ise_lvn@ujn.edu.cn

Abstract. Skeleton-based action recognition has achieved remarkable progress by employing graph convolutional neural networks (GCNs) to model correlations among body joints. However, GCNs have limitations in establishing long-term dependencies and are constrained by the natural connections of human body joints. To overcome these issues, we propose a Graph relative TRansformer (GTR) that captures temporal features through learnable topology and invariant joint adjacency graphs. The GTR provides a high-level representation of the structure of the spatial skeleton, seamlessly integrated into the time series. Moreover, we introduce a Multi-Stream Graph Transformer (MS-GTR) to integrate various dynamic information for an end-to-end human action recognition task. The MS-GTR applies a double-branch structure, where the GTR is implemented as the main branch to extract long-term dynamic features, and an auxiliary branch processes short-term kinematic content. Finally, we use cross-attention as an inter-branch interaction mediator. Experimental results on the HDM05, NTU RGB+D, and NTU RGB+D 120 datasets demonstrate the potential of the proposed MS-GTR model for improving action recognition.

Keywords: Action recognition · Transformer · Skeleton-based · Graph

1 Introduction

Given its potential applications in video surveillance [13] and virtual reality [11], human action recognition has garnered significant interest from academia and industry. Compared to the original video data, skeleton data offers several advantages, including mitigating complex background interference and adapting to dynamic changes. Consequently, researchers have developed various skeleton-based action recognition methods. While existing action recognition methods exhibit diversity, there is a consensus that extracting sufficient spatial-temporal information is crucial. Traditional approaches commonly use handcrafted features to model the spatial human joint framework and dynamic information in the temporal dimension. However, these exquisitely designed features are tailored to specific data and applications but are difficult to generalize. Deep learning techniques have rapidly evolved in recent years and are widely used for autonomous feature extraction. Representative networks include convolutional neural networks (CNNs) for processing static images and recurrent neural networks (RNNs) for modeling long-term contextual information in sequential data, such as joint coordinate sequences. In virtue of the peculiarity of the non-Euclidean data format of the natural physical connection of the skeleton structure, Yan et al. [32] pioneered graph-based approaches to model joints and their contacts for skeleton-based action recognition using graph convolutional neural networks (GCNs) and temporal convolution. Since then, GCNs have become the dominant deep neural network architecture for skeleton-based action recognition. Despite their success, GCNs still struggle to establish long-term temporal dependencies and often overlook joint cooperative relationships in motion. For instance, the "clapping" motion heavily relies on the cooperation between the left and right hands, but consciously focusing on the joint-to-joint relationship can lead to computational problems in the model.

In this paper, we proposed a novel framework for skeleton-based action recognition called Multi-Stream Graph Transformer (MS-GTR), as illustrated in Fig. 1. This framework enables effective multi-scale processing of skeleton information and extraction of representative spatio-temporal features. Concretely, we improve the transformer not only to model sequence context dependencies but also to incorporate the graph structure of the skeleton in action recognition. Additionally, we extract diverse information from the joint trajectories to enrich the range of expressions. We divide the data into the main and auxiliary branches to avoid computational complexity. While the main branch is always involved in feature extraction, various extra streams, *e.g.*, self-similarity matrices(SSM) and difference, provide dynamic short-range information to support the main feature extractor. We employ cross-attention for information exchange between the branches to facilitate the efficient integration of motion features across different scales.

As depicted in Fig. 1, the main unit provides only a token representing global information and interacts with the feature conveyed by the auxiliary branch using cross-attention. This token has absorbed the supplemental information, returns to the main unit, and undergoes subsequent operations. We conducted experiments on several human action datasets, including HDM05, NTU RGB+D, and NTU RGB+D 120, and the obtained results validate the value of our approach in improving action recognition performance.

Our main contributions to this work are summarized as follows:

1. A novel graph Transformer architecture is proposed to represent action sequences' higher-order spatial-temporal features and eliminate the redundant dependencies associated with fixed body connectivity.
2. We propose the multi-stream model called MS-GTR that consists of two distinct branches. The main branch is designed to extract the long-term dynamic features from the joint data directly. The auxiliary branch provides short-term information.

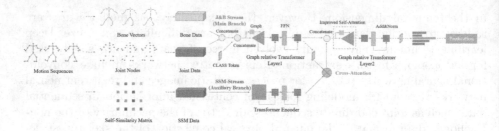

Fig. 1. Illustration of the proposed Multi-Stream Graph Transformer.

2 Related Work

2.1 Vision Transformer

The transformer [29] is a famous attention-based neural network architecture initially proposed for natural language processing. In addition to its success in NLP, the transformer has also proven its excellence for many fundamental computer vision tasks, *e.g.* classification [2,8,35], detection [1,12], and segmentation [30,36]. In particular, Zhang et al. [35] introduced the Video Transformer (VidTr) with spatio-temporal separable attention, which outperformed convolutional-based approaches for video classification. Sun et al. [27] built a multi-stream transformer network to model motion at different scales, taking advantage of the transformer's ability to capture long-range time dependencies. Chen et al. [2] applied a dual-branch vision transformer to complete the task of multi-scale feature extraction and image classification. Moreover, a simple and practical information exchange scheme between branches was proposed based on cross-attention. Inspired by their work, we offer a novel network to provide supplementary information for motion sequences at different scales through cross-attention. EAPT [47] proposes Deformable Attention, which learns offsets for each position in patches to obtain non-fixed attention information that can cover various visual elements.

2.2 Skeleton-Based Action Recognition

Skeleton-based action recognition aims to identify action through the human skeleton sequence. The most significant advantage of the first category of networks is that they take complete account of the long-term contextual associations in action. For example, Du et al. [9] fed the hierarchical structure of the human skeleton into an end-to-end hierarchical RNN, and the parts were reused and spliced together as the number of layers in the network increased. Two-stream temporal convolution networks proposed by Jia et al. [15] fully used inter-frame and intra-frame action characteristics. Xie et al. [18] proposed a temporal-then-spatial recalibration scheme that introduced the attention mechanism to recalibrate the temporal attention of frames and then further process using a convolutional neural network.

The above methods for skeleton-based action recognition primarily focused on capturing temporal features from human skeleton sequences. Still, they struggled to extract spatial characteristics from the topology of the connections between joints. Graph convolutional networks (GCNs) have emerged as a promising solution to this challenge. Yan et al. [32] were the first to apply GCNs to model dynamic skeletons for this task, but the graph topology heavily influenced the expressiveness of the model. Compared to manually setting fixed graph topology, Shi et al. [25] developed an adaptive GCN to learn the graph topology uniformly or individually. Cheng et al. [5] used parameterized topology for channel groups, but their model was bloated. Going a step further, Chen et al. [4] proposed a channel-wise graph convolution that shared a learnable topology as a generic prior for all channels and learned each channel-specific topology in a refinement way, which overcomes the inflexibility of previous methods like 2s-AGCN [25]. The adaptive graph convolutional block used in our proposed model to capture the spatial features is similar to the channel-wise methods. GAT [48] utilizes velocity information in a data-driven manner to learn discriminative spatial-temporal motion features from the sequence of skeleton graphs.

3   Method

3.1   Graph Relative Transformer

Motivation. Expressing higher-order spatial topology, adequately capturing contextual relationships, and effectively modeling spatial-temporal dependencies are essential for the signature representation of human action. However, unbiased modeling of long-term joint relationships can limit reliance on fixed natural connections in the human body, resulting in redundant dependency problems. In other words, due to the model's excessive focus on the genuine relationships of the body, the potential interactions between joints are easily overlooked. At the same time, the extraction of temporal features is over-reliant on the temporal convolution module. Adopting a fixed convolution kernel for feature extraction cannot adapt to feature changes in different periods, resulting in inadequate local feature extraction. As shown in Fig. 2, we aim to develop a graph topology that goes beyond the natural connectivity of the human body and can represent potential information of human pose. We use this topology to participate in the spatial-temporal feature with the improved Transformer. The goal is to capture long-term dependencies while retaining constraints on the higher-order spatial information of the skeleton in a lightweight manner.

Implementation of Graph. We attempt to find a reasonable and relatively accessible graph topology to guide us in constructing the spatial information of the skeleton. Our model involves two forms of graph convolution units to gather spatial details in a single frame. In the first approach, we follow the critical design of the spatial graph convolutional neural network proposed by [32]. The difference is that the sampling function is redefined using attention scores instead

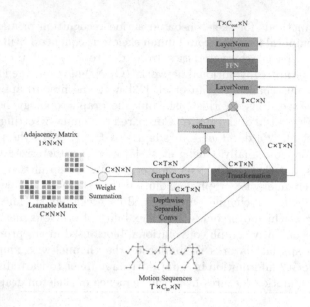

Fig. 2. Illustration of the proposed graph relative transformer.

of inter-joint connections, and the partition strategy is redesigned by manually setting thresholds to extract different scales of joint information. We determine the attention score among vertices as follows:

$$a_{ij} = \mathbf{x}_i \mathbf{w}_i \cdot (\mathbf{x}_j \mathbf{w}_j)^T \tag{1}$$

where $\mathbf{w}$ is the weight parameter. After normalization we end up with a $N \times N$ attention scores matrix and partition the vertex neighborhood by thresholds. This partition strategy can filter the vertices that are more related to a certain vertex as:

$$N(v_i) = \{v_j | threshold_{low} < a_{ij} \le threshold_{up}\} \tag{2}$$

where $threshold_{up}$ and $threshold_{low}$ are the upper and lower limits of the thresholds, respectively. However, this approach dramatically increases the computational complexity of the model when calculating the attention scores, resulting in a waste of computational resources, and it does not show the expected effect during the experiment as shown in Sect. 4.3.

Inspired by [4], we aim to capture potential dependencies between joints in a manner that extends beyond the channels of the original spatial coordinates. Therefore, we designed a learnable matrix to represent the degree of association between joints, unlike the attention score matrix, which is parameterized and obtained through model optimization. However, as this solution may lead to the loss of some graph structure features by operating globally, we also add the adjacency matrix as a guide to natural connection to complement it. Another advantage of our approach is that the channels are grouped and globally averaged within the group pooling, which helps simplify the network model. As shown in

Fig. 2, relying on the joint association relationships provided by the learnable and adjacency matrices, we apply a graph convolutional operation on the features extracted by the depthwise separable convolution block to obtain an update of the nodal expression features. The obtained feature vectors will be directly involved in extracting the inter-frame dependencies.

Improved Transformer. The standard transformer is the backbone of our model, which we improve to achieve better performance and establish a baseline for subsequent experiments. To incorporate the spatial details of the skeleton, we reconstruct the query vector in the following way:

$$\mathbf{q}_i^t = \sum_{v_j^t \in N(v_i^t)} a_{ij}^t \phi_q(\mathbf{x}_j^t) \tag{3}$$

where a_{ij}^t denotes the weight coefficient of vertex i and vertex j at time t in the generalized sense. After fully considering the spatial feature map, we obtain each frame's corresponding key-value vector pairs by transforming the channel features using Eqs. (4) and (5):

$$\mathbf{k}_i^t = \phi_k(\mathbf{x}_i^t) \tag{4}$$

$$\mathbf{v}_i^t = \phi_v(\mathbf{x}_i^t) \tag{5}$$

In the temporal dimension, the focus is on modeling the frame-to-frame dependencies to obtain a representative feature map that incorporates the attention mechanism of the transformer:

$$\alpha_n^{ij} = \mathbf{q}_n^i \cdot \mathbf{k}_n^{j\,T} \tag{6}$$

where i, j is the frame number of the action sequence, and n is the index number of the joint node. The joint characteristics of a given frame are updated based on information shared from the same joint in other frames, which establishes a strong long-term dependency. A global information token is introduced to summarize events for the entire time sequence, similar to the approach used in natural language processing. The update equation for a joint node's features in a given frame is as follows:

$$y_n^i = \sum \sigma(\frac{\alpha_n^{ij}}{\sqrt{d_k}})v_n^j \tag{7}$$

where σ is an activation function that normalizes the input. After all the frames have been aggregated, the subsequent feed-forward layer can adjust the dimensions of the output, adding additional capabilities to the model.

3.2   Multi-stream Model Architecture

Based on GTR, we have constructed a robust MS-GTR model for integrating a variety of dynamic information streams toward skeleton-based action recognition. The overall model architecture is shown in Fig. 1. The proposed algorithm operates on an action sequence $S = \{s^1, \ldots, s^t, \ldots, s^T\}$, consisting of T frames where each element $s^t \in \mathbb{R}^{N \times 3}$ represents the 3D coordinates of all available captured joints at a particular frame. We introduce the main and auxiliary branches in the model to capture a broader range of action details.

The main branch is concerned with the long-term dynamic information representation in the joint and bone data. Long-term dynamic information representation refers to a change in motion over long periods, usually in terms of modeling sequence contextual relationships. Specifically, we introduce bone representation as an interpretation of inter-joint connection to obtain directly from the original joint coordinates, which is then fed into the main branch along with the underlying joint features. To calculate bone vectors, which describe the relationship between two joints, we adopt the same approach as in [25]. Given a pair of head joint $J_i = \{x_i, y_i, z_i\}$ and tail joint $J_j = \{x_j, y_j, z_j\}$, we calculate the second-order information as $B_{i,j} = \{x_j - x_i, y_j - y_i, z_j - z_i\}$.

The auxiliary branch, in contrast, captures short-term features, such as the self-similarity matrix (SSM) and the difference between frames(also known as velocity). Given a set of joint features $J = \{J_1, J_2, \ldots, J_N\}$, we construct the self-similarity matrix $M_{ssm} \in \mathbb{R}^{N \times N}$ by comparing all the elements in the joint feature set with each other using the calculation formula $M(i, j) = SSM(J_i, J_j)$. The dot product of elements with each other is the simplest way to calculate the self-similarity matrix. This SSM data is used as the input of the auxiliary branch and as an additional information stream to the main branch regarding joint tightness. Likewise, the motion velocity of joints contains a wealth of action features. The velocity of a particular joint can be calculated as $\nu^t = s^{t+1} - s^t$, where ν^t is a vector reflecting the difference between two continuous frames in the original action sequence. This velocity information can be input into an auxiliary branch to support the main component regarding speed characteristics.

To ensure simplicity and fluency, we limit the role of the auxiliary branch to information transfer and rely on the main branch for capturing the most useful action features. To facilitate interaction between the main and auxiliary branches, we employ cross-attention. The remaining streams provide additional supplements to the main branch through the participation of a token related to global information. Specifically, the token of the main branch, $token_{main}$, is concatenated with the sequence data $S_{auxiliary} = \{s^1_{aux}, \ldots, s^T_{aux}\}$ arising from the auxiliary branch. Subsequently, a self-attention mechanism is implemented on the updated sequence $S_{fresh} = \{token_{main}, s^1_{aux}, \ldots, s^T_{aux}\}$, allowing the $token_{main}$ also to detect the characteristics of the auxiliary branch.

4   Experiments

4.1   Datasets

HDM05. HDM05 [22] is captured using optical marker-based technology, which helps to reduce noise interference in the motion capture data. It contains trajectories for 31 joints from 130 motion classes performed by five actors. And among these 130 categories, some can be grouped into one category due to the same expression meaning, so we finally get the data of 65 action categories.

NTU RGB+D. The NTU RGB+D [23] involves the capture of motion sequences using three synchronized Microsoft Kinect v2 devices. The dataset contains 56,880 clips from 40 subjects, with each action organized into one of 60 action categories(including 11 multiplayer action categories). The skeleton data includes the 3D coordinates of 25 major joints at each frame. The dataset offers two evaluation criteria for action recognition methods: **Cross-View** is based on the camera's viewpoint that captured the action. The training set consists of 37,920 samples captured from a 45-degree view from the left and right, while the test set contains 18,960 samples captured from the front view. **Cross-Subject** validates the model in terms of different subjects. The experiment had 40 subjects categorized into training and test groups, each containing 20 actors. The training and test sets contain 40,320 and 16,560 samples, respectively.

NTU RGB+D 120. The NTU RGB+D 120 [40] is a large-scale dataset expended from the NTU RGB+D dataset. In addition to the 60 categories in the previous dataset, this dataset has an additional 60 types (i.e., 120 classes in NTU RGB+D 120). This dataset comprises 114,480 action clips captured from 155 camera views with 106 subjects. The authors of this dataset likewise recommend two benchmarks: Cross-Subject, similar to the previous dataset, are grouped by subjects, with 53 subjects in each group (63,026 samples for training and 50,922 clips for validation). **Cross-Set** is based on the setup made at the cameras' height and distance to the subjects to construct the training and testing set. The training set consists of 54,471 samples, while the test set contains 59,477 samples. The dataset includes 56,880 RGB+D video samples from 40 subjects, with each action classified into one of 60 action categories (including 11 multiplayer action categories).

4.2 Implementation Details

The implementation of our model is based on PyTorch and was run on an NVIDIA GeForce RTX 3090 GPU. We use gradient descent to update the model parameters. Specifically, we employed a stochastic gradient descent (SGD) optimizer with a momentum of 0.9 and a weight decay of 0.0004. We set the maximum number of training epochs to 120 and the size of each batch to 64. The initial learning rate is set to 0.01 and decays to 0.1 of the previous at epochs 45, 75, and 90. We employed the cross-entropy function as the loss function and added label smoothing to alleviate over-fitting and improve the model's generalization ability.

4.3   Ablation Study

We can demonstrate the contributions of the proposed components in GTR to achieve the goal of action recognition through a series of relevant experiments on the Cross-View benchmark of the NTU RGB+D dataset.

Graph Relative Transformer Block. First, we need to confirm whether it is necessary to use graph convolution to construct skeletal spatial guidelines instead of using transformers for the intuitive processing of time series. As previously mentioned, we feed the features extracted by the standard transformer to the classifier for action recognition and compare the result. Additionally, this section will discuss the implications of aggregating and updating graph nodes. As shown in Table 1, the experiment result indicates that combining the initial transformer model with the graph-related blocks significantly improves performance. Therefore, the most effective GTR associated with channels is selected as the foundational component for later model upgrades.

Table 1. Comparisons of the action recognition accuracy on Transformer with and without graph dependencies.

Methods	Accuracy (%)
Standard transformer	81.17
GTR (Threshold-dependent)	87.66
GTR (Learnable-matrix)	**89.74**

Table 2. Comparison of the effect of the presence or absence of auxiliary branch and different action input modalities on recognition results.

Joint	Bone	SSM	Difference	Accuracy (%)
√	×	×	×	90.33
×	√	×	×	88.06
√	√	×	×	90.32
×	×	√	×	90.68
√	×	√	×	91.19
×	×	×	√	85.17
√	√	√	×	**92.25**

Multi-stream Framework. To improve the representation and generalization ability of the model, we introduce an auxiliary branch to provide different forms of action implications to supplement the main unit. We conducted experiments by blocking the auxiliary streams and comparing their effects with those of the main branch alone. The results in Table 2 show that the fusion of information between branches can provide better semantic support for recognition. We also measured the strength of the different action dynamic expressions introduced to the main branch for recognition. When only difference is available, the model performance is most unsatisfactory. Although the joint flow alone can improve the model to 90.33%, adding the self-similarity matrix to the main branch as an auxiliary information flow improves the recognition accuracy by 0.86%. It indicates that the collaboration of multi-stream information is more beneficial for the final action recognition.

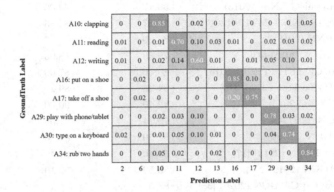

Fig. 3. Confusion matrix of skeleton-based action recognition with MS-GTR building on the cross View validation of NTU RGB+D dataset.

4.4   Confusion Matrix Analysis

As shown in Fig. 3, we visualized the confusion matrix of the cross-view benchmark results on the NTU RGB+D dataset to identify the categories that caused substantial interference leading to false recognition. Two situations can cause confusion between classification categories. The first set included categories where the inability to capture the reference led to some inaccuracy in recognition, including "A11:reading", "A12:writing", "A29:playing with phone or tablet", and "A30:type on a keyboard". These actions all involved manipulating the hands, and the specific tools used varied between the categories. The second set of confusing categories was the inverse order of each other, such as the pair of action

Table 3. Performance comparison on HDM05.

Methods	Accuracy (%)
Hierarchical RNNs (2015)	96.92
Deep LSTM (2016)	96.80
DHMR (2021) [39]	98.30
MANs (2021)	99.04
GTR (Ours)	**99.34**

sequences "A16:put on a shoe" and "A17:take off a shoe". We provided an explanation that as the network goes deeper, location information appears to become less significant.

Table 4. Performance comparison on NTU RGB+D dataset.

Methods	NTU RGB+D	
	Cross Subject (%)	Cross View (%)
Hierarchical RNNs (2015)	59.10	64.00
Clips + CNN + MTLN (2017) [16]	79.57	84.83
IndRNN (2018)	81.80	87.97
VA-RNN (2019) [33]	79.80	88.90
AMCGC-LSTM (2020) [31]	80.10	87.60
RGB+Skeleton (2020) [10]	84.23	89.27
TS-TCNs (2020)	82.40	90.20
MANs (2021)	79.74	91.55
ST-GCN (2018)	81.50	88.30
AM-STGCN (2019) [17]	83.40	91.40
2s-AGCN (2019)	88.50	95.10
Advanced CA-GCN (2020) [38]	83.5	91.4
LSGM+GTSC (2020) [14]	84.71	91.74
MS-G3D (2020) [41]	91.50	96.20
MST-GCN (2021) [42]	91.50	96.60
FV-GCN (2022) [28]	81.70	89.80
STAR (2021) [24]	83.40	89.00
MS-GTR (Ours)	84.50	92.25

Table 5. Performance comparison on NTU RGB+D 120 dataset.

Methods	NTU RGB+D 120	
	Cross Subject (%)	Cross Setup (%)
ST-LSTM (2016)	55.7	57.9
GCA-LSTM (2017)	61.2	63.3
FSNet (2019)	59.9	62.4
ST-GCN (2018)	70.7	73.2
2s-AGCN (2019)	82.9	84.9
MS-G3D (2020)	86.9	88.4
SGN (2020) [46]	77.9	78.5
MST-GCN (2021)	87.5	88.8
EfficientGCN (2022) [43]	88.3	89.1
PGT (2022) [45]	86.5	88.8
KA-AGTN (2022) [44]	86.1	88.0
MS-GTR (Ours)	78.3	80.8

4.5   Comparison to the State of the Art

To visually verify the feasibility and effectiveness of our model on action recognition, we conducted experiments on the HDM05 dataset (Table 3), the NTU RGB+D dataset (Table 4), and the NTU RGB+D 120 dataset (Table 5).

Notably, on the HDM05 dataset, we are currently at the forefront with a result of 99.34%. Whether it is the NTU RGB+D or the extended version, our model always has an advantage in recognition accuracy compared to the recurrent approaches, which indicates that our baseline model extracts superior features when establishing temporal dependencies. However, we still have a long way to go regarding a series of graph convolution variants of the method. Although our model is slightly less effective than 2 s-AGCN, we get a more significant improvement when we introduce the adaptive graph convolutional block, which proves the values of embedding the topology with the Transformer as the baseline model. For STAR [24], which was designed with the same intention as our baseline model, we used a graph structure to compensate for the lack of purely self-attention mechanisms to capture spatial features. Compared to this model, our recognition accuracy improved by 3.25% on Cross View and 0.75% on Cross Subject. In particular, taking KA-AGTN as an example, this model is also positioned as a graph transformer, but its model takes 2 s-AGCN as the baseline model and interpolates the attention layer for enhancing the dependence of local neighboring joints while preserving the spatio-temporal graph convolution layer. Our model starts from the most basic Transformer rather than using the currently available models as a baseline model to improve recognition accuracy, which results in us not fully utilizing the computational resources to represent the capabilities of our model. Therefore, to improve the model's generalization ability, we can use the existing pre-trained model to participate in the task, which is the direction we can improve in the future.

5   Conclusion

In this work, we propose a novel approach called GTR, which utilizes a transformer to efficiently capture the temporal features of action progression instead of solely relying on graph convolution neural networks. The proposed GTR involves a graph based on the natural connection of body parts in the expression update, which enhances the model expression diversification by motion features of different scales and makes the results more credible. We also introduce motion features with various expression meanings while reducing the complexity of model operations. In contrast to the direct fusion of action information from different scales, MS-GTR involves auxiliary input under the guidance of the main branch without introducing additional calculation costs. Our proposed MS-GTR achieves state-of-the-art performance on datasets captured by motion capture devices with widely varying accuracy and notably achieves leading recognition accuracy on the HDM05 dataset.

References

1. Carion, N., Massa, F., Synnaeve, G., Usunier, N., Kirillov, A., Zagoruyko, S.: End-to-end object detection with transformers. In: Vedaldi, A., Bischof, H., Brox, T., Frahm, J.-M. (eds.) ECCV 2020. LNCS, vol. 12346, pp. 213–229. Springer, Cham (2020). https://doi.org/10.1007/978-3-030-58452-8_13
2. Chen, C.F.R., Fan, Q., Panda, R.: CrossViT: cross-attention multi-scale vision transformer for image classification. In: Proceedings of the IEEE/CVF International Conference on Computer Vision, pp. 357–366 (2021)
3. Chen, Y., Zhang, Z., Yuan, C., Li, B., Deng, Y., Hu, W.: Channel-wise topology refinement graph convolution for skeleton-based action recognition. In: Proceedings of the IEEE/CVF International Conference on Computer Vision (ICCV), pp. 13359–13368 (2021)
4. Chen, Y., Zhang, Z., Yuan, C., Li, B., Deng, Y., Hu, W.: Channel-wise topology refinement graph convolution for skeleton-based action recognition. In: Proceedings of the IEEE/CVF International Conference on Computer Vision, pp. 13359–13368 (2021)
5. Cheng, K., Zhang, Y., Cao, C., Shi, L., Cheng, J., Lu, H.: Decoupling GCN with DropGraph module for skeleton-based action recognition. In: Vedaldi, A., Bischof, H., Brox, T., Frahm, J.-M. (eds.) ECCV 2020. LNCS, vol. 12369, pp. 536–553. Springer, Cham (2020). https://doi.org/10.1007/978-3-030-58586-0_32
6. Cho, S., Maqbool, M., Liu, F., Foroosh, H.: Self-attention network for skeleton-based human action recognition. In: Proceedings of the IEEE/CVF Winter Conference on Applications of Computer Vision, pp. 635–644 (2020)
7. Devlin, J., Chang, M.W., Lee, K., Toutanova, K.: BERT: pre-training of deep bidirectional transformers for language understanding. arXiv preprint arXiv:1810.04805 (2018)
8. Dosovitskiy, A., et al.: An image is worth 16×16 words: transformers for image recognition at scale. arXiv preprint arXiv:2010.11929 (2020)
9. Du, Y., Wang, W., Wang, L.: Hierarchical recurrent neural network for skeleton based action recognition. In: Proceedings of the IEEE Conference on Computer Vision and Pattern Recognition, pp. 1110–1118 (2015)
10. Fan, Y., Weng, S., Zhang, Y., Shi, B., Zhang, Y.: Context-aware cross-attention for skeleton-based human action recognition. IEEE Access **8**, 15280–15290 (2020)
11. Fangbemi, A.S., Liu, B., Yu, N.H., Zhang, Y.: Efficient human action recognition interface for augmented and virtual reality applications based on binary descriptor. In: De Paolis, L.T., Bourdot, P. (eds.) AVR 2018. LNCS, vol. 10850, pp. 252–260. Springer, Cham (2018). https://doi.org/10.1007/978-3-319-95270-3_21
12. Gao, P., Zheng, M., Wang, X., Dai, J., Li, H.: Fast convergence of DETR with spatially modulated co-attention. In: Proceedings of the IEEE/CVF International Conference on Computer Vision, pp. 3621–3630 (2021)
13. Han, Y., Zhang, P., Zhuo, T., Huang, W., Zhang, Y.: Going deeper with two-stream ConvNets for action recognition in video surveillance. Pattern Recogn. Lett. **107**, 83–90 (2018)
14. Huang, J., Xiang, X., Gong, X., Zhang, B., et al.: Long-short graph memory network for skeleton-based action recognition. In: Proceedings of the IEEE/CVF Winter Conference on Applications of Computer Vision, pp. 645–652 (2020)
15. Jia, J.G., Zhou, Y.F., Hao, X.W., Li, F., Desrosiers, C., Zhang, C.M.: Two-stream temporal convolutional networks for skeleton-based human action recognition. J. Comput. Sci. Technol. **35**(3), 538–550 (2020). https://doi.org/10.1007/s11390-020-0405-6

16. Ke, Q., Bennamoun, M., An, S., Sohel, F., Boussaid, F.: A new representation of skeleton sequences for 3D action recognition. In: Proceedings of the IEEE Conference on Computer Vision and Pattern Recognition, pp. 3288–3297 (2017)
17. Kong, Y., Li, L., Zhang, K., Ni, Q., Han, J.: Attention module-based spatial-temporal graph convolutional networks for skeleton-based action recognition. J. Electron. Imaging **28**(4), 043032 (2019)
18. Li, C., Xie, C., Zhang, B., Han, J., Zhen, X., Chen, J.: Memory attention networks for skeleton-based action recognition. IEEE Trans. Neural Netw. Learn. Syst. **33**(9), 4800–4814 (2021)
19. Li, M., Chen, S., Chen, X., Zhang, Y., Wang, Y., Tian, Q.: Actional-structural graph convolutional networks for skeleton-based action recognition. In: Proceedings of the IEEE/CVF Conference on Computer Vision and Pattern Recognition, pp. 3595–3603 (2019)
20. Li, S., Li, W., Cook, C., Zhu, C., Gao, Y.: Independently recurrent neural network (IndRNN): building a longer and deeper RNN. In: Proceedings of the IEEE Conference on Computer Vision and Pattern Recognition, pp. 5457–5466 (2018)
21. Liu, J., Shahroudy, A., Perez, M., Wang, G., Duan, L.Y., Kot, A.C.: NTU RGB+D 120: a large-scale benchmark for 3D human activity understanding. IEEE Trans. Pattern Anal. Mach. Intell. **42**(10), 2684–2701 (2020)
22. Müller, M., Röder, T., Clausen, M., Eberhardt, B., Krüger, B., Weber, A.: Documentation mocap database HDM05 (2007)
23. Shahroudy, A., Liu, J., Ng, T.T., Wang, G.: NTU RGB+D: a large scale dataset for 3D human activity analysis. In: Proceedings of the IEEE Conference on Computer Vision and Pattern Recognition, pp. 1010–1019 (2016)
24. Shi, F., et al.: STAR: sparse transformer-based action recognition. arXiv preprint arXiv:2107.07089 (2021)
25. Shi, L., Zhang, Y., Cheng, J., Lu, H.: Two-stream adaptive graph convolutional networks for skeleton-based action recognition. In: Proceedings of the IEEE/CVF Conference on Computer Vision and Pattern Recognition (CVPR) (2019)
26. Song, Y.F., Zhang, Z., Shan, C., Wang, L.: Constructing stronger and faster baselines for skeleton-based action recognition. IEEE Trans. Pattern Anal. Mach. Intell. **45**(2), 1474–1488 (2022)
27. Sun, Y., Shen, Y., Ma, L.: MSST-RT: multi-stream spatial-temporal relative transformer for skeleton-based action recognition. Sensors **21**(16), 5339 (2021)
28. Tang, J., Wang, Y., Fu, S., Liu, B., Liu, W.: A graph convolutional neural network model with Fisher vector encoding and channel-wise spatial-temporal aggregation for skeleton-based action recognition. IET Image Proc. **16**(5), 1433–1443 (2022)
29. Vaswani, A., et al.: Attention is all you need. In: Advances in Neural Information Processing Systems, vol. 30 (2017)
30. Xie, E., Wang, W., Yu, Z., Anandkumar, A., Alvarez, J.M., Luo, P.: SegFormer: simple and efficient design for semantic segmentation with transformers. In: Advances in Neural Information Processing Systems, vol. 34 (2021)
31. Xu, S., et al.: Attention-based multilevel co-occurrence graph convolutional LSTM for 3-D action recognition. IEEE Internet Things J. **8**(21), 15990–16001 (2020)
32. Yan, S., Xiong, Y., Lin, D.: Spatial temporal graph convolutional networks for skeleton-based action recognition. In: Thirty-Second AAAI Conference on Artificial Intelligence (2018)
33. Zhang, P., Lan, C., Xing, J., Zeng, W., Xue, J., Zheng, N.: View adaptive neural networks for high performance skeleton-based human action recognition. IEEE Trans. Pattern Anal. Mach. Intell. **41**(8), 1963–1978 (2019)

34. Zhang, X., Xu, C., Tian, X., Tao, D.: Graph edge convolutional neural networks for skeleton-based action recognition. IEEE Trans. Neural Netw. Learn. Syst. **31**(8), 3047–3060 (2019)
35. Zhang, Y., et al.: VidTr: video transformer without convolutions. In: Proceedings of the IEEE/CVF International Conference on Computer Vision, pp. 13577–13587 (2021)
36. Zheng, S., et al.: Rethinking semantic segmentation from a sequence-to-sequence perspective with transformers. In: Proceedings of the IEEE/CVF Conference on Computer Vision and Pattern Recognition, pp. 6881–6890 (2021)
37. Zhu, W., et al.: Co-occurrence feature learning for skeleton based action recognition using regularized deep LSTM networks. In: Proceedings of the AAAI Conference on Artificial Intelligence, vol. 30 (2016)
38. Zhang, X, Xu, C, Tao, D.: Context aware graph convolution for skeleton-based action recognition. In: Proceedings of the IEEE/CVF Conference on Computer Vision and Pattern Recognition, pp. 14333–14342 (2020)
39. Lv, N., Wang, Y., Feng, Z., Peng, J.: Deep hashing for motion capture data retrieval. In: ICASSP 2021–2021 IEEE International Conference on Acoustics, Speech and Signal Processing (ICASSP), pp. 2215–2219. IEEE (2021)
40. Liu, J., Shahroudy, A., Perez, M., Wang, G., Duan, L., Kot, A.: NTU RGB+ D 120: a large-scale benchmark for 3D human activity understanding. IEEE Trans. Pattern Anal. Mach. Intell. **42**(10), 2684–2701 (2019)
41. Liu, Z., Zhang, H., Chen, Z., Wang, Z., Ouyang, W.: Disentangling and unifying graph convolutions for skeleton-based action recognition. In: Proceedings of the IEEE/CVF Conference on Computer Vision and Pattern Recognition, pp. 143–152 (2020)
42. Chen, Z., Li, S., Yang, B., Li, Q., Liu, H.: Multi-scale spatial temporal graph convolutional network for skeleton-based action recognition. In: Proceedings of the AAAI Conference on Artificial Intelligence, pp. 1113–1122 (2021)
43. Song, Y., Zhang, Z., Shan, C., Wang, L.: Constructing stronger and faster baselines for skeleton-based action recognition. IEEE Trans. Pattern Anal. Mach. Intell. **45**(2), 1474–1488 (2022)
44. Liu, Y., Zhang, H., Xu, D., He, K.: Graph transformer network with temporal kernel attention for skeleton-based action recognition. Knowl.-Based Syst. **240**, 108146 (2022)
45. Chen, S., Xu, K., Jiang, X., Sun, T.: Pyramid spatial-temporal graph transformer for skeleton-based action recognition. Appl. Sci. **12**(18), 9229 (2022)
46. Zhang, P., Lan, C., Zeng, W., Xing, J., Xue, J., Zheng, N.: Semantics-guided neural networks for efficient skeleton-based human action recognition. In: Proceedings of the IEEE/CVF Conference on Computer Vision and Pattern Recognition, pp. 1112–1121 (2020)
47. Lin, X., Sun, S., Huang, W.: EAPT: efficient attention pyramid transformer for image processing. IEEE Trans. Multimedia **25**, 50–61 (2021)
48. Zhang, J., Xie, W., Wang, C.: Graph-aware transformer for skeleton-based action recognition. Vis. Comput. **39**, 4501–4512 (2023). https://doi.org/10.1007/s00371-022-02603-1

GFENet: Group-Free Enhancement Network for Indoor Scene 3D Object Detection

Feng Zhou[1], Ju Dai[2(✉)], Junjun Pan[2,3], Mengxiao Zhu[1], Xingquan Cai[1], Bin Huang[4], and Chen Wang[5]

[1] North China University of Technology, Beijing, China
{zhoufeng,zhumx,caixingquan}@ncut.edu.cn
[2] Peng Cheng Laboratory, Shenzhen, China
daij@pcl.ac.cn
[3] State Key Laboratory of Virtual Reality Technology and Systems, Beihang University, Beijing, China
pan_junjun@buaa.edu.cn
[4] AI Research Center, Hangzhou Innovation Institute, Beihang University, Hangzhou, China
marshuangbin@buaa.edu.cn
[5] Beijing Technology and Business University, Beijing, China
wangc@btbu.edu.cn

Abstract. The state-of-the-art group-free network (GFNet) has achieved superior performance for indoor scene 3D object detection. However, we find there is still room for improvement in the following three aspects. Firstly, seed point features extracted by multi-layer perception (MLP) in the backbone (PointNet++) neglect to consider the different importance of each level feature. Second, the single-scale transformer module in GFNet to handle hand-crafted grouping via Hough Voting cannot adequately model the relationship between points and objects. Finally, GFNet directly utilizes the decoders to predict detection results disregarding the different contributions of decoders at each stage. In this paper, we propose the group-free enhancement network (GFENet) to tackle the above issues. Specifically, our network mainly consists of three lifting modules: the weighted MLP (WMLP) module, the hierarchical-aware module, and the stage-aware module. The WMLP module adaptively combines features of different levels in the backbone before max-pooling for informative feature learning. The hierarchical-aware module formulates a hierarchical way to mitigate the negative impact of insufficient modeling of points and objects. The stage-aware module aggregates multi-stage predictions adaptively for better detection performance. Extensive experiments on ScanNet V2 and SUN RGB-D datasets demonstrate the effectiveness and advantages of our method against existing 3D object detection methods.

Keywords: 3D Object Detection · Point Cloud · Transformers · Hough Voting · Group-free

1 Introduction

3D object detection from point clouds is an active research task and is receiving increasing attention in the computer community due to the progressive development of commercial depth cameras [1–4]. It is designed to simultaneously localize and recognize

B. Sheng et al. (Eds.): CGI 2023, LNCS 14497, pp. 119–136, 2024.
https://doi.org/10.1007/978-3-031-50075-6_10

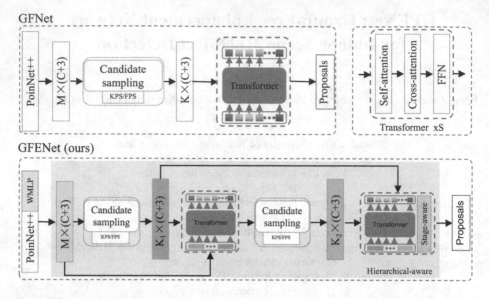

Fig. 1. The overall architecture of our GFENet model. GFENet is built based on GFNet with three new modules: 1) the WMLP module aims to automatically weight different level features for obtaining better seed point features; 2) the hierarchical-aware module concentrates on hierarchically modeling global context dependencies between seed points and candidate objects for extracting more plausible feature representations, as shown in the light sky blue area; 3) the stage-aware module is utilized for adaptively combining the prediction results of different stages. For better comparison with the baseline, the framework of GFNet is also provided. Best viewed in color. (Color figure online)

3D objects from the input point clouds. As a core technology in 3D scene understanding tasks, 3D object detection plays a wide range of applications in virtual reality, autonomous driving, and other fields.

With the breakthrough of deep convolutional neural networks (DCNNs), significant progress has been made in 2D object detection. Different from the 2D task, 3D object detection takes irregular, disordered, and sparse point clouds as input. Because of the intrinsic complexities and variations of expressions of point cloud data, it is challenging to exploit the powerful capabilities of DCNNs directly.

To tackle the discrepancy between images and point clouds, earlier works adopt parametric min-cut [5], Exemplar-SVM [6] and many other hand-crafted feature representations to deal with 3D object detection. Some studies focus on projecting point clouds into new spaces, where the projected data has regular structures. These works can be roughly divided into grid projection-based [7,8] and voxelization-based [9–12]. The grid projection-based methods project point cloud data into a bird's-eye-view, while the voxelization-based approaches convert input data into 3D-grid voxels. Point cloud features will then be extracted using standard 2D or 3D convolutional operations on the transformed space. Nevertheless, the projected data damage the important spatial structural details of the point cloud.

Another technical branch is to extract expressive representations directly from original point cloud data based on PointNet/PointNet++ [13, 14]. Because of these pioneering exploratory works, it becomes a prevalence for point cloud based object detection, and extensive endeavors have been devoted [15–19]. In particular, the deep hough voting network [20], with the PointNet++ as backbone, attempts to vote on object centroids directly from point clouds and learns to aggregate votes from their features. It transfers the classic traditional hough voting scheme to a regression task and reproduces it through deep neural networks. However, the hand-crafted grouping scheme in VoteNet cannot effectively model spatial dependencies of the votes.

To tackle the above problem, GFNet [21] leverages the self-attention and cross-attention mechanism to utilize all points to vote. Although more plausible results have been achieved, we observe that the following modifications can be used for performance improvement. Firstly, in the PointNet++-based backbone, features of seed points are obtained by simply max-pooling and then fed into the next MLP without considering the different contributions of different level features. Secondly, to address the limitation of the hand-crafted grouping scheme, GFNet utilizes Transformer mechanism, which leverages all points to model relationship between points and objects for voting. However, GFNet only relies on a single-scale transformer module, which cannot effectively model the spatial dependencies between points and objects. Thirdly, GFNet fuses object features from different stages to produce more accurate object detection results. However, directly integrating predictions from different decoders is not sufficient. Different decodes will provide different information for the final predictions.

This paper discusses the task of indoor scene 3D object detection based on the point cloud. In particular, we adopt GFNet [21] as our baseline, based on which a WMLP module, a hierarchical-aware module, and a stage-aware module are proposed to address the above three bottlenecks. As shown in bottom-left PointNet++ block in Fig. 1, the proposed WMLP module learns a weighted mask for each extracted feature level before the max-pooling operation. Features of different levels are then multiplied by the corresponding masks to generate a weighted aware feature representation. Towards the second problem, inspired by [22], a hierarchical-aware module is introduced to model the spatial dependencies hierarchically, which is as shown in the sky-blue part in Fig. 1. For the third issue, a stage-aware module is proposed to complement the above two modules, which can adaptively combine different stages prediction results for performance improvement, as shown in the bottom-right transformer block in Fig. 1. Experiment on ScanNet V2 [23] and SUN RGB-D [24] validate the superior performance of our method against state-of-the-arts. The main contributions can be summarized as follows:

- We propose a novel GFENet based on GFNet, involving a WMLP, a hierarchical-aware module, and a stage-aware module to obtain performance gains for 3D object detection in indoor scenes.
- The WMLP module is used to enhance seed point features by considering the different contributions of each level feature. The hierarchical-aware module is designed to model spatial dependencies between point and object hierarchically. The stage-aware module is leveraged to adaptive ensemble prediction results from each stage.
- Experiments on ScanNet V2 and SUN RGB-D datasets demonstrate the effectiveness and superiority of our three modification modules compared with GFNet.

The rest of the paper is organized as follows. Section 2 briefly reviews the most related literature. We then elaborate on the GFENet in Sect. 3. Experimental results and depth analysis are provided in Sect. 4. Finally, the conclusions are drawn in Sect. 5.

2 Related Work

3D Object Detection. Thanks to the development of deep neural networks, great progress has been made in 2D image object detection [25–30]. However, 2D object detection neglects the depth information of detected targets. 3D object detection outperforms 2D tasks in terms of spatial perception and more consistent with human visual cognition. Therefore, the 3D object detection task based on point clouds has become the new prevalence.

Due to the inherent irregularity, disorder, and sparsity of point cloud data, it is unsuitable for directly leveraging the advantages of the DCNN methods. Many methods try to project point clouds into 2D or bird's-eye-view plans or voxel and then extract feature representations using the 2D image methods [7, 8, 31] or 3D convolutional methods [9–11]. These methods show convincing for both 2D and 3D object detection. However, projection-based methods can damage the original structural information of the point clouds.

PointNet-Based 3D Object Detection. Thanks to the powerful abilities of PointNet [13] and PointNet++ [14], informative features can be extracted from raw point clouds. Based on the advanced explorations [13, 14] and inspired by the Hough voting strategy in 2D image object detection, VoteNet [20] proposes an end-to-end framework for 3D point cloud object detection, achieving state-of-the-art results at the time. However, VoteNet neglects geometric primitives, which is beneficial for the task. After then, H3DNet [15] and MCGNet [32] present a 4-way network to utilize these geometric primitives information, and it obtains more plausible results. Although superior performance have been achieved, methods with PointNet/PointNet++ as the backbone neglect to consider the varied contributions of different level features, as the seed point features are obtained by merely MLP and then fed into the next max-pooling.

To address the above problems, Huang *et al.* [33] propose a Combined-MLP (CMLP) with a different level max-pooling structure to extract different level representations and concatenate them to form the final feature. However, the simple concatenation strategy considers different hierarchical features equally important regardless of their different contributions to the final prediction. VENet [17] adopts an attention mechanism with an Attentive MLP (AMLP) to enhance seed point feature description via adaptively considering multi-layer information in MLP. Nevertheless, AMLP treats the features from each level separately. To comprehensively utilize the different level features of seed points, we propose the WMLP module, which adaptively weighted different level features to attain expressive representations.

Transformer-Based 3D Object Detection. Recently, Transformer has gained incredible standout performance in natural language processing [34] and various vision tasks [35–41]. Due to the attention mechanism, Transformer has powerful abilities to model global context information. Therefore, extensive efforts have applied Transformer to point cloud data analysis [21,42,43]. For instance, Misra *et al.* [42] propose the first end-to-end transformer-based framework for 3D object detection. GFNet [21] leverages a simple yet powerful transformer module to replace the proposal head in VoteNet [20] and has achieved superior performance. Based on GFNet [21], this paper also resorts to the Transformer and formulates a hierarchical-aware module to build spatial context dependencies among different level features and the same level feature. Furthermore, we design the stage-aware module to automatically ensemble the prediction results of different stages, different from GFNet [21] to directly aggregate the detections from all stages.

3   Our Approach

The proposed GFENet is inspired by the GFNet [21], aiming to enhance the seed point representation abilities, model the spatial dependencies between seed points and candidate objects, and adaptively ensemble predictions of different stages. To achieve the goals, we formulate three new modules based on GFNet [21], *i.e.,* the WMLP module, the hierarchical-aware module, and the stage-aware module. This section elaborates on the details of GFENet, and the overall framework is shown in Fig. 1. The input to GFENet is point cloud data $P = \{p_1, ..., p_N\} \in \mathcal{R}^{N \times 3}$ without color and other information. N is the number of the input point cloud. The output of the 3D object detection is to generate proposals for each object for the input, giving the oriented 3D bounding boxes and associated semantic labels.

3.1   Backgrounds

PointNet++ [14] is a hierarchical network consisting of several set-abstraction and upsampling layers to process point cloud data. This network is usually leveraged as a backbone to extract point cloud features for downstream tasks.

Based on PointNet++ [14], VoteNet [20] formulates a trainable network for 3D object detection that combines interest point generation, vote generation, vote aggregation, and object proposal schemes into a single but powerful end-to-end model. It contains three main parts: point cloud feature learning through a backbone network, hough voting from seed points, and proposal generation and classification. VoteNet [20] adopts PointNet++ [14] as the backbone to obtain seed point features which an MLP generates, and each seed point produces one vote. When votes are obtained, they are sampled and grouped based on spatial proximity.

GFNet [21] is built based on VoteNet. Its framework is displayed in Fig. 1. It employs PointNet++ as the backbone to extract point features and then utilizes k-Closest Points Sampling (KPS) to classify each point on the input point cloud to be a real object candidate or not. In the end, GFNet leverages the self-attention mechanism to model interactions between object features and uses the cross-attention insight to model relationships between objects and points to obtain detection results. For more details about GFNet, please refer to [21].

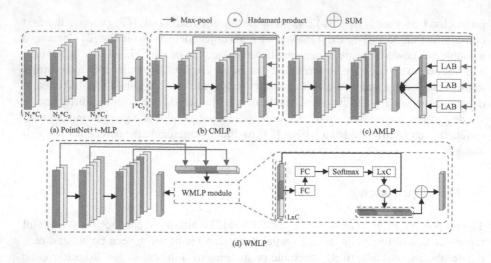

Fig. 2. Comparison of different MLP-based point cloud feature extraction, the feature vector is pooled from each of the layers for each point. (a) PointNet++-MLP adopts the last layer to extract feature vector; (b) CMLP leverages different layers to extract feature vector; (c) AMLP learns weights for different level feature to obtain more plausible representation; (d) the proposed WMLP combines the feature from different layers through a learned weight map. Best viewed in color. (Color figure online)

3.2 WMLP Module

In the classical MLP of PointNet++ [14] based backbone, the feature vectors of seed points depend on the neighboring points and are obtained by a max pooling operation, as illustrated in Fig. 2(a). However, such a scheme ignores the low-level and middle-level features, only considering features of the last layer. Concerning this issue, two improved MLPs, *i.e.*, CMLP [33] and AMLP [17], are integrated into PointNet++ to attain more expressive seed point representations. CMLP pools each feature at different levels and combines different levels of pooled features to form the final feature, as shown in Fig. 2(b). However, CMLP ignores the contribution of each feature at different levels. To address this problem, AMLP attempts to learn the weight of each level feature before concatenation, as shown in Fig. 2(c). Nevertheless, AMLP does not consider the relationships among the features at different levels, as it pools the feature separately. We argue that the combination of multi-level features may be more adaptive and ingenious. Therefore, we propose a WMLP module, which concatenates the features together and then feeds the features to a softmax layer to produce a weighted map. Each channel of the weighted map is used for each level of features, as illustrated in Fig. 2(d) WMLP.

Specifically, for input point cloud data $\mathbf{P}$, it is assumed that there are L layers in the MLP, and the feature of each layer is $\mathbf{F}_k$. Instead of directly concatenating the pooled features like CMLP [33], or pooling the feature individually as AMLP [17], we concatenate the features $\mathbf{F}_k$ together to form the feature $\mathbf{F}_c$ and then feed $\mathbf{F}_c$ into two FC (fully connected) layers. Then we normalize the computed features using softmax to obtain a weighted map $\mathbf{F}_m$. The detail of this module is as shown in the green dash bounding box in Fig. 2(d). The WMLP features are calculated as follows:

$$\mathbf{F}_v = \text{softmax}(\text{FC}_2(\text{FC}_1(\sum_{j=1}^{L} \mathbf{F}_{c_j} \odot \mathbf{F}_{m_j}))) \tag{1}$$

where the operator $\odot$ represents the Hadamard product. In this way, the proposed WMLP module enhances the feature representations of the generated seed points.

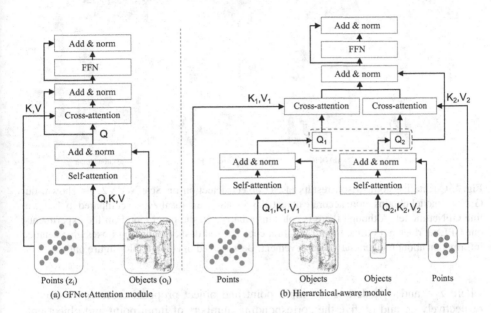

(a) GFNet Attention module   (b) Hierarchical-aware module

Fig. 3. Comparison of different attention-based module. (a) the attention module from GFNet adopts self-attention and cross-attention modules to model the relationship between the input points and the generated objects; (b) the hierarchical-aware module which extents (a) to a hierarchical way, to build a more reasonable and reliable relationships between the points and objects. Best viewed in color. (Color figure online)

3.3   Hierarchical-Aware Module

In VoteNet [20], initial candidates are generated by a farthest point sampling scheme, and then candidates are obtained by hand-crafted grouping. However, GFNet [21] proves that the hand-crafted strategy is not sufficient for the cluster indoor scenes. Hence, GFNet formulates a transformer-based object proposal decoder to utilize all points on the input point cloud to compute features. Due to the standard transformer are used in an auto-regressive manner to implement machine translation [34], GFNet modifies the transformer to predict object proposals in parallel. For the multi-head attention of the transformer decoder in GFNet, the query set $\mathbf{Q}$, key set $\mathbf{K}$, and value set $\mathbf{V}$ are set as follows:

$$\mathbf{Q} = \{\mathbf{z}_i^{(s)}\}_{i=1}^{Z}, \mathbf{K} = \{\mathbf{o}_i^{(s)}\}_{i=1}^{O}, \mathbf{V} = \mathbf{K} \tag{2}$$

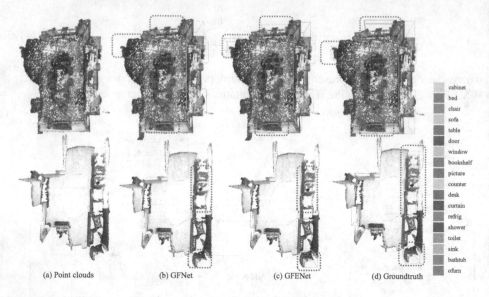

(a) Point clouds   (b) GFNet   (c) GFENet   (d) Groundtruth

Fig. 4. Qualitative comparison results of 3D object detection on ScanNet V2. As shown, our GFENet model obtains more accurate object classification and localization compared to the baseline GFNet model. Although there is color information on the point cloud, in the experiments, our GFENet does not utilize the information cue. The red dashed bounding boxes give detailed information about the qualitative improvement. Best viewed in color. (Color figure online)

where $z_i^{(s)}$ and $o_i^{(s)}$ denote the input point and object proposal features at stage s, respectively. Z and O give the corresponding numbers of input point and object proposals. Q, K, V are fed into a self-attention module to compute the interaction between object features and then fed into a cross-attention module to leverage the obtained point features to compute the object features. GFNet [21] classifies each point an object or not based on two rules: (1) it is inside a ground-truth object box; (2) it is one of the K-closet points to the object center.

Although the above attention-guided grouping strategy in GFNet [21] outperforms the hand-crafted grouping, it only considers the single-scale relationships between points and objects, which is actually not sufficient enough. Inspired by [22], we adopt multiple attention blocks to build a hierarchical scale scheme (shown in Fig. 3(b)) to address the issue. The structure of our hierarchical-aware module is very similar to the GFNet attention module (shown in Fig. 3(a)). We adopt two-level hierarchical attention blocks to model the relationship between points and objects, where Q_1, K_1, and V_1 denote the query set, key set, and value set in the first level, and Q_2, K_2, and V_2 denotes the corresponding sets in the second level. In Fig. 3(b), the points and the objects on the left are denoted as the first level cue, and then we use FPS/KPS to sample the points and objects to obtain the second level cue, as shown on the right. Our module could model more plausible relationships between points and objects through the hierarchical structure.

3.4 Stage-Aware Module

Aggregating multi-stage predictions is an efficient strategy to improve object detection performance, which has been confirmed in vision tasks [44]. Therefore, GFNet [21] attempts to integrate the prediction results of multiple stages. However, since not all stages contribute equally to the final prediction, directly assembling multi-stage results is considered inefficient.

In this paper, we propose a stage-aware module to learn weighted maps for each stage. Assume there are S-stage decoders in the last transformer block, and then S-channel weighted maps are learned. Each channel of the weighted map represents the importance of the current stage decoder. After obtaining the weighted maps, we split them into S channels. We take a Hadamard product between the split weighted maps and the decoder results, then add them to generate the final results. Specifically, for input point cloud $\mathbf{P}$, it is assumed that the prediction results in the stage s are $\mathbf{Y}_s$, the learned S-stage weighted map is $\mathbf{W}_s$. Instead of directly ensemble the results in all stages like GFNet [21], we split the $\mathbf{W}_s$ into S-channel maps, and then each channel is multiplied by the results in the corresponding stage. The ensemble results are calculated as follows:

$$\mathbf{R} = \sum_{s=1}^{S} \mathbf{W}_s \odot \mathbf{Y}_s \tag{3}$$

where S is set to 6 in the experiments, the operator $\odot$ represents the Hadamard product.

4 Experiments and Discussions

4.1 Dataset

We evaluate our GFENet on two large datasets with real 3D scans, ScanNet V2 [23] and SUN RGB-D [24]. The ScanNet V2 is a well-known public indoor scene dataset with richly-annotated 3D reconstructions. It contains 1513 indoor scene per-point annotated instances, semantic labels, and 3D bounding boxes. The 3D bounding boxes are classified into 18 categories. We employ the standard evaluation protocols [20] to measure our proposed model by using mean average precision (mAP) at 0.25 and 0.5 IoU thresholds.

The SUN RGB-D dataset is a recent single-view RGB-D benchmark for indoor scene understanding. It possesses approximately 10,355 pairs of RGB and depth images captured by four consumer depth cammers, Intel Realsence, Asus Xtion, Kinect v1, and Kinect v2. 5285 pairs are used for training, and the rest are used for validation. The RGB-D of each scene should be converted to a point cloud representation of annotated indoor objects before training and validation. The ground-truth 3D bounding box of each object in the converted scene is provided.

Table 1. Performance comparison on ScanNet V2 validation set with state-of-the-arts. The top two results are shown in **bold** and *italic* respectively.

Methods	Presented at	cabinet	bed	chair	sofa	table	door	window	bookshelf	picture	counter	desk	curtain	refrigerator	showercurtain	toilet	sink	bathtub	ofurn	mAP@0.25	mAP@0.5
VoteNet [20]	ICCV'19	36.27	87.92	88.71	89.62	58.77	47.32	38.1	44.62	7.83	56.13	71.69	47.23	45.37	57.13	94.94	54.7	92.11	37.2	58.6	33.5
GRNet [45]	ISPRS'20	39.45	88.78	89.18	88.34	58.16	48.46	32.7	46.97	4.94	63.48	69.81	48.46	49.06	66.37	94.07	49.7	90.9	35.6	59.1	39.1
Griffiths [46]	ECCV'20	43.0	70.8	58.3	16.0	44.6	28.0	13.4	58.2	4.9	69.9	74.0	75.0	36.0	58.9	79.0	47.0	77.9	48.2	50.2	–
SPOT [47]	ECCV'20	–	–	–	–	–	–	–	–	–	–	–	–	–	–	–	–	–	–	59.8	40.4
GSDN [48]	ECCV'20	41.58	82.5	92.14	86.95	61.05	42.41	40.66	51.14	10.23	64.18	71.06	54.92	40.0	70.54	**99.97**	*75.5*	93.23	53.07	62.8	34.8
H3DNet [15]	ECCV'20	49.4	88.6	91.8	90.2	64.9	61.0	51.9	54.9	18.6	62.0	75.9	57.3	57.2	75.3	97.9	67.4	92.5	53.6	67.2	48.1
HGNet [49]	CVPR'20	–	–	–	–	–	–	–	–	–	–	–	–	–	–	–	–	–	–	61.3	34.4
SESS [50]	CVPR'20	–	–	–	–	–	–	–	–	–	–	–	–	–	–	–	–	–	–	62.1	–
DOPS [51]	CVPR'20	53.2	83.3	91.6	82.6	60.5	54.8	45.2	41.0	**26.3**	51.9	73.7	53.9	49.2	64.7	98.0	71.3	86.6	**59.2**	63.7	38.2
MLCVNet [16]	CVPR'20	42.45	88.48	88.98	87.4	63.5	56.93	46.98	56.94	11.94	63.94	76.05	63.94	60.86	65.91	98.33	59.18	87.22	47.89	64.5	41.4
VENet [17]	ICCV'21	50.4	87.7	92.7	88.1	68.6	60.7	46.0	55.2	18.2	**70.2**	77.5	59.9	58.4	75.9	95.1	67.2	92.3	54.4	67.7	–
GFNet(L6, O256) [21]	ICCV'21	–	–	–	–	–	–	–	–	–	–	–	–	–	–	–	–	–	–	67.3(66.3)	48.9(48.5)
GFNet(L12, O512) [21]	ICCV'21	52.1	**92.9**	*93.6*	88.0	70.7	60.7	*53.7*	**62.4**	16.1	58.5	80.9	67.9	47.0	76.3	99.6	72.0	**95.3**	56.4	69.1(68.6)	52.8(51.8)
Hyper3D [52]	CVPR'22	–	–	–	–	–	–	–	–	–	–	–	–	–	–	–	–	–	–	70.9	57.2
RBGNet(R66, O256) [53]	CVPR'22	–	–	–	–	–	–	–	–	–	–	–	–	–	–	–	–	–	–	70.2(69.6)	54.2(53.6)
RBGNet(R66, O512) [53]	CVPR'22	–	–	–	–	–	–	–	–	–	–	–	–	–	–	–	–	–	–	70.6(69.9)	55.2(54.7)
Our GFENet(L6, O256)	–	52.4	90.9	91.8	*91.9*	69.9	64.1	53.2	49.9	20.4	59.1	75.9	62.1	*61.1*	*83.1*	97.9	65.9	91.9	54.2	68.7(67.9)	52.2(52.0)
Our GFENet(L12, O512)	–	**54.1**	*91.4*	91.9	**92.2**	70.7	**66.4**	**55.1**	50.8	22.4	58.9	**82.1**	66.0	**62.3**	**84.2**	97.8	66.3	*94.9*	58.2	70.3(69.1)	**56.1(54.6)**

4.2 Training Details

The proposed GFENet is optimized using the AdamW optimizer with a batch size of 16 for ScanNet V2 and 8 for SUN RGB-D. All the experiments are implemented on RTX P6000 GPU by the PyTorch platform. We set the base learning rate as 0.01 and 0.001 for ScanNet V2 and SUN RGB-D datasets, respectively, and decay it by 0.1 at the step of 280 and 340. The network is trained for 400 epochs on both datasets. Due to the transformer block being unstable and hard to train, there is some slight variance with the evaluated mAP. Therefore, we adopt the same setting as VENet [17] and GFNet [21]. Each setting of the experiments is trained three times, and we also test each training trial three times. To illustrate the randomness of the algorithm, the average performance of these 9 trials is reported.

Regarding the parameters of the backbone, we keep the same settings as VoteNet [20]. There are four set abstraction layers and two feature propagation layers. The input point number is set to 50,000 for ScanNet V2 and 20,000 for SUN RGB-D. Then points are sub-sampled to 2048, 1024, 512, and 256 and up-sampled to 512 and 1024 by two feature propagation layers. For larger model GFNet (L12, O512), careful parameter tuning and time-consuming optimization are necessary. Therefore, ablation studies are conducted on smaller model GFNet (L6, O256). About the parameters in the transformer decoder, for each transformer in the decoder, we follow the setting in GFNet [21] using six and twelve attention modules to predict the bounding boxes of objects.

4.3 Comparisons with the State-of-the-Art Methods

To demonstrate the effectiveness and superiority of the proposed GFENet, we implement experiments on ScanNet V2 [23] and SUN RGB-D [24] and make comparisons with recent state-of-the-art methods.

Experiments on ScanNet V2 [23]. We first evaluate our method on the ScanNet V2 dataset using the same 18 object categories as in VoteNet [20]. Quantitative comparisons with the representative Feng [54], Griffiths [46], VoteNet [20], GRNet [45] and others are provided in Table 1. From the results, we can see that our method achieves better overall performance than most state-of-the-arts. Furthermore, our

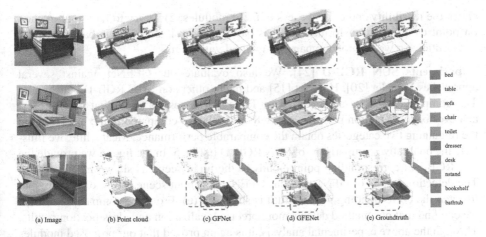

(a) Image   (b) Point cloud   (c) GFNet   (d) GFENet   (e) Groundtruth

Fig. 5. Qualitative comparison results of 3D object detection on SUN RGB-D. As shown, our GFENet model obtains more accurate object classification and localization compared to the baseline GFNet model. Although there is color information on the point cloud, in the experiments, our GFENet does not utilize the information cue. The red dashed bounding boxes give detailed information about the qualitative improvement. Best viewed in color. (Color figure online)

Table 2. Performance comparison on SUN RGB-D validation set with state-of-the-arts. The top two results are shown in **bold** and *italic* respectively.

Methods	Presented at	table	sofa	bookshelf	chair	desk	dresser	nightstand	bed	bathtub	toilet	mAP@0.25
VoteNet [20]	ICCV'19	47.3	64.0	28.8	75.3	22.0	29.8	62.2	83.0	74.4	90.1	57.7
GRNet [45]	ISPRS'20	51.1	64.8	29.3	76.2	26.0	26.1	59.2	84.3	76.8	90.4	58.4
MLCVNet [16]	CVPR'20	50.4	66.3	31.9	75.8	26.5	31.3	61.5	85.8	79.2	89.1	59.8
H3DNet [15]	ECCV'20	50.8	66.5	31.0	76.7	29.6	33.4	65.5	85.6	73.8	88.2	60.1
GFNet [21]	ICCV'21	*53.8*	**70.0**	32.5	*79.4*	32.6	36.0	66.7	87.8	*80.0*	–	63.0 (62.6)
Hyper3D [52]	CVPR'22	–	–	–	–	–	–	–	–	–	–	63.5
RGBNet [53]	CVPR'22	–	–	–	–	–	–	–	–	–	–	*64.1 (63.6)*
FCAF3D [18]	ECCV'22	53.0	69.7	*33.0*	**81.1**	**34.0**	**40.1**	**71.9**	**88.3**	79.0	*91.3*	**64.2 (63.8)**
Our GFENet	–	**54.1**	*69.9*	**35.2**	78.9	*33.5*	*37.2*	66.9	*87.9*	**81.1**	**91.9**	*64.1 (63.7)*

GFENet achieves the best results in 7 of 18 classes. The results demonstrate that the proposed GFENet can effectively improve subsequent object localization and classification tasks. We also illustrate the qualitative comparisons in Fig. 4. In the Figure, we provide the raw point clouds, the visualization results of GFNet and our GFENet, as well as the ground truth of the corresponding scenes. By comparing the visualization results, especially the red dashed bounding box in the Figure, it can be seen that our method obtains a more reasonable detection performance. For example, in the second scene, GFNet ignores the door object due to less surrounding information, while our GFENet considers hierarchical information, which makes our method achieve better results. There are many other superior methods which are better than ours, such as [12] and [18]. We did not compare our method with them, mainly for the following reasons: 1) we take [21] as our baseline, and therefore tested three proposed modules on [21] to check the feasibility and effectiveness of these modules; 2) we try to focus our method on point cloud and transformers, [12] is based on voxels and [18] is based on fully convolution, so we did not compare our method with them.

Experiments SUN RGB-D [24]. We also evaluate our GFENet against several approaches VoteNet [20], H3DNet [15] and many others on SUN RGB-D benchmark. The comparison results are reported in Table 2. The results show that our GFENet achieves better detection performance in 8 of 10 classes compared to the baseline, and the remaining two categories obtain the comparable performance. Meanwhile, we illustrate the qualitative comparisons of SUN RGB-D in Fig. 5. In the figure, we provide the raw RGB and corresponding point clouds of the input scene as shown in (a) and (b). The detection results of GFNet and our GFENet for input scenes are shown in (c) and (d), and the corresponding ground truth is shown in (e). From the comparison results, we can find that our method detects more precise localization and classification results. Through the above experimental analysis, it is again proved that our proposed modules are effective for improving the performance of cloud object detection.

4.4   Ablation Study and Qualitative Results

Effectiveness of the WMLP module. To demonstrate the effectiveness of the WMLP module, we provide the results of the position of votes in Fig. 7(a). From the results, we can find that the WMLP module can provide more plausible votes, the generation of votes are more concentrated near the object, which helps reduce the noise information and focus on the object itself, thus improving the object detection performance. Furthermore, to demonstrate that the WMLP does not depend on any particular architecture, we embed this module into VoteNet. We provide the quantitative results on the ScanNet V2 dataset in Table 3. The performance of VoteNet using CMLP and AMLP is provided in VENet [17]. From the results, we can see that our proposed WMLP has more powerful feature extraction abilities.

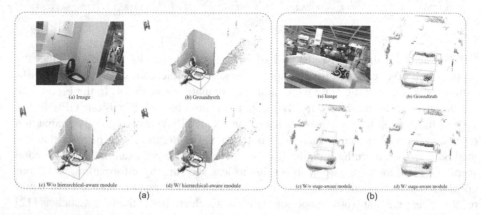

Fig. 6. (a) Comparison with and without the proposed hierarchical-aware module. (b) Comparison with and without the proposed stage-aware module. Best viewed in color. (Color figure online)

Table 3. Performance on different architecture methods of our WMLP module.

Methods	mAP
VoteNet [20]	59.6
VoteNet + CMLP [33]	61.1
VoteNet + AMLP [17]	62.3
VoteNet + WMLP	62.6

Table 4. Comparison on realistic inference speed on ScanNet V2.

Methods	mAP@0.25	mAP@0.5	frames/s
MLCVNet [16]	64.5	41.4	5.37
BRNet [19]	66.1	50.9	7.37
H3DNet [15]	67.2	48.1	3.75
GFNet (L6, 256) [21]	67.3	48.9	6.64
RBGNet (R66, O256) [53]	70.2	54.2	4.75
Our GFENet (L6, O256)	68.7	52.2	6.21
Our GFENet (L12, O512)	70.3	56.1	4.19

Table 5. Ablation study of our GFENet on ScanNet V2 dataset. W, H, and S denote WMLP module, hierarchical-aware module, stage-aware module respectively.

Methods	mAP@0.25
a. GFNet (L6, O256)	67.3
b. GFNet (L6, O256) + W	67.6
c. GFNet (L6, O256) + $W + H$	68.1
d. GFNet (L6, O256) + $W + S$	68.3
e. GFNet (L6, O256) + $W + H + S$	68.7
f. GFNet (L12, O512) + $W + H + S$	70.3

Effectiveness of the Hierarchical-Aware Module. To validate the advantage of the hierarchical-aware module, we provide the visualization results with and without the module on the SUN RGB-D dataset, as shown in Fig. 6(a). From the results, we can find that using the hierarchical-aware module, our GFENet could learn more specific feature representations. Since the hierarchical-aware module utilizes different scale information, different scales could provide different levels of dependency information. This information would strengthen the relationship between objects to provide a more reliable proposal, which is valuable and practical for object localization where there are many objects around.

Effectiveness of the Stage-Aware Module. Finally, we conduct experiments with and without the stage-aware module on the SUN RGB-D dataset to verify its effectiveness. The qualitative results are shown in Fig. 6(b). Since each stage of the decoders in GFNet [21] provides a set of 3D bounding boxes, the author ensembles all the boxes in different stages to obtain better detection performance. However, different stages would provide disparate information. As can be observed in Fig. 6(a) of (a), the white sofa in the front is close to the camera, while the black sofa in the back is far from the camera, which is mostly blocked by the white sofa in front. The stage which holds the white sofa feature would provide a good prediction, whereas this stage would offer little valuable information for the black sofa. Therefore, we utilize a stage-aware module to automatically select the prediction results of each stage to improve the final performance. As shown in Fig. 6(a) of (c) and (d), we give the results on the SUN RGB-D dataset with and without the proposed stage-aware module. By comparison, we can find that the module can provide more precise location results.

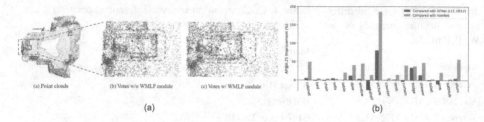

(a)   (b)

Fig. 7. (a) Voting comparison with and without the proposed WMLP module. (b) Performance Analysis. Per-class AP@0.25 improvement of our GFENet model over the VoteNet and GFNet on ScanNet V2 dataset. Best viewed in color. (Color figure online)

Quantitative Depth Analyses. In Table 5, we present the quantitative comparisons with and without our GFENet components on the ScanNet V2 dataset. The comparison results from (b) to (e) demonstrate that each component in the proposed GFENet will benefit the detection performance. Since each experiment in the paper needs to go through 9 trains and tests to get the results, this is very time-consuming and labor-intensive. Therefore, we do not use a permutation and combination to design our ablation study. In Table 5, we only provide the combined performance of the WMLP module with the hierarchical-aware module and stage-aware module. e represents our GFENet (L6, O256) performance, and f represents our final performance on ScanNet V2.

In Table 6, we compare our method with the proposed GFNet [21] furtherly. From the results, it can be seen that our model does not increase the parameter size of the baseline too much. Our approach gives a more plausible results compared to our baseline GFNet [21].

Table 6. Comparison with GFNet [21] with various configurations on the ScanNet V2.

Model	backbone	params	mAP@0.25
GFNet (L6, O256)	PointNet++	14.5M	67.3
GFNet (L12, O512)	PointNet++w2×	29.6M	69.1
GFENet (L6, O256)	PointNet++	17.6M	68.7
GFENet (L12, O512)	PointNet++w2×	36.1M	70.3

The realistic inference speed of our method is competitive with other state-of-the-art methods, which is shown in Table 4. To better understand the proposed GFENet model, we further implement experiments on the ScanNet V2 dataset and provide the performance gains of per-class over VoteNet and GFNet in terms of the AP@0.25 criteria in Fig. 7(b). As can be seen from the statistics result, our GFENet is superior to the VoteNet in all classes. Although our method degrades performance in some classes compared to the GFNet approach, our GFENet achieves performance improvements in 12 out of 18 classes.

5 Conclusion

In this paper, we propose a novel GFENet to tackle the challenging task of 3D object detection in indoor scenes. Our method is inspired by GFNet, based on which we propose the WMLP, hierarchical-aware, and stage-aware modules to improve detection performance. The WMLP module combines features from different levels in the backbone before the max-pooling operation in an adaptive manner to obtain more expressive seed point features. The hierarchical-aware module proposes a hierarchical strategy to mitigate the adverse effects of the baseline transformer module in GFNet. The stage-aware module is leveraged to adaptively aggregate multi-stage predictions to attain better performance. Qualitative and quantitative experimental results on the public ScanNet V2 and SUN RGB-D datasets demonstrate that our GFENet can achieve plausible performance gains for 3D object detection compared with state-of-the-arts.

Acknowledgements. This work was supported by Beijing Natural Science Foundation (4232023), R&D Program of Beijing Municipal Education Commission (KM202310009002), and National Natural Science Foundation of China (62102208). The authors also thank the editor and all the reviewers for their very helpful comments to improve this paper.

References

1. Wu, Q., Yu, Y., Luo, T., Lu, P.: GridPointNet: grid and point-based 3D object detection from point cloud. In: Sun, F., Hu, D., Wermter, S., Yang, L., Liu, H., Fang, B. (eds.) ICCSIP 2021. CCIS, vol. 1515, pp. 191–199. Springer, Singapore (2022). https://doi.org/10.1007/978-981-16-9247-5_14

2. Lian, Q., Xu, Y., Yao, W., Chen, Y., Zhang, T.: Semi-supervised monocular 3D object detection by multi-view consistency. In: Avidan, S., Brostow, G., Cissé, M., Farinella, G.M., Hassner, T. (eds.) ECCV 2022. LNCS, vol. 13668, pp. 715–731. Springer, Cham (2022). https://doi.org/10.1007/978-3-031-20074-8_41

3. Qin, Y., Chi, X., Sheng, B., Lau, R.W.: GuideRender: large-scale scene navigation based on multi-modal view frustum movement prediction. Vis. Comput. **39**, 3597–3607 (2023). https://doi.org/10.1007/s00371-023-02922-x

4. Li, J., et al.: Automatic detection and classification system of domestic waste via multimodel cascaded convolutional neural network. IEEE Trans. Ind. Inf. **18**(1), 163–173 (2021)

5. Lin, D., Fidler, S., Urtasun, R.: Holistic scene understanding for 3D object detection with RGBD cameras. In: IEEE International Conference on Computer Vision, pp. 1417–1424 (2013)

6. Song, S., Xiao, J.: Sliding shapes for 3D object detection in depth images. In: Fleet, D., Pajdla, T., Schiele, B., Tuytelaars, T. (eds.) ECCV 2014. LNCS, vol. 8694, pp. 634–651. Springer, Cham (2014). https://doi.org/10.1007/978-3-319-10599-4_41

7. Ku, J., Mozifian, M., Lee, J., Harakeh, A., Waslander, S.L.: Joint 3D proposal generation and object detection from view aggregation. In: IEEE International Conference on Intelligent Robots and Systems, pp. 1–8 (2018)

8. Liang, M., Yang, B., Wang, S., Urtasun, R.: Deep continuous fusion for multi-sensor 3D object detection. In: Ferrari, V., Hebert, M., Sminchisescu, C., Weiss, Y. (eds.) ECCV 2018. LNCS, vol. 11220, pp. 663–678. Springer, Cham (2018). https://doi.org/10.1007/978-3-030-01270-0_39

9. Hou, J., Dai, A., Nießner, M.: 3D-SIS: 3D semantic instance segmentation of RGB-D scans. In: IEEE Conference on Computer Vision and Pattern Recognition, pp. 4421–4430 (2019)

10. Shi, S., Wang, Z., Shi, J., Wang, X., Li, H.: From points to parts: 3D object detection from point cloud with part-aware and part-aggregation network. IEEE Trans. Pattern Anal. Mach. Intell. **43**(8), 2647–2664 (2020)

11. Lang, A.H., Vora, S., Caesar, H., Zhou, L., Yang, J., Beijbom, O.: PointPillars: fast encoders for object detection from point clouds. In: IEEE Conference on Computer Vision and Pattern Recognition, pp. 12697–12705 (2019)

12. Vu, T., Kim, K., Luu, T.M., Nguyen, X.T., Yoo, C.D.: Softgroup for 3D instance segmentation on 3D point clouds. In: IEEE Conference on Computer Vision and Pattern Recognition, pp. 2708–2717 (2022)

13. Qi, C.R., Su, H., Mo, K., Guibas, L.J.: PointNet: deep learning on point sets for 3D classification and segmentation. In: IEEE Conference on Computer Vision and Pattern Recognition, pp. 652–660 (2017)

14. Qi, C.R., Yi, L., Su, H., Guibas, L.J.: PointNet++: deep hierarchical feature learning on point sets in a metric space. In: Advances in Neural Information Processing Systems, vol. 30 (2017)

15. Zhang, Z., Sun, B., Yang, H., Huang, Q.: H3DNet: 3D object detection using hybrid geometric primitives. In: Vedaldi, A., Bischof, H., Brox, T., Frahm, J.-M. (eds.) ECCV 2020. LNCS, vol. 12357, pp. 311–329. Springer, Cham (2020). https://doi.org/10.1007/978-3-030-58610-2_19

16. Xie, Q., et al.: MLCVNet: multi-level context VoteNet for 3D object detection. In: IEEE Conference on Computer Vision and Pattern Recognition, pp. 10447–10456 (2020)

17. Xie, Q., et al.: VENet: voting enhancement network for 3D object detection. In: IEEE International Conference on Computer Vision, pp. 3712–3721 (2021)

18. Rukhovich, D., Vorontsova, A., Konushin, A.: FCAF3D: fully convolutional anchor-free 3D object detection. In: Avidan, S., Brostow, G., Cissé, M., Farinella, G.M., Hassner, T. (eds.) ECCV 2022. LNCS, vol. 13670, pp. 477–493. Springer, Cham (2022). https://doi.org/10.1007/978-3-031-20080-9_28

19. Cheng, B., Sheng, L., Shi, S., Yang, M., Xu, D.: Back-tracing representative points for voting-based 3D object detection in point clouds. In: IEEE International Conference on Computer Vision, pp. 8963–8972 (2021)

20. Qi, C.R., Litany, O., He, K., Guibas, L.J.: Deep hough voting for 3D object detection in point clouds. In: IEEE International Conference on Computer Vision, pp. 9277–9286 (2019)

21. Liu, Z., Zhang, Z., Cao, Y., Hu, H., Tong, X.: Group-free 3D object detection via transformers. In: IEEE International Conference on Computer Vision, pp. 2949–2958 (2021)

22. Chen, H., et al.: Learning to match features with seeded graph matching network. In: IEEE International Conference on Computer Vision, pp. 6301–6310 (2021)

23. Dai, A., Chang, A.X., Savva, M., Halber, M., Funkhouser, T., Nießner, M.: ScanNet: richly-annotated 3D reconstructions of indoor scenes. In: IEEE Conference on Computer Vision and Pattern Recognition (2017)

24. Song, S., Lichtenberg, S.P., Xiao, J.: SUN RGB-D: a RGB-D scene understanding benchmark suite. In: IEEE Conference on Computer Vision and Pattern Recognition, pp. 567–576 (2015)

25. Ren, S., He, K., Girshick, R., Sun, J.: Faster R-CNN: towards real-time object detection with region proposal networks. In: Advances in Neural Information Processing Systems, vol. 28, pp. 91–99 (2015)

26. Zhu, X., Su, W., Lu, L., Li, B., Wang, X., Dai, J.: Deformable DETR: deformable transformers for end-to-end object detection. In: International Conference on Learning Representations (2021)

27. Song, G., Liu, Y., Wang, X.: Revisiting the sibling head in object detector. In: IEEE Conference on Computer Vision and Pattern Recognition, pp. 11563–11572 (2020)
28. Li, Y., et al.: Should all proposals be treated equally in object detection? In: Avidan, S., Brostow, G., Cissé, M., Farinella, G.M., Hassner, T. (eds.) ECCV 2022. LNCS, vol. 13685, pp. 556–572. Springer, Cham (2022). https://doi.org/10.1007/978-3-031-19806-9_32
29. Wang, S.Y., Qu, Z., Li, C.J., Gao, L.Y.: BANet: small and multi-object detection with a bidirectional attention network for traffic scenes. Eng. Appl. Artif. Intell. **117**, 105504 (2023)
30. Guo, J., Feng, H., Xu, H., Yu, W., Shuzhi Ge, S.: D3-Net: integrated multi-task convolutional neural network for water surface deblurring, dehazing and object detection. Eng. Appl. Artif. Intell. **117**, 105558 (2023)
31. Song, S., Xiao, J.: Deep sliding shapes for amodal 3D object detection in RGB-D images. In: IEEE Conference on Computer Vision and Pattern Recognition, pp. 808–816 (2016)
32. Chen, K., Zhou, F., Dai, J., Shen, P., Cai, X., Zhang, F.: MCGNet: multi-level context-aware and geometric-aware network for 3D object detection. In: IEEE International Conference on Image Processing, pp. 1846–1850 (2022)
33. Huang, Z., Yu, Y., Xu, J., Ni, F., Le, X.: PF-Net: point fractal network for 3D point cloud completion. In: IEEE Conference on Computer Vision and Pattern Recognition, pp. 7662–7670 (2020)
34. Vaswani, A., et al.: Attention is all you need. In: Conference and Workshop on Neural Information Processing Systems, pp. 5998–6008 (2017)
35. Zhao, B., Gong, M., Li, X.: Hierarchical multimodal transformer to summarize videos. Neurocomputing **468**, 360–369 (2022)
36. Yuan, L., et al.: Tokens-to-Token ViT: training vision transformers from scratch on ImageNet. In: IEEE International Conference on Computer Vision, pp. 558–567 (2021)
37. Liu, X., Wang, L., Han, X.: Transformer with peak suppression and knowledge guidance for fine-grained image recognition. Neurocomputing **492**, 137–149 (2022)
38. Park, C., Jeong, Y., Cho, M., Park, J.: Fast point transformer. In: IEEE Conference on Computer Vision and Pattern Recognition, pp. 16949–16958 (2022)
39. Chen, Y., Yang, Z., Zheng, X., Chang, Y., Li, X.: PointFormer: a dual perception attention-based network for point cloud classification. In: Proceedings of the Asian Conference on Computer Vision, pp. 3291–3307 (2022)
40. Wu, X., Lao, Y., Jiang, L., Liu, X., Zhao, H.: Point Transformer V2: grouped vector attention and partition-based pooling. In: Advances in Neural Information Processing Systems (2022)
41. Lai, X., et al.: Stratified transformer for 3D point cloud segmentation. In: IEEE Conference on Computer Vision and Pattern Recognition, pp. 8500–8509 (2022)
42. Misra, I., Girdhar, R., Joulin, A.: An end-to-end transformer model for 3D object detection. In: IEEE International Conference on Computer Vision, pp. 2906–2917 (2021)
43. Pan, X., Xia, Z., Song, S., Li, L.E., Huang, G.: 3D object detection with pointformer. In: IEEE Conference on Computer Vision and Pattern Recognition, pp. 7463–7472 (2021)
44. Lin, T.Y., Dollár, P., Girshick, R., He, K., Hariharan, B., Belongie, S.: Feature pyramid networks for object detection. In: IEEE Conference on Computer Vision and Pattern Recognition, pp. 2117–2125 (2017)
45. Li, Y., Ma, L., Tan, W., Sun, C., Cao, D., Li, J.: GRNet: geometric relation network for 3D object detection from point clouds. ISPRS J. Photogramm. Remote. Sens. **165**, 43–53 (2020)
46. Griffiths, D., Boehm, J., Ritschel, T.: Finding your (3D) center: 3D object detection using a learned loss. In: Vedaldi, A., Bischof, H., Brox, T., Frahm, J.-M. (eds.) ECCV 2020. LNCS, vol. 12363, pp. 70–85. Springer, Cham (2020). https://doi.org/10.1007/978-3-030-58523-5_5
47. Du, H., Li, L., Liu, B., Vasconcelos, N.: SPOT: selective point cloud voting for better proposal in point cloud object detection. In: Vedaldi, A., Bischof, H., Brox, T., Frahm, J.-M.

(eds.) ECCV 2020. LNCS, vol. 12356, pp. 230–247. Springer, Cham (2020). https://doi.org/10.1007/978-3-030-58621-8_14

48. Gwak, J.Y., Choy, C., Savarese, S.: Generative sparse detection networks for 3D single-shot object detection. In: Vedaldi, A., Bischof, H., Brox, T., Frahm, J.-M. (eds.) ECCV 2020. LNCS, vol. 12349, pp. 297–313. Springer, Cham (2020). https://doi.org/10.1007/978-3-030-58548-8_18

49. Chen, J., Lei, B., Song, Q., Ying, H., Chen, D.Z., Wu, J.: A hierarchical graph network for 3D object detection on point clouds. In: IEEE Conference on Computer Vision and Pattern Recognition, pp. 392–401 (2020)

50. Zhao, N., Chua, T.S., Lee, G.H.: SESS: self-ensembling semi-supervised 3D object detection. In: IEEE Conference on Computer Vision and Pattern Recognition, pp. 11079–11087 (2020)

51. Najibi, M., et al.: DOPS: learning to detect 3D objects and predict their 3D shapes. In: IEEE Conference on Computer Vision and Pattern Recognition, pp. 11913–11922 (2020)

52. Zheng, Y., Duan, Y., Lu, J., Zhou, J., Tian, Q.: HyperDet3D: learning a scene-conditioned 3D object detector. In: IEEE Conference on Computer Vision and Pattern Recognition, pp. 5585–5594 (2022)

53. Wang, H., et al.: RBGNet: ray-based grouping for 3D object detection. In: IEEE Conference on Computer Vision and Pattern Recognition, pp. 1110–1119 (2022)

54. Feng, M., Gilani, S.Z., Wang, Y., Zhang, L., Mian, A.: Relation graph network for 3D object detection in point clouds. IEEE Trans. Image Process. **30**, 92–107 (2021)

Research on Fabric Defect Detection Technology Based on RDN-LTE and Improved DINO

Li Yao, Zhongqin Chen, and Yan Wan[✉]

Donghua University, Shanghai 201620, China
winniewan@dhu.edu.cn

Abstract. In order to solve the problem of detecting various types of complex fabric defects such as different scale sizes, high fusion with the background and extreme aspect ratios generated in actual production environment, this paper proposes a defect detection method that combines super-resolution reconstruction technology with object detection technology. Firstly, the dataset is reconstructed using the super-resolution reconstruction technology RDN-LTE, which effectively solve the problem of high fusion between defects and background. Furthermore, the copy-paste technology is employed for data augmentation to enhance model robustness. Then the dataset is fed into the detection network DINO for training. To improve the receptive field of the model, Swim Transformer is used as the backbone network of the model instead of ResNet-50, and the scale features extracted by the model are increased from 4 to 5. The deformable attention mechanism is also introduced in the third and fourth stages of Swim Transformer to enhance the global relationship modeling. Finally, multi-scale training method is introduced to capture the defect features at different scales to further improve the model detection effect and training speed. The results of the three kinds of comparative experiments show that the method based on RDN-LTE and improved DINO has a better overall recognition rate for multiple kinds of fabric defects than other current methods.

Keywords: Fabric defect detection · RDN-LTE · DINO · Swim Transformer · Copy-paste

1 Introduction

The textile industry plays an important role in China's economic development, and the quality of fabrics has a great impact on the economic benefits of the textile industry. Statistics show that defective fabrics can cost enterprises 45% to 65% of their profits [1], so the accurate detection of defects is a crucial step in enterprise production. The types of defects are complex and diverse, for example, some types of defects are extremely small, and some types of defects are highly integrated with the background. Even experienced workers may have problems such as missed detection, false detection, slow detection speed, long time consumption. Object detection algorithms have been applied in many fields, such as [2,3], effectively saving labor and improving enterprise profits, so it is necessary to research automated defect detection.

In the model-based method, [4] constructed a new low rank decomposition model to handle defects. [5] first preprocessed the dataset with denoising, and then used the Gaussian Markov random field (GMRF) model to model fabric texture features. However, model-based methods have the problem of difficulty in identifying small defects and high computational complexity.

In the statistical analysis method, [6] obtained the set of fabric texture feature vectors based on Haralick parameters. However, statistical analysis requires a large number of defect datasets, and it is difficult to accurately describe defects with complex background.

In the spectrum analysis method, [7] proposed a new method for local tuning of amplitude spectrum to preserve defect areas while suppressing background patterns. [8] used Gabor filters to enhance the contrast between defects and surrounding background textures, while obtaining the Histogram of Oriented Gradient (HOG) features of the background image, and identified defects based on the differences between defect features and HOG features.

In the one-stage algorithm based on deep learning, [9] added deformable convolution network (DCN) to the backbone of YOLOv4 in order to improve the ability of the model to describe geometric changes. Although the one-stage algorithm is fast in detection, the detection accuracy is low due to the absence of the link to generate candidate regions.

In the two-stage algorithm, [10] used the cascade approach to first identify defects as bars or blocks in the Inception-ResNet-v2 network, and then adjusted the anchor frame ratio to detect them in the Faster R-CNN network. The detected defect categories were not comprehensive and did not have generalization ability.

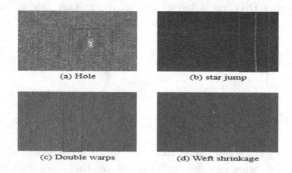

(a) Hole   (b) star jump

(c) Double warps   (d) Weft shrinkage

Fig. 1. Comparison of hard-to-detect defects and easy-to-detect defects.

Although the above methods can achieve the detection of some obvious defect types, as shown in (a) and (b) in Fig. 1, the detection effect is not good for complex defect types with different scale sizes, high fusion with background, and extreme aspect ratios, as shown in (c) and (d) in Fig. 1, and these types of defects are also common, this paper proposes a universal method for detecting multiple types of defects in actual production environments. Firstly, to effectively address the issue of high fusion between defects and background, RDN-LTE fabric defect image reconstruction model is proposed, thus obtaining a clearer texture dataset for fabric defects. Further utilizing copy-paste [11] technology for data augmentation to enhance the robustness of the model. Then the enhanced dataset is input into the detection network DINO [12] for training. In order to increase the receptive field of the model, the original backbone network ResNet-50 [13] is replaced by Swim Transformer [14]. At the same time, in order to better capture the shape and size characteristics of different types of defects, and enhance global relationship modeling, deformable attention [15] is introduced in the third and fourth stages of Swim Transformer. And increase the scale features extracted by the model from 4 to 5, in order to obtain more rich and diverse representation of defect features. Finally, multi-scale training is introduced to capture the defect features at different scales to improve the model detection effect and training speed. This paper detects 20 common types of fabric defects provided by the Alibaba Cloud Tianchi platform. The experiment proves that our method has a good improvement in the detection accuracy of different types of defects, especially for difficult to identify defect types. The three sets of comparative experiments demonstrate that our method is superior to other methods, the average detection accuracy reaches 86.7%.

2 Model Structure Based on RDN-LTE and Improved DINO

In response to the above issues, this paper proposes a fabric defect detection method based on RDN-LTE and improved DINO, with the model structure shown in Fig. 2.

The main idea of the model is to first solve the problem of high fusion between defects and background, which is a major difficulty in defect detection. Therefore, it is necessary to study the super-resolution reconstruction technology. The study found that compared to the Deeply-Recursive Convolutional Network (DRCN) [16], the local residual learning and dense feature fusion mechanism of the Residual Dense Network (RDN) [17] can better adapt to different types of defects and fully learn the texture features of the defects. Moreover, the introduction of Local Texture Estimator (LTE) [18] algorithm into RDN can further enhance the local texture feature representation of defects, help the model quickly capture the main frequency information of defects, thus accelerating the model convergence. Therefore, this paper proposes the RDN-LTE fabric defect image reconstruction model. Furthermore, copy-paste technology is used for data augmentation, allowing the model to better adapt to new datasets and enhance its robustness. The enhanced dataset is then fed into the detection network DINO. The receptive field of the original backbone network ResNet-50 is

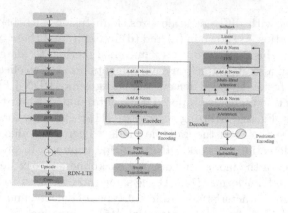

Fig. 2. Network structure based on RDN-LTE and improved DINO.

limited, which can only focus on local features of the defective images. It cannot fully learn the relationships between global features, making it prone to information loss. The study found that the adaptive pooling layer in Swim Transformer can dynamically adjust the pooling size based on the sizes of different defective images, thereby increasing the receptive field. In addition, the grouping convolution and cross layer connection technology in Swim Transformer can also be used. The grouping convolution can divide the defect feature map into multiple subgroups, and each subgroup can be convolved, thus further increasing the receptive field while keeping the model parameters unchanged. The cross layer connection technology can connect the shallow and deep defect feature maps, so that broader context information can be learned. Therefore this paper uses Swim Transformer as the backbone network instead of ResNet-50, and increases the scale features extracted from the model from 4 to 5 to capture more abundant defect features. However, during the model training process, it was found that Window-based Multi-head Self-Attention (W-MSA) in Swim Transformer perceives local defect information well, but may ignore the correlation between global features, and the Shifted Window-based Multi-head Self-Attention (SW-MSA) cannot self-adapt to defects of different scales due to the fixed size of the shifted window. Through experiments, it was found that deformable attention can enable the model to adaptively adjust the size and shape of the receptive field, flexibly adapt to different types of defects with different scale sizes, and can also enhance global relationship modeling, to a certain extent, reducing the computational complexity of the model. Therefore, deformable attention is introduced in the third and fourth stages of Swim Transformer. Finally, the introduction of multi-scale training methods can not only enable the model to learn defect features of different scales, improve the detection performance and robustness of the model, but also improve the computational efficiency of the model and accelerate its convergence.

2.1 RDN-LTE Network

This paper studies the RDN model and improves it to adapt to the fabric defect dataset. In order to adapt to the complex and diverse types of defects, this paper deepens shallow feature extraction network by adding a layer of convolution on top of the original structure. Then the extracted shallow defect features are input into residual dense block (RDB) for further processing, by utilizing dense connections in RDB modules, defect features of different scales can be obtained, and local feature fusion and residual learning mechanisms are utilized to enhance the representation of defect features. Subsequently, defect dense feature fusion is performed in the dense feature fusion (DFF) layer. Research has found that introducing the LTE algorithm into RDN model can effectively detect and repair local defect texture features, enhance the local expression ability of defect features, and learn the dominant frequency information of defects faster, thereby accelerating model convergence. Finally, the upsampling layer utilizes grouped sub-pixel convolution to generate high-resolution defect images. The RDN-LTE model is shown in Fig. 3.

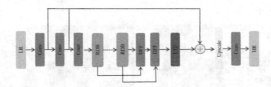

Fig. 3. Network structure of RDN-LTE.

Introducing LTE Algorithm. In order to further enhance the local texture feature representation of defects, this paper introduces the LTE algorithm, which estimates the Fourier coefficients corresponding to high-frequency defect texture information to assist RDN in obtaining more precise texture features during fabric defect image reconstruction. The LTE algorithm is shown in formula (1), Where θ represents the trainable weight of MLP, χ represents two-dimensional coordinates in continuous image domain, S denotes the predictive value space function of the decoder, ψ is used to estimate the principal frequency and the corresponding Fourier coefficients, $\mathbf{I}_\uparrow^{\mathbf{LR}}$ indicates a jump connection between the low-resolution defective image and the decoder.

$$\hat{s}\left(\mathbf{x}\right) = s\left(\mathbf{x}, \mathbf{I}^{\mathbf{LR}}; \Theta, \psi\right) + \mathbf{I}_\uparrow^{\mathbf{LR}}\left(\mathbf{x}\right) \tag{1}$$

The original dataset is used as the high-resolution image, and the 2× downsampling is used as the low-resolution image, and the dataset is made in DIV2K format and trained in the RDN-LTE model, the PSNR is continuously adjusted to obtain the desired image, and the model with LTE has a shorter training time. Figure 4 shows a comparison of the effects before and after reconstruction.

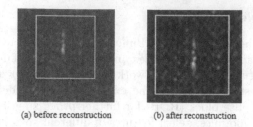

(a) before reconstruction   (b) after reconstruction

Fig. 4. Comparison of three silk type defect before and after reconstruction.

2.2 Copy-Paste Data Augmentation

In order to improve the robustness of the model, this paper uses copy-paste data augmentation technology to expand the dataset by randomly copying each type of defect and performing random horizontal or vertical flipping, random zooming in and out, and randomly adjusting the contrast within a certain range. Figure 5 shows a comparison of the effects before and after copy-paste.

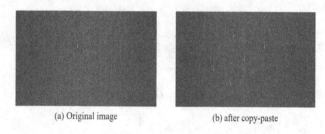

(a) Original image   (b) after copy-paste

Fig. 5. Comparison of before and after copy-paste.

2.3 Improved DINO

The original DINO model consists of a backbone network, multi-layer Transformer encoder, multi-layer Transformer decoder, and multiple prediction head modules. First, the fabric defect image is input to the backbone network for feature extraction, and the backbone network ResNet-50 is commonly used to extract the features of 4 scales, and then enter the multi-layer transformer encoder for feature enhancement and global relationship modeling. At this stage, the contrast noise reduction training method of the DINO model is fully utilized, specifically, adding noise to the edge of the anchor frame of the defect, research has found that using this contrastive denoising training method can enable the model to better handle noise interference and increase its adaptability to defects of different shapes and sizes. Then, the hybrid query and look forward twice algorithm are simultaneously used in the decoder to obtain defect context information and optimize the size and position of the defect anchor box. Finally, perform the final defect classification and regression in the prediction header module.

However, the types of defects are complex and diverse, and the resolution of the reconstructed image becomes larger. The receptive field of ResNet-50 is limited, and it can only focus on the local features of the defective image, unable to fully learn the relationship between the global features, and prone to information loss, resulting in poor detection effect of the model. Therefore, the backbone network needs to be improved.

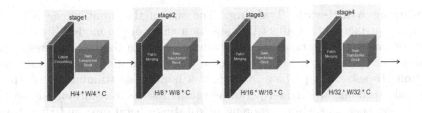

Fig. 6. Network structure of Swim Transformer.

Using Swim Transformer as Backbone Network. Research has found that Swim Transformer, through its flexible hierarchical structure and shifted window design, can obtain defect features at different scales while maintaining the same model parameter quantity, and weighted fuse shallow and deep features. In addition, the adaptive pooling layer of Swim Transformer can dynamically adjust the pool size according to different defect sizes, thus increasing the receptive field, which is very suitable for training multi-species fabric defect dataset. The model structure of Swim Transformer is shown in Fig. 6, which consists of four stages, in each stage the images are downsampled by 4×, 8×, 16× and 32×, and the sampled images are subjected to Patch_Embedding operation, while each individual patch is subjected to W-MSA computation, and then global information connection is established by shifted window, this structure can better adapt to defects of different scale sizes.

Introducing Deformable Attention Mechanism. The main attention mechanisms used in Swim Transformer are W-MSA and SW-MSA. Although W-MSA is able to reduce the computational complexity relative to the global attention mechanism, its slow receptive field growth rate limits the model's ability to model the reconstructed defect images. In addition, SW-MSA focuses on the spatial location of the defect, while ignoring the differences in the specific shape and size of defects. In contrast, the deformable attention mechanism can learn the shape and size differences of defects through the deformation module, while enhancing the connection between local and global receptive fields. This paper introduced deformable attention in the third and fourth stages of Swim Transformer, and the results showed a certain improvement in the detection effect for each type of defect. The deformable attention mechanism is shown in formula (2), where $x \in R^{C*H*W}$, p_q is the two-dimensional reference point for the query element, K represents the sampling point, m represents the attention head, $Amqk$ and $\triangle pmqk$ represent the attention weight and offset of the k-th sampling point in the m-th attention head, respectively.

$$DeformAttn\left(z_q, p_q, x\right) = \sum_{m=1}^{M} W_m \left[\sum_{k=1}^{K} A_{mqk} * W_m' x\left(p_q + \triangle p_{mqk}\right)\right] \quad (2)$$

Introducing Multi-scale Training. The size of the input image is one of the important factors that affect the detection effect of the model. If the image size is too small, it is difficult for the model to capture the key features, while the image size is too large, it will increase the computation and memory consumption. To solve this problem, we adopt a multi-scale training approach. In multi-scale training, the model performs random scale transformations on the input image, such as scaling, cropping or rotating operations, and then trains on the transformed data. In this way, the model can learn features at different scales, thus improving its robustness and generalization ability.

3 Experiments

3.1 Experimental Environment and Dataset

All the experiments are based on the computing cloud platform, and the server uses two V100-SXM2-32 GB graphics cards. During the experiment, the learning rate is continuously adjusted, we try to set the learning rate to 1e−4, 1e−5 and 5e−5 respectively, and the results show that the best training effect is achieved when the learning rate is set to 5e−5. All experiments were conducted using multi-scale training methods.

The experimental dataset is derived from the publicly available fabric defect dataset on the Tianchi platform, containing 9576 data samples, of which there are 5913 images with defects, each containing one or more different defects. In this paper, we re-clean the dataset, and the defects are classified into 20 categories according to their characteristics, the category names are shown in Table 2, and the numbers 1 to 20 are used to indicate the corresponding categories in order.

3.2 Experiments Process and Results

The first experiment inputs the original dataset without any processing into the original DINO model with ResNet-50 as the backbone network to extract 4 scale features. The second experiment with Swim-L as the backbone network to extract 5 scale features. The third experiment reconstructed the dataset based on the second experiment. The fourth experiment uses copy-paste data augmentation technology. The fifth experiment introduces deformable attention mechanism. The detection results of each experiment are shown in Table 1. Table 2 shows the detection results for each type of defect in each round of experiments.

Table 1. Experimental results of each step of our algorithm.

Object detection algorithm	mAP@[IoU = 0.5]
(a) DINO (ResNet-50) Baseline	**65.9%**
(b) DINO+Swim-L	70.4%
(c) DINO+Swim-L+RDN-LTE	77.9%
(d) DINO+Swim-L+RDN-LTE+copy-paste	83.8%
(e) DINO+Swim-L+RDN-LTE+copy-paste+Deformable Attention	**86.7%**

Figure 7 shows the detection results of a representative defect type after each improvement experiment, with labels (a), (b), (c), (d), and (e) corresponding to each experiment in Table 1.

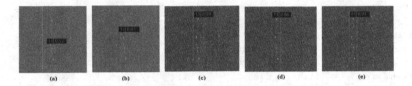

Fig. 7. The detection effect of hanging warp type defect in each step of our method.

3.3   Comparison Experiments

In order to verify the superiority of the method proposed in this paper, comparative experiments are conducted using Transformer based object detection algorithm Deformable DETR, one-stage algorithm YOLOv4, and two-stage algorithm Cascade R-CNN. The experimental results are shown in Table 3.

According to the comparative experimental results, our method performs better than other methods in fabric defect detection tasks. Figure 8 shows the comparison of our method with other methods in detecting knot defect. This type of defect has a small area, irregular shape, and high fusion with the background. In order to display the differences more clearly, we enlarged the image. It can be observed from the comparison graph that the detection effects of other methods are not satisfactory, and Yolov4 even produces false detection. This is because other methods require the design of appropriate anchor frame ratios, which makes it difficult to cover various defect shapes, especially for irregularly shaped defects. In addition, it is difficult for the model to learn effective defect features because the defect occupies a small area and is highly integrated with the background. In contrast, our method automatically determines the anchor box during the training process and first performs super-resolution reconstruction on the defect image to solve the problem of high fusion between the defect and the background. In addition, we introduce Swim Transformer, which can adaptively adjust the size of the pool based on the characteristics of defects, and better perceive the specific shape and size of defects by introducing deformable attention

Table 2. Detection results of each type of defect in each round of experiments.

Defect Type	experiments 1	experiments 2	experiments 3	experiments 4	experiments 5
Hole	95.5%	95.7%	96.4%	97.0%	97.1%
Water stains	51.9%	58.4%	69.5%	72.7%	75.5%
Three threads	76.6%	80.5%	86.3%	90.1%	93.1%
Knot	71.5%	73.6%	79.9%	85.9%	90.0%
Flower board jump	67.9%	70.4%	81.4%	86.9%	89.8%
Hundred feet	62.2%	71.3%	77.0%	81.8%	82.1%
coarse grain	56.8%	62.2%	70.7%	79.3%	83.9%
Thick warp	85.1%	85.8%	87.2%	93.8%	94.6%
loose warp	63.9%	66.1%	73.7%	79.0%	81.2%
Broken warp	44.2%	50.3%	66.2%	72.5%	77.2%
Hanging warp	51.6%	62.1%	77.8%	88.8%	90.5%
Thick weft	63.9%	70.5%	77.1%	75.9%	80.8%
Weft shrinkage	45.2%	48.1%	57.8%	77.0%	81.3%
Pulp spot	88.1%	88.5%	87.1%	91.6%	94.0%
Warping knot	72.5%	74.8%	78.1%	84.2%	92.9%
star jump	84.4%	85.6%	89.1%	99.2%	98.6%
Broken spandex	77.1%	80.5%	82.3%	84.5%	84.2%
Thin and dense paths	43.7%	50.1%	60.1%	68.4%	76.0%
Wear mark	60.6%	63.5%	81.1%	83.3%	83.1%
Double warps	55.1%	69.8%	79.1%	84.8%	88.2%

Table 3. Comparison with mainstream methods.

Object detection algorithm	mAP@[IoU = 0.5]
Deformable DETR (ResNet-50)Baseline	**51.5%**
Deformable DETR + Swim-L	66.7%
Deformable DETR + Swim-L+RDN-LTE	69.1%
Deformable DETR + Swim-L+RDN-LTE+copy-paste	72.7%
Deformable DETR + Swim-L+RDN-LTE+copy-paste+Deformable Attention	75.8%
Cascade R-CNN(ResNet-50)Baseline	**52.7%**
Cascade R-CNN + Swim-L	55.4%
Cascade R-CNN + Swim-L+RDN-LTE	59.7%
Cascade R-CNN + Swim-L+RDN-LTE+copy-paste	64%
Cascade R-CNN + Swim-L+RDN-LTE+copy-paste+Deformable Attention	66.7%
YOLOv4 (CSPDarknet53)	**54.3%**
YOLOv4+ Swim-L	50.7%
YOLOv4+ Swim-L+RDN-LTE	55.6%
YOLOv4+ Swim-L+RDN-LTE+copy-paste	61%
YOLOv4+ Swim-L+RDN-LTE+copy-paste+Deformable Attention	62.8%
Our method	**86.7%**

mechanisms. Finally, we also use multi-scale training to capture defect features at different scales, enabling the model to fully learn the features of defects. Therefore, our method has made significant improvements in defect detection.

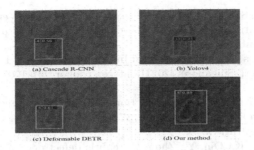

Fig. 8. Comparison of detection effects of knot type defect in different methods.

4 Conclusion

This paper proposes a detection method for various common defects in the actual environment of fabric production. Firstly, the defect dataset is reconstructed using super-resolution reconstruction technology RDN-LTE to solve the problem of high fusion between defects and background. Then, copy-paste technology is used to enhance the dataset and improve the robustness of the model. Finally, the processed dataset is input into the DINO detection model. In the DINO model, the Swim Transformer is introduced as the backbone network, and the deformable attention mechanism is introduced in the third and fourth stages of the network. In addition, multi-scale training is used to capture different scale defect features to improve the detection effect. Three sets of comparison experiments show that the method in this paper is better than other methods. However, due to the high performance requirements for GPU, high memory consumption, and long training time of the super-resolution reconstruction technology, further improvement is needed in subsequent work.

References

1. Selvi, S.S.T., Nasira, G.: An effective automatic fabric defect detection system using digital image processing. J. Environ. Nanotechnol. **6**(1), 79–85 (2017)
2. Chen, Z., Qiu, J., Sheng, B., Li, P., Wu, E.: GPSD: generative parking spot detection using multi-clue recovery model. Vis. Comput. **37**(9–11), 2657–2669 (2021). https://doi.org/10.1007/s00371-021-02199-y
3. Li, J., et al.: Automatic detection and classification system of domestic waste via multimodel cascaded convolutional neural network. IEEE Trans. Ind. Inf. **18**(1), 163–173 (2021)
4. Liu, G., Li, F.: Fabric defect detection based on low-rank decomposition with structural constraints Vis. Comput. **38**(2), 639–653 (2022). https://doi.org/10.1007/s00371-020-02040-y
5. Xu, Y., Meng, F., Wang, L., Zhang, M., Wu, C.: Fabric surface defect detection based on GMRF model. In: 2021 2nd International Conference on Artificial Intelligence and Information Systems, pp. 1–4 (2021)

6. Tola, S., Sarkar, S., Chandra, J.K., Sarkar, G.: Sparse auto-encoder improvised texture-based statistical feature estimation for the detection of defects in woven fabric. In: Chakraborty, M., Jha, R.K., Balas, V.E., Sur, S.N., Kandar, D. (eds.) Trends in Wireless Communication and Information Security. LNEE, vol. 740, pp. 143–151. Springer, Singapore (2021). https://doi.org/10.1007/978-981-33-6393-9_16

7. Liu, G., Zheng, X.: Fabric defect detection based on information entropy and frequency domain saliency. Vis. Comput. **37**(3), 515–528 (2021). https://doi.org/10.1007/s00371-020-01820-w

8. Tang, X., Huang, K., Qin, Y., Zhou, C.: Fabric defect detection based on Gabor Filter and HOG feature. Comput. Measur. Control **26**(9), 39–47 (2018)

9. Liu, T., Chen, S.: YOLOv4-DCN-based fabric defect detection algorithm. In: 2022 37th Youth Academic Annual Conference of Chinese Association of Automation (YAC), pp. 710–715. IEEE (2022)

10. Zhao, Z., Gui, K., Wang, P.: Fabric defect detection based on cascade faster R-CNN. In: Proceedings of the 4th International Conference on Computer Science and Application Engineering, pp. 1–6 (2020)

11. Ghiasi, G., et al.: Simple copy-paste is a strong data augmentation method for instance segmentation. In: Proceedings of the IEEE/CVF Conference on Computer Vision and Pattern Recognition, pp. 2918–2928 (2021)

12. Zhang, H., et al.: DINO: DETR with improved denoising anchor boxes for end-to-end object detection. In: The Eleventh International Conference on Learning Representations (2022)

13. He, K., Zhang, X., Ren, S., Sun, J.: Deep residual learning for image recognition. In: 2016 IEEE Conference on Computer Vision and Pattern Recognition (CVPR), pp. 770–778 (2016). https://doi.org/10.1109/CVPR.2016.90

14. Liu, Z., et al.: Swin transformer: hierarchical vision transformer using shifted windows. In: Proceedings of the IEEE/CVF International Conference on Computer Vision, pp. 10012–10022 (2021)

15. Xia, Z., Pan, X., Song, S., Li, L.E., Huang, G.: Vision transformer with deformable attention. In: Proceedings of the IEEE/CVF Conference on Computer Vision and Pattern Recognition, pp. 4794–4803 (2022)

16. Kim, J., Lee, J.K., Lee, K.M.: Deeply-recursive convolutional network for image super-resolution. IEEE (2016)

17. Zhang, Y., Tian, Y., Kong, Y., Zhong, B., Fu, Y.: Residual dense network for image super-resolution. In: Proceedings of the IEEE Conference on Computer Vision and Pattern Recognition, pp. 2472–2481 (2018)

18. Lee, J., Jin, K.H.: Local texture estimator for implicit representation function. In: Proceedings of the IEEE/CVF Conference on Computer Vision and Pattern Recognition, pp. 1929–1938 (2022)

Anomaly Detection of Industrial Products Considering Both Texture and Shape Information

Shaojiang Yuan[1] , Li Li[1,2,3]([✉]) , Neng Yu[1], Tao Peng[1,2,3], Xinrong Hu[1,2,3], and Xiong Pan[1,2,3]

[1] School of Computer Science and Artificial Intelligence,
Wuhan Textile University, Wuhan 430200, China
[2] Engineering Research Center of Hubei Province for Clothing Information,
Wuhan 430200, China
lli@wtu.edu.cn
[3] Hubei Provincial Engineering Research Center for Intelligent Textile and Fashion,
Wuhan 430200, China

Abstract. Anomaly detection of industrial products is an important issue of the modern industrial production in the case of shortage of abnormal samples. In this work we design a novel framework for unsupervised anomaly detection and localization. Our method aims to learn global and compact distribution from image-level and feature-level processing of normal images. For image-level information, we present a self-supervised shape-biased module (SBM) aimed at fine-tuning the pre-trained model to recognize object shape information. As for feature-level information, our research proposes a pretrained feature attentive module (PFAM) to extract multi-level information from features. Moreover, given the limited and relatively small amount of texture-based class feature information in existing datasets, we prepare a multi-textured leather anomaly Detection (MTL AD) dataset with both the texture and shape information to shed a new light in this research field. Finally, by integrating our method with multiple state-of-the-art neural models for anomaly detection, we are able to achieve significant improvements in both the MVTec AD dataset and the MTL AD dataset. Our code and dataset are publicly available at https://github.com/DiagoAlaraviz/JigsawBlock.

Keywords: Anomaly detection · Self-supervised learning · Attention mechanism · Jigsaw puzzle

1 Introduction

With the advent of industry 4.0 [16], production intelligence has become more and more important. Due to the difficulty of obtaining defects, the traditional

---

Supported by National Natural Science Foundation of China with No. 61901308.

B. Sheng et al. (Eds.): CGI 2023, LNCS 14497, pp. 149–160, 2024.
https://doi.org/10.1007/978-3-031-50075-6_12

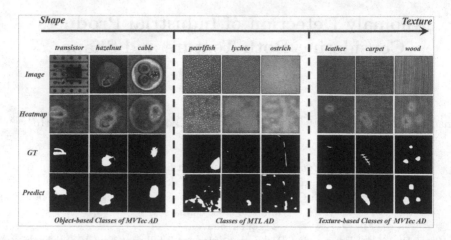

Fig. 1. The visualization results of the PaDiM [9] method on the two datasets (Image, Heatmap, GT, Predict anomaly mask). The top and bottom of the image are texture-based and object-based classes of MVTec AD respectively, and the middle of the image is our MTL AD dataset, which incorporates texture and shape features. The predict results show that the model cannot handle our MTL AD dataset effectively.

defect detection system based on a large amount of data also needs to be dynamically changed. It is urgent to apply unsupervised or few-shot reliable methods to solve the problem of industrial product defect detection.

With the in-depth study of pretrained models [11,12], the convolutional neural network tend to have a preference for local texture information [1,4,15,19], and make judgments only by these. As shown in Fig. 1, high-precision tasks often require the features extracted by the model to be more comprehensive and in line with the characteristics of specific task. In the unsupervised anomaly detection task, it is necessary to obtain high-level abstract features as much as possible. This information extraction capability is a great challenge to the existing ImageNet-based convolutional neural network framework.

To balance the shape and texture information, as shown in Fig. 2, we propose a novel framework to learn global and compact distribution from image-level and feature-level processing of normal images. For shape-based class images, we introduce a shape-biased module (SBM) composed of a defect synthesis block and a defect jigsaw block to fine-tune the pre-trained network for global information recognition. We use the pre-trained feature attentive module (PFAM) to apply different processing to multi-level features extracted by the model. The MFCSAM attention mechanism is introduced to aggregate multi-channel and long-distance information, allowing the model to focus on global shape information. In addition, since the texture-based class feature information in the existing anomaly detection datasets is relatively small and simple, we especially collect a large leather texture dataset MTL AD dataset with both texture information and shape information. We combine our method with various state-of-the-art anomaly detection methods and conduct extensive experiments on MTL AD

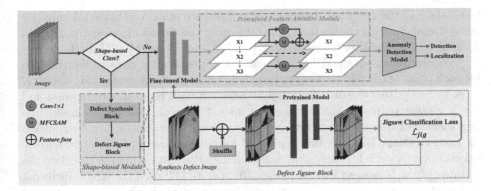

Fig. 2. The overview of our anomaly detection framework. The shape-biased module (SBM) fine-tunes the pretrained model at the image level, enhancing the model's ability to perceive the global shape information. The pretrained feature attentive module (PFAM) processes the features at the feature level, acquiring richer contextual semantic information. Incorporating these two modules can mitigate the issue of convolutional locality in existing anomaly detection models and improve the effect of anomaly detection.

and MVTec AD datasets [6]. Our experimental results show that the method can bring significant improvements in both anomaly detection and localization.

In summary, the main innovations of our work are listed as follows:

1) We propose a unique jigsaw block to adapt the pretrained model to shape information, helping the pretrained features overcome the local shape bias of the pretrained network in anomaly detection.
2) We integrate our method into several state-of-the-art models [9,17,24] for anomaly detection, showing significant performance improvements across multiple models and baselines.
3) We prepare a Multi-Textured Leather Anomaly Detection (MTL AD) dataset with both the texture and shape information to effectively expand the authenticity and diversity of anomaly detection datasets.

2 Related Work

Anomaly detection models learn feature representation from normal data and apply it to both normal and abnormal data during testing due to the large amount of unstructured and unlabeled data of real-world abnormal samples. Depending on the representation learning models used, anomaly detection models can be divided into discriminative models based on pretrained models and generative models based on AE/GAN.

2.1 Discrimination Models Based on Pretrained Feature

The anomaly detection model learns discriminant features in nominal data through their own unique methods, and then compares the distribution of the test data and the extracted feature in the inference stage to obtain an anomaly score. Depending on the method of establishing the distribution, it can be subdivided into probability-based [9,10,26] and distance-based [5,22] methods.

Probability-based algorithm calculates the probability density distribution for each point of the feature map to form a distribution map, and obtain anomaly score by computing the distribution difference between the test feature point and the K closest points in the distribution map. Shi et al. [26] use normalization flow instead of Gaussian distribution to compute a richer probability distribution for each location. Distance-based method finds the most representative feature information for each feature point, and then uses the feature map to calculate the distance of the K nearest feature points. Reiss et al. [22] used the KNN clustering method to collect the core features to establish a memory bank. Bergman et al. [5] used the nearest neighbor algorithm to calculate the distance of test features after reducing the feature dimension, and Roth et al. [24] introduced the coreset selection method on the basis of [22] to optimize the steps of establishing a memory bank.

2.2 Generative Models Based on Autoencoder and GAN

Generative models such as autoencoder [14] and GAN [13], directly encode the original information of the image to obtain latent space features, and learn the feature distribution of nominal data, then finally compare the test information and the generated features at the image level or pixel level in the inference stage to obtain abnormal results. Zhou et al. [29] used a deep autoencoder to introduce deep learning and some nonlinear activation functions to learn image feature information more robustly. After the GAN was proposed, the field of anomaly detection gradually began to use that network with a stronger generative effect instead of the autoencoder [25]. However, the disadvantage of simply using GAN is that it is irreversible, i.e. it cannot use the generated image to infer the latent space input that generated this image. Liang et al. [20] reconstructed images from multiple scales using multiple frequency components, making the image reconstruction more effective.

3 Methodology

First of all, we emphasize that our framework is an embeddable model enhancement method. For different data categories, we have designed different methods. As shown in Fig. 2, for texture-based classes, we have designed PFAM to help the model obtain richer feature information; For shape-based classes, on the basis of PFAM, we also designed shape-biased module (SBM) to fine-tune its pretrained model to help it learn shape information better. Next, we will introduce the component of the proposed method in detail. It needs to be explained in advance that our method only preprocesses pretrained models and features, and does not involve specific anomaly detection methods.

3.1   Shape-Biased Module

Inspired by [3], we design a shape-biased module (SBM) for the shape bias of pretrained model, which focuses on the global shape information by making the pretrained model solve the jigsaw puzzle while reducing the local texture preference. In terms of input data, compared with the general classification problem using jigsaw [7,8], the amount of nominal data available for training of a single category in industrial data is less, and the feature information is often relatively fixed, which makes the model easy to overfit. Hence, we refer to the method in [28] and use deformation and texture noise to act on nominal data to obtain synthetic anomaly data with complex feature information in the defect synthesis block. Then we combine this data with nominal data as input data for defect jigsaw block.

Let us assume to observe the t class from MVTec AD datasets, with the class containing N_{nom}^t images. After the augmenting of these images, we can get N_{syn}^t synthetic anomaly images, and we merge them into N^t images. Then, we use a regular $n \times n$ grid of patches to crop the source images and shuffled them into one of the n^2 grid positions. In the $n^2!$ possible permutations, we randomly select a set of P elements and assign an index to each patch. Then we define a jigsaw classification task on N^t labeled instances $\{(z_i^t, p_i^t)\}_{i=1}^{N_t}$, where z_i^t indicates the recomposed samples and $p_i^t \in \{1, \ldots, P\}$ is the related permutation index. The objective of defect jigsaw block is to minimize the jigsaw loss $\mathcal{L}_c\left(h\left(z \mid \theta_f, \theta_p\right), p\right)$ that measures the errors between the true permutation index and the index predicted by pretrained model function h, parametrized by θ_f and θ_p. These parameters define the feature embedding space and the final classifier, respectively for the convolutional network and fully connected layer dedicated to permutation recognition. We trained the defect jigsaw block to obtain the shape-adapted model, where $\mathcal{L}_{jig}$ is a standard cross-entropy loss:

$$\operatorname*{argmin}_{\theta_f, \theta_p} \sum_{i=1}^{N^t} \mathcal{L}_{jig}\left(h\left(z_i^t \mid \theta_f, \theta_p\right), p_i^t\right) \tag{1}$$

3.2   Pretrained Feature Attentive Module

This study introduces pretrained feature attentive module (PFAM) to learn the feature. The module integrates low-level and high-level pretrained features through Multi-scale Frequency Channel Self-Attention Module (MFCSAM) to enhance features, mitigate shape bias in the pretrained features, and facilitate the model in obtaining richer information from the global context.

For a given input image I, we denote the output features of the last three stages of pretrained backbone network as:

$$X^I = \{X_1, X_2, X_3\} \tag{2}$$

As shown in Fig. 2, we employ specialized operations for different features. For the feature X_1, since it contains a large number of low-level information

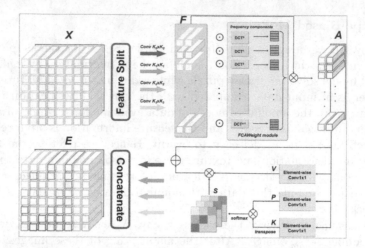

Fig. 3. The schematic diagram of the MFCSAM module is shown above. The module takes as input the pretrained features and first splits them into different scales using dedicated convolutional kernels. Next, frequency-domain attention and self-attention are applied to each scale to enable global feature learning, followed by the fusion of the multi-scale features to produce the final output.

that can guide small-size defects detection and shape features, we use a 1×1 convolution kernel to obtain its deeper information, and use MFCSAM to obtain its global information from multiple channels and different dimensions, Then, the two sets are combined as far as possible to obtain low-level information without the interference of useless information. For features X_2 and X_3, under the consideration of balancing parameters and effects, only use MFCSAM for the last layer of feature X_3 to obtain its highest level and richest information.

Multi-scale Frequency Channel Self-attention. For feature information, our motivation is to build a more global and effective attention mechanism. Therefore, a novel Multi-scale Frequency Channel Self-Attention module is proposed. As illustrated in Fig. 3, the MFCSAM is mainly implemented in three steps.

In the multi-scale implementation, we use convolution kernels of different sizes, so the features of a single scale can be expressed as follows:

$$F_i = \text{Conv} \left(k_i \times k_i \right) \left(X_i \right), \quad i = 0, 1, 2 \ldots S - 1 \tag{3}$$

where the i-th kernel size $k_i = 2 \times (i + 1) + 1$, and $F_i \in \mathbb{R}^{C' \times H \times W}$ denotes the feature map with different scales. By introducing frequency components to extract channel information from feature maps of each scale, the attention weight vectors of frequency channels at different scales can be obtained. Mathematically, the vector of channel attention vector can be represented as:

$$A_i = \text{FCAWeight} \left(F_i \right) \tag{4}$$

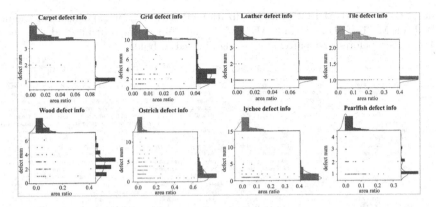

Fig. 4. Individual information of annotated bounding box for each of the 8 classes, including the proportion of defect area of this category and the number of defects in each image.

where $A_i \in \mathbb{R}^{C' \times H \times W}$ is the split frequency channel attention vector, the FCAWeight module is used to generate frequency channel attention weights. After gaining frequency channel attention, we feed A_i into three convolution layers to generate three new feature maps P, K and V, respectively, where $\{P, K, V\} \in \mathbb{R}^{C' \times H \times W}$. Then we transpose and reshape them to $\mathbb{R}^{C' \times N}$, where $N = H \times W$ is the number of pixels. After that we perform a matrix multiplication between the transpose of K and P, and apply a softmax layer to calculate the position attention map $S \in \mathbb{R}^{N \times N}$:

$$s_{ji} = \frac{\exp\left(P_i \cdot K_j\right)}{\sum_{i=1}^{N} \exp\left(P_i \cdot K_j\right)} \tag{5}$$

where S_{ji} represents the i_{th} position's impact on j_{th} positions. Meanwhile, we perform a matrix multiplication between V and the transpose of S. After a leaky ReLU layer, we multiply it by a scale parameter and perform a element-wise sum operation with the feature A to obtain the output $E_j \in \mathbb{R}^{C' \times H \times W}$ as follows:

$$E_j = \alpha \sum_{i=1}^{N} (s_{ji} V_i) + A_j, \quad j = 0, 1, 2 \cdots S - 1 \tag{6}$$

where α is initialized as 0 and gradually learns to assign more weight. From this, we obtain features with channel and position attention, which come from fully convolutional layers without information loss, thus improving the consistency of anomaly detection classification and segmentation. Finally, we re-concatenate the split part as the output of MFCSAM, the final output can be represented by:

$$E = E_0 \oplus E_1 \oplus \ldots \oplus E_{s-1} \tag{7}$$

Table 1. Detection (I-AUROC) and localization (P-AUROC) (in %) of state-of-the-art methods on MVTec AD and MTL AD, before and after adding our method. The best result for each before-versus-after pair is highlighted in bold.

Dataset	Class	DRAEM +SSPCAB [23]	ViTLnet [27]	GLAD [2]	Pyramidflow [18]	PaDiM [9]	+Our method	PatchCore [24]	+Our method	CFA [17]	+Our method
Texture-based	Carpet	(98.2, 95.0)	(-, 98.9)	(99.0, 97.8)	(-, 97.4)	(99.5, 99.1)	(99.7, 99)	(98.4, 98.8)	(99.2, 98.7)	(99.5, 98.7)	(99.5, 99.1)
	Grid	(100, 99.5)	(-, 97.8)	(98.7, 99.7)	(-, 95.7)	(94.2, 97)	(95.6, 97.4)	(95.9, 96.8)	(98, 97.6)	(99.2, 97.8)	(99.6, 98.6)
	Leather	(100, 99.5)	(-, 99.7)	(100, 99.8)	(-, 98.7)	(100, 99.3)	(100, 99.1)	(100, 99.1)	(100, 99)	(100, 99.1)	(100, 99.5)
	Tile	(100, 99.3)	(-, 97.5)	(99.6, 96.1)	(-, 97.1)	(97.4, 95.5)	(98.2, 94.9)	(100, 96.1)	(100, 95.4)	(99.4, 95.8)	(100, 97.1)
	Wood	(99.5, 96.8)	(-, 97.4)	(99.1, 95.8)	(-, 97.0)	(99.3, 95.7)	(99.2, 95)	(98.9, 93.4)	(99.2, 95.1)	(99.7, 94.8)	(100,96.4)
	Average	(99.54, 98.02)	(-, 98.3)	(99.1, 97.8)	(-, 97.18)	(98.08, 97.28)	(98.54, 97.08)	(98.64, 96.84)	(99.28, 97.16)	(99.56, 97.24)	(99.82, 98.14)
object-based	Bottle	(98.4, 98.8)	(-, -)	(100, 96.9)	(-, 97.8)	(99.9,98.5)	(100,98.7)	(100,98.4)	(100,98.8)	(100,98.6)	(100,98.6)
	Cable	(96.9, 96.0)	(-, -)	(99.8, 98.6)	(-, 91.8)	(87.8, 97.0)	(91.8,98.0)	(99.0, 98.8)	(99.2,98.7)	(99.8,98.7)	(99.9,98.6)
	Capsule	(90.3, 93.1)	(-, -)	(97.8, 98.7)	(-, 98.6)	(92.7,98.8)	(92.2,99.0)	(98.2,98.8)	(97.4,99.2)	(97.3,98.9)	(98.2,98.9)
	Hazelnut	(100, 99.8)	(-, -)	(99.8, 98.2)	(-, 98.1)	(96.4, 98.5)	(96.2,98.6)	(100,98.7)	(100,98.9)	(100,98.6)	(100,98.6)
	Metal_nut	(100, 98.9)	(-, -)	(99.4, 96.2)	(-, 97.2)	(98.9, 98.2)	(99.2,98.6)	(100, 96.1)	(98.6,99.3)	(100,98.8)	(99.6,98.7)
	Pill	(99.8, 97.5)	(-, -)	(96.3, 96.2)	(-, 96.1)	(93.9, 96.6)	(94.7,96.8)	(92.4,98)	(92.5,97.0)	(97.9,98.6)	(98.7, 98.2)
	Screw	(97.9, 99.8)	(-, -)	(97.9, 99.9)	(-, 94.6)	(84.5, 98.8)	(87.2,98.9)	(96.0,98.9)	(96.2, 98.5)	(97.3,99.0)	(97.3,98.9)
	Toothbrush	(100, 98.1)	(-, -)	(100, 98.9)	(-, 98.5)	(94.2, 99.1)	(99.7,99.2)	(93.3,98.8)	(100,99.0)	(100,98.8)	(99.7,98.9)
	Transistor	(92.9, 87.0)	(-, -)	(99.6, 96.5)	(-, 96.9)	(97.6, 97.6)	(94.3,98.7)	(100,98.1)	(97.3,97.8)	(100,98.3)	(100,98.4)
	Zipper	(100, 99.0)	(-, -)	(99.9, 99.1)	(-, 96.6)	(88.2, 98.6)	(91.0,98.8)	(98.2,98.3)	(96.4,99.0)	(99.6,98.6)	(99.7,98.8)
	Average	(98.52, 96.8)	(-, -)	(99.0, 97.9)	(-, 96.62)	(93.41, 98.17)	(94.55,98.29)	(97.65, 98.57)	(97.76, 98.72)	(99.19,98.69)	(99.31,98.66)
Overall		(98.86, 97.20)	(-, -)	(99.1, 97.9)	(-, 96.80)	(95.,97.9)	(95.93,98.04)	(98, 98)	(98.27, 98.20)	(99.3,98.2)	(99.48, 98.48)
MTL AD Dataset	Ostrich	(-, -)	(-, -)	(-, -)	(-, -)	(72.7, 74.8)	(73.7, 75.6)	(84.8, 82.3)	(86.9, 80.8)	(91.3, 86.7)	(93.2, 86.4)
	Lychee	(-, -)	(-, -)	(-, -)	(-, -)	(87.9, 91.6)	(87.5, 92.7)	(75.2, 89.4)	(73.9, 89.9)	(87.7, 93.9)	(93.6, 94.8)
	Pearlfish	(-, -)	(-, -)	(-, -)	(-, -)	(71.4, 82.9)	(73.4, 84.9)	(75.3, 87.5)	(81.2, 90.9)	(79.5, 91.3)	(82.8, 91.8)
	Average	(-, -)	(-, -)	(-, -)	(-, -)	(77.33, 83.10)	(78.20, 84.40)	(78.43 86.40)	(80.67, 87.20)	(86.17, 90.63)	(89.86, 91)

4   Results and Discussion

4.1   DataSets

In this paper, we use MVTec AD dataset and our own MTL AD dataset to conduct experiments of our proposed method. MVTec AD dataset is a commonly used anomaly detection dataset, which contains images from 10 object categories and 5 texture categories. The number and size distribution of MTL AD dataset is shown in Fig. 4. From the size comparison, we can see that the size of defects in our dataset is more diverse and in line with the actual situation, while the defects in MVTec AD data set are generally larger and easier to identify.

4.2   Experimental Setup

Since the input image size of this experiment is generally larger than 900×900, in order to reduce the amount of calculation, we resize the image and center cropped it to 224×224. The GPU is Nvidia RTX 3080Ti, and the CPU is 12th Gen Intel(R) Core(TM) i7-12700 to measure the throughput of the proposed method. Anomaly detection is generally divided into defect detection and localization. Referring to previous methods [9,24], we adopt Area Under the Receiver Operator Curve (AUROC), and then evaluated the performance of the proposed method in terms of anomaly detection and localization.

4.3   Quantitative Results

Benchmark. We choose PaDiM [9], PatchCore [24] and CFA [17] models as benchmark models for anomaly detection. In addition, we introduce state-of-the-art algorithms for result comparison, including sspcab [23], PyramidFlow [18], GLAD [2], and ViTALnet [27].

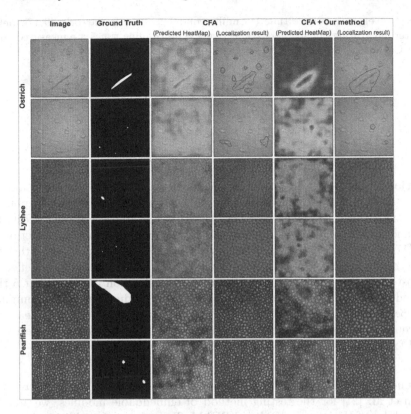

Fig. 5. Results on the MTL AD Dataset using the CFA model and adding our method. From left to right, each column is the predicted heatmap and localization results of the original image, GT, and the original CFA model (represented by the red line) and the predicted heatmap and localization results of the CFA model after adding our method (represented by the red line). (Color figure online)

Results. We present our results in Table 1. From the results of texture-based classes of both MVTec AD and MTL AD datasets, it can be seen that except for the 0.2% loss in the localization effect of the PaDiM [9] model, the rest of the models all have a certain degree of improvement after adding our method, among PatchCore [24] model achieved a 0.64% improvement in the detection effect of MVTec AD data set. For the CFA [17] model, since the model utilizes the features of all layers and is adaptive to specific tasks, it is more suitable for our tasks for texture and shape, and the performance is also the best: the detection effect for MTL AD is improved by 3.69% and the detection effect for MVTec AD is improved by 0.18% overall. Moreover, compared to the state-of-the-art methods, the CFA algorithm with our proposed enhancements achieves the optimal results in almost every category. Except for a 0.16 lower score in texture-based categories compared to ViTLnet, which is a specialized algorithm for texture-based categories.

Table 2. Average inference time (in milliseconds) for two frameworks [9,17], before and after integrating our method, respectively. The running times are measured on an Nvidia GeForce GTX 3080Ti GPU with 12 GB of VRAM.

Method	Time (ms)	
	Baseline	+Our method
PaDiM [9]	503	507
CFA [17]	129	131

Ablation Study. To illustrate the effectiveness of the proposed method, we use the CFA [17] model for ablation experiments. We added the components of our method, i.e., SBM and PFAM, to the model to see the final effect. For SBM and PFAM, in Table 1, we show the detection and localization effect of the CFA [17] model in texture-based and object-based classes according to the idea of whether to use our method. The results proves that our method is effective on most classes. It can also be seen from the visualization results in Fig. 5 that our module can better locate and detect industrial product defects. In summary, the experimental results prove that our method has a good ability to deal with the problem of shape-bias, and can more comprehensively utilize the pretrained model for anomaly detection on the surface of industrial products.

Inference Time. Regardless of the underlying framework [9,17], referring to Madan et al. [21] for the testing method of embeddable modules, we add the two modules of this paper, SBM and PFAM. To evaluate the additional amount of time for adding modules in this paper, we show the running time before and after integrating our method into two state-of-the-art frameworks [9,17] in Table 2. For both baseline models, the time after adding our method is at most 0.5 ms higher. Furthermore, the computation time of CFA differs by no more than 0.2 ms relative to the original baseline.

5   Conclusion

Most anomaly detection methods use pretrained convolutional models to extract nominal data features. Due to the shape-bias, these features can have side effects when faced with shape or texture products. In this paper, We propose a novel framework to remove local bias without reducing the features of convolutional layers. To show the superiority of our method, we combine it with current state-of-the-art models [9,17,24]. We demonstrate that each module in the method is necessary through extensive experiments on MVTec AD [6] and MTL AD dataset. Although a certain amount of computation is increased, our method can overcome shape-bias from pretrained model to a certain extent, and can achieve improvements at the image/pixel level of anomaly detection. In future work, we will continue to study the anomaly detection of industrial product defects, and explore how to improve the detection effect with as less computational cost as possible.

References

1. Ali, S.G., et al.: Experimental protocol designed to employ Nd: YAG laser surgery for anterior chamber glaucoma detection via UBM. IET Image Process. **16**(8), 2171–2179 (2022)
2. Artola, A., Kolodziej, Y., Morel, J.M., Ehret, T.: GLAD: a global-to-local anomaly detector. In: Proceedings of the IEEE/CVF Winter Conference on Applications of Computer Vision, pp. 5501–5510 (2023)
3. Asadi, N., Sarfi, A.M., Hosseinzadeh, M., Karimpour, Z., Eftekhari, M.: Towards shape biased unsupervised representation learning for domain generalization. arXiv preprint arXiv:1909.08245 (2019)
4. Bahroun, S., Abed, R., Zagrouba, E.: Deep 3D-LBP: CNN-based fusion of shape modeling and texture descriptors for accurate face recognition. Vis. Comput. **39**, 239–254 (2023). https://doi.org/10.1007/s00371-021-02324-x
5. Bergman, L., Cohen, N., Hoshen, Y.: Deep nearest neighbor anomaly detection. arXiv preprint arXiv:2002.10445 (2020)
6. Bergmann, P., Fauser, M., Sattlegger, D., Steger, C.: MVTec AD-a comprehensive real-world dataset for unsupervised anomaly detection. In: Proceedings of the IEEE/CVF Conference on Computer Vision and Pattern Recognition, pp. 9592–9600 (2019)
7. Carlucci, F.M., D'Innocente, A., Bucci, S., Caputo, B., Tommasi, T.: Domain generalization by solving Jigsaw puzzles. In: Proceedings of the IEEE/CVF Conference on Computer Vision and Pattern Recognition, pp. 2229–2238 (2019)
8. Chen, P., Liu, S., Jia, J.: Jigsaw clustering for unsupervised visual representation learning. In: Proceedings of the IEEE/CVF Conference on Computer Vision and Pattern Recognition, pp. 11526–11535 (2021)
9. Defard, T., Setkov, A., Loesch, A., Audigier, R.: PaDiM: a patch distribution modeling framework for anomaly detection and localization. In: Del Bimbo, A., et al. (eds.) ICPR 2021. LNCS, vol. 12664, pp. 475–489. Springer, Cham (2021). https://doi.org/10.1007/978-3-030-68799-1_35
10. Feng, Y., Yuan, Y., Lu, X.: Learning deep event models for crowd anomaly detection. Neurocomputing **219**, 548–556 (2017)
11. Fu, J., et al.: Dual attention network for scene segmentation. In: Proceedings of the IEEE/CVF Conference on Computer Vision and Pattern Recognition, pp. 3146–3154 (2019)
12. Geirhos, R., Rubisch, P., Michaelis, C., Bethge, M., Wichmann, F.A., Brendel, W.: ImageNet-trained CNNs are biased towards texture; increasing shape bias improves accuracy and robustness. arXiv preprint arXiv:1811.12231 (2018)
13. Goodfellow, I., et al.: Generative adversarial networks. Commun. ACM **63**(11), 139–144 (2020)
14. Hinton, G.E., Salakhutdinov, R.R.: Reducing the dimensionality of data with neural networks. Science **313**(5786), 504–507 (2006)
15. Hu, X., Zheng, C., Huang, J., Luo, R., Liu, J., Peng, T.: Cloth texture preserving image-based 3D virtual try-on. Vis. Comput. **39**(8), 3347–3357 (2023). https://doi.org/10.1007/s00371-023-02999-4
16. Lasi, H., Fettke, P., Kemper, H.G., Feld, T., Hoffmann, M.: Industry 4.0. Bus. Inf. Syst. Eng. **6**(4), 239–242 (2014). https://doi.org/10.1007/s12599-014-0334-4
17. Lee, S., Lee, S., Song, B.C.: CFA: coupled-hypersphere-based feature adaptation for target-oriented anomaly localization. arXiv preprint arXiv:2206.04325 (2022)

18. Lei, J., Hu, X., Wang, Y., Liu, D.: PyramidFlow: high-resolution defect contrastive localization using pyramid normalizing flow. In: Proceedings of the IEEE/CVF Conference on Computer Vision and Pattern Recognition, pp. 14143–14152 (2023)

19. Li, J., et al.: Automatic detection and classification system of domestic waste via multimodel cascaded convolutional neural network. IEEE Trans. Ind. Inf. **18**(1), 163–173 (2021)

20. Liang, Y., Zhang, J., Zhao, S., Wu, R., Liu, Y., Pan, S.: Omni-frequency channel-selection representations for unsupervised anomaly detection. arXiv preprint arXiv:2203.00259 (2022)

21. Madan, N., et al.: Self-supervised masked convolutional transformer block for anomaly detection. arXiv preprint arXiv:2209.12148 (2022)

22. Reiss, T., Cohen, N., Bergman, L., Hoshen, Y.: PANDA: adapting pretrained features for anomaly detection and segmentation. In: Proceedings of the IEEE/CVF Conference on Computer Vision and Pattern Recognition, pp. 2806–2814 (2021)

23. Ristea, N.C., et al.: Self-supervised predictive convolutional attentive block for anomaly detection. In: Proceedings of the IEEE/CVF Conference on Computer Vision and Pattern Recognition, pp. 13576–13586 (2022)

24. Roth, K., Pemula, L., Zepeda, J., Schölkopf, B., Brox, T., Gehler, P.: Towards total recall in industrial anomaly detection. In: Proceedings of the IEEE/CVF Conference on Computer Vision and Pattern Recognition, pp. 14318–14328 (2022)

25. Schlegl, T., Seeböck, P., Waldstein, S.M., Schmidt-Erfurth, U., Langs, G.: Unsupervised anomaly detection with generative adversarial networks to guide marker discovery. In: Niethammer, M., et al. (eds.) IPMI 2017. LNCS, vol. 10265, pp. 146–157. Springer, Cham (2017). https://doi.org/10.1007/978-3-319-59050-9_12

26. Shi, H., Zhou, Y., Yang, K., Yin, X., Wang, K.: CSFlow: learning optical flow via cross strip correlation for autonomous driving. arXiv preprint arXiv:2202.00909 (2022)

27. Tao, X., Adak, C., Chun, P.J., Yan, S., Liu, H.: ViTALnet: anomaly on industrial textured surfaces with hybrid transformer. IEEE Trans. Instrum. Meas. **72**, 1–13 (2023)

28. Yang, M., Wu, P., Liu, J., Feng, H.: MemSeg: a semi-supervised method for image surface defect detection using differences and commonalities. arXiv preprint arXiv:2205.00908 (2022)

29. Zhou, C., Paffenroth, R.C.: Anomaly detection with robust deep autoencoders. In: Proceedings of the 23rd ACM SIGKDD International Conference on Knowledge Discovery and Data Mining, pp. 665–674 (2017)

An Interpretability Case Study of Unknown Unknowns Taking Clothes Image Classification CNNs as an Example

Huan Li and Yue Wang[✉]

School of Information, Central University of Finance and Economics, Beijing, China
yuelwang@163.com

Abstract. "Unknown unknowns" are instances predicted models assign incorrect labels with high confidence, greatly reducing the generalization ability of models. In practical applications, unknown unknowns may lead to significant decision-making mistakes and reduce the application value of models. As unknown unknowns are agnostic to models, it is extremely difficult to figure out why models would make highly confident but incorrect predictions. In this paper, based on identification of unknown unknowns, we investigate the interpretability of unknown unknowns arising from convolutional neural network models in image classification tasks by interpretable methods. We employ visualization methods to interpret prediction results on unknown unknowns, further understand predictive models and analyze the predictive basis of unknown unknowns. We focus the application scenario of interpretability of unknown unknowns on a clothes category recognition task (dress vs shorts) in e-commerce platforms, and observe some patterns of models making wrong classifications that lead to unknown unknowns, which indicates that a CNN model that lacks of common sense can make mistakes even for a large dataset. Besides, we observe some interesting phenomena: certain correct predictions of instances are unreliable due to wrongly identified features by CNNs.

Keywords: Unknown unknowns · CNN Interpretability · CNN Visualization

1 Introduction

Unknown unknowns refer to image data that are misclassified with high confidence in image classification tasks, revealing the models' inability to detect these errors. There are various reasons for unknown unknowns, such as the limitation of datasets, the emergence of new categories, etc. "Unknown unknowns" problem can be disastrous in some special application scenarios. e.g., in the medical field, exist where the categories or certain features of these cases are absent from previous datasets. As a result, medical predictive models may fail to diagnose or misdiagnose, leading to significant and tragic consequences in disease decision-making. Therefore, addressing the "unknown unknowns" problem is crucial for enhancing the accuracy and generalizability of predictive models in image classification.

B. Sheng et al. (Eds.): CGI 2023, LNCS 14497, pp. 161–173, 2024.
https://doi.org/10.1007/978-3-031-50075-6_13

Nowadays image classification has become a focus in the field of machine learning. Convolutional Neural Networks (CNNs) [1] has emerged as a classic and high-performing model for image classification. As image classification continues to evolve, model interpretability has garnered widespread attention. Interpretability research aims to convert the output of black-box deep learning models' image predictions into human-understanding formats, using specific methods and techniques. Despite significant progress, the interpretability research faces challenges, one of which is unknown unknowns, resulting from factors like incomplete datasets and poorly extracted features. Due to their negative impact on apparel classification in e-commerce platforms, it is crucial to ensure accurate and reliable image recognition technology. Hence, we focus on clothes image classification in e-commerce platforms as a specific application scenario for our interpretability research.

To tackle unknown unknowns in clothes classification, we train two CNN model (VGG [2] and ResNet [3]), identify the unknown unknowns and visualize their prediction results using interpretable methods, which allows us to gain insights into their inner mechanisms. We also compare the performance of two different CNNs. Finally, we investigate how the resolution of image data affects model performance and the occurrence of unknown unknowns.

Using two interpretation methods (Class Activation Mapping [4] and Local Interpretable Model-agnostic Explanations [5]), we uncover valuable facts: unreliable correct predictions of instances (not uncommon for key areas to differ between methods on the same instances), which have been previously overlooked. e.g., an instance is correctly classified as "shorts", but the CAM result highlights the vest as the key area instead of the shorts. This unreliable correct prediction is probably attributed to similar edge characteristics between them. Additionally, models may erroneously focus on irrelevant aspects, such as distinct edges or human body parts, as key areas.

2   Related Work

This section provides an overview of prior research on CNN semantic problems in identifying unknown unknowns. The distinction of previous work is that we identify the semantics problems of interpretability areas for unknown unknowns (images correctly predicted but having unknown wrongly classification features).

2.1   Semantics Problems in CNNs

Network dissection is a pioneer paper which investigates the roles of neurons in CNNs [6]. Following this line, Fong et al. [7] find that in most cases multiple neurons encode a concept, and a single neuron can encode multiple concepts. Mu et al. [8] employ beam search to generate logical forms of primitive concepts and investigate their connection to neurons. They discover that in image classification, some neurons learn highly abstract and semantically coherent visual concepts, while others detect unrelated features. Olah et al. [9] propose a microscopic approach to studying interpretability by carefully examining neurons and circuits, similar to using microscopes to study microorganisms in history. Surprisingly, they report an instance where a car detector spreads its car feature to a dog detector in the next layer. They also observe equivariance, a term borrowed from biology, where multiple neurons can detect different posed dog faces [10]. Hohman et al. [11] introduce an interactive system called SUMMIT that provides a summary and visualization of the features learned by a deep learning model.

2.2 Identify Unknown Unknowns

Lakkaraju et al. [12] propose a two-phase method using descriptive space partitioning (DSP) and Bandit for Unknown Unknowns (UUB), which shows progress in semi-automatic identification. Bansal et al. [13] introduce a utility model based on coverage, encouraging exploration in high-density regions not adjacent to discovered unknown unknowns. Compared to DSP + UUP, this method discovers diverse unknown unknowns and achieves a more evenly distributed effect in their discovery. Subsequently, Dong and Dong et al. [14] present a region selection model using unsupervised learning for improved generalization and robustness in image classification tasks.

2.3 Improve Accuracy for Specific Application Scenarios

Various novel methods have been employed to improve classification accuracy in specific image classification applications. The FSCAP model [15] consists of multiple functional modules to enhance the accuracy of fashion sub-category and attribute prediction. Shajini et al. [16] propose an attention-driven technique that enables the model to capture multiscale contextual information of landmarks, thereby improving classification performance. Li et al. [17] utilize a teacher–student (T–S) pair model in a semi-supervised multi-task learning approach on unlabeled clothing datasets. Additionally, a multimodel cascaded convolutional neural network (MCCNN) [18] is introduced for garbage classification, effectively suppressing false-positive predicts.

3 Experiments

We now present the details of the experiments of training model, discovering unknown unknowns and visualizing the interpretation results.

3.1 Experiment Preparation

In our experiment, we use the DeepFashion dataset [19], which offers detailed classification with numerous categories. e.g., the original dataset includes specific dress categories based on features like tightness, prints, plaid, logos, and dress styles. However, the original dataset contains a limited number of images per category (around 20 to 50), which is insufficient for clothes recognition requiring a larger number of samples.

To adapt the DeepFashion dataset for our application, we integrate and reorganize the image data. We consolidate subcategories within the same clothes category, ensure correct labels, and renumber the images based on their sequence, thereby creating a binary classification dataset comprised of approximately 5000 image samples, with a focus on the categories of dresses and shorts.

3.2 Experiment Process

Construct Two CNNs and Evaluate Their Performance. We construct and train VGG16 [2] and ResNet18 [3], both known for their excellent performance. Additionally, we add an adaptive average pooling layer (AdaptiveAvgPool2d) to VGG16 for subsequent visualization research using the CAM method.

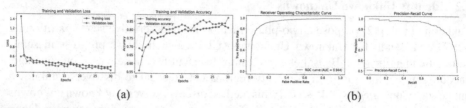

(a)   (b)

Fig. 1. (a): Loss and accuracy of VGG16 on training set and test set; (b): ROC curve and PR curve of VGG16 on test set.

As shown in Fig. 1, the model achieves approximately 85% accuracy on the validation set after several iterations. The loss consistently decreases, and the accuracy converges to around 85% from the third round. These results indicate the VGG16 model demonstrates robust classification performance on this dataset.

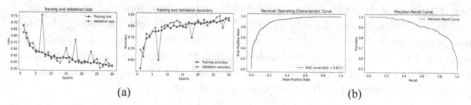

(a)   (b)

Fig. 2. (a): Loss and accuracy of ResNet18 on training set and test set; (b): ROC curve and PR curve of ResNet18 on test set.

The ResNet18 model achieves the highest accuracy of approximately 84% on the validation set in the final iteration, which is similar to VGG16. Figure 2 shows significant fluctuations in loss and accuracy on both sets during the 7th and 18th iterations, but overall, the model's classification performance steadily improves.

Compare Performance of Two Models in Clothes Classification. Table 1 shows VGG16 outperforms ResNet18 in AUC, Accuracy, F1 score, and Precision, though ResNet18 has a slightly better Recall score. Figure 3 indicates a larger area under the ROC and PR curves for VGG16 compared to ResNet18, demonstrating that VGG16 exhibits better classification performance on this dataset. Consequently, we use the prediction results of VGG16 for subsequent interpretability research.

According to the reference paper, unknown unknowns are misclassified image data with high confidence. For our experiment, we set a confidence threshold (α) of 0.65 to identify unknown unknowns.

Table 1. Various classification performance indicators of VGG16 and ResNet18.

Indicators	ResNet18	VGG16
AUC	0.917	0.944
Accuracy	0.794	0.812
Precision	0.788	0.820
Recall	0.811	0.794
F1	0.787	0.802

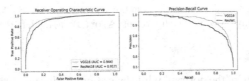

Fig. 3. ROC curve and PR curve of VGG16 and ResNet18.

Employ two Interpretability Methods for Prediction Visualization. Based on the pretrained VGG16, we implement the CAM method [4] to obtain a weighted average feature map where each pixel represents the intensity of the effect of that location on the target category. A heat map is created by retaining the pixels with values over zero, normalizing them, and scaling to the original image size. Finally, the heat map is converted to RGB format and superimposed onto the original image to visualize significantly influential areas.

Additionally, we employ the LIME method [5] for visual interpretation. We obtain the output vector and prediction result by inputting image data into the pretrained model. We construct the LIME image interpreter, adjust parameters, and apply the resulting mask to the original image for visualization. LIME is a model-agnostic method that can be applied to any CNN model, such as VGG16. However, it necessitates the definition of a prediction function that is compatible with LIME.

4 Results

4.1 Interpretable Results of CAM Method

Visualize and Analyze the Visualization Results of Two Unknown Unknowns. The visualization result is obtained by overlaying the CAM diagram and the original image. (a) displays the original heat map. (b) displays the heat map converted to RGB. (c) displays the original image. And (d) displays the overlay diagram of the heat map and the original image. Different colors in (d) represent varying levels of attention given by the model to different areas of the image during classification. Colors closer to red indicate areas where the model pays more attention.

The true label of unknown unknown A is "dress", but the model predicts it as "shorts" with a confidence level of up to 82%. In Fig. 4(A)–(d), the model focuses more on the

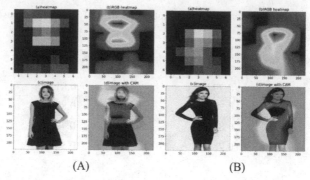

(A)   (B)

Fig. 4. (A): Visualization result of unknown unknown A with CAM; (B): Visualization result of unknown unknown B with CAM. For the figures of (A) or (B): (a) top left, (b) top right, (c) bottom left, (d) bottom right.

shoulders and abdomen of the portrait, while bright-colored areas are mainly in the upper part of the clothes. This indicates A's key area interpreted by CAM is concentrated in the upper part of the clothes, whereas the lower part of the clothes is actually crucial for recognizing whether it is a dress. The misalignment between the key area and the actual distinguishing features of clothes could be latent reason for the occurrence of unknown unknowns.

The true label of unknown unknown B is "dress", but the model incorrectly predicts it as "shorts" with a confidence level of 93%. In Fig. 4(B)–(d), the red area represents the chest of the portrait, while the bright-colored area is mainly distributed in the upper part and right edge of the dress. The model focuses on most areas of the clothes for the prediction but gives more attention to the upper part, similar to unknown unknown A. The model also considers the edge of the lower part of the clothes. However, due to the tight-fitting nature of the dress, it may exhibit characteristics resembling the edge lines of shorts, which could be another possible reason for unknown unknowns.

Sample and Compare Visualized Results of Unknown Unknowns with the Correctly Classified Data by CAM Method. 11 unknown unknowns and 5 correctly classified data are randomly sampled for visual comparison, which makes the experiment more rigorous and comprehensive.

In Table 2, the key areas of unknown unknowns 1 and 2, similar to A and B, concentrate on the upper part of clothes. Unknown unknown 3's key area is limited to the hem of the clothes, suggesting a poor capture of overall features. The key area of unknown unknown 4 is the environment with prominent edges, unrelated to clothes features. The key areas of unknown unknowns 5, 6, 7, 8, and 9 are clothes edges close to the environment, indicating sensitivity to obvious edge features. Unknown unknown 10 focuses on the hem of clothes and human body, which resembles the unknown unknown 3.

For correctly classified data, key area of data 1 remains at the dress edge, correctly predicting it as "dress". Unknown unknowns 5, 6, 7, 8, and 9 also focus on the dress edge but incorrectly predict shorts as "dress", which is interesting finding that a potential relationship between the dress edge and the model's predictions of "dress". The key area of data 2 covers most of the clothes, obtaining the correct prediction. Though

Table 2. Visual results of CAM method for unknown unknowns and classified correct data sampling (UU for unknown unknowns, CC for correctly classified data).

Type	N O.	Interpretation results	The key areas	Type	N O.	Interpretation results	The key areas
UU	1		Upper part of clothes	UU	9		Edge of clothes and human body
UU	2		Upper part of clothes	UU	10		Hem and human body
UU	3		Hem	UU	11		Upper part of clothes
UU	4		Environment	CC	1		Edge of clothes
UU	5		Environment and edge of clothes	CC	2		Edge of clothes
UU	6		Edge of clothes and human body	CC	3		Vest
UU	7		Edge of clothes and human body	CC	4		Shorts
UU	8		Edge of clothes and environment	CC	5		Shorts

correctly classified, the model predicts data 3 as "shorts", with its key area being the vest, suggesting some unreliable prediction results for correctly classified data. The key areas of data 4 and 5 represent shorts, consistent with their prediction results. These two predictions are reliable.

4.2 Interpretable Results of LIME Method

Visualize and Analyze the Visualization Results of Two Unknown Unknowns. We use LIME method to visualize model's prediction results. (a) displays the top 2 features with significant impact. (b) displays the top 5 features with significant impact. (c) displays the top 5 features comprehensively considering positive and negative contributions. Positive features contribute to results (e.g., the clothes parts), while negative features contribute nothing or may confound (e.g., the human body parts). (d) displays a visualization where features with weights < 0.1 are excluded, thereby omitting irrelevant features.

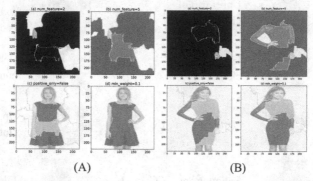

Fig. 5. (A): Visualization result of unknown unknown A with LIME; (B): Visualization result of unknown unknown B with LIME. For the figures of (A) or (B): (a) top left, (b) top right, (c) bottom left, (d) bottom right.

Figure 5(A)-(a) shows that the key areas are the middle part of the dress and the environment. Whereas key area in Fig. 5(A)-(b) covers larger clothes area than that of Fig. 5(A)-(a), indicating poor performance in extracting the first two features. In Fig. 5(A)-(c), positive and negative features are illustrated, where the green area represents the positive contribution to the prediction result, mainly focusing on the middle part of the dress, while the red area covers the face, which is not a significant factor in differentiating between dresses and shorts. When examining Fig. 5(A)-(d), only the human face, which represents the negative area, has feature with weight > 0.1. It should be noted that the interpretable results of the LIME method for A are not entirely consistent with those obtained from the CAM method.

In Fig. 5(B)-(a), the top 2 important features, the upper part of the clothes and the human hand, are similar to those interpreted by the CAM method for B. Compared to Fig. 5(B)-(a), Fig. 5(B)-(b) extends the key area to include the left edge of the clothes. Figure 5(B)-(c) shows more comprehensive interpretation, where the green area represents interpretable positive features for classification, and the red area represents interpretable negative features, indicating that the area of the human head is irrelevant to the classification result. When we ignore features with weights < 0.1 in Fig. 5(B)-(d), the green area still highlights the model's focus on the upper part of the clothes instead of the lower part.

Sample and Compare Visualized Results of Unknown Unknowns with the Correctly Classified Data by LIME Method. We interpret the prediction results of 16 instances sampled, including 11 unknown unknowns and 5 correctly classified data, using the LIME method. We also analyze and compare the results of LIME and CAM.

Table 3. Visual results of LIME method for unknown unknowns and classified correct data sampling (UU for unknown unknowns, CC for correctly classified data).

Type	N O.	Interpretation results	The key areas	Type	N O.	Interpretation results	The key areas
UU	1		Left side of clothes and environment	UU	9		Edge of clothes and environment
UU	2		Waist	UU	10		Left side of clothes
UU	3		Right side of clothes	UU	11		Part of clothes
UU	4		Lower part of clothes	CC	1		Human body
UU	5		Middle part of the clothes	CC	2		Left side of clothes
UU	6		Upper part of clothes	CC	3		Vest and environment
UU	7		Left side of clothes and environment	CC	4		Environment and vest
UU	8		Part of clothes and environment	CC	5		Shorts and human body

In Table 3, the key area for unknown unknown 1 is the left side of the dress and the environment. However, CAM result for unknown unknowns 1 focus on the upper part of the dress, which is different from LIME result. The key area for unknown unknown 2 is the waist of the dress, while CAM result is the upper part of dress, indicating both methods interpret similar key areas. The key area for unknown unknown 3 is only the right side of the dress. But CAM result is the hem of the dress. There is no overlap between the key areas interpreted by the two methods. The key area for unknown unknown 4 is the lower part of the dress. It significantly differs from the CAM result (the environment). The key area for unknown unknown 5 is the body of the dress, covers most but not edges. Despite the contribution of result to the prediction decision, unknown unknown 5 is incorrectly predicted. The key area for unknown unknown 6 is the upper part of the clothes, while the key area of CAM is the edge of the clothes and the human body. Both sets of results indicate that the model focuses on the upper part of the clothes when classifying. The key area for unknown unknown 7 is the left side of the shorts and the environment. Yet, CAM result for unknown unknown 7 is the edge of the clothes and the human body. The overlapping key areas are located at the left edge of the vest, confirming that the model focuses on edge features. The key areas for unknown unknown 8 is the body of the clothes and the environment, including part of the edge, which is the same as the key areas interpreted by the CAM. The key area for unknown unknown 9 is the environment close to dress edge, which matches CAM method result, confirming the model focuses on edge again. The key area for unknown unknown 10 is the right part of the dress, but CAM result is the hem of the dress and the human body. The key area for unknown unknown 11 is a small portion of middle of dress, differs from CAM method's key area as upper part of dress.

The key area for correctly classified data 1 is the human body, whereas the CAM result focuses on the edge of the clothes. They are completely different results. We suspect that the top 2 features are insufficient for a comprehensive interpretation or that the model is unable to extract key features effectively. The key area for data 2 is the left side of the clothes, differs from CAM result that covers most of the clothes. The key area for data 3 is the upper part of the clothes and the environment, which is consistent with CAM result. However, the expected key area is the lower part of the clothes, indicating that the prediction results may be unreliable. The key area for data 4 is the human body and the upper part of the clothes, different from CAM method. Similar to correctly classified data 1, LIME result on correctly classified data 4 is unrelated to shorts but predicted correctly. There are possible reasons: unreliable LIME interpretations (different from CAM results) or inappropriate selection of the top 2 features (more features needed for interpretation). The key area data 5 is the shorts and the human body, same as CAM result. The model seems to focus excessively on shape of the human body, as the key area.

4.3 Impact of Image Resolution on Classification Performance and Unknown Unknowns

In the initial experiments, we use low-resolution images. However, high-resolution images provide more information and yield better classification performance during model training. To investigate the impact of image resolution on classification performance and unknown unknowns, experiments are performed using HD image data from the same dataset, processed in a similar manner.

As shown in Fig. 6, the model achieves an accuracy of 86% on the high-resolution dataset, slightly higher than that on the low-resolution dataset by one percentage point after around 30 rounds of convergence. Table 4 shows the VGG16 model performs better in terms of AUC and recall scores, while the VGG16 HD model exhibits higher accuracy, F1 score, and precision score. The ROC and PR curves in Fig. 6 demonstrate similarities between the two models. Overall, image resolution appears to have minimal impact on the models' classification performance in this particular task. Additionally,

Table 4. Various classification performance indicators of VGG16 on low-resolution image data and VGG16 HD on high-resolution image data.

Indicators	VGG16 HD	VGG16
AUC	0.942	0.944
Accuracy	0.820	0.812
Precision	0.815	0.820
Recall	0.721	0.794
F1	0.818	0.802

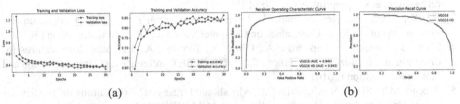

(a)   (b)

Fig. 6. (a): Loss and accuracy of VGG16 HD model on high-resolution training set and test set; (b): ROC curve and PR curve of VGG16 and VGG16 HD on HD image data.

when sampling unknown unknowns from the VGG HD model, we find overlap with those from the VGG model, suggesting no significant correlation between image resolution and unknown unknowns. However, further rigorous experiments are necessary to establish conclusive results.

5 Conclusion and Future Work

In our study, we find some interesting facts that we believe are valuable to the community of CNN researchers taking the clothes classification CNNs in E-Commerce as an example: We explain unknown unknowns by classic interpretability methods CAM and LIME, that is, the correct predictions of some instances are not always reliable. e.g., a pair of shorts is predicted correctly, but the key part interpreted by CAM or LIME is that of a vest. This confusion may be due to similar edges features present in both items, as evidenced by some visualized image samples. Our work contributes to a deeper understanding of the internal mechanisms behind the predictive decisions made by black-box CNN models, showing their lack of common sense from the perspective of unknown unknowns. We test VGG and ResNet CNNs which are widely used and trusted in the current practice (especially ResNet) due to good classification performances. However, the interpretive results highlight issues with these models when they are used solely for binary classification tasks (dress vs shorts). And we use the standard interpretation models CAM and LIME. They are widely used in current research and have been demonstrated to deliver reasonably good interpretative performance across various studies. In the future, we shall test more recent CNN models such SOTA by some new designed interpretation models.

Acknowledgements. This work is supported by: National Defense Science and Technology Innovation Special Zone Project (No. 18-163-11-ZT-002-045-04); Engineering Research Center of State Financial Security, Ministry of Education, Central University of Finance and Economics, Beijing, 102206, China. The code is at: https://github.com/marcherwang/cgi2023_unknown_unknown_paper.

References

1. LeCun, Y., Bottou, L., Bengio, Y., Haffner, P.: Gradient-based learning applied to document recognition. Proc. IEEE **86**(11), 2278–2324 (1998)
2. Simonyan, K., Zisserman, A.: Very deep convolutional networks for large-scale image recognition. arXiv preprint arXiv:1409.1556 (2014)
3. He, K., Zhang, X., Ren, S., Sun, J.: Deep residual learning for image recognition. In: Proceedings of the IEEE Conference on Computer Vision and Pattern Recognition (2016)
4. Zhou, B., Khosla, A., Lapedriza, A., Oliva, A., Torralba, A.: Learning deep features for discriminative localization. In: Proceedings of the IEEE Conference on Computer Vision and Pattern Recognition (2016)
5. Ribeiro, M.T., Singh, S., Guestrin, C.: "Why should I trust you? " Explaining the predictions of any classifier. In: Proceedings of the 22nd ACM SIGKDD International Conference on Knowledge Discovery and Data Mining (2016)
6. Bau, D., Zhou, B., Khosla, A., Oliva, A., Torralba, A.: Network dissection: quantifying interpretability of deep visual representations. In: Proceedings of the IEEE Conference on Computer Vision and Pattern Recognition (2017)
7. Fong, R., Vedaldi, A.: Net2vec: quantifying and explaining how concepts are encoded by filters in deep neural networks. In: Proceedings of the IEEE Conference on Computer Vision and Pattern Recognition (2018)
8. Mu, J., Andreas, J.: Compositional explanations of neurons. Adv. Neural. Inf. Process. Syst. **33**, 17153–17163 (2020)
9. Olah, C., Cammarata, N., Schubert, L., Goh, G., Petrov, M., Carter, S.: Zoom in: An introduction to circuits. Distill **5**(3), e00024-001 (2020)
10. Olah, C., Cammarata, N., Voss, C., Schubert, L., Goh, G.: Naturally occurring equivariance in neural networks. Distill **5**(12), e00024-004 (2020)
11. Hohman, F., Park, H., Robinson, C., Chau, D.H.P.: Summit: scaling deep learning interpretability by visualizing activation and attribution summarizations. IEEE Trans. Visual Comput. Graphics **26**(1), 1096–1106 (2019)
12. Lakkaraju, H., Kamar, E., Caruana, R., Horvitz, E.: Identifying unknown unknowns in the open world: Representations and policies for guided exploration. Proc. AAAI Conf. Arti. Intell. **31**(1), 2125–2132 (2017)
13. Bansal, G., Weld, D.: A coverage-based utility model for identifying unknown unknowns. Proc. AAAI Conf. Artif. Intell. **32**(1) (2018)
14. Dong, X., Zhang, H., Demartini, G.: A region selection model to identify unknown unknowns in image datasets. In: ECAI 2020, pp. 474–481. IOS Press (2020)
15. Amin, M.S., Wang, C., Jabeen, S.: Fashion sub-categories and attributes prediction model using deep learning. Vis. Comput. **39**(6), 3851–3864 (2023)
16. Shajini, M., Ramanan, A.: An improved landmark-driven and spatial-channel attentive convolutional neural network for fashion clothes classification. Vis. Comput. **37**(6), 1517–1526 (2021)
17. Li, J., et al.: Automatic detection and classification system of domestic waste via multimodel cascaded convolutional neural network. IEEE Trans. Ind. Informatics **18**(1), 163–173 (2022)

18. Shajini, M., Ramanan, A.: A knowledge-sharing semi-supervised approach for fashion clothes classification and attribute prediction. Vis. Comput. **38**, 3551–3561 (2022)
19. Liu, Z., Luo, P., Qiu, S., Wang, X., Tang, X.: Deepfashion: Powering robust clothes recognition and retrieval with rich annotations. In: Proceedings of the IEEE Conference on Computer Vision and Pattern Recognition (CVPR) (2016)

Classification of Toric Surface Patches

Lanyin Sun[1][(✉)] and Chungang Zhu[2]

[1] School of Mathematics and Statistics, Xinyang Normal University,
Xinyang 464000, People's Republic of China
lysun@xynu.edu.cn
[2] School of Mathematical Sciences, Dalian University of Technology,
Dalian 116023, People's Republic of China
cgzhu@dlut.edu.cn

Abstract. Triangular Bézier patch and tensor-product Bézier patch are widely used in Computer Aided Design (CAD). Toric surface patch is a multi-sided generalization of Bézier patch. In this paper, we study the classification of toric surface patches with the theory of equivalent polygons from Combinatorics, and get different types of toric surface patches. Moreover, an recursive algorithm is proposed to get the lists of arbitrary toric surface patches. Furthermore, several geometrical models are given to present shape possibilities of toric surface patches in Computer Aided Geometric Design (CAGD).

Keywords: Bézier patch · Toric surface patch · Geometric modeling · CAGD · Equivalent polygons

1 Introduction

The triangular and tensor-product Bézier patches are effectively applied in many areas of CAGD and CAD [4]. The multi-sided surface patches are often required to design freeform surfaces in manufacturing industry and parameterize the computational domains in isogeometric analysis (IGA for short) [6,20,21]. Loop and DeRose [12] introduced S-patches which generalize triangular Bézier patches by allowing patches to be defined over any convex polygonal domains. Sabin [14] described a pair of non-rectangular surfaces for inclusions in B-splines. Warren [19] created multi-sided Bézier patches using bases points. Vàrady et al. [17] proposed a method to construct n-sided surfaces interpolating so-called tangential ribbons based on transfinite surface interpolation scheme. In 2002, Krasauskas [9] presented a kind of multi-sided surface patches, called toric patches, which generalize classical Bézier patches. Moreover, many real rational surfaces which are actively used in CAGD are found to be toric surface patches [8].

Toric surface patches have attracted many scholars' attentions from their appearance. Garcia et al. [5] applied toric geometry to explain how the geometric properties of toric surface patches are related with the control points. Krasauskas

This work is partly supported by Program for Science Technology Innovation Talents in Universities of Henan Province (No. 22HASTIT021), the Science and Technology Project of Henan Province (No. 212102210394).

B. Sheng et al. (Eds.): CGI 2023, LNCS 14497, pp. 174–185, 2024.
https://doi.org/10.1007/978-3-031-50075-6_14

[10] developed several algorithms for toric surface patches with depth, including de Casteljau pyramid evaluation algorithm, blossoming and so on. Sun and Zhu [15,16] studied the geometrical continuity of toric patches via toric degenerations. The number of regular control surfaces of toric surface patch was given by Wang et al. [18]. In 2020, Zhu et al. [22] used toric surface patches in isogeometric analysis and reached the optimized convergence rate. Toric spline patches share the advantages of isogeometric continuum elements, in that they can exactly model the geometry and can be implemented in standard finite-element code architectures. Dai et al. [3] proposed a novel attention-based approach to fulluse the information of mesh data and exploit comprehensive features for more accurate classification. Ali et al. [1] introduced a system for 360° overview of iridocorneal angle of anterior chamber via Ultrasound Biomicroscopy. Li et al. [11] proposed a pipeline for the accurate segmentation and extraction of rural road surface objects in 3D lidar point-cloud.

The parametric domains of toric surface patches are arbitrary convex lattice polygons. In Combinatorics, convex lattice polygons can be classified into equivalent classes via unimodular transformations [7]. Arkinstall [2] proved there is just one convex lattice hexagon containing a single interior lattice point up to equivalent polygons. In 1989, Rabinowitz [13] extend Arkinstall's results by finding all convex lattice polygons with at most one interior lattice point. Those results about lattice polygons are useful in the classifications of multi-sided parametric surfaces. As we all know, the classical Bézier patches are classified as triangular Bézier patches and tensor-product Bézier patches. In this paper, we study the classification of toric surface patches with unimodular transformations of parametric domains, and demonstrate the equivalent classes of toric patches with at most one interior control point.

The structure of this paper is organized as follows. In Sect. 2, we review the definition and properties of toric surface patches. In Sect. 3, we recall the unimodular transformations and demonstrate the equivalent classes of polygons with at most one interior point. In Sect. 4, we study the classification of toric surface patches, and different types of toric surface patches are given. In Sect. 5, several geometrical models are proposed to present the shape possibilities of toric patches in CAGD. Finally, the paper ends with a conclusion.

2 Previous Work

2.1 Toric Surface Patches

Consider a convex polygon Δ in the real affine plane $\mathbb{R}^2$, if its vertices are in the plane $\mathbb{Z}^2$, the polygon Δ is called a lattice polygon. Suppose the edges Γ_k of Λ defines line equations $l_k(u,v) = a_k u + b_k v + c_k, k = 1, \cdots, n$. Normalize these linear forms so that every normal vector (a_k, b_k) satisfies the following two additional conditions:

(1) the normal vector (a_k, b_k) is inward oriented;
(2) (a_k, b_k) is a primitive lattice vector, that is, it is the shortest vector in this direction with integer coordinates.

For each lattice point **a** of $\mathcal{A} = \Delta \cap \mathbb{Z}^2$, Krasauskas [9] defined toric Bernstein basis functions

$$\beta_{\mathbf{a}}(u,v) = c_{\mathbf{a}}l_1(u,v)^{l_1(\mathbf{a})} \cdots l_n(u,v)^{l_n(\mathbf{a})}, \quad (u,v) \in \Delta,$$

where the coefficients $c_{\mathbf{a}} > 0$.

Definition 1 [9]. *A toric surface patch defined on lattice polygon Δ is a piece of a surface parameterized by the map $\mathcal{T} : \Delta \to \mathbb{R}^3$*

$$\mathcal{T}(u,v) = \frac{\sum_{\mathbf{a} \in \mathcal{A}} \beta_{\mathbf{a}}(u,v)\omega_{\mathbf{a}}\boldsymbol{p}_{\mathbf{a}}}{\sum_{\mathbf{a} \in \mathcal{A}} \beta_{\mathbf{a}}(u,v)\omega_{\mathbf{a}}}, \quad (u,v) \in \Delta, \tag{1}$$

where $\{\beta_{\mathbf{a}}(u,v)|\mathbf{a} \in \mathcal{A}\}$ are the toric Bernstein basis functions, and $\{\omega_{\mathbf{a}} \geq 0|\mathbf{a} \in \mathcal{A}\}$ and $\{\boldsymbol{p}_{\mathbf{a}}|\mathbf{a} \in \mathcal{A}\}$ are the corresponding weights and control points.

Remark 1. If Δ is a triangle or rectangle, toric Bernstein basis functions are exactly the classical triangular or tensor-product Bernstein basis functions by taking proper values for $c_{\mathbf{a}}$ and parametric transformation, then toric surface patches are degenerated to the classical triangular or tensor-product Bézier patches [9].

The toric Bernstein basis functions characterize the geometry aspects of toric surface patches and the convex lattice set $\Delta \cap \mathbb{Z}^2$ describes the topology structure of the control nets. For toric surface patches, the geometry aspects and the combinatorial structure of the lattice nets are closely related [10]. The classifications of convex lattice polygons imply the types of parametric surfaces. It also turns out that the toric surface patches have many good geometric properties analogous to the classical Bézier patches listed as follows [9].

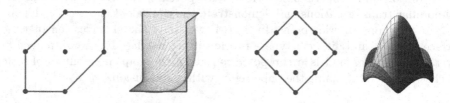

Fig. 1. Toric surface patches

- Affine invariance: Affine transformations such as translation, scaling and rotation can be applied on the toric surface patch by applying the respective transform on the control points.
- Corner points interpolation: The patch $\mathcal{T}(u,v)$ interpolates the control points indexed by corner points of Δ.
- Convex hull property: The patch $\mathcal{T}(u,v)$ is contained in the convex hull of its control points.
- Boundary property: The restriction of $\mathcal{T}(u,v)$ on a boundary of Δ is a rational Bézier curve, defined by control points and weights indexed by points on the boundary of Δ.

Next we illustrate the constructions of toric surface patches by an example.

Example 1. Let Δ_1 be a convex hexagon containing the following point set

$$\mathcal{A}_1 = \{[-1,0],[-1,-1],[0,-1],[0,0],[0,1],[1,0],[1,1]\},$$

i.e., $\Delta_1 = Conv\{\mathcal{A}_1\}$, shown in the left of Fig. 1. The edges of Δ_1 are defined by

$$l_1(u,v) = u+1; l_2(u,v) = u-v+1; l_3(u,v) = 1-v;$$
$$l_4(u,v) = -u+1; l_5(u,v) = -u+v+1; l_6(u,v) = v+1.$$

For each point $(u_0,v_0) \in \mathcal{A}_1$, toric Bernstein basis functions $\beta_{(u_0,v_0)}(u,v)$ is

$$\beta_{(u_0,v_0)}(u,v) = c_{(u_0,v_0)}l_1(u,v)^{l_1(u_0,v_0)}l_2(u,v)^{l_2(u_0,v_0)}\cdots l_6(u,v)^{l_6(u_0,v_0)}.$$

Given control points,

$$\mathbf{P}_{(-1,0)} = [-1,0,0]; \mathbf{P}_{(-1,-1)} = [-0.5,-0.5,-1]; \mathbf{P}_{(0,-1)} = [0,-1,0];$$
$$\mathbf{P}_{(0,0)} = [0,-2,8]; \mathbf{P}_{(0,1)} = [0,1,0]; \mathbf{P}_{(1,0)} = [1,0,0]; \mathbf{P}_{(1,1)} = [0.5,0.5,1],$$

and corresponding weights $\omega = \{1,1,1,1,1,1,1\}$, we get the toric surface patch defined on Δ_1 (see the left two configurations of Fig. 1). Similarly, consider a convex rhombus Δ_2 contains the following points set

$$\mathcal{A}_2 = \{[-2,0],[-1,-1],[-1,0],[-1,1],[0,-2],[0,-1],[0,0],$$
$$[0,1],[0,2],[1,-1],[1,0],[1,1],[2,0]\}$$

i.e., $\Delta_2 = Conv\{\mathcal{A}_2\}$ (see the third in Fig. 1). Then, the edges of Δ_2 and toric Bernstein basis functions can be obtained with the same method, we will omit the details here. Given a set of control points and weights, a toric surface patch defined on Δ_2 is shown in the last one of Fig. 1.

In contrast to classical Bézier patches, however, it is possible to have singular points in vertices for general toric surface patches. As usual, a singular point on a parametric surface implies there is no tangent plane at this point [4]. Given a convex lattice polygon Δ, for every corner $\mathbf{v}$ of Δ, we define a lattice triangle $\Delta_\mathbf{v}$ with three vertices: $\mathbf{v}$ and the two nearest lattice points on the adjacent boundary edges.

Theorem 1. *For a toric surface patch $T(u,v)$ defined on Δ, a corner points $\mathbf{v} \in \Delta$ is non-singular if and only if the area of lattice triangle $\Delta_\mathbf{v}$ of corner points $\mathbf{v}$ equals $1/2$.*

The proof and more details can be found in [9]. In Example 1, for convex hexagon parametric domain Δ_1, it is easy to check the areas of six lattice triangle all equals $1/2$, that is to say, every vertex of toric surface patches is non-singular. But for rhombus parametric domain Δ_2, area of lattice triangle of every corner is 1 which implies those vertices are singular points of corresponding toric surface patches. Singular points may be useful for specific purposes in geometric modeling, we will explain them in Results and discussions section.

2.2   Equivalent Polygons and Unimodular Transformations

The parametric domains of toric surface patches are arbitrary convex lattice polygons. Since the properties of parametric surfaces are closely related with parametric domains. To get the classifications of toric surface patches, it is necessary to study the types of parametric domains. In this section, we explain unimodular transformations and demonstrate the equivalent classes of polygons with at most one interior lattice point.

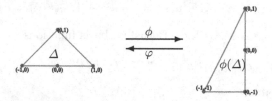

Fig. 2. Unimodular transformations

To understand when two lattice polygons are "equivalent", we firstly review some definitions concerning standard transformations of the plane. An affine transformation is a linear transformation followed by a translation. Unimodular transformation preserves areas of lattice polygons and has a matrix with integer entries and determinant ± 1.

Definition 2. *Two lattice polygons Δ_1 and Δ_2 are called equivalent if there exists an uimodular transformation ϕ, such that $\phi(\Delta_1) = \Delta_2$.*

Example 2. In this example, we illustrate unimodular transformations and equivalent polygons. Given a lattice triangles $\Delta = Conv\{(1,0),(0,1),(-1,0)\}$ and let $\phi((1,0)) = (0,1)$, $\phi((0,1)) = -(1,0) - (0,1) = (-1,-1)$. Obviously, it's a unimodular transformation. Imposed the unidmodular transformation ϕ on Δ,

$$\phi(\Delta) = Conv\{(0,1),(-1,-1),(0,-1)\}.$$

Figure 2 shows triangles Δ and $\phi(\Delta)$. Actually, let φ denote the inverse map of ϕ, i.e., $\varphi((-1,-1)) = (0,1)$, $\varphi((0,1)) = (1,0)$, then

$$\varphi(\phi(\Delta)) = \Delta.$$

It is easy to verify that φ is also an unimodular transformation.

Theorem 2 [13]. *If Δ is a convex lattice polygon without interior lattice point, then Δ is equivalent to one of the following polygons:*

(1) A triangle with vertices $(0,0),(n,0),(0,1)$ (see Fig. 3(a)).
(2) A triangle with vertices $(0,0),(2,0),(0,2)$ (see Fig. 3(b)).
(3) A polygon with vertices $(0,0),(n,0),(m,1),(0,1), n \geq m \geq 1$ (see Fig. 3(c)).

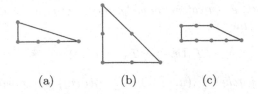

Fig. 3. Polygons without interior lattice point

From the above result, there are only three kinds of convex lattice polygon without interior lattice point.

Theorem 3 [7]. *A polygon with one internal lattice point is precisely equivalent to one of the following 16 polygons which are all not equivalent to each other.*

1. *Triangles with one interior point (see Fig. 4(a)–(e));*
2. *Quadrangles with one interior point (see Fig. 4(f)–(l));*
3. *Pentagons with one interior point (see Fig. 4(m)–(o));*
4. *Hexagons with one interior point (see Fig. 4(p)).*

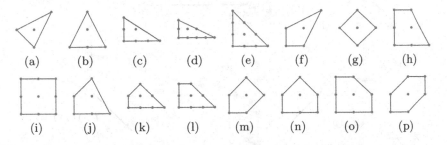

Fig. 4. Polygons with one interior lattice point

The proof and more detailed classifications of convex lattice polygons can be found in Chap. 4 of [7].

3 Classifications of Toric Surface Patches

3.1 Toric Surface Patches with at Most One Interior Control Point

In this subsection, we classify toric surface patches in the sense of reparameterization according to the number of interior control points.

Definition 3. *Let $\mathcal{T}' : \Lambda' \to \mathbb{R}^3$ be a parametric surface, and $\phi . \Delta \to \Delta'$ be a smooth bijective map with a smooth inverse map. Then surface $\mathcal{T} = \mathcal{T}' \circ \phi : \Delta \to \mathbb{R}^3$ is called a reparametrization of $\mathcal{T}'$.*

Lemma 1. *Given two toric surface patches $\mathcal{T}_\Delta(u, v)$ and $\mathcal{T}_{\Delta'}(u, v)$ with the same control points and weights, defined on the lattice polygons Δ and Δ' respectively,* *if Δ and Δ' are lattice equivalent, namely, there exists an unimodular transformation $\phi(\Delta) = \Delta'$, then*

$$\mathcal{T}_{\Delta}(u,v) = \mathcal{T}_{\Delta'}(\phi(u,v)), \tag{2}$$

i.e., toric surface patches $\mathcal{T}_{\Delta}(u,v)$ and $\mathcal{T}_{\Delta'}(\phi(u,v))$ are reparametrizations of each other.

Proof. The linear forms $l_k(u,v), k = 1, 2, \cdots, n$ of Δ satisfy two conditions, i.e., the normal vector (a_k, b_k) is inward oriented and (a_k, b_k) is a primitive lattice vector. Obviously, the unimodular transformations ϕ preserves inward orientation and primitivity properties of (a_k, b_k). Therefore, $\phi(l_k(u,v)) = l'_k(u,v), k = 1, 2, \cdots, n$ for linear forms $l_k(u,v)$ and $l'_k(u,v)$ associated with Δ and Δ' (see Fig. 5), then $\beta_{\phi(\mathbf{a})}(u,v) = \beta_{\mathbf{a}'}(u,v)$, that is to say, their toric Bernstein basis functions are identical. Given weights $\{\omega_{\mathbf{a}} \geq 0 | \mathbf{a} \in \Delta \cap \mathbb{Z}^2\}$ and control points $\{p_{\mathbf{a}} | \mathbf{a} \in \Delta \cap \mathbb{Z}^2\}$, then Eq. (2) holds.

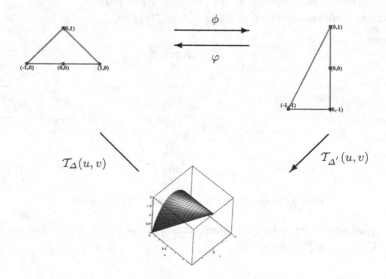

Fig. 5. Reparametrization

By combining above Lemma 1 with Theorem 2 and Theorem 3, we get the following results about the classification of toric surface patches with at most one interior control point.

Theorem 4. *If $\mathcal{T}(u,v)$ is a toric surface patch defined on lattice polygon Δ without interior lattice point, then there are three types for toric surface patches $\mathcal{T}(u,v)$ listed below in the sense of reparametrizations:*

(1) Toric surface patch defined on a triangle with vertices $(0,0), (n,0), (0,1)$;
(2) Toric surface patch defined on a triangle with vertices $(0,0), (2,0), (0,2)$;
(3) Toric surface patch defined on a polygon with vertices $(0,0), (n,0), (m,1), (0,1), n \geq m \geq 1$.

Proof. Since the domain Δ of toric surface patch $\mathcal{T}(u,v)$ has no interior lattice point, according to Theorem 2, Δ is equivalent to three kinds of polygons without interior lattice point. Therefore, in the sense of reparametrization, $\mathcal{T}(u,v)$ is equivalent to three kinds of toric surface patches presented in the above theorem.

Fig. 6. Toric surface patches without interior control point

We show above three kinds of equivalent toric surface patches with some representative surfaces in Fig. 6, whose parametric domains are associated with polygons in Fig. 3, respectively. Similarly, for toric surface patches defined on lattice polygons with one interior lattice point, an analogous result holds.

Theorem 5. *For toric surface patches with one interior control point, there are 16 types of surface patches shown in Fig. 7 in the sense of reparametrization.*

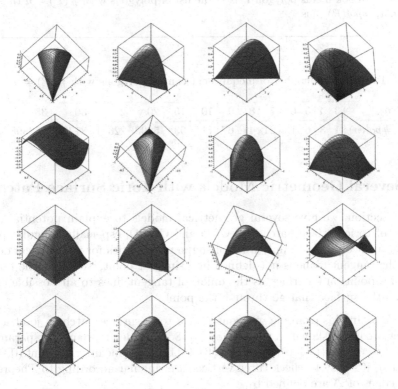

Fig. 7. Toric surface patches with one interior control point

3.2   Classification of Arbitrary Toric Surface Patches

In this subsection, we give a recursive algorithm to get the lists of arbitrary toric surface patches according to the number of control points of toric surface patches.

For a polygon P in $\mathbb{R}^n$, let $\#(P)$ be the number of points of $\mathbb{Z}^n$ in P and $\#pol(n)$ be the number of inequivalent convex polygons P such that $\#(P) = n$. For $n = 3$, there is only one such polygon. Algorithm 1 gives the outline of recursive algorithm to get all types of arbitrary toric surface patches. It is great to display all these polygons, but there are too many to show them here. More interesting is the number of inequivalent convex polygons P with $\#(P) = n$ for a given n. The number of inequivalent convex polygons is shown in Table 1.

Algorithm 1. Outline of recursive algorithm to get the number and lists of arbitrary toric surface patches P with $\#(P) = n$ for a given n

---

For $n = 3$, $\#pol(n) = 1$.
For $n > 3$, suppose we have a list of polygons P' with $\#(P') = \#(P) - 1$
Step 1: Find all points Q whose distance is 1 from Q to edges of polygons P'.
Step 2: Determine the convex hull P of point Q and polygon P'.
Step 3: Look if this polygon P is in the list of polygons with $\#(P) = n$ till so far, if not, $\#pol(P)$ plus 1.

Table 1. the number of inequivalent convex polygons with $\#(P) = n$

n	3	4	5	6	7	8	9	10	15	20	25	30	35
$\#pol(n)$	1	3	6	13	21	41	67	111	938	5293	22641	81300	252898

4   Several Geometric Models with Toric Surface Patches

In this section, we give several geometrical models to explain potential applications of toric surface patches in CAD and CAGD, especially, singular points of toric surface patches imply a lot of shape possibilities for geometrical design. Since the tangent plane is not defined in a singular point, we define the tangent cone of a point on a surface as the union of tangent lines to all possible curves lying on the surface that go through the point.

Example 3. In this example, we construct a toric surface patch to joint a cube missing a corner, shown in the left of Fig. 8. Consider a triangular parametric domain $\Delta = Conv\{(-1, 0), (0, -1), (0, 0), (1, 1)\}$ with one interior point $(0, 0)$(see Fig. 8(b)), it's easy to check three vertices are singular according to Theorem 1. Three edges of Δ are defined by

$$l_1(u, v) = u + v + 1; l_2(u, v) = u - 2v + 1; l_3(u, v) = -2u + v + 1.$$

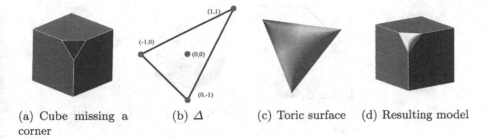

(a) Cube missing a   (b) Δ (c) Toric surface   (d) Resulting model
corner

Fig. 8. Toric surface patches jointing with cube

For each point (u_0, v_0) in $\Delta \cap \mathbb{Z}^2$, toric Bernstein basis function is

$$\beta_{(u_0,v_0)}(u,v) = c_{(u_0,v_0)} l_1(u,v)^{l_1(u_0,v_0)} l_2(u,v)^{l_2(u_0,v_0)} l_3(u,v)^{l_3(u_0,v_0)}.$$

Given the control points

$$\mathbf{P}_{(-1,0)} = [1, 0.4, 1]; \mathbf{P}_{(-1,-1)} = [1, 1, 0.4]; \mathbf{P}_{(0,-1)} = [1, 1, 1]; \mathbf{P}_{(0,0)} = [0.4, 1, 1],$$

we get corresponding toric surface patch, shown in Fig. 8(c). Here three vertices $(1,1), (-1,0), (0,-1)$ are singular points and their tangent cone are pairs of planes which coincide with the corresponding faces of the cube.

In this example, there are three singular vertices $(1,1), (-1,0), (0,-1)$. Compared with toric surface patch, when we use a triangular Bézier patch to blend the cube, it's impossible to get the tangent cones on these vertices since tangent planes of Bézier surface patch are defined on these vertices.

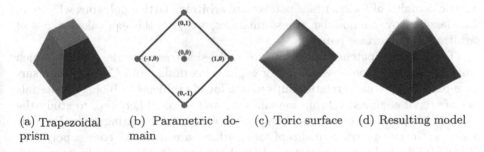

(a) Trapezoidal   (b) Parametric do-   (c) Toric surface   (d) Resulting model
prism   main

Fig. 9. Toric surface patch jointing with trapezoidal prism

Example 4. In this example, a 4-sided toric surface patches is constructed to joint a trapezoidal prism, shown in Fig. 9(a). Here a 4-sided parametric domain is given (see Fig. 9(b)) and four vertices are singular points whose tangent cone are pairs of planes. The corresponding toric surface patch and resulting model are shown in the last two of Fig. 9.

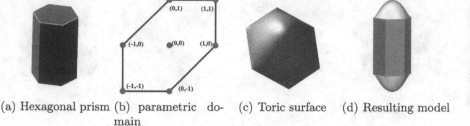

(a) Hexagonal prism (b) parametric do- (c) Toric surface (d) Resulting model
main

Fig. 10. Toric surface patch jointing with hexagonal prism

Example 5. As can be seen in Fig. 10(a), there is a hexagonal prism. We construct two 6-sided toric surface patches defined on hexagonal parametric domain (see Fig. 10(b)) to joint the prism. The toric surface patches and resulting model are presented in the Fig. 10(c) and (d).

By contrast, in this example, while using Bézeir surfaces to blend the hexagonal prism, it's necessary to partition hexagonal parametric domains and joint several Bézier surface patches together to get the resulting surfaces. Compared with Bézier surface patches, toric surface patches are multi-sided which implies it's feasible to use the hexagonal convex domain as a whole parametric domain to construct a corresponding toric surface patch which reduces the complexity of computation.

5   Conclusions and Future Work

In this paper, we consider classification of toric surface patches. Since the parametric domains of toric surface patches are arbitrary lattice polygons which can be classified by unimodular transformations, we give the equivalent types of arbitrary toric surface patches.

Toric surface patches are a kind of multi-sided parametric surfaces which implies a lot of shape possibilities for engineering design and CAGD. Toric surface patches have close relationships with a lot of problems in biology, materials science, civil engineering, ship manufacture and so on. Therefore, to study the potential application of toric surface patches is a very interesting topic. Furthermore, as the parametric domains of toric surfaces are arbitrary convex polygons, it is useful to study the parameterization of computational domain in isogeometric analysis with toric surfaces.

References

1. Ali, S.G., et al.: Cost-effective broad learning-based ultrasound biomicroscopy with 3D reconstruction for ocular anterior segmentation. Multimed. Tools Appl. **80**, 35105–35122 (2021)

2. Arkinstall, J.R.: Minimal requirements for Minkowski's theorem in the plane I. Bull. Aust. Math. Soc. **22**(2), 275–283 (1980)
3. Dai, J., Fan, R., Song, Y., Guo, Q., He, F.: MEAN: an attention-based approach for 3D mesh shape classification. Vis. Comput. 1–14 (2023)
4. Farin, G.: Curves and Surfaces for CAD. Morgan Kaufmann (2002)
5. Garcia-Puente, L.D., Sottile, F., Zhu, C.G.: Toric degenerations of Bézier patches. ACM Trans. Graph. **30**(5), Article 110 (2011)
6. Ji, Y., Li, J.G., Yu, Y.Y., Zhu, C.G.: H-refinement method for toric parameterization of planar multi-sided computational domain in isogeometric analysis. Comput. Aided Geom. Design **93**, Article 102065 (2022)
7. Koelman, R.: The Number of Moduli of Families of Curves on Toric Surfaces. [S.l. : s.n.] (1991)
8. Krasauskas, R.: Shape of toric surfaces. In: IEEE, Computer Graphics, Spring Conference, pp. 55–62 (2001)
9. Krasauskas, R.: Toric surface patches. Adv. Comput. Math. **17**(1–2), 89–113 (2002)
10. Krasauskas, R., Goldman, R.: Toric Bézier patches with depth. Contemp. Math. **334**, 65–91 (2003)
11. Li, H.T., Todd, Z., Bielski, N., Carroll, F.: 3D lidar point-cloud projection operator and transfer machine learning for effective road surface features detection and segmentation. Vis. Comput. **38**(5), 1759–1774 (2022)
12. Loop, C.T., DeRose, T.D.: A multisided generalization of Bézier surfaces. ACM Trans. Graph. (TOG) **8**(3), 204–234 (1989)
13. Rabinowitz, S.: A census of convex lattice polygons with at most one interior lattice point. Ars Combin. **28**, 83–96 (1989)
14. Sabin, M.: Non-rectangular surface patches suitable for inclusion in a B-spline surface. In: Eurographics Conference Proceedings, pp. 57–79. The Eurographics Association (1983)
15. Sun, L.Y., Zhu, C.G.: G^1 continuity between toric surface patches. Comput. Aided Geom. Design **35–36**, 255–267 (2015)
16. Sun, L.Y., Zhu, C.G.: Curvature continuity conditions between adjacent toric surface patches. Comput. Graph. Forum **37**(7), 469–477 (2018)
17. Várady, T., Rockwood, A., Salvi, P.: Transfinite surface interpolation over irregular N-sided domains. Comput. Aided Des. **43**(11), 1330–1340 (2011)
18. Wang, H., Zhu, C.G., Zhao, X.Y.: The number of regular control surfaces of toric patch. J. Comput. Appl. Math. **329**, 280–293 (2018)
19. Warren, J.: Creating multisided rational Bézier surfaces using base points. ACM Trans. Graph. **11**(2), 127–139 (1992)
20. Xu, G., Li, M., Mourrain, B., Rabczuk, T., Xu, J., Bordas, S.P.: Constructing IGA-suitable planar parameterization from complex CAD boundary by domain partition and global/local optimization. Comput. Methods Appl. Mech. Eng. **328**, 175–200 (2018)
21. Xu, G., Mourrain, B., Duvigneau, R., Galligo, A.: Parameterization of computational domain in isogeometric analysis: methods and comparison. Comput. Methods Appl. Mech. Eng. **200**(23–24), 2021–2031 (2011)
22. Zhu, X., Ji, Y., Zhu, C., Hu, P., Ma, Z.D.: Isogeometric analysis for trimmed cad surfaces using multi-sided toric surface patches. Comput. Aided Geom. Design **79**, Article 101847 (2020)

Integrate Depth Information to Enhance the Robustness of Object Level SLAM

Shinan Huang and Jianyong Chen[✉]

College of Computer Science and Software Engineering,
Shenzhen University, Shenzhen, China
jychen@szu.edu.cn

Abstract. vSLAM (Visual Simultaneous Localization and Mapping) is a fundamental function in various robot applications. With the development of downstream applications, there is an increasing challenge for scene semantic understanding and stable operation in different scenarios. In this paper, we propose an object-level RGBD SLAM system that reconstructs objects using quadric surfaces and extracts planar information with lower measurement noise compared to point features. These extracted planes and original point features are tightly coupled as landmarks in the system to enhances the robustness of the system in different scenarios. Moreover, we utilize the edges of planes to inference unseen planes to obtain more structured constraints. The experiments conducted on publicly available datasets demonstrate the competitive performance of our framework when compared to state-of-the-art object-based algorithms. Code is available in github.com/DemoShiNan/RGBDOBJ/tree/master.

Keywords: Object level SLAM · RGB-D · Plane feature · Structured constraints

1 Introduction

With the rapid advancement of robot applications such as path planning and object grasping, the vSLAM algorithm, as a vision system for robots, needs to fulfill not only the responsibility of self-localization, but also become the primary gateway for understanding and interacting with the environment. In order to serve specific applications, the algorithm faces the challenge to provide accurate, stable, and even real-time localization information when facing unknown environments. Meanwhile, it should extract semantic information from input data as much as possible to enhance scene comprehension.

To solve these problems, various algorithms have been developed to extract feature points from RGB images in unknown environments and perform localization based on feature point detection and correlation [1,2]. These algorithms yield reasonably accurate localization information and generate maps in different forms. These representations only accomplish the most basic scene construction

B. Sheng et al. (Eds.): CGI 2023, LNCS 14497, pp. 186–197, 2024.
https://doi.org/10.1007/978-3-031-50075-6_15

and lack semantic information. Additionally, in many challenging scenes, like texture-less scenes, system robustness is still unsatisfactory.

To further advance towards the goal of scene comprehension and interaction, there has been increasing attention on incorporating and utilizing semantic information, Dense semantic mapping SLAM algorithms, such as Suma++ [3], have been developed. Moreover, the emergence of Nerf has initiated the development of Nice-SLAM [4] and Nicer-SLAM [5], which are based on neural networks for dense semantic mapping. However, these methods currently face challenges in terms of real-time performance and model deployment compared to traditional SLAM methods. As a result, object-based SLAM approaches [6,7] in sparse semantics domain have gained attention.

However, the tracking robustness of most object-based algorithms ultimately relies on the stability of tracking point features. Once point tracking is lost, the objects established in the map themselves struggle to maintain tracking. Prior studies have demonstrated that plane features extracted from depth images have lower noise and can achieve higher accuracy compared to pure point features. Therefore, it is worthwhile to investigate the improvement of tracking robustness in non-dense semantic SLAM by integrating planar features. We propose an improved SLAM system with points features and planar features tightly coupled, using both point and planar constraints during matching and optimization.

To sum up, our main contributions are as follows:

· We propose a tightly coupled object-level SLAM framework, which can track planes, objects, and feature points simultaneously.
· We propose an innovative method which integrate depth information to extract planar features, enabling the inference of occluded planes and yielding a more structured map.
· We evaluated the tracking stability and map building capabilities of the proposed algorithm on challenging scenarios in publicly available dataset. The results outperform the state-of-the-art methods.

2   Related Work

2.1   Object-Based SLAM

By using deep learning detectors, it is possible to obtain continuous frame-by-frame object detection boxes. By leveraging the relationship between feature points and the detection boxes, the feature points belonging to the tracked objects can be bulit as objects in map. This forms the basic construction logic of object-level SLAM.

Recently, Zins et al. [8] proposed a SLAM system builds upon the ellipsoid-based representation method of EAO-SLAM [9] and proposed an object track-based approach for robust relocalization. In the relocalization process, it calculates the optimal score through potential matches between objects to determine the best match and recover the pose. This approach improves the algorithm's robustness in relocalization.

2.2 RGB-D SLAM

RGB-D SLAM has been extensively studied due to its ability to improve algorithm accuracy by utilizing depth information from depth cameras. Chen et al. [10] proposed a tightly-coupled framework that jointly optimizes keyframe poses, IMU states, and parameters of points and planes. Li et al. [11] extracted lines and planes from depth maps to aid in estimating camera rotations. While all these methods effectively utilize depth information, the constructed maps contain only structural information without deeper semantic understanding.

Hosseinzadeh et al. [12] introduces object-plane tangency constraints. However, it does not tightly couple the plane features into the system to enhance operational robustness. Furthermore, it lacks the capability to reconstruct occluded planes or planes temporarily out of view due to viewpoint issues. In our work, we not only tightly couple various features, but also infer the hidden planes based on known plane edges to supplement the features.

3 Framework

3.1 Overview

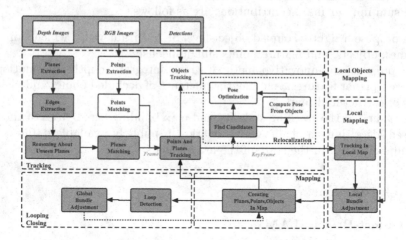

Fig. 1. System overview: Newly added or modified parts are marked with green (Color figure online)

Figure 1 displays the detailed structure of our system which is based on OA-SLAM [8]. Tracking thread serves as the frontend of the algorithm, receiving input and performing feature extraction and matching on the image stream to maintain tracking. It ultimately accomplishes the initial pose estimation, while the relocalization component helps the system automatically recover tracking when it is lost. The local mapping and local object mapping threads, as the backend of the system, receive the keyframe structures created by the frontend. They utilize various information and constraints within these keyframes to construct an optimization problem that optimizes the pose while updating the information in the keyframes. The mapping thread is responsible for map construction, map updates, and visualization using these keyframes. The loopclosing thread, which runs periodically as an independent thread, detects similarities between the information in the map and the current observations. When a similar scene is detected, it builds loop closure constraints using the associations of keyframes. These constraints are then incorporated into the optimization problem to mitigate accumulated drift.

Innovatively, RGB-D images and detections obtained by YOLO [13] are received by the front-end tracking thread. Depth images will be used to construct a point cloud for plane extraction, edge extraction, and unseen planes inference, which will be explained in Sect. 3.2. Then the obtained planes are matched with the previous frame through association. Meanwhile, the extraction and matching of point features are also carried out on RGB images. Only if successful association is made, the system will create a new frame to store the tracked information. The information, including points, planes, and pose-related data, will be used to compute the camera pose for the current frame. Meanwhile, the input detections are used for objects tracking. Then, the pose of both points and planes in the frame will be optimized, as described in Sect. 3.3 and Sect. 3.4.

In the event of tracking loss, which means that the data association has failed for a period of time. The improved relocalization approach will be triggered which is briefly introduced in Sect. 3.5. Normally, frames will be used to calculate disparity and make a determination on whether to create a keyframe, which are designed to reduce computation. These keyframes are stored in a queue for transmission and passed to the back-end local mapping thread for local bundle adjustment, which will be described in Sect. 3.6.

3.2   Object and Plane Detection

We use YOLO [13] to obtain detection boxes for each frame and only adopt objects with confidence greater than 0.5.

For planar features, we estimate small planes for each point in the ordered structural point cloud and then distinguish and merge small planes based on their differences to calculate plane parameters. When using the implementation in pcl library, the execution time of this process is less than 10 ms. It is worth noting that we can also obtain a set of plane contours at the same time during this process.

Figure 2(a) shows a dark, low-textured cabinet, while Fig. 2(b) displays the map reconstructed by our system on this cabinet scene. System reconstructs the occluded planes with only three visible planes in the depicted viewpoint, even before the camera observes its hidden planes. By using the edges of planes, we can infer hidden planes that are not displayed in the current view. Meanwhile, In the scene of Fig. 2(c), the zig-zag structure which is one meter high is built from wooden panels and fully wrapped in a white plastic foil with little to no texture. Figure 2(d) shows the map built on this scene. When the system perspective cannot see the plane between two parallel planes (green and pink) after initialization, it can still infer that there may be a plane (purple) at this position through edge point inference. We use RANSAC to extract lines from contours and assume that the edges of planes are the intersection lines of two perpendicular planes. Then we can infer one plane from another plane through one of its edges.

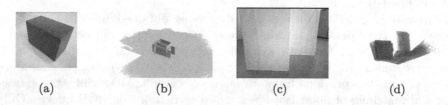

(a)   (b)   (c)   (d)

Fig. 2. Plane inference (Color figure online)

3.3 Data Association

The data association includes landmarks building and association. During the tracking process, the data association of the object uses the detection box between frames, and the successfully tracked object obtains long-term data association by reconstructing an ellipsoid. As for planes, after the extraction of planar features, planes are treated as a level of data along with the feature points for tracking and reconstructing. During the detection phase, the planes adhere to the Manhattan-world assumption and are classified as horizontal or vertical based on a certain threshold. The matching and association of planar features between consecutive frames primarily rely on the comparison of their plane parameters and categories.

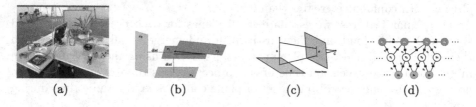

(a)   (b)   (c)   (d)

Fig. 3. (a) Object association, (b) plane association, (c) normal vector projection and (d) factor graph for pose optimization (Color figure online)

As for object association, as shown in the Fig. 3(a), only the successfully reconstructed object will be projected into the current frame during tracking and matched with the detection box using Hungarian optimal matching [14] to obtain the optimal matching solution.

For the representation of planes in building process, we construct a 3D point cloud from the depth map and extract planes from it. The planes are then parameterized in Hessian form:

$$\pi = (n^T, d)^T, \tag{1}$$

where $n = (n_x, n_y, n_z)^T$ is the unit normal vector of the plane, and d is the distance from the origin to the plane. In addition to directly extracting planes from the point cloud, we infer the observability of partially occluded planes by incorporating edge constraints from the extracted planes. This ensures the observability of planes that are not fully visible from certain viewpoints.

In the phase of associating planes with the map, the matching planes are obtained by comparing the intersecting angles and distances. Considering the specific range of planes in the map, we calculate distances using the points p_j extracted from the plane contour C_p during the semantic extraction process and the planes $\pi_i = (n_i^T, d_i)^T$ in the map. The formula for distance calculation is as follows.

$$dist = \min \left\{ \left| n_i^T \cdot p_j + d_i \right| \right\}, \quad p_j \in C_p. \tag{2}$$

It is important to note that in this process, we strive to find a corresponding plane π_2, the nearest perpendicular plane π_3, and a parallel plane π_4 for each observed plane π_1 in the map, as Fig. 3(b) shows. The orthogonal and parallel relationships between planes are also established as constraints in subsequent optimizations. The contour points of the planes also play a role in assisting the computation of distances between planes.

3.4   Pose Refinement

The fusion of objects and the optimization of object poses are performed in the local object mapping thread, which is consistent with OA-SLAM [8]. When a new keyframe observes an object that already exists, a least squares problem will be constructed by projecting the inscribed ellipses of consecutive detection boxes, aiming to fit the parameters of the ellipse.

For the optimization of plane parameters, when a new keyframe is created and passed to the local mapping thread, the data association phase allows us to establish correspondences between plane features in the keyframe and those in the local map. Subsequently, the plane features are optimized by minimizing the projection error of their normal vectors.

To project the plane normal vectors from the map coordinates to the camera coordinate system as Fig. 3(c), the camera's pose is utilized, which is also an esti-mated value subject to optimization. In the core technology of SLAM, this task is typically accomplished by constructing a factor graph to describe and solve the problem. Estimated variables are represented as nodes in the graph, and con-straints are represented as edges. The optimization process involves minimizing the error associated with both camera poses and other parameters.

As shown in Fig. 3(d), circular symbols represent nodes, while connecting lines represent constraints between nodes. White color represents camera poses, green color represents planar landmarks, and orange color represents point landmarks. The constraints between cameras and points are denoted as X_i, the constraints between cameras and planes are denoted as Y_i, and the structured constraints between planes are denoted as Z_i.

In order to reduce the number of parameters, the expression uses the representation of Euler angles with the following conversion method:

$$q(\pi) = (\arctan{(n_y/n_x)}, \arcsin{n_z}, d)^T. \tag{3}$$

We can define the factor for planes:

$$f_Y(\pi_w, T_{cw}) = \sum_i \|q(\pi_i) - q(T_{cw}{}^{-T}\pi_w)\|, \tag{4}$$

where π_i means the plane observed in the current frame, and $T_{cw}{}^{-T}\pi_w$ means the plane translated from the world coordinate system to the camera coordinate system. Meanwhile, the constraint factor between planes have the similar form:

$$f_Z(\pi_w, T_{cw}) = \sum_j \|q_n(n_j) - q_n(R_{cw}n_w)\|, \tag{5}$$

where n represents the normal vector of the plane. q_n represents the first two terms in the transformation formula related to the normal vector. R_{cw} represents the rotation of the current frame.

3.5 Relocalization

Tracking is inevitably lost due to some reasons during the tracking process. At this time, a relocation algorithm is needed to help the system recover tracking.

During the relocalization process, in our innovative work, plane features are also included in the relocalization matching process. It not only matches object categories but also confirms that the variation in distance between the object and several nearby planes is not significant. Once the matching pairs are determined, camera pose estimation is performed, and a score is calculated based on the reprojection error of points and plane normals. The best match is selected based on the highest score. Finally, a global optimization is conducted to refine the plane parameters, camera poses, and map points. This improves the relocalization performance. Details are shown in the Algorithm 1.

By incorporating both objects and plane features in the relocalization process, the system benefits from a more comprehensive and robust matching scheme, enhancing the ability to recognize and relocalize in the same scene even under challenging conditions.

Algorithm 1 Relocalization from planes and objects

Input: Current Frame detections (**Det, Det_category**), current Frame Planes **Cur_Pls**, current Frame Points **Cur_Pts**, objects and planes closest to the object in map (**E, E_category, E_Pls**), points in map **Map_Pts**, camera extrinsics **K**.
Output: Estimated pose of camera **P**.
  Initialization:
  BestMactch $= \emptyset$, **MaxScore** $= 0$, **BestPose** $= \mathbf{I}$;
  // Stage 1: Objects Matching and P3P_ransac problem solving.
  for each $(\mathbf{D}_i, \mathbf{DC}_i)$ in (**Det, Det_category**) **do**
    for each $(\mathbf{E}_j, \mathbf{EC}_j)$ in (**E, E_category**) **do**
      if $\mathbf{DC}_i == \mathbf{EC}_j$ **then**
        for each **p** in **Cur_pls do**
          Compute **dist** of $\mathbf{E}_j$ and **p** according to Eq.(2);
        end for
        The Top-3 **p** with the smallest **dist** are matched with **E_Pls**;
        if matched **then**
          Compute guess pose **G_pose** by center of $\mathbf{E}_j$ and geometry center of **p**;
          Project all **E, E_Pls** to examine coherence by **K** and **G_pose**;
          Compute score from 2D iou of **Det** and projected **E**, and normal angle of **Cur_pls** and projected **E_Pls**;
          Update **MaxScore**;
          Update **BestMactch** with $\mathbf{D}_i$, $\mathbf{E}_j$;
        end if
      end if
    end for
    Update the **BestPose** obtained by objects and planes match;
  end for
  // Stage 2: Refine pose.
  Optimize by minimizing the projection error of **Det** and projected **E**;
  Optimize by minimizing projection error of features (**Cur_Pts, Cur_Pls**) and (**Map_Pts, E_Pls**).

3.6 Local Bundle Adjustment

When the tracking process of the system is smooth, the Local Mapping thread will process the keyframe queue and maintain the local map. The system will optimize camera poses, map points, and plane parameters through the construction of a local map factor graph. This is achieved by projecting the features in the local map to the camera coordinate system based on the camera poses corresponding to the keyframes, and then calculating the reprojection error to form constraints.

In this work, we supplement the plane feature observation constraint based on object observation constraint and point feature observation constraint on the basis of OA-SLAM [8]. The supplemented cost function also uses the same method as the Eq. (4) in pose refinement Sect. 3.4. At the same time, this process also completes the redundancy check and elimination of keyframes.

4   Experiments

To evaluate the effectiveness of our system, we conducted a series of experiments on a publicly available dataset. For the hardware setup, we run on a laptop computer with i7-7700HQ 2.80 GHz CPU, 24 GB RAM.

4.1   Dataset

The widely accessible TUM dataset provides synchronized RGB images and corresponding depth maps, acquired from a variety of indoor and outdoor scenes. These scenes cover diverse environmental conditions, such as varying lighting conditions, textures, and object arrangements.

The dataset utilized in this study is derived from the TUM dataset, specifically designed for RGB-D applications. It encompasses RGB images, depth maps, and ground truth poses for the complete sequence. The dataset encompasses a diverse range of scenes, such as large_cabinet and large_with_loop. These scenes contain both structured features and images with less prominent textures.

4.2   Tracking Stability in Challenging Scenes

Our method demonstrates significant superiority over the distance estimation method of OA-SLAM [8] in the testing process on the TUM dataset. It exhibits better reconstruction capability of the scene and greater stability in feature and object tracking. To showcase the accuracy level of our algorithm, we compare it with the widely used RGBD form of ORB-SLAM2 [1] and SP-SLAM [15], both of which utilize planar features. The results are shown in Table 1 (Fig. 4).

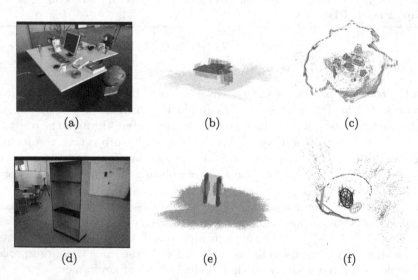

(a)   (b)   (c)

(d)   (e)   (f)

Fig. 4. (a) Desktop scene containing (b) Plane map and (c) Object map, and (d) Large_cabinet scene containing (e) Plane map and (f) Object map.

(a)   (b)

Fig. 5. Comparison of tracking performance between (a) SP-SLAM and (b) ours in Large_with_loop scene

Table 1. RMSE (m) of frames Relative Trajectory Error (median value obtained on 20 runs)

Scene/Data	ORB-RGBD [1]	SP-SLAM [15]	OA-SLAM [8]	Ours
desk	0.003579	**0.003547**	0.107680	0.003834
cabinet	–	0.009878	–	**0.007818**
large_cabinet	–	0.023082	–	**0.019522**
str_notex_far	**0.008855**	0.011074	–	0.013235
large_with_loop	0.029688	0.023154	–	**0.021448**

The last scene, shown in Fig. 5(a) named large_with_loop, is a warehouse scene containing loop closure frames. It includes frames with significant variations in lighting and walls with minimal texture. The scene also features a teddy bear and a potted plant, which serve as landmarks detectable by object detectors. This sequence is well-suited for validating the effectiveness of the system. As shown in Fig. 5(b), complete tracking of this scene still requires the incorporation of depth information. However, due to the excessive reliance on planar surfaces for loop closure, SP-SLAM fails to close the loop and eliminate accumulated errors. In contrast, our proposed method successfully completes the loop closure.

4.3 Relocalization Capability

To validate the improvement in relocalization capability, we perform experiments on the large_with_loop scene. We divide the scene into two segments.

We prebuilt the map on slice1 and then ran the system on slice2 to make it recover tracking in the map of slice1. Our experimental results in Fig. 6 demonstrate that the inclusion of structured features enhances the loop closure capability of the system, particularly in scenes with significant variations in viewing angles and a small number of objects.

Fig. 6. Results: Pre_built map and performance of OA-SLAM and ours

4.4 Runtime Analysis

Our system additionally extracts plane features from the depth map and tracks them, which takes some time. The plane extraction and inference plane generation takes about 10–15 ms. However, due to the sparsity of plane features and the simplicity of normal vector expression, the time consumption of system feature matching and tracking is basically the same as that of simple point feature tracking. The time consumption of object matching and tracking is about 15 ms, and the average tracking time of each frame is about 60 ms, which can reach a running speed of about 15 frames per second.

5 Conclusion

In conclusion, our research proposed a tightly coupled SLAM framework for monocular object-level SLAM domain, to track planes, objects, and feature points simultaneously which can perform feature matching, camera relocalization and pose optimization. By incorporating depth information and leveraging planar features, our algorithm significantly improves the inference of occluded planes, leading to a more comprehensive and detailed map representation. This framework surpasses the performance of state-of-the-art object SLAM methods, demonstrating superior mapping capabilities and tracking stability.

Acknowledgements. This work is supported by the National Nature Science Foundation of China under Grant U2013201.

References

1. Mur-Artal, R., Tardós, J.D.: ORB-SLAM2: an open-source slam system for monocular, stereo, and RGB-D cameras. IEEE Trans. Robot. **33**(5), 1255–1262 (2017)
2. Engel, J., Sturm, J., Cremers, D.: Semi-dense visual odometry for a monocular camera. In: Proceedings of the IEEE International Conference on Computer Vision, pp. 1449–1456 (2013). https://doi.org/10.1109/iccv.2013.183
3. Chen, X., Milioto, A., Palazzolo, E., Giguère, P., Behley, J., Stachniss, C.: SuMa++: efficient lidar-based semantic SLAM. In: 2019 IEEE/RSJ International Conference on Intelligent Robots and Systems (IROS), pp. 4530–4537 (2019). https://doi.org/10.1109/IROS40897.2019.8967704

4. Zhu, Z., et al.: NICE-SLAM: neural implicit scalable encoding for SLAM. In: Proceedings of the IEEE/CVF Conference on Computer Vision and Pattern Recognition (CVPR), pp. 12786–12796 (2022)

5. Zhu, Z., et al.: NICER-SLAM: neural implicit scene encoding for RGB SLAM. arXiv preprint arXiv:2302.03594 (2023)

6. Tian, R., et al.: Accurate and robust object SLAM with 3D quadric landmark reconstruction in outdoors. IEEE Robot. Autom. Lett. **7**(2), 1534–1541 (2021). https://doi.org/10.1109/lra.2021.3137896

7. Cao, Z.Z., et al.: Object-aware SLAM based on efficient quadric initialization and joint data association. IEEE Robot. Autom. Lett. **7**(4), 9802–9809 (2022). https://doi.org/10.1109/lra.2022.3190622

8. Zins, M., Simon, G., Berger, M.O.: OA-SLAM: leveraging objects for camera relocalization in visual SLAM. In: 2022 IEEE International Symposium on Mixed and Augmented Reality (ISMAR), pp. 720–728 (2022). https://doi.org/10.1109/ISMAR55827.2022.00090

9. Wu, Y., Zhang, Y., Zhu, D., Feng, Y., Coleman, S., Kerr, D.: EAO-SLAM: monocular semi-dense object SLAM based on ensemble data association. In: 2020 IEEE/RSJ International Conference on Intelligent Robots and Systems (IROS), pp. 4966–4973 (2021). https://doi.org/10.1109/iros45743.2020.9341757

10. Chen, D., et al.: VIP-SLAM: an efficient tightly-coupled RGB-D visual inertial planar SLAM. In: 2022 International Conference on Robotics and Automation (ICRA), pp. 5615–5621. IEEE (2022)

11. Li, Y., Yunus, R., Brasch, N., Navab, N., Tombari, F.: RGB-D SLAM with structural regularities. In: 2021 IEEE International Conference on Robotics and Automation (ICRA), pp. 11581–11587 (2021). https://doi.org/10.1109/icra48506.2021.9561560

12. Hosseinzadeh, M., Latif, Y., Pham, T., Suenderhauf, N., Reid, I.: Structure aware SLAM using quadrics and planes. In: Jawahar, C.V., Li, H., Mori, G., Schindler, K. (eds.) ACCV 2018. LNCS, vol. 11363, pp. 410–426. Springer, Cham (2019). https://doi.org/10.1007/978-3-030-20893-6_26

13. Redmon, J., Divvala, S., Girshick, R., Farhadi, A.: You only look once: unified, real-time object detection. In: 2016 IEEE Conference on Computer Vision and Pattern Recognition (CVPR), pp. 779–788 (2016). https://doi.org/10.1109/CVPR.2016.91

14. Kuhn, H.W.: The Hungarian method for the assignment problem. Naval Res. Logist. Q. **2**(1–2), 83–97 (2007). https://doi.org/10.1002/nav.3800020109

15. Cho, H.M., Jo, H., Kim, E.: SP-SLAM: surfel-point simultaneous localization and mapping. IEEE/ASME Trans. Mechatron. **27**(5), 2568–2579 (2021). https://doi.org/10.1109/tmech.2021.3118719

Multi-attention Integration Mechanism for Region Destruction Detection of Remote Sensing Images

Hang Sun[1] , Yunyun Sun[2] , Peng Li[1,3]([email]) , and He Xu[1,3]

[1] School of Computer Science, Nanjing University of Posts and Telecommunications, Nanjing 210023, China
lipeng@njupt.edu.cn
[2] School of Internet of Things, Nanjing University of Posts and Telecommunications, Nanjing 210023, China
[3] Institute of Cyberspace Security and Information Computing, Nanjing University of Posts and Telecommunications, Nanjing 130012, China

Abstract. In the existing remote sensing image recognition, the problems of poor imaging quality, small sample size, and the difficulty of using a single attention mechanism to fully extract the hidden distinguishing features in the image, this paper proposes a method for detecting regional destruction in remote sensing images based on MA-CapsNet (multi-attention capsule encoder-decoder network) network. The method firstly adopts the BSRGAN model for image super-resolution processing of the original destruction data, and adopts various data enhancement operations for data expansion of the processed image, and then adopts the MA-CapsNet network proposed in this paper for further processing, using Swin-transformer and Convolutional Block The lower level features are extracted using a cascading attention mechanism consisting of Swin-transformer and Convolutional Block Attention Module (CBAM); finally, the feature map is fed into the classifier to complete the detection of the destroyed area after the precise target features are captured by the CapsNet module (CapsNet). In the destruction area detection experiment carried out in the remote sensing images after the 2010 Haiti earthquake, the accuracy of the MA-CapsNet model in area destruction detection reaches 99.64%, which is better than that of the current state-of-the-art models such as ResNet, Vision Transformer (VIT), and the ablation experimental network model. This method improves the model's characterization ability and solves the problem of low accuracy of remote sensing image destruction area detection under complex background, which is of theoretical guidance significance for quickly grasping remote sensing image destruction and damage assessment.

Keywords: Attention Mechanism · Remote Sensing Image · Destruction Detection · MA-CapsNet

1   Introduction

High-resolution remote sensing images contain rich texture, structure, neighborhood relationship and other information, which can fully extract the contextual semantic information of the features and improve the image classification from pixel level to object level. High-resolution remote sensing images are therefore used in many fields such as urban planning, earthquake detection, etc., and play a crucial role [1].

Image classification, as a method of destruction detection, can achieve rapid identification and detection of destroyed areas based on feature information such as color and texture in post-earthquake remote sensing images. Most of the traditional image classification methods use image processing algorithms to extract a single underlying feature such as the corresponding texture or color, and perform mathematical statistical analysis of these features or use classifiers to output classification results [2]. Nowadays, deep learning [3] technology is booming, which is known for its high accuracy and stable performance, and the deep neural network, as a representative, has achieved better results in the fields of feature target recognition and damage assessment of high-resolution remote sensing images. Liu [4] et al. proposed a sea-land segmentation method based on multi-scale fully convolutional networks to solve the problem of near-shore ship detection. Muhammad [5] et al. proposed a lightweight CNN to achieve precise location of fire and accurate identification of monitored objects. Shao [6] et al. proposed building residual refinement network for accurate and complete extraction of buildings. Peiqi Yang [7] et al. proposed an exactly defined contour loss (CL) for remote sensing interpretation with Residual Attention U-Net (RA U-Net) as the main framework. Jiajia Li [8] et al. proposed a multi-model cascaded convolutional neural network (MCCNN) for domestic waste image detection and classification. Deep learning has shown excellent performance in the field of image recognition, but insufficient data volume will lead to problems such as overfitting of the model [9]. As one of the most widely used "components" in the field of deep learning, the attention mechanism has been applied to remote sensing images to solve the phenomenon of homogeneous and heterogeneous, focusing on relevant information and ignoring irrelevant information from a wide range of remote sensing images [10, 11]. In the research based on the combination of attention mechanism and deep learning models, Li [12] et al. proposed a fire detection method based on multi-scale feature extraction, implicit deep supervision and channel attention mechanism, which achieves a better trade-off between accuracy, model size and speed. Chen [13] et al. proposed a new deep learning based Multi-Resolution Attention and Balance network to recognize bridges in SAR images, which solves the problem of false alarms and omissions in bridge detection in SAR images. Chen [14] et al. proposed an improved YOLOv3 based on an attention mechanism, which solves the detection of ships with different scales and different motion states in complex backgrounds. All of the above methods are related studies based on a single attention mechanism, and although they can effectively represent the extracted features, the visual appearance of different objects and scenes is very different, and a single attention mechanism is not sufficient to fully extract this information [15].

To address this problem, this paper proposes a regional destruction detection method for remote sensing images based on MA-CapsNet model, and the innovations of this paper are mainly reflected in the following aspects:

(1) By integrating Windows Multi-head Self-Attention (W-MSA), Shifted Windows Multi-Head Self-Attention (SW-MSA), Channel Attention and Spatial Attention mechanisms into MA-CapsNet, and joining Spatial Feature Extraction. This enables the network to better obtain information on the channel axis, spatial axis characteristics of the image, and solves the problems of difficult training, low recognition accuracy and poor generalization ability of remote sensing image classification models.

(2) This paper proposes a remote sensing image region destruction detection method based on MA-CapsNet model for the first time to apply remote sensing technology fused attention mechanism to region destruction detection and verifies the feasibility of the attention mechanism in region destruction detection, which has theoretical guidance significance for the research and development of high precision remote sensing image region destruction detection technology.

2 MA-CapsNet Model for Region Destruction Detection of Remote Sensing Images

In this paper, super-resolution image processing is performed on the raw data, and the processed images are expanded with various data enhancement operations. The MA-CapsNet model proposed in this paper adopts Swin-transformer as the backbone network and linearly combines CBAM containing Channel Attention Module, Spatial Attention Module as the feature extractor, and finally embeds the CapsNet network structure. In the procedure of model training, this paper uses Margin Loss in SVM as the loss function and AdamW as the optimizer to optimize the MA-CapsNet network.

2.1 Pre-Processing and Data Augmentation

In this paper, BSRGAN super-resolution model is adopted for image super-resolution processing of the raw data, and multiple data augmentation operations are applied to the processed images for data expansion, such as rotation and Gaussian blurring.

BSRGAN Super-Resolution Pre-processing. Constrained by the external conditions such as sensor jitter during remote sensing image acquisition, resulting in low accuracy of the acquired data, this paper adopts the BSRGAN super-resolution model to improve the quality of remote sensing images. BSRGAN needs to learn how to reverse the effects of the degraded model on image quality to recover high quality images The degradation model it designed uses random mixing degradation to synthesize LR images, and the degradation model is schematically shown in Fig. 1. It adopts includes random mixing and shuffling blurring, downsampling and noise degradation, and moreover, it involves degradation and shuffling strategy [16]. The core idea adopted to construct a degradation model that can be practically applied is:

$$y = (x * k) \downarrow s + n \tag{1}$$

where k is the fuzzy kernel, the convolution kernel is k, $\downarrow_s$ is the downsampling with scale factor s, n is the noise.

The BSRGAN model, as a derivative network of the GAN [17] network, consists of two parts, the generator G and the discriminator D. The two are trained by continuously playing the competition until a Nash equilibrium is reached, and then a better estimation of the distribution of the target samples can be obtained. GAN networks are now widely used in data augmentation, image style migration, image super-resolution [18, 19], text image generation, and other fields.

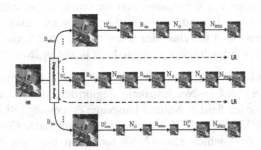

Fig. 1. Schematic diagram of degradation model.   **Fig. 2.** Experimentally augmented data

Data Augmentation Processing. In this paper, data augmentation processing is performed on the data, and the image blocks processed by BSRGAN are rotated by 90°, rotated by 180°, mirrored, added with Gaussian noise, bright processing, dark processing and Gaussian blurring processing to form the dataset used for the experiment, as shown in Fig. 2, which increases the amount of data for training, solves the problem of little sample data of remote sensing images and improves the generalization ability of the model; the noise data is added to improve the robustness of the model.

2.2 MA-CapsNet Attentional Mechanisms Model

The MA-CapsNet network model proposed in this paper integrates W-MSA, SW-MSA, Channel Attention and Spatial Attention mechanisms into a unified network The overall framework of MA-CapsNet network is shown in Fig. 3.

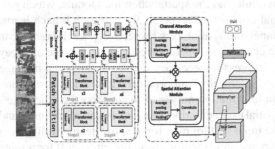
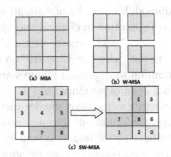

Fig. 3. MA-CapsNet network structure diagram   **Fig. 4.** Module structure diagram

The MA-CapsNet network structure is described as follows: first, the image is input to the Patch Partition module for chunking, i.e., every 4×4 neighboring pixels is a Patch, and then it is flattened in the channel direction, and the input image features are downsampled using the four stages of the Swin-transformer model to extract the underlying image features. The four stages of Swin-transformer model are used to downsample the input image features in order to extract the underlying features, and its repeated stacking Swin Transformer Block, two consecutive Block detailed structure is shown in Fig. 3, then the Attention mechanism is processed in the channel and the space, respectively; and finally, the CapsNet network structure is used for the further feature extraction to extract deeper information of the image and the classifier along the CapsNet network structure.The model code is available at https://github.com/sunhang1998/CapsNet.git.

Swin-Transformer Attention Module.   Swin-transformer attention module for feature extraction of remote sensing images in MA-CapsNet destruction region detection model. Transformer [20] initially appeared for the field of Natural Language Processing (NLP) and with the Vision Transformer [21] (VIT) appeared, Transformer was applied to Computer Vision (CV) field with great success, which adopts MSA for feature map, and the module structure is shown in Fig. 2-a. Later, Swin-transformer [22] network appeared, which is another collision of Transformer model in CV Another collision in the field, which utilizes the concepts of W-MSA and SW-MSA, with the structure diagrams in Fig. 4-b, 4-c. And an efficient computation method is proposed: Efficient batch computation for shifted configuration. The SW-MSA module uses a multi-head self-attention mechanism, in which the information of each pixel is processed by several different self-attention heads, and then the outputs of these heads are merged together, allowing the model to capture richer information and improve the expressive power of the model, which can be effectively applied to remote sensing image area destruction detection.

CBAM Convolutional Attention Module.   CBAM [23] performs feature extraction of remote sensing images in the MA-CapsNet region destruction detection model. CBAM belongs to the hybrid domain lightweight attentional mechanism, and the main idea is to introduce the attentional mechanism at the level of the feature map, so that the model can pay more attention to important regions in the image, containing two sequential sub-modules: channel attentional module and spatial attentional module, which perform Attention in the channel and spatial dimensions respectively, and each branch can learn "what" on the channel and spatial axes respectively. CBAM contains two sequential submodules: the channel attention module and the spatial attention module, which perform Attention in channel and spatial dimensions respectively, and each branch learns the "what" and "where" on the channel and spatial axes respectively. Each branch can learn the "what" and "where" on the channel and spatial axes, and at the same time pay attention to important features and suppress unnecessary features, which can help the flow of information within the network, and it is important for the region destruction detection to focus on the destruction information only, and to suppress the other interfering information. (channel and spatial) sequentially inferring the attention map and multiplying the attention map by the input feature map for adaptive feature refinement saves parameters and computational power, and greatly saves computing cost for remote sensing imagery, so in this paper, this module is integrated into the proposed network. For a given feature map as input, CBAM uses this to infer 1D channel attention map and

2D spatial attention map. The whole attention process can be summarized as:

$$F' = M_C(F) \otimes F, \quad F'' = M_S(F') \otimes F' \tag{2}$$

where $\otimes$ denotes element $-$ by $-$ element multiplication and F'' as the final output.

CapsNet Network Architecture. CapsNet network structure [24] performs feature extraction and classification of remote sensing images in the MA-CapsNet region destruction detection model. Traditional neural networks focus on the extraction and recognition of target features, but do not pay attention to the attributes and internal connections of images such as direction, size, orientation, etc. To address the various shortcomings of neural networks, CapsNet comes into being, whose key element, Capsule, is a set of neurons capturing various parameters of specific features, and the internal mechanism of Capsule is illustrated in Fig. 5.

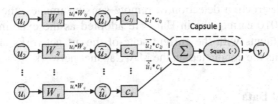

Fig. 5. Capsule internal mechanism diagram

The capsule network connects in the same way as the full connection neural network, where the neural network learns the weights of neurons by backpropagation, while the capsule network updates the coupling coefficient c_{ij} through the "dynamic routing" algorithm to determine which higher-level capsule is output from the lower-level capsule i. The coupling coefficient c_{ij} is calculated as follows,

$$\hat{u}_{j|i} = W_{ij} \cdot u_i, \, b_{ij} = b_{ij} + \hat{u}_{j|i} \cdot v_j, \, c_{ij} = \frac{e^{b_{ij}}}{\sum_k e^{b_{ik}}} \tag{3}$$

where $\hat{u}_{j|i}$ is the prediction vector, W_{ij} is the weight, u_i is the output of last layer of the capsule network, v_j is the vector output of capsule j, and b_{ij} is initialized to 0.

2.3 Model Training and Optimization

In the remote sensing image region destruction detection network, the loss function is the basis for determining the prediction of the model, which significantly depends on the convergence effect of the model. Adopting an appropriate loss function to obtain better detection accuracy can greatly optimize the performance of the network model. In this paper, the loss function of the CapsNet network structure is followed and Margin Loss in SVM is adopted to calculate the loss value in terms of the Euclidean distance between the reconstructed image and the input image re-generated from the prediction category of the input image, denoted by L_i, which is defined by,

$$L_i = T_i \max\left(0, m^+ - \|V_i\|\right)^2 + \varepsilon(1 - T_i) \max\left(0, \|V_i\| - m^-\right)^2 \tag{4}$$

where $T_i = 1$ when the image belongs to category i, otherwise $T_i = 0$, $m^+ = 0.9$, $m^- = 0.1$, $\varepsilon = 0.5$, and the mode of V_i is the L2 distance of the vector.

In remote sensing image region destruction detection, in order to cope with the overfitting phenomenon caused by the insufficient amount of sample data, and to solve the problem that the adaptive learning rate optimizer does not work well after using L2 regularization. In this paper, AdamW [25] is adopted based on Adam improved optimizer, which adds weight decay to Adam, and decouples between the initial learning rate parameters to bring lower training and testing errors to the MA-CapsNet network model with better generalization performance.

3   Experiment and Analysis

To verify the feasibility and robustness of the MA-CapsNet model proposed in this paper for region destruction detection of remote sensing images, the remote sensing images after the 2010 earthquake in Haiti are adopted as the experimental data, and comparison experiments with the current state-of-the-art networks are designed and ablation experiments are conducted on the MA-Capsnet network.

3.1   Experimental Data

In this paper, the remote sensing images of the Jacmel region of Haiti after the 2010 earthquake are used to train and validate the proposed model. Its remote sensing images can be obtained from http://www.haiti-patrimoine.org/. The experimental data used are shown in Fig. 6, after cropping, 2426 samples of size 128×128 are uniformly selected from these two remote sensing images, which are labeled as de-stroyed and un-destroyed regions one by one. Figure 7 shows an example of dam-aged area data and Fig. 8 shows an example of indestructed area data.

3.2   Region Destruction Detection of Remote Sensing Images

To guarantee the credibility of the experimental results, this experiment detects 8 regional sample blocks of destruction regions to avoid the influence of accidental events on the experimental results. Finally, comparison experiments are executed with the current state-of-the-art networks and ablation experiments are executed on the MA-Capsnet network to analyze the performance of the MA-CapsNet proposed in this paper in remote sensing image region destruction detection.

Model Training and Evaluation Results. In order to evaluate the performance of MA-CapsNet network, 19,408 remote sensing images were chosen to train the MA-CapsNet model during the training process, and the training and validation sets were divided according to the ratio of 8:2. The variation of region destruction classification accuracy of MA-CapsNet model curves and loss function convergence curves are shown in Fig. 9.

Fig. 6. Remote sensing images after the 2010 earthquake in the Jacmel region of Haiti

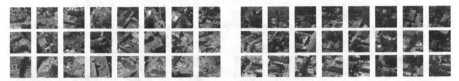

Fig. 7. Destruction region data   **Fig. 8.** Non-destruction region data

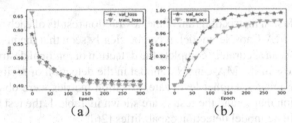

(a)   (b)

Fig. 9. MA-CapsNet model region destruction classification accuracy change curve and loss function convergence curve

Figure 9(a) is a graph of the convergence curve of the loss function of regional destruction classification of the MA-CapsNet model, which tends to converge with the increase of the number of iterations; Fig. 9(b) is a curve of the change of the accuracy rate of regional destruction classification of the MA-CapsNet model, and the accuracy rate reaches 99.64% when the number of iterations is about 300 times.

Utilizing the above trained MA-CapsNet model to classify the test set, the results of the MA-CapsNet model detecting the destruction of sample blocks in eight regions are shown in Fig. 10. In Fig. 10, red areas are correctly detected damaged areas, blue areas are correctly detected undamaged areas, green areas are incorrectly detected undamaged areas, and yellow areas are incorrectly detected damaged areas.

In order to observe the effect of MA-CapsNet model more intuitively for destruction detection in samples, this paper visualizes the results of the above MA-Capsnet model for detecting destruction in eight regional sample blocks, and its confusion matrix heat map is shown in Fig. 11.

Fig. 10. MA-CapsNet model detects the destruction results of 8 regional sample blocks

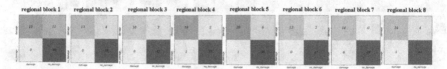

Fig. 11. Confusion matrix of damage results for MA-CapsNet detection areas

From the confusion matrix diagram of the destruction results of each regional sample block detected by MA-CapsNet model, it can be clearly seen that the number of TP and TN is more, which can accurately complete the detection of regional destruction, indicating the effectiveness of the MA-CapsNet model in the detection of regional destruction of remote sensing images. Higher level categorization metrics were obtained based on the above confusion matrix and the results are shown in Table 1, the test uses F1 scores, recall, etc. to evaluate model detection capabilities [26].

Table 1. MA-CapsNet model detection of destruction region index results (%)

regional block	Accuracy	Recall	Specificity	F1-score	IOU$_{damage}$
1	94.64	100.00	93.48	86.96	76.92
2	92.86	100.00	90.70	86.67	76.47
3	80.36	100.00	73.17	73.17	57.69
4	94.64	94.74	94.59	92.31	85.71
5	100.00	100.00	100.00	100.00	100.00
6	95.24	100.00	94.00	89.66	81.25
7	88.89	95.24	85.71	85.11	74.07
8	92.06	93.33	91.67	84.85	73.68

The 8 regional sample blocks divided in this paper contain 476 image blocks, and 440 image blocks are accurately detected using the MA-CapsNet model proposed in this paper and the detection accuracy is 92.4%.

Comparison Experiments. To further validate the effectiveness of MA-CapsNet model on destruction detection in remote sensing image area, convolutional network framework such as ResNet and VIT attention mechanism framework are selected in this section. The destruction classification accuracy comparison results are shown in Table 2, and MA-Capsnet model accuracy reaches the highest 99.64% at ACC300. The model framework in this paper can effectively capture the texture features and spatial structure information of remote sensing images by combining the attention mechanism and capsule network module to achieve better classification accuracy.

Table 2. Comparison of experimental destruction classification accuracy results

method	$ACC_{100}(\%)$	$ACC_{200}(\%)$	$ACC_{300}(\%)$	method	$ACC_{100}(\%)$	$ACC_{200}(\%)$	$ACC_{300}(\%)$
MobileViT	95.95	97.16	97.70	ConvNeXt	98.19	98.68	98.84
GoogLeNet	95.65	96.47	96.68	CapsNet	86.94	86.94	86.94
ShufflleNet	98.20	98.69	98.89	VggNet	94.41	95.47	95.90
Swin-Transformer	97.70	99.17	99.58	ResNet	98.02	98.04	98.04
Vision Transformer	88.46	88.46	88.46	RegNet	**99.28**	**99.43**	99.54
MA-CapsNet	97.86	99.41	**99.64**	AlexNet	94.28	95.59	96.01

As shown in Table 2, the detection accuracy of the MA-CapsNet model is higher than that of the basic model CapsNet, which fully reflects the flexibility and superiority of the attention mechanism, and significantly improves the performance of the model in destruction detection tasks, bringing the model to an advanced level.

Ablation Experiments. Ablation experiments are usually used for relatively complex neural networks to understand the network by deleting part of the network and studying the performance of the network. In this paper, the proposed MA-CapsNet network is subjected to ablation experiments, and the ablation experiment destruction classification accuracies are shown in Table 3, and the change curve of regional destruction classification accuracy is shown in Fig. 12.

Table 3. Accuracy of ablation experimental destruction classification

model	BSRGAN + Data Augmentation	Swin-Transformer	CBAM	CapsNet	Accuracy (%)
ablation model 1		√	√	√	76.97
ablation model 2	√	√		√	99.59
MA-CapsNet	√	√	√	√	99.64

1. Evaluation of BSRGAN pre-processing and data augmentation module

The BSRGAN preprocessing and data enhancement module was removed from the MA-CapsNet network model with a view to improving the spatial and channel contribution and reducing the interference of useless channels. The destruction classification accuracy of the ablation experiment is shown in Table 3, and the destruction

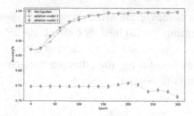

Fig. 12. Variation curve of destruction classification accuracy in the ablation experiment region

classification accuracy of removing the BSRGAN preprocessing and data enhancement module is only 76.97%, which performs worse than the 99.64% of the MA-CapsNet model, and overfitting occurs as shown in Fig. 12, which shows that the BSRGAN preprocessing and data enhancement module enables the data to contain richer texture information, effectively improves the quality of remote sensing images and data expansion, which can effectively prevent the overfitting phenomenon.

2. Evaluation of CBAM module

The CBAM module was removed from the MA-CapsNet model with a view to enhancing the contribution of attributes such as image orientation, size, and internal linkages. Experiments were conducted with the same training and validation sets, and the ablation experimental destruction classification accuracy is shown in Table 3. The destruction classification accuracy after removing the CBAM module was 99.59%, which performed slightly worse than the 99.64% of the MA-CapsNet network model. It can be observed that the CBAM module can enhance feature channels through channel attention mechanism and spatial attention mechanism, thereby improving feature expression while suppressing unnecessary features.

4 Conclusion

Aiming at the problems of poor imaging quality and small sample size of remote sensing images in regional destruction detection, and the difficulty of fully extracting the hidden distinguishing features in the images by using a single attention mechanism, this paper carries out the research on deep learning image classification method based on multi-attention mechanism, and proposes a remote sensing image regional destruction detection method based on MA-CapsNet model, which integrates the W-MSA, SW-MSA, channel Attention and Spatial Attention multi-attention mechanisms, achieving a high detection accuracy of 99.64%. Therefore, the proposed remote sensing image region destruction detection method integrating the attention mechanism and capsule network module can accurately identify the destroyed regions in remote sensing images, and provide a reference for remote sensing image destruction information statistics and damage assessment.

Acknowledgement. The subject is sponsored by the National Natural Science Foundation of P. R. China (No. 62102194 and No. 62102196), Six Talent Peaks Project of Jiangsu Province (No. RJFW-111), Postgraduate Research and Practice Innovation Program of Jiangsu Province (No. KYCX20_0759, No. KYCX21_0787, No. KYCX21_0788, No. KYCX21_0799, and KYCX22_1019).

References

1. Li, W., et al.: Classification of high-spatial-resolution remote sensing scenes method using transfer learning and deep convolutional neural network. IEEE J. Sel. Top. Appl. Earth Observations Remote Sens. **13**, 1986–1995 (2020)
2. Lv, W., Wang, X.: Overview of hyperspectral image classification. J. Sens. **2020**, 1–13 (2020)
3. Hinton Geoffrey, E., Salakhutdinov, R.R.: Reducing the dimensionality of data with neural networks. Science **313**(5786), 504–507 (2006)
4. Liu, L., et al.: Inshore ship detection in sar images based on deep neural networks. In: IEEE International Geoscience and Remote Sensing Symposium, pp. 25–28 (2018)
5. Khan, M., Jamil, A., Lv, Z., et al.: Efficient deep CNN-based fire detection and localization in video surveillance applications. IEEE Trans. Syst. Man Cybern. Syst. **49**(7), 1419–1434 (2019)
6. Shao, Z., Tang, P., Wang, Z., et al.: BRRNet: a fully convolutional neural network for automatic building extraction from high-resolution remote sensing images. Remote Sens. **12**(6), 1050 (2020)
7. Yang, P., Wang, M., Yuan, H., He, C., Cong, L.: Using contour loss constraining residual attention U-net on optical remote sensing interpretation. Vis. Comput. **39**(9), 4279–4291 (2022)
8. Li, J., et al.: Automatic detection and classification system of domestic waste via multimodel cascaded convolutional neural network. IEEE Trans. **18**(1), 163–173 (2022)
9. Soto, P.J., Costa, G.A.O.P., Feitosa, R.Q., et al.: Domain adaptation with cyclegan for change detection in the amazon forest. ISPRS Arch. **43**(B3), 1635–1643 (2020)
10. Gianni, B., Frasincar, F.: A general survey on attention mechanisms in deep learning. IEEE Trans. Know. Data Eng. **35**, 3279–3298 (2021)
11. Lin, X., Sun, S., Huang, W., Sheng, B., Li, P., Feng, D.D.: EAPT: efficient attention pyramid transformer for image processing. IEEE Trans. **25**, 50–61 (2023)
12. Li, S., Yan, Q., Liu, P.: An efficient fire detection method based on multiscale feature extraction, implicit deep supervision and channel attention mechanism. IEEE Trans. Image Process. **29**, 8467–8475 (2020)
13. Chen, L., Weng, T., Jin, X., et al.: A new deep learning network for automatic bridge detection from SAR images based on balanced and attention mechanism. Remote Sens. **12**(3), 441 (2020)
14. Chen, L., et al.: Improved YOLOv3 based on attention mechanism for fast and accurate ship detection in optical remote sensing images. Remote Sens. **13**(4), 660 (2021)
15. Wang, P., Liu, L., Shen, C., et al.: Multi-attention network for one shot learning. In: IEEE Conference on Computer Vision and Pattern Recognition, pp. 6212–6220 (2017)
16. Zhang, K., et al.: Designing a practical degradation model for deep blind image super-resolution. In: IEEE International Conference on Computer Vision, pp. 4771–4780 (2021)
17. Gui, J., Sun, Z., Wen, Y., et al.: A review on generative adversarial networks: algorithms, theory, and applications. IEEE Trans. Knowl. Data Eng. **14**(8), 1–28 (2021)
18. Christian, L., Lucas, T., Ferenc, H., et al.: Photo-realistic single image super-resolution using a generative adversarial network. In: IEEE Conference on Computer Vision and Pattern Recognition, pp. 105–114 (2017)
19. Bulat, A., et al.: To learn image super-resolution, use a GAN to learn how to do image degradation first. In: Ferrari, V., Hebert, M., Sminchisescu, C., Weiss, Y. (eds.) ECCV 2018. LNCS, vol. 11210, pp. 187–202. Springer, Cham (2018). https://doi.org/10.1007/978-3-030-01231-1_12
20. Ashish, V., Noam, S., Niki, P., et al.: Attention is all you need. In: Annual Conference on Neural Information Processing Systems, pp. 5998–6008 (2017)

21. Alexey, D., et al.: An image is worth 16x16 words: transformers for image recognition at scale. In: 9th International Conference on Learning Representations (2021)
22. Liu, Z., Lin, Y., et al.: Swin transformer: hierarchical vision transformer using shifted windows. In: IEEE International Conference on Computer Vision, pp. 9992–10002 (2021)
23. Woo, S., Park, J., Lee, J.-Y., Kweon, I.S.: CBAM: convolutional block attention module. In: Ferrari, V., Hebert, M., Sminchisescu, C., Weiss, Y. (eds.) ECCV 2018. LNCS, vol. 11211, pp. 3–19. Springer, Cham (2018). https://doi.org/10.1007/978-3-030-01234-2_1
24. Sara, S., Nicholas, F., Hinton, G.E.: Dynamic routing between capsules. In: Annual Conference on Neural Information Processing Systems, pp. 3856–3866 (2017)
25. Ilya, L., Hutter, F.: Decoupled weight decay regularization. In: 7th International Conference on Learning Representations (2019)
26. Chen, H., Han, Q., Li, Q., Tong, X.: A novel general blind detection model for image forensics based on DNN. Vis. Comput. **39**(1), 27–42 (2021)

Visual Analytics and Modeling

Visual Analytics of CO₂ Emissions from Individuals' Daily Travel Based on Large-Scale Taxi Trajectories

Dongliang Ma[1] , Song Wang[1]([⊠]) , Liang Liu[1,2] , and Hao Hu[1]

[1] School of Computer Science and Technology,
Southwest University of Science and Technology, Mianyang, China
`wangsong@swust.edu.cn`
[2] School of Computer Science and Technology,
Chongqing University of Posts and Telecommunications, Chongqing, China

Abstract. Understanding the patterns of traffic-related carbon dioxide (CO_2) emissions from different trip purposes is of great significance for the development of low-carbon transportation. However, most existing research ignores the traffic-related CO_2 emissions from daily trip. Accurately inferring trip purposes is a prerequisite for analyzing the patterns of traffic-related CO_2 emissions from daily trip. The existing research on inferring trip purposes has been proven effective, but it ignores door-to-door service (DTD) and the time-varying characteristics of the attractiveness of Points of Interest (POIs). In this paper, we propose a Bayesian-based method to infer trip purposes. It identifies DTD through spatial relation operations and constructs the dynamic function of POIs attractiveness using kernel density estimation (KDE). A visual analysis system is also developed to help users explore the spatio-temporal patterns of traffic-related CO_2 emissions from daily trip. Finally, the effectiveness of the method and the system is verified through case study based on real data and positive feedback from experts.

Keywords: Trip purpose inference · CO_2 emissions · Taxi trajectories · Visualization and visual analytics · Spatio-temporal patterns

1 Introduction

With the rapid growth in the number of private cars and the development of ride-hailing services, the traffic-related CO_2 emissions related to daily trip have become a key issue for urban low-carbon development.

Existing research related to traffic-related CO_2 emissions mainly focuses on the calculation of road CO_2 emissions et al. [8]. The impact of daily trip on traffic-related CO_2 emissions has been rarely discussed. In order to study the relationship between daily trip and traffic-related CO_2 emissions, We assign trip purposes as the semantic meaning for the CO2 emissions of each trajectory, thereby combining the previously separate calculations of trajectory CO2 emissions with residents' daily trip. Hence, the key to be addressed is how to infer trip purposes based on residents' travel data. Previous inferring methods based on machine learning [7], probability [4,19], and rules [3] have been proven effective, but they have the following shortcomings: a) Generally, the drop-off point is as close as possible to the destination (i.e., DTD). However, DTD is ignored in existing studies; b) When calculating the probability of accessing candidate POIs, existing means ignore that POIs attractiveness will change over time.

In this paper, we meet two challenges.

1) **Identifying DTD.** POIs that do not meet the DTD should be filtered out [2,15]. Hence, a method is needed to determine whether passengers need to cross the road from the drop-off point to a points-of-interest (POI).
2) **Constructing the dynamic function of POIs attractiveness.** The probability of accessing a POI is closely related to its current level of attractiveness, which changes over time. Therefore, the dynamic function that reflects the changing attractiveness of POIs needs to be constructed.

Our contributions are summarized as follows:

1) We propose a method to identify DTD based on spatial relationship operations.
2) We implement a method for constructing the dynamic function of POIs attractiveness with the help of KDE.
3) We develop a visual analytics system (called TCDEVis) that can assist users in analyzing the spatio-temporal patterns of traffic-related CO_2 emissions from different trip purposes.

2   Related Work

2.1   Traffic-Related CO_2 Emissions

Traffic-related CO_2 emissions accounted for twenty-three percent of the total global emissions [12]. As a result, efforts have been made to study traffic-related CO_2 emissions [1,6,16,17]. Pucher et al. [11] utilized floating vehicle data to analyze the spatio-temporal distribution of traffic-related CO_2 emissions. Improving the control algorithm of traffic lights to shorten the waiting time of vehicles can also reduce traffic-related CO_2 emissions [18]. Accurate calculation models of traffic-related CO_2 emissions have been designed to probe the status of road CO_2 emissions [21]. The CO_2 emissions of different roads and the strategies of peak CO_2 emissions on road were discussed [20]. However, there is little research that uses taxi trajectory data to probe the impact of different trip purposes on traffic-related CO_2 emissions.

2.2 Trip Purpose Inference

Existing methods of inferring trip purposes can fall into three categories: machine learning, probability, and rule-based methods. In machine learning methods, trip characteristics (i.e., trip time, trip distance, etc.) were used as training sets to train models. Lee et al. [7] trained a decision tree model using POIs data, land use data, and the spatial-temporal characteristics of cycling trips. [9] proposed the Dual-Flow Attentive Network for inferring trip purposes based on trip chains. Probability-based methods infer trip purposes by matching the drop-off point to a POI using the Bayesian model [4]. To improve the inference accuracy, Zhao et al. [19] incorporated POIs attractiveness into traditional Bayesian methods. Rule-based methods match features from GPS, GIS, and survey data with pre-defined rules for inferring trip purposes. Chen [3] and Stopher et al. [14] inferred trip purposes based on the rules established with the help of land use data and the frequency of accessing POIs. However, previous research has not taken into account DTD and has ignored the time-varying characteristics of POIs attractiveness. In this paper, DTD is identified via spatial operations. Based on POIs check-in data, the dynamic function of POIs attractiveness is constructed using KDE.

3 Overview

3.1 Data and Trip Purpose Description

We utilize three types of data from Nanchang city, China. **(1) Road network data** includes 59,306 road segments and 41,398 vertices (i.e., road intersections). **(2) Taxi trajectory data**. The trajectories of approximately 4,530 taxis within a week are covered in the dataset. **(3) POIs check-in data** contains 22,408 points. Based on previous studies [5], we set up ten categories of trip purposes (Table 1).

Table 1. The categories of trip purpose

Trip purpose	POIs types
Traffic	Vehicle service, Traffic facilities
Shop	Shopping mall, Sales center
Dining	Restaurant
Service	Bank, Communal facilities
Pastime	Scenic area, Leisure facility
Medical	Hospital, Clinic
Lodging	Hotel
Home	Residence
Work	Company, Governmental agency
School	University, Middle and primary school

3.2 Requirement Analysis

R1: Display Spatio-Temporal Distribution. What are the time-frequency distribution characteristics of different types of trips? How does the temporal distribution of CO_2 emissions from different types of trips relate to their time-frequency distribution? How are the spatial distributions of trip trajectories and CO_2 emissions?

R2: Analyze the Impact of Driving Situation on CO_2 Emissions. The driving situation of vehicles (i.e., driving distance, driving time, driving speed, etc.) has a significant impact on their CO_2 emissions. Therefore, we need to compare and analyze the driving situation of vehicles with their corresponding CO_2 emissions, to help experts understand how driving situation affect CO_2 emissions.

R3: Explore OD (Origin-Destination) CO_2 Emissions. OD CO_2 emissions refer to the CO_2 emissions generated by residents' trips from the origin region (i.e., O) to the destination region (i.e., D). Besides the spatial distribution of OD CO_2 emissions, experts are also interested in the following tasks: which road sections are primarily used for trajectories from region A to region B? Which road sections have the highest CO_2 emissions? (Fig. 1).

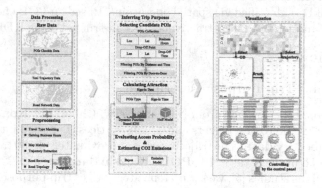

Fig. 1. The pipeline of analysis framework.

3.3   Workflow

The Data Processing Module. We match POIs to corresponding trip purposes based on the Table 1. Map matching is used to correct the drifted GPS coordinates of taxi to the road network. We only study the main roads in Nanchang, hence it is necessary to filter out the road network outside Nanchang and minor road segments through filtering operations. The topology of road network is stored in PostgreSQL.

The Inferring Trip Purpose Module consists of three main steps: (1) the target set of POIs is obtained by screening POIs based on the distance and the opening hours of POIs. We then pick up the set of candidate POIs by identifying DTD. (2) we construct the dynamic function of POIs attractiveness using KDE and calculate the comprehensive attractiveness using the Huff model. (3) the accessing probabilities of each candidate POI are worked out via the Bayesian model.

The Visualization Module provides an interactive analysis tool with dynamic update capability for experts.

4 Inferring Trip Purposes

4.1 Filtering POIs

We filter POIs first by time and distance (Fig. 2). A POI and the drop-off point are represented as $p_i = ((lon_i, lat_i), t_i)$ and $drop = ((lon, lat), t)$, respectively, where (lon_i, lat_i) and (lon, lat) are separately the coordinates of p_i and the drop-off point, t_i is the business hours of p_i, and t is the drop-off time. $d(p_i, drop)$ is the Euclidean distance (denoted as d in Fig. 2) between the drop-off point and p_i. R (denoted as R in Fig. 2) is the maximum walking distance (MWD) of passengers, and is set to $500m$ in this paper according to [13]. POIs that are in business at time t and have the $d(p_i, drop)$ less than R are added to the set $C = \{p_1, p_2, \ldots, p_n\}$. Finally, only the purple and green POIs are added to the set C, in Fig. 2.

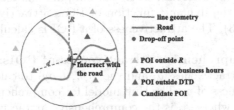

Fig. 2. The schematic diagram of filtering candidate POIs.

4.2 Selecting Candidate POIs

Further, we screen the POIs in the set C through DTD. POIs that meet DTD are selected as candidate POIs. We first create a spatial line geometry connecting the drop-off point and a POI. Subsequently, we use spatial relation operators in PostgreSQL to determine whether the spatial line geometry intersects with the road network. If there is no intersection, the corresponding POI will be added to the set $Can = \{Can_1, Can_2, \ldots, Can_m\}$ of candidate POIs. Finally, only the green POIs are added to the set Can, in Fig. 2.

4.3 Calculating POIs Attractiveness

1) **Classifying POIs:** According to Table 1, we classify POIs based on trip purposes. Each trip purpose corresponds to a set of POIs, denoted as $trip_{poi} = \{p_1, p_2, \ldots, p_n\}$.
2) **Extracting time feature:** Subsequently, we extract the check-in times for each POI in the $trip_{poi}$ to obtain the feature vector of check-in time $trip_t = (t_1, t_2, \ldots, t_n)$.

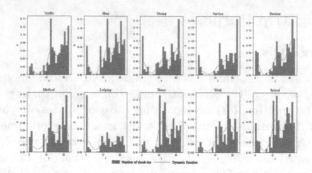

Fig. 3. The dynamic function of POIs attractiveness based on KDE.

3) **Constructing dynamic function of POIs attractiveness:** We first slice the $trip_t$ in one-hour intervals. Then we compute the distribution of check-in times. Finally, the dynamic function of POIs attractiveness, $f(t) = a$, is constructed (Fig. 3). The attractiveness of a POI is calculated using $f(t)$, at time t.

4) **Calculating comprehensive attractiveness of POIs:** We consider both the time-based attractiveness a_i and the $d(p_i, drop)$ to calculate the comprehensive attractiveness of p_i. The Huff model for comprehensive attractiveness is shown in Eq. 1, where A_i is the comprehensive attractiveness of p_i. The μ and λ are set to 1 and 2 respectively, based on previous research. n is the number of candidate POIs.

$$A_i = \frac{a_i^{\mu}/d(p_i, drop)^{\mu}}{\sum_{j=1}^{n} a_j^{\mu}/d(p_j, drop)^{\lambda}} \qquad (1)$$

4.4 Evaluating the Accessing Probability of POIs

The accessing probability of POIs is figured out by the Bayesian model. The accessing probability from the drop-off point $drop = ((lon, lat), t)$ to candidate POI Can_i is as follows:

$$Pr(Can_i|(lon, lat), t) = \frac{Pr((lon, lat)|Can_i, t) \cdot Pr(Can_i|t) \cdot Pr(t)}{Pr((lon, lat), t)} \qquad (2)$$

In general, the location and the time of the drop-off point are conditionally independent given the candidate POI Can_i. Thus $Pr((lon, lat)|Can_i, t) = Pr((lon, lat)|Can_i)$. We consider the influence of distance and POIs attractiveness on the accessing probability, as shown in Eq. 3, where A_i is the comprehensive attractiveness of Can_i. $d((lon, lat), Can_i)$ is the Euclidean distance from the drop-off point to Can_i. β is the decay factor of distance. Previous research [19] has shown that the optimal value of β ranges from 1 to 2. In this paper, we set $\beta = 1.5$.

$$Pr((lon, lat)|Can_i) \propto A_i d((lon, lat), Can_i)^{-\beta} \qquad (3)$$

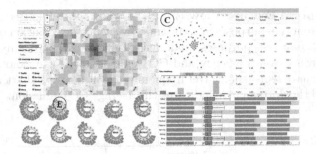

Fig. 4. The system interface.

Finally, the accessing probability of candidate POIs Can_i can be calculated as follows:

$$Pr(Can_i|(lon, lat), t) = \frac{A_i d((lon, lat), Can_i)^{-\beta} \cdot Pr(Can_i|t)}{\sum_{j=1}^n A_j d((lon, lat), Can_j)^{-\beta} Pr(Can_j|t)} \quad (4)$$

4.5 Estimating the CO_2 Emissions of Trip Trajectory

The length of each trajectory (i.e., driving distance) be denoted as l. The starting time of each trajectory is represented as T_{start}, and the arrival time of each trajectory is marked as T_{end}. The driving time $T = T_{end} - T_{start}$. Based on the taxi trajectory data, we obtain the speed sequence $v = (v_1, v_2, ..., v_n)$, where v_i is the speed at the ith GPS point of a trajectory. Finally, we construct a feature set $F = \{l, T, v\}$ for each trajectory.

We use the Oguchi [10] emission model (Eq. 3) to calculate the CO_2 emissions for each trajectory. In this equation, $CO2_{trip}$ represents the CO_2 emissions for trajectories (in kg). $F = 0.002322kg$ is the emission factor. T and l are driving time and driving distance respectively. n is the total number of GPS points for each trajectory. v_i represents driving speed at the ith GPS point. $\delta_i = 0(v_{i+1} \leq v_i)$ or $1(v_{i+1} > v_i)$.

$$CO2_{trip} = F(0.3T + 0.028l + 0.056 \sum_{i=1}^{n-1} \delta_i(v_{i+1}^2 - v_i^2)) \quad (5)$$

5 Visual Design

The OD Trajectory View (Fig. 4(C)) describes the characteristics of the trajectories from the O area to the D area (R3). We utilize t-SNE for dimensionality reduction on trajectory features (including the CO2 emissions of trajectory, average speed at al). Each point represents a trajectory. The color of points encodes different trip purposes. The Time Heatmap view shows the time distribution of trajectories. The Number of Travel view shows the number of trajectories in different trip purposes.

The **Temporal Feature View** (Fig. 4(E)) shows the time-frequency distribution of different trip purposes and the time-frequency distribution of CO_2 emissions from different trip purposes, making it easy for users to analyze the relationship between travel frequency and CO_2 emissions (R1). As shown in Fig. 5, the outer bar chart represents travel frequency, the radial area chart reveals CO_2 emissions, and the dotted circle indicates the average CO_2 emission.

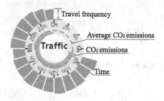

Fig. 5. The design of temporal feature glyph.

6   Case Study

6.1   Evaluation of the Proposed Method

By the means of the Tencent questionnaire platform, we distribute online questionnaires to residents in the study area. Three non-sensitive trip purposes (i.e., Dining, Work, and School) are selected as the options in questionnaire. Users are required to type in the trip purposes. The time that is used as check-in time and the location coordinates of a questionnaire are automatically obtained by the platform. In the end, we pick up 732 records of data. Then, the data is classified according to trip purposes. Subsequently, the proposed method, traditional bayes, and closest assignment are used to infer the trip purposes for each category. The accuracy of three methods is shown in Table 2, which validates the effectiveness of our method.

6.2   Case1: Uncovering Spatio-Temporal Patterns (R1)

In the Control Panel View, we select three common travel types to explore the spatio-temporal patterns of CO_2 emissions (Fig. 6). The CO_2 emissions from the Bayi Bridge etc. are found to be notably high for all three trip purposes. Specifically, as depicted in Fig. 6(1), the CO_2 emissions related to Home are prominently high along the Hongguzhong Road. Figure 6(2) reveals that the Shanghaibei Road exhibit a high level of CO_2 emissions associated with School. In addition, Fig. 6(3) demonstrates that the CO_2 emissions related to Work are significantly high along the Yanjiangzhong Road. The temporal feature glyph in Fig. 6 describes the time-frequency distribution of travel frequency and CO_2 emissions for travel types.

6.3   Case2: Probing CO_2 Emissions Based on Driving Behavior (R2)

Based on Fig. 7(1), the average driving speed is $15-18$ m/s, indicating medium-high speed trip. The average driving distance and the average driving time are $5-7$ km and $0.3-0.5$ h, respectively, indicating short-distance trip. The average CO_2 emissions mostly range from $2-3$ kg. In general, as average driving speed,

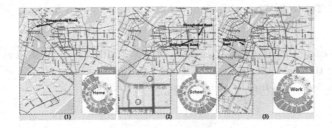

Fig. 6. Uncovering spatio-temporal patterns.

Fig. 7. Probing CO_2 emissions based on driving behavior.

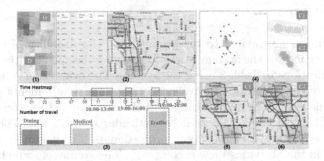

Fig. 8. Analyzing OD CO_2 emissions.

average driving distance, CO_2 emissions etc. also tend to increase. According to the Fig. 7(2), the high values of driving speed, driving distance, driving time, and CO_2 emissions are concentrated in Shop, School, and Work. On the contrary, the low values are concentrated in Dining and Medical.

6.4 Case3: Analyzing OD CO_2 Emissions (R3)

We then select the O/D regions (Fig. 8(1)) on the Map View based on the OD heatmap. The Time Heatmap view (Fig. 8(3)) indicates that the starting time of trajectories from region O to region D are concentrated at 10:00AM-13:00PM

Table 2. The assessment result of the proposed method

Trip purpose	Proposed method	Traditional bayes	Closest assignment
Dining	89.94%	62.49%	60.15%
Work	85.79%	73.37%	52.68%
School	93.57%	88.69%	65.33%

Table 3. The assessment result of the proposed method

No	Question
Q1	Redo case study, then if user requirements (R1, R2 and R3) can be resolved by the system
Q2	Explore on their own using the system, if topics that interest them can be met
Q3	The system has a user-friendly visualization and interaction

at al. The Number of Travel view (Fig. 8(3)) reveals that Dining, Medical, and Traffic are the main trip purposes. Subsequently, the top ten trajectories are selected (left table in v 8(2)). The distribution of characteristics of all trajectories is presented in Fig. 8(4). We brush the two clusters (C1 and C2 in Fig. 8(4)). Figure 8(6) shows that high CO_2 emission trajectories for Dining mainly distribute on the Bayi Road, the Fuhe Road etc. High CO_2 emissions roads for Medical (Fig. 8(5)) also include the Ruzi Road and the Jiefang Road.

7 Evaluation

Twenty volunteers are invited to further evaluate the usability of our system. Firstly, we explain how the system works for users. Subsequently, the volunteers explore the questions in Table 3 using the system. The evaluation results (Fig. 9) indicate that our system can effectively meet the user requirements (Q1). Most volunteers believe that the system can assist them in exploring topics that interest them (Q2). Most users hold positive attitudes towards Q3. The volunteer with a disagree attitude for Q3 is a non-professionals. The volunteer deems that "the box plot in the Statistics View is complex". The volunteers who hold unsure opinion for Q3 note that "when we explore OD CO_2 emissions, if we select a large O/D region on the map, the system may not render the results immediately". The reason is that more time will be spent to compute the results, when the volume of data is large.

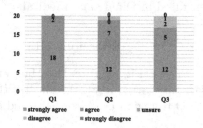

Fig. 9. The evaluation questionnaire results.

8 Conclusion

In this paper, we propose a novel approach for inferring trip purposes to support the analysis of CO_2 emissions from daily trip. Through in-depth discussions with experts, The user requirements are acquired. Based on the user requirements, we developed an interactive visual analytics system (TCDEVis). The spatiotemporal patterns of CO_2 emissions from daily trip can be explored via this system. A case study based on real data and positive feedback from experts validate the effectiveness of this system.

Acknowledgements. This work was supported by Natural Science Foundation of Sichuan Province (Grant No. 2022NSFSC0961) the Ph.D. Research Foundation of Southwest University of Science and Technology (Grant No. 19zx7144) the Special Research Foundation of China (Mianyang) Science and Technology City Network Emergency Management Research Center (Grant No. WLYJGL2023ZD04).

References

1. Cha, J., Park, J., Lee, H., Chon, M.S.: A study of prediction based on regression analysis for real-world CO2 emissions with light-duty diesel vehicles. Int. J. Automot. Technol. **22**(3), 569–577 (2021)
2. Chen, C., Jiao, S., Zhang, S., Liu, W., Feng, L., Wang, Y.: Tripimputor: real-time imputing taxi trip purpose leveraging multi-sourced urban data. IEEE Trans. Intell. Transp. Syst. **19**(10), 3292–3304 (2018). https://doi.org/10.1109/TITS.2017.2771231
3. Chen, C., Gong, H., Lawson, C., Bialostozky, E.: Evaluating the feasibility of a passive travel survey collection in a complex urban environment: lessons learned from the New York city case study. Transp. Res. Part A: Policy Pract. **44**(10), 830–840 (2010)
4. Dhananjaya, D., Sivakumar, T.: Inferring the purposes of taxi trips using GPS and poi data considering the destination context. In: 2021 International Conference on Data Analytics for Business and Industry (ICDABI), pp. 295–300. IEEE (2021)
5. Huang, L., Li, Q., Yue, Y.: Activity identification from GPS trajectories using spatial temporal POIs' attractiveness. In: Proceedings of the 2nd ACM SIGSPATIAL International Workshop on Location Based Social Networks, pp. 27–30 (2010)
6. Kuga, K., Ito, K.: Integrated modeling of CO2 transport from indoor to alveolar region for elucidating human CO2 emission mechanism. In: Wang, L.L., et al. (eds.) COBEE 2022. Environmental Science and Engineering, pp. 1997–2000. Springer, Singapore (2022). https://doi.org/10.1007/978-981-19-9822-5_210
7. Lee, J., Yu, K., Kim, J.: Public bike trip purpose inference using point-of-interest data. ISPRS Int. J. Geo Inf. **10**(5), 352 (2021)
8. Liu, J., et al.: Multi-scale urban passenger transportation CO2 emission calculation platform for smart mobility management. Appl. Energy **331**, 120407 (2023)
9. Lyu, S., Han, T., Li, P., Luo, X., Kusakabe, T.: A dual-flow attentive network with feature crossing for chained trip purpose inference. IEEE Trans. Intell. Transp. Syst. **24**, 631–644 (2022)
10. Oguchi, T., Katakura, M., Taniguchi, M.: Carbondioxide emission model in actual urban road vehicular traffic conditions. Doboku Gakkai Ronbunshu **2002**(695), 125–136 (2002)

11. Pucher, G.: Deriving traffic-related CO2 emission factors with high spatiotemporal resolution from extended floating car data. In: Ivan, I., Singleton, A., Horák, J., Inspektor, T. (eds.) The Rise of Big Spatial Data. LNGC, pp. 55–68. Springer, Cham (2017). https://doi.org/10.1007/978-3-319-45123-7_5
12. Schipper, L., Leather, J., Fabian, H.: Transport and carbon dioxide emissions: forecasts, options analysis, and evaluation (2009)
13. Song, C., Koren, T., Wang, P., Barabási, A.L.: Modelling the scaling properties of human mobility. Nat. Phys. **6**(10), 818–823 (2010)
14. Stopher, P., Clifford, E., Zhang, J., FitzGerald, C.: Deducing mode and purpose from GPS data (2008)
15. Tahmasbi, B., Haghshenas, H.: Public transport accessibility measure based on weighted door to door travel time. Comput. Environ. Urban Syst. **76**, 163–177 (2019). https://doi.org/https://doi.org/10.1016/j.compenvurbsys.2019.05.002. https://www.sciencedirect.com/science/article/pii/S019897151830214X
16. Wang, W., Tang, Q., Gao, B.: Exploration of CO2 emission reduction pathways: identification of influencing factors of CO2 emission and CO2 emission reduction potential of power industry. Clean Technol. Environ. Policy **25**(5), 1589–1603 (2023)
17. Wu, J., Abban, O.J., Boadi, A.D., Charles, O.: The effects of energy price, spatial spillover of CO2 emissions, and economic freedom on CO2 emissions in Europe: a spatial econometrics approach. Environ. Sci. Pollut. Res. **29**(42), 63782–63798 (2022)
18. Xiao, Z., Xiao, Z., Wang, D., Li, X.: An intelligent traffic light control approach for reducing vehicles CO2 emissions in VANET. In: 2015 12th International Conference on Fuzzy Systems and Knowledge Discovery (FSKD), pp. 2070–2075. IEEE (2015)
19. Zhao, P., Kwan, M.P., Qin, K.: Uncovering the spatiotemporal patterns of CO2 emissions by taxis based on individuals' daily travel. J. Transp. Geogr. **62**, 122–135 (2017)
20. Zheng, J., Dong, S., Hu, Y., Li, Y.: Comparative analysis of the CO2 emissions of expressway and arterial road traffic: a case in Beijing. PLoS ONE **15**(4), e0231536 (2020)
21. Zhou, X., Wang, H., Huang, Z., Bao, Y., Zhou, G., Liu, Y.: Identifying spatiotemporal characteristics and driving factors for road traffic co2 emissions. Sci. Total Environ. **834**, 155270 (2022)

Visual Analytics of Air Pollution Transmission Among Urban Agglomerations

Shijie Chen, Song Wang(✉), Yipan Liu, Dongliang Ma, and Hao Hu

School of Computer Science and Technology, Southwest University of Science and Technology, Mianyang 621010, Sichuan, China
wangsong@swust.edu.cn

Abstract. In field of air quality research, it is essential to scientifically reflect the internal structure of air quality distribution and reveal the dynamic evolution of air pollution. In this study, a novel visual analytics method is proposed to address these challenges. Initially, the spatio-temporal features of air quality data are mined to complete urban agglomeration division based on dimensionality reduction and clustering. Subsequently, the air pollution transmission network (APTN) is constructed through particle transport and correlation analysis. A progressive exploration analysis method based on multidimensional space transformation is then employed to explore the process of air pollution transmission. Furthermore, a visual analytics system is developed to facilitate the interpretation of the results. Finally, we demonstrate the effectiveness of our proposed methodology using real data sets and case studies, and receive positive feedback from domain experts.

Keywords: Air pollution · Urban agglomerations · Air pollution transmission network · Multidimensional space transformation · Visual analytics

1 Introduction

Air quality data are analysed using traditional data analysis methods based on the statistical learning paradigm. Theoretically, the relationship between meteorological parameters such as atmospheric visibility, relative humidity and air pollution factors can be analysed [1]. Spatial clustering is utilised to explore city clusters with similar time-series characteristics to facilitate regional management [2]. In addition, the combination of data mining and intelligent decision-making can identify the transport sources of pollution sources [3,4]. Data visualization restores or enhances the structure and details of the data, helping users understand information. Several studies propose innovative methods and techniques, including new glyph designs and time-correlated partitioning (TCP) trees [5,7], for representing correlations in air quality variables. Extracting and interpreting

B. Sheng et al. (Eds.): CGI 2023, LNCS 14497, pp. 225–237, 2024.
https://doi.org/10.1007/978-3-031-50075-6_18

uncertain air pollution transport patterns through the development of a visual analysis system also proves to be an effective approach [6]. However, current research lacks the process of exploring from overview to details, which makes the dynamic analysis of air pollution lack basic technical guidance and core technical support.

In this paper, visual analysis process design to overcome the challenges facing the Air Quality Institute. Specifically, we employ a spatio-temporal clustering algorithm to divide cities into different spatial clusters. In addition, we propose an air pollution transmission network model (APTN) and introduce a progressive exploration and analysis method based on multi-dimensional spatial transformation to investigate the pollution transmission process between cities. The main contributions of the paper are as follows:

- We propose a new concept of air pollution in urban agglomerations that enhances joint regional efforts to combat it.
- We develop the air pollution transmission network (APTN) to gain valuable insights into air pollution propagation analysis.
- A progressive visual analysis system based on multidimensional spatial transformations is developed to improve analysis efficiency.

2   Related Work

2.1   Air Pollution Data Mining

In the field of air pollution analysis, various approaches have been applied, including pattern-assisted graphical causality analysis [8], complex network modeling [9], Lagrange dispersion model (LDM) usage [10–12], co-occurrence pattern mining [13], and self-adaptive spatio-temporal event pattern mining [14]. These methods have contributed to studying the relationship between different regions, simulating pollutant diffusion, extracting spatial relations, and identifying drivers for the occurrence of geographical events. To address the opacity and interpretation challenges in air quality research utilizing data mining or machine learning methods, researchers turned to visualization techniques.

2.2   Visual Analytics of Air Pollution

In air pollution data analysis, information visualization and visual analytics technologies have been widely applied by researchers. Wang et al. [15] introduced a visual method using the parallel coordinate system to process multidimensional time-varying data, enabling effective exploration of hidden regularities. Zhou et al. [16] utilized hierarchical clustering for spatial clustering and employed Voronoi diagrams for visualizing and interacting with these clusters. Sun et al. [17] proposed a stacked map with embedded lines to analyze the spatial and temporal patterns of urban clusters found in large air quality datasets. In addition, some researchers have studied air pollution in other ways [21–24]. While visual analytics techniques have greatly benefited air quality data analysis, previous work has lacked the capability to explore spatial and temporal patterns of air pollution from an overview to a detailed level.

3   Overview

The interactive visual analytics pipeline is shown in Fig. 1. Furthermore, after consulting domain experts, we identify three tasks for exploring the visual analytics of urban air quality data.

- T1: Urban agglomeration division. By exploring the spatial and temporal characteristics of air pollution, urban agglomerations are effectively classified.
- T2: Urban agglomeration pollution analysis. A clear visual method is developed to investigate the air pollution differences among urban agglomerations and to analyze the temporal trends of air pollution.
- T3: Air pollution propagation analysis among cities. Analysis of the impact of air pollution on different cities can help to develop joint regional management programmes.

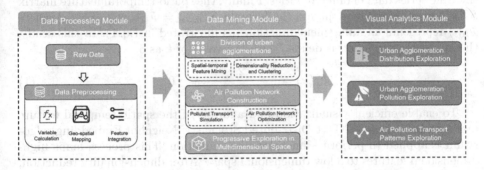

Fig. 1. Visual analytics process of air pollution propagation among urban agglomerations

4   Methodology

4.1   Urban Agglomeration Division

Figure 2 demonstrates the process of urban agglomeration classification, which involves extracting time-series features to identify similar temporal trends in air pollutant evolution across different cities.

To analyze the temporal evolution of air pollutants in different cities, a set $C_m = \{C_1, C_2, ..., C_m\}$ is defined, where m represents the total number of cities and C_i denotes the time-series data of a specific city. Each C_i consists of pollutant values at different timestamps, i.e., $C_i = \{p_1, p_2, ..., p_{t-1}, p_t\}$, where p_i indicates the pollutant content at timestamp t. The time period T is divided into multiple time slices, denoted as $T = \{t_1, t_2, ..., t_{n-1}, t_n\}$. The enhanced CORT (Coefficient of Rank Truncated) method is utilized to compute the similarity coefficient matrix $A_{m \times n}$ for the set C_m within the time period T. A higher

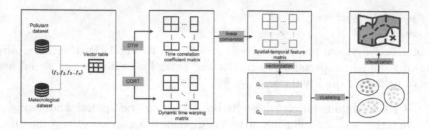

Fig. 2. The workflow of dividing urban agglomerations.

CORT value close to 1 implies similar trends between two time series. Next, the Dynamic Time Warping (DTW) technique is employed to measure the similarity of volatility between two distinct time-series. Using DTW, the similarity distance matrix $D_{m\times n}$ is calculated, effectively capturing fluctuations and variations in the time-series data of different cities. Finally, the spatio-temporal feature matrix $ST_{m\times n}$ is obtained by applying the formula $ST_{m\times n} = \Phi[A_{m\times n}] \cdot D_{m\times n}$, where $\Phi_k(\cdot)$ represents an adjustment function (as illustrated in Eq. 1). In this study, the adjustment function is defined with the value of k as 5.

$$\Phi_k(u) = \frac{2}{1 + \exp(ku)}, k \geq 0 \tag{1}$$

To enable efficient visualization and analysis of the spatio-temporal feature matrix $ST_{m\times n}$, the t-SNE (t-Distributed Stochastic Neighbor Embedding) algorithm is applied to perform dimensionality reduction. This process maps high-dimensional features to a low-dimensional space. After dimensionality reduction, the Kmeans clustering algorithm is used to group urban agglomerations based on their similarity in terms of air quality and meteorological data. The optimal number of clusters is determined using the elbow rule, which indicates that 5 clusters should be used for K value.

4.2 Construction of Air Pollution Transmission Network (APTN)

To incorporate the impact of meteorological factors on air pollution propagation, we employ a particle tracking method [18] and introduce the angle of wind direction as an innovative approach to construct an initial pollution propagation network.

In Fig. 3, we address the uncertainty in air pollutant transport between two regions caused by variable wind fields. To simulate the motion of air parcels, we employ a quantitative sampling method. The positions of the air parcels are updated iteratively based on meteorological conditions, such as wind speed and direction. Furthermore, we propose an enhanced particle transport algorithm that incorporates the wind direction angle. This allows us to determine the direction of pollutant transmission paths. The algorithm terminates when the lifespan of pollutant particles reaches 0. We also set a maximum motion time threshold (τ) within the algorithm.

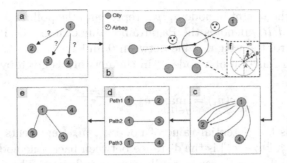

Fig. 3. Transport simulation of pollutant particles: (a) Station 1 may cause air pollution in surrounding cities. (b) The iterative update of the airbag locations. (c) The quantitative sampling method. (d) The extracted transport paths. (e) The primary APTN. (f) Schematic diagram of wind direction angle

The resulting network is represented as a graph G = (V, E), where nodes symbolize urban monitoring stations, edges represent paths of pollutant transmission, and the direction of these edges is determined by wind direction. To assess the relationship between connected stations, we compute the Pearson Correlation Coefficient (PCC) for the time-series of pollutants.

4.3   Exploration of Pollution Transmission Mode Based on Multi-dimension

The multi-dimensional progressive interactive exploration method is an effective approach for analyzing large-scale network topologies [19]. It divides the exploration and analysis of such networks into three levels (Fig. 4). This method enables multi-level interactive exploration, reducing the difficulty for users to explore and analyze the data. Clustering is performed on the air pollution transmission network to extract the community structure of the network backbone, creating the air pollution transport community network. To extract important nodes accurately, we calculated the weight of each node using the formula:

$$w_{ni} = \alpha p_{ni} + \beta PR_{ni} + \lambda \tag{2}$$

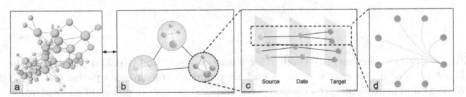

Fig. 4. Multi-dimensional exploration and analysis process: (a) The APTN topology in 3D space. (b) The APTN community structure in 3D space. (c) The APTN topology of a specific community in 2.5D space. (d) The topology of the selected network in 2D space.

Here, w_{ni} is the weight of node n_i, p_{ni} represents the pollutant concentration on node n_i, and PR_{ni} denotes the PageRank value of node n_i. The coefficients α, β, and λ control the weight value between 0 and 1.

The potential function of a node n_i in the network is given by:

$$\varphi(n_i) = \max_{j \in [1,k]} m_{c_j} e^{-(\frac{\|n_i - c_j\|}{\sigma})^2} \tag{3}$$

Here, $\varphi(n_i)$ is the potential value of node n_i, m_{c_j} represents the quality of backbone node c_j, $\|n_i - c_j\|$ is the distance between backbone node c_j and node p_i, and σ is an influence factor controlling node influence. The potential value $\varphi(n_i)$ determines the cluster to which node p_i belongs.

By merging nodes in the same cluster into a community node and preserving connecting edges between communities, the air pollution transmission network is transformed into a community network for further analysis.

5 Case Studies

5.1 System Overview

The system provides three functions to enhance the reliability and effectiveness of our method, which includes parameter selection, urban agglomeration analysis, air pollution transmission analysis.

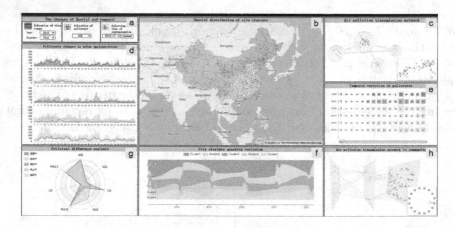

Fig. 5. System overview: (a) Toolbar for parameter selection. (b) Map displaying the distribution of urban agglomerations and air pollution transmission paths. (c) APTN topology and community presentation. (d) Temporal changes in pollutant concentration in urban agglomerations. (e) Air pollution barometer for exploring air pollution movement. (f) Temporal changes in the total number of cities in urban agglomerations. (g) Visualization of pollutant concentration in urban agglomerations. (h) Network topology of a community in 2.5D space and specific air pollution transmission relationships among cities in 2D space.

5.2   Urban Agglomeration Division and Pollution Exploration

To demonstrate the accuracy of urban agglomeration division, we conducted an analysis of PM2.5 pollutant levels during Q1 2018. Figure 6 displays the spatial distribution of urban agglomerations (**T1**) across five regions: the North China Plain, southwest, northwest and northern minority regions, southern coastal region, and middle and lower reaches of the Yangtze River plain. The radar views of pollutants in urban clusters (Fig. 6) reveal substantial disparities in air quality between urban agglomerations. AQI, PM10, and PM2.5 were notably elevated in urban agglomerations I, III, IV, and V, while CO levels were relatively low. Urban agglomerations I, II, III, and V exhibited significantly high O3 content, indicating a major contributor to the development of photochemical pollution. SO2 levels were high in urban agglomerations II and III during the quarter.

Further analysis revealed that urban agglomeration I in the North China Plain experienced severe air pollution due to tall mountains and the presence of heavy industries emitting exhaust gases. Urban agglomeration II in the less developed southwest, northwest, and northern minority regions of China experienced relatively low air pollution. Urban agglomeration III in the southern coastal region experienced moderate levels of pollution due to high temperatures, humidity, and bustling industry and traffic. Urban agglomeration IV in the Northeast Plain and surrounding mountain areas experienced air pollution from heating emissions, but wetlands helped to mitigate the issue. Finally, urban agglomeration V in south of the middle and lower reaches of the Yangtze River plain also experienced severe air pollution due to high humidity and heavy traffic emissions.

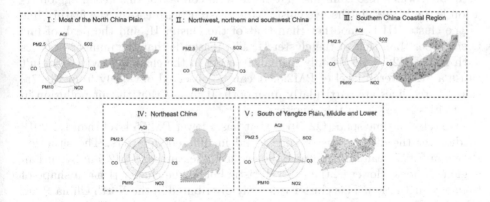

Fig. 6. Urban agglomeration distribution and pollutant concentration.

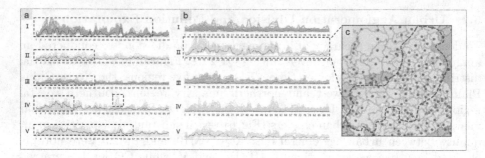

Fig. 7. (a) Pollutant evolution among urban agglomerations in Q1 2018. (b) Pollutant evolution among urban agglomerations in Q2 2018. (c) Spatial distribution of urban agglomeration II in Q2 2018.

5.3   Analysis of Pollution Evolution Among Urban Agglomerations

We apply the theme river view to explore the dynamic evolution of urban agglomerations from 2013 to 2018 (**T2**). As shown in Fig. 5f, the number of cities in the high-pollution cluster increases in January and peaks in February each year. This is reasonable because the high incidence of air pollution occurs in January and February each year in China. The air pollutants show specific trends with different seasons. Consequently, our system employs the stacked view of pollutant evolution to present the trends of the pollutants (Fig. 7d), where the red lines represent the evolution feature of PM2.5 in different clusters. The feature lines of five urban agglomerations are extremely unstable in the first quarter of 2018 in (Fig. 7a). In the cluster I, the PM2.5 content reaches an extraordinarily high level, which also confirms that the PM2.5 content of this urban agglomeration is the highest in the five cluster. Inconsistent with case 1, the feature line of the cluster III is smoother than that of the cluster II, and the peak of line is smoother than that of the cluster II. The reason is that the number of cities with high PM2.5 levels is only a small fraction in the cluster II, which doesn't cause a high overall level of PM2.5. It can be observed obviously from Fig. 7a, that the red lines are particularly unsmooth. It means that the air pollution in most cities is serious in this quarter.

We select a time-span (Q2 2018) that has a lower PM2.5 level than Q1 2018 to discover the distinctions of time trend in different quarters. The situation shown in Fig. 7b can further prove the evolution features of PM2.5 in five urban agglomerations. However, the characteristic line of the cluster II has a shape of frequent fluctuation. This cluster is mainly distributed in the North China Plain (Fig. 7c). The air pollution in this area is extremely serious in China. Though concentrating the Q2 2018, it can be seen that the air quality in this quarter is better than in Q1 2018.

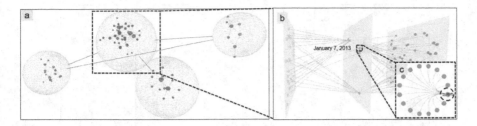

Fig. 8. Multidimensional transformation analysis of air pollution transmission: (a) The APTN community structure in 3D space. (b) The community internal topology in 2.5D space. (c) The specific pollution relationship among cities in 2D space.

5.4 Exploration of Air Pollution Transmission

As shown in Fig. 8a, a clustering algorithm is used to complete the clustering of the network topology, and it is presented in 3-dimensional space (**T3**). It can be observed that the community under analysis and several other communities have air pollution transmission, and this community contains the largest number of nodes. The social network is presented in 2.5-dimensional space for further exploration and analysis. The pollution transmission in the first half of January 2013 is presented in the 2.5-dimensional space, and it is found that the total pollution days in the first half of the month reach five days. Next, we select the specific pollution transmission path on January 7, 2013 and present it in 2-dimensional space. It is found that Shanghai is the only source of pollution and has an impact on the air pollution in the surrounding cities. To obtain further analysis results, we select Changzhou, Zhenjiang, Chuzhou, Nanjing, and other cities for verification, as shown in Fig. 9a. It can be found that Shanghai is the origin city, and Changzhou, Zhenjiang, Chuzhou, Nanjing, and Yangzhou are the destinations of pollution. As depicted in Fig. 9b, the rectangle size of PM2.5 in six cities gradually increases. The five destination cities are in accordance with Shanghai in terms of wind direction, and the five polluted cities are located in the northwest of Shanghai.

Shanghai is a first-tier city in China, with a developed economy and industry, and located in a coastal area. As a result, it remains as a major source of pollution, and pollutants are transmitted to surrounding cities by certain wind directions. Therefore, effective air pollution prevention and control can be formulated for Shanghai to prevent the next large-scale air pollution transmission event.

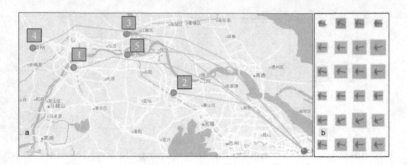

Fig. 9. Case of air pollution based on Shanghai: (a) The air pollution transmission paths. (b) The barometer of air pollution transmission

6 User Evaluation

To verify the effectiveness of the proposed method, we invited 12 volunteers to take part in the assessment, included three experts in air pollution research, six individuals involved in data visualization research, and three experienced big data researchers. Before the experimentation phase, all participants received a practical demonstration of the system's interactive process. Afterward, they were given thirty minutes to independently complete their respective experimental tasks. Once completed, the twelve participants were invited to evaluate the experimental results and provide feedback on user satisfaction through a questionnaire. The participants were divided into three groups based on their area of expertise.

Table 1. Evaluation questionnaire

No	Problem description
Q1	Is it reasonable about the division of urban agglomerations based on temporal and spatial characteristics?
Q2	Is it reasonable about the pollution transmission analysis based on the pollution transmission network?
Q3	Is it reasonable about association between views and system interaction?

In this study, we employed a likert scale to evaluate the system, which comprised five levels: "very reasonable (5 points)", "more reasonable (4 points)", "reasonable (3 points)", "unreasonable (2 points)", and "very unreasonable (1 point)". The scoring outcomes are depicted in Fig. 10. The evaluations mainly included the following points:

Visual Design. Our work confirmed the capability of our system to accurately depict comprehensive information on air pollution in both spatial and temporal dimensions. Our system used visualization technology to show the complex transmission process of air pollution.

Interactions of the System. The specialists lauded the clarity and comprehensibility of the interactions within our system. Experts pointed out that exploring air pollution transmission through system interaction was a very effective method.

Practicability. The feasibility of our system was validated by experts. In addition, one of the experts recommended enhancing the transportation simulation of pollutants by integrating additional variables, which would ultimately benefit the overall functionality of the system.

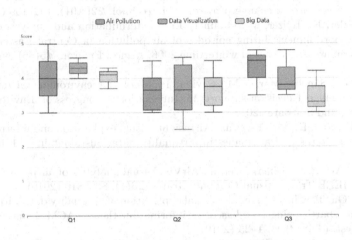

Fig. 10. Results of user evaluation.

7   Discussion and Conclusion

In this paper, we introduce the concept of urban agglomeration and employs spatio-temporal data mining to analyze air quality data. This approach is effective for joint air pollution control. Additionally, an air pollution transmission network is established and a progressive exploration and analysis method is introduced to study the transmission process of air pollution within the region. The accuracy of the method is demonstrated, there are numerous factors contributing to air pollution transmission, and thus, the air pollution transmission network requires further refinement. Expert evaluation of our work is positive, with considerable effectiveness noted. However, experts suggest that we design richer interactions based on existing work to explore deeper information. In response, we will incorporate expert feedback to further improve our work in the future.

Acknowledgements. This study was supported by the Natural Science Foundation of Sichuan Province (Grant No. 2022NSFSC0961), the Doctoral Foundation of Southwest University of Science and Technology (Grant No. 19zx7144), and the Special Research Fund of the Research Centre for Network Emergency Management in China (Mianyang) Science and Technology City (Grant No. WLYJGL2023ZD04).

References

1. Fan, X., Sun, Z., Su, M.: A new method to discern haze using meteorological parameters and air pollution factors. In: 2009 First International Conference on Information Science and Engineering, pp. 4650–4656. IEEE (2009)
2. Yuan, B., Xiao, S., Jiang, D.: Air pollution of city clusters in China and its characteristics on seasonal change. Environ. Sci. Technol. **22**(A01), 102–106 (2009)
3. Juda-Rezler, K., Reizer, M., Oudinet, J.P.: Determination and analysis of PM10 source apportionment during episodes of air pollution in Central Eastern European urban areas: the case of wintertime 2006. Atmos. Environ. **45**(36), 6557–6566 (2011)
4. Gibert, K., Sànchez-Marrè, M., Sevilla, B.: Tools for environmental data mining and intelligent decision support. In: International Congress on Environmental Modelling and Software (2012)
5. Zhang, H., Ren, K., Lin, Y., et al.: AirInsight: visual exploration and interpretation of latent patterns and anomalies in air quality data. Sustainability **11**(10), 2944 (2019)
6. Deng, Z., Weng, D., Chen, J., et al.: AirVis: Visual analytics of air pollution propagation. IEEE Trans. Visual Comput. Graph. **26**(1), 800–810 (2019)
7. Guo, F., Gu, T., Chen, W., et al.: Visual exploration of air quality data with a time-correlation-partitioning tree based on information theory. ACM Trans. Interact. Intell. Syst. (TiiS) **9**(1), 1–23 (2019)
8. Zhu, J.Y., Zhang, C., Zhang, H., et al.: pg-causality: identifying spatiotemporal causal pathways for air pollutants with urban big data. IEEE Trans. Big Data **4**(4), 571–585 (2017)
9. Zhao, G., Huang, G., He, H., Wang, Q.: Innovative Spatio-temporal network modeling and analysis method of air quality. IEEE Access **7**, 26241–26254 (2019). https://doi.org/10.1109/ACCESS.2019.2900997
10. Bahiraei, M., Hosseinalipour, S.M.: Thermal dispersion model compared with Euler-Lagrange approach in simulation of convective heat transfer for nanoparticle suspensions, dispersion. Sci. Technol. **34**(12), 1778–1789 (2013)
11. Carvalho, J.C., De Vilhena, M.T.M.B.: Pollutant dispersion simulation for low wind speed condition by the ILS method. Atmos. Environ. **39**(34), 6282–6288 (2005)
12. Manomaiphiboon, K., Russell, A.G.: Effects of uncertainties in parameters of a Lagrangian particle model on mean ground-level concentrations under stable conditions. Atmos. Environ. **38**(33), 5529–5543 (2004)
13. Akbari, M., Samadzadegan, F., Weibel, R.: A generic regional spatio-temporal co-occurrence pattern mining model: a case study for air pollution. J. Geogr. Syst. **17**(3), 249–274 (2015)
14. He, Z., Deng, M., Cai, J., et al.: Mining spatiotemporal association patterns from complex geographic phenomena. Int. J. Geogr. Inf. Sci. **34**(6), 1162–1187 (2020)

15. Wang, Z., Haihong, E., Song, M., Ren, Z.: Time-varying data visual analysis method based on parallel coordinate system. In: 2019 IEEE 3rd Information Technology, Networking, Electronic and Automation Control Conference (ITNEC), pp. 1256-1260 (2019). https://doi.org/10.1109/ITNEC.2019.8728990.

16. Zhou, Z., Ye, Z., Liu, Y., Liu, F., Tao, Y., Su, W.: Visual analytics for spatial clusters of air-quality data. IEEE Comput. Graph. Appl. **37**(5), 98–105 (2017)

17. Sun, G., Hu, Y., Jiang, L., et al.: Urban agglomerations-based visual analysis of air quality data. J. Comput.-Aided Des. Comput. Graph. **29**(1), 17–26 (2017)

18. Ren, K., Wu, Y., Zhang, H., Fu, J., Qu, D., Lin, X.: Visual analytics of air pollution propagation through dynamic network analysis. IEEE Access **8**, 205289–205306 (2020)

19. Wang, S., Chen, S., Cai, T., et al.: MULTI-NETVIS: visual analytics for multivariate network. Appl. Sci. **12**(17), 8405 (2022)

20. Zou, T., Wang, S., Li, H., Wu, Y.: Hybrid traffic route visual recommendation based on multilayer complex networks. In: 2022 IEEE 15th Pacific Visualization Symposium (PacificVis), pp. 186–190. IEEE (2022)

21. Li, J., Bi, C.: Visual analysis of air pollution spatio-temporal patterns. Vis. Comput. 1–12 (2023)

22. Manu, C.M., Sreeni, K.G.: GANID: a novel generative adversarial network for image dehazing. Vis. Comput. 1–14 (2022)

23. France, S.L., Akkucuk, U.: A review, framework, and R toolkit for exploring, evaluating, and comparing visualization methods. Vis. Comput. **37**(3), 457–475 (2021)

24. Qin, Y., Chi, X., Sheng, B., lau, R.W.H.: GuideRender: large-scale scene navigation based on multi-modal view frustum movement prediction. Vis. Comput. 1–11 (2023)

Visual Analysis of Machine Tool Operation Mode Correlation Based on Parameter Category Coding

Jinxin Long[1], Lijuan Peng[1(✉)], Xuejun Li[1], Kaiming Ma[1], and Feng Qiu[2]

[1] School of Computer Science and Technology, Southwest University of Science and Technology, Mianyang, China
plj@swust.edu.cn
[2] Automation Research Institute Co., Ltd. of China South Industries Group Corporation, Mianyang, China

Abstract. Aiming at the problem that the machine tool operation data has many dimensions, the parameters relationship is complex, and its abnormal patterns and hidden correlation information are difficult to fully excavate, this paper proposed a visual analysis method for the correlation of CNC machine tool operation mode. Firstly, the parameter category encoding is carried out from the two aspects of the sliding window and time point of the machine tool operation data, and then the multi-parameter category encoding combination is clustered and association rule mining is carried out to extract the machine tool operation mode and parameter state association mode, and establish visual map. Integrating ease of use, flexibility, and interpretability, the visual analysis system MachineVis is further constructed, and a variety of interactive methods are designed to support users in discovering abnormal patterns of machine tool data, analyzing the changes of various parameters of machine tool data and capturing the relationship between each parameter. Finally, the validity and practicability of the system are proved by case studies.

Keywords: symbolic aggregate approximation · association rules · machine tool operation data · visual analysis

1 Introduction

CNC machine tools play a vital role in the industrial field, which can control machine movements through digital commands to complete various complex parts processing tasks, and are widely used in military equipment, automobile manufacturing, mold processing, aerospace and other fields. However, breakdowns in the operation of machine tool equipment can cause multiple problems, including damage to the equipment itself, loss of productivity, economic losses and safety accidents. Therefore, abnormality detection and condition monitoring of machine tools are increasingly becoming a hot research topic. Most of the existing anomaly detection methods are constructed based on machine learning models, which are largely applied to feature extraction of sensor signals and

B. Sheng et al. (Eds.): CGI 2023, LNCS 14497, pp. 238–249, 2024.
https://doi.org/10.1007/978-3-031-50075-6_19

equipment fault diagnosis, with little comprehensive analysis and deep exploration of machine tool anomaly data, while providing very limited knowledge in the interpretation of anomaly causes.

With the development of digital promotion work, a variety of sensors and recorders and other equipment can record and detect machine tool production operation status in real time, and accumulate a large amount of machine tool operation data. This data contains valuable domain knowledge such as the changing patterns and correlation characteristics of the machine's operating conditions. In-depth analysis and utilization of equipment operation history data will help to control, analyze and make decisions on the operation status of machine tools. However, machine operation data has multiple dimensions, operation status has multiple categories, and is time-dynamic, which makes machine operation data analysis very difficult.

The rapid development of visualization and visual analytics technology provides an effective way to solve the above problems. Use visualization tools and techniques to quickly visualize machine operation data for more intuitive observation and analysis of changes in machine operating conditions. In addition, visual analytics allows users to interactively select production segments of interest and drill down, layer by layer, to analyze and explore the impact of each parameter in the segment on equipment operation and the relationships between parameters, which not only helps to understand abnormal machine problems, but also helps to uncover potential correlations and patterns in machine operation data to better prevent failures and improve machine productivity and quality.

2 Related Works

The analysis of machine tool operation data is actually the analysis of time series data. Symbolization technology can refer to complex and variable time series data with simpler symbols, weaken the influence of local data fluctuations, and is widely used in time series data analysis. The symbolic aggregate approximation (SAX) [1] is used more, which divides the time series into segments based on the piecewise aggregation approximation method (PAA) [2], and calculates mean of each segment and mapped to different signs on the standard normal distribution. Georgoulas et al. used the method of symbol aggregation approximation and related intelligent icon representation to extract the features of the bearing vibration records, and input the features into the classifier to realize the fault diagnosis [3]. Park et al. apply symbol aggregation approximation to represent time series and use association rule mining to discover frequent rules between symbols of anomalous events [4]. Shi et al. used a symbolic aggregation approximation method to represent the consumer's load curve, and clustered the load curve, and finally analyzed and mined the typical power consumption behavior of the user [5]. Yin et al. proposed an improved Lempel-Ziv method based on a symbolic aggregation approximation method, which can realize early fault diagnosis of bearings [6]. Li et al. proposed an equiprobable association rule mining method on the basis of symbol aggregation approximation, and used it for fault classification and defect severity identification [7]. In terms of correlation modeling, Lv et al. design a region-based adaptive association learning framework that well improves the performance of scene recognition [8]. Gao et al. proposed a dynamic correlation model and an improved fuzzy clustering algorithm for solving the inaccuracy problem in complex image segmentation [9]. Xie et al. proposed a new extensive attention graph fusion network to efficiently perform complex higher-order feature interactions at the granularity of feature dimensions and verified its effectiveness [10].

As an important technology for understanding complex data, visualization is frequently introduced into industrial data analysis [11], and it can efficiently help researchers analyze problems in many industrial application scenarios. Liu et al. designed a novel interactive system ECoalVis, which enables experts to intuitively analyze the control strategies of coal-fired power plants extracted from historical sensors [12]. Eirich et al. proposed the visual analysis system IRVINE, which can help analyze acoustic data in order to detect and understand unknown errors in motor manufacturing [13]. The visualization system designed by Musleh et al. supports local and global exploration of multivariate time-series data generated by blow molding machine sensors [14]. Wu et al. proposed a visual analysis method for factory equipment condition monitoring [15]. The visual analysis system designed by Zhang et al. supports interactive exploration of fault propagation patterns in power grid simulation data [16]. Li et al. designed an automatic household waste detection and sorting system that helps to improve the efficiency of waste recycling [17].

Therefore, this paper proposes a CNC machine tool operation mode association visual analysis method, using sliding window technology, symbolic aggregation approximation, association rule mining and clustering methods to extract the association modes and operation modes in the machine tool operation data, and designing an interactive visual analysis system MachineVis that contains five views: control panel view, global view, local view, parameter state association view, and contrast view.

3 Task Analysis

In order to fully explore the machine operation data, assist users to analyze the machine operation data from the whole to the details, and realize the all-round visual presentation of the operation data. Accordingly, the design tasks for the MachineVis interactive visual analysis system were derived as follows:

- T1: Supports visual exploration of anomalous patterns in historical machine tool operating data. It also helps users to deeply investigate the abnormal pattern of machine operation data.
- T2: Supports visual analysis of the relationships between machine parameters. Users can better understand the relationship between parameters in different modes.
- T3: Supports users in efficiently exploring historical machine operation data and provides flexible interaction.

In this paper, we encode parameter categories and extract symbolic features for machine operation data in terms of sliding windows and time points, and then clustering and association rules are mined for the combination of multiple parameter category codes to extract machine operation patterns and parameter state association patterns (T1, T2), and an interactive visual analysis system MachineVis (T1, T2, T3) is further constructed, as shown in Fig. 1.

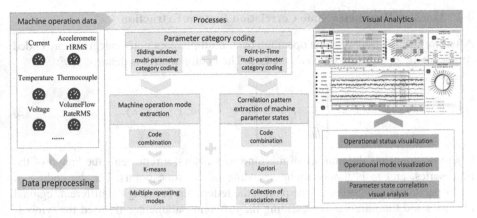

Fig. 1. MachineVis interactive visual analysis system architecture

4 Methodology Overview

4.1 Machine Operation Mode Extraction

In order to detect changes and trends in the data in a timely manner, the SAX method was used to categorize and code the sliding window multiparameter data. A matrix consisting of multidimensional time series can be obtained by first normalizing multiple subsequences of machine tool operation data using z-score. The multidimensional time series matrix is segmented according to the segmentation method of fixed sliding window, and the mean value of each sliding window is extracted for symbol coding, and the coding matrix E is obtained according to SAX coding, denoted as:

$$E = \left\{ \begin{array}{ccc} e_{11} & \cdots & e_{1(n-w+1)} \\ \vdots & e_{ij} & \vdots \\ e_{m1} & \cdots & e_{m(n-w+1)} \end{array} \right\} (1 \leq i \leq m, 1 \leq j \leq n - w + 1) \qquad (1)$$

where e_{ij} is the symbolic encoding of the mean, n is the length of the time series, m is the number of machine parameters, and w is the sliding window length. According to SAX, it can be obtained that when the number of letters is 4, there are three breakpoints of -0.67, 0 and 0.67 which are divided into 4 regions. For the values of these 4 regions, the letters a, b, c and d are used from lowest to highest, respectively.

By extracting the multi-parameter class coding combinations at the same moment and performing cluster analysis on the multi-parameter class coding combinations at different moments. Thus, the similar multi-parameter category codes are combined into the same cluster, and finally the machine operation mode is recognized. In this paper, we use the K-means clustering algorithm (K-means) [18]. Specifically, the multi-parameter category coding combinations in each column of the coding matrix sequence E are extracted and de-duplicated as data samples, and the samples are clustered using the K-means algorithm.

4.2 Machine Parameter State Correlation Pattern Extraction

After normalizing the machine operation data, multiple parameter categories are coded for each time point using the SAX method. The coding matrix is denoted as F:

$$F = \begin{Bmatrix} f_{11} \cdots f_{1n} \\ \vdots \quad f_{ij} \quad \vdots \\ f_{m1} \cdots f_{mn} \end{Bmatrix} (1 \leq i \leq m, 1 \leq j \leq n) \tag{2}$$

where m represents the number of machine parameters, n represents the length of the time series, and f_{ij} is the symbolic encoding of the time points. For the coding of multi-parameter categories at time points, the letters representing the different regional divisions and the numbers representing the different parameters are used for symbolization. For example, the code combination in the first column $\{f_{11}, f_{21}, f_{31}, f_{41}\} = \{d_1, c_2, b_3, a_4\}$, it indicates that at the first second, the first parameter is in state d; the second and third parameters are in states c and b, respectively; and the fourth parameter is in state a.

The Apriori [19] algorithm is a common association rule mining algorithm. For each column in the encoding matrix sequence F with a combination of multi-parameter class encoding at time points, the Apriori association rule algorithm is applied to generate the set of parameter state association rules. It consists of two components, which are support and confidence. Users can set their own support and confidence thresholds according to actual needs and data characteristics.

5 Interactive Visual Analytics System Design

This section introduces the five key views of the MachineVis interactive visual analysis system (Fig. 2), which are the control panel view, the global view, the local view, the contrast view and the parameter state association view.

5.1 Control Panel View

In Fig. 2(a), three options are included from top to bottom: selection data, support level, and confidence level. The selection data is used to determine the machine operation data to be analyzed. The settings of support and confidence are related to the extraction of correlation patterns of machine parameter states.

5.2 Global View

In Fig. 2(b), line graphs are used to show the machine operation data, and the shaded areas of the line graphs represent the fluctuation size and duration of the data. The background color of the mouse position represents the current running state of the machine tool. When the user clicks on the state of a certain time point, the global view can search and highlight other time points that are the same as the current machine running state.

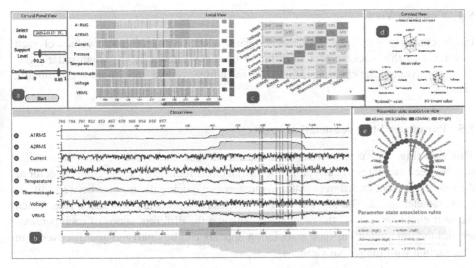

Fig. 2. MachineVis interactive visual analysis system

According to the clustering results, different clusters can represent different operating modes in the machine tool work, and different clusters are mapped with different colors. Below the line graph shows the change of the machine operating mode.

In addition, in the global view, you can adjust the range of the local view by dragging the slider. The light green histogram at the bottom of the view shows the one-dimensional data characteristics of the machine tool operation data after PCA dimensionality reduction. The higher the height of the bars in the bar chart represents the more obvious changes in the data at the current moment, which helps to observe the changes in the overall machine operation status.

5.3 Local View

The left part of the partial view (Fig. 2(c)) shows the detailed changes of each parameter data in the selected time period. If the number of symbol letters is 4, symbol a is represented by red, which means the current parameter data is high; symbol d is represented by blue, which represents the current parameter data is low; symbol b and symbol c are represented by light gray and dark gray, representing that the current data is in a stable range.

This view provides a comparison of the state at a certain point in time with the previous state. Put the mouse at a certain time point, the two small rectangles on the left will display the running status of the previous second and the previous two seconds, and the large rectangle represents the current running status of the mouse positioning. Additionally, a heatmap represents the correlation between different parameters over a selected time period.

5.4 Contrast View

In the contrast view (Fig. 2(d)) the comparison of the characteristic values of each parameter of the machine tool in different operation modes is shown in radar plots, the comparison of the characteristic values including average, maximum and minimum values.

5.5 Parameter State Association View

This view (Fig. 2(e)) uses a circular relationship diagram and a table to show the correlation between the states of each parameter. Each circle represents a state, and the color of the circle represents a different state, so the user can quickly distinguish between different parameter states. The line between the circles represents an association rule. When the user clicks on a state, the association between the different states of each parameter and the time when the state association appears can be analyzed and discovered in conjunction with the global view.

6 Case Studies and User Evaluations

6.1 Data Sets and Data Preprocessing

This paper uses the publicly available dataset SKAB, which is a multivariate time series collected from sensors mounted on a motor test bench and contains eight parameters, namely Accelerometer1RMS, Accelerometer2RMS, Current, Pressure, Temperature, Thermocouple, Voltage and VolumeFlowRateRMS. The data is recorded for each second from 2020-02-08 17:27:19 to 2020-02-08 17:47:18 and is 1144 in length.

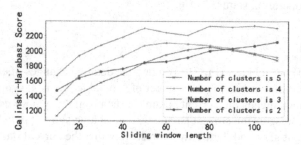

Fig. 3. Cluster comparison of different values

The data first needs to be z-score normalized, using a number of letters of 4. For the number of clusters and different sliding window lengths, this paper uses the Calinski-Harabasz Score clustering model evaluation metric to evaluate, with larger metrics indicating better clustering results [20]. In our experiments, we consider the case where the number of clusters is between [2–5] and the sliding window length is between [10–110] with a step size of 10. As shown in Fig. 3, it can be found that the evaluation metric is greatest when the sliding window length is taken as 80 and the number of clusters is 3.

Therefore, in this paper, the sliding window length of 80 and the number of clusters of 3 are used to extract the machine operation mode. In order to find the rules of strong correlation of parameter states in machine operation data, the support is set to 0.25 and the confidence level is set to 0.85.

6.2 Anomaly Analysis

In Fig. 4, the color rectangle bar below the global view shows that the rectangle colors are mapped to three different colors, so the machine operation mode is divided into three modes.

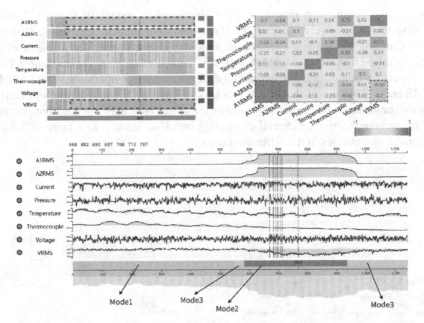

Fig. 4. Anomaly analysis

In the view you can see that the light green bar at the bottom rises in height and lasts longer in the middle and late stages, representing a greater change in parameter status from the previous one. Also in operation Mode 2, it is clearly observed that the parameters A1RMS (abbreviation for Accelerometer1RM1), A2RMS (abbreviation for Accelerometer1RM2) and VRMS (abbreviation for VolumeFlowRateRMS) have a large shadow area, indicating that the parameters fluctuate greatly during this time period and that an abnormal condition is likely to have occurred. Therefore, special attention needs to be paid to the distribution of these parameter states during this time period. By dragging the time brush in the global view and positioning the time range in operation mode 2, it can be seen by looking at the local view that the red area of A1RMS and A2RMS covers a wider area and the blue area of VRMS occupies most of the area. This indicates that most of the data for A1RMS and A2RMS were relatively high during this time period, while most of the data for VRMS were relatively low, allowing for greater certainty that A1RMS, A2RMS, and VRMS were anomalous during the Mode 2.

By looking at the correlation heat map on the right side of the local view, a positive correlation is found between A1RMS and A2RMS in operation mode 2, and there is also a high negative correlation between A1RMS and A2RMS and VRMS. Where when clicking on the state at the 767th second in the anomaly mode, it was found that the state also appeared at the moments 668, 682, 690, 697, 706 and 712, indicating that a similar anomalous state appeared at these moments.

6.3 Sensitive Parametric Analysis

The radar plot comparison reveals that the characteristic values of Current, Voltage and Pressure are relatively close in the three operation modes (Fig. 5(a)). It shows that the Current, Voltage and Pressure are in a stable state during the whole working process. However, A1RMS, A2RMS, VRMS, Temperature and Thermocouple have large disparities in multiple eigenvalues in different modes of operation. The A1RMS, A2RMS and VRMS are probably due to a lack of stability in the machine's operating conditions or to abnormal factors, as judged by the global view in Fig. 4. And Temperature and Thermocouple show an overall decreasing trend, so leading to a large difference between the eigenvalues in the different modes.

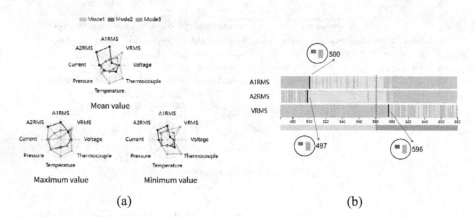

(a)   (b)

Fig. 5. Discovering sensitive features and sensitive state changes

The three anomalous sequences A1RMS, A2RMS and VRMS are analyzed in detail in the local view (Fig. 5(b)). it is found that before the anomaly occurred in the machine (before the red dashed line in the figure), it was found that the color combination of the rectangular bars of A1RMS and A2RMS changed considerably in the first period. Combined with the change in the size rectangle and the positioning of the mouse, it was found that the state of A2RMS and A1RMS changed considerably from the 497th and 500th seconds respectively. We can then deduce that the persistent elevation of A1RMS and A2RMS may have been the cause of the abnormal occurrence of the machine to the extent that it caused the VRMS to become abnormal.

6.4 Parameter State Correlation Analysis

In the parameter state association view (Fig. 6), it is found that A1RMS(d), A2RMS(d) and VRMS(a) are associated with each other and that a mouse clicks on one of the states shows the location of the individual state appearances in the global view. We found that the regions where the correlation states of A1RMS(d), A2RMS(d), and VRMS(a) occur are mostly within the anomaly interval, i.e., we can infer that A1RMS, A2RMS, and VRMS usually produce anomalies together and that VRMS is lower when A1RMS and A2RMS are higher.

Where A1RMS(a) and A2RMS(a) are also correlated with each other, indicating that when A1RMS is lower in Operation Mode 1 and Operation Mode 3, A2RMS is also lower. It was also found that both Temperature(d) and Thermocouple(d) point to A1RMS(a), indicating that within Operation Mode 1, when Temperature and Thermocouple are higher, A1RMS is also typically lower.

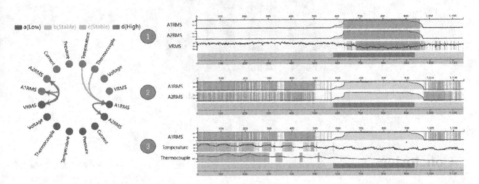

Fig. 6. Parameter state association pattern analysis

6.5 User Evaluation and Feedback

To further verify the effectiveness and usability of the system, eight volunteers were invited to evaluate the system. Two of the experts are from the field of machine automation research, three from the field of visualization and three from the field of industrial data analysis. We first designed a questionnaire:

- Q1: The system is able to distinguish between different machine operation modes.
- Q2: The system is able to observe machine operation in detail and quickly identify abnormalities.
- Q3: The system is able to clearly show machine parameter state correlations
- Q4: The system offers flexible ways to help users explore machine operation data.

The volunteers were then explained how the system works, and finally a Likert scale was used, with volunteers scoring from 1 (strongly disagree) to 10 (strongly agree).

The results of the evaluation (Fig. 7) show that for each question the average score is above 8.5, indicating that our system is a good solution to the user's needs. After completing the evaluation, a return visit was made to experts in the field of machine automation research to discuss the usability and visualization design of the system, and the following are the valuable optimization suggestions made by the experts in the field:

1. Further comparative analysis of abnormal patterns can be achieved for multiple possible abnormal patterns.
2. The presentation of parameter status correlation information can be further enriched, allowing the user to quickly access parameter correlation information in different operating modes from multiple perspectives.

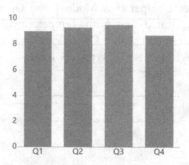

Fig. 7. Questionnaire result

7 Conclusion

This paper's interactive visual analysis system MachineVis, is used in a case study on the dataset. Through the visual mapping of the correlations among machine operating modes, machine operating states, and machine parameter states and the interactive linkage of multiple views, it is demonstrated that MachineVis can easily detect and analyze anomalies, and can fully explore the interactions, correlations, and their hidden correlation information among machine parameters. In future usage scenarios, we hope that the methods in this paper can be applied to different types of industrial systems to provide references for deeper mining and analysis of their anomaly patterns.

References

1. Lin, J., Keogh, E., Lonardi, S., Chiu, B.: A symbolic representation of time series, with implications for streaming algorithms. In: Proceedings of the 8th ACM SIGMOD Workshop on Research Issues in Data Mining and Knowledge Discovery, pp. 2–11 (2003)
2. Keogh, E., Chakrabarti, K., Pazzani, M., Mehrotra, S.: Dimensionality reduction for fast similarity search in large time series databases. Knowl. Inf. Syst. **3**, 263–286 (2001)
3. Georgoulas, G., Karvelis, P., Loutas, T., Stylios, C.D.: Rolling element bearings diagnostics using the Symbolic Aggregate approXimation. Mech. Syst. Signal Process. **60**, 229–242 (2015)

4. Park, H., Jung, J.-Y.: SAX-ARM: Deviant event pattern discovery from multivariate time series using symbolic aggregate approximation and association rule mining. Expert Syst. Appl. **141**, 112950 (2020)
5. Shi, Y., Yu, T., Liu, Q., Zhu, H., Li, F., Wu, Y.: An approach of electrical load profile analysis based on time series data mining. IEEE Access. **8**, 209915–209925 (2020)
6. Yin, J., Xu, M., Zheng, H.: Fault diagnosis of bearing based on symbolic aggregate approXimation and Lempel-Ziv. Measurement **138**, 206–216 (2019)
7. Li, Y., et al.: Association rule-based feature mining for automated fault diagnosis of rolling bearing. Shock Vibr. **2019**, 1–12 (2019)
8. Lv, G., Dong, L., Zhang, W., Xu, W.: Region-based adaptive association learning for robust image scene recognition. Vis. Comput. **39**, 1629–1649 (2023)
9. Gao, X., Zhang, Y., Wang, H., Sun, Y., Zhao, F., Zhang, X.: A modified fuzzy clustering algorithm based on dynamic relatedness model for image segmentation. Vis. Comput. **39**, 1583–1596 (2023)
10. Xie, Z., Zhang, W., Sheng, B., Li, P., Chen, C.P.: BaGFN: broad attentive graph fusion network for high-order feature interactions. IEEE Trans. Neural Netw. Learn. Syst. **34**, 4499–4513 (2021)
11. Zhou, F., et al.: A survey of visualization for smart manufacturing. J. Vis. **22**, 419–435 (2019)
12. Liu, S., et al.: ECoalVis: visual analysis of control strategies in coal-fired power plants. IEEE Trans. Visual Comput. Graphics **29**, 1091–1101 (2022)
13. Eirich, J., et al.: IRVINE: a design study on analyzing correlation patterns of electrical engines. IEEE Trans. Visual Comput. Graphics **28**, 11–21 (2021)
14. Musleh, M., Chatzimparmpas, A., Jusufi, I.: Visual analysis of blow molding machine multivariate time series data. J. Vis. **25**, 1329–1342 (2022)
15. Wu, W., Zheng, Y., Chen, K., Wang, X., Cao, N.: A visual analytics approach for equipment condition monitoring in smart factories of process industry. In: 2018 IEEE Pacific Visualization Symposium (PacificVis), pp. 140–149. IEEE (2018)
16. Zhang, T., Chen, Z., Zhao, Z., Luo, X., Zheng, W., Chen, W.: FaultTracer: interactive visual exploration of fault propagation patterns in power grid simulation data. J. Vis. **24**, 1051–1064 (2021)
17. Li, J., et al.: Automatic detection and classification system of domestic waste via multimodel cascaded convolutional neural network. IEEE Trans. Industr. Inf. **18**, 163–173 (2021)
18. Hartigan, J.A., Wong, M.A.: Algorithm AS 136: A k-means clustering algorithm. J. Roy. Stat. Soc. Ser. C (Appl. Stat.) **28**, 100–108 (1979)
19. Agrawal, R., et al.: Fast algorithms for mining association rules. In: Proceedings of the 20th International Conference very large data bases, VLDB, pp. 487–499. Santiago, Chile (1994)
20. Caliński, T., Harabasz, J.: A dendrite method for cluster analysis. Commun. Stat.-Theory Methods **3**, 1–27 (1974)

CAGviz: A Visual Analysis Method to Explore Cyber Asset Graphs of Cybercrime Gangs

Yinuo Liu[1], Yifan Li[2], Binhao Zhao[3], Tianyi Zhou[4], Shengtao Chen[4], and Xiaoju Dong[4(✉)]

[1] SJTU Paris Elite Institute of Technology, Shanghai Jiao Tong University, Shanghai 200240, China
[2] University of Michigan-Shanghai Jiao Tong University Joint Institute, Shanghai Jiao Tong University, Shanghai 200240, China
[3] School of Environmental Science and Engineering, Shanghai Jiao Tong University, Shanghai 200240, China
[4] Department of Computer Science, Shanghai Jiao Tong University, Shanghai 200240, China
xjdong@sjtu.edu.cn

Abstract. In recent decades, cybercrime has become more and more frequent in people's lives, causing serious consequences. Cybercrime groups usually hold a range of large and complex cyber assets to support the operation of their industries. Analyzing information about the cyber assets and the relationships among them can help people better understand the mechanism of cybercrime gangs. In this paper, based on an open-source cybercrime gang asset dataset, we propose a visual analysis system: CAGviz. The system helps to achieve tasks such as mining subgraphs of gang assets and extracting important assets. In addition, it also allows users to interactively view and analyze cyber asset information through a visual interface. Finally, a scenario analysis and user studies illustrate the effectiveness of the system.

Keywords: Visual analytics · Cyber asset · Graph search algorithm · Interaction design

1 Introduction

In recent years, cybercrime is becoming increasingly serious. Relying on computer technology and the Internet, cybercrime gangs carry out well-organized illegal activities, which threaten the life and property safety of Internet users [6]. Cybercrime covers a wide range of activities, including computer fraud, financial crimes, scams, cybersex trafficking, and ad fraud.

A *cyber asset* is any data, device, or other component of the environment that supports information-related activities [9]. Cybercrime groups usually hold a large and complex association of multiple cyber assets to support the operation

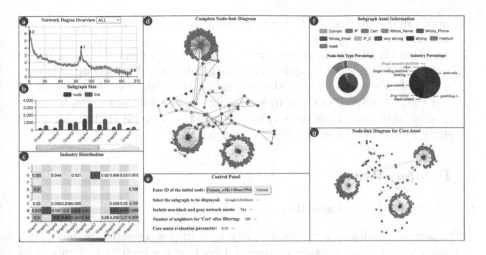

Fig. 1. The interface of CAGviz system.

of the industry chain. Some of these assets are related to the operation of many other cyber assets or associated with multiple lines of business. These cyber assets are called *core cyber assets*. In-depth analysis of core cyber assets enables people to explore the connection between multiple assets or businesses, which can help restore the entire industry chain and even discover clues to the real criminals behind the virtual network world. However, in the face of the massive amount of cyber security data, there is a lack of solutions that can integrate and visually present cyber asset information for people to understand and analyze cyber crime groups.

Visualization and visual analytics technologies that have emerged in recent years combine machine intelligence with human intelligence, providing new means to understand and analyze complex problems [8]. They have been widely used in all aspects of life, such as detection and classification of household waste [18], soccer matches [24], analysis of spatial and temporal patterns of air pollution [19] and so on. In this paper, we present CAGviz (Fig. 1), an interactive visual analysis system that supports automated mining and display of asset information of cybercriminal groups and is able to extract core cyber assets and critical correlation information from them. Users can explore interactively through the system. The system can thus give data support to relevant authorities so as to better understand and combat Internet criminal gangs.

The main contributions of this paper are as follows:

(1) We propose a subgraph mining algorithm that supports finding cyber assets associated with one particular asset that is given by the user. It also supports finding new subgraphs by node degree analysis and community detection methods in the absence of information given by users.

(2) After obtaining relevant cyber asset subgraphs, we propose a core cyber asset and critical link identification algorithm to help users quickly find the

most valuable assets and the association relationships among these important assets.

(3) Based on the above algorithms, we design and implement a visual analysis
system CAGviz, which supports automatic mining and display of asset subgraphs of cybercrime groups, showing information such as core cyber assets
and critical links. Users can interactively explore and analyze cybercrime
groups' assets and their associations. Finally, a scenario analysis and user
studies illustrate the effectiveness of the system.

2   Related Work

2.1   Graph Search Algorithm

Graph search algorithms have been widely used in past research for tasks such
as path planning and subgraph mining. Depth-first search (DFS) moves as
fast as possible toward the goal and searches the path until it reaches a dead
end. Extended depth-first search (EDFS) algorithm allows faster exploration of
smaller search spaces and reduces the cost [17]. Moore proposed the breadth-first
search algorithm (BFS) in 1957. It is a systematic search algorithm because it
first expands the shallow nodes by searching all the next level nodes of the path
before proceeding to the next step. Dijkstra [10] introduced the search algorithm
for a system to find an optimal path between the initial point and all other points
in the graph based on the cost associated with traversal. Recent imporvements
include Bi-directional A*, LSS-LRTA*, etc. However, there is a lack of practical search algorithms that combine cybercrime domain knowledge and business
rules for the study of cyber asset graphs.

2.2   Graph Layout Technique

Graph layout is very important for graph visualization. The two main categories
of graph layout techniques are force-directed layout and dimension reduction layout [11]. Force-directed algorithms include Noack's LinLog layout [21,22], Gephi
[3]'s ForceAtlas [13], etc. Dimensional reduction in graph layout include multidimensional scaling (MDS), linear dimensionality reduction, and self-organizing
graphs. Harel and Koren [12] proposed a high-dimensional embedding (HDE).
Bonabeau's [4,5] method can be used as a stand-alone graph layout or as
a preprocessing step to provide the initial layout. Meyer's [20] Inverted Self-
Organizing Map (ISOM) adapts graph theory to Euclidean distances and uses
the SOM method to layout the graph. In this paper, we choose to use force-
directed graphs to demonstrate the cyber assets of criminal groups, where the
nodes represent cyber assets and the edges represent the relationships among
the assets.

2.3   Cyber Security Visualization

Visualization techniques can be used to present data and information in the cybersecurity domain. Noel et al. [23] proposed a multiple collaborative view approach to present cyber attack graphs, and Leichtnam et al. [16] developed a 3D graphical data exploration platform called Starlord for visualizing different correlated security data. Koike et al. [15], on the other hand, used an IP matrix to visualize the network attack paths. In addition, some visualization methods can help to solve cybersecurity problems. For example, Ali et al. [2] proposed a visual analytics-based intrusion detection framework that enables traffic-based security monitoring in high-speed networks. Chen et al. [7] proposed a distributed network attack visualization method that clearly shows the scale and distribution form of attacks by segmenting, aggregating, and visualizing the attack data. Knijnenburg et al. [14] applied self-organizing maps (SOM) to the visualization of network behaviors by using the clustering algorithm of SOM to present a large amount of data in the form of images to visualize the behavior patterns in the network.

3   CAGviz Approach

3.1   Pipeline and Dataset

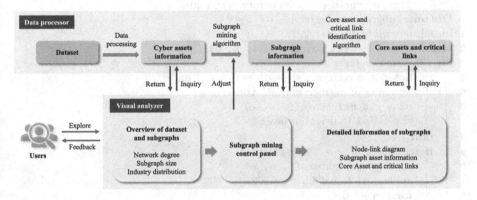

Fig. 2. The pipeline of CAGviz.

CAGviz is an interactive visual analysis system. Its workflow is shown in Fig. 2. The system comprises a data processor and a visual analyzer. The data processor first performs preliminary cleaning and processing for the dataset. Then, through the subgraph mining algorithm, subgraphs of different criminal groups' cyber assets can be extracted from the processed data. Finally, through the core asset and critical link identification algorithm, we can obtain the important asset information in the subgraph. After data processing, users can view and explore the cyber asset graphs of cybercrime gangs through the visual analyzer and interact with it through the control panel. A short video demo is available.[1]

---

[1] https://drive.google.com/file/d/1uXhDcOAh71pusOgKlJRnd493bkbs6RiL/view? usp=drive_link.

The dataset chosen for the system is an open-source cyber asset graph dataset [25], which consists of 2.37 million nodes and 3.28 million edges. As we have mentioned before, the nodes represent cyber assets, and the edges represent the relationships among them. There are 8 types of nodes: website domain, IP address, SSL security certificate, registrant's name, registrant's phone number, registrant's email, c-segment of the IP and autonomous domain of the IP. According to the dataset, the first three are *very important*. The three types of information for the registrant are *important*. And the last two are of *average* importance. There are 11 types of edges, and their association strengths are classified as *very strong, strong, average* and *weak* according to cybersecurity domain knowledge.

3.2   Algorithms

In this section, we introduce three algorithms used in the data processor for subgraph mining, core asset identification, and critical link identification, respectively.

Algorithm 1: Get the subgraph of node A

Input: node A, nodes and links information, maximum neighbor number for Cert: n, whether contain empty type nodes: e

Output: subgraph nodes of A

1 Initialize $neighbor layers 1, 2, 3$
2 neighbor layer 1 = get_neighbors(A, n, e)
3 **for** i *in neighbor layer 1* **do**
4   relation = the relation's strength between A and i
5   **if** *relation is of average strength* **then**
6         $n1$ = get_neighbors(i, n, e)
7   append $n1$ to neighbor layer 2
8   **end**
9   **if** *relation is of strong strength* **then**
10         $n1$ = get_neighbors(i, n, e)
11   append $n1$ to neighbor layer 2
12   **for** j *in n1* **do**
13   relation_layer 2 = the relation' strength between i and j
14   **if** *relation_layer 2 is of strong type* **then**
15                 $n2$ = get_neighbors(j, n, e)
16   append $n2$ to neighbor layer 3
17   **end**
18   **end**
19   **end**
20 **end**
21 subgraph nodes = sum of neighbor layers 1, 2, 3
22 return subgraph nodes

Subgraph Mining. The subgraph mining algorithm needs to extract the cyber assets associated with the given nodes. Considering the relevant domain knowledge and the characteristics of the dataset, we follow the rules below in our algorithm:

(1) The cyber asset subgraph is mined mainly within 3 hops of the starting node.
(2) For target nodes pointed by edges with weak (W) association strength, we mine the nodes within 1 hop; for target nodes pointed by edges with average (A) association strength, we mine the nodes within 2 hops.
(3) For nodes of type Cert, since the number of neighboring nodes is generally very large, we only consider part of the neighbors. So users can customize the parameter to limit the number of neighbors.
(4) Since some subgraphs are too large, the user can customize the parameter that determines whether to remove nodes with empty industry types when mining the subgraphs. If set to False, the nodes with empty industry type will be removed when mining the second and third level neighbor nodes.

According to the above rules, we first find the neighbors of a given node. Then we can further extract the whole cyber asset subgraph, which is implemented by the subgraph mining function, whose pseudo code is shown in Algorithm 1. For the above function, the parameters n and e are user-defined and can be adjusted according to the actual situation to obtain a subgraph of cyber assets of suitable size. If the users do not offer the starting node, we mine new subgraphs by node degree analysis and community detection methods.

Core Asset Identification. After obtaining the relevant subgraphs of cyber assets, we are required to identify the core cyber assets in order to facilitate the analysis of the operation mechanism of cybercrime groups. When determining the core cyber assets, we follow the following three rules:

(1) A cyber asset is not considered as a core network asset if more than 50% of its neighbors have weak association strength.
(2) Multiple IP addresses associated with Domain type cyber assets are not considered as core network assets. Specifically, Domain type assets that are associated with two or more IP addresses at the same time are likely to be using content distribution networks, and their associated IP addresses are also not considered as core cyber assets.
(3) Provided that rules 1 and 2 are satisfied, the more neighbors a cyber asset has, the more possible it is considered as a core cyber asset.

In order to put the first two rules into practice, we propose the core asset identification function is_core(A,G). For the third rule, since there is no fixed limit on the number of associated edges, we take a user-defined approach. We first find the node with the highest number of associated edges in the subgraph and the number of associated edges ($maxDegree$). Then, we set a user-defined parameter $ratio$ that helps to identify core asset. Therefore, we can transform

---

Algorithm 2: Get the core assets of G

Input: *ratio*, subgraph G
Output: core assets of G
1 $maxDegree$ = the max degree among all nodes in G
2 centers = nodes with degree greater or equal to $maxDegree \times ratio$
3 **for** *every node A in centers* **do**
4 | **if** $is\_core(A,G)$ **then**
5 | | append A to core assets
6 | **end**
7 **end**
8 return core assets

---

rule 3 into: a cyber asset is considered as a core cyber asset when the number of associated edges is greater than or equal to $maxDegree \times ratio$, provided that the first two rules are satisfied. This is achieved by Algorithm 2.

Critical Link Identification. After identifying the core assets of the subgraphs, we are required to find the critical links (or correlations). In this way, by combining the core assets with the critical links, users can analyze the operation mechanism of the cybercrime groups. When identifying critical links, we follow the rules below:

(1) The critical link path does not exceed 4 hops.
(2) The shorter the path between two core cyber assets, the more important it is.
(3) The stronger the association strength between two core cyber assets, the more important it is.

We first filter each edge of the core cyber asset based on the number of hops and importance when traversing it. For hop count, we use python's igraph [1] library to obtain the shortest path between two points and eliminate paths with hop count greater than 4 on this basis. In terms of importance, we only keep the paths with the strongest importance between two nodes. The returned value is the critical link of the subgraph. As the identification of critical links is closely related to the core cyber assets, it is particularly important to select the right number and type of assets. Thus, it is recommended that the users pay attention to the nature of the filtered core cyber assets when adjusting the parameter *ratio*.

To sum up, in this section we propose three algorithms which enable users to obtain the subgraph of each cybercrime group, and to identify the core assets and critical links in the subgraph. The workflow of the algorithms is shown in Fig. 3.

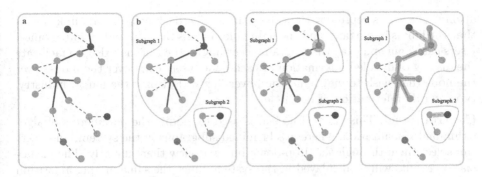

Fig. 3. The workflow of our algorithms. **a** Cyber asset community. **b** Result of the subgraph mining algorithm (3.2.1). **c** Result of the core asset identification algorithm (3.2.2). **d** Result of the critical link identification algorithm (3.2.3).

3.3 Visual Design

The visual interface of CAGviz consists of the following views: network degree overview, subgraph size view, industry distribution, complete node-link diagram, control panel, subgraph asset information and node-link diagram for core asset.

Network Degree Overview. The network node degree overview (Fig. 1-a) is used to show the correlation between the degree of various nodes and the corresponding number of nodes. Users can click the drop-down box to select different node types. The horizontal axis corresponds to the degree of nodes, and the vertical axis represents the number of nodes (after logarithm).

Subgraph Size View. The subgraph size view (Fig. 1-b) shows the number of nodes and edges of the 11 mined subgraphs. The scale of the cybercrime groups can be judged based on this view. Users can also find out the ratio of edges to nodes for each subgraph. In the interaction design, the sliders are designed to stretch the subgraphs in view of the need to cover a total of 11 subgraphs. The number of nodes and links in any subgraph can be viewed when the mouse hovers over the corresponding bar.

Industry Distribution. The industry distribution view (Fig. 1-c) uses a heat map to show the percentage of each cybercrime industry in the 11 mined subplots. The horizontal axis shows each subgraph and the vertical axis shows the label of each industry. As for interaction design, in addition to the mouse-over hoverbox effect, users can also select a range of values on the bottom heat value bar so that only the corresponding values within that range are displayed on the graph.

Complete Node-Link Diagram. In the complete node-link diagram (Fig. 1-d), we use a force-directed diagram to show the complete subgraph. The node type is identified by the node's color and name. The name is the type abbreviation[2]. The edges represent the correlations. The dark color of the link means that the link is important, and the light color means that it is of low importance. Users can zoom and drag the diagram according to their needs. Also, to facilitate the display of detailed information of each node, users can hover the mouse over the node they wish to view, and the hover box will display the name, industry, type and ID information of the node.

Control Panel. This panel (Fig. 1-e) is used to modify the parameters of algorithm and visualization. There are 11 mined subgraphs in the system, and users can select them through the drop-down box and view them directly. The visualization results will be displayed in the system. Since the same mining algorithm has different effects on different subgraphs, users can change the three parameters to obtain different visualization result of the same cybercrime gang. The modified results will be updated in the relevant views. In addition to the 11 subgraphs that have been mined, users can also view other subgraphs using free search. In order to achieve this, users need to select the *Search* in the drop-down box, type the ID of node in the search box, and then select the appropriate parameters.

Subgraph Asset Information. In the subgraph asset information view (Fig. 1-f), the left sector displays the node type outside and the corresponding node strength inside. The right sector displays the node's industry type. After the user chooses to switch to the selected subgraph in the control panel, the information of this view will be updated. As for interaction design, users can point specific legend to hide its information.

Node-link Diagram for Core Asset. In this view (Fig. 1-g), the core assets and critical links are displayed using force-directed graph. The implementation and presentation is the same as the complete node-link diagram.

4 Scenario Analysis

Through the visual analyzer, users are able to observe and interactively analyze the cybercrime gangs in the dataset. Here's an example of medieum-sized gang involving the gambling industry.

According to our proposed subgraph mining method, we mined and visualized the subgraph with a given starting node[3]. This group is a medium-sized group, containing 311 nodes and 1459 edges in total. The complete subgraph is shown in Fig. 4.

Then, we performed the association strength statistics of edges. Among them, there are 900 links with strong association strength, such as security certificates used by domain names, subdomains, jumping relationships, corresponding IP addresses, etc. With the help of subgraph asset information view, we find that this group involves only one type of cybercrime industry: gambling.

---

[2] Type-abbreviation: IP-IP, IP_C-_C, Domain-D, Cert-C, ASN-A, Whois_Phone-P, Whois_Name-N, Whois_Email-E.

[3] node ID: $IP\_400c19e584976ff2a35950659d4d148a3d146f1b71692468132b849b0eb8702c$.

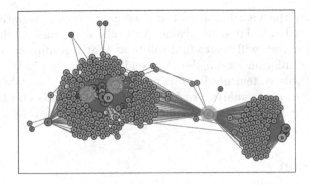

Fig. 4. The cyber asset subgraph (The core assets are highlighted).

We then identified and analyzed the core cyber assets and critical links of the gang. We found that the group contains three core cyber assets and 30 critical links. The three core assets are all SSL security certificates shared by the group's multiple business websites. Security certificates, as a necessary condition for the downstream payment link of the cybercrime gang's industry chain, support the operation of the industry chain and are essential in the process of gambling-related crimes. So we recommend relevant regulatory authorities to block the three core assets, so that the business websites associated with them fall into security risks and this may therefore cause high recovery costs for the crime group.

5   Discussion

5.1   Usability

We invited three users from different majors to use our system to complete the analysis task. One of the users had some knowledge about cybersecurity, while the other two users did not have any knowledge about the field. All three users understood the functionality of the visual analyzer in less than seven minutes, and roughly understood the meaning of the parameters that the user could adjust and enter in the control panel. This shows that our method is of low learning cost and can be used by users who do not have knowledge of the cybersecurity. One user stated that she could use the system to complete her analysis tasks with relative ease, and that the different views gave her intuitive information about how a cybercrime group operates. The other two users said they could use the system to complete assigned analysis tasks, find the criminal group they needed to understand, and learn about the criminal industry involved in the group as well as its size.

5.2   Limitations and Future Work

In order to shorten the time spent on displaying information in the interface of CAGviz, we calculated and stored the data of 11 gangs in advance. So users can call to view the visualization of any gang as needed. However, the data not processed and calculated in advance will take more time to display in the system. Therefore, we will try to find solutions that can improve the instantaneous display of information on the front end for future work. In addition, the extensibility of this system needs to be further improved. Apart from exploring cybercrime gangs, other analysis tasks involving cyber assets and their associations may also be helped by this system. The potential of this area needs to be further explored.

6   Conclusion

In this paper, we present CAGviz, an visual analysis system that supports automated mining and display of asset information of cybercrime gangs. The system is made up of a data processor, where three algorithms we proposed help to achieve the tasks of subgraph mining, core assets and critical links identification; and of a visual analyzer, which contains 7 views to display the global and local information of our dataset, supporting users' interaction and adjustment of parameters. At last, the scenario analysis shows the analysis process and results.

Acknowledgements. The paper is supported by National Nature Science Foundation of China (Grant No. 61100053) and Research Grant from Intel Asia-Pacific Research and Development Co., Ltd.

References

1. Akhtar, N.: Social network analysis tools. In: 2014 Fourth International Conference on Communication Systems and Network Technologies, pp. 388–392. IEEE (2014)
2. Ali, S., Mahmood, N., Hussain, M., Khan, S.U., Ahmed, E.: Visual analytics for intrusion detection in backbone network. IEEE Trans. Visual Comput. Graph. **23**(1), 251–260 (2017)
3. Bastian, M., Heymann, S., Jacomy, M.: Gephi: an open source software for exploring and manipulating networks. In: Proceedings of the International AAAI Conference on Web and Social Media, vol. 3, pp. 361–362 (2009)
4. Bonabeau, E.: Graph multidimensional scaling with self-organizing maps. Inf. Sci. **143**(1–4), 159–180 (2002)
5. Bonabeau, E., Hénaux, F.: Self-organizing maps for drawing large graphs. Inf. Process. Lett. **67**(4), 177–184 (1998)
6. Bossler, A.M., Berenblum, T.: Introduction: new directions in cybercrime research. J. Crim. Justice **42**(5), 495–499 (2019)
7. Chen, W., Wu, X., He, J., Chen, E., Yip, K.H.: Visualizing large-scale cyber attacks with distributed segmentation and aggregation. IEEE Trans. Visual Comput. Graph. **18**(12), 2251–2260 (2012)
8. Chen, Y., Guan, Z., Zhang, R., Du, X., Wang, Y.: A survey on visualization approaches for exploring association relationships in graph data. J. Vis. **22**, 625–639 (2019)
9. D'Amico, A., Buchanan, L., Goodall, J., Walczak, P.: Mission impact of cyber events: scenarios and ontology to express the relationships between cyber assets, missions, and users. Technical report, Applied Visions Inc Northport NY (2009)

10. Dijkstra, E.W.: A note on two problems in connexion with graphs. In: Edsger Wybe Dijkstra: His Life, Work, and Legacy, pp. 287–290 (2022)
11. Gibson, H., Faith, J., Vickers, P.: A survey of two-dimensional graph layout techniques for information visualisation. Inf. Vis. **12**(3–4), 324–357 (2013)
12. Harel, D., Koren, Y.: Graph drawing by high-dimensional embedding. J. Graph. Algorithms Appl. **8**, 195–214 (2006)
13. Jacomy, M., Venturini, T., Heymann, S., Bastian, M.: Forceatlas2, a continuous graph layout algorithm for handy network visualization designed for the Gephi software. PLoS ONE **9**(6), e98679 (2014)
14. Knijnenburg, B.P., Willemsen, M.C., Gantner, Z., Van Hoof, J., Frens, J., Tintarev, N.: Visualizing network behavior with self-organizing maps. IEEE Trans. Visual Comput. Graph. **17**(12), 2021–2030 (2011)
15. Koike, H., Ohno, K., Koizumi, K.: Visualizing cyber attacks using IP matrix. In: IEEE Workshop on Visualization for Computer Security, 2005, (VizSEC 2005). IEEE (2005)
16. Leichtnam, L., Wu, H.Y., Deshpande, A., Ghani, R.: STARLORD: linked security data exploration in a 3d graph. In: 2017 IEEE Symposium on Visualization for Cyber Security (VizSec). IEEE (2017)
17. Li, C., Ueno, M.: An extended depth-first search algorithm for optimal triangulation of Bayesian networks. Int. J. Approximate Reason. **80**, 294–312 (2017)
18. Li, J., et al.: Automatic detection and classification system of domestic waste via multimodel cascaded convolutional neural network. IEEE Trans. Industr. Inf. **18**(1), 163–173 (2021)
19. Li, J., Bi, C.: Visual analysis of air pollution spatio-temporal patterns. Visual Comput., 1–12 (2023)
20. Meyer, B.: Competitive learning of network diagram layout. In: Proceedings 1998 IEEE Symposium on Visual Languages (Cat. No. 98TB100254), pp. 56–63. IEEE (1998)
21. Noack, A.: An energy model for visual graph clustering. In: Liotta, G. (ed.) GD 2003. LNCS, vol. 2912, pp. 425–436. Springer, Heidelberg (2004). https://doi.org/10.1007/978-3-540-24595-7_40
22. Noack, A.: Energy models for graph clustering. J. Graph Algorithms Appl. **11**(2), 453–480 (2007)
23. Noel, S., Weaver, C., Diggory, J., Heath, C., Pooch, U., Jakobsson, M.: Multiple coordinated views for network attack graphs. In: IEEE Workshop on Visualization for Computer Security, 2005, (VizSEC 05). IEEE (2005)
24. Sheng, B., Li, P., Zhang, Y., Mao, L., Chen, C.P.: GreenSea: visual soccer analysis using broad learning system. IEEE Trans. Cybern. **51**(3), 1463–1477 (2020)
25. Zhao Ying, F.S., Xin, Z.: Constructing and visualizing cyber asset graphs of cybercrime gangs. J. Comput.-Aided Des. Comput. Graph

KDEM: A Knowledge-Driven Exploration Model for Indoor Crowd Evacuation Simulation

Yuji Shen[1], Bohao Zhang[1], Chen Li[1], Changbo Wang[1], and Gaoqi He[1,2(✉)]

[1] East China Normal University, Shanghai 200062, China
yjshen@stu.ecnu.edu.cn
[2] Chongqing Key Laboratory of Precision Optics, Chongqing Institute of East China Normal University, Chongqing, China
gqhe@cs.ecnu.edu.cn

Abstract. Knowledge plays an important role in the indoor crowd evacuation. However, most evacuation simulation models assume that the agent is familiar with the simulation scene and does not apply the posterior knowledge to the simulation. This also makes it difficult for these models to judge the real situation of unfamiliar and complex scenes effectively. This study proposes a Knowledge-Driven Evacuation Model (KDEM), focusing on indoor crowd evacuation. In order to adapt the model to more complex scenarios, we refine the building structure knowledge and add bridge knowledge, and clarify the role of building object knowledge of safety signs and dangerous sources. The SEIR model is used to construct the function of knowledge dissemination and decay, and knowledge discovery is proposed as another way of knowledge acquisition. An exploration module is proposed, using Dijkstra and ORCA models, to help agents plan goals and paths and avoid obstacles in action. The experimental results show that the KDEM model conforms to the real situation and can provide practical guidance for public safety.

Keywords: Crowd Simulation · Crowd Evacuation · Knowledge-Driven · Knowledge Dissemination · Exploration Planning

1 Introduction

Crowd simulation has always been an important area of computer graphics. With the development of crowd simulation, it plays an important role in more fields such as the metaverse [4], architectural design, and urban planning [5]. The agent-based motion model is the most commonly used model in crowd simulation. Recently, data-based [3,10] and rules-based [15] models which are agent-based motion models have been continuously proposed, and methods such as collision avoidance [1] and route planning [9,19] have been continuously improved.

Supplementary Information The online version contains supplementary material available at https://doi.org/10.1007/978-3-031-50075-6_21.

These models and methods have made outstanding contributions to real security, robots, and game fields.

However, most crowd simulation models endow knowledge to agents in advance. This makes the agent only act according to the given prior knowledge or rules, and cannot obtain and use the posterior knowledge in the scene. Meanwhile, some knowledge-driven crowd simulation models often have issues such as monotonous knowledge acquisition methods, no systematic establishment of knowledge application modules, and no consideration of knowledge decline.

Regarding the issue above, this paper proposes a Knowledge-Driven Exploration Model (KDEM), as shown in Fig. 1. It is essentially a knowledge-driven model in which the internal knowledge of the agent dominates the external actions. KDEM builds knowledge and exploration modules for each agent. The knowledge module only deals with knowledge and mainly includes functions such as knowledge dissemination, knowledge discovery, and knowledge decay. Knowledge dissemination and knowledge discovery are two ways to acquire knowledge, while knowledge decay is the process of knowledge being forgotten. Among them, the SEIR model is used for knowledge dissemination, and the Ebbinghaus forgetting curve is used for knowledge decay. The exploration module is a specific module for knowledge application. It uses knowledge to find the implementation module that explores and escapes. Goal planning is carried out through the knowledge possessed by the agent and the current location. According to the goal, Dijkstra is used for route planning, and the ORCA model completes the action and collision avoidance of the agent.

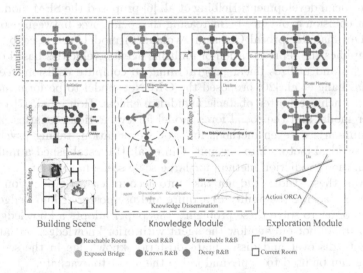

Fig. 1. The KDEM model is composed of architectural scenes, knowledge modules, and exploration modules, respectively located in three blue solid line boxes. The simulated scene is located in the orange-dotted box. The simulated scene shows the acquired knowledge and scope of action of the agent. The lower part of the figure shows the legend of the simulated scene. (Color figure online)

The main contributions of this paper are as follows:

- A novel KDEM model is proposed for simulating crowds to use knowledge to explore and find exits in unfamiliar scenes. Makes the simulation results more realistic, observes the phenomenon of group evacuation and crowd merging in unfamiliar scenes in results;
- A novel knowledge module covering knowledge dissemination, knowledge discovery, and knowledge decay is proposed to solve the problem that it is difficult for agents to acquire posterior knowledge of building scenes. Proposes an exploration module solves the problem that knowledge and action are difficult to interact with;
- A new building structure knowledge named bridge is proposed to realize the combination of building structure knowledge and path planning. Enriching the types of building object knowledge, experiments found that this building object knowledge significantly affects the path and evacuation time of the simulation results.

2   Related Work

2.1   Agent-Based Motion Model and Crowd Evacuation

Over the past few decades, crowd simulation has undergone significant advancements and has rapidly developed in areas such as route planning, obstacle avoidance models, and emergency evacuation. Many of these technologies have been applied to social development. Helbing et al. [6] proposed the SFM model, which is used for collision avoidance by increasing the social force between people. The ORCA (Optimal Reciprocal Collision Avoidance) model, proposed by Berg et al. [1] simplifies the representation of multiple agents' velocities based on velocity obstacles and utilizes linear programming to compute collision-free motion velocities. Zhang et al. [20] proposed the ORCNet model to perform parameter inversion to achieve better obstacle avoidance effects. Hou et al. [7] combined the leader model and the social force model for evacuation scenarios. Zheng et al. [22] summarized seven methods for crowd evacuation, taking psychological and physiological factors into account. Qin et al. [14] established a multimodal frustum motion prediction method for large-scale scene navigation.

However, these studies did not take into account crowd evacuation in unfamiliar scenes, lacking the ability to acquire and use posterior knowledge in simulation. In order to solve these problems, this paper adopts a knowledge-driven approach. It can not only endow the agent with prior knowledge, but also allow the agent to discover and disseminate posterior knowledge in the scene. This knowledge can be used to apply and guide the agent to evacuate.

2.2   Knowledge Dissemination

Knowledge dissemination, typically considered as a part of communication studies, has evolved with different methods and effects across different eras. Research on knowledge dissemination is beneficial for individuals to acquire knowledge and skills more rapidly. Jaap et al. [11] simulated the classic forgetting curve proposed by Ebbinghaus in 1880 using the savings method and investigated which mathematical equations yield better fits. Su et al. [8] utilized the SEIR (Susceptible-Exposed-Infectious-Recovered) virus propagation model to simulate knowledge dissemination and studied the impact of factors such as the distribution of disseminators and individual differences. Tian et al. [16] employed a dual-driver approach combining knowledge and emotion to simulate crowd evacuation, incorporating knowledge and emotion contagion in the simulation.

3   Methodology

We identify the rules for building structures to generate corresponding structural knowledge, and propose the role of knowledge of dangerous sources and safety signs within buildings. Establish a complete knowledge module through knowledge dissemination, knowledge discovery and knowledge decay. Use knowledge to guide goal planning and route planning, make exploration decisions and act. By organically combining the knowledge module and the exploration module to form the KDEM model, the dynamic escape process of knowledge and exploration interaction is realized.

As Fig. 1 shows. The building scene, mainly includes building structures and building objects, all of which have corresponding knowledge. Among them, the architectural structure can be converted into the corresponding node graph, and the node graph can be used for the initialization of agent scene knowledge. In the knowledge module, there are the main functions of knowledge dissemination, knowledge decay, and knowledge discovery. Knowledge dissemination adopts the SEIR model, knowledge decay adopts the Ebbinghaus forgetting curve model, and knowledge discovery will obtain the knowledge of the agent's current room and surrounding bridges. The exploration module mainly includes goal planning, path planning, and action. Goal planning chooses to explore reachable rooms and corresponding bridges. Path planning finds a feasible path from the current room to the goal room, and ORCA completes obstacle avoidance and action. After completing a step of exploration, knowledge discovery will be carried out again until the exit is reached.

3.1   Building Scene and Knowledge Representation

The evacuation scenarios in this paper are mainly large indoor evacuation scenes, such as shopping malls, city halls, museums, and other places. Most of the people in this type of building are not familiar with the complete appearance of the building, or even unfamiliar. Moreover, such buildings often have multiple exits, and there will be more complicated relationships between regions. This increases the complexity of crowd evacuation and puts forward higher requirements for the simulation model. Therefore, when considering the evacuation scene, the knowledge of the structure of the building and building objects becomes the main consideration. In the model, only the types and functions of knowledge are defined, and the knowledge is not directly endowed. The agent needs to explore and use knowledge.

Table 1. Kinds of building structure knowledge and object knowledge

knowledge name	knowledge effect
Bridge	Provides the location and distance of the rooms at both ends
Room	Provides the number and location of bridges in the room
Dangerous Sources	Keep the agent away from the danger source location
Safety Sign	Indicate the direction of the nearest exit

Building structure knowledge including bridge and room knowledge. The room is bounded by walls and bridges. Bridges are connections between rooms, and in this building scene, bridges can be doors, aisles, and exits. An aisle is generally an extension of a wall. A bridge is a binary structure in that it connects one and only two rooms. The room is multi-dimensional, and there can be one bridge or multiple bridges. So when considering the basic unit of knowledge, the stable binary structure of the bridge is the most appropriate. According to the characteristics of a bridge, it can be compared to an edge, and the basic value of an edge is the distance between two rooms passing through the bridge. A room can be compared to a node, connected by multiple edges. See the bridges and rooms in Table 1 for details.

Knowledge of building objects mainly includes dangerous sources and safety signs. Dangerous sources are places that the agent avoids as much as possible in the simulation. The safety sign is an object in the evacuation scene that reminds the agent of the exit. See the dangerous sources and safety signs in Table 1 for details.

3.2   Knowledge Acquisition and Decay

This section is the main part of the knowledge module, including knowledge dissemination, knowledge decay, and knowledge discovery. As shown in Fig. 2, it is a scene of knowledge dissemination and discovery of a blue bridge. The agent in state I will spread knowledge to the agent in state S and R within the transmission range. The smaller the distance between agents, the better the effect. The agent in state S and R can also directly find the corresponding knowledge in the room.

Knowledge Dissemination. Knowledge dissemination and knowledge discovery are two ways for agents to acquire knowledge. Among them, knowledge dissemination is the most efficient way to acquire knowledge. Knowledge dissemination also plays a key role in real-world evacuations, with a huge impact

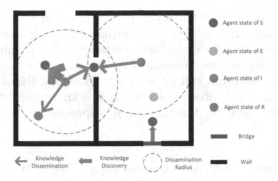

Fig. 2. The process of knowledge dissemination and knowledge discovery represented by the blue bridge in the scene. The size of the arrow for knowledge dissemination indicates the strength of the dissemination. (Color figure online)

on evacuation times. This article uses the SEIR infectious disease model for knowledge dissemination, where S represents the population that has not fully acquired knowledge; E represents the population that has acquired knowledge but is not disseminating and using it; and I represents the population that can use knowledge and spread it to others; finally, R represents people who gradually forget their knowledge. In order to adapt to the dissemination of individual knowledge, the original SEIR model function is changed and differentiated, and the following formula is obtained:

$$A_{b,t+1}^{S} = A_{b,t}^{S} + \sum_{I}^{i} \lambda_{si}, \text{if } A_{b,t+1}^{S} \geq 1, A_{b,t+1}^{S} \rightarrow A_{b,t+1}^{E} \tag{1}$$

$$A_{b,t+1}^{E} = A_{b,t}^{E} + \delta, \quad \text{if } A_{b,t+1}^{E} \geq 1, \quad A_{b,t+1}^{E} \rightarrow A_{b,t+1}^{I} \tag{2}$$

$$A_{b,t+1}^{I} = A_{b,t}^{I} + \mu, \quad \text{if } A_{b,t+1}^{I} \geq 1, \quad A_{b,t+1}^{I} \rightarrow A_{b,t+1}^{R} \tag{3}$$

Here, A represents a specific intelligent agent, and S, E, I, and R represent the states of knowledge as unknown, acquired, capable of dissemination and utilization, and declined respectively. This t represents the time step, and b represents knowledge of a bridge. The λ represents the transmission coefficient between the intelligent agent A^S with the current status s and the intelligent agent A^I with the status i. It can be defined as $\lambda = f_1(d_{si})$, where d_{si} represents the distance between the two agents. The value of λ decreases as the distance between the agents increases, and vice versa, which aligns with real-world logic. The δ represents the time parameter required for the transformation from A^E, indicating the acquired knowledge, to A^I, indicating the ability to disseminate and utilize knowledge. This parameter is a constant. Similarly, μ represents the time parameter required for the transformation from A^I to A^R, indicating the transition of knowledge into the knowledge decay phase.

Knowledge Decay. Knowledge decay is very common in reality. Knowledge does not remain fully remembered all the time and decays over time. Therefore, it is also considered in evacuation scenarios. After acquiring knowledge, this knowledge starts to decay over time. At this stage, the knowledge loses its dissemination capability, but still retains its applicability. Based on the Ebbinghaus forgetting curve and subsequent studies, it is known that memory exhibits exponential decay. The decay function can be expressed as:

$$A_{b,t+1}^{R} = A_{b,t}^{R} e^{-\frac{1}{\rho}} \tag{4}$$

Here, ρ represents the speed of memory decline, which is a constant parameter.

Knowledge Discovery. Knowledge discovery is a channel for acquiring knowledge that is different from knowledge dissemination. The essence of knowledge discovery is what you see is what you get. Every time a room is reached, the agent will update or obtain the knowledge of the room and the corresponding bridge knowledge. as shown in the following formula:

$$A_{b,t}^{\{S,R\}} \rightarrow A_{\tilde{b},t}^{E}, \text{if } A_{pos} \text{ in } Room_i \tag{5}$$

$$\tilde{b} \in \{b \mid b \text{ connect } Room_i, b \in B\} \tag{6}$$

Here, A_{pos} represents the location of the agent. $Room_i$ represents the room numbered i. The $\tilde{b}$ belongs to the set of bridges connected to $Room_i$. B represents the set of all bridges.

3.3   Exploration and Knowledge Application

The ultimate goal of exploration is to find the exit and evacuate. However, the existing knowledge in an unfamiliar scene may not be able to find an exit, so the staged goal is to acquire more knowledge faster. The agent can discover knowledge by exploring unknown rooms, and it will also receive knowledge from others during the exploration process. Therefore, the agent needs to continue to explore until it finds the exit and escapes.

Goal Planning. Goal planning requires the selection of a target room for exploration based on current knowledge. Because of the binary structure of the bridge, the target room can be selected by selecting the bridge. Remove the bridge set with unreachable rooms at both ends, then remove the bridge set with known rooms at both ends and select the target in the unknown and reachable bridge set. A room is known when all connected bridges of the room are known and the number of bridges the room has been known. The goal planning formula is as follows:

$$B_{arr} = B \cap \overline{B}_{una} \tag{7}$$

$$B_{cho} = B_{arr} - B_{rkn} \tag{8}$$

Here, B_{arr} represents the set of bridges that can be reached, and B_{una} is the unreachable bridge set. There can be determined using Dijkstra's algorithm. B_{rkn} is the set of bridges for which both rooms at each end are known. Removing this set helps avoid meaningless exploration. Within B_{cho} which is the bridges that can be selected, bridges are selected randomly using a probability function:

$$P(X = b) = \frac{f_2(P_b, P_{my})}{\sum_i f_2(P_i, P_{my})}, \quad \{b \in B_{cho}\} \tag{9}$$

Here, $f_2(P_b, P_{my})$ represents a distance function between P_b and P_{my}. The closer the distance, the larger the value, and thus the higher the probability of being selected. This aligns with normal exploration logic.

Route Planning. After determining the target room, the existing building structure knowledge is required to compose the node graph. Route planning is based on the node graph to find the optimal path. When the agent's knowledge about a bridge is in the state of A_b^I, the value of the edge V_b is the actual distance d_b between the two rooms connected by the bridge. When the agent's knowledge about the bridge is in the state of A_b^R, the value of the edge is:

$$V_b = d_b \times f_3(A_{b,t}^R) \tag{10}$$

Here, $f_3(A_{b,t}^R)$ represents a function that determines the familiarity of the agent with the knowledge of the bridge at the current time. As the familiarity increases, the function tends to 1, otherwise, it is larger.

Action and Avoidance. In terms of specific actions, the agent needs to use the node given by the path planning as a navigation point to reach the planned goal location. In this process, ORCA is used for collision avoidance and as the carrier of the specific actions of the agent. We consider the heterogeneity of agents, different ORCA parameters is assigned to each agent.

$$A_{orca} \sim U(0.8A_{def}, 1.2A_{def}) \tag{11}$$

4   Experiment and Analysis

4.1   Experimental Settings

The main building map is 50×50 meters. See Fig. 3(a) for details. It can be transformed into a node graph as shown in Fig. 3(b). The width of the door in the scene is generally $3\,\mathrm{m}$, and the width of the exit is $4\,\mathrm{m}$. Safety signs or sources of danger can be added in Building scenes to increase realism. For example, escape signs are added to the two joints Room 12 and Room 8, and the escape signs point to the nearest exit; hazard signs are added to Room 7 to indicate that there is danger here. When the agent gets the message, it will try to avoid the area as much as possible. Other experimental settings and parameters can be found in Sect. 1 of the supplementary material.

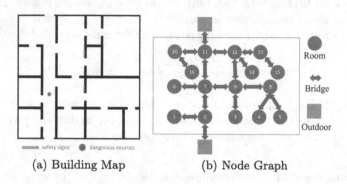

(a) Building Map   (b) Node Graph

Fig. 3. Building Map(a) shows the building plan of 50 × 50 m, the black part is the wall, the red part is a dangerous source, and the green part is a safety sign. Node Graph(b) is an abstract graph of nodes and edges transformed from the room and bridge structures of Building Map(a). (Color figure online)

4.2   Results and Analysis

Evacuation in Unfamiliar Scenes. In unfamiliar scenes, the agent has little initial knowledge and it is difficult to obtain knowledge. It needs to disseminate and acquire knowledge through exploration to obtain enough knowledge to find the escape route. This scenario is also called the unfamiliar mode. We can also more easily observe which factors affect the behavior of the agent through the unfamiliar mode. There are 100 random initial positions in the scene. Figure 4(a) shows the relationship between the number of evacuated people and the evacuation time in this scenario. The curve is stepped, and a large number of agents gather together to evacuate, which is also in line with the characteristics of crowds gathering during evacuation [2,13]. As shown in Fig. 4(b) and t = 90 s, it can be found that when two streams of people converge, there will be a confluence phenomenon. In essence, after individuals or groups of people with rich knowledge spread knowledge to others, others will make a decision closer to the communicator, choose the same path, and merge. So this merging is not just a merging of physical locations, but also a merging of knowledge. This is similar to the leader-follower model [12,18], but the leader in the knowledge-driven model is not constant, it is the person or group who is knowledgeable and transmits the most knowledge to others.

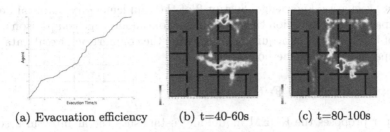

(a) Evacuation efficiency   (b) t=40-60s   (c) t=80-100s

Fig. 4. Evacuation efficiency(a) shows the relationship between the number of evacuated people and evacuated time in the unfamiliar mode. Heat maps at different time steps in unfamiliar mode. It can be seen that the two crowd streams in different positions when t = 40–60 s (b) and gradually merged when t = 80–100 s (c).

Evacuation Routes. The evacuation path is compared with the additional hazard mode, and the walking preference of the agent under the four modes is compared. Figure 5 shows four heat maps, which are determined by the position of the agent every 2.5 s. In the unfamiliar mode Fig. 5(a), the agent prefers to go to the bottom exit, and the rooms 7, 8, 9, and 12 pass by more people. It can be found that in the unfamiliar mode, the rooms with more bridges have more agents passing by. Compared with Fig. 5(b) of the heat map of the safety sign mode, the number of agents evacuating to the top exit has increased significantly, and the routes are more concentrated in the middle area. Comparing the unfamiliar mode Fig. 5(a) with the dangerous source mode Fig. 5(c), there are still more people passing through the rooms 8, 9, and 12. However, in room 7 where the source of danger is located, the room heat value is greatly reduced, and there are very few agents evacuated from the bottom exit. Proof that knowledge of hazard sources has a strong influence on the agent's choice of evacuation routes. In addition, under the omniscient mode Fig. 5(d), the heat value presents an obvious linear peak, indicating that the crowd will behave more orderly when they have

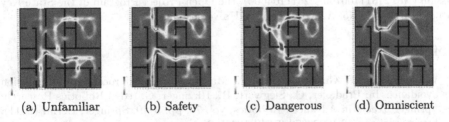

(a) Unfamiliar   (b) Safety   (c) Dangerous   (d) Omniscient

Fig. 5. Four model heat map. In Unfamiliar mode(a), the trajectories are widely distributed, and the color of the exit position is not obvious. In Safety sign mode(b), the color of the exit position becomes darker, showing a clear trajectory. In Dangerous source mode(c) the color fades near the dangerous source. In Omniscient mode(d), the trajectory is clearly visible as a bifurcation.

sufficient evacuation knowledge. Section 2 of the supplementary material details the comparison of evacuation time among the four modes, the comparison of the effects of the two ways of acquiring knowledge, the comparison of real data, and the comparison of other methods.

5 Conclusion and Future Work

This paper proposes the KDEM model and establishes the architectural scene, knowledge module and exploration module respectively. Among them, the architectural scene module converts architectural structures into architectural structural knowledge, and proposes that bridges are the most basic unit of architectural structural knowledge. Extract information such as safety signs and hazard sources of building objects to form building object knowledge, which has a significant impact on simulation results. In the knowledge module, knowledge discovery is proposed, the SEIR model is used to improve the knowledge dissemination model, and the Ebbinghaus forgetting curve is used to propose knowledge decay. The exploration module is essentially the application of knowledge, using known knowledge for goal planning and path planning. The experiment found that the building structure knowledge setting is reasonable and the building object knowledge effect is obvious. Both the amount of knowledge and the way it is acquired have an impact on evacuation time. The exploration module plays an important role in the simulation of unfamiliar scenes.

The knowledge-driven model in this article cannot be used across domains. Proposing more general knowledge categories and more complete knowledge application methods is necessary. In future work, the types of knowledge can be expanded, and computer vision methods [17,21] can be used to identify crowds and establish machine learning models trained with data so that the models can give action strategies to agents.

Acknowledgements. This work was supported in part by Natural Science Foundation Project of CQ (No. CSTB2022NSCQ-MSX0552), National Natural Science Foundation of China (No. 62002121 and 62072183), Shanghai Science and Technology Commission (No. 21511100700, 22511104600), the Open Project Program of the State Key Lab of CAD&CG (No. A2203), Zhejiang University.

References

1. van den Berg, J., Guy, S.J., Lin, M., Manocha, D.: Reciprocal n-body collision avoidance. In: Pradalier, C., Siegwart, R., Hirzinger, G. (eds.) Robotics Research. Springer Tracts in Advanced Robotics, vol. 70, pp. 3–19. Springer, Berlin (2011). https://doi.org/10.1007/978-3-642-19457-3_1
2. Bonomi, A., Manzoni, S., Pisano, A., Vizzari, G.: Experimenting situated cellular agents in indoor scenario: pedestrian dynamics during lecture hall evacuation, vol. 3, pp. 591–594 (2009). https://doi.org/10.1109/WI-IAT.2009.357
3. Duan, J., Liu, H., Gong, W., Lyu, L.: Crowd evacuation under real data: a crowd congestion control method based on sensors and knowledge graph. IEEE Sens. J. **23**(8), 8923–8931 (2023). https://doi.org/10.1109/JSEN.2023.3255217

4. Gu, J., Wang, J., Guo, X., Liu, G., Qin, S., Bi, Z.: A metaverse-based teaching building evacuation training system with deep reinforcement learning. IEEE Trans. Syst. Man Cybern.: Syst. **53**(4), 2209–2219 (2023). https://doi.org/10.1109/TSMC.2022.3231299

5. He, F., Xiang, Y., Zhao, X., Wang, H.: Informative scene decomposition for crowd analysis, comparison and simulation guidance. ACM Trans. Graph. (TOG) **39**(4), 50–1 (2020)

6. Helbing, D., Molnár, P.: Social force model for pedestrian dynamics. Phys. Rev. E **51**, 4282–4286 (1995). https://doi.org/10.1103/PhysRevE.51.4282

7. Hou, L., Liu, J.G., Pan, X., Wang, B.H.: A social force evacuation model with the leadership effect. Phys. A **400**, 93–99 (2014). https://doi.org/10.1016/j.physa.2013.12.049

8. Jiafu, S., Xuefeng, Z., Jiaquan, Y., Xiaoduo, Q.: Modelling and simulating knowledge diffusion in knowledge collaboration organisations using improved cellular automata. J. Simul. **13**(3), 181–194 (2019). https://doi.org/10.1080/17477778.2018.1508937

9. Jindal, A., Agarwal, V., Chanak, P.: Emergency evacuation system for clogging-free and shortest-safe path navigation with IoT-enabled WSNs. IEEE Internet Things J. **9**(13), 10424–10433 (2022). https://doi.org/10.1109/JIOT.2021.3123189

10. Jordao, K., Pettré, J., Christie, M., Cani, M.P.: Crowd sculpting: A space-time sculpting method for populating virtual environments, vol. 33, no. 2, pp. 351–360 (2014)

11. Murre, J.M., Dros, J.: Replication and analysis of Ebbinghaus' forgetting curve. PLoS ONE **10**(7), e0120644 (2015)

12. Pelechano, N., Badler, N.I.: Modeling crowd and trained leader behavior during building evacuation. IEEE Comput. Graphics Appl. **26**(6), 80–86 (2006). https://doi.org/10.1109/MCG.2006.133

13. Qin, X., Liu, H., Zhang, H., Liu, B.: A collective motion model based on two-layer relationship mechanism for bi-direction pedestrian flow simulation. Simul. Model. Pract. Theory **84**, 268–285 (2018). https://doi.org/10.1016/j.simpat.2018.03.005

14. Qin, Y., Chi, X., Sheng, B., Lau, R.W.: Guiderender: large-scale scene navigation based on multi-modal view frustum movement prediction. Vis. Comput., 1–11 (2023)

15. Reynolds, C.W.: Flocks, herds and schools: a distributed behavioral model, pp. 25–34 (1987)

16. Tian, Z., Zhang, G., Hu, C., Lu, D., Liu, H.: Knowledge and emotion dual-driven method for crowd evacuation. Knowl.-Based Syst. **208**, 106451 (2020). https://doi.org/10.1016/j.knosys.2020.106451

17. Wang, Y., Xu, K., Chai, Y., Jiang, Y., Qi, G.: Semantic consistent feature construction and multi-granularity feature learning for visible-infrared person re-identification. Vis. Comput., 1–17 (2023)

18. Xie, W., Lee, E.W.M., Lee, Y.Y.: Simulation of spontaneous leader-follower behaviour in crowd evacuation. Autom. Constr. **134**, 104100 (2022). https://doi.org/10.1016/j.autcon.2021.104100

19. Yuan, J., Chen, R., Yu, P.: Application of navigation grid corner point algorithm in virtual reality simulation images of indoor fire evacuation. Internet Things **22**, 100716 (2023). https://doi.org/10.1016/j.iot.2023.100716

20. Zhang, J., Li, C., Wang, C., He, G.: ORCANet: differentiable multi-parameter learning for crowd simulation. Comput. Animation Virtual Worlds **34**(1), e2114 (2023)

21. Zhao, Y., Zhou, H., Cheng, H., Huang, C.: Cross-modal pedestrian re-recognition based on attention mechanism. Vis. Comput., 1–14 (2023)
22. Zheng, X., Zhong, T., Liu, M.: Modeling crowd evacuation of a building based on seven methodological approaches. Build. Environ. **44**(3), 437–445 (2009). https://doi.org/10.1016/j.buildenv.2008.04.002

GVPM: Garment Simulation from Video Based on Priori Movements

Jiazhe Miao[1], Tao Peng[1,2](✉), Fei Fang[1,2], Xinrong Hu[1,2], Ping Zhu[1,2], Feng Yu[1,2], and Minghua Jiang[1,2]

[1] Wuhan Textile University, Wuhan 430200, Hubei, China
pt@wtu.edu.cn
[2] Engineering Research Center of Hubei Province for Clothing Information, Wuhan 430200, Hubei, China

Abstract. Garment simulation plays an essential role in the virtual try-on and film industries. Our proposed GVPM method is more cost-effective and easier to deploy than the physical simulation-based method for 3D garment animation. Previous methods generated videos with uneven transitions between the adjacent frames. Therefore, we propose to solve this problem using a priori motion-generation model. The motion sequences are then passed to the physics-based garment model we established, which recovers the pose from monocular video frames. Thus, unlike some methods that use 2D images as input, GVPM is unaffected by body proportion and posture, resulting in diverse simulated garment results. Finally, combined with our temporal cue attention optimization module, the movements, joints, and forms are optimized to create dynamic garment deformations.

Keywords: Garment simulation · Garment animation · Physical simulation-based · Attention mechanism

1 Introduction

Simulation based on physics principles is the most mature approach to modeling garments [6,15], but its deployment needs improvement because of high computational costs and the deviation from reality. While attempting to narrow the gap, existing methods only apply to small fabric pieces [14] and need to be more manipulable. Moreover, conventional methods are not applicable to loosely-fitting garments. To address these challenges, we introduce GVPM: A novel approach for learning 3D garment deformation models from monocular videos captured by mobile devices, which bridges the gap between simulation and reality. Our proposed motion module addresses the issue of unsmoothness

---

Supported by organization x.

Supplementary Information The online version contains supplementary material available at https://doi.org/10.1007/978-3-031-50075-6_22.

between consecutive frames in a video by effectively reconstructing the 3D geometry of a garment from monocular video frames and utilizing it to construct a comprehensive dataset. We then use this reconstructed data to train a regression model that precisely predicts the deformation of the garment in response to the underlying body pose. Our main contributions are:

- In order to mitigate the issue of inconsistent motion between neighboring frames, we introduce a priori motion-sequence module which leverages similar poses as a point of reference for expected motion. This module is trained to produce seamless and natural motion sequences.
- By incorporating physical factors such as joint shape optimization, per-frame pose, and mask weights, we present a physics-based model for deep garment deformation.
- To enhance the dynamic deformation of the garment, we have proposed a spatiotemporal cue attention module that incorporates collision constraints.

2   Related Work

Several physics-based techniques have been previously proposed that can generate realistic deformations of fabric [5,9,23]. While these simulators produce fabric simulations of high quality, they incur significant computational costs. Tailor-Net [16] and DeepDraper [20] are two methods that use garment parameters and learn garment displacement based on body pose, shape, and garment style hierarchies. However, these methods are tailored to specific garments, and therefore, necessitate retraining the model to accommodate new types of garments. Currently, some learning-based methods [1,2,4,8,16,19,20] want to reduce the computational time. [7,17] proposed a learning method for garment pose space deformation based on temporal features. However, these techniques require retraining for unfamiliar apparel and do not take into account fabric properties and the relative motion of the body. PERGAMO [3] is a technique designed for the explicit reconstruction of 3D garment layers from a single viewpoint, which can be further leveraged to learn deformable models. However, this approach does not incorporate an explicit model for garment self-collision, which may result in residual collisions in regions with high deformation. Additionally, the method is only capable of reconstructing garment meshes similar to those used in the experiments, and does not account for variations in body shape. Conversely, while GarSim [21] can simultaneously learn the deformation of multiple clothing types, there is a possibility of collision issues when simulating long dresses.

3   Our Approach

We used a video-based method to reconstruct garments and generate 3D mesh data, from which we extracted motion information about the body and clothing. To address the issue of unsmooth transitions between frames, we proposed a priori motion sequence module. The resulting motion sequences were then used in the garment module, where we introduced a physics-based deep clothing model. This model allowed us to train regression quantities that represent the offset of the 3D garment while accounting for the underlying body parameters and movements, as well as physically relevant variables. To optimize dynamic clothing deformation, including motions, joints, force, and form, we introduced a temporal cue attention mechanism. Additionally, collision constraints were implemented to prevent self-collision. As a result, our proposed GVPM approach can accurately predict garment deformation caused by changes in human pose in a video, while also achieving generalization and natural dynamic deformation of the garment. Figure 1 provides an overview of the implementation.

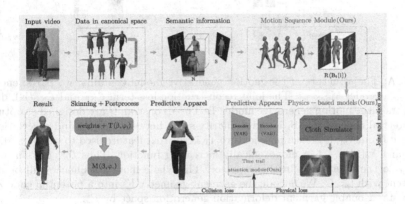

Fig. 1. Starting from the RGB frames of the input video. To extract the semantic data about the body and clothing, we first preprocess the garment dataset to mimic different body forms and turn them into a normalized space. We use the predicted body geometry and texture avatars as the base body, obtain the action sequences and pass them to the garment module, add a space-time attention mechanism module to optimize, and then mask them to produce the final result.

3.1 Frame Feature Information Extraction

The combination of image features associated with the human body is first extracted from each frame(Frame_t) of the input video. We use the recent image parsing method [10] to assign pixel labels to the input frame (Frame_t) to obtain a set of binary segmentation masks(Mask_i). Each label corresponds to a body part or garment type, such as a T-shirt, pants, thighs, and arms. Then use based on the work of [18] to estimate the surface normal N for each pixel of the input image Frame_t. We define a model of a clothed body and use the body model SMPL [11] to capture the full body shape and pose changes. We added a set of joint point offsets $\xi \in R^{n_v \times 3}$ to capture local geometric details to increase the flexibility of the human model. The model is defined as

$$M(\beta, \theta, \Psi, \xi) = L[(T + \xi + U(\beta, \theta, \Psi)), J(\beta), \theta, \mathcal{W}]$$
$$U(\beta, \theta, \Psi) = B_S(\beta, S) + B_P(\theta, \mathcal{P}) + B_E(\Psi, \varepsilon) \tag{1}$$

Where the linear hybrid skinning function L uses the hybrid skinning weights $\mathcal{W} \in R^{n_k \times n_v}$, $T \in R^{n_v \times 3}$, is the template for the stationary pose. $J \in R^{n_k \times 3}$ is the n_k shape related joints, $B_S(\beta, S)$ is the identity fusion morphology, $B_P(\theta, P)$ is the pose morphology, and $B_E(\Psi, \varepsilon)$ is the hybrid morphology of the learned body, pose, and other expressions. In conjunction with Sect. 3.3, to fit the garment model to the frame(Frame$_t$), we force the normal of the fitted garment to match the predicted normal N.

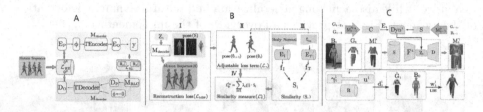

Fig. 2. A: The structure of the motion generative model contains two parts: encoder $M_{encoder}$, decoder $M_{decoder}$. The joint reconstruction loss term $\mathcal{L}_{RE}$ and $\mathcal{L}_{KL}$(KL divergence) train the motion generative model. B: Three constraints are designed to optimize the potential code M_{RLC}. S_i is the similarity score between pose θ_i and description of the input frame t_m, f_I is each pose feature, f_T is the text feature used to select candidate poses, and $\lambda_c(i) = \frac{i}{L}$ is a monotonically increasing function. Thus $\mathcal{L}_\theta^{tm}$ gives a higher penalty to the later poses in the sequence. The whole motion sequence will be more consistent with t_m. C: We encode the garment geometry F^ε into a potential code Z_t to achieve a reasonable garment deformation generation space by F^ε.

3.2   A Priori Action Sequence Module

Making smooth transitions between consecutive frames is also a problem that needs to be solved. Thus, we propose priori motion sequence module. This module can use similar poses as a reference to generate the expected motion, and is described as follows.

We propose a new approach to encode the pose as $Z \in R^{d_P}$ and then use K-Means to dimensionally reduce the pose data $P_Z = R^{k \times d_P}$ decoded by VPoser to obtain the pose P_θ. Given the motion description tm of the input frame, we construct the candidate pose set S by computing the similarity between t_m and each pose $P_\theta[i]$ in P_θ as a reference for generating the motion sequence in the next stage. We use a pre-trained motion generative model with two components: a motion encoder $M_{encoder}$ and a motion decoder $M_{decoder}$. A motion sequence of length L with $\theta^E \in R^{L \times 24 \times 6}$ is shown in Fig. 2A. $\mu = R_\mu(y), \sigma = R_\sigma(y)$, R_μ, R_σ are fully connected layers that compute the mean μ and standard deviation σ of the distribution, respectively. random latent codes M_{RLC} are sampled under the distribution $N(\mu, \sigma)$ using structural reparameterization. The latent code is further decoded by $M_{decoder}$. D_P and D_O are fully connected layers, and 0 is the zero vector. TDecoder contains the converter decoder layer.

The motion encoder $M_{encoder}$ contains a projection layer, a position embedding layer, a converter encoder layer, and an output layer. It can be defined as: $y = M_{encoder} (\theta') = E_0 (TEncoder (\varphi (E_p (\theta'))))$, where E_P and E_O are fully connected layers and φ denotes the position embedding operation. TEncoder denotes the converter encoder layer. $M_{decoder}$ is decoded and can be defined as $\theta^D = M_{decoder} (M_{RLC}) = D_0 (TDecoder (D_P (M_{RLC}), \varphi(0)))$, where D_P and D_O are fully connected layers, and 0 is the zero vector. TDecoder contains the layer for decoding converters. We define two loss functions for training the generative motion model, which is as follows:

$$\Omega_{VAE_M} = \gamma \times \mathcal{L}_{KL} + \mathcal{L}_{RE} \qquad (2)$$

Where γ is the hyperparameter of the balanced two terms. $\mathcal{L}_{KL}$ calculates the KL divergence to enforce the distribution assumption. $\mathcal{L}_{RE}$ is the mean squared error between θ^D and θ^D of the motion sequence reconstruction.

3.3 Deep Physical-Based Garment Model

The mesh data, semantic information, and action sequences generated from Sects. 3.1 and 3.2 are exported to the fabric simulation module to generate the natural geometry of the garment. Next, the garment appearance model is applied to the simulated geometry. The final results are generated by introducing the temporal cues attention mechanism module.

According to the SMPL function $M_i(\beta, \theta, \Psi, \xi)$ defined in Sect. 3.1. The SMPL mask weight closest to the body vertex is then borrowed to define $\mathcal{W}_G$. We developed a new fabric generation model that infers deformations related to poses. We convert the reconstructed mesh dataset into a dataset with the displacement of each vertex relative to the T morphology in the template mesh. For each mesh in our dataset, we computed its ground truth displacements $\Delta_D = \Lambda(M, \theta, \mathcal{W}, \xi) - \overline{T}$, where Λ is the inverse mask transformation, θ is the pose parameter, and $\overline{T}$ is the initial garment of the dataset.

Given the garment geometry G_t and body B_t, $P_t^i = g_t^i - b_t^j (j \in J)$. We encode each garment vertex g_t^j and sampled point b_t^j on the body. Encoding the information in UV space exploits the local nature of 2D convolution and helps capture neighborhood information [12]. We output the potential vector $(Z_t \in R^{64}) = F^\varepsilon(S(M_t^P))$ using a feature map encoder F^ε consisting of a convolutional layer S and a linear perceptron layer that maps M_t^P to a predefined feature dimension $S(M_t^P)$. Input Z_t, we use a symmetric decoder D with an encoder F^ε to decode the geometric feature map $M_t^\gamma \in R^{w \times h \times 128}(M_t^\gamma = D(Z_t))$. Then, we obtain vertex-by-vertex geometric features σ_t^i by bilinear interpolation. Next, we input these features into an (MLP)R to predict the local displacement $d_t^i(d_t^i = R(\sigma_t^i, u^i))$, as shown in the network architecture in Fig. 2C.

3.4 Time Trail Attention Module

We use the frame-processing mechanism as the basic building block and embed it in the loop structure, while using the attention layer to provide context and

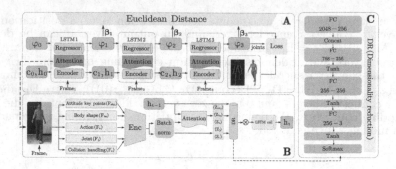

Fig. 3. Schematic diagram of the method: Block A is used for the loop setting, with as many LSTM units as the length of the clip sharing the encoder and regressor weights. An additional collective loss is defined on β_t for geometric consistency across frames. Block B illustrates the details related to the attention layer in video processing. Attention mechanisms are merged to encode contextual information from low-level visual features to refresh the loop state conditionally. Block C is the descending layer.

enhance geometric consistency across frames. The shared encoder and regressor weights are embedded in the loop structure, as in Fig. 3a. For the input video clip Frame$_t$, the same encoder extracts visual features from each Frame. As in Fig. 3b, the attention layer f_{att} and the multilayer perceptron (MLP) used to implement the context vector $z_t^{\wedge}$ of the Frame. Then encode the annotation vector a_t. The reduced dimensional layer is shown in Fig. 3c. $h_t = \Omega(i_t)$ is the LSTM cell function we set. We set up an LSTM recurrent neural network to control the entry and exit of information at each time step. We refine the temporal features of the current frame using a hierarchical attention integration to enhance temporal correlation and generate the final refined z_t by gradually integrating the temporal features in adjacent frames.

3.5   Loss Function

We use various loss terms to train our approach and obtain realistic results that conform to physical constraints. Motion sequence loss, spatio-temporal cues attention loss, and collision loss in physical loss are the new losses that we propose, and the other losses are our work focusing on optimizing the baseline.

- Motion sequence loss: We propose three optimization constraints to synthesize the motion sequence $\theta = M_{decoder}(M_{RLC})$, as shown in Fig. 2B. $\mathcal{L}_{MDP}$ is the reconstruction loss term between the decoded motion sequence θ and the candidate pose S. Coefficient $\lambda_p(i) = \frac{k-i-1}{k}$ to filter the candidate poses with higher similarity. The expressions are as follows:

$$\mathcal{L}_{MDP} = \sum_{i=1}^{k} \lambda_p(i) \min_j \{\|\theta_i - \theta_j\|\} \tag{3}$$

In order to generate motions with a more extensive range of motion, we designed a range-of-motion term $\mathcal{L}_\tau$ to measure the smoothness of adjacent poses:

$$\mathcal{L}_\tau = -\sum_{i=1}^{L-1} \|\theta_i - \theta_{i+1}\| \tag{4}$$

Supervision pose ordering with bootstrap loss terms $\mathcal{L}_\theta^{t_m}$:

$$\mathcal{L}_\theta^{t_m} = \sum_{i=1}^{L} \lambda_c(i) \cdot (1 - n(f_I) \cdot n(f_T)) \tag{5}$$

The final loss of motion is as follows:

$$\mathcal{L}_M = \mathcal{L}_{MDP} + \lambda_\tau \mathcal{L}_\tau + \lambda_\theta \mathcal{L}_\theta^{t_m} \tag{6}$$

- Spatio-temporal cues attention loss:

$$\mathcal{L}_f = \sum_t^T \lambda \left((\mathcal{L}_P)_t + \xi (\mathcal{L}_{3D})_t \right) + \mathcal{L}_s \tag{7}$$

Where $\mathcal{L}_p = \sum_i \|\eta_i (J_i - J_i^\wedge)\|_1$ is the projection loss, and $\eta()$ is a masking parameter that forces the invisible joints in the real 2D skeleton to zero. $\mathcal{L}_{3D} = \sum_i \|X_i (J_i - J_i^\wedge)\|_2^2$ is the 3D joint loss. The additional shape smoothing loss is $\mathcal{L}_s = \sum_t^{T-1} \|\beta_{t+1} - \beta_t\|_2^2$ that we suggest in order to allow the projected posture sequences to strengthen the geometric consistency. For the recurrent network, β_t denotes the loss obtained from the regressor at the t time stamp. In the cyclic structure, this loss encompasses all frames in the video clip. We use the attention mechanism to capture the spatial information of individual frames more effectively. At the same time, we embed spatial cues into the recurrent network to exploit video-level temporal constraints. The advantages of both paradigms are integrated to improve both the final spatial accuracy and temporal consistency.

- Physical loss:

We define the collision loss for collision detection: $\mathcal{L}_\theta = \sum_i \text{Relu}\left(-o_t^{i,k}\right)$. $o_t^{i,k}$ is the signed distance we compute between the garment vertex g_t^i and the tangent plane defined by the vertex average $n_t^{b,k}$ on nearest body vertex b_t^k. When predicting the dynamic garment sequence (considering the prediction in the previous frame as the input to the current frame), we set a threshold ε for the collision loss $\mathcal{L}_\theta$. When a collision occurs($\mathcal{L}_\theta > \varepsilon$), we optimize the displacement map θ to minimize the following objective function:

$$\mathcal{L}_{Phy} = \left\|\ddot{G}_t - G_t\right\|_1 + \left\|\Delta\ddot{G}_t - \Delta G_t\right\|_1 + \lambda_3 \mathcal{L}_\theta \tag{8}$$

The corresponding loss balance weights are directly related to the properties of the fabric we want to simulate. When we optimize for frame t, the resulting garment geometry will be used as input to the network for the next frame.

4 Experiment

4.1 Datasets

We reconstruct garments from monocular videos taken by devices such as cell phones and use them to build a garment dataset from monocular videos. We go through the obtained dataset to train the clothing model, which can be generalized to other motion capture datasets. We created a clothing reconstruction dataset using CLOTH3D [1]. We aim to demonstrate that our model can generate realistic garment animations for arbitrary motion inputs. To this end, we also used motion sequences from the AMASS [13] datasets and fed them into the trained regressor.

4.2 Quantitative Evaluation

To evaluate the performance of our method, we compared it with GarSim [21], PBNS [2] and SNUG [19] for motion loss. We retrained GarSim [21], PBNS [2] and SNUG [19] to obtain meaningful comparative results. Our method consistently produced lower error values in the AMASS [13] test sequence. Table 1 shows the improvement of our method over the baseline method tested on six garment datasets.

Table 1. We have divided and tested the dataset into six categories based on different garment structures. GVPM shows good stability and scalability on different garments.

Methods		Tshirt	Top	Dress	Trousers	Tank top	Shorts
PBNS [2]	Euclidean	17.08	66.54	49.05	16.14	87.08	69.65
SNUG [19]	error	16.57	15.47	32.33	15.24	34.77	17.68
GarSim [21]	(mm)	15.37	14.12	26.33	12.31	24.62	13.68
Ours		**12.58**	**12.46**	**12.49**	**11.33**	**13.35**	**10.65**
PBNS [2]	Edge	0.69	0.46	0.89	0.56	1.24	0.33
SNUG [19]		0.71	**0.37**	0.76	**0.46**	0.65	0.42
GarSim [21]		**0.63**	0.52	1.14	0.62	0.58	**0.21**
Ours		0.66	0.43	**0.75**	0.53	**0.44**	0.26
PBNS [2]	Bend	0.063	0.052	0.076	0.092	0.069	0.119
SNUG [19]		**0.038**	**0.019**	0.069	0.063	0.097	0.075
GarSim [21]		0.047	0.035	**0.037**	**0.019**	0.041	0.013
Ours		0.044	0.038	0.042	0.027	**0.012**	**0.006**
PBNS [2]	Strain	0.144	0.231	0.043	0.331	0.117	0.041
SNUG [19]		0.066	0.183	0.058	**0.065**	0.102	**0.026**
GarSim [21]		**0.053**	0.296	**0.022**	0.256	0.136	0.038
Ours		0.078	**0.083**	0.031	0.081	**0.069**	0.029
PBNS [2]	Collision(%)	0.95	1.13	1.33	1.34	1.27	1.47
SNUG [19]		**0.36**	0.78	1.68	**0.45**	1.62	1.67
GarSim [21]		0.69	**0.49**	**1.12**	0.66	1.56	0.88
Ours		0.41	0.53	1.19	0.61	**0.69**	0.51

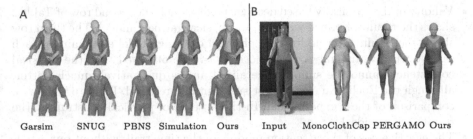

Fig. 4. A: By comparing the garment deformation results of the four methods. They have problems predicting the poor quality of cloth and the collision of the garment with the body. Our method produces significantly better pose deformation. B: Compared to MonoClothCap [22] and PERGAMO [3], our method can recover finer garment deformation details.

4.3 Qualitative Evaluation

- Based on physical constraints, we conducted comparative experiments and compared them to PBNS [2]. Our method considers inertia terms and employs a more complex material model, resulting in a more realistic and natural deformation of our garment and the ability to deform naturally with changes in body posture and adapt to different shapes. In contrast to SNUG [19]'s unsupervised approach, our method considers more dynamic deformations (as shown in Fig. 4A) and predicts them based on body-garment interactions and body-related garment geometry. GarSim [21] learns the fabric and poses aware deformations of garments. While able to handle bodice collisions to a large extent, it has the same limitations as all SOTA methods. There are more collisions in skirts and no pleat details in tops.
- Comparison with MonoClothCap [22] and PERGAMO [3]: MonoClothCap is a monocular reconstruction method that outputs a dressed incarnation encoded in a single mesh, which is unsuitable for garment modeling. The PERGAMO [3] method reconstructs the garments with poor detail and only reconstructs them for the grid they set up. As Fig. 4B shows, our approach can recover finer details of the folds.

4.4 Ablation Study

- Effectiveness of motion sequence generation module: the existing methods cannot evaluate the smoothness of motion sequences, and it is challenging to generate smooth motion sequences. Our proposed motion sequence generation module plays a crucial role in the pre-and post-frame overload of the video by further introducing the construction of candidate pose sets as a reference for the next stage of generating motion sequences. Figure 5 and the supplementary video show that our motion sequence generation module makes the generated 3D human movements and the corresponding clothing deformations smoother.

- Validity of the physically based deep garment model: the second row of Table 2 shows the results obtained without our physical garment model. The third row shows the results after adding the physical clothing model and training each sample with a randomly chosen pose. It can be observed that the physical consistency cannot be simply generalized and is qualitatively much better, although the Euclidean error is not substantially reduced. Figure 6A shows a comparison of these experiments. In the absence of physical constraints, the results are not ideal.
- The effectiveness of the attention module of the time trail: without our attention module, there would be problems with wearing the mold, incorrect pose calibration, stiff costume effects, etc. Adding our attention module allows for a smoother garment animation effect. As shown in Fig. 6B and the ablation experiment in the supplemental video.

Fig. 5. Smooth video frames: Reconstruction detail the effect of the same garment under different movement changes.

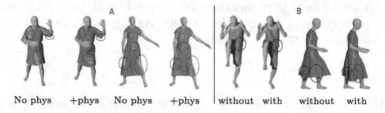

No phys   +phys   No phys   +phys   without   with   without   with

Fig. 6. The figure A shows that adding our physics module will have a good deformation effect, and a slightly more complex action (such as lifting the leg) can also be handled better. The figure B shows adding our spatiotemporal cue module will have a smoother effect and can handle self-collision well. A more reasonable sagging effect can be produced at the cuffs, and a more reasonable deformation pleat can be produced at the skirt.

Table 2. We have compared the physical terms with and without our physical garment model. The table shows that our method produces deformations more in line with the physics-based simulator. As well as validating the superiority of the loss combination.

Physical	Strain	Bend	Collision	Error
No phys	0.438	0.121	3.05%	18.23
+phys	0.062	0.023	0.69%	16.67

Loss Combinations	Collision	Error
No Loss	6.17%	25.69
$\mathcal{L}_{Phy}$	5.64%	18.17
$\mathcal{L}_{Phy} + \mathcal{L}_f$	2.16%	13.23
$\mathcal{L}_{Phy} + \mathcal{L}_f + \mathcal{L}_m$	0.66%	11.61

5   Conclusions and Limitations

We propose a method called GVPM to learn 3D garment deformable models from monocular videos, mainly through our proposed a priori motion sequences, optimization of spatiotemporal cue attention mechanism, and physical constraints. These enable us to achieve smooth video playback and joint training of multiple garments with different topologies, fabrics, and looseness. We realistically reproduce the details of the garments while following changes in the body. Compared with existing methods, our approach can accurately predict the deformation of garments in videos and achieve matching garments with different styles of the human body in videos. This way, we can achieve virtual and real-world similarities in 3D garment simulations while extracting unknown body motions from other motion capture datasets.

Despite the progress of our method in 3D clothing modeling and animation simulation, it still has some limitations. First, generating candidate poses outside the distribution is challenging, which limits the ability to generate complex motions. Second, although we normalize the 3D deformation to avoid artifacts, it still falls short in some areas prone to creases (e.g., underarms and behind the knees).

Acknowledgements. The author would like to express gratitude to the individuals who provided the dataset. In addition, we are also thankful for the comments and suggestions from anonymous reviewers.

Funding. This work was supported by Ningbo Cixing Co.(Grant No. 2021Z069) and National Natural Science Foundation of China, and Engineering Research Center of Hubei Province for Clothing Information.

References

1. Bertiche, H., Madadi, M., Escalera, S.: CLOTH3D: clothed 3D humans. In: Vedaldi, A., Bischof, H., Brox, T., Frahm, J.-M. (eds.) ECCV 2020. LNCS, vol. 12365, pp. 344–359. Springer, Cham (2020). https://doi.org/10.1007/978-3-030-58565-5_21

2. Bertiche, H., Madadi, M., Escalera, S.: PBNS: physically based neural simulator for unsupervised garment pose space deformation. arXiv preprint arXiv:2012.11310 (2020)
3. Casado-Elvira, A., Trinidad, M.C., Casas, D.: PERGAMO: personalized 3d garments from monocular video. arXiv preprint arXiv:2210.15040 (2022)
4. Cha, I.H., Ko, H.S.: BLI-resolver: resolving the boundary-loop-interior type intersections for clothing simulation. Vis. Comput. **38**(4), 1359–1368 (2022)
5. Chen, Z., et al.: Three stages of 3d virtual try-on network with appearance flow and shape field. Vis. Comput., 1–15 (2023)
6. Cirio, G., Lopez-Moreno, J., Miraut, D., Otaduy, M.A.: Yarn-level simulation of woven cloth. ACM Trans. Graph. (TOG) **33**(6), 1–11 (2014)
7. Lahner, Z., Cremers, D., Tung, T.: Deepwrinkles: accurate and realistic clothing modeling. In: Proceedings of the European Conference on Computer Vision (ECCV), pp. 667–684 (2018)
8. Lee, S.B., Lee, K.W., Ko, H.S.: Regularly striped preconditioner for implicit clothing simulation. Vis. Comput. **38**(8), 2827–2838 (2022)
9. Li, J., et al.: An implicit frictional contact solver for adaptive cloth simulation. ACM Trans. Graph. (TOG) **37**(4), 1–15 (2018)
10. Li, P., Xu, Y., Wei, Y., Yang, Y.: Self-correction for human parsing. IEEE Trans. Pattern Anal. Mach. Intell. **44**(6), 3260–3271 (2020)
11. Loper, M., Mahmood, N., Romero, J., Pons-Moll, G., Black, M.J.: SMPL: a skinned multi-person linear model. ACM Trans. Graph. (TOG) **34**(6), 1–16 (2015)
12. Ma, Q., Saito, S., Yang, J., Tang, S., Black, M.J.: Scale: modeling clothed humans with a surface codec of articulated local elements. In: Proceedings of the IEEE/CVF Conference on Computer Vision and Pattern Recognition, pp. 16082–16093 (2021)
13. Mahmood, N., Ghorbani, N., Troje, N.F., Pons-Moll, G., Black, M.J.: Amass: archive of motion capture as surface shapes. In: Proceedings of the IEEE/CVF International Conference on Computer Vision, pp. 5442–5451 (2019)
14. Miguel, E., et al.: Data-driven estimation of cloth simulation models. In: Computer Graphics Forum, vol. 31, pp. 519–528. Wiley Online Library (2012)
15. Narain, R., Samii, A., O'brien, J.F.: Adaptive anisotropic remeshing for cloth simulation. ACM Trans. Graph. (TOG) **31**(6), 1–10 (2012)
16. Patel, C., Liao, Z., Pons-Moll, G.: TailorNet: predicting clothing in 3d as a function of human pose, shape and garment style. In: Proceedings of the IEEE/CVF Conference on Computer Vision and Pattern Recognition, pp. 7365–7375 (2020)
17. Qin, Y., Chi, X., Sheng, B., Lau, R.W.: GuideRender: large-scale scene navigation based on multi-modal view frustum movement prediction. Vis. Comput., 1–11 (2023)
18. Saito, S., Simon, T., Saragih, J., Joo, H.: PIFuHD: multi-level pixel-aligned implicit function for high-resolution 3d human digitization. In: Proceedings of the IEEE/CVF Conference on Computer Vision and Pattern Recognition, pp. 84–93 (2020)
19. Santesteban, I., Otaduy, M.A., Casas, D.: SNUG: self-supervised neural dynamic garments. In: Proceedings of the IEEE/CVF Conference on Computer Vision and Pattern Recognition, pp. 8140–8150 (2022)
20. Tiwari, L., Bhowmick, B.: DeepDraper: fast and accurate 3d garment draping over a 3d human body. In: Proceedings of the IEEE/CVF International Conference on Computer Vision, pp. 1416–1426 (2021)

21. Tiwari, L., Bhowmick, B.: GarSim: particle based neural garment simulator. In: Proceedings of the IEEE/CVF Winter Conference on Applications of Computer Vision, pp. 4472–4481 (2023)
22. Xiang, D., Prada, F., Wu, C., Hodgins, J.: MonoClothcap: towards temporally coherent clothing capture from monocular RGB video. In: 2020 International Conference on 3D Vision (3DV), pp. 322–332. IEEE (2020)
23. Zeller, C.: Cloth simulation on the GPU. In: ACM SIGGRAPH 2005 Sketches, pp. 39-es (2005)

Deep Reinforced Navigation of Agents in 2D Platform Video Games

Emanuele Balloni$^{(\boxtimes)}$ ⓘ, Marco Mameli ⓘ, Adriano Mancini ⓘ,
and Primo Zingaretti ⓘ

Università Politecnica delle Marche, Ancona, Italy
e.balloni@pm.univpm.it

Abstract. The use of Artificial Intelligence in Computer Graphics can be applied to video games to a great extent, from human-computer interaction to character animation. The development of increasingly complex environments and, consequently, ever increasing state-spaces, brought the necessity of new AI approaches. This is why Deep Reinforcement Learning is becoming widespread also in this domain, by enabling training of agents capable of out-performing humans. This work aims to develop a methodology to train intelligent agents, allowing them to perform the task of interacting and navigating through complex 2D environments, achieving different goals. Two platform video games have been examined: one is a level-based platformer, which provides a "static" environment, while the other is an endless-type video game, in which elements change randomly every game, making the environment more "dynamic". Different experiments have been performed, with different configuration settings; in both cases, trained agents showed good performance results, proving the effectiveness of the proposed method. In particular, in both scenarios the stable cumulative reward achieved corresponds to the highest value of all the trainings performed, and the policy and value loss obtained show really low values.

Keywords: Human-Computer Interaction · Environment exploration · Character animation · Deep Reinforcement Learning · Video games

1 Introduction

Computer Graphics (CG) and Artificial Intelligence (AI) are two rapidly growing fields that are changing the way we interact with technology. The interaction between these two fields is leading to the development of new and innovative technologies that are changing the way we interact with computers and the world around us. For example, computer graphics can be used to create realistic and interactive environments for AI systems to operate in [33,34,36], and AI can be used to enhance and interpret models generated by computer graphics [16,28]. This interaction has the potential to revolutionize fields such as gaming, entertainment and education, and has limitless applications in fields such as medicine, robotics and engineering.

B. Sheng et al. (Eds.): CGI 2023, LNCS 14497, pp. 288–308, 2024.
https://doi.org/10.1007/978-3-031-50075-6_23

Concerning the video games field, AI has been leveraged in many scenarios: to create realistic character animations [2,17], to improve performances in games [1,32] or to achieve in-game performances comparable to that of a human being [6]. The latter focuses predominantly on the study of the complex interactions between humans and computers and between agents and game environments [27]. The variety of environments and problems to be solved make video games a perfect field for AI research. AI in video games is based on perception, exploration and decision-making within a game environment. There are several challenges in this field: the state-space can be very large, especially in strategic games, learning a policy to make the right decisions in environments with unknown dynamics is not an easy task and transferring AI skills from one game to another is a significant challenge.

These challenges were solved through Reinforcement Learning (RL) for a long time. In recent years, we have witnessed the development of Deep Learning (DL), capable of achieving remarkable results in areas such as computer vision and natural language processing. The combination of RL and DL has led to the development of Deep Reinforcement Learning (DRL), which has made it possible to train agents in high-dimensional spaces, drastically increasing the generalization and scalability of classical RL algorithms. In particular, in the video game and simulation domain, DRL has made significant progress, also thanks to the development of both general (e.g., ALE, OpenAI Gym, ML-Agents) and game-specific (e.g., ViZDoom, StarCraft, Dota 2) benchmarking platforms.

In this context, the aim of this work is to develop a methodology to enable agents to efficiently and effectively navigate in goal-oriented environments, by leveraging DRL. More specifically, 2D platform video games have been taken into account, aiming to reach and exceed human performances by training intelligent agents. To achieve such objectives, two environments have been chosen, the first one being a level-based platformer, which provide a more "static" environment, and the second one being an endless runner platformer, which has more "dynamic" aspects, due to the randomness of its environment. The development of intelligent agents can enable more realistic human-computer interactions, e.g., smart game assistants that can interact with players by giving them advices to progress in a level or to overcome certain obstacles. Also, trained agents can be used to take over character's control to aid players in case of difficulties. Animations play an important role in this context, as they are strictly tied to actions that the agent can perform and, by increasing or changing actions in the training phase, the number or type of animations can increase accordingly. This final aspect has not been the focus of this work, but it can be certainly explored in future developments.

The main contributions of this work can be identified as follows:

- The creation of 2 different environments, both suitable for DRL training, starting from existing 2D platform video games
- The creation of the general DRL pipeline (choosing observations, actions and rewards) for both video games

- The development of modification to the video games, to make them suitable for DRL; in particular, in the second video game, a checkpoint system has been created from scratch, which was essential for the correct training of the agent
- The development of DRL neural networks able to overcome challenges in the aforementioned environments.

The paper is structured as follows: Sect. 2 presents an overview on video game platforms suitable for DRL and the state-of-the-art DRL techniques. Furthermore, Unity Machine Learning Agents Toolkit is introduced, along with its DRL cycle. Section 3 introduces the case studies and the metrics used for the evaluation. In Sect. 4 the settings used, the experiments performed and the results obtained are shown, discussing and comparing them. Finally, Sect. 5 includes concluding notes on the work and possible future developments.

2 State-of-the-Art

2.1 DRL in Video Games

DRL is based on the complementary use of Deep Learning and Reinforcement Learning. In recent years, there has been an increasing interest in DRL within the video game industry. Several training and benchmark platforms have been created over time. In particular, they can be divided into general platforms and specific platforms (focused on a single video game).

Among the available platforms, we have Arcade Learning Environment (ALE) [5], which includes a multitude of Atari 2600 games; OpenAI Gym [7], which contains a variety of Atari games, board games, 2D and 3D robots (development has been recently handed to an external team[1]); OpenAI Universe, which includes a wide range of video games; OpenAI Gym Retro, which extends Gym with NEC, Nintendo and Sega video games; DeepMind Lab [4], which is a first-person learning environment; Unity ML-Agents Toolkit [13], which is a tool to create and integrate simulation environments. This is the platform chosen for the experiments. Despite not being specific to a single video game, each of these platforms specializes in a different category or genre of video games; for example, ALE only handles Atari 2600 games, and DeepMind Lab first-person games. Unity ML-Agents Toolkit, on the other hand, can handle pretty much every game created in Unity; this flexibility compared to the others is part of the reason why it was chosen for the experiments.

Among the specific platforms we can find first-person games platforms, such as Malmo [12], which presents an environment based on the video game Minecraft, TORCS [9], which is a racing simulator and ViZDoom [14], which is a platform based on the first-person shooter game Doom. Real-time strategy (RTS) video games are another popular genre in this field, counting different benchmark environments, such as TorchCraft [30], which is a platform created

---

[1] https://gymnasium.farama.org/.

by Facebook for the videogame StarCraft I, and DeepMind [31], which presents an environment for training networks in StarCraft II. Finally, Google introduced Google Research Football [15], an environment based on the open-source video game Gameplay Football. These platforms focus on a single video game, with the advantage of being able to create a training environment that is tailored to that specific game; on the other hand, they do not offer the choice and flexibility provided by general platforms such as OpenAI Gym or Unity ML-Agents Toolkit.

2.2 DRL Methods

We can distinguish 3 main categories of methods within DRL in literature: value-based, model-based and policy-based.

Value-based DRL algorithms learn based on the state or state-action pair. They act by following the best action in the state. The most famous algorithm is Deep Q-network (DQN) [19], which receives raw pixels as input and outputs a value function to estimate future rewards. Some recent algorithms include: Rainbow [11], which combines 6 of the DQN-based algorithms, showing how each contributes to improving overall performance; RUDDER [3], used to deal with finite MDPs with delayed rewards, which proposes two methods to bring future rewards toward zero, attempting, in this way, to remove the problems of bias and high variance; Ape-X DQfD [21], which uses a new transformed Bellman operator to process variable density and scale rewards, an auxiliary loss to extend the planning horizon and human demonstrations to guide the agent to higher reward states; Soft DQN [23], which is a version of Q-learning for entropy-regularized environments.

Model-based DRL algorithms create a model of the environment and they use it to learn. Some recent algorithms in this category include: World Model [10], which trains a generative RNN via unsupervised learning to model RL environments through compressed spatiotemporal representations. The extracted features are inserted into simple and compact policies and trained through evolution; Value Propagation (VProp) [20], which is based on value iteration and is a set of efficient differential planning modules; MuZero [22], which is an algorithm that combines tree-based search with a trained model; when applied iteratively it succeeds in predicting rewards, action selection policy and the value function.

Policy-based DRL algorithms (also called policy gradient) [35] directly learn the policy function that maps the state to the action and act on the basis of the best policy, always trying to improve it. The Actor-Critic algorithm [29] improves the policy gradient with a value-based evaluation. Asynchronous Advantage Actor-Critic (A3C) [18] improves Actor-Critic by implementing parallel training, by which multiple agents in parallel environments update a global value function, thereby increasing the efficiency and effectiveness of the state-space exploration. Trust Region Policy Optimization (TRPO) [24] is a policy optimization algorithm that guarantees monotonic improvements. It uses Actor-Critic in its A2C version. TRPO computes an ascending direction to improve the policy gradient and this can ensure small changes in the policy distribution. Proximal Policy

Optimization (PPO) [26] enhances TRPO by clipping the objective function. PPO will be mentioned again in later sections, as it is the algorithm chosen for the experiments, due to its balance between ease of implementation, sample complexity and efficiency.

2.3 Unity Machine Learning Agents Toolkit

Unity Machine Learning Agents Toolkit (ML-Agents) [13] is an open-source platform created by Unity that enables video games and simulations to be used as environments for training intelligent agents. It provides, via Python APIs, implementations of some state-of-the-art algorithms in DRL (PPO, SAC, MA-POCA, self-play) for single-agent, cooperative multi-agent and competitive multi-agent training. In particular, PPO uses a neural network to approximate an ideal function that maps an agent's observations to the best action the agent can take in a given state. The algorithm is implemented in PyTorch and is executed in a separate Python process, communicating with Unity via socket.

2.4 Unity ML-Agents Toolkit DRL Cycle

An agent is an entity that can observe its environment, decide the best action to take based on these observations, and execute it. The learning cycle of an agent in ML-Agents consists of 4 key components[2]: observations, decision, action and reward.

Observations are information an agent has about the environment. In ML-Agents there are 4 types of observations:

- Vector observations: these are lists of `floats` that contain variables the agent should know (e.g., the position of the agent, the position of the target to be reached). They also include a parameter, called *stacked vectors*, which indicates the number of states to be stored before feeding them to the neural network, giving the agent a "memory". It can be set with a value ≥ 1, where the number indicates the amount of states to be stored (by default it is 1, i.e., no "memory").
- Visual observations: they use a *CameraSensor* object to capture images and transform them into a 3D tensor that is processed by the policy CNN. This is the least efficient and slowest type of observation in training.
- Raycast observations: these are rays emitted from the agent's position, allowing it to observe its surroundings. Figure 1 shows an example of raycasts emitted from the agent in the video game Red Runner.
  Various sensor parameters can be customized, including objects to consider and ignore, number of rays, direction and length. As with vector observations, the parameter *stacked raycasts* allows to store multiple states before feeding them to the network.

---

[2] Components are implemented in Unity ML-Agents through pre-defined classes.

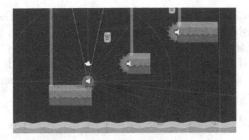

Fig. 1. 2D raycast observations example (red rays) in the game Red Runner (Color figure online)

- Grid observations: they combine visual and raycast observations; in particular, the sensor uses a grid to split the environment into cubes and has a 2D top-down view of the agent. During the agent's movement, the sensor detects the presence of objects in cells near the agent's and passes the information of each cell to a 3D tensor that will be processed by the policy CNN.

A decision is made based on a policy to which the agent passes observations. Decisions can be made at regular intervals or at specific times, through code.

An action is an instruction executed by an agent based on the decision made by the policy. Neither the policy nor the training algorithm knows the meaning of the actions; the algorithm simply tests them and observes how the cumulative rewards change over time and episodes. There are 2 types of actions in ML-Agents: continuous and discrete. Continuous actions are a customizable length array containing `float` values. Discrete actions are arrays of integers of customizable length; these can be divided into *branches*: each *branch* is an array of integers and the "parent" *branch* defines the number of possible values for each *branch*. This division is useful in case the agent needs to perform several operations at once (e.g., move and jump).

A reward is given to an agent for performing a correct action; it is also possible for an action to result in no reward, or in negative rewards (i.e., penalties). Rewards are the evaluation metric used by the PPO algorithm to learn; in particular, the algorithm operates by optimizing the choices made so that an agent earns the highest average cumulative reward possible over time.

Rewards can be divided into extrinsic and intrinsic rewards: the first ones are the rewards defined by the environment, i.e., defined externally to the learning algorithm; the second ones are defined externally to the environment; they are, therefore internal to the algorithm itself. The cumulative reward represents the average of the two types of reward. The logic of assignment of the extrinsic rewards is defined by the programmer and is a fundamental element for a correct learning. As far as intrinsic rewards, within ML-Agents there are 4 algorithms for their assignment: Generative Adversarial Imitation Learning (GAIL), Behavioral Cloning (BC), curiosity and Random Network Distillation (RND). The first two use Imitation Learning: they base their learning on trying to replicate demonstrations, i.e., actions pre-recorded by the developer; in particular, GAIL uses an adversarial generative network where a second network, the discriminator, is trained to distinguish the actions of the demonstrations from those of the agent; BC tries to copy exactly the actions in the demonstrations. Curiosity and RND are two algorithms that can be used in cases of sparse rewards, i.e., points where the agent needs a lot of exploration before receiving a compensation.

3 Materials and Methods

Two different 2D platform video games have been explored: Super Sparty Bros[3] and Red Runner[4]. Several reasons led to the choice of these two video games: first of all, they are open-source video games developed in Unity. Secondly, testing the application of DRL on already developed video games allows to understand their ease of adaptation to DRL; it is essential to consider its implementation flexibility in products already on the market (or already in an advanced stage of development) rather than in products created specifically for this task, as adaptability is an important factor. This choice also brought to light the need to make changes to the code and structure of the original games to make them compatible with the DRL process and to speed up agent training. Moreover, the two video games have been chosen because they are good representations of different categories within the same genre: in particular, Super Sparty Bros is a 2D level-based platform, which provides a more "static" environment (i.e., the level structure and elements are the same in every game), while Red Runner is an endless runner 2D platform, which means that there is no real ending to the level, but the player tries to go on as much as possible, overcoming obstacles in a procedurally generated environment, (i.e., different at each game). This randomness of environment, obstacles and terrain generation provides a more "dynamic" environment. The strategy chosen for the implementation of the DRL pipeline can be considered general, as the main elements (observations, actions and rewards) remain the same in both video games.

3.1 Evaluation Metrics

The metrics that are present in ML-Agents and are used to evaluate the goodness of the approach are as follows:

- Cumulative Reward: as discussed earlier, this represents the agent's learning metric, combining extrinsic and intrinsic rewards. It is expected to increase over time until it stabilizes when training is complete
- Policy loss: this represents the mean loss of the policy function; it shows how much the policy changes over episodes. It is expected to decrease during training
- Value loss: this metric represents the mean loss of the value function update; it shows how correctly the model can predict the value of each state. It is expected to increase during learning and decrease when the reward stabilizes

---

[3] https://github.com/Zj-Lan/Unity_Platform-game.
[4] https://github.com/BayatGames/RedRunner.

- Entropy: determines how arbitrary the decisions are. It is expected to decrease slowly during training
- Extrinsic reward: it represents the average value of the extrinsic rewards only
- Extrinsic value estimate (EVE): represents the average value estimated for all the states visited by the agent. It is expected to grow during learning

3.2 Level-Based Video Game: Super Sparty Bros

Super Sparty Bros. is an open-source video game developed in Unity. It is a 2D horizontal scrolling level-based platformer in which a character, controlled by the player, must move around an environment to reach and touch an object (a rose) to win the level, collecting coins along the way. Enemies are present (both still and moving) and deadly drop points; touching enemies or falling into one of the points causes an instant game over. The inputs the player can give are: movement to the right, movement to the left and jump (with the possibility of a double jump). The player can also jump on top of an enemy to temporarily stun them (Fig. 2).

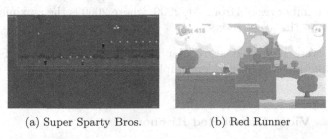

(a) Super Sparty Bros.   (b) Red Runner

Fig. 2. Examples of the training environments

Some changes have been made to the original structure of the game to adapt it to the use of ML-Agents and to improve the training itself, as well as fix some bugs that were present in the original game.

Subsequently, to manage the agent, its behaviour and the DRL process, a `CharacterAgent` class has been created, defining all the learning logic, including observations, actions and rewards. The class has been integrated as a component of the object representing the character.

As for the observations, vector observations and raycast observations have been used. 7 vector observations have been defined, consisting of:

- the (x, y, z) coordinates related to the position of the character,
- the (x, y, z) coordinates related to the position of the rose (the objective to reach)
- a value representing the number of available jumps (used to assist the agent in learning how to double jump).

Concerning raycast observations, 7 tags (which represent the objects the sensor is interested in) have been used: coins, drop zone, ground, fixed platforms, mobile platforms and enemies. 20 rays were used with a maximum amplitude of 180°, a length equal to 20 and a radius of the balls size at the end of the ray of 0.15.

As for the actions, only discrete ones were used; in particular, 2 *branches* of 3 actions each were inserted: the first represents the movement of the agent (0 = stop, 1 = movement to the right, −1 = movement to the left), the second the state of the jump (0 = not jumping, 1 = the jump button is pressed, 2 = the jump button is released, the latter being necessary due to how the game was coded in the first place). In addition, the existing class that managed movement and jump mechanics has been modified to make it compatible with the use of these actions.

Regarding rewards, they have been distributed as follows:

- +0.1 for each coin taken,
- +5 for reaching the goal,
- −1 for a game over (by either contact with enemies or fall),
- −0.0005 per step, as an existential penalty to stimulate the agent's movement (to prevent the agent from deciding that standing still was the best action to take). This number results from −1/2000, where 2000 is the maximum number of steps before the agent resets.

Decisions were requested at regular intervals (at each step). Finally, the `Heuristic` function was overridden, implementing manual input of actions for testing purposes.

3.3   Endless Video Game: Red Runner

The second video game explored for the task of learning through DRL with ML-Agents is Red Runner. It is an open-source game developed in Unity. It shares with Super Sparty Bros the characteristic of being a 2D horizontal scrolling platform. The big difference is that it is part of the "endless runner" subgenre, i.e., video games where the goal is to go on as much as possible without losing; therefore, there is not a final state of victory (there is no objective to reach). The environment is procedurally generated, that means it is created randomly every playthrough, thus creating an ever-changing challenge. Due to these elements, the network is required to have a greater generalization ability.

There are several obstacles that the character must overcome or avoid, such as water, spikes, blades (fixed and moving), falling objects and more. In this environment, the objective is for the agent to cover the longest distance before losing. The game is structured to have 17 "blocks", with each block representing a possible part of the infinite path to generate; the first block is fixed as it is the starting point, the other 16 are randomly chosen to be added to the path as the character continues to progress. Each block has the same probability of being selected and can be selected multiple times.

Some changes and additions to the game code have been made in this case too, to make it suitable for DRL training with ML-Agents.

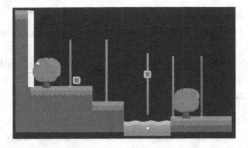

Fig. 3. Example of checkpoints (green vertical rectangles) created in the starting area (Color figure online)

The approach used to train the agent in this environment involves the creation of a checkpoint system, used to give rewards to the agent based on its progression (Fig. 3). Every checkpoint in a block has been grouped in a GameObject *Checkpoints*. The class *CheckpointSingle* communicates with another one (*TrackCheckpoints*, also created for this purpose), which keeps track of the checkpoints that have been passed and notices if the agent makes a mistake (e.g., it goes back and touches a checkpoint already passed before). This last class was inserted as a component of the block itself. Finally, to manage the agent and the DRL process, including the assignment of rewards (or penalties) when passing through a right (or wrong) checkpoint, a third class, *RedAgent*, was created and inserted as a component of the agent.

Regarding observations, vector observations and raycast observations have been used. There are 4 vector observations: the (x, y, z) coordinates related to the agent's position and the velocity on the agent's x axis. Concerning raycast observations, 8 tags have been used; they monitor: terrain, water, spikes, objects from above, circular saws, checkpoints, coins and some specifically created zones that trigger a game over, used to facilitate training. The values of the raycast parameters differ from those used in Super Sparty Bros as the environment is very different; in particular, 15 rays have been used (decreased from the 20 of the other game because in this case the obstacles are larger and, therefore, fewer rays are needed to detect them) with a maximum amplitude of 180°, a length equal to 69 (length increased because the environment is larger) and a radius of 0.4 (also increased because the obstacles are larger).

As for the actions, 1 continuous action was used and a *branch* of 3 for the discrete ones; in particular, the continuous one is a *float* value between -1 and 1 that signifies the direction of movement of the agent ($0 = $ stop, $> 0 = $ moving right, $< 0 = $ moving left), the discrete one represents the state of the jump ($0 = $ not jumping, $1 = $ jumping).

As for rewards, the following have been defined:

- $+1$ for each correct checkpoint passed,
- -1 for passing on a wrong checkpoint (note: a game over is generated after the penalty is assigned),

E. Balloni et al.

298   E. Balloni et al.

- −1 for collision with obstacles,
- −0.0005 at each step, as existential penalty to stimulate the movement of the agent (same as in Super Sparty Bros),
- −0.1 per jump (in order to stimulate the agent to jump only when necessary, since some obstacles can be overcome only by acquiring a certain speed, which is increased by running without jumping)

In addition, the environment is reset if the agent does not pass through a checkpoint within 2000 steps. Decisions were requested at each step. Finally, the *Heuristic* function was overridden, implementing manual input of actions for testing purposes.

4 Experiments and Results

4.1 Hyperparameters and Experiments Settings

One of the most important processes for training a neural network is the choice of hyperparameters; a correct selection is crucial to create a network that satisfies the required task. The most relevant parameters in ML-Agents are:

- *Gamma*: it represents the discount factor for future rewards
- *Lambda*: it is the parameter used to calculate the Generalized Advantage Estimate (GAE) [25] (which is part of PPO), which shows how dependent an agent is on the current value estimate relative to the current reward
- *Buffer size*: it is the amount of experience (agent observations, actions and rewards obtained) that should be acquired before updating the model
- *Batch size*: it is the number of experiences used for an iteration of the gradient descent udpate
- *Number of epochs*: it is the number of passes through the experience buffer during the gradient descent
- *Learning rate*: it represents the intensity of each step of gradient descent update
- *Beta*: it corresponds to the intensity of entropy regularization, used to make the agent properly explore the action space during training
- *Epsilon*: it is the acceptable threshold value in the divergence between the old and the new policy during the gradient descent update
- *Number of layers*: it is the number of hidden layers present after the input observations (or after CNN encoding of the visual observations)
- *Hidden ynits*: it represents the number of Fully Connected units per layer of the neural network
- *Normalize*: it allows to choose whether to normalize the input vector observations or not

Several experiments were performed on both environments, with the aim of searching for the best combination of network hyperparameters.

In both cases, *Learning rate*, *Beta* and *Epsilon* have linear scheduling, i.e., they descend linearly during the training process from the set value. This is due to a ML-Agents limitation, which allows for constant or linear scheduling only. In addition, *stacked vectors* were set to 2 and *stacked raycasts* to 1.

11 tests have been performed on Super Sparty Bros. The constant hyperparameters in each experiment were:

- *Lambda*: 0.95
- *Normalize*: true

Table 1 shows the hyperparameters used for each experiment.

14 tests have been performed on Red Runner. The constant hyperparameters in each experiment were:

- Batch size: 512
- Buffer size: 5120
- Lambda: 0.95
- Normalize: true

Table 2 shows the hyperparameters used for each experiment.

4.2 Results

The results obtained from the experiments carried out are reported below in Fig. 4, 5, 6. The best results were chosen based on cumulative reward, policy loss, value loss, entropy and extrinsic value estimate. The extrinsic reward was not taken into account due to the fact that intrinsic rewards were not used in the experiments, as they were not suitable for the video games taken into consideration. The latter metric corresponds, therefore, to the cumulative reward (it is therefore not replicated within the results graphs). No manual tweaking, instruction or routing of the agents has been performed.

4.2.1 Super Sparty Bros Results

As for Super Sparty Bros, the game was initially not structured to support DRL at all, with code choices that impacted both the efficiency and effectiveness of the training. For a complete solving of this issue it would have been necessary to rewrite a large part of the game code, which was outside the scope of the experiments. Therefore, choices were made in the creation (and modification) of the code for the DRL implementation, which were a trade-off between the initial code logic of the game and a correct implementation, in order to generate a neural network that works and makes the correct decisions.

Table 3 summarizes the results in terms of the final metrics. The best results obtained for Super Sparty Bros. are those of test 11, as shown in Fig. 4; in particular, it can be seen that the second training (in blue) presents an almost constant cumulative reward for every steps; this implies that the network has no possibility of further improvement. The final cumulative reward of the second training has a value of 2.061 (highest value of all the trainings performed). The goodness of the training is confirmed also by the policy loss and the value loss, whose final values are respectively of 0.03338 and 0.01346, which are really low values. Also the final entropy value is low, standing at 0.4845; the final extrinsic value estimate is 1.446, with a trend in line with the cumulative reward.

The average training time was estimated at 3 h and 15 min for 1 million steps, using a machine with an NVIDIA Quadro P3200 GPU and 32 GB of RAM.

4.2.2   Red Runner Results

As for Red Runner, the training was definitely more complex than Super Sparty Bros, not so much due to the initial structure that the game code presented (more articulated but better implemented than Super Sparty Bros) but mainly because of the very nature of the game to present a procedurally generated environment (which changes with each game), making, therefore, the ability for the network to generalize a must-have.

Table 4 summarizes the results in terms of the final metrics. Given the complexity of the environment, many experiments were performed, resulting in more than one satisfactory configuration. In particular, tests 9 (Fig. 5) and 10 (Fig. 6) turned out to be the best models, with a cumulative reward of 22.9 and 22.24 respectively. It should be noted that tests 3, 4, 5 and 6 exceed the previous ones solely in terms of cumulative reward. These experiments were done subsequently (i.e., starting with test 3, networks in tests 4, 5 and 6 were trained each from the previous one). Despite the high cumulative reward, the agent does not behave correctly, as it is confirmed by the really high value loss.

The average training time has been estimated in 4 h and 51 min for 1 million steps, using a machine with NVIDIA RTX 2070 SUPER GPU and 16 GB of RAM.

4.3   Results Discussion

The results obtained and shown in Sect. 4.2 are discussed below, highlighting the best ones and the reasons behind their behaviour.

4.3.1   Super Sparty Bros Results Discussion

As highlighted in the previous sections, the best result was obtained in test 11 (Fig. 4). None of the other tests have metrics on par. The behaviour of the agent in inference and an evaluation of the hyperparameters used for each experiment is reported:

- Test 1: not working; interaction too low to understand the scene. Batch size and buffer size are too low (they do not allow to reach rewards), beta is too high (agent explores the space too superficially), epsilon is too low (slows down the training), layers number is too low (does not allow deep learning by the agent)
- Test 2: fails to get on the first platform. Beta too high, epsilon too low, layers number too low (same parameter problems as in test 1)
- Test 3: not working. Batch size and buffer size too small, beta too high (makes actions too random)

Table 1. Super Sparty Bros. hyperparameter settings

Test	1	2	3	4	5	6	7	8	9	10	11
Batch size	128	512	128	128	512	512	512	512	1024	1024	512
Buffer size	1280	5120	2560	2560	5120	5120	5120	5120	10240	10240	5120
Learning rate	$3 \cdot 10^{-4}$	$3 \cdot 10^{-5}$	$3 \cdot 10^{-5}$	$3 \cdot 10^{-5}$	$3 \cdot 10^{-5}$	$3 \cdot 10^{-5}$	$3 \cdot 10^{-5}$	$3 \cdot 10^{-5}$	$3 \cdot 10^{-3}$	$1 \cdot 10^{-3}$	$3 \cdot 10^{-5}$
Beta	0.005	0.005	0.01	0.0001	0.001	0.001	0.001	0.001	0.001	0.001	0.001
Epsilon	0.2	0.2	0.3	0.3	0.3	0.3	0.3	0.3	0.4	0.4	0.3
Epochs	3	3	3	3	3	3	3	3	25	25	3
Hidden units	128	256	256	256	256	256	256	256	256	256	256
Layers	2	3	5	4	4	4	4	4	10	10	4

Table 2. Red Runner hyperparameter settings. Tests 4 and 5 were performed starting from the network trained in configuration 3; test 6 was performed starting from the network with configuration 5

Test	1	2	3	4	5	6	7	8	9	10	11	12	13	14
Learning rate	$3 \cdot 10^{-5}$	$3 \cdot 10^{-6}$	$3 \cdot 10^{-5}$	$3 \cdot 10^{-5}$	$3 \cdot 10^{-5}$	$3 \cdot 10^{-5}$	$3 \cdot 10^{-5}$	$3 \cdot 10^{-5}$	$3 \cdot 10^{-5}$	$3 \cdot 10^{-5}$	$3 \cdot 10^{-5}$	$3 \cdot 10^{-3}$	$3 \cdot 10^{-3}$	$3 \cdot 10^{-5}$
Beta	0.005	0.005	0.005	0.0001	0.01	0.01	0.01	0.01	0.01	0.01	0.01	0.01	0.01	0.01
Epsilon	0.2	0.2	0.2	0.2	0.2	0.3	0.3	0.3	0.3	0.3	0.3	0.3	0.3	0.3
Epochs	3	3	3	3	3	3	3	3	3	3	5	5	5	3
Hidden units	256	256	256	256	256	256	256	256	256	512	512	512	256	512
Layers	2	2	2	2	2	2	4	4	4	5	5	5	10	10

- Test 4: the agent takes the first coins and then moves in place. Batch size and buffer size are too low (they do not allow to reach all rewards), beta is too low (exploration is too slow)
- Test 5, 6, 7, 8: the agent takes the first coins then voluntarily collides with the enemy; possibility of the network falling in a local minimum. Due to a limitation of ML-Agents, it was not possible to change the learning rate from linear scheduling, so changes had to be made to the placement of rewards
- Test 9: agent jumps in place without moving. Batch size and buffer size too large (too much time passes between a model update and the next one), learning rate too high (makes training unstable), epsilon too high (induces policy changes too drastic, leading to unstable training), number of epochs and number of layers too high (slows down training)
- Test 10: not working. Batch size and buffer size too large, learning rate too high (even if lower than test 9), epsilon too high, number of epochs and number of layers too high (like test 9)
- Test 11: working network. Correct parameters

The game also has a second level, on which some tests were carried out (both using a network trained on the first level and starting from scratch); unfortunately, given the different structure that this level presents in comparison to the first one, in particular regarding the placement of objects (coins, enemies, platforms, etc.) and the subsequent associated rewards, the results obtained were not satisfactory.

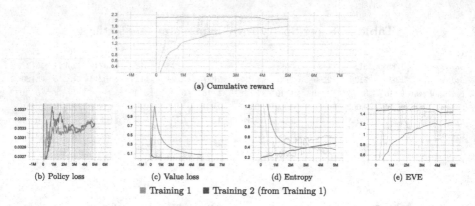

(a) Cumulative reward

(b) Policy loss   (c) Value loss   (d) Entropy   (e) EVE

■ Training 1   ■ Training 2 (from Training 1)

Fig. 4. Super Sparty Bros test 11 results on 5 million steps. Training 2 is performed starting from Training 1

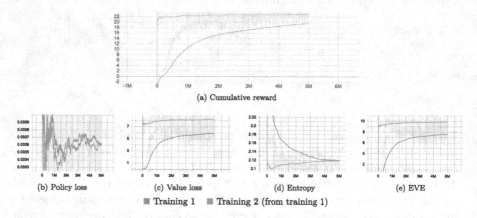

(a) Cumulative reward

(b) Policy loss   (c) Value loss   (d) Entropy   (e) EVE

■ Training 1   ■ Training 2 (from training 1)

Fig. 5. Red Runner test 9 results on 5 million steps. Training 2 is performed starting from training 1

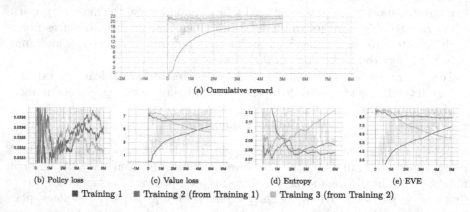

(a) Cumulative reward

(b) Policy loss   (c) Value loss   (d) Entropy   (e) EVE

■ Training 1   ■ Training 2 (from Training 1)   ■ Training 3 (from Training 2)

Fig. 6. Red Runner test 10 results on 5 million steps. Training 2 and 3 are performed starting from the previous ones

4.3.2 Red Runner Results Discussion

In Fig. 7, a direct comparison between the training of the two best networks (test 9 and 10) is reported; as it can be seen, the cumulative rewards are both high and very similar (22.9 for test 9, 22.24 for test 10), slightly favouring the network in test 9; the policy loss is remarkably similar too, standing at 0.03361 for test 9 and 0.03332 for test 10, both relatively low values and in line with the other tests performed. The value loss is pretty stable but relatively high (8.25) for test 9, while it decreases and is about half (4.632) in test 10, thus favouring the latter. The final entropy for test 9 is 2.119, with a downward trend, while it is 2.123 for test 10, with a slightly upward trend (however, both are below the mean values found in the experiments); in this case, therefore, test 9 is better. Finally, the extrinsic value estimate is 9.854 for test 9, with a slightly increasing trend, and 6.102 for test 10, with a slightly decreasing trend. In this case, test 9 is favoured, as it shows a more significant learning margin than test 10.

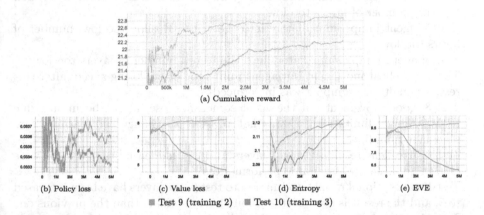

(a) Cumulative reward

(b) Policy loss   (c) Value loss   (d) Entropy   (e) EVE

■ Test 9 (training 2)   ■ Test 10 (training 3)

Fig. 7. Comparison between Red Runner test 9 and 10 on 5 million steps

As it can be inferred from the comparison carried out, both the models present some strengths and weaknesses in their trend in comparison to each other. They are, however, very similar and also their behaviour in inference turns out to be almost the same, being able to overcome various obstacles. Using the model from test 10, the agent was able to run for 93 m before losing.

The behaviour of the agent in inference and an evaluation of the hyperparameters used are reported for each experiment:

- Test 1: agent jumps too often and thus does not pick up speed. Beta is too low (the state space is not explored at its best), epsilon too low (slows down the training), number of layers too low (the problem is complex, a network with more hidden layers is needed)
- Test 2: agent jumps and moves in place without taking any checkpoint. Learning rate too low (does not learn correctly), beta too low, epsilon too low, number of layers too low

Table 3. Super Sparty Bros. metrics results

Test	Cumulative reward	Policy loss	Value loss	Entropy	EVE
1	1.637	0.067	0.234	0.611	1.131
2	0.038	0.034	2.026	2.093	4.338
3	0.996	0.067	7.844	0.692	0.391
4	0.863	0.067	4.112	0.572	0.292
5	1.737	0.033	0.262	0.364	1.206
6	0.639	0.034	8.108	1.127	0.136
7	0.603	0.033	4.392	1.351	0.098
8	0.608	0.033	1.711	0.686	0.109
9	0.078	0.027	34.96	0.158	0.044
10	0.929	0.037	0.28	0.505	0.617
11	2.061	0.033	0.013	0.485	1.446

Table 4. Red Runner metrics results

Test	Cumulative reward	Policy loss	Value loss	Entropy	EVE
1	6.407	0.033	1.834	2.47	3.65
2	1.6	0.033	0.379	2.518	0.787
3	22.87	0.034	10.13	2.285	11.6
4	22.96	0.033	10.22	2.246	11.63
5	23.52	0.034	10.34	2.302	11.73
6	23.75	0.033	10.31	2.298	11.75
7	18.71	0.033	3.913	2.086	5.754
8	15.2	0.034	2.338	2.136	3.764
9	22.9	0.034	8.25	2.119	9.854
10	22.24	0.033	4.632	2.123	6.102
11	9.454	0.033	0.371	2.02	0.957
12	−0.42	0.123	192.9	16.95	−0.09
13	−6.57	0.13	19.62	3.834	−2.78
14	10.83	0.034	1.529	1.946	3.176

- Test 3 and 4: agent jumps immediately into the water. Beta too low, epsilon too low, number of layers too low
- Test 5: agent jumps immediately into the water. Epsilon too low, number of layers too low
- Test 6: agent jumps immediately into the water. number of layers too low
- Test 7: excellent movement but agent jumps too often, losing speed; after this test, a penalty for jumping was introduced
- Test 8: good movement but the agent sometimes loses at the beginning; due to ML-Agents limitations, it was not possible to change the learning rate scheduler from linear
- Test 9: excellent results. Using 4 layers and 256 hidden units, 3 epochs were enough to achieve outstanding performances
- Test 10: exceptional results. Compared to test 9, the layers have been increased to 5, and the result is even better (though very similar) than the previous one
- Test 11: agent reluctant to cross obstacles, jumping in place when he encounters one he does not think he can pass. Increasing the number of epochs from 3 to 5 only worsened the performance of the network, making it more unstable
- Test 12: in this and the following two experiments *stacked vectors* and *stacked raycasts* were set to 4, with unsatisfactory results. In particular, in this test, the agent falls into a local minimum, trying to end the episode as soon as possible by losing immediately. The learning rate was found to be too high (making the training unstable), and the number of layers was too high too
- Test 13: same behaviour of the agent of the previous test. The number of layers is too high (slowing down the training too much)
- Test 14: the agent hesitates to cross the obstacles until the end of the episode. Number of layers too high

To further test the results obtained, the environment has been modified by changing the position of some elements. Figure 8 shows some examples of original and modified positions of the elements: in the first case (Fig. 8a, b), the vertical spike was previously positioned on a raised block, while in the new configuration the block has been removed and the spike has been positioned at ground level; in

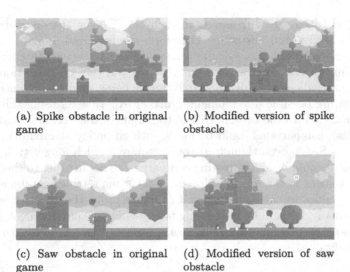

(a) Spike obstacle in original game

(b) Modified version of spike obstacle

(c) Saw obstacle in original game

(d) Modified version of saw obstacle

Fig. 8. Red Runner character overcoming obstacles before and after environment changes

the second case (Fig. 8c, d), the circular saw that was previously positioned in front of the character has been positioned directly on the ground. Even with said modification of the environment, using the network from test 10, the character was able to identify the best approach to overcome obstacles without additional training, thanks to the network that drives him. By manually tuning the environment scene to spawn these new elements only, the character was able to travel a total of 37 m before losing.

Tests were also performed in Red Runner using the best network trained in Super Sparty Bros. As expected, the network's performance was not satisfactory, as the two environments present many differences, starting from the objective to the obstacles and movement.

5   Conclusion and Future Developments

AI and Deep Learning are leveraged more and more in the Computer Graphics area, with DRL being a prominent example. This work aimed at studying the possibilities given by DRL in video games environments concerning the 2D platform genre. In particular, a methodology to train intelligent agents in different scenarios has been developed, showing that, in both the video games analyzed, it is possible to train effective networks with satisfactory results. This can enable the creation of tools for human-computer interaction, such as smart game assistants that aim to help players by giving hints for correct pathing and obstacles overcoming. Furthermore, these results can be considered as a baseline for future DRL approaches. It has also been proved how the two video games produce models that are different from each other, given the diversity of environments, objective and obstacles. Therefore, a generalized model is very hard (if not impossible) to obtain. Generalization could be achieved in environments with matching observations, actions and rewards; but the generalization problem is still a main challenge of DRL and one that is being studied currently [8].

As for future possible developments, further experiments using this environment as a base are a valid option, to test the limits of the networks and improve on them; also, comparisons could be made with off-policy algorithms (e.g., Soft Actor Critic - SAC), even though it would require a much longer training time; nevertheless, it could be an interesting comparison to do, in order to check if there is an improvement in the results. Moreover, the same settings can be applied to other video games in the same genre, to further prove the effectiveness of the networks. Finally, it could be interesting to test the same environment (or a similar one) in other benchmarking platforms, such as OpenAI Gym, to compare the results obtained.

References

1. Introducing NVIDIA DLSS 3 (2022). https://www.nvidia.com/en-us/geforce/news/dlss3-ai-powered-neural-graphics-innovations/
2. Aouaidjia, K., Sheng, B., Li, P., Kim, J., Feng, D.D.: Efficient body motion quantification and similarity evaluation using 3-D joints skeleton coordinates. IEEE Trans. Syst. Man Cybern. Syst. **51**(5), 2774–2788 (2021). https://doi.org/10.1109/TSMC.2019.2916896
3. Arjona-Medina, J.A., Gillhofer, M., Widrich, M., Unterthiner, T., Brandstetter, J., Hochreiter, S.: Rudder: return decomposition for delayed rewards (2019)
4. Beattie, C., et al.: Deepmind lab (2016)
5. Bellemare, M.G., Naddaf, Y., Veness, J., Bowling, M.: The arcade learning environment: an evaluation platform for general agents. J. Artif. Intell. Res. **47**, 253–279 (2013). https://doi.org/10.1613/jair.3912
6. Berner, C., et al.: DOTA 2 with large scale deep reinforcement learning. arXiv preprint arXiv:1912.06680 (2019)
7. Brockman, G., et al.: OpenAI gym (2016)
8. ElDahshan, K.A., Farouk, H., Mofreh, E.: Deep reinforcement learning based video games: a review. In: 2022 2nd International Mobile, Intelligent, and Ubiquitous Computing Conference (MIUCC), pp. 302–309 (2022). https://doi.org/10.1109/MIUCC55081.2022.9781752
9. Espié, E., Guionneau, C., Wymann, B., Dimitrakakis, C., Coulom, R., Sumner, A.: TORCS, the open racing car simulator (2005)
10. Ha, D., Schmidhuber, J.: Recurrent world models facilitate policy evolution. In: Bengio, S., Wallach, H., Larochelle, H., Grauman, K., Cesa-Bianch, N., Garnett, R. (eds.) Advances in Neural Information Processing Systems, vol. 31. Curran Associates, Inc. (2018)
11. Hessel, M., et al.: Rainbow: combining improvements in deep reinforcement learning. In: Proceedings of the AAAI Conference on Artificial Intelligence, vol. 32, no. 1 (2018). https://ojs.aaai.org/index.php/AAAI/article/view/11796

12. Johnson, M., Hofmann, K., Hutton, T., Bignell, D., Hofmann, K.: The Malmo platform for artificial intelligence experimentation. In: 25th International Joint Conference on Artificial Intelligence (IJCAI 2016). AAAI - Association for the Advancement of Artificial Intelligence (2016)
13. Juliani, A., et al.: Unity: a general platform for intelligent agents (2020)
14. Kempka, M., Wydmuch, M., Runc, G., Toczek, J., Jaśkowski, W.: ViZDoom: a doom-based AI research platform for visual reinforcement learning. In: 2016 IEEE Conference on Computational Intelligence and Games (CIG), pp. 1–8 (2016). https://doi.org/10.1109/CIG.2016.7860433
15. Kurach, K., et al.: Google research football: a novel reinforcement learning environment (2020)
16. Liu, Y., Long, W., Shu, Z., Yi, S., Xin, S.: Voxel-based 3D shape segmentation using deep volumetric convolutional neural networks. In: Magnenat-Thalmann, N., et al. (eds.) CGI 2022. LNCS, vol. 13443, pp. 489–500. Springer, Cham (2022). https://doi.org/10.1007/978-3-031-23473-6_38
17. Mirzaei, M.S., Meshgi, K., Frigo, E., Nishida, T.: Animgan: a spatiotemporally-conditioned generative adversarial network for character animation. In: 2020 IEEE International Conference on Image Processing (ICIP), pp. 2286–2290 (2020). https://doi.org/10.1109/ICIP40778.2020.9190871
18. Mnih, V., et al.: Asynchronous methods for deep reinforcement learning. In: Proceedings of the 33rd International Conference on International Conference on Machine Learning - Volume 48, ICML 2016, pp. 1928–1937. JMLR.org (2016)
19. Mnih, V., et al.: Human-level control through deep reinforcement learning. Nature 518(7540), 529 (2015). https://doi.org/10.1038/nature14236
20. Nardelli, N., Synnaeve, G., Lin, Z., Kohli, P., Torr, P.H., Usunier, N.: Value propagation networks (2019)
21. Pohlen, T., et al.: Observe and look further: achieving consistent performance on atari (2018)
22. Schrittwieser, J., et al.: Mastering atari, go, chess and shogi by planning with a learned model. Nature 588(7839), 604–609 (2020). https://doi.org/10.1038/s41586-020-03051-4
23. Schulman, J., Chen, X., Abbeel, P.: Equivalence between policy gradients and soft Q-learning (2018)
24. Schulman, J., Levine, S., Abbeel, P., Jordan, M., Moritz, P.: Trust region policy optimization. In: F. Bach, D. Blei (eds.) Proceedings of the 32nd International Conference on Machine Learning, Proceedings of Machine Learning Research, Lille, France, vol. 37, pp. 1889–1897. PMLR (2015). https://proceedings.mlr.press/v37/schulman15.html
25. Schulman, J., Moritz, P., Levine, S., Jordan, M., Abbeel, P.: High-dimensional continuous control using generalized advantage estimation (2018)
26. Schulman, J., Wolski, F., Dhariwal, P., Radford, A., Klimov, O.: Proximal policy optimization algorithms (2017)
27. Shao, K., Tang, Z., Zhu, Y., Li, N., Zhao, D.: A survey of deep reinforcement learning in video games, p. 2 (2019)
28. Suta, A., Hlavacs, H.: Comparing traditional rendering techniques to deep learning based super-resolution in fire and smoke animations. In: Magnenat-Thalmann, N., Zhang, J., Kim, J., Papagiannakis, G., Sheng, B., Thalmann, D., Gavrilova, M. (eds.) CGI 2022. LNCS, vol. 13443, pp. 199–210. Springer, Cham (2022). https://doi.org/10.1007/978-3-031-23473-6_16
29. Sutton, R.S., Barto, A.G.: Reinforcement Learning: An Introduction. The MIT Press, Cambridge (1998)

30. Synnaeve, G., et al.: Torchcraft: a library for machine learning research on real-time strategy games (2016)
31. Vinyals, O., et al.: StarCraft II: a new challenge for reinforcement learning (2017)
32. Wang, J., Xiang, N., Kukreja, N., Yu, L., Liang, H.N.: LVDIF: a framework for real-time interaction with large volume data. Vis. Comput. **39**(8), 3373–3386 (2023). https://doi.org/10.1007/s00371-023-02976-x
33. Wang, S., Jiang, H., Wang, Z.: Resilient navigation among dynamic agents with hierarchical reinforcement learning. In: Magnenat-Thalmann, N., et al. (eds.) CGI 2021. LNCS, vol. 13002, pp. 504–516. Springer, Cham (2021). https://doi.org/10.1007/978-3-030-89029-2_39
34. Wen, Y., et al.: Structure-aware motion deblurring using multi-adversarial optimized CycleGAN. IEEE Trans. Image Process. **30**, 6142–6155 (2021). https://doi.org/10.1109/TIP.2021.3092814
35. Williams, R.J.: Simple statistical gradient-following algorithms for connectionist reinforcement learning. Mach. Learn. **8**(3–4), 229–256 (1992). https://doi.org/10.1007/BF00992696
36. Yadav, K.S., Kirupakaran, A.M., Laskar, R.H.: End-to-end bare-hand localization system for human–computer interaction: a comprehensive analysis and viable solution. Vis. Comput. (2023). https://doi.org/10.1007/s00371-023-02837-7

A Novel Approach to Curved Layer Slicing and Path Planning for Multi-degree-of-Freedom 3D Printing

Yuqin Zeng[1,2], Zhen Chen[1,2], Weihao Zhang[1,2], Jiapeng Wang[1,2], and Shuqian Fan[1,3(✉)] (iD)

[1] Chongqing Institute of Green and Intelligent Technology, Chinese Academy of Sciences, Chongqing 400714, China
`fansq@cigit.ac.cn`
[2] Chongqing School, University of Chinese Academy of Sciences, Chongqing 400714, China
[3] Chongqing Key Laboratory of Additive Manufacturing Technology and Systems, Chongqing 400714, China

Abstract. In this study, we propose a novel approach to overcome the limitations of traditional 3D printing, including restricted degrees of freedom, the staircase effect, and the need for additional support for manufacturing overhanging features. Our method includes a curved layer slicing algorithm and a surface path planning algorithm. This work presents five key contributions: (1) it reduces most of the staircase effect commonly seen in 3D printing; (2) it eliminates most of the need for support structures typically required by traditional 3D printing; (3) its property of reducing most of the staircase effect and the need for support structures is applicable to complex topological shapes, including 1-loss models; (4) it achieves B-spline interpolation through Equidistant arc-length sampling, which is more efficient than Gauss-Legendre and other existing methods; and (5) it has a collision-free path planning strategy based on hierarchical priority to prevent collisions between the printing nozzle and the model being printed. Through rigorous simulation and comparison with other state-of-the-art algorithms, we have validated the feasibility and effectiveness of our approach.

Keywords: 3D Printing · Curved Layer Slicing · Path Planning

1 Introduction

Additive manufacturing has become a widely adopted technology in numerous industries [17]. The most popular 3D printing technologies currently used are Stereolithography (SLA), Fused Deposition Modeling (FDM), Selective Laser Sintering (SLS), and Laser Deposition Manufacturing (LDM). However, these traditional 3D printing methods are limited in terms of degrees of freedom and can only print parts in one direction. One issue with traditional 3D printing is the

B. Sheng et al. (Eds.): CGI 2023, LNCS 14497, pp. 309–320, 2024.
https://doi.org/10.1007/978-3-031-50075-6_24

need to add supporting structures(as shown in Fig. 1(b)) for overhanging features such as holes and edges, which results in increased time (32%–48%) and material (30%–60%) consumption [18]. When the supporting structure is removed, the joint surface between the support structure and the model may be damaged. Additionally, the staircase effect (as shown in Fig. 1(a)) would occur and negatively impact the molding accuracy [13]. The currently proposed dual extrusion and water-soluble polyvinyl alcohol [8] are solutions to weaken the staircase effect and provide additional support, but they consume time and increase material waste. In addition, in large-scale additive restoration projects, especially in complex working conditions [12], desktop 3D printing methods such as dual extrusion and water-soluble polyvinyl alcohol are very difficult to implement and have certain limitations. With the advent of industrial robots, the integration of 3D printing and industrial robots has given rise to a novel approach to 3D printing with multiple degrees of freedom surpassing the conventional three degrees. This advanced technique, known as multi-degree-of-freedom 3D printing, offers enhanced flexibility in motion trajectories and printing strategies. Consequently, it effectively addresses challenges that are beyond the scope of traditional 3D printing methodologies. Chakraborty et al. put forward a 3D printing method of melt deposition on the curved layer that makes full use of 3 degrees of freedom [4], but the algorithms in the early time realize layer slicing by offsetting the layer, which will lead to self-intersection, non-uniqueness of normal direction and so on. In this paper, we propose a curved layer slicing algorithm by solving Eikonal equation. In addition, we design a geodesic-based surface path planning strategy. Finally, we output the data in G code format and simulate the path of the test model using simulation software. The simulation results indicate that the track meets the expected requirements and there are no collisions in the simulation process, thereby verifying the feasibility of our proposed approach.

2   Related Work

Dai et al. [7] voxelized the 3D model and utilized a greedy strategy to establish a growth field for the convex hull. They employed the dual contour method to extract isosurfaces, achieving surface layering. However, voxelization necessitated significant computational resources. Xu et al. [19] proposed an algorithm based on the geodesic field to extract isovalued contour line trajectories for surface layering. However, when the slice layer thickness is small, surface intersections occur, and the internal structure points are not adequately represented. Moreover, Etienne et al. [9] proposed the utilization of slightly curved layers to enhance the quality and strength of 3-axis printed objects. Shan et al. [16] presented a method for generating curved layers based on the isothermal surface of 3D models, reducing the staircase effect and improving the surface quality of printed objects. Zhang et al. [20] deformed the model based on local printing directions and generated curved layers to improve print quality. In this article, our key contribution is the hierarchical slicing algorithm based on the Eikonal equation, inspired by physical principles. This algorithm can be conceptualized as the propagation of waves from one of the model's starting points. In comparison to the aforementioned approaches, our method requires minimal preprocessing and mathematical assumptions, eliminates intersecting surfaces, and ensures the acquisition of the surface normal vector for the model boundary and any internal point after layering. To optimize the robot arm's jerk and ensure smoother trajectory, Dai et al. [6] proposed a method based on sampling. Fang et al. [10] employed a vector field-based approach to calculate printing directions and a graph-based algorithm to plan tool motions. Bhatt et al. [2] employed the ball fitting algorithm to detect the collision between the printing platform and the printing head, and utilized a neural network to compensate for trajectory error.

3   Our Method

3.1   Solving Eikonal Equation Based on Tetrahedron

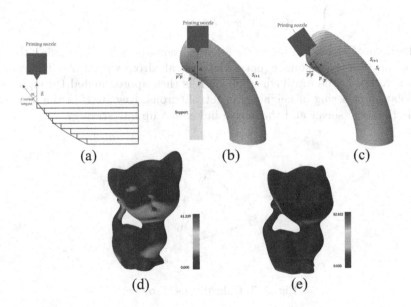

Fig. 1. (a) Staircase effect (b) Additional support for traditional 3D printing (c) 3D printing process using our curved Layer slicing algorithm based on the Eikonal equation (d) Distribution of overhang angles with planar slicing (e) Distribution of overhang angles with our curved Layer slicing algorithm

The requirement for support structures is directly influenced by the overhang angle, which is the angle between the tangent of the model's profile curve and the printing nozzle. If the overhang angle exceeds a certain threshold, typically 45°, there is a risk of the printing material falling off and causing printing failure. Consequently, in traditional printing modes, support structures are generated at locations with significant overhang angles. However, the addition of support structures leads to increased printing time, material wastage, and surface damage to the part, which can adversely affect its quality when the supports are removed. Moreover, higher overhang angles result in a more pronounced staircase effect. In this study, we propose a novel surface slicing algorithm based on the Eikonal equation, as depicted in Fig. 1(c). Our primary contribution lies in ensuring that the model's boundary and any internal point are preserved after layering, along with the surface's normal vector. By aligning the printing head's direction with the normal vector on the slice layer containing point p, we significantly reduce the overhang angle (as demonstrated in Table 1, Sect. 4.1 of the paper). With our algorithm, the overhang angle above 45° virtually disappears, thus enabling the elimination of a substantial portion of the support structures and mitigating the staircase effect. When the velocity function $f(x) = 1$, the form of Eikonal equation in three-dimensional space is:

$$\begin{cases} |\nabla\varphi(x)| = \dfrac{1}{f(x)}, x \in \Omega \in R^n, f(x) > 0 \\ \varphi(x) = 0, x \in \partial\Omega \end{cases} \tag{1}$$

The Eikonal algorithm based on tetrahedrons works by discretizing the spatial domain Ω of the Eikonal equation into tetrahedrons within Ω_T. The solution for each vertex in the tetrahedron element is then approximated through linear interpolation of a ring of neighboring tetrahedrons. Key steps in the algorithm include the local solver and the active linked-list update strategy.

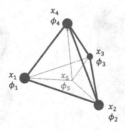

Fig. 2. Tetrahedral local solver

Local Solver. The proposed solution approach for the tetrahedral Eikonal equation involves defining a local solver that employs a fast iterative method to calculate the equation in each tetrahedron. Figure 2 shows the local solver used. Assuming that the given solutions $\varphi 1$, $\varphi 2$, and $\varphi 3$ in the tetrahedral element with linear characteristics adhere to the causal properties of the Eikonal solution [14], the local solver utilizes an upwind method to calculate the unknown solution $\varphi 4$. The velocity function in the tetrahedron is assumed to be constant, and the time for the traveling wave to reach vertex $x4$ depends on the line segment $e54$ connecting point $x5$ and vertex $x4$ in triangle T_{123}, with e_{54} being along the wavefront normal. The time taken to reach vertex x_4 is minimum when e_{54} is minimum. Then, we need to determine the coordinates of the intersection point x_5 between the traveling wave and the plane defined by triangle T_{123}. If point x_5 is not inside triangle T_{123}, it is projected onto the nearest edge of T_{123} to ensure the causal nature of the Eikonal solution. Finally, the local solver obtains the nonlinear equations in the last step:

$$\begin{cases} \phi_{1,3}\sqrt{\lambda^T M' \lambda} = \lambda^T \alpha \\ \phi_{2,3}\lambda^T \alpha = \phi_{1,3}\lambda^T \beta \end{cases} \quad (2)$$

λ and ϕ_4 can be obtained by solving Eqs. 2.

Active Linked List Update Strategy. The Eikonal algorithm based on tetrahedron uses a fast iterative method that employs an active linked list data structure. In each iteration, the middle vertex or tetrahedron of the active list can be updated in parallel. The algorithm consists of two main steps: initialization and update. The initialization step sets the initial values of the solutions for all tetrahedrons in the mesh. The update step iteratively calculates the solution at each vertex by selecting the minimum solution value from the neighboring tetrahedrons, updating the solution value at the vertex, and adding the neighboring vertices to the active list if their solution values are affected by the update.

Generate Shape Constrained Signed Distance Field. To achieve surface stratification of the 3D model, the Eikonal equation solution - traveling wave's shortest time in the spatial domain is used as a metric. We define the metric from any point in the space domain T_M (transformed from tetrahedron M) to the reference point S_{base} as a shape-constrained signed distance field (SCSDF). Mathematically, SCSDF can be expressed as:

$$\text{SCSDF}(S_{\text{base}}, v) = \phi_v, v \in T_M \quad (3)$$

Extracting Isosurface and Mesh Optimization. After the tetrahedron model establishes SCSDF, the set of isosurface points SP_{ϕ_i} is defined:

$$SP_{\phi_i} = \{v \mid \text{SCSDF}(S_{\text{base}}, v) = \phi_i\}$$
$$0 \le \phi_i \le \phi_{\max}, v \in T_M \quad (4)$$

To obtain the set of isosurface points SP_{ϕ_i}, the algorithm traverses each tetrahedral element and uses linear interpolation to find the intersection point within the tetrahedron. After obtaining the set of isosurface points SP_{ϕ_i}, it is necessary to determine the connection relationship between them. Therefore, for each tetrahedral element, if there are intersection points, connecting them can generate one or two triangular patches. Connecting all the triangular isosurface patches can form an isosurface. To avoid duplicated intersection points due to shared edges, the algorithm sets up an EdgeToPoint mapping table between the edge of the tetrahedron and interpolation points, which is used to check whether the edge has interpolation points in each iteration. Then we applied the isotropic Remeshing algorithm [3] with five iterations to optimize the curved layer mesh.

3.2   Path Planning of Multi-DOF 3D Printing

Extracting Equidistant Contour Geodesics. Geodesic is a measure of the shortest path between two points on a curved layer. We establish a geodesic field based on heat flow method [5], and the Varadhan formula is shown in the equation below:

$$\phi(x, y) = \lim_{t \to 0} \sqrt{-4t \log k_{t,x}(y)} \tag{5}$$

The thermonuclear function $k_{t,x}(y)$ is used to measure the heat transferred from source point x to y after time t. This function serves as a kernel function for calculating geodesic distance between any two points on the manifold surface by propagating thermonuclear point-by-point. The 3D model is sliced into a series of curved layers using the Eikonal equation, which results in curved layer boundaries. With the curved layer edges as boundary conditions, the curved layer boundary geodesic field (CSBGF) can be obtained using Algorithm 1.

Algorithm 1. HeatMethod

1: Integrate the heat flow $\dot{u} = \Delta u$ for some fixed time t
2: Evaluate the vector field $X = -\nabla u_t / |\nabla u_t|$
3: Solve The Poisson equation $\Delta \phi = \nabla \cdot X$

Define the equidistant contour geodesic C_d from the edge contour d as:

$$C_d = \{p \mid \text{CSBGF}(p) = d\} \tag{6}$$

To extract the equidistant geodesic point set from the curved contour geodesic field, we use the linear interpolation method to interpolate the triangle. Let ϕ_1, ϕ_2, and ϕ_3 be the geodesic values of the vertices of triangle T_{123}. If $\phi_1 > d$, $\phi_2 < d$, and $\phi_3 < d$, where d is the distance threshold, then the interpolation point can be obtained using linear interpolation:

$$\begin{cases} v_{p_1} = x_2 + \frac{d - \phi_2}{\phi_1 - \phi_2}(x_1 - x_2) \\ v_{p_2} = x_3 + \frac{d - \phi_3}{\phi_1 - \phi_3}(x_1 - x_3) \end{cases} \tag{7}$$

To avoid interpolation duplication, an EdgeToPoint mapping table is established to ensure that each edge is interpolated only once. However, in some cases, path truncation may occur, especially when the triangular patch is located at the tip of the contour edge and its three vertices have the same geodesic value.

This can result in multiple loops in the path, which can be eliminated by finding the vertex with the smallest index, keeping the edge connected with it, and removing its opposite edge.

Finally, the ordered vertices are obtained using the depth-first search algorithm, and the equidistant geodesic contour curves are obtained by connecting them. The results of this process are shown in Fig. 3(a).

B-spline Interpolation. Let $s(a,t) = \int_a^t |r'(t)| \, dt$ be the arc length of the curve. Assuming a sampling distance of d, the problem of equal arc length sampling is transformed into:

$$
\begin{cases}
s\,(0, u_0) = d \\
s\,(u_0, u_1) = d \\
\quad \cdots \\
s\,(u_{n-1}, u_n) = d \\
\quad s\,(u_n, 1) \leq d
\end{cases}
\tag{8}
$$

The unsolved $\{u_0, u_1, \ldots, u_n\}$ is the parameter space of the spline and represents the set of vectors of nodes in the spline. If conventional numerical integration calculation methods such as Gauss-Legendre are used to solve them one by one, the efficiency is very low. This paper uses a novel algorithm that shown in Algorithm 2 and Fig. 3 as a result to improve the efficiency.

Algorithm 2. Equidistant arc-length sampling

Require: Regular curve $r(t)$; Allowable error; sampling distance d
Ensure: Parameter space of the spline curve: $U = \{u_0, u_1, \ldots, u_n\}$
1: Divide the parameter space of a B-spline into n equal parts
2: Create an array to record the interval point parameters and the arc length from the point to the starting point to speed up the computation below
3: **for** each u_x in U **do**
4:    Get u_i and u_j by finding $d_i < d < d_j$ in the array
5:    Input u_i and u_j to use binary search algorithm 3 times to iterate to a value close to u_x
6:    **while** error of u_x is larger than allowable error **do**
7:       Use binary search algorithm to iterate u_x
8:    **end while**
9: **end for**

KNN Normal Extraction. Depending on the distribution and hierarchy of the 3D model [15], this paper proposes using the k-nearest neighbors (KNN) algorithm to find a suitable substitute point in the next layer that is supported by the substitute point and takes the direction from the suspended point to the substitute point as the orientation of the printing nozzle.

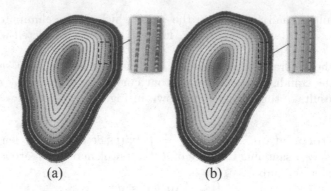

Fig. 3. Equidistant arc-length sampling: (a) Initial curves (b) Equidistant arc-length sampling

Collision-Free Path Planning. To prevent collisions between the printing nozzle and the printing model, this paper proposes a collision-free path planning approach based on hierarchical priority. In situations where multiple connected subgraphs exist on the equivalence surface, an octree is created to sample the subconnected graphs of the next layer. The closest Euclidean distance is then used to determine the inter-layer connection for the intersecting subconnected graph.

4   Experiment and Results

4.1   Experiment of Curved Layer Slicing

The time complexity of the fast iterative method for solving the Eikonal equation based on tetrahedron and extracting isosurface is O(N). The Maximum size (mm^3) of Stanford bunny, Cat and Bended pipe are 103*79*100, 60*135*168, and 98*89*146, respectively. And the Number of triangular patches of Stanford bunny, Cat and Bended pipe are 11094, 18806, and 7696, respectively. All algorithms were implemented in C++, and the experiments were conducted on a WIN10 (64-bit) machine equipped with an Intel (r) Xeon (r) CPU @ 3.7ghz (8 CPUs) and 16 GB memory. To compare with traditional 3D printing, the overhang area of the test model is calculated and the distribution of overhang angles is counted, with a threshold of 45°. The results, shown in Fig. 1(d), indicate that overhanging areas are concentrated in positions with large curvature of the curved layer. Meanwhile, the percentage of overhang angles, as shown in Fig. 1(e), indicates that the range of overhang angle distribution is significantly reduced and is concentrated in positions with larger local curvature.

Table 1 presents a comparison of the interval distribution of the overhang angles α between the horizontal planar slicing and curved layer slicing. The results indicate that the proposed curved layer slicing algorithm is more effective in reducing overhang angles larger than 45° compared to the traditional

Table 1. Overhang angle α interval distribution of planar slicing and curved layer slicing(bold)

Test model	$\alpha = 0$		$0 < \alpha < \pi/4$		$\alpha >= \pi/4$	
Stanford bunny	60.4%	**74.1%**	33.7%	**25.9%**	5.9%	**0.0%**
Cat	54.6%	**71.3%**	38.4%	**28.7%**	7.0%	**0.0%**
Bended pipe	60.3%	**64.8%**	36.1%	**35.2%**	3.6%	**0.0%**

horizontal planar slicing method. Additionally, the algorithm compresses the overhang angle to a smaller range, enabling unsupported or less supported 3D printing. Moreover, our another analysis showed that the interlayer deviations varied for different geometric models, and using an appropriate layer thickness could avoid the occurrence of maximum deviation. Increasing the layer thickness could effectively reduce the percentage of interlayer deviation. Notably, in the 1-genus model cat, the maximum deviation of the vertex reached 0.891, with a maximum deviation ratio of 0.891. The reason for this was that the point was located at the intersection of the model's branches and suspended below it, making it far away from the surface below.

The test model was sliced with a thickness of 1mm, and the information of surface slices of the Eikonal equation based on the tetrahedron was tabulated in Table 2. Our analysis in Table 2 shows that the elbow model has the largest number of tetrahedral elements and slice layers. However, its surface optimization time is significantly shorter than that of the cat model because of its regular shape and fewer small surfaces. Table 3 presents the running time comparison of various curved layer slicing algorithms. In summary, the proposed curved layer slicing algorithm based on the Eikonal equation effectively reduces the distribution range of overhanging angles and the number of large overhanging angles, thus weakening the staircase effect, eliminating most supporting structures, and realizing unsupported or less supported 3D printing. Our algorithm is well-suited for complex topological shape models such as 0-genus and 1-genus, and compared with other algorithms, it exhibits higher efficiency.

Table 2. Statistics of curved layers (tetrahedral number: N_t, number of plies: N_p, tetrahedral transformation (s): t_{trans}, solving time of Eikonal equation (s): $t_{Eikonal}$, Slice time (s): t_{slice}, and surface optimization time (s): t_{opt})

Model	t_{trans}	N_p	t_{trans}	$t_{Eikonal}$	t_{slice}	t_{Opt}
Stanford bunny	291697	113	3.920	4.190	7.498	24.350
Cat	547478	149	7.678	6.064	17.073	42.894
Bended pipe	629966	177	9.023	6.269	19.581	32.664

Table 3. Running time comparison (Number of slice layers: N_{slice}). We have enlarged our 3D model for robotic arm simulation. For example, the tetrahedron numbers of stanford bunny and cat models in our approach are 4.7 and 9.4 times that of Li et al.'s algorithm [11]. Compared with Li et al.'s algorithm [11], we scale up on our 3D original model, so it doesn't seem to be dominant. In fact, our 3D original model is more complicated. Notably, even though we scale up the model, our curved layer slicing algorithm based on Eikonal demonstrated significantly better efficiency than Xu et al.'s [19] algorithm.

Methods	Model	N_{slice}	Slicing time (s)
Xu et al. [19]	Stanford bunny	60	693
	Cat	61	310
Li et al. [11]	Stanford bunny	152	55
	Cat	153	52
Ours	Stanford bunny	113	**40**
	Cat	149	**71**

4.2 Path Planning Simulation Experiment

The path planning for the three models was performed with a slice thickness of 1mm, a contour geodesic offset interval of 3mm, and an interval equal arc length sampling of 1mm. In the path planning process, the time complexity of extracting geodesics with equidistant contours, B-spline interpolation, and equal arc length sampling is O(N). Additionally, the time complexity of the KNN algorithm based on octree is O(logN). The final step of the path planning process is to output the data in the form of G-code, which is then imported into the robot simulation software RobotDK to simulate the motion of the test model. The robot arm used in the simulation is the ABB IRB 2600-20/1.65. Figure 4 depicts the simulation process of the printing of the rabbit model. The simulation shows that there are no collisions during the printing process. In Fig. 5, the final printing simulation diagram of the test model is presented. The blue track represents the empty stroke of the printing nozzle. The simulation results validate the accuracy and effectiveness of the curved layer slicing based on the Eikonal equation and the surface path planning based on the geodesic. The absence of any collision during the printing process demonstrates that the algorithm is capable of generating a feasible printing path without requiring additional supports.

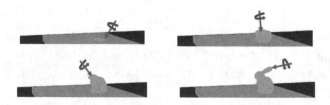

Fig. 4. 3D printing simulation process of bunny model

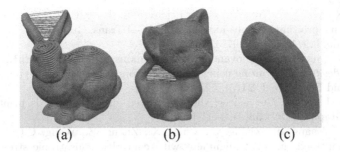

(a)   (b)   (c)

Fig. 5. 3D printing simulation

5 Conclusion and Future Work

This paper proposes a comprehensive solution for curved layer slicing and path planning of multi-degree-of-freedom additive manufacturing, which is verified by comparative experiments and simulation tests. Our algorithm is suitable for 6DOF devices and 3+2DOF devices. However, for 4DOF devices, the normal vector of the print head to any point on the layer cannot be guaranteed due to the lack of flexibility of the nozzle. Additionally, different layer thicknesses require the real-time adjustment of the powder-feeding rate of the printing nozzle. In future work, we will conduct more verifications on various types of real multi-DOF devices experiment. Additionally, developing an algorithm to couple the powder feeding equipment and the trajectory of the robotic arm [1] is essential to realize the real-time adjustment of the powder feeding rate.

References

1. Aouaidjia, K., Sheng, B., Li, P., Kim, J., Feng, D.D.: Efficient body motion quantification and similarity evaluation using 3-D joints skeleton coordinates. IEEE Trans. Syst. Man Cybern. Syst. **51**(5), 2774–2788 (2019)
2. Bhatt, P.M., Malhan, R.K., Shembekar, A.V., Yoon, Y.J., Gupta, S.K.: Expanding capabilities of additive manufacturing through use of robotics technologies: a survey. Addit. Manuf. **31**, 100933 (2020). https://doi.org/10.1016/j.addma.2019.100933
3. Botsch, M., Kobbelt, L.: A remeshing approach to multiresolution modeling. In: Proceedings of the 2004 Eurographics/ACM SIGGRAPH Symposium on Geometry Processing, pp. 185–192 (2004)
4. Chakraborty, D., Reddy, B.A., Choudhury, A.R.: Extruder path generation for curved layer fused deposition modeling. Comput. Aided Des. **40**(2), 235–243 (2008). https://doi.org/10.1016/j.cad.2007.10.014
5. Crane, K., Weischedel, C., Wardetzky, M.: The heat method for distance computation. Commun. ACM **60**(11), 90–99 (2017). https://doi.org/10.1145/3131280
6. Dai, C.K., Lefebvre, S., Yu, K.M., Geraedts, J.M.P., Wang, C.C.L.: Planning jerk-optimized trajectory with discrete time constraints for redundant robots. IEEE Trans. Autom. Sci. Eng. **17**(4), 1711–1724 (2020). https://doi.org/10.1109/tase.2020.2974771

7. Dai, C.K., Wang, C.C.L., Wu, C.M., Lefebvre, S., Fang, G.X., Liu, Y.J.: Support-free volume printing by multi-axis motion. ACM Trans. Graph. **37**(4), 1–14 (2018). https://doi.org/10.1145/3197517.3201342

8. Duran, C., Subbian, V., Giovanetti, M.T., Simkins, J.R., Beyette, F.R., Jr.: Experimental desktop 3D printing using dual extrusion and water-soluble polyvinyl alcohol. Rapid Prototyp. J. **21**(5), 528–534 (2015)

9. Etienne, J., et al.: Curvislicer: slightly curved slicing for 3-axis printers. ACM Trans. Graph. (TOG) **38**(4), 1–11 (2019)

10. Fang, G., Zhang, T., Zhong, S., Chen, X., Zhong, Z., Wang, C.C.: Reinforced FDM: multi-axis filament alignment with controlled anisotropic strength. ACM Trans. Graph. (TOG) **39**(6), 1–15 (2020)

11. Li, Y., He, D., Wang, X., Tang, K.: Geodesic distance field-based curved layer volume decomposition for multi-axis support-free printing. arXiv preprint arXiv:2003.05938 (2020)

12. Liu, M., Yang, W.: Optimizing the design process of 3D printing services for personal customization. In: Marcus, A., Rosenzweig, E., Soares, M.M. (eds.) HCII 2023. LNCS, vol. 14031, pp. 497–513. Springer, Cham (2023). https://doi.org/10.1007/978-3-031-35696-4_36

13. Pandey, P.M., Reddy, N.V., Dhande, S.G.: Slicing procedures in layered manufacturing: a review. Rapid Prototyp. J. **9**(5), 274–288 (2003). https://doi.org/10.1108/13552540310502185

14. Qian, J.L., Zhang, Y.T., Zhao, H.K.: Fast sweeping methods for eikonal equations on triangular meshes. SIAM J. Numer. Anal. **45**(1), 83–107 (2007). https://doi.org/10.1137/050627083

15. Qin, Y., Chi, X., Sheng, B., Lau, R.W.: Guiderender: large-scale scene navigation based on multi-modal view frustum movement prediction. Vis. Comput. 1–11 (2023)

16. Shan, Y., Gan, D., Mao, H.: Curved layer slicing based on isothermal surface. Procedia Manufact. **53**, 484–491 (2021)

17. Szydlo, T., Sendorek, J., Windak, M., Brzoza-Woch, R.: Dataset for anomalies detection in 3D printing. In: Paszynski, M., Kranzlmüller, D., Krzhizhanovskaya, V.V., Dongarra, J.J., Sloot, P.M.A. (eds.) ICCS 2021. LNCS, vol. 12745, pp. 647–653. Springer, Cham (2021). https://doi.org/10.1007/978-3-030-77970-2_50

18. Wang, M.Q., Zhang, H.G., Hu, Q.X., Liu, D., Herfried, L.: Research and implementation of a non-supporting 3D printing method based on 5-axis dynamic slice algorithm. Robot. Comput.-Integr. Manuf. **57**, 496–505 (2019). https://doi.org/10.1016/j.rcim.2019.01.007

19. Xu, K., Li, Y.G., Chen, L.F., Tang, K.: Curved layer based process planning for multi-axis volume printing of freeform parts. Comput.-Aided Des. **114**, 51–63 (2019). https://doi.org/10.1016/j.cad.2019.05.007

20. Zhang, T., et al.: S3-slicer: a general slicing framework for multi-axis 3D printing. ACM Trans. Graph. (TOG) **41**(6), 1–15 (2022)

Graphics and AR/VR

Human Joint Localization Method for Virtual Reality Based on Multi-device Data Fusion

Zihan Chang, Xiaofei Di[✉], Xiaoping Che, Haiming Liu, Jingxi Su, and Chenxin Qu

School of Software Engineering, Beijing Jiaotong University, Beijing 100044, China
xfdi@bjtu.edu.cn

Abstract. Virtual reality (VR) utilizes computer vision, artificial intelligence and other techniques to enable interaction between users and virtual environments. In order to solve the problems of human joint localization based on single device, multi-device data fusion technology has been adopted. In this paper, a multi-device data fusion method is proposed based on HTC Vive and Kinect. Firstly, two devices are utilized to separately capture motion data of human joints and the two sets of data are aligned temporally and unified in coordinates. Then the weights are respectively assigned to the two sets of data based on the different location of the human body. Next, particle filtering is adopted to combine the two sets of data. Finally, a bidirectional long short-term memory (Bi-LSTM) neural network model is deployed, where the bone length loss is incorporated into the loss function to further improve the localization accuracy. Experiment results show that the localization accuracy of the proposed multi-device data fusion-based localization method outperforms that of the single device method.

Keywords: Virtual reality · Data fusion · Human joint localization · Kinect · HTC Vive

1 Introduction

Virtual reality (VR) has attracted wide attention from industry and academia. Human joint localization is one important technology of VR, which refers to the process of tracking the user joints in virtual environments. Human joint localization has a wide range of applications in film production, interactive scenarios and so on [1–3].

Traditional single VR device-based methods for human joint localization have limitations in accuracy due to noise, environmental factors, and invisibility. So multi-device-based methods have been proposed. In [4–6], the methods using the same type of devices have been studied. Dual Kinects were deployed for adaptive weighted data fusion to track human parts [4]. Multiple Kinects were combined with a Leap Motion controller for hand tracking [5]. The method using inertial sensors for human body motion capture was investigated, but it required wearing a suit with multiple sensors and suffered from drift issues [6].

Furthermore, human localization methods using multiple different devices are also proposed. A real-time motion tracking method combining Kinect and inertial sensors

B. Sheng et al. (Eds.): CGI 2023, LNCS 14497, pp. 323–335, 2024.
https://doi.org/10.1007/978-3-031-50075-6_25

was proposed [7], but it didn't consider human biology constraints. In [8]. An extended Kalman filter was adopted to fuse inertial sensor and visual data for tracking, but it just had very limited applications. In [9], a robot with a laser range scanner was used to accompany the tracked person, which utilized densely placed inertial sensor clusters for human localization.

The existing methods based on multiple devices either use the same devices or suffer from small tracking range and excessive number of devices. In this paper, a data fusion method based on Kinect and HTC Vive is proposed, where the Kinect device collects visual data and the HTC Vive device collects non-visual data. The data of the two devices are fused to improve the accuracy of human joint localization.

Our main contributions are summarized as follows. Firstly, an adaptive weighting approach for location data from two devices is proposed and then weighted location data are fused by particle filtering to improve the reliability of the data. Secondly, a bidirectional long short-term memory (Bi-LSTM) model with bone length constraint is deployed to enhance the human joint localization accuracy. Thirdly, experiments are performed across multiple motion fragment sequences and results show that the localization accuracy of the proposed method outperforms that of the single device method.

2 Data Collection and Pre-processing

The 3D skeleton model is suitable for representing the data format of human motion [10, 11]. So, we utilized the skeleton model for analysis. In this section, both HTC Vive and Kinect are first deployed to collect human joint location data, and then the data from two devices are aligned temporally and unified in coordinates.

The collected data includes locations of joint points from Kinect device and HTC Vive, as well as user bone length. In order to facilitate the description of the motion trajectory and jitter of the two devices for human joint point tracking, 8×10 grids of size 50×50 cm is marked on a floor with an area of about 20 m^2, as shown in Fig. 1(a).

Kinect Data Collection. Kinect is a motion capture-based controller, which uses depth cameras and infrared sensors to capture the user's motion. The Kinect is located at the x-axis with x = 2 m and fixed at a horizontal height of 1 m. The human motion images are acquired using the OpenCV library. The PyKinect2 library is then utilized to access Kinect's depth data and obtain the 3D coordinates of joints. The orientation of the Kinect coordinate system is shown in Fig. 1(b).

HTC Vive Data Collection. The HTC Vive consists of two base stations (Lighthouses), one head-mounted display (HMD), three trackers, and two wireless controllers for hand interaction. The two lighthouses of HTC Vive are placed at the diagonal positions of the grids, one is located at x = 4 m, z = 0 m and the other is at x = 0 m, z = 5 m. The two lighthouses are set to be 2.5 m high and tilted downward by 40°.

The computer is connected to the HMD through SteamVR and OpenVR libraries, and the 3D coordinates of the HMD, three trackers and two controllers and the acceleration in six joint points and three directions are obtained in real time. In the HTC Vive coordinate system, the lighthouse is located at the origin, facing left as the x-axis, facing upward as the y-axis, and facing forward as the z-axis.

User Bone Length Collection. The identical tape is adopted to measure the bone length of all the volunteers and the collected information is shown in Table 1.

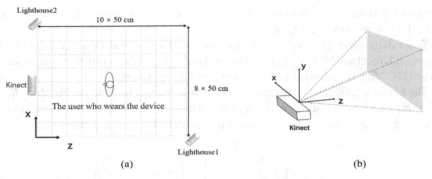

Fig. 1. (a) Experimental environment diagram. (b) The Kinect coordinate system is a Cartesian coordinate system centered on the Kinect infrared sensor, with the x-axis facing left, the y-axis facing up and the z-axis facing forward.

Table 1. User bone measurement description

Bone length	Description
Height	Top of head to ankle
Shoulder width	Left shoulder joint point to right shoulder joint point
Forearm length	Elbow joint to wrist
Arm length	Shoulder joint to elbow joint
Calf length	Knee joint to ankle
Thigh length	Hip joint to knee joint

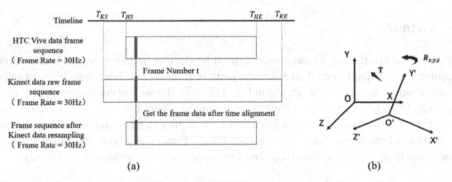

Fig. 2. (a) Time alignment of Kinect and HTC Vive. (b) Diagram of the coordinate system transformation.

Time Alignment. The sampling frequency of Kinect is about 30 frames per second. The sampling frequency of HTC Vive can be set independently in the program, and for the convenience of processing, it is set to 30 frames per second. Since the sampling frequency of the Kinect is unstable, the time domain of the HTC Vive is selected as a reference for time synchronization. HTC Vive turns on later than Kinect and turns off before Kinect, as shown in Fig. 2(a).

Space Alignment. In order to facilitate data comparison and fusion, the coordinate systems of Kinect and HTC Vive are unified and in this paper the coordinate data collected by the HTC Vive is converted to the Kinect coordinate system.

The transformation between the two coordinate systems is shown in Fig. 2(b). $R_{x,y,z}$ and T represent the rotation matrix and translation vector of the coordinate system, respectively. The corresponding 3D coordinate conversion can be expressed as

$$\begin{pmatrix} x' \\ y' \\ z' \end{pmatrix} = R_{x,y,z} \begin{pmatrix} x \\ y \\ z \end{pmatrix} + T, \tag{1}$$

The coordinates change around the axes in Z-Y-X order. The rotation matrix can be expressed as

$$R_{x,y,z} = R_z R_y R_x$$
$$= \begin{pmatrix} cos\theta_z & -sin\theta_z & 0 \\ sin\theta_z & cos\theta_z & 0 \\ 0 & 0 & 1 \end{pmatrix} \begin{pmatrix} cos\theta_y & 0 & -sin\theta_y \\ 0 & 1 & 0 \\ sin\theta_y & 0 & cos\theta_y \end{pmatrix} \begin{pmatrix} 1 & 0 & 0 \\ 0 & cos\theta_x & -sin\theta_x \\ 0 & sin\theta_x & cos\theta_x \end{pmatrix} \tag{2}$$

where θ_x, θ_y, θ_z are rotation angles of the HTC Vive along x-axis, y-axis and z-axis. R_x, R_y, R_z are the rotation matrices for rotating around x-axis, y-axis and z-axis.

Since the y-axis of the coordinate system of both Kinect and HTC Vive are fixed to point to the top, only the x-axis and z-axis coordinates need to be rotated. In this experiment, θ_y can be obtained based on the fixed placement of the two devices. Similarly, the translation vector T can be obtained.

3   Method

In order to solve the localization errors caused by devices and improve the localization accuracy, a localization method based on particle filtering and bone-length constraints is proposed in this section, as shown in Fig. 3. Firstly, the weight coefficients of the two data sets from Kinect and HTC Vive are determined. Then, the data of the two sets are weighted and summed to obtain a fused value. Next, this value is used as an observation of particle filtering to enhance the data reliability. Finally, the bone length serves as a constraint to optimize the fused data and further improve the localization accuracy.

3.1   Adaptive Weight Assignment

The weights of Kinect and HTC Vive are assigned to improve the reliability of data, according to the different actions and joint positions of the user at each moment.

The position of the i-th joint obtained by HTC Vive is denoted as g_h^i, $i = 1, 2, \cdots, 6$, where g_h^i denotes the 3D coordinate (x_h^i, y_h^i, z_h^i) of the i-th joint. The data state is divided into two types: successfully detected and unsuccessfully detected. The weight of the

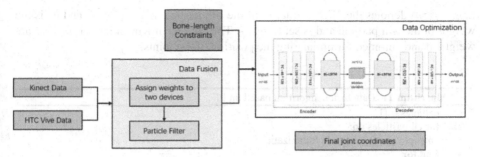

Fig. 3. The localization method based on particle filtering and bone-length constraints.

successfully track device is set to be 1 and the weight of the unsuccessfully track device is set to be 0.

The position of the i-th joint obtained by Kinect is represented as g_k^i, $i = 1, 2, \cdots, 25$, where g_k^i denotes the 3D coordinate (x_k^i, y_k^i, z_k^i) of the i-th joint. The data of six joints identical to HTC Vive is selected to perform data fusion.

Then the weighted 3D coordinate (x_i, y_i, z_i) of the i-th joint point is expressed as

$$g_i = w_k^i g_k^i + w_h^i g_h^i, \tag{3}$$

where w_k^i and w_h^i denotes the weight of the i-th joint point of the Kinect and HTC Vive, respectively.

The weights of each joint are set according to the distance of the human body from the sensor's position. In the experiment, the height of Kinect is set to be 1 m. It is assumed that the shortest distance that Kinect can completely detect the human is l_{min}, the longest distance is l_{max}. In this experiment, $l_{min} = 1.5$ m, $l_{max} = 4.5$ m, $\frac{l_{min}+l_{max}}{2} = 3$ m. The best distance is set at $\frac{l_{min}+l_{max}}{2}$ to balance sensitivity and blurriness, optimizing joint localization accuracy across different distances. Moreover, according to [12], this distance is within the minimum error range of positioning accuracy.

The distance between the k-th human body and Kinect is l_k, so the data weight detected by the Kinect w_k^i is $\frac{1}{2}(1 - |l_k - l_{best}|/(|l_{max} - l_{min}|))$, and the weight of HTC Vive w_h^i is $\frac{1}{2}(1 + |l_k - l_{best}|/(|l_{max} - l_{min}|))$.

3.2 Data Fusion Based on Particle Filtering

The motion of human joints is a nonlinear and non-Gaussian system model, which is difficult to describe using fixed motion models. Therefore, the particle filter (PF) algorithm is adopted to fuse the data of the two devices to perform state estimation in dynamic systems and smooth the trajectory [13].

The proposed algorithm based on PF is shown in Algorithm 1. For the six joint points of the head, two hands, two feet and waist, the weighted summed positions g_i ($i = 1, 2, \ldots 6$) of Kinect and HTC Vive are used as observations in the PF algorithm.

Particle Initialization. In the initialization phase, the experiment creates N particles, where N is set to be 100. The state quantity of each particle is $(x_{Ji}, y_{Ji}, z_{Ji}, w_i)$, where

(x_{Ji}, y_{Ji}, z_{Ji}) denotes the 3D coordinates of the i-th particle at the joint J, and w_i is the weight of the i-th particle and is set to be $\frac{1}{N}$. The data from Kinect and HTC Vive are weighted and summed for initializing the position of the joints.

Algorithm 1: Data fusion algorithm based on PF

---
1.   particles = []
2.   **for** all particles **do:**
3.   particle. init() // Particle Initialization
4.   **End for**
5.   **for** all timesteps **do:**
6.   Obtain observations from two devices
7.   **for** all particles **do:**
8.   Predict_state(particle) // Particle Position Update
9. $w_i = \frac{1}{\sqrt{2\pi}\sigma} \exp\left(\frac{-d_i^2}{2\sigma^2}\right)$ // Particle Weight Update
10. **End for**
11. $w_i' = \frac{w_i}{\sum_{l=1}^{N} w_l}$ // Weight Normalization
12. **If** $N_{eff} < \frac{2}{3}N$
13.   resample_particles(particles)
14. **End if**
15. **End for**
16. Obtain the ultimate position by weighting and summing all particles

---

Particle Position Update. The position update of particles depends on the information such as joint acceleration given by HTC Vive. When the joint position changes, all particles are updated according to the moving direction of the joint and the acceleration in all directions.

Particle Weight Update. The observations of the particle filter are the localization results from the weighted sum of the Kinect and HTC Vive. Depending on the magnitude of the error, a normal distribution with zero mean is also used to calculate the particle weights in this paper. The distance between the current observation and the i-th particle is d_i, and the particle weight is

$$w_i = \frac{1}{\sqrt{2\pi}\sigma} \exp\left(\frac{-d_i^2}{2\sigma^2}\right), \tag{4}$$

where σ is standard deviation of normal distribution. According to the normal distribution, the smaller the σ is, the greater the effect of the observations on the particle weights is. To this end, σ is set to be 0.55 in this paper.

Weight Normalization. After updating the particle positions and weights, all the weights need to be normalized, and the normalization is performed as

$$w_i' = \frac{w_i}{\sum_{k=1}^{N} w_k}. \tag{5}$$

Particle Resampling. Since particle degradation occurs in particle filtering, resampling of particles is required. The particles with higher weights have a high probability of being copied. The number of effective particles is defined as

$$N_{eff} = \frac{1}{\sum_{i=1}^{N} w_i^2},$$ (6)

where N_{eff} decreases when there are some particles with too large weights. The threshold value of the number of particles for resampling is set to $2N/3$. When N_{eff} is less than the threshold value, the particle population is resampled by using the roulette wheel approach, and each replicated particle is assigned to the identical weight $1/N$.

3.3 Positioning Optimization

Long Short-Term Memory (LSTM) is a deep learning method for processing time series. Bidirectional Long Short-Term Memory (Bi-LSTM) is an extension of LSTM that can be trained in both forward and backward directions, and thus can improve contextual relevance and prediction accuracy. In the field of motion data processing, mapping motion sequences to latent variable space can make motion sequences smoother [14]. So, a bidirectional LSTM model incorporating a bone-length constraint (BC-Bi-LSTM) is proposed for motion data optimization based on [15].

Model Structure. The model consists of an encoder and a decoder, where the encoder projects the input motion sequence into the hidden units, and the decoder projects the hidden cell back to the motion sequence in the same dimension. The encoder and decoder have a symmetric structure, as shown in Fig. 4. The fully connected layers facilitate the prediction of motion data and defect repair [15].

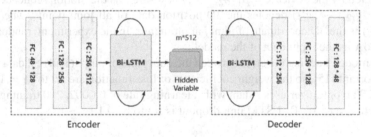

Fig. 4. Neural network model structure adding skeletal constraints

In the encoder, the human joint coordinates are input in the format $(m, 48)$, where 48 represents the 3D positions of the 16 joints in the 48 dimensions and m represents, where m denotes the number of frames of the motion segment. For example, if the length of the motion segment is 4 s, then $m = 30$ Hz $\times$ 4 s $= 120$. The input data passes through three fully connected layers of the encoder and Bi-LSTM units, reaching the hidden variables. Three fully connected layers convert the number of parameters per frame to 128, 256 and 512, respectively. The input size of the Bi-LSTM unit is a sequence of $m \times 512$. The output of the encoder is then passed to the hidden units and finally the data is recovered through the decoder.

Loss Function. The experiments in the literature [16] show that the output motion sequences are jittered if only the position loss is considered. To this end, in this paper, the bone length is also considered as an important constraint.

Output data after data fusion process is Y, and the label data is real motion data fragment X. The mean square error (MSE) represents the error between the network output's position coordinates and the real position coordinates, which is denoted as

$$Loss_p = \frac{1}{n} \sum_{i=1}^{n} (Y_i - X_i)^2, \tag{7}$$

where n is the total number of frames of training data, and n is set to be 120.

In frame i, the coordinates of the corresponding position of the two end joints of the bone b are assumed to be $p_{bi}^{(1)}$ and $p_{bi}^{(2)}$, and thus the bone length can be calculated as $l_{bi} = ||p_{bi}^{(1)} - p_{bi}^{(2)}||$. The real length of skeleton b is l_b'. The number of joint nodes is J and thus the number of bones is $J - 1$. Then the loss function $Loss_b$ on the bone length is expressed as

$$Loss_b = \frac{1}{n \times (J-1)} \sum_{i=1}^{n} \sum_{b=0}^{J-1} |l_{bi} - l_b'| \tag{8}$$

By imposing the two types of loss functions above, the final loss function can be expressed as

$$Loss = \lambda_1 Loss_p + \lambda_2 Loss_b, \tag{9}$$

where λ_1 and λ_2 denote the weight coefficients of the two loss functions, respectively.

Model Training. In this paper, the model is trained using motion data pairs of noisy data and real data. In the training process, the input of the network is the motion sequence data collected by the device $x = p_1, p_2, \cdots, p_L$, where L is the motion sequence length. $p_t = (g_{t1}, g_{t2}, \cdots, g_{tJ})$ denotes the 3D position data of all joint points, where $g_{tj} = (x_{tj}, y_{tj}, z_{tj})$ is the 3D coordinate of joint j at moment t. In the experiment, random noise is added to x as the input data of the model.

In the model, keeping the error between the data pairs of output and real data small is more important [15], so the weight coefficients of loss function are set to $\lambda_1 = 1$ and $\lambda_2 = 0.0001$. The optimizer uses Adam with a learning rate of 0.0002, 200 training rounds and a batch size of 16. Bi-LSTM unit dropout is set to be 0.1.

4 Experiments and Discussion

The experimental setup consists of a Kinect and a set of HTC Vive devices, as shown in Fig. 1(a). The hardware environment consisted of an Intel(R) Core (TM) i5-8265U CPU @ 1.60 GHz 1.80 GHz processor and 8.00 GB of memory. The experiment is conducted using the Windows 11 Home Chinese version operating system and developed within the environment of Python 3.6.13 Ananconda3 (64-bit) and PyTorch 1.7.01.

4.1 Datasets

User Skeleton Data. In the experiment, nine volunteers are invited to participate in data collection. The bone length of each volunteer is measured by using an identical tape and the collected data is shown in Table 2.

Kinect and HTC Vive Data. A total of 9 fixed actions such as arm swing and body rotation are specified in the experiment. In order to improve the data usability, each volunteer tests the same action four times with a sampling frequency of 30 Hz. In total, more than 300,000 frames of data are collected, and each person records about 14 min of movement. An example is given in Fig. 5, where the skeleton and joint points tracked by the Kinect are shown when a volunteer performs one of the motion sequences. It is worth noting that only 16 joint points are used as the skeleton constraint in the neural network model. The joints obtained by HTC Vive except waist correspond to the joint points of Kinect, and the position collected by the tracker on the waist corresponds to the base of the spine collected by Kinect.

Table 2. Results of bone length measurements of volunteers. The table shows the height, shoulder width, forearm length, upper arm length, lower leg length, and thigh length of 9 volunteers.

No	Height/cm	Shoulder/cm	Forearm/cm	Arm/cm	Calf/cm	Thigh/cm
1	163	41	26	29	39	40
2	173	43	27	29	41	45
3	180	46	33	35	44	50
4	180	46	32	33	44	50
5	184	48	36	39	45	51
6	181	49	33	35	46	53
7	166	39	26	28	39	40
8	171	43	28	28	40	43
9	178	49	33	34	45	49

Fig. 5. Skeleton map generated by Kinect joint point tracking

In order to ensure the generalization of the training set data and the generality of the recognition results, the proportion of the training set should be as large as possible. So, the proportions of training set and test set are set to be 70% and 30%, respectively.

4.2 Evaluation Metric

In this paper, the localization accuracy of each joint is used to evaluate the performance of the proposed method. For each frame, let the coordinates of the i-th human joint point obtained by the proposed method be $g_{oi}(x_{oi}, y_{oi}, z_{oi})$, and the coordinates of the true position be $g_{ri}(x_{ri}, y_{ri}, z_{ri})$. The error of the positioning of the i-th human joint point in this frame can be expressed as

$$err_i = \sqrt{ex_i^2 + ey_i^2 + ez_i^2},$$
(10)

where $ex_i = x_{oi} - x_{ri}$, $ey_i = y_{oi} - y_{ri}$, $ez_i = z_{oi} - z_{ri}$. When err_i is less than 4 mm, the joint point i is recorded as accurate positioning, and its accuracy acc_i is 1, and 0 otherwise. Then the accuracy of the frame is expressed as

$$accuracy = \frac{\sum_{i=1}^{N} acc_i}{N},$$
(11)

where N represents the number of all joint points.

Finally, the average value of the localization accuracy of all frames is referred to as the final performance evaluation index. The closer the accuracy is to 1, the better the performance is.

4.3 Performance Comparison

Figure 6 shows the motion trajectory of the left and right hands, the left and right ankles on a motion segment. The orange curve represents the real trajectory specified by the experiment and the blue curve represents the trajectory obtained by the proposed method (BC-Bi-LSTM).

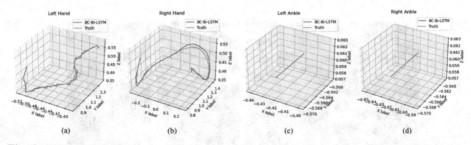

Fig. 6. The real and predicted trajectories of the left hand, right hand, left ankle, and right ankle.

From Fig. 6(a) and Fig. 6(b), it can be seen that the motion trajectories of the positioning of the left and right hands are close to the true trajectories, but there are still errors due to the complex and unstable hand movement. From Fig. 6(c) and Fig. 6(d). The positioning trajectory of both ankles aligns well with the real motion trajectory.

In order to evaluate the localization performance, the proposed method is compared with four other positioning methods, that is, only using Kinect, only using HTC Vive, only using PF fusion and using the model with only position constraints but no bone length constraints (Bi-LSTM). The experiment randomly selects 100 frames of 9 kinds of motion sequences for prediction, and calculates the positioning accuracy of each method. The localization accuracy data is shown in Table 3.

From the location accuracies of the above nine kinds of motion sequence, it can be found that the localization accuracy only using PF fusion is almost the same as that of single device localization accuracy. Through Bi-LSTM model processing, the accuracy is improved by 1% to 8% on each motion sequence. Further, the localization accuracy of the proposed BC-Bi-LSTM model is generally higher than that of using a single device. Motion sequence 3 and 4 are fiercer, where the posture is more complex and joint movement speed is faster than other sequences. In these two sequences, the average accuracy of the proposed BC-Bi-LSTM method is 16% and 12% higher than that of Kinect, and 1% and 9% higher than that of HTC Vive. In motion sequence 6 and 9, the posture of is simple and the motion is gentle, the proposed method have similar performance with the method only using a single device.

Table 3. Localization accuracy of nine motion sequences performed by different methods

Method Sequence	Kinect	HTC Vive	PF	Bi-LSTM	BC-Bi-LSTM
1	0.8842	0.8904	0.9013	0.9132	0.9314
2	0.8931	0.8842	0.8874	0.9014	0.9354
3	0.7623	0.8213	0.8516	0.8748	0.9262
4	0.8078	0.8379	0.8445	0.8761	0.9213
5	0.8473	0.8625	0.8524	0.8713	0.8910
6	0.9298	0.9183	0.9331	0.9389	0.9277
7	0.8983	0.9013	0.9145	0.9214	0.9145
8	0.9621	0.9152	0.9013	0.9413	0.9364
9	0.9323	0.9355	0.9209	0.9317	0.9309

The location accuracies of the five methods on the nine motion sequences are averaged and compared. As shown in Fig. 7, the average location accuracy of the proposed method (BC-Bi-LSTM) based on two kinds of devices achieves 0.9239, which is about 6% higher than that of the method only using Kinect, and about 4% higher than that of the method only using HTC Vive.

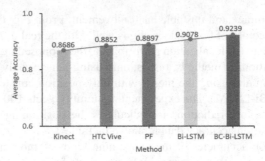

Fig. 7. Comparison of average accuracy.

5 Conclusion

In this paper, a human joint localization method based on Kinect and HTC Vive is proposed. An adaptive weighting method is firstly designed to improve data creditability. Then, the particle filter is used for data fusion of the two devices. The localization results are further optimized using bone length constraints. The experimental results show that this proposed method has achieved the better positioning accuracy.

Acknowledgements. This work was supported by the Fundamental Research Funds for the Central Universities (Grant No. 2022XKRC004 and 2021RC258), by the National Natural Science Foundation of China (Grant No. 61801155), and by the China Postdoctoral Science Foundation (Grant No. 2021M700366).

References

1. Kyriakou, M., Pan, X., Chrysanthou, Y.: Interaction with virtual crowd in Immersive and semi-Immersive Virtual Reality systems. Computer Animation and Virtual Worlds **28**(5), e1729 (2017)
2. Yiming, Q., Xiaoyu, C., Bin, S., et al.: GuideRender: İarge-scale scene navigation based on multi-modal view frustum movement prediction. Vis. Comput. **39**(8), 3597–3607 (2023)
3. Gonzalez-Toledo, D., Cuevas-Rodriguez, M., Molina-Tanco, L., et al.: Still room for improvement in traditional 3D interaction: selecting the fixed axis in the virtual trackball. Vis. Comput. **39**, 1149–1162 (2023)
4. Yao, S., Li, L., Wang, Y., et al.: Whole-body motion capture method based on adaptive weighted data fusion of dual Kinect. J. Chongqing Univ. Technol. (Natural Science) **33**(9), 109–117 (2019)
5. Leoncini, P., Sikorski, B., Baraniello, V., et al.: Multiple NUI device approach to full body tracking for collaborative virtual environments. In: Augmented Reality, Virtual Reality, and Computer Graphics: 4th International Conference, pp. 131–147. Springer, Italy (2017)
6. Roetenberg, D., Luinge, H., Slycke, P.: Xsens MVN: Full 6DOF human motion tracking using miniature inertial sensors. Xsens Motion Technologies BV **3**, 1–7 (2009)
7. Helten, T., Müller, M., Seidel, H., et al.: Real-Time body tracking with one depth camera and inertial sensors. In: 2013 IEEE International Conference on Computer Vision, pp. 1105–1112. IEEE, Australia (2013)

8. Tao, Y., Hu, H., Zhou, H.: Integration of vision and inertial sensors for 3D arm motion tracking in home-based rehabilitation. The Int. J. Robot. Res. **26**(6), 607–624 (2007)

9. Ziegler, J., Kretzschmar, H., Stachniss, C., et al.: Accurate human motion capture in large areas by combining IMU- and laser-based people tracking. In: 2011 IEEE/RSJ International Conference on Intelligent Robots and Systems, pp. 86–91. IEEE, USA (2011)

10. Aouaidjia, K., Bin, S., Ping, L., et al.: Efficient body motion quantification and similarity evaluation using 3-D joints skeleton coordinates. IEEE Trans. Sys. Man, and Cybernetics: Sys. **51**(5), 2774–2788 (2021)

11. Zhang, Q., Chen, Y.: Spatial and contextual aware network based on multi-resolution for human pose estimation. Vis. Comput. **39**, 651–662 (2023)

12. Yang, L., Zhang, L., Dong, H., et al.: Evaluating and improving the depth accuracy of Kinect for Windows v2. IEEE Sens. J. **15**(8), 4275–4285 (2015)

13. Jiang, X., Zhu, L., Liu, J., et al.: A SLAM-based 6DoF controller with smooth auto-calibration for virtual reality. Vis. Comput. **39**, 3873–3886 (2023)

14. Holden, D., Saito, J., Komura, T.: A deep learning framework for character motion synthesis and editing. ACM Transactions on Graphics (TOG) **35**(4), 1–11 (2016)

15. Li, S., Zhou, Y., Zhu, H., et al.: Bidirectional recurrent autoencoder for 3D skeleton motion data refinement. Comput. Graph. **81**, 92–103 (2019)

16. Holden, D., Saito, J., Komura, T., et al.: Learning motion manifolds with convolutional autoencoders. In: Proceedings of the SIGGRAPH Asia Technical Briefs, pp. 1–4. ACM (2015)

VRGestures: Controller and Hand Gesture Datasets for Virtual Reality

Georgios Papadopoulos[✉]⬛, Alexandros Doumanoglou⬛,
and Dimitrios Zarpalas⬛

Centre for Research and Technology Hellas, Thessaloniki, Greece
{giorgospap,aldoum,zarpalas}@iti.gr
https://vcl.iti.gr/

Abstract. Gesture Recognition is attracting increasingly more attention over the years and has been adopted in main applications in the real
world and the Virtual one. New generation Virtual Reality (VR) head-
sets like the Meta Quest 2 support hand tracking very efficiently and
are challenging the research community for more breakthrough discover-
ies in Hand Gesture Recognition. What has also been quietly improved
recently are the VR controllers, which have become wireless and also
more practical to use. However, when it comes to VR gesture datasets,
and especially controller gesture datasets there are limited data available.
Point-And-Click methods are widely accepted, which is why gestures are
being neglected, combined with the shortage of available datasets. To
address this gap we provide two datasets one with controller gestures
and one with hand gestures, capable of recording with either controller
or hand and even with both hands simultaneously. We created two VR
applications to record for controllers and hands the position and the orientation and also each timestamp that we record data. Then we trained
off-the-shelf time series classifiers to test our data, export metrics, and
compare different subsets of our datasets between them. Hand gesture
recognition is far more complicated than controller gesture recognition
as we take almost thrice input and the difference is being analyzed and
discussed with findings and metrics. The datasets are available online
https://doi.org/10.5281/zenodo.8027807.

Keywords: Hand Gestures · Controller Gestures · Virtual Reality ·
Machine Learning · Dataset

1 Introduction

A technology that supports highly accurate and effective Gesture Recognition
(GR) in Virtual Reality (VR) environments has been envisioned in many popular
sci-fi movies, from a long time ago. So many years after those movies, it is now
the time, that finally the technology has just begun to become mature enough

Centre for Research and Technology Hellas - Information Technologies Institute.

B. Sheng et al. (Eds.): CGI 2023, LNCS 14497, pp. 336–350, 2024.
https://doi.org/10.1007/978-3-031-50075-6_26

for those visions to become a reality. VR devices have rapidly evolved over the last decade and massively increased their capabilities and potential. Improved features, wireless equipment, better resolution, and lower market price are just a few of the major upgrades. New research horizons have broadened the Artificial Intelligence field, unlocking possibilities that were abandoned before due to the lack of methods and equipment. The recently released Meta's Quest 2[1], is the first standalone VR device, which supports bare hand tracking, wireless controllers, and wireless head-mounted display (HMD). As of now, hand tracking has been a milestone, that has not been conquered entirely. Machine learning models were unable to handle big datasets with many features and for that reason, deep learning methods were used to address the hand gesture recognition research field. VR controllers have also experienced revolutionary changes, cabled HMDs are outdated and are being replaced by wireless ones. What is common between controllers and hands is the Human-Computer-Interaction, which is achieved with Point and Click. This method is widely accepted by the users resulting in gestures being neglected on many occasions even where they could be extremely meaningful. We grounded on these flaws to contribute with two datasets to fill some gaps in the bibliography and provide two solemn tools for researchers to work with in future gesture recognition systems. Introducing gestures in a VR application consists of disproportionate sizes in terms of usability and effort required and that, precisely, is the main reason for gestures to be neglected, in combination with the shortage of available datasets, regarding controller and hand gestures. Collecting a dataset is a high effort time-consuming task, with large ambiguities even between samples of the same gesture class (Fig. 1). However, without this effort, one can not train a machine-learning algorithm to identify dynamic movements as gestures. After all, gesture recognition whether with controllers or bare hands ends up being a time series classification problem and we will research whether the state-of-the-art time series classifiers with machine learning can achieve high accuracy or deep learning methods are truly required. Our contribution concerns the creation and publication of two completely different datasets, the former with controller gestures and the latter with hand static and dynamic gestures, supporting both left or right controller and hand. Additionally, we created a benchmark with off-the-shelf time-series algorithms from Sktime [15,16] and will showcase a large diversity of subsets and metrics. We will discuss the findings and share some thoughts on future work, what else we could try to get different results, and what conclusions we finally concluded.

---

[1] meta.com/quest/products/quest-2.

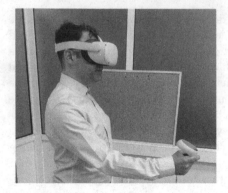

Fig. 1. Subjects while recording controller and hand gestures with the Meta Quest 2.

2   Related Work

The literature should be divided into two parts, one for controller gestures and one for hand gesture recognition. While the former seems more user-friendly, the latter draws more attention due to its potential. To begin with, not so long ago the standard way to record hand gestures in real time [28] was either with a camera [13] or a depth sensor [12]. There are also approaches to classifying gestures outside VR [6] from video and image recordings [17,18]. Rather similar research interest has been shown by [8], focusing on user experience and what is preferable either controllers or hands. A static Hand Gesture research work [21] using a publicly open hand dataset with grayscale images of hand poses demonstrates high accuracy in short-time recognition. Meanwhile, combining gestures with deep learning [2,5,32] in real-time has recently been a trend [3,9,31]. In this work [21] 10 static gestures can be recognized by using a camera as a tracking device. Gesture classifiers have been researched in other fields, including neuroscience [14,22,30] with prosthetic devices like armbands and sensors to create a human-machine interaction for higher gesture recognition [20,27]. What should be mentioned here is that having gestures with both controllers or hands is not common. Attention is being drawn to one-handed gestures, especially with the right hand. A similar work [24] demonstrates an application of one-handed dynamic gestures to perform tasks in VR or even Augmented Reality (AR) and showcases why this kind of dataset needs to exist and improve. Another recent work [1] with gestures using the same equipment as us. In the aforementioned paper, a new game-based application with gesture interaction was created and the users had to perform gestures to proceed to the next stages of the game. Skeleton-based data [19] is being used to analyze patterns and train new convolutional neural networks [10,11]. These data have been widely used for action recognition [25] and extended to other research areas like human-robot-collaboration [26]. Finally, datasets are rare to find and differ vastly in gesture classes, design, and recording methods. One of the most recent papers [4] extends the NVIDIA [7] dataset to provide a new dataset with video recordings.

3 Gap Analysis and Motivation

The existing literature provides valuable insights into gesture recognition, although there are gaps that need to be addressed. We built upon existing work while also contributing with some new perspectives. As of now, there is limited availability in VR gesture datasets especially regarding controller gestures. To the best of our knowledge, these datasets are unique regarding the open access availability they provide, together with details on which hand was used. With respect to other existing datasets, we introduced a diversity allowing the user to draw a gesture with either hand or controller, concerning the user's preferred hand and we imported not only static gestures but also dynamic ones. Our datasets take into consideration the case of both controllers or hands being used simultaneously to draw a gesture. We are recording detailed information on hand position and orientation through time, as one unified object but also as a union of 24 joints with respect to the wrist. Our participants are relative to computer science, the age variance is 25–40 years old and previous VR experience with hand tracking is little to none. Our motivation arises from the fact that already existing datasets are short in terms of information, mostly by ignoring some details that could be meaningful and essential to others and are limited to one-handed gestures and only with a specific hand. We take a novel approach that combines all the aforementioned work, reinforcing the existing literature with a VR controller dataset and publishing a VR hand dataset with respect to both hands and the HMD. We argue that the aforementioned datasets provide unique dynamic two-handed VR gestures and also natural hand and controller movements. For the hand dataset, gestures are common actions resembling grabbing or pushing with either hand, and for the controller dataset, gestures are easily memorable as they resemble symbols that are being used daily. Taking into account the HMD relocation is crucial for VR applications as it is also pretty elegant to have access to each recording. New subsets can be created with great flexibility as one can choose to create subsets only from a specific hand or with limited classes or even a combination of both. It should be mentioned that despite having information on which controller or hand was used, the sampling methods were completely anonymous and could not be matched to the subjects participating in the experiment.

4 Applications

To record the two datasets we created two different applications one for recording controller gestures and one for hand gestures. The controller recording application is tracking both the controllers' position and rotation and each recording timestamp. It is built using the Steam VR SDK[2]. In Fig. 2 there are examples of gestures being recorded. The user can observe what he records from these white spawning spheres. The hand gesture recording application is built on a different

---

[2] store.steampowered.com/app/250820/SteamVR.

Fig. 2. Screenshots from the VR controller gesture recording application, showing how gestures were recorded. On top are gestures drawn with the left controller and examples with the right controller in the bottom row. All gestures could be drawn with either controller.

principle. We used the Voice SDK[3] deployed by meta so that the user activates the recording with his speech. There was a hand resembling figure on the left of the user's VR view which was performing on repeat the gesture the user should draw, as presented in Fig. 3 and Fig. 4. The user could start the process by saying a predefined word, then he would get optical feedback and an indication that recording is active. While in recording mode, the user performs one gesture and says a second predefined word to stop the recording and save the gesture. In our application, there is visual feedback on when the subject was recorded, a hand animation on one side to describe the gesture that should be drawn, and a newly created hand animation after the gesture was stored to observe what was recorded.

With the Meta Quest Developer Hub[4] application, we can monitor the user in both applications, guide him if necessary and make sure the recordings were performed under the same conditions for all the subjects. After each recording, the data were evaluated and reviewed concerning their quality, we retained some gestures where the HMD lost tracking momentarily, since this may occur in real-time applications as well. In an attempt to preserve the authenticity of the dataset, we asked the participants to perform each repetition slightly differently each time and only removed recordings that did not resemble the target gesture.

---

[3] assetstore.unity.com/packages/tools/integration/oculus-integration-82022.
[4] developer.oculus.com/downloads/package/oculus-developer-hub-win.

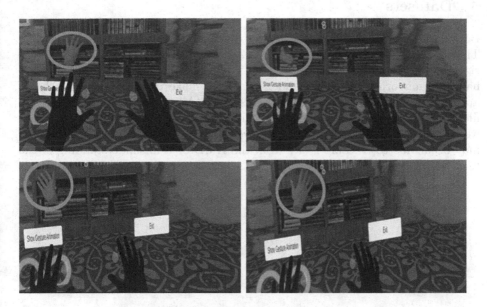

Fig. 3. The circled game object resembles a hand performing on repeat a gesture the user should draw. This figure portrays the RightInfinity gesture.

Fig. 4. After observing the motion of Fig. 3 the user attempts to replicate the gesture, activating the gesture recorder with voice commands.

5   Datasets

Both datasets were recorded using the left-handed coordinate system of Unity3D. The VR device used was the Meta Quest 2. Drawing Controller gestures with the right and left hand are completely identical, while hand gestures with the left hand are mirroring the right hand gestures, to make them more approachable and easy to perform naturally and realistically. All gestures are stored in .bin files. To ensure that everything was recorded properly and labeled as it should, we created animation methods to observe and remove wrong recordings, which may occur due to tracking issues from the HMD or a misunderstanding of the task (Fig. 5).

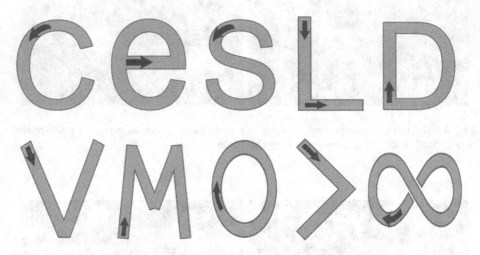

Fig. 5. Controller Gestures Vocabulary. The arrows are indicating the starting point and the route that should be followed.

To create our controller gesture dataset we recorded 16 subjects, 12 of which were right-handed and 4 were left-handed. Each participant was asked to draw some sample controller gestures with his preferred hand for 10 min. We collected samples from 15 different classes, 12 of them were English letters and 3 were symbols, with an average of 570 samples per class for right-handed gestures and 120 for left-handed. Our gesture names are L, O, I, U, V, e, S, D, Z, C, N, M, >, <, INFINITY. These symbols were chosen because there is no repetition in patterns when designed, to be easily memorable and useful in actions with a starting letter the same as the gesture name. These gestures were created and applied to the H2020 EC project INFINITY. They were tested under real-time conditions by end-users who did not participate in the collection of the dataset and were successfully integrated into different environments. Some of these gestures are similar, to evaluate the performance in ambiguous cases and others differ to assure the generality of the dataset. To draw a gesture, the user must press and hold the trigger button of the controller and perform the desired gesture which resembles either letters of the English alphabet or common symbols. Upon release, we write down on the .bin file the subject tag, the gesture class, which hand was used, and discard the other. Each time, a dictionary is created with numpy arrays containing the position of the controller and HMD (X, Y, Z), the orientation of both of them (Qx, Qy, Qz, Qw), and each timestamp that was recorded. The subjects had been told to draw each gesture in a similar pattern and yet with many tiny differences in gesture shape, size, and controller orientation. Hand Recordings were trickier. Since there is no trigger button, somehow we should record the hand motion only for the duration of the gesture. As said before, we used voice commands to start/stop recording the gestures and even erase them if they did not respond to the desired one. We split the hand into 24 joints as placed by Oculus SDK in Unity3D[5] and recorded each joint for each hand. For one-handed gestures, we emptied the numpy array of the non-dominant hand. Similarly to the controller dataset, we record the position and orientation of each joint, of each hand as a whole object, and of the HMD. Finally, we recorded an array of timestamps for each recording frame, to access the duration of each gesture. For our Hand Gesture dataset, we collected samples from 34 subjects, 25 were right-handed and 9 were left-handed. Hand Gestures were either dynamic or static. 11 different gestures were recorded for either hand and two additional gestures with both hands drawing at the same time, which are included in the dataset but were not used in the benchmark. We collected an average of 307 samples per gesture with the right hand, 226 samples with the left, and 266 from both-handed gestures. Our 11 one-handed gesture names are: Back, Click, Close, Grab, Home, Infinity, OpenPalm, Point, Push, Rotate, and Scroll each with a prefix in front of the name, for example, the actual name is RightBack, LeftClick, etc. The sampling procedures were monitored and the samples have been cleared of wrong labeling or different design pattern. This way ensures that each sample in each class is a correctly drawn gesture and yet not quite identical to the rest of the samples in the same class. It must be emphasized that the datasets were designed consistently for the recognizer to achieve maximum accuracy. All participants were informed of the procedures and signed an informed consent form before the experiment.

6 Benchmarking

Sktime provides state-of-the-art transformers and classifiers for time-series classification and forecasting in pandas data frames. It is an open-source python library that provides a unified API, compatible with scikit-learn, in terms of methods fit and transforms to train time-series data. The selected algorithms offer a variety of different options and although they manage time-series data as input, the inner processing varies vastly and could be manipulated to produce a ton of different results based on the selected hyperparameters. Our data format takes as input a pandas dataframe with features and samples as columns

---

[5] docs.unity3d.com/Manual/index.html.

and rows respectively but with different dimensions in the two datasets. For the controller dataset, the features are 3 positions (X Y Z) and 1 timestamp, which equals 4. For each cell, which is called a panda series, a new one-dimensional numpy array is being stored, the length of which depends on the duration of the gesture, in other words, how many timestamps were recorded. The hand dataset is more complex. Each feature consists of 3 positions (X Y Z), 24 more positions for each X, Y, Z calculating each joint position and 1 timestamp, which equals 76, and, similarly, with the controller dataset, each panda series is calculated for every timestamp of each sample. What is important to mention here is that each sample has an equal length of X, Y, Z and timestamps but the length may vary between samples. For instance, a sample contains 80 timestamps recorded, which means that it also contains 80 X, Y, Z matching each one of these times-tamps, and that is one row of the pandas dataframe while another sample/row consists of 150 recorded timestamps and equally X, Y, Z. Unfortunately, this is not functional for our classifiers, for it is a necessity the pandas series to have the same length in the whole dataframe. To resolve this issue we applied a prepro-cess interpolation step, TSInterpolator from sktime, to our benchmark so that each sample duration is fixed to 180 timestamps. This essentially means that a sample with fewer than 180 timestamps will be stretched and another sample with 200 timestamps will be compressed so that all the samples of the dataframe have the same length of 180 for each panda series. To achieve translation invari-ance, we perform a pre-processing step before interpolation. In particular, before providing the input feature time series to the classifiers, we position the center of the feature space at the location of the first element in the time series, by subtracting from the X,Y,Z controller/hand/joint coordinates of frame t, the X,Y,Z controller/hand/joint coordinates of frame 0. This method allows us to calculate only the movement of the controller/hand/joint without distractions, like a possible head movement while recording, that could insert noise and weird angles. For simplicity reasons, we did not include orientation recordings as fea-tures to our benchmark although orientation has been recorded to both datasets as quaternions (Qx, Qy, Qz, Qw) for each recorded timestamp of controllers and hands and also for each of the 24 hand joints.

7   Experiments

We split our data to 70–30% train-test and we performed 5-fold cross-validation to sweep our data with the nevergrad optimizer and find the best hyperparame-ters from a selected range for our classifiers on the training set then we applied these hyperparameters to the test set to compare our classifiers. To implement the Sktime off-the-shelf algorithms for experiment tracking of our results we used mlflow[6], an open source platform, to access our experiments, be able to repro-duce them and find the best hyperparameters for each algorithm and concerning the evaluation metrics, which could be used to export results and findings. More-over, to parse our data and be able to manipulate our code with minimal changes

---

[6] mlflow.org.

we used another Python framework, Hydra [29] which was combined with nevergrad [23] to sweep and find the best optimization parameters in a rapid and elegant approach. Our sweeper optimizer was set to NGOpt, which offers several settings to work within each run. A challenging task to increase the accuracy was not only to find the best algorithm for the complete datasets but also to divide them into subsets, explore the different metrics of each one of them and try to justify why this is the case on each subset. Defining a subset with gestures without many similarities between them is the best choice, but what is critical is to compare classifiers on gesture vocabularies containing gestures that are hard to distinguish. For the controller dataset, we tested our classifiers at first with 5 controller gestures (L, e, S, >, INFINITY) and then we added 5 more gestures (O, V, D, C, M). We wanted to test the accuracy of our classifier on a small dataset compared to one with a bigger gesture vocabulary, in an attempt to research their learning capacity. This metric was chosen to evaluate the performance of the gesture recognizer and not the quality of the data itself, to keep the authenticity of the dataset intact. All hyperparameters were set the same but the budget was doubled for the bigger dataset to achieve a fair comparison between the datasets. For the hand dataset, we used a subset of 5 gestures (Infinity, Scroll, Back, Grab, Point) with both the left and the right hand and we will showcase the best results for each classifier. For both datasets, we used 4 classifiers (Catch22, IndividualTDE, KNeighborsTimeSeries, RocketClassifier) that take as input different hyperparameters. The range of the hyperparameters that were used for the controller gesture subsets is presented in Table 1. With MLflow we got the best hyperparameters for each classifier. Table 2 presents the best hyperparameters as found for the small controller dataset while Table 3 contains those of the bigger one. The next step is to set these hyperparameters to the models to extract some metrics and compare the classifiers. Table 4 and Table 5 present the results of the test set on both controller datasets that we tested. The same process has been done for the hand gestures in the aforementioned subset of 5 hand gestures and we present the metrics of the right-hand gesture subset as the findings were better than the ones of the corresponding left. Table 6 presents the range of the hyperparameters that were tested, which is slightly different due to the increased complexity of the input of the hand data. Finally, Table 7 presents the best hyperparameters after the sweep, and Table 8 compares the classifier's metrics after testing on unseen data with the best hyperparameters for each of them.

8   Discussion

The findings are indicating that controller gesture recognition can be handled extremely well with the already existing classifiers being able to achieve the highest accuracy reaching out next to perfect classification on unseen data. The accuracy was almost the same whether with a small subset or two times bigger. On the contrary, even state-of-the-art machine learning algorithms are being confused when it comes to classifying hand gestures with many features. Deep

Table 1. Hyperparameters tested for each classifier for our controller subsets. The budget was set to 15 for the small subset and 30 for the bigger subset. The NGOpt sweeps random values in the given range of each hyperparameter for each classifier with respect to the budget.

Catch22	IndividualTDE	KNeighborsTimeSeries	RocketClassifier
n_estimators: range 20–100	Window_Size: range 5–20	n_neighbors: range 1 -20	num_kernels: range 20–200
outlier_norm: True or False	norm: True or False	weights: Uniform or Distance	max_dilations: range 1–50
	igb: True or False	algorithm: brute or ball_tree or kd_tree	n_features: range 1–3
	bigrams: True or False	distance: dtw or euclidean	
	alphabet_size: range 2–10	leaf_size: range 10–30	
	dim_threshold: range 0.7–1.0		
	max_dims: range 5–30		

Table 2. Best hyperparameters for each classifier of the 5 gesture Controller dataset

Catch22	IndividualTDE	KNeighborsTimeSeries	RocketClassifier
n_estimators: 58	window_size: 11	n_neighbors: 9	num_kernels: 142
outlier_norm: false	norm: false	weights: uniform	max_dilations_per_kernel: 46
	igb: false	algorithm: brute	n_features_per_kernel: 3
	alphabet_size: 5	distance: euclidean	
	bigrams: false	leaf_size: 20	
	dim_threshold: 0.824		
	max_dims: 14		

Table 3. Best hyperparameters for each classifier of the 10 gesture Controller dataset

Catch22	IndividualTDE	KNeighborsTimeSeries	RocketClassifier
n_estimators: 60	window_size: 15	n_neighbors: 13	num_kernels: 155
outlier_norm: true	norm: false	weights: distance	max_dilations_per_kernel: 16
	igb: false	algorithm: brute	n_features_per_kernel: 2
	alphabet_size: 5	distance: dtw	
	bigrams: true	leaf_size: 22	
	dim_threshold: 0.924		
	max_dims: 22		

Table 4. Best metrics on unseen data with the best hyperparameters for each classifier on the 5 gestures controller subset.

Classifiers	accuracy	balanced_accuracy	precision	f1 score	recall
Catch22	0.995	0.995	0.995	0.995	0.995
IndividualTDE	0.899	0.895	0.894	0.902	0.895
KNeighborsTimeSeries	0.992	0.992	0.992	0.992	0.992
RocketClassifier	0.997	0.997	0.997	0.997	0.997

Table 5. Best metrics on unseen data with the best hyperparameters for each classifier on the 10 gestures controller subset.

Classifiers	accuracy	balanced_accuracy	precision	f1 score	recall
Catch22	0.992	0.993	0.993	0.993	0.993
IndividualTDE	0.862	0.86	0.86	0.862	0.86
KNeighborsTimeSeries	0.992	0.992	0.992	0.992	0.992
RocketClassifier	0.994	0.994	0.994	0.994	0.994

Table 6. Hyperparameters tested for each classifier for our hand subset. The budget was set to 30.

Catch22	IndividualTDE	KNeighborsTimeSeries	RocketClassifier
n_estimators: range 20–100	Window_Size: range 5–20	n_neighbors: range 1 -20	num_kernels: range 5–500
outlier_norm: True or False	norm: True or False	weights: Uniform or Distance	max_dilations: range 1–50
	igb: True or False	algorithm: brute or ball_tree or kd_tree	n_features: range 1–3
	bigrams: True or False	distance: dtw or euclidean	
	alphabet_size: range 2–10	leaf_size: range 10–30	
	dim_threshold: range 0.7–1.0		
	max_dims: range 5–30		

Table 7. Best hyperparameters for each classifier of the 5 gesture Hand dataset

Catch22	IndividualTDE	KNeighborsTimeSeries	RocketClassifier
n_estimators: 100	window_size: 14	n_neighbors: 16	num_kernels: 329
outlier_norm: true	norm: false	weights: uniform	max_dilations_per_kernel: 35
	igb: true	algorithm: brute	n_features_per_kernel: 3
	alphabet_size: 7	distance: dtw	
	bigrams: true	leaf_size: 22	
	dim_threshold: 0.7		
	max_dims: 12		

Table 8. Best metrics on unseen data with the best hyperparameters for each classifier on the 5 gestures hand subset.

Classifiers	accuracy	balanced_accuracy	precision	f1 score	recall
Catch22	0.753	0.747	0.744	0.754	0.555
IndividualTDE	0.559	0.555	0.556	0.557	0.555
KNeighborsTimeSeries	0.368	0.364	0.353	0.359	0.364
RocketClassifier	0.692	0.685	0.673	0.675	0.685

learning algorithms are necessary to have a decent accuracy score. Particularly left-handed gestures failed to handle the ambiguity between the samples because the left-hand dataset was way smaller than the one with the right-hand gestures. Adding more hand gestures further confused the classifiers and they were not able to return worth showing results. The fact that in all the subsets used, the accuracy was almost equal to the balanced accuracy indicates that all the gestures are about equally important and the samples are distributed desirably.

9   Conclusion and Future Work

Gesture Recognition provides a shortcut to add another extra feature to VR applications. What we offer are two completely different datasets, containing all the information needed to make good use of them, which are also capable to function with either controller or hand allowing the user the choice to perform a gesture in any way that suits him better. Having also recorded the HMD position and orientation through time we are able to get out of the equation some random unintended head movements. What is an essential task in gesture recognition is to not recognize falsely the gestures. A drawing is preferred to be labeled as unknown rather than labeled incorrectly and perform the mapped action, which may lead to a domino of undesired sequential actions, causing discomfort to the user. In future research, we will focus on using these datasets to integrate them into a gesture-based application and achieve the same high results that we obtained in our experiments. What could also be researched in the future is a step between, which gives feedback to the user on the percentage of gesture recognition accuracy while drawing the gesture. It is meaningful to import an online/continuous recognition feature, to track the hands continuously and recognize when a pattern was drawn mid-air that is mapped to a predefined gesture. Another interesting topic to research would be Gesture Elicitation, giving the privilege the user to create gestures based on his preferences and map them to actions. Interesting as it may be to test our controller dataset with even smaller subsets even creating subsets by tag, to try deep learning methods with few-shot learning or one-shot learning, and try to trace the point where the accuracy of the controller gesture recognition is being reduced significantly, However, this is a challenging task to train the recognizer with limited samples of a gesture, because disambiguate issues will occur that require special treatment to make sure the precision of the recognizer is not affected deeply by the new inducted samples.

Acknowledgements. We also acknowledge financial support by the H2020 EC project INFINITY under contract 883293. We thank Athanasios Ntovas for his help with the experiment setup, and the subjects recorded in our datasets for their participation.

References

1. Arendttorp, E.M.N., Rodil, K., Winschiers-Theophilus, H., Magoath, C.: Overcoming legacy bias: re-designing gesture interactions in virtual reality with a san community in Namibia. In: Proceedings of the 2022 CHI Conference on Human Factors in Computing Systems, CHI 2022. Association for Computing Machinery, New York (2022)
2. Bhaumik, G., Verma, M., Govil, M.C., Vipparthi, S.K.: HyFiNet: hybrid feature attention network for hand gesture recognition. Multimedia Tools Appl. **82**(4), 4863–4882 (2023)
3. D'Eusanio, A., Simoni, A., Pini, S., Borghi, G., Vezzani, R., Cucchiara, R.: A transformer-based network for dynamic hand gesture recognition. In: 2020 International Conference on 3D Vision (3DV), pp. 623–632 (2020). https://doi.org/10.1109/3DV50981.2020.00072
4. Fronteddu, G., Porcu, S., Floris, A., Atzori, L.: A dynamic hand gesture recognition dataset for human-computer interfaces. Comput. Netw. **205**, 108781 (2022)
5. Gnanapriya, S., Rahimunnisa, K.: A hybrid deep learning model for real time hand gestures recognition. Intell. Autom. Soft Comput. **36**(1) (2023)
6. Guo, L., Lu, Z., Yao, L.: Human-machine interaction sensing technology based on hand gesture recognition: a review. IEEE Trans. Hum.-Mach. Syst. **51**(4), 300–309 (2021). https://doi.org/10.1109/THMS.2021.3086003
7. Gupta, P., Kautz, K., et al.: Online detection and classification of dynamic hand gestures with recurrent 3D convolutional neural networks. In: CVPR, vol. 1, p. 3 (2016)
8. Huang, Y.J., Liu, K.Y., Lee, S.S., Yeh, I.C.: Evaluation of a hybrid of hand gesture and controller inputs in virtual reality. Int. J. Hum.-Comput. Interact. **37**(2), 169–180 (2021)
9. Jiang, S., Kang, P., Song, X., Lo, B.P., Shull, P.B.: Emerging wearable interfaces and algorithms for hand gesture recognition: a survey. IEEE Rev. Biomed. Eng. **15**, 85–102 (2022). https://doi.org/10.1109/RBME.2021.3078190
10. Jiang, X., Zhu, L., Liu, J., Song, A.: A slam-based 6dof controller with smooth auto-calibration for virtual reality. Vis. Comput. 1–14 (2022)
11. Köpüklü, O., Gunduz, A., Kose, N., Rigoll, G.: Real-time hand gesture detection and classification using convolutional neural networks. In: 2019 14th IEEE International Conference on Automatic Face & Gesture Recognition (FG 2019), pp. 1–8. IEEE (2019)
12. Kurakin, A., Zhang, Z., Liu, Z.: A real time system for dynamic hand gesture recognition with a depth sensor. In: 2012 Proceedings of the 20th European Signal Processing Conference (EUSIPCO), pp. 1975–1979. IEEE (2012)
13. Lai, H.Y., Lai, H.J.: Real-time dynamic hand gesture recognition. In: 2014 International Symposium on Computer, Consumer and Control, pp. 658–661 (2014)
14. Li, J., Wei, L., Wen, Y., Liu, X., Wang, H.: An approach to continuous hand movement recognition using sEMG based on features fusion. Vis. Comput. **39**(5), 2065–2079 (2023)
15. Löning, M., Bagnall, A., Ganesh, S., Kazakov, V., Lines, J., Király, F.J.: sktime: a unified interface for machine learning with time series. arXiv preprint arXiv:1909.07872 (2019)
16. Löning, M., et al.: sktime/sktime: v0.13.4 (2022)
17. Materzynska, J., Berger, G., Bax, I., Memisevic, R.: The jester dataset: a large-scale video dataset of human gestures. In: Proceedings of the IEEE/CVF International Conference on Computer Vision (ICCV) Workshops (2019)

18. Mujahid, A., et al.: Real-time hand gesture recognition based on deep learning YOLOv3 model. Appl. Sci. **11**(9), 4164 (2021). https://doi.org/10.3390/app11094164. https://www.mdpi.com/2076-3417/11/9/4164
19. Nguyen, X.S., Brun, L., Lezoray, O., Bougleux, S.: A neural network based on SPD manifold learning for skeleton-based hand gesture recognition. In: Proceedings of the IEEE/CVF Conference on Computer Vision and Pattern Recognition (CVPR) (2019)
20. Ntovas, A., Lazaridis, L., Papadimitriou, A., Psaltis, A., Axenopoulos, A., Daras, P.: Data-driven haptic feedback utilizing an object manipulation data-set. In: IEEE Conference on Computer Vision and Pattern Recognition Workshops (CVPRW) (2021)
21. Núñez-Fernández, D.: Development of a hand gesture based control interface using deep learning. In: Lossio-Ventura, J.A., Condori-Fernandez, N., Valverde-Rebaza, J.C. (eds.) SIMBig 2019. CCIS, vol. 1070, pp. 143–150. Springer, Cham (2020). https://doi.org/10.1007/978-3-030-46140-9_14
22. Rahimian, E., Zabihi, S., Asif, A., Farina, D., Atashzar, S.F., Mohammadi, A.: FS-HGR: few-shot learning for hand gesture recognition via electromyography. IEEE Trans. Neural Syst. Rehabil. Eng. **29**, 1004–1015 (2021). https://doi.org/10.1109/TNSRE.2021.3077413
23. Rapin, J., Teytaud, O.: Nevergrad - A gradient-free optimization platform (2018). https://GitHub.com/FacebookResearch/Nevergrad
24. Schäfer, A., Reis, G., Stricker, D.: Anygesture: arbitrary one-handed gestures for augmented, virtual, and mixed reality applications. Appl. Sci. **12**(4), 1888 (2022)
25. Shi, L., Zhang, Y., Cheng, J., Lu, H.: Skeleton-based action recognition with directed graph neural networks. In: Proceedings of the IEEE/CVF Conference on Computer Vision and Pattern Recognition (CVPR) (2019)
26. Terreran, M., Lazzaretto, M., Ghidoni, S.: Skeleton-based action and gesture recognition for human-robot collaboration. In: Petrovic, I., Menegatti, E., Marković, I. (eds.) IAS 2017, vol. 577, pp. 29–45. Springer, Cham (2023). https://doi.org/10.1007/978-3-031-22216-0_3
27. Toro-Ossaba, A., et al.: LSTM recurrent neural network for hand gesture recognition using EMG signals. Appl. Sci. **12**(19), 9700 (2022)
28. Wang, Y., Hu, Z., Yao, S., Liu, H.: Using visual feedback to improve hand movement accuracy in confined-occluded spaces in virtual reality. Vis. Comput. **39**(4), 1485–1501 (2023)
29. Yadan, O.: Hydra - a framework for elegantly configuring complex applications. Github (2019). https://github.com/facebookresearch/hydra
30. Zabihi, S., Rahimian, E., Asif, A., Mohammadi, A.: TraHGR: transformer for hand gesture recognition via electromyography (2022)
31. Zeghoud, S., et al.: Real-time spatial normalization for dynamic gesture classification. Vis. Comput. 1345–1357 (2022)
32. Zou, Y., Cheng, L.: A transfer learning model for gesture recognition based on the deep features extracted by CNN. IEEE Trans. Artif. Intell. **2**(5), 447–458 (2021). https://doi.org/10.1109/TAI.2021.3098253

Mobile AR-Based Robot Motion Control from Sparse Finger Joints

Di Wu[1,2], Shengzhe Chen[3], Meiheng Wang[1,2], and Zhanglin Cheng[1(✉)]

1 Shenzhen VisuCA Key Lab, SIAT, Shenzhen, China
`zl.cheng@siat.ac.cn`
2 University of Chinese Academy of Sciences, Beijing, China
3 School of Mathematical Sciences, Beijing Normal University, Beijing, China

Abstract. Human-robot interaction plays a crucial role in the field of robot motion control. Recent advancements in Augmented Reality (AR) devices have opened up new possibilities for enhancing natural interaction. This paper explores the potential of utilizing AR devices as both sensors and interfaces for controlling robot motion. We present an intuitive and lightweight robot motion control system that enables users to manipulate a robot's motion using hand gestures represented by 3D sparse finger joints. Our approach begins with the predefinition of primitive robot motions and their corresponding user gestures. Subsequently, we train a neural network to map 3D finger joints to specific robot motions. To enhance the accuracy of hand gesture recognition, we incorporate floating calibration and anchor-joint alignment techniques. An ablation experiment is devised to evaluate our proposed data alignment method, followed by a usability study conducted in real-world environments. Experimental results demonstrate the effectiveness of our approach in terms of accurate hand gesture recognition and intuitive control of robot motion.

Keywords: Robot Motion Control · Augmented Reality · Hand Gesture Recognition · Human-Robot Interaction

1 Introduction

Designing a flexible and natural robot control system for applications in an unknown environment is the goal of human-robot interaction. Among possible choices of control signals, it has been proven a creative and intuitive idea to use hand gesture as the input of control system [15]. For example, Zhang and Wu [22] recognize gestures from 2D images as commands to control robots. However, this method has a huge gap between an ideal experiment and a real environment; the accuracy is difficult to guarantee in that the potential occlusions and complicated backgrounds of in-the-wild images may lead to the mis-recognition of hand gestures. To tackle this challenge, depth images and other 3D information have

---

Supplementary Information The online version contains supplementary material available at https://doi.org/10.1007/978-3-031-50075-6_27.

been considered as input [18]. It is evident that 3D inputs offer greater expressiveness compared to 2D images. Recent advancements include the utilization of the human body skeleton captured by Microsoft Kinect to construct a control system for robot motion [8]. Nonetheless, due to the tedious configuration of captured equipment, the human skeleton driven strategy may not work in those scenarios that full body motions cannot be acquired, particularly in situations such as dangerous disasters or critical emergencies. Furthermore, not all joint movements of the entire body contribute to the human-robot interaction. These limitations motivate us to develop a flexible and lightweight robot motion control system that can be effectively implemented in real-world environments.

In recent years, the rapid advancement of visual reality (VR) and augmented reality (AR) technologies has ushered in a new era of more intuitive and promising human-computer interactions [5,9,14,16]. With remarkable progress in sensors, processors, and algorithms seamlessly integrated into portable devices, AR has emerged as a potent tool within the realm of robotics. It not only presents opportunities to enhance human-robot interaction but also to facilitate the exchange of visual information in this domain [3]. For example, Makhataeva et al. [13] have utilized AR to develop a system that enhances a robot operator's perception of potential dangers. Therefore, our primary objective is to explore the potential of utilizing AR devices for achieving natural and intuitive control of robot motion.

Fig. 1. Our mobile AR-based robot motion control system is capable of mapping captured 3D gestures, represented by sparse finger joints, into corresponding robot motions. The first row shows scenes of users controlling robot motions; the second row displays detailed gestures observed from the perspective of the AR device.

In this paper, we propose a novel lightweight robot motion control system based on mobile AR, which enables users to control the motion of a robot with high accuracy and great mobility. To alleviate the burden of redundant inputs to the robot motion control system, we employ only six finger joints as the interactive input, inspired by Yi's sparse IMU sensor [20]. However, recognizing gestures based on sparse finger joints poses significant challenges. While Kim's scheme [8] can easily differentiate whole skeleton joint actions, distinguishing the motion of local finger joints is ambiguous in our case, particularly when the palm is flipped. To overcome this ambiguity, we introduce an anchor-joint alignment module as the first component in our pipeline, enhancing the distinguishing characteristics of each gesture. Through this approach, we demonstrate that only 6 finger joints are sufficient for controlling robot motion. In addition to addressing the challenge of sparse inputs, mobility is another key consideration. AR devices establish variable coordinate systems at the initiation of each session, depending on the specific positions and orientations of the users. This makes the recognition of captured 3D gestures difficult due to non-uniform scales. To tackle this issue, we devise floating calibration as the second component in our system, aiming to unify the captured gestures into a consistent coordinate system. By combining both components, user gestures can be more distinctive, resulting in a high-accuracy and robust control system. Furthermore, our system offers greater mobility compared to Kim's scheme, which restricts robot control to a fixed area. Our system allows users to control the robot remotely from any position and direction, making it suitable for unforeseen scenarios. The diverse results of robot control presented in Fig. 1 demonstrate the high accuracy achieved in real-world environments. The main contributions of our method include:

- An intuitive and lightweight robot motion control system that leverages AR devices as both the sensor and the interface.
- A novel human-robot interaction strategy that utilizes only six sparse 3D finger joints as inputs.
- Floating calibration and anchor-joint alignment techniques to improve hand gesture recognition accuracy.

2   Related Work

Gesture Recognition. Gestures have long been considered as a natural, creative and intuitive human-robot interaction technique [6,15]. From the perspective of acquiring gesture, gesture recognition can be classified as vision-based and sensor-based approaches [4]. The vision-based methods mainly obtain gesture information through various cameras, including single camera, stereo-camera, and the camera of motion capture system such as Microsoft Kinect and Leap Motion; the sensor-based devices usually involve data glove, acceleration sensor, multi-touch screen which uses several detectors. From the perspective of representing gesture, gesture recognition can be categorized as 2D appearance-based and 3D model-based [4]. In 2D space, the difference in viewpoints causes the gesture (even for the same gesture) to appear differently [4,15]. There could be vital information lost in the process. However, complete representation means that gestures are constructed as 3D models of voxels, geometries, or skeletons, which is another complex problem. In our work, we do not utilize 2D appearance with missing information nor consider time-consuming and labor-intensive hand reconstruction. For convenience, we choose to represent a specific gesture using 5 fingertip joints and 1 wrist joint sampled from the hand model of HoloLens2. Therefore, our gesture model can be referred to as a 6-joint-based model.

Mobile Robot Control. Robots (terrestrial ones) are classified in fixed-place robots and mobile robots [17]. Unlike fixed-place robots, mobile robots can move from one place to another. Traditional robot control researches normally focus on robot kinematics. With the development of deep learning, neural network control [10] has become a popular direction and leads it to an interdisciplinary field. What's more, vision-based control, especially with the burst of augmented reality (AR), also shows great potential. Equipped with deep learning and AR, researchers begin to consider more intuitive and natural robot control ways. For instance, Kim et al. [8] develops a control policy using supervised learning and reinforcement learning. However, this work overly pursues motion imitation and deviates from the original intention of robot motion control. In fact, a specific task can be operated based on a limited number of primitive motions, so it is not necessary to imitate every human motion. Moreover, spatial limitations caused by capture device change a mobile robot into a fixed-area robot whose mobility is weakened. Therefore, we propose a flexible AR-based [12] control system as a better solution, which allows user to control robot motion with great mobility.

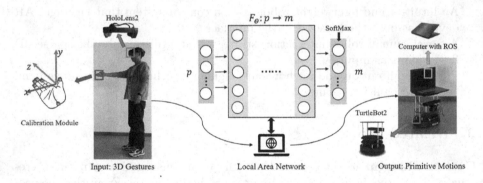

Fig. 2. System overview. Our system takes the 3D joint poses as the input in mobile AR and the primitive motions as the output to achieve robot control via deep learning network $F_\Theta : p \mapsto m$.

3 System Overview

To tackle the burdensome inputs and mobility issues of aforementioned methods, we develop a system for controlling robot with sparse finger joints obtained by mobile AR. Our system receives 3D gestures from any motion capture device (which is HoloLens2 in our case), then maps them into robot motions. First, five primitive motions of robot and corresponding gestures are predefined as outputs and inputs of the system respectively (Sect. 3.1). Once the relationships of gestures and motions are determined, we proceed to collect dataset of 3D coordinates of finger joints (Sect. 3.2) to train the mapping network. Although there are many 2D and 3D gesture recognition datasets, they mainly sample dense finger joints as inputs. Therefore, we present the first dataset with sparse finger joints as the inputs. To obtain the correct mapping, the data calibration module (Sect. 3.3) is applied to unify the captured finger joints scale by depriving their inconsistent coordinate system. Further, we adopt anchor-joint alignment method of re-centering a set of finger joints to make data more separable. In the end, the neural network is trained on the calibrated data to represent the mapping, and it converts the captured gestures into primitive motions to control robot (Sect. 3.4). We illustrate the system overview in Fig. 2.

Table 1. The robot primitive motions and the corresponding gestures. Forward: 5 fingers all point forward. Backward: 4 fingers point back. Turn right: 3 fingers point right. Turn left: 2 fingers point left. Stop: No fingers point any direction.

Forward	*Backward*	*Turn right*	*Turn left*	*Stop*

3.1 Predefined Motions and Gestures

In this section, we adopt the strategy of predefining primitive motions, as referred to Iba's work [7]. Hence, we design five primitive motions which are: *forward, backward, turn right, turn left and stop*. Although these motions are simple, different movement trends, directions, start or stop states have already been included. Based on these primitives, the robot can generate more complex actions according to various tasks. On the other hand, our aim is to acquire gestures that are associated with the intended meaning of robot motion. Although Hololens2 has indeed achieved some basic gestures can be recognized for interacting with objects in the virtual world, such as tapping and pinching, the rigid application of these gestures to robot control fails to meet the intuitive requirements and exhibits a weak connection with robot movements. Therefore, we propose a custom gesture approach and set the direction of fingers to determine the trend of robot movement. For example, we make the gesture of 5 fingers pointing forward to represent the forward movement of the robot, other gestures and more details are shown in Table 1. Additionally, we validate in our user experiments that our gesture design is smooth and aligns with human habits. For instance, when users switch between *turn left* and *turn right* gestures according to their control purposes, they can perceive a fluid and intuitive control process, which also achieves a low learning cost.

3.2 Data Preparation

In Sect. 3.1, we predefine five gestures and assign them to certain robot motions. Then we still need to identify arbitrary gestures as one of the five to send the motion instructions. The captured 3D gestures is represented only by 6 finger joints, which are 5 fingertip joints and 1 wrist joint. Thus what we identify is meaningless pose of sparse finger joints. We use the concatenated coordinates of the 6 joints $(j_1, j_2, \ldots, j_6)$ denoted as p to represent a gesture. As revealed in Fig. 3, we denote a joint coordinate by $j_k = (x_k, y_k, z_k), k \in \{1, 2, \ldots, 6\}$. We aim to develop a function $F_\Theta : p \mapsto m$, which takes finger joints pose p as input and maps it into the corresponding robot motion m.

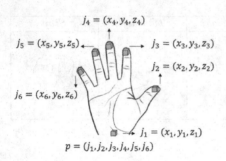

$$j_4 = (x_4, y_4, z_4)$$
$$j_5 = (x_5, y_5, z_5)$$
$$j_3 = (x_3, y_3, z_3)$$
$$j_2 = (x_2, y_2, z_2)$$
$$j_6 = (x_6, y_6, z_6)$$
$$j_1 = (x_1, y_1, z_1)$$
$$p = (j_1, j_2, j_3, j_4, j_5, j_6)$$

Fig. 3. 6 finger joints on the hand.

Once the input and output are defined, we need to prepare the dataset D to train the mapping network F_Θ. To accomplish this, we perform the standard gestures corresponding to the predefined robot primitive motions, and label and record these poses using HoloLens2. Each input pose is a tuple of 18 elements obtained by concatenating the coordinates of the 6 joints. Additionally, we visualize the distribution of spatial pose data in Fig. 4, which supports our data analysis and processing in Sect. 3.3.

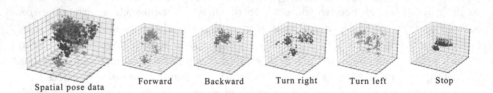

Spatial pose data   Forward   Backward   Turn right   Turn left   Stop

Fig. 4. Visualization of the spatial pose data. The point cloud of raw data bunches up.

3.3 Data Calibration

To begin with, the mobility issue arises from the fact that the pose coordinates are recorded by the captured device. Each time the HoloLens2 is started, it generates a new origin of the coordinate system, resulting in inconsistent scales of the captured poses. As a result, effective robot control is limited to a fixed area where the HoloLens2 was previously started, thereby hindering the mobility of system. To enable users to control the robot in any position and orientation, we propose a floating calibration strategy that maintains a local coordinate system of the hand.

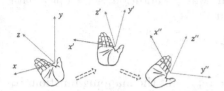

The wrist joint   The little finger joint

Fig. 5. The floating calibration module ensures the recording of gesture poses on a uniform scale.

Fig. 6. Comparison of two anchor-joint alignment methods for improving pose data separability.

In HoloLens2, we creatively utilize the camera sensor's coordinate system as the proxy for the floating coordinate system, with all captured joints being sub-objects of this proxy. This approach achieves a uniform scale without the need for an additional complex localization module. As shown in Fig. 5, the coordinate system is independently established and always implicitly floats above the user's hand. When the palm is naturally flattened, the positive directions of the x, y, and z axes correspond to the left side of the palm, the direction perpendicular to the palm, and the direction of the four fingers, respectively. As the hand moves, the axes switch to $(x', y', z'), (x'', y'', z'') \ldots$ in accordance with the movements. With the floating coordinate system, users have the ability to control the robot with unlimited mobility.

Next, the separability of the spatial pose data also needs to be confirmed. Figure 4 shows that the raw data is linearly inseparable. Misalignment, overlap, and replacement of finger joints pose will lead to errors in gesture recognition. Therefore, performing data alignment helps [19]. In our case, we propose an anchor-joint alignment strategy that is to move all the captured pose to the same center based on a characteristic joint, namely anchor-joint. We pick two candidate joints: the wrist joint and the little finger joint, since previous gestures design in Sect. 3.1 indicates that the little finger joint moves in a maximum amplitude and the wrist joint moves in a minimum amplitude. All gesture poses are relocated by anchoring one of the two joints. In detail, we calculate the mean coordinate of the little finger joint $\bar{j}_l = (\bar{x}_l, \bar{y}_l, \bar{z}_l)$ or the wrist joint $\bar{j}_w = (\bar{x}_w, \bar{y}_w, \bar{z}_w)$ undor floating coordinate system from dataset D as the anchor-joint. Then, for a new input pose p, we pick its litter finger and wrist joint coordinate $j_l = (x_l, y_l, z_l), j_w = (x_w, y_w, z_w)$ and calculate its gap from the anchor-joint, namely $\Delta j_i = (x_i - \bar{x}_i, y_i - \bar{y}_i, z_i - \bar{z}_i), i \in \{l, w\}$. In the end, we let all joints coordinates of the pose p minus the gap so that the pose is re-centered to the anchor-joint.

$$p \leftarrow p - \Delta j_i := (j_1 - \Delta j_i, \ldots, j_6 - \Delta j_i), i \in \{l, w\} \tag{1}$$

As shown in Fig. 6, the anchor-joint alignment makes the raw data more separable. It is easier for the mapping to learn the features and identify gestures to achieve high-accuracy recognition. In summary, based on the floating calibration, we realize the robot control in a mobile way. In addition, we adopt a data alignment strategy to prepare for the training.

3.4 Motion Control

We use the multi-layer perceptron (MLP) to represent the mapping function F_Θ and train the model from the given dataset D, which maps finger joint poses to predefined robot motions. Our MLP consists of seven ReLU layers of 256 dimensions and one final softmax layer of 5 dimensions. The loss terms used to train our model is a cross-entropy loss. Additionally, our training dataset D consists of 5 classes of gestures, each class has 35 samples. To our knowledge, this is the first sparse finger joints for robot control dataset. Note that our strategy of anchor-joint alignment makes the spatial pose data more separable (Sect. 3.3), thus improves the accuracy of the model. The performance comparison of the two anchor-joints will be showed in Sect. 4.

With the trained model, we set up a local area network and configure a computer to access the network for TurtleBot2. The computer receives the finger joint coordinates transmitted by HoloLens2, processes the data using the model, and subsequently maps these poses to corresponding instructions. Meanwhile, the robot operating system (ROS) translates the instructions into speeds and angles, driving the TurtleBot2 according to the user intention.

4 Experimental Results

We devise and execute quantitative experiments as well as a usability study to comprehensively evaluate our proposed system from multiple perspectives. First, we calculate the recognition accuracy of the system and evaluate the efficacy of two anchor-joint alignment strategies which are critical components of the system. Second, we design four complex tasks for user to control robot in real environment, in order to demonstrate the practicality of our system. Finally, we conduct a small-scale usability study to assess the system's effectiveness and the user experience.

4.1   Gesture Recognition

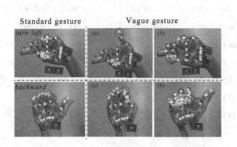

Standard gesture   Vague gesture

Fig. 7. The vague gesture is transformation of standard gesture with some wrong joints marked with red circles. (Color figure online)

To evaluate the accuracy of the model, we collect two test sets when the HoloLens2 start at different time and space, which are Test set 1 and Test set 2. Moreover, when collecting Test set 2, we deliberately make some vague finger joint poses trying to simulate a real environment. Figure 7 visually shows two instances of vague gesture. We use vagueness indicates how confusing the gestures are. It is defined as $V = \sum_{p \in D} \|p - p_s\|_2$, p_s is the mean of standard gesture joint poses. In this case, our model still performs very robust, and the accuracy rate is more than 98%. These results powerfully prove that our calibrated sparse input are characteristic enough to be identified and adequate for the robot control system.

In this part, we train the model based on two candidates of anchor-joint respectively which are the wrist joint and the little finger joint. As analysed in Sect. 3.3, designed gestures (Table 1) indicates that the little finger joint represents maximum motion amplitude and the other is minimum in our case. If we aim to make our spatial pose data better separable, the little finger joint should be chosen as the anchor. Based on the above assumption, we carry out further experimental verification. The accuracy comparison is showed in Table 2. It turns out choosing the little finger joint better satisfies our expectation, and the model achieves higher accuracy. We also directly train a model without any alignment, and it proves anchor-joint alignment is the key of high accuracy in our system.

Table 2. The accuracy of alignments in Test set 1 & 2.

Dataset	Size	Vagueness	Accuracy		
			None	The wrist	The little finger
Test set 1	175	12.39	82.67%	98.00%	99.33%
Test set 2	175	15.48	83.33%	95.33%	98.67%

We compare the performance of our system with state-of-the-art methods, and the results are presented in Table 3. The column labeled "Robot" in the table indicates whether a given method involves robot control. For instance, Zeng et al. [21], Liu et al. [11], and Bao et al. [1] primarily focus on gesture recognition without applying it to develop a robot control system. In contrast, Zhang and

Table 3. Comparison with state-of-the-art methods.

Method	Sensing	Algorithm	Recognition	Robot	Accuracy(%)
[21]	Leap Motion	RBF	Numbers/Alphabets	No	95.10/92.90
[11]	Kinect	RBF	Numbers/Alphabets	No	97.25/92.63
[1]	RGB Camera	CNN	2D hand gestures	No	85.30
[22]	RGB Camera	PCA-HOG, Dlib	2D hand gestures	Yes	–
[18]	Kinect	Threshold	3D body skeletons	Yes	> 96.00
[8]	Kinect	RL	3D body motions	Yes	–
Ours	Hololens2	CNN	3D hand gestures	Yes	98.67

Wu [22] adopt existing OpenCV-related algorithms for both gesture recognition and robot control. These methods are capable of recognizing gestures such as 10 Arabic numbers, 26 English alphabets or custom gestures with semantic information, but they are limited to 2D information. Regarding 3D inputs, Wang et al. [18] calculate the distance between current body pose and predefined gestures to identify control signals using a threshold. On the other hand, Kim et al. [8] employ deep reinforcement learning (RL) on 3D body motions, but this approach imposes a heavy burden on the system. Both of these approaches rely on Kinect for their operations. In comparison, our method, which is based on Hololens2, achieves an impressive recognition accuracy of 98.67% for 5 custom gestures. These high precision levels ensure our system's ability to effectively control the robot's motion, showcasing its practicality and potential for real-world applications.

4.2   Motion Control Performance

In the real environment, we also achieve real-time control that the robot moves smoothly according to user gestures. To demonstrate the effectiveness of our proposed system, we present the results of four complex human-robot interaction tasks, along with their corresponding action scenes and time durations, as depicted in supplement video. The detailed instructions for each task are as follows: Obstacle avoidance takes 18 s; Fire detection takes 21 s; Object delivery takes 15 s; Load following takes 26 s.

In summary, the extensive experimental results of all the complex tasks demonstrate that our system has four significant advantages: (1) it enables one-handed control, allowing the user to engage in other activities simultaneously; (2) it leverages human intelligence to handle unknown situations; (3) it reduces the burden of the user who has other tasks to perform; and (4) it provides the flexibility for both the user and the robot to move freely, without being limited by fixed positions.

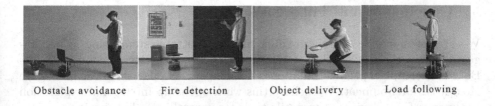

| Obstacle avoidance | Fire detection | Object delivery | Load following |

Fig. 8. Four human-robot interaction tasks.

4.3 Usability Study

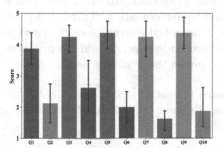

Fig. 9. The mean and standard deviation of SUS questions.

To evaluate the effectiveness of our system and gather user feedback, we invite eight university students to participate in a study on robot control using the proposed system. Prior to the study, a training session is conducted to familiarize the participants with the Hololens2 and ensure their comfort with this AR device. Then, each participant controls the Turtlebot2 in Hololens2 and is required to perform the four tasks presented in Sect. 4.2, with a total time limit of 120 s. At the end of the study, participants are asked to complete a questionnaire based on the five-point System Usability Scale (SUS, 1 = strongly disagree to 5 = strongly agree) [2], to appraise the usability of the system.

In terms of subjective measurements, we calculate the mean and standard deviation of the questionnaire responses. Figure 9 presents a histogram with a 95% confidence interval for visual analysis. The SUS score is computed using a standard formula based on the mean scores of the questions. Our system receives a score of 80 out of 100, corresponding to a B rating on the grading scale, indicating excellent system usability. Furthermore, an analysis of individual question reveals that Q1, Q3, Q5, Q7, and Q9 all receive high scores, with an average of 4.225, while Q2, Q4, Q6, Q8, and Q10 receive lower scores, with an average of 2.05. This further confirms the strong usability of our system.

After analyzing the questionnaire results, we observe that Q4 has a slightly higher standard deviation of over 1, indicating that participants' choices for this question are widely distributed. Upon interviewing participants, we discover that the primary issue is their lack of confidence in operating AR devices. Participants feel that the tutorial training provided for the Hololens2 is necessary, which causes some disagreement on the question. Nonetheless, we maintain an optimistic outlook on this matter, as the increasing prevalence of AR technology is expected to alleviate this problem over time.

5   Conclusion and Future Work

We present a mobile AR-based robot motion control system using sparse finger joints as the input. This system allows user to effectively control Turtle-Bot2 to accomplish primitive motions and complex actions within the immersive HoloLens2 environment. We believe this work opens up intentional exploration of the use of AR devices as versatile tools for controlling robot motion.

Our work has a few limitations. First, our approach relies on directly pre-defined gestures, which may overlook individual variations and habits. To overcome this limitation, we plan to conduct a user pre-experiment to gather a more diverse set of popular gestures, accommodating a wider range of user preferences. Second, requiring users to perform highly standardized gestures for issuing commands may be too strict, we plan to implement a threshold approach, which allows commands for gestures closely resembling the standard ones, but prompt users to adjust their gestures in cases of significant deviation. Third, the delay from HoloLens2 to TurtleBot2 introduces a potential source of error, particularly in hazardous environments. In our future endeavors, we aim to minimize this delay and ensure that it does not compromise the system's performance.

Acknowledgements. This work was supported in part by NSFC (No. U21A20515, 61972388) and Shenzhen Science and Technology Program (GJHZ20210705141402008).

References

1. Bao, P., Maqueda, A.I., del Blanco, C.R., García, N.: Tiny hand gesture recognition without localization via a deep convolutional network. IEEE Trans. Consum. Electron. **63**(3), 251–257 (2017)
2. Brooke, J., et al.: SUS-a quick and dirty usability scale. In: Usability Evaluation in Industry, vol. 189, no. 194, pp. 4–7 (1996)
3. Chandan, K., Kudalkar, V., Li, X., Zhang, S.: Arroch: augmented reality for robots collaborating with a human. In: 2021 IEEE International Conference on Robotics and Automation (ICRA), pp. 3787–3793. IEEE (2021)
4. Cheok, M.J., Omar, Z., Jaward, M.H.: A review of hand gesture and sign language recognition techniques. Int. J. Mach. Learn. Cybern. **10**(1), 131–153 (2019)
5. Chung, S., Lee, T., Jeong, B., Jeong, J., Kang, H.: VRCAT: VR collision alarming technique for user safety. Vis. Comput. **39**(7), 3145–3159 (2023)
6. Guo, L., Lu, Z., Yao, L.: Human-machine interaction sensing technology based on hand gesture recognition: a review. IEEE Trans. Hum.-Mach. Syst. **51**(4), 300–309 (2021)
7. Iba, S., Paredis, C.J.J., Khosla, P.K.: Interactive multi-modal robot programming. In: Ang, M.H., Khatib, O. (eds.) Experimental Robotics IX. STAR, vol. 21, pp. 503–513. Springer, Heidelberg (2006). https://doi.org/10.1007/11552246_48
8. Kim, S., Sorokin, M., Lee, J., Ha, S.: Humanconquad: human motion control of quadrupedal robots using deep reinforcement learning. In: SIGGRAPH Asia 2022 Emerging Technologies, pp. 1–2. Association for Computing Machinery (2022)
9. Kim, T., Kim, G.J.: Real-time and on-line removal of moving human figures in hand-held mobile augmented reality. Vis. Comput. **39**(7), 2571–2582 (2023)

10. Lin, H.I., Hsu, M.H., Chen, W.K.: Human hand gesture recognition using a convolution neural network. In: 2014 IEEE International Conference on Automation Science and Engineering (CASE), pp. 1038–1043. IEEE (2014)
11. Liu, F., Zeng, W., Yuan, C., Wang, Q., Wang, Y.: Kinect-based hand gesture recognition using trajectory information, hand motion dynamics and neural networks. Artif. Intell. Rev. **52**, 563–583 (2019)
12. Makhataeva, Z., Varol, H.A.: Augmented reality for robotics: a review. Robotics **9**(2), 21 (2020)
13. Makhataeva, Z., Zhakatayev, A., Varol, H.A.: Safety aura visualization for variable impedance actuated robots. In: 2019 IEEE/SICE International Symposium on System Integration (SII), pp. 805–810. IEEE (2019)
14. Qin, Y., Chi, X., Sheng, B., Lau, R.W.: Guiderender: large-scale scene navigation based on multi-modal view frustum movement prediction. Vis. Comput. 1–11 (2023)
15. Rautaray, S.S., Agrawal, A.: Vision based hand gesture recognition for human computer interaction: a survey. Artif. Intell. Rev. **43**(1), 1–54 (2015)
16. Rudolph, C., Brunnett, G., Bretschneider, M., Meyer, B., Asbrock, F.: Technosapiens: merging humans with technology in augmented reality. Vis. Comput. 1–16 (2023)
17. Tzafestas, S.G.: Mobile robot control and navigation: a global overview. J. Intell. Robot. Syst. **91**(1), 35–58 (2018)
18. Wang, Y., Song, G., Qiao, G., Zhang, Y., Zhang, J., Wang, W.: Wheeled robot control based on gesture recognition using the kinect sensor. In: 2013 IEEE International Conference on Robotics and Biomimetics (ROBIO), pp. 378–383. IEEE (2013)
19. Wu, D., Jiang, X., Peng, R.: Transfer learning for motor imagery based brain-computer interfaces: a tutorial. Neural Netw. **153**, 235–253 (2022)
20. Yi, X., et al.: Physical inertial poser (PIP): physics-aware real-time human motion tracking from sparse inertial sensors. In: Proceedings of the IEEE/CVF Conference on Computer Vision and Pattern Recognition, pp. 13167–13178 (2022)
21. Zeng, W., Wang, C., Wang, Q.: Hand gesture recognition using leap motion via deterministic learning. Multimedia Tools Appl. **77**, 28185–28206 (2018)
22. Zhang, X., Wu, X.: Robotic control of dynamic and static gesture recognition. In: 2019 2nd World Conference on Mechanical Engineering and Intelligent Manufacturing (WCMEIM), pp. 474–478. IEEE (2019)

The Role of the Field Dependence-Independence Construct on the Curvature Gain of Redirected Walking Technology in Virtual Reality

Rui Jing[1], Gaorong Lv[1(✉)], Hongqiu Luan[1], Wei Gai[1(✉)], Shengzun Song[2(✉)], and Chenglei Yang[1]

[1] Shandong University, Ji'nan, China
15953173765@163.com, gw@sdu.edu.cn
[2] The National Police University for Criminal Justice, Baoding, China
songshenzun@163.com

Abstract. Redirected walking (RDW) enables users to physically stay inside a limited area while moving in large-scale virtual environments by purposefully introducing scene motions. Utilizing the curvature gain could improve the effectiveness of redirection. User's thresholds of curvature gain may be influenced by field dependence-independence (FDI) cognitive style and gender. In order to conduct a more thorough investigation of how FDI structure and gender affect thresholds of curvature gain, we have created three different virtual reality (VR) experimental scenes, evaluated thresholds of curvature gain using the psychophysical "limit method", and conducted correlational and hierarchical multiple regression analysis. The results reveal a significant association between FDI structure and the threshold of curvature gain, with gender acting as a moderator in this relationship in complex scene. These findings provide valuable insights for the personalized design of RDW systems.

Keywords: Redirected walk · Curvature gain · FDI structure · Gender

1 Introduction

Real walking in virtual space can provide a more natural user experience in terms of presence and immersion in virtual reality (VR), compared to walking-in-place and joystick-based locomotion [10,28]. However, there are difficulties in roaming virtual scenes in a vast region [20], partly due to the limited scale of the actual space. Therefore the directed walking (RDW) method is presented to address the issue of the non-isometric mapping of the virtual and real space, which partially overcomes this limitation [18,19]. Immersive roaming takes users out of reality and can be dangerous [5], so research on the RDW approach has made significant advances in exploring wider environments, multi-user interactions, collision avoidance, and other topics [9,29,30].

The principle of the RDW is to make use of the tolerable deviation between the user's visual perception and proprioception, so that the user's action in the actual environment is different from the perceived action in the virtual environment. Currently RDW methods mainly use four main operations, namely rotation gain, translation gain, curvature gain and bending gain, to control the user's motion in the real space [19]. Among them, the fundamental concept of curvature gain is to introduce a tolerable rotation during the user's forward movement. This creates the illusion that the user is moving in a straight line within the virtual space, while actually walking along a curved path in the real world. This occurs because the user subconsciously compensates for the minor discrepancy between the physical path and the perceived virtual path while walking [15,18]. Some studies have proposed the concept of detection thresholds to quantify this "tolerable amount of deviation" [11,18]. However, existing studies show that the estimation of detection threshold of curvature gain does not consider the influence of individual differences, and the results are inconsistent [4,11,15,18,26].

Field dependence-independence (FDI) is used to describe an individual's cognitive style and may affect the curvature gain threshold. Prior research has indicated that diverse cognitive styles can influence how users allocate their attentional resources to the surrounding environment and spatial orientation [3,11,16,28]. These variations in attentional focus can impact individuals' perception of self-motion within virtual environments [23], potentially influencing their sensitivity to curvature gain in such settings. In addition, in view of gender difference in spatial orientation ability, it is speculated that the relationship between field cognitive style and curvature gain may be affected by gender [31], which needs to be verified to provide specific suggestions. Motivated by these, we categorized individuals into two groups based on their cognitive styles: field-dependent and field-independent types. By devising experiments to detect curvature gain thresholds, we aimed to analyze the obtained results and explore the impacts of cognitive style and gender on individuals' sensitivity to curvature gain in redirected walking.

The major contribution of this paper is to make up for the measurement of curvature gain for people with different cognitive styles and gender in redirected walking technology. This provides suggestions for the personalized setting of redirected walking curvature gain parameters in virtual reality technology, so that to achieve higher efficiency and usability.

2   Related Work

2.1   FDI Structure

FDI structure is one of the most widely studied cognitive style dimensions in the literature. Field dependent type (FD) and field independent type (FI) are polar structures that describe cognitive styles [12]. FI individuals regard themselves as the reference of behavior and are not easily disturbed by irrelevant clues in the environment. FD individuals, take the environment as a reference for their behavior and are easily affected by irrelevants clues in the environment [12,14]. FDI is a stable dimension of individual functioning that is not easily changed [27].

Previous research has shown that people can be distracted by factors unrelated to the content of the scene [13]. Moreover, the FDI structure affects the way people process distracted and selective attention, and FD individuals are more likely to be distracted than FI individuals [12,17]. Therefore, FD individuals and FI individuals differ in the allocation of attention resources. FI individuals are more likely to be influenced by internal rather than external cues [6,22,33], and can complete key tasks faster [3]. FD individuals are opposite.

Common methods to determine whether a subject is FD or FI include Group Embedded Figures Test (GEFT) and Rod-frame Test (RFT). GEFT is the original and traditional "paper-and-pencil" instrument used to classify people as FD or FI. It asked subjects to assess their cognitive style by looking for simple patterns in complex shapes [3,21]. RFT is commonly used to assess the degree to which subjects rely on the visual frame of reference to perceive vertical, and use it to assess the subject's cognitive style (FDI Structure) [1]. In this study, we used the RFT test because it is simpler and more objective.

The development of virtual reality technologies such as Augmented reality (AR), Virtual reality (VR) and Mixed reality (MR) provides people with immersive and richer visual experiences, including visual attention, search, processing and understanding of task triggering [24,25]. Since FD and FI individuals differ in the way they perceive and process visual information [16,22,25], it is possible that the sensitivity of an individual to curvature gain in a virtual environment may also be related to their cognitive style, which will be discussed further in this paper.

2.2   Curvature Gain

Curvature gain is a gain method for redirected walking, which generally involves adding a continuous offset to the user's virtual rotation when walking in real physical space [19,26], and for the user to still think they are staying oriented to the intended target, so they unconsciously adjust their body rotation (rotating their head or torso) to correct their current orientation, thus correcting this offset [15]. When the virtual offset is quite small, the user will unknowingly walk along a curve in real space, while feeling straight ahead in virtual space [15]. Ideally, if the actual walking area is large enough, the curvature gain enables the user to walk along a circular path in the real environment while walking infinitely along a straight path in the virtual environment. In the experiments, the value of curvature gain g is $1/r$ (r is the radius of the ideal circle corresponding to walking in real physical space), when no curvature gain is performed, i.e., $r = +\infty$, at which time the curvature gain $g = 0(m^{-1})$.

An important component of evaluating detection thresholds is the estimation method that describes the rules for selecting the level of stimulus (In this paper, it refers to the curvature gain) to be tested in each trial. The "limit method" can specifically explain the meaning of threshold [7,15]. In the "limit method", the stimulus value changes in small steps up or down in each round of experiments, and the interval of each stimulus is equal until the turning point perceived by the subjects is detected [15]. After the completion of multiple test sequences, the average value of all turns is obtained, namely the perceived threshold of the subjects. In this way, we can intuitively study the changing characteristics of people's perception of curvature gain [15].

In previous studies, the curvature gain threshold has been used as a fixed parameter in many existing redirected walking methods [8]. Threshold detection studies of curvature gain still vary widely [4,11,18,26]. Later studies have reestimated the curvature gain threshold [15], but did not consider the influence of cognitive style (FDI structure) and gender.

3   Experiment

3.1   Participants

A total of 35 participants (17 males and 18 females), aged 22–35 years participated in the experiment. All participants were right-handed, with normal or corrected normal vision and no other visual impairment. None of our participants reported a balance disorder. Before participating in the formal experiment, all participants were adequately practiced and familiarized with the virtual reality environment. Every participant received a present as a reward (it worth about 7 dollars) for participation.

3.2   Design

The design of the experiment was divided into two stages: first, the cognitive style of the subjects was evaluated by the Rod-frame Test (see Sect. 3.3 for details); second, the user's threshold was detected by the curvature gain detection experiment (see Sect. 3.3 for details). In order to control the irrelevant interference of real space on subjects' perception, the experiment was conducted in a quiet room with uniform light.

3.3   Procedure

Rod-Frame Test. The experimental requirements and procedures of Rod-frame Test are as follows: (1) Before each round of experiment, the experimenter adjusted the frame to a certain Angle and returned the Angle of the rod to zero; (2) Through observation and judgment, the subjects adjusted the rod to the vertical direction; (3) Record the deviation between the Angle of the rod adjusted by the subject and the true vertical direction; (4) The experiment was conducted for 10 rounds. Subjects adjusted the frame Angle ($0°$, $10°$, $20°$, $30°$, $40°$, $50°$, $60°$, $70°$, $80°$, $90°$), and took the average deviation as the quantitative index of cognitive style score [32].

As shown in Fig. 1, the subject is performing a Rod-frame test. It can be seen in Fig. 1(c) that the Angle of the rod he adjusted is $87°$ (red dotted line), the vertical direction is $90°$ (green dotted line), the Angle of the frame is $70°$ (yellow dotted line), so the deviation from the vertical direction is $90°–87° = 3°$.

The greater the deviation is tested, the more likely the subject is to be field-dependence. The participants were given a 3-min break in every two rounds to avoid errors caused by visual strain and muscle memory.

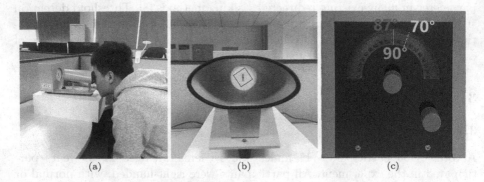

Fig. 1. (a) A subject was testing, (b) The state of the rod adjusted by the participant, (c) Test result. (Color figure online)

Curvature Gain Threshold Detection Experiment. In this experiment, we utilized the HTC Vive device to develop a virtual reality system specifically designed to measure the curvature gain threshold. Our system involved mapping a virtual straight path onto a circular path in the real physical space. All parameters of curvature gain are adjustable, including bending direction, travel distance and offset Angle. Due to the limitation of HTC Vive positioning and tracking system, we chose 4 m × 4 m experiment space and required participants to minimize head movement to control errors.

He experimental scenes were mostly simple indoor scenes [9,15] or outdoor path scenes [29]. However, in a virtual environment, people's perceptual sensitivity may be affected by complexity of scene, visual distance and other factors. Therefore, in order to more fully explore the general differences in curvature gain sensitivity of individuals with different cognitive styles in the redirected walking method, three different experimental scenes were selected in this paper to avoid the contingency of the single-scene experiment.

As shown in Fig. 2, the three scenes are museum exhibition hall, desert walking path and snowy mountain forest. The scene of museum exhibition hall simulates indoor scenes with short visual distance; The desert path and the snowy mountain forest simulate the outdoor scene with long visual distance, but the snowy mountain forest is more complex; Through these three scenes, we can evaluate the relationship between the curvature gain and FDI in different scenes more comprehensively, which is helpful to the generalization of the results.

Before the formal experiment, the purpose of the experiment was explained to the subjects, and the subjects were told that all the curvature gains were random. They were asked to answer their true feelings without making any

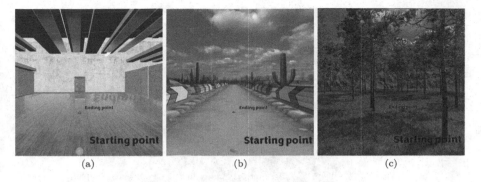

Fig. 2. Three experimental scenes: (a) Museum exhibition hall scene, (b) Desert walking path scene, (c) Snowy mountain forest scene.

guesses. All subjects underwent training experiments before the experiment to adapt to the experimental environment.

The specific experimental operation was as follows: the tester setted different curvature gain conditions in ascending or descending order, and asked the subjects to walk a straight line at a slow and uniform speed (from the start-point to the end-point) in the virtual environment. After the end, the tester asked subjects to report their feelings (did they feel the direction of walking is curved?), and recorded it using the "+" (yes) and "−" (no) symbols. The average value was calculated as the subject's threshold of curvature gain after all tests were completed. In order to avoid the possible sequential effect of the experimental design of two-factor subjects, all the ascending and descending experimental sequences were balanced by ABBA sequential design [15]. Taking left-rotation gain as an example, the test result of one of the subjects in scene 1 is shown in Fig. 3, with red lines showing all the turning points. Using the "limit method", his curvature gain threshold is the average of all the turning points ($g = 0.109\,\mathrm{m}^{-1}$).

Curvature gain	SCENE 1									
	1	2	3	4	5	6	7	8	9	10
	↑	↓	↓	↑	↑	↓	↓	↑	↑	↓
0.13526		+	+			+	+			+
0.12872		+	+			+	+			+
0.12217		+	+			+	-			+
0.11563		-	+			+				+
0.10908			-	+	-	-				-
0.10254	+			+	-					
0.09599	-			-	-				+	
0.08945	-			-	-				-	
0.08290	-			-	-			+	-	
0.07636	-			-	-			"	"	
...	-			-	-			-	-	
0.00000	-			-	-			-	-	

Fig. 3. Result of one of the subjects in scene 1. Red lines indicate the turning point. (Color figure online)

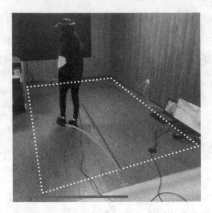

Fig. 4. A subject was performing a curvature gain threshold detection experiment.

The Fig. 4 shows the path taken by a subject during an experiment, the solid red line is the virtual path and the solid green line is the actual walking path. The subject walked a straight line in the virtual environment, but actually walked a curve.

Data Analysis. For all data, a Shapiro-Wilk test for normality was performed. The test found that all data were normal (all $P > 0.05$). The mean scores of curvature gain threshold in different categories of sociodemographic were tested by Student's t test or one-way ANOVA. Pearson's correlation analysis was used to analyze the correlation between FDI and curvature gain threshold. Hierarchical multiple regression analyses were applied to explore the moderating of gender on the relationship between FDI and curvature gain threshold. The p-value of <0.05 was considered significant.

4   Experimental Results

4.1   Results of RFT

It is worth noting that the perception of FDI is not a dichotomous category; it is a continuum (or dimension) that exists for all people [2]. We calculated a mean deviation value of 2.14° for the 35 subjects. Thus, we used this value to divide the 35 subjects into two categories: FI group had 18 subjects ($<2.14°$), and FD group had 17 subjects ($>2.14°$) [32].

4.2   Results of Mean Curvature Gain Threshold

Using the "limit method", we tested the average threshold of the curvature gain for users of two cognitive styles (FI group, FD group). The statistical results are as follows:

As shown in Fig. 5, in experimental scene 1 (museum exhibition hall), the mean curvature gain threshold of FI group was $0.1065 \, m^{-1}$, the mean curvature gain threshold of FD group was $0.1459 \, m^{-1}$; in experimental scene 2 (desert walking path), the mean curvature gain threshold of FI group was $0.1162 \, m^{-1}$, the mean curvature gain threshold of FD group was $0.1484 \, m^{-1}$; in experimental scene 3 (snowy mountain forest), the mean curvature gain threshold of FI group was $0.1126 \, m^{-1}$, the mean curvature gain threshold of FD group was $0.1445 \, m^{-1}$. Then, we conducted independent samples t-tests on the detection thresholds of the two groups in the FD group and FI group in each of the three scenes. The results were as follows: $Scene1: t = -4.807, P < 0.001, df = 33; Scene2: t = -4.258, P < 0.001, df = 33; Scene3: t = -5.564, P < 0.001, df = 33$. It showed that FI individuals had significantly lower detection thresholds than FD individuals.

4.3 Curvature Gain Threshold Difference in the Three Scenes

The mean curvature gain threshold results of all people in the three scenarios are shown in Fig. 5: $Scene1 : 0.1257 \, m^{-1}, Scene2 : 0.1318 \, m^{-1}, Scene3 : 0.1281 \, m^{-1}$. The result of one-way ANOVA ($F = 0.451, P = 0.638, partical \, \eta^2(eta) = 0.009$) showed that there are no difference in thresholds among three scenes. It shows that the results found in this study was reliable and stable.

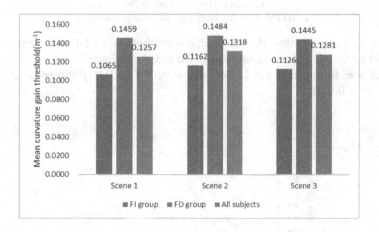

Fig. 5. Curvature gain threshold of subjects in three scenes.

4.4 Correlation Analyses of the Relationship Between FDI and Curvature Gain Threshold

The bivariate correlations for the assessed variables are presented. The FDI scores were positively related to curvature gain threshold of scene 1 ($r =$

0.811, $P < 0.001$), curvature gain threshold of scene 2 ($r = 0.779$, $P < 0.001$), and curvature gain threshold of scene 3 ($r = 0.764$, $P < 0.001$).

4.5 Moderation Effect of Gender on Relationship Between FDI and Curvature Gain Threshold

First, independent variables were mean centered to minimize multi-collinearity. Then, multiple linear regression analysis was used to test the moderating effect of gender on relationship between FDI and curvature gain threshold among different scenes. The results are shown in Table 1. The interaction between gender and FDI in scene 3 was significant (Beta $= -0.360$, $P = 0.009$).

Table 1. Hierarchical linear regression predicting curvature gain threshold

	Variables	Beta	t	P
Scene1	Gender	−0.110	−1.065	0.295
	FDI	0.785	6.044	0.000
	Gender×FDI	−0.026	0.198	0.845
Scene2	Gender	−0.072	−0.422	0.527
	FDI	0.774	−0.640	0.000
	Gender×FDI	−0.005	−0.036	0.972
Scene3	Gender	−0.078	−0.760	0.453
	FDI	0.538	0.538	0.000
	Gender×FDI	−0.360	2.790	0.009

• NOTE: FDI: Field Dependence-independence

The Fig. 6 is presented that the correlation between FDI and curvature gain threshold of female is lower compared with male. However, no moderating effect of gender was found in scene 1 (Beta $= -0.026$, $P > 0.05$) and scene 2 (Beta $= -0.005$, $P > 0.05$).

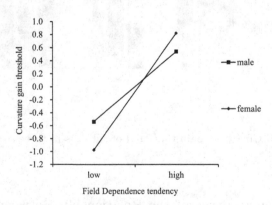

Fig. 6. Moderation effect of gender on relationship between FDI and curvature gain threshold.

5   Discussion

In this paper, the differences in the detection thresholds of curvature gain of users with different genders and cognitive styles are discussed.

The experimental results showed that the curvature gain threshold of FD individuals was significantly greater than that of FI individuals in three different scenes, and the threshold of curvature gain of users is positively correlated with its field dependence in VR redirected walking. It may be because the higher the field dependence an individual have, the more likely he is to be disturbed by the surrounding environment, resulting in a lower allocation of attention to his own spatial positioning ability. Therefore, he can accept a higher curvature gain threshold. We calculated the average curvature gain threshold for all participants, and the total average curvature gain ($g = 0.1252\,\mathrm{m}^{-1}$) is similar to the measurements in a previous study [15], indicating that our results have some credibility.

The moderating effect of gender was found in the scene 3. Compared with male, the field independence of female was more correlated with curvature gain threshold, that is, the higher field independence female have, the easier it was to perceive the rotation in physical space [31]. This finding may be related to gender advantage. According to social gender theory, men tend to have higher sense of direction and spatial orientation ability than women, and have a higher grasp of space [31]. The Snowy mountain forest is more complicated and needs more spatial orientation to walk in it. Therefore, men's high spatial recognition may present obvious advantages [31].

Our test environment was arranged in a $4\,\mathrm{m} \times 4\,\mathrm{m}$ area, using a small area to maintain the VR experience for the participants. However, whether the "large space, long-distance" test region affects human perception of curvature gain thresholds still needs further study. In this study, VR symptoms, car sickness and motion sickness were not considered. Although no participants reported vertigo in the experiment, such symptoms may affect participants' sensitivity to threshold perception of curvature gain, which we will continue to investigate in future work.

6   Conclusion

This study experimentally explored the detection threshold of curvature gain for users with different cognitive styles. Analysis of the experimental results demonstrated that the cognitive styles of participants had significant effects on the detection threshold of curvature gain, and the threshold of curvature gain of the FD individuals was significantly higher than that of the FI individuals. In addition, in complex VR scene (scene 3), gender can Moderate the relationship between cognitive styles (FDI structure) and curvature gain threshold, and male individuals with field-independence have lower thresholds. This provides suggestions for the personalized setting of redirected walking curvature gain parameters in virtual reality technology, so that the curvature gain intensity can be more accurately controlled according to the user's gender and pre-assessed cognitive styles (FDI structure), so as to achieve higher efficiency and usability.

Acknowledgement. We would like to thank all reviewers for their valuable comments. This work is supported by National Key R&D Program of China (2022ZD0118002), and the National Natural Science Foundation of China under Grant (61972233, 62007021, 62277035).

References

1. Bagust, J., Docherty, S., Haynes, W., Telford, R., Isableu, B.: Changes in rod and frame test scores recorded in schoolchildren during development - a longitudinal study. PLoS ONE **8**(5), e65321–e65321 (2013)
2. Baran, M., Chignell, M.: Differences in cognitive ability and preference mediate effects of interruptions on simulated driving performance. Hum. Factors Ergon. Soc. Annu. Meet. Proc. **50**(17), 2008–2011 (2006)
3. Bian, Y., Zhou, C., Chen, Y., Zhao, Y., Yang, C.: The role of the field dependence-independence construct on the flow-performance link in virtual reality. In: I3D 2020: Symposium on Interactive 3D Graphics and Games (2020)
4. Bruder, G., Interrante, V., Phillips, L., Steinicke, F.: Redirecting walking and driving for natural navigation in immersive virtual environments. IEEE Trans. Visual. Comput. Graphics **18**(4), 538–545 (2012)
5. Chung, S., Lee, T., Jeong, B., Jeong, J., Kang, H.: VRCAT: VR collision alarming technique for user safety. Vis. Comput. **39**, 3145–3159 (2022)
6. Couñago, M.A.G.: Field dependence-independence (FDI) cognitive style: an analysis of attentional functioning. Psicothema **19**(4), 572–577 (2007)
7. Damasceno, B.: Sensation and perception. In: Damasceno, B. (ed.) Research on Cognition Disorders, pp. 15–24. Springer, Cham (2020). https://doi.org/10.1007/978-3-030-57267-9_2
8. Bachmann, E.R., Hodgson, E., Hoffbauer, C., Messinger, J.: Multi-user redirected walking and resetting using artificial potential fields. IEEE Trans. Visual. Comput. Graphics **25**(5), 2022–2031 (2019)
9. Fan, C.W., Xu, S.Z., Yu, P., Zhang, F.L., Zhang, S.H.: Redirected walking based on historical user walking data. In: 2023 IEEE Conference Virtual Reality and 3D User Interfaces (VR), pp. 53–62 (2023)
10. Gai, W., et al.: Supporting easy physical-to-virtual creation of mobile VR maze games: a new genre. In: Proceedings of the 2017 CHI Conference on Human Factors in Computing Systems, CHI 2017, pp. 5016–5028. Association for Computing Machinery, New York (2017)
11. Grechkin, T., Thomas, J., Azmandian, M., Bolas, M., Suma, E.: Revisiting detection thresholds for redirected walking: combining translation and curvature gains. In: Proceedings of the ACM Symposium on Applied Perception, pp. 113–120 (2016)
12. Jolly, E.J., Reardon, R.: Cognitive differentiation, automaticity, and interruptions of automatized behaviors. Pers. Soc. Psychol. Bull. **11**(3), 301–314 (1985)
13. Kim, T., Kim, G.J.: Real-time and on-line removal of moving human figures in hand-held mobile augmented reality. Vis. Comput. **39**, 2571–2582 (2022)
14. Kozhevnikov, M.: Cognitive styles in the context of modern psychology: toward an integrated framework of cognitive style. Psychol. Bull. **133**(3), 464 (2007)

15. Li, H., et al.: Estimation of human sensitivity for curvature gain of redirected walking technology (2021)
16. Mayer, R.E., Massa, L.J.: Three facets of visual and verbal learners: cognitive ability, cognitive style, and learning preference. J. Educ. Psychol. **95**(4), 833 (2003)
17. Meys, H.L., Sanderson, P.M.: The effect of individual differences on how people handle interruptions. Proc. Hum. Factors Ergon. Soc. Annu. Meet. **57**(1), 868–872 (2013)
18. Neth, C.T., Souman, J.L., Engel, D., Kloos, U., Mohler, B.J.: Velocity-dependent dynamic curvature gain for redirected walking. In: IEEE Virtual Reality Conference, VR 2011, Singapore, 19–23 March 2011 (2011)
19. Nilsson, N.C., et al.: 15 years of research on redirected walking in immersive virtual environments. IEEE Comput. Graphics Appl. **38**(2), 44–56 (2018)
20. Qin, Y., Chi, X., Sheng, B., Lau, R.W.H.: Guiderender: large-scale scene navigation based on multi-modal view frustum movement prediction. Vis. Comput. **39**, 3597–3607 (2023)
21. Raptis, G.E., Fidas, C., Avouris, N.: Effects of mixed-reality on players' behaviour and immersion in a cultural tourism game: a cognitive processing perspective. Int. J. Hum Comput Stud. **114**, 69–79 (2018)
22. Riding, R., Cheema, I.: Cognitive styles-an overview and integration. Educ. Psychol. **11**(3), 193–215 (1991)
23. Rudolph, C., Brunnett, G., Bretschneider, M., Meyer, B., Asbrock, F.: Technosapiens: merging humans with technology in augmented reality. Vis. Comput. (2023)
24. Sharples, S., Cobb, S., Moody, A., Wilson, J.R.: Virtual reality induced symptoms and effects (VRISE): comparison of head mounted display (HMD), desktop and projection display systems. Displays **29**(2), 58–69 (2008)
25. Sousa Santos, B., et al.: Head-mounted display versus desktop for 3D navigation in virtual reality: a user study. Multimedia Tools Appl. **41**, 161–181 (2009)
26. Steinicke, F., Bruder, G., Jerald, J., Frenz, H., Lappe, M.: Estimation of detection thresholds for redirected walking techniques. IEEE Trans. Vis. Comput. Graph. **16**(1), 17–27 (2010)
27. Teghil, A., Boccia, M., Guariglia, C.: Field dependence-independence differently affects retrospective time estimation and flicker-induced time dilation. Exp. Brain Res. **237**(4), 1019–1029 (2019)
28. Usoh, M., et al.: Walking> walking-in-place> flying, in virtual environments. In: Proceedings of the 26th Annual Conference on Computer Graphics and Interactive Techniques, pp. 359–364 (1999)
29. Xu, S.Z., Liu, J.H., Wang, M., Zhang, F.L., Zhang, S.H.: Multi-user redirected walking in separate physical spaces for online VR scenarios. IEEE Trans. Visual. Comput. Graphics 1–11 (2023)
30. Xu, S.Z., Lv, T., He, G., Chen, C.H., Zhang, F.L., Zhang, S.H.: Optimal pose guided redirected walking with pose score precomputation. In: 2022 IEEE Conference on Virtual Reality and 3D User Interfaces (VR), pp. 655–663 (2022)
31. Xueyuan, G., Weihua, D., Yiyi, T., Diyang, C.: Study on the influence of field cognitive style, gender and spatial terminology on geographical spatial orientation ability. based on experiments in virtual space. J. Geo-Inf. Sci. **18**(11), 9 (2016)
32. Yan, L., Xiaohong, L., Youqin, J., Yingchun, B.: Psychological factors influencing individual seasickness. Acad. J. Second Mil. Univ. **27**(12), 3 (2006)
33. Zhang, L.F.: Field-dependence/independence: cognitive style or perceptual ability?-validating against thinking styles and academic achievement. Pers. Individ. Differ. **37**(6), 1295–1311 (2004)

A New Camera Calibration Algorithm Based on Adaptive Image Selection

Huang Jian and Zeng Shan[(⊠)]

The College of Mathematics and Computer Science, Wuhan Polytechnic University, Wuhan, China
zengshan1981@whpu.edu.cn

Abstract. Camera calibration plays an important role in the 3D reconstruction task. However, in the calibration process, users need to select some key images from a large number of calibration board images for further performing the maximum likelihood estimation of camera model parameters. Due to the subjectivity of this estimation, it is difficult to guarantee the consistency of the results obtained by different testers. In this paper, a new camera calibration image selection algorithm is proposed to obtain high accuracy intrinsic parameters. Users only need to acquire a series of checkerboard image sequences, randomly select one image from the image sequence each time, and determine whether the image can be used for camera calibration by calculating the angle error of single frame checkerboard corner. This method can adaptively select a small number of images from the image sequence for camera calibration. The experimental results show that this self-built calibration algorithm is not only simple in the operation process, but also has higher accuracy and consistency in calibration results when compared with traditional calibration method.

Keywords: Camera calibration · Intrinsic parameters evaluation · Image filtering

1 Introduction

Camera calibration is the process of determining the internal geometric and optical properties (intrinsic parameters) of the camera and acquiring the position and direction (external parameters) of the camera optical center in the world coordinate system [1]. It determines the camera parameters by the real coordinates of the three-dimensional object and corresponding two-dimensional image coordinates. The camera parameters obtained by camera calibration determine a mapping relationship between points on the image and corresponding points on the space surface of object. Accurate camera calibration has become an important part of 3D reconstruction in the task.

The application of 3D reconstruction [2] depends on the accuracy of camera calibration to a great extent. When using a planar calibration plate to calibrate the camera, the accuracy of obtained calibration results primarily depends on the attitude of captured images. It is high likely that there is a degraded posture in the set of manually selected recording postures [3]. Based on the theories of degenerate camera poses [3–8], it is of

B. Sheng et al. (Eds.): CGI 2023, LNCS 14497, pp. 376–387, 2024.
https://doi.org/10.1007/978-3-031-50075-6_29

great significance to change the direction (rotation) of the camera and enable captured image set to cover the entire visual field of the camera both in the process of image collection. Therefore, the selection of calibration images constitutes an important part of camera calibration.

Scientific researchers have studied the influencing factors of camera calibration results. Triggs [9] found that the angular spread affected the estimation of camera focal length, and further proved the angular spread should be more than 5° for its accurate estimation. Sturm et al. [3] further distinguished the estimation of principal point coordinates and focal length. More importantly, the singularity that may exist in camera calibration was discussed and linked to individual camera parameters, such as the focal length cannot be estimated when the picture is parallel to the image plane. Sun et al. [10] evaluated the sensitivity of the camera model to noise, and the influence of image number and model complexity on accuracy. However, only the reprojection error on the training dataset was measured in their work, resulting in potential risks of overfitting in the calibration results. In order to overcome this problem, Richardson et al. [11] introduced the maximum expected reprojection error (Max ERE) to measure the error, and this measure method was related to the error of test dataset.

The current calibration toolbox requires users to place calibration boards (checkerboard, circular grid pattern, AprilTag, etc.) at different positions for taking images, and then use optimization algorithms to optimize the estimated parameters and calculate the maximum likelihood calibration parameters. Tan et al. [12] proposed to use a monitor to display the camera posture, but the selection of the best shooting posture was not determined in the study. The previous works have guided users to place the camera correctly. In photogrammetry, the offline determination of placing a given number of cameras was used to obtain 3D reconstruction results with higher accuracy [13, 14]. The optimal posture of camera calibration was calculated in the study [15], but this method was only based on constrained camera movement. The Robot Operating System (ROS) [16] monocular camera calibration toolbox provided text descriptions for users to obtain better camera calibration images. Recently, the ZED stereo system of StereoLabs completed interactive guidance for users to maintain a good shooting posture during the calibration process. However, a specific cube calibration system was used in the process, contributing to the incompatibility of other calibration system. Richardson et al. [11] came up with a posture selection method for interactive calibration that automatically calculated the next best posture and guided users to place the calibration plate corrodingly. However, these poses searched from a fixed set of approximate 60 candidate images were evenly distributed in the perspective of the camera, and this method relied on good posture initialization without considering the rotation angle and degraded pose. Rojtberg et al. [17] proposed a method called Pose selection that optimized the camera intrinsic parameters and distortion coefficients separately, and defined two different pose selection methods based on intrinsic parameters and distortion coefficients. The variance of each parameter in current calibration results was calculated to determine which pose selection method is used for specific situation. Pen et al. [18] presented a method called Wizard, which optimized the pose by using some algorithms such as simulated annealing to minimize the uncertainty of intrinsic parameters expectation, and obtained the final calibration results based on optimized pose.

2 Preliminaries

2.1 Overview of Pinhole Camera Model

The calibration method in pinhole camera model [19] obtains the intrinsic parameters of the camera through a relationship between the actual spatial position of the checkerboard and the imaging position. Arbitrary three-dimensional world coordinate points are expressed as $P = [X,Y,Z]$, corresponding two-dimensional image pixel coordinates are expressed as $p = [u,v]$, their homogeneous coordinates are expressed as $\tilde{P} = [X,Y,Z,1]$ and $\tilde{p} = [u,v,1]$. Their geometric relationship can be expressed as the following equation:

$$s\tilde{p} = K\Delta([Rt]\tilde{P}) \tag{1}$$

where s is the scale factor, $[Rt]$ is the rotation and translation between world coordinate system and camera coordinate system, K is the intrinsic parameters matrix, and $\Delta(.)$ is the distortion operator.

The intrinsic matrix K is expressed as follows:

$$K = \begin{bmatrix} f_x & 0 & c_x \\ 0 & f_y & c_y \\ 0 & 0 & 1 \end{bmatrix} \tag{2}$$

where f_x, f_y represent the focal length of the camera, and c_x, c_y represent the principal point coordinates.

The distortion operator $\Delta(.)$ can be expressed by the following formula:

$$\begin{cases} x_1 = x(1 + k_1 r^2 + k_2 r^4 + k_3 r^6) + 2p_1 xy + p_2(r^2 + 2x^2) \\ y_1 = y(1 + k_1 r^2 + k_2 r^4 + k_3 r^6) + 2p_2 xy + p_1(r^2 + 2y^2) \\ r^2 = x^2 + y^2 \end{cases} \tag{3}$$

where k_1, k_2, k_3 represent the radial distortion coefficients, p_1, p_2 represent the tangential distortion coefficients, (x,y) represents the coordinates of distortion image, (x_1,y_1) represents the image coordinates without distortion.

Through nonlinear optimization algorithm, the intrinsic and external parameters of the camera are optimized to minimize the reprojection error. The reprojection error is expressed as the following equation:

$$E_r = \sum_i^N \sum_j^M (\left\| u_i^j - \tilde{u}\left(C, \Pi_i, P_i^j\right) \right\|) + (\left\| v_i^j - \tilde{v}\left(C, \Pi_i, P_i^j\right) \right\|) \tag{4}$$

where (u_i^j, v_i^j) denotes the two-dimensional pixel coordinates of the j_{th} ($j = 1,2,...,M$) point of the i_{th} ($i = 1,2,...,N$) image, which can be obtained by various corner detectors. $(\tilde{u}, \tilde{v})$ represents the reprojection coordinates of three-dimensional point coordinates corresponding to (u_i^j, v_i^j). P_i^j represents the three-dimensional world coordinates of the j_{th} point on the i_{th} image. The three-dimensional coordinates are preset before calculating internal parameters, and the Z-axis coordinates are set to zero when using the plane calibrator. C represents the parameter set of intrinsic parameters and distortion coefficients, and Π_i represents the parameter set of rotation matrix R and translation vector t of the i_{th} image.Parameter variance of camera calibration

3 Methods

3.1 Camera Calibration Process Based on Adaptive Image Filtering

This paper takes a series of image sequences of checkerboard calibration board and randomly selects a picture from the image sequence each time. The corner detection function [20] in OpenCV is used to determine the corner coordinates of the checkerboard on the picture. Then, the angle error is calculated by the corner coordinates, and is further used to judge whether the image can be used for camera calibration. The above operations adaptively select a small number of key frames from the image sequence for camera calibration. The process of camera calibration in this paper is mainly divided into two parts including camera intrinsic parameter initialization and key frame selection. The overall process is shown in Fig. 1.

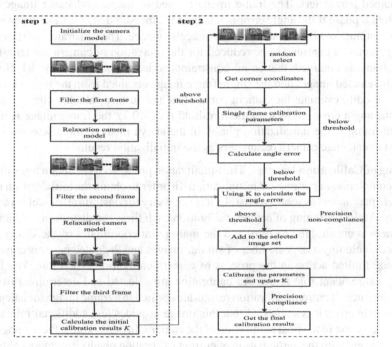

Fig. 1. The flowchart of camera calibration in self-built algorithm

Parameter Initialization. The initialization phase needs to obtain three pictures for the completion of parameters initialization. In order to obtain the initialization results of camera parameters as soon as possible, it is necessary to constrain all model parameters properly. At the beginning of camera calibration each time, the distortion coefficient of the camera is constrained to zero, and the main point coordinates of the camera locate in the center of the image, making it easier to acquire the initialization results of focal length by a single picture. The constrain is then reduced gradually in camera model, that is, no constrain in the coordinates of the main point and distortion.

As for the initial stage of camera calibration, better images need to be selected for obtaining initialization results. Firstly, the camera model is initialized, the principal point coordinates of the camera model are set to the image center, and the distortion coefficient is set to zero. At next, key images are selected from the image sequence, the intrinsic parameters are estimated individually by using the frame image, and the angle error of the frame image is calculated by the method mentioned in Sect. 3.2. The frame is taken as the first valid frame if the angle error is less than the threshold th_1 (< 0.2), otherwise, the image is continued to be obtained from the image sequence. After obtaining the first frame image, the constrain of the camera model parameters is reduced to relax the camera model, only setting the distortion coefficient to zero, and the image is then obtained from the image sequence. The camera parameters are estimated by both using the currently selected frame and the single frame image obtained from the image sequence, and the angle error of single frame image is calculated by using the obtained parameters. The frame image is used as the second frame image in the initialization phase if the angle error is less than the threshold th_1 (<0.2), otherwise, the picture continues to be obtained from the image sequence. The constraints of the camera model parameters continue to be reduced for the relaxation of camera model after the second frame is obtained, that is, no constraints added to the camera model. Both the currently selected images and the single frame image obtained from the image sequence are then used to estimate the camera parameters and further calculate the angle error. When the angle error is less than the threshold th_1 (<0.2), the frame image is used as the third frame in the initialization phase. In the above method, three selected images are used to calculate camera parameters as the initialization results.

Filtering of Calibration Images. The initialization phase needs to obtain three pictures for the completion of parameters initialization. In order to obtain the initialization results of camera parameters as soon as possible, it is necessary to constrain all model parameters properly. At the beginning of camera calibration each time, the distortion coefficient of the camera is constrained to zero, and the main point coordinates of the Using image sequences including a large number of similar images and degraded poses is considered to provide limited action in the process of camera calibration. Therefore, key frames playing a significant role in camera calibration are selected and determined from the image sequence. If current calibration results are applied to a frame image for calculating smaller angle error, it is suggested that this image provides less additional information and limited action in the final calibration of the camera. In other words, these images that are inconsistent with the participation of current calibration results in camera calibration are preferred to be obtained, and thereby allowing more universality in the results of camera calibration.

After obtaining initial model parameters, the subsequent images are evaluated to determine their effectiveness in camera calibration. At first, an image is obtained from the image sequence, this frame image is used to estimate the parameters of camera model, and these obtained parameter estimation results are then used to calculate the angle error of this frame image. If the angle error is less than the threshold th_3 (<0.6), the current frame is believed to be an effective high-quality image with benefits in the model converge. The angle error of current frame is then calculated by using the parameter estimation results obtained from all currently selected frames. If the angle error is greater than the threshold th_2 (>0.2), it is demonstrated that the current frame is helpful to optimize the model parameters, and this frame image is placed in the selected image set. The above process is repeated for image filtering. The selection of key frames should be stopped until the accuracy of camera parameters meets the requirements.

3.2 Camera Parameter Evaluation Index Based on Rectangular Information

The method in this paper directly uses the corner pixel coordinates of calibration plate in the picture to evaluate the calibration results. Using the rectangular information of the checkerboard, the points on the image are directly projected into three-dimensional coordinates in the camera coordinate system, and whether three-dimensional points in the camera coordinate system meet the rectangular condition is judged.

In the pinhole imaging model, it is assumed that the model has no distortion, and the image pixel coordinates of four corners in a rectangle are expressed as follows:

$$a(u_1, v_1), b(u_2, v_2), c(u_3, v_3), d(u_4, v_4) \tag{5}$$

The formula for converting pixel coordinates into normalized coordinates is:

$$\begin{cases} x = (u - c_x)/f_x \\ y = (v - c_y)/f_y \end{cases} \tag{6}$$

where (x, y) represents the normalized coordinate, (u, v) represents the pixel coordinate, f_x, f_y represents the focal length, and c_x, c_y represents the principal point coordinate. The Eq. (6) is used to convert a, b, c, d in Eq. (5) into normalized coordinates as follows:

$$A(x_1, y_1, 1), B(x_2, y_2, 1), C(x_3, y_3, 1), D(x_4, y_4, 1) \tag{7}$$

Assuming that the coordinate origin O (0,0,0) represents the three-dimensional coordinates of the camera, there is the following relationship:

$$\begin{cases} \overrightarrow{OA} = t_1\overrightarrow{OA} \\ \overrightarrow{OB} = t_2\overrightarrow{OB} \\ \overrightarrow{OC} = t_3\overrightarrow{OC} \\ \overrightarrow{OD} = t_4\overrightarrow{OD} \end{cases} \tag{8}$$

where t_1, t_2, t_3, t_4 represent the proportional coefficient and $\tilde{A}, \tilde{B}, \tilde{C}, \tilde{D}$ represent the three-dimensional coordinates of four corners (A, B, C, D in a rectangle) in the camera coordinate system.

Since $\tilde{A}, \tilde{B}, \tilde{C}, \tilde{D}$ represent four corners of the same checkerboard grid, it is found that $\overrightarrow{\tilde{A}\tilde{B}} = \overrightarrow{\tilde{C}\tilde{D}}$. The homogeneous linear equations are obtained as following:

$$\begin{cases} -x_1t_1 + x_2t_2 + x_3t_3 - x_4t_4 = 0 \\ -y_1t_1 + y_2t_2 + y_3t_3 - y_4t_4 = 0 \\ -t_1 + t_2 + t_3 - t_4 = 0 \end{cases} \tag{9}$$

From the above equation, the freedom degree of the solution of equation groups is one, as following:

$$\begin{cases} t_1 = at \\ t_2 = bt \\ t_3 = ct \\ t_4 = dt \end{cases} \tag{10}$$

where a, b, c, d are known constants, which can be calculated by Eq. (18).

Based on the characteristics of checkerboard rectangle, the angle between two vectors $\vec{AB}$ and $\vec{AC}$ should be 90 degrees. The evaluation indicators are defined as follows:

$$\varepsilon_{error} = degress(\vec{AB}, \vec{AC}) - \pi/2 \tag{11}$$

where degress (.) represents the angle function, which is used to calculate the angle between two vectors. This error is called angle error.

4 Experiments

This paper evaluates a new self-built method of camera calibration from multiple perspectives. Firstly, its stability of multi-channel parallelism is tested. At second, the ability of different image selection methods to select key frames is compared on a basis of real data, and the accuracy of this camera calibration method is compared with other camera calibration methods or tools. The experiment in this paper is based on 200 checkerboard image sequences collected from the same camera without changing the focal length in the same field of view space.

4.1 Multi-channel Parallel Experiment

In order to verify the stability of the camera calibration method in this paper, 20 groups of image sets are generated in parallel, and then the mean and standard deviation of calibration results of each group of image sets are calculated. Their results are further compared with the mean and standard deviation of calibration results obtained from 20 groups of randomly selected pictures.

Table 1. Comparison of calibration results

	f_x(mean/std)	f_y(mean/std)	c_x(mean/std)	c_y(mean/std)	k_1(mean/std)	k_2(mean/std)
Random	986.15 ± 7.59	985.34 ± 8.66	637.71 ± 7.51	340.09 ± 7.98	0.023 ± 0.044	-0.139 ± 0.276
Angle error	989.61 ± 4.06	988.22 ± 4.17	636.08 ± 1.97	344.65 ± 1.41	0.019 ± 0.008	-0.091 ± 0.029

From Table 1, although the mean value of camera parameters obtained from multi-channel parallel results by the self-built camera calibration method in this paper is not much different from that obtained by the random selection method, the standard deviation of camera parameters obtained by the self-built method is significantly smaller than that obtained by the random selection method. The results show that this self-built method can adaptively establish a better image selection path when filtering different initial images, and its calibration results are demonstrated to possess higher stability.

4.2 Accuracy Comparison of Different Image Screening Methods

This paper compares the mean reprojection error (MRE) of camera calibration results from three different methods including random screening, minimizing parameter variance, and angle error proposed in this paper.

Previous calibration methods are used to calculate the MRE on all images used for camera calibration. In this paper, 60 images are selected carefully and further used as the test dataset, and these images contain various angles and distortion areas. Some images in the test dataset are shown in Fig. 2.

Fig. 2. Sample images in the test dataset

Due to unknown pose in each image of test dataset, the PNP algorithm uses current calibration results as the input to calculate the image posture. This method is utilized to optimize external parameters of the camera based on calibration results of internal parameters, which possibly leads to a lower value of MRE calculated by test dataset. However, it is guaranteed that fair assessment is still performed on the calibration results. In the experiment, three image filtering methods are used to select 20 groups of different images from the same image sequence, and then the MRE of 20 times of calibration results obtained by image filtering methods on the same image from test dataset is calculated, and the MRE on all images from test dataset is compared under three various image filtering methods.

Table 2 shows the MRE of 20 filtering results on the test set according to three image screening methods. The method based on angle error reaches a smaller MRE when comparing with the results of Table 2. Angle error is used to evaluate the calibration results of the camera. To be more specific, detected corners in checkerboard image are mapped into camera coordinates system by calibration results of internal parameters. Mapping points of checkerboard in camera coordinates system meet the rectangular conditions, contributing to the generation of small angle error. The larger value of angle

Table 2. Accuracy comparison of three image filtering methods

	MRE(max)	MRE(min)	MRE(mean)
Random	0.8404	0.2046	**0.3804**
Minimize var	0.6670	0.1623	**0.3774**
Angle error	0.7487	0.1644	**0.3614**

error represents the calibration results with lower accuracy. The application of angle error is able to avoid the influence of external parameters estimation based on images in the evaluation of calibration results. It is worth noting that the maximum MRE on the test dataset obtained by minimizing the parameter variance method is smaller than that of the angle error method in this paper. This is because it is easier to select images with checkerboards at the edge of the field of view space or with large rotation angles when using the method of minimizing the parameter variance for image filtering. Calibration results therefore have good performance on images with large checkerboard rotation angles in test set. However, the self-built method based on angle error selects images with more universality, and thereby having slightly worse performance on these extreme images in the test set.

4.3 Comparison of Different Camera Calibration Methods and Tool Results

Other camera calibration methods and tools are also compared in this paper. Different calibration tools are used for 20 times of calibration experiments. The MRE from the results of each calibration method on the test set is compared and shown in Table 3.

Table 3. Accuracy comparison of different camera calibration methods and tools

	MRE(max)	MRE(min)	MRE(mean)
OpenCV [20]	0.9833	0.1785	**0.4199**
Pose selection [17]	0.7831	0.2183	**0.4167**
Wizard [18]	1.001	0.196	**0.3941**
Image filtering	0.7148	0.1630	**0.3601**

In Table 3, the calibration results obtained by the method based on image filtering proposed in this paper have the smallest average MRE on images of test set when compared with other calibration methods and tools, indicating that calibration results based on this method have higher accuracy than other calibration methods and tools. Meanwhile, the calibration results of this method show the smallest value of maximum MRE on the test set, indicating that the calibration results are superior to other calibration methods and tools in abnormal pose.

The mean and standard deviation of focal length, optical center and distortion coefficient in 20 experiments are shown in Table 4.

Table 4. Comparison of calibration results from different camera calibration methods and tools

	f_x(mean/std)	f_y(mean/std)	c_x(mean/std)	c_y(mean/std)	k_1(mean/std)	k_2(mean/std)
OpenCV [20]	982.97 ± 8.66	982.38 ± 8.48	629.92 ± 9.57	341.31 ± 8.14	0.041 ± 0.029	−0.217 ± 0.157
Pose selection [17]	947.56 ± 3.28	946.03 ± 3.04	626.95 ± 1.83	346.78 ± 1.06	0.007 ± 0.002	−0.149 ± 0.032
Wizard [18]	991.68 ± 6.52	984.04 ± 5.73	611.16 ± 4.67	349.49 ± 2.18	−0.014 ± 0.023	−0.116 ± 0.073
Image filtering	987.61 ± 4.79	987.42 ± 4.13	635.86 ± 2.75	343.47 ± 2.19	0.023 ± 0.016	−0.125 ± 0.065

In Table 4, the difference of image dataset obtained every time is small due to the Pose selection method using the same standard to generate the pose, so the standard deviation of each parameter is the smallest and the results are relatively stable. Moreover, the standard deviation of each parameter from calibration results based on image filtering is smaller than OpenCV and Wizard, and its results are more stable. As a result, the self-built camera calibration algorithm provides: 1) smaller reprojection error, indicating that the calibration results possess higher accuracy; 2) the calibration method with high stability and reproducibility, which is proved by small parameter estimation variance in calibration results obtained from different experiments.

4.4 Structure from Motion Test

The calibration parameters were evaluated by the 3D reconstruction results of SfM. The object of the reconstruction is the stone statue of Confucius, as shown in Fig. 3.

Fig. 3. The stone statue of Confucius

We took 30 images of Confucius statues and then reconstructed them using SfM algorithm. The reconstructed results were optimized using BA algorithm. The reconstruction error of calibration results obtained by different methods on the same set of views and the time consuming of BA algorithm are compared. The result are shown in Table 5.

As can be seen from Table 5, the calibration results in our paper can accelerate the running time of BA and reduce the reconstruction error.

Table 5. Reconstruction error and BA time of different algorithms

	BA time(s)	Reconstruction error(pix)
OpenCV [20]	63.5839	20.2581
Pose selection [17]	28.4661	16.6339
Wizard [18]	24.3586	17.3621
Image filtering	23.2713	15.5649

5 Conclusion

The camera calibration method based on adaptive image filtering proposed in this paper selects non-singular pose images by angle error. Its stability is verified by multiple parallel experiments, and its calibration results with higher accuracy is also demonstrated by comparing with other camera calibration methods and tools. At the same time, this paper also proposes a new evaluation index named angle error, achieving the evaluation of camera calibration results in test dataset. More importantly, using angle error can avoid the influence caused by external parameters estimation of test set images in the calibration results evaluation when compared with conventional MRE.

References

1. Tsai, R.: A versatile camera calibration technique for high-accuracy 3D machine vision metrology using off-the-shelf TV cameras and lenses. IEEE J. Robot. Autom. **3**(4), 323–344 (1987)
2. Geiger, A., Ziegler, J., Stiller, C.: Stereoscan: dense 3d reconstruction in real-time. In: Proceedings of the 2011 IEEE intelligent vehicles symposium (IV), pp. 963–968. IEEE (2011)
3. Sturm, P., Maybank, S.: On plane-based camera calibration: A general algorithm, singularities, applications. In: Proceedings of the 1999 IEEE Computer Society Conference on Computer Vision & Pattern Recognition, pp. 432–437. IEEE (1999)
4. Zhang, Z.: Flexible camera calibration by viewing a plane from unknown orientations. In: Proceedings of the seventh IEEE international conference on computer vision, pp. 666–673. IEEE (1999)
5. Hammarstedt, P., Sturm, P., Heyden, A.: Degenerate cases and closed-form solutions for camera calibration with one-dimensional objects. In: Proceedings of the Tenth IEEE International Conference on Computer Vision (ICCV'05), pp. 317–324. IEEE (2005)
6. Sturm, P.: A case against Kruppa's equations for camera self-calibration. IEEE Trans. Pattern Anal. Mach. Intell. **22**(10), 1199–1204 (2000)
7. Buchanan, T.: The twisted cubic and camera calibration. Computer Vision, Graphics, and Image Processing **42**(1), 130–132 (1988)
8. Ren, Y., Hu, F.: Camera calibration with pose guidance. In: Proceedings of the ICASSP 2021-2021 IEEE International Conference on Acoustics, Speech and Signal Processing (ICASSP), pp. 2180–2184. IEEE (2021)
9. Triggs, B.: Autocalibration from planar scenes. In: Proceedings of the Computer Vision—ECCV'98: 5th European Conference on Computer Vision Freiburg, Germany, June, e pp. 89–105. Springer Berlin Heidelberg (1998)

10. Sun, W., Cooperstock, J.: Requirements for camera calibration: must accuracy come with a high price?. In: Proceedings of the Seventh IEEE Workshops on Applications of Computer Vision, pp. 356–361. IEEE (2005)
11. Richardson, A., Strom, J., Olson, E.: AprilCal: assisted and repeatable camera calibration. In: Proceedings of the IEEE/RSJ International Conference on Intelligent Robots and Systems, pp. 1814–1821. IEEE (2013)
12. Tan, L., Wang, Y., Yu, H., Zhu, J.: Automatic camera calibration using active displays of a virtual pattern. Sensors 17(4), 685–698 (2017)
13. Mason, S., Grün, A.: Automatic sensor placement for accurate dimensional inspection. Comput. Vis. Image Underst. 61(3), 454–467 (1995)
14. Gonzalez-Barbosa, J., Garcia-Ramirez, T., Salas, J., Hurtado-Ramos, J.: Optimal camera placement for total coverage. In: Proceedings of the IEEE International Conference on Robotics and Automation, pp. 844–848. IEEE (2009)
15. Ricolfe-Viala, C., Sanchez-Salmeron, A.: Camera calibration under optimal conditions. Opt. Express 19(11), 10769–10775 (2011)
16. Quigley, M., et al.: ROS: an open-source Robot Operating System. In: Proceedings of the ICRA workshop on open source software (2009)
17. Rojtberg, P., Kuijper, A.: Efficient pose selection for interactive camera calibration. In: Proceedings of the IEEE International Symposium on Mixed and Augmented Reality (ISMAR), pp. 31–36. IEEE (2018)
18. Peng, S., Sturm, P.: Calibration wizard: a guidance system for camera calibration based on modelling geometric and corner uncertainty. In: Proceedings of the IEEE/CVF International Conference on Computer Vision, pp. 1497–1505 (2019)
19. Forsyth, D.A., Ponce, J.: Computer vision: a modern approach. A modern approach 17, 21–48 (2003)
20. Bradski, G.: The openCV library. Dr. Dobb's Journal: Software Tools for the Professional Programmer 25(11), 120–123 (2000)

Hybrid Prior-Based Diminished Reality for Indoor Panoramic Images

Jiashu Liu[1], Qiudan Zhang[1], Xuelin Shen[3], Wenhui Wu[2], and Xu Wang[1(✉)]

[1] College of Computer Science and Software Engineering, Shenzhen University,
Shenzhen 518060, China
`wangxu@szu.edu.cn`
[2] College of Electronics and Information Engineering, Shenzhen University,
Shenzhen 518060, China
[3] Guangdong Laboratory of Artificial Intelligence and Digital Economy,
Shenzhen 518132, China

Abstract. Due to the advancement of hardware technology, *e.g.* head-mounted display devices, augmented reality (AR) has been widely used. In AR, virtual objects added to the real environment may partially overlap with objects in the real world, leading to a degraded display. Thus, except for adding virtual objects to the real world, diminished reality (DR) is an urgent task that virtually removes, hides, and sees through real objects from panoramas. In this paper, we propose a pipeline for diminished reality in indoor panoramic images with rich prior information. Especially, to restore the structure information, a structure restoration module is developed to aggregate the layout boundary features of the masked panoramic image. Subsequently, we design a structured region texture extraction module to assist the real texture restoration after removing the target object. Ultimately, to explore the relations among structure and texture, we design a fast Fourier convolution fusion module to generate inpainting results respecting real-world structures and textures. Moreover, we also create a structured panoramic image diminished reality dataset (SD) for the diminished reality task. Extensive experiments illustrate that the proposed pipeline is capable of producing more realistic results, which is also consistent with the human eye's perception of structural changes in indoor panoramic images.

Keywords: Diminished Reality · Image Inpainting · Structure Prior · Semantic Prior

1 Introduction

AR is a real-time interactive visualization method that uses computer technology and graphics methods to add virtual objects to the real world so that they exist in the same image or space. Diminished reality (DR), as an auxiliary method of AR, refers to the removal of physical objects in the real world from users' visual perception, making AR technology more effective in interior design applications. If we use AR technology to directly add the designed virtual model to the real world, it will lead to model penetration, thus the effectiveness of AR will be greatly reduced. Therefore, in addition to adding virtual objects in the real space, it is also necessary to virtually remove the objects in the real space, namely DR. DR is achieved by filling the target area to be removed from the original image according to the surrounding environment, and restoring the background texture of the target area in the original image. This rendering operation is called image inpainting in image processing terminology.

Image inpainting is a method of filling missing regions of a damaged input image with additional textures to achieve visual realism. Traditional 2D image inpainting methods focus on generating realistic textures via nearest neighbor search or replicating relevant patches. With the development of deep neural networks, the task is modeled as a conditional generation problem of learning a functional mapping between the damaged image and the input original uncorrupted image [12]. These methods can learn meaningful semantics in 2D images and generate coherent structures and textures for missing regions, but the resulting images lack realism.

For the DR task, we need to respect the context in a more strict way to produce padding that is close to the real background. Previous image inpainting methods performed well on 2D natural perspective images. Panoramic images, especially indoor scenes, usually contain complex structure and texture. Most existing inpainting methods cannot accurately extract features from them to guide the inpainting process. As shown in Fig. 1, the results generated by the most advanced deep learning-based methods cannot align image structure along the layout boundary, leading to the restored results with blurred structures and unreal textures.

In this paper, we propose a hybrid prior-based diminished reality method for indoor panoramic images based on the existing 2D image inpainting network. To learn the overall structure of indoor panoramic images, a structure restoration module is designed to extract the structural layout features. Subsequently, we introduce a structured region texture extraction module to aggregate local textural features to restore regions of removed objects. Ultimately, in order to reduce color differences and blur artifacts at the boundary between the filled and background regions, we develop a fast Fourier convolution fusion module to explore the complementary among the structure and texture by merging the local textural features and structure layout features. Furthermore, to facilitate training and evaluation, a large-scale dataset of 14527 groups of indoor panoramic images SD is constructed. Experimental results demonstrate that our proposed method significantly outperforms state-of-the-art inpainting models over the created dataset. The main contributions of this paper are as follows:

- We propose a novel hybrid prior-based diminished reality model for the indoor panoramic image by exploiting structure feature and texture features, which preserves the structural and textural consistency among the inpainted region and the image background.
- We create a new challenging dataset, structured panoramic image diminished reality dataset (SD) for further research and evaluation of panoramic image diminished reality.

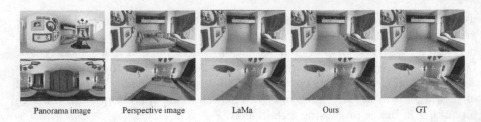

Panorama image   Perspective image   LaMa   Ours   GT

Fig. 1. The figure compares the diminished reality effect of LaMa and Ours in the VR perspective after removing the target object, and it can be clearly felt that the missing or blurred of indoor structure has an important impact on visual realism.

- Experimental results illustrate that the proposed method outperforms other methods in terms of structural consistency and textural realism in recovering the removed object regions of indoor panoramic images.

2   Related Work

2.1   Diminished Reality of Indoor Scenes

DR Application for indoor scenes can hide, eliminate and see through objects while sensing the environment. In indoor scenes, the most basic operation is to remove indoor clutter furniture and other non-permanent objects [2,20–22], and the removed target objects can be defined by interactive masks [1], semantic and instance segmentation [18]. Earlier studies synthesized hidden backgrounds by re-projection and different frame methods. But our work focuses on interior design applications, where the background behind the removed object is unknown, so the multi-camera approach is unsuitable for our task. A number of recent data-driven methods leveraged the concepts of data-driven inpainting and image-to-image translation [2] to recover not only the color but also the geometry of an empty scene in the form of a depth map [7]. It is noteworthy that structure inference is important for DR indoor scenes, which improves texture re-projection [3] and parallax effects [4] and provides a basis for image editing operations.

2.2   Data-Driven Image Inpainting

In data-driven 2D image inpainting methods, conditional information such as semantics and structure are increasingly used for inpainting tasks. Recognizing the importance of edge-preserving structure generation, Nazeri *et al.* [5] divided the image inpainting problem into structure prediction and image completion, and then predicted the image structure of missing regions in the form of edge mapping. Dong *et al.* [6] added prior information incrementally to the trained inpainting model without retraining. Suvorov *et al.* [11] proposed a high-resolution robust large mask inpainting based on Fourier convolution, which increases the receptive field of the inpainting network, and repairs images in large blank regions. Since most panoramic images are of high resolution, the method based on diffusion [13] provides the possibility of inpainting super-resolution images. However, due to the structural distortion problem caused by ERP, these methods can't get the best result of the model in the panorama. Additionally, for the image inpainting task of panoramic images, Gkitsas et al. [2] guided the generation of the hollow background in the same scene by predicting the indoor structure, so as to achieve the purpose of background content reconstruction.

2.3 Image-to-Image Translation

DR can also be regarded as an image-to-image translation task, since it maps the texture part of the indoor scene in the image to the mask part. The traditional image-to-image translation method PatchMatch [17], utilized the continuity of the image to search for the nearest neighbor patch in the translation area, and greatly reduces the search range by utilizing the continuity of the image to ensure that most points converge quickly through iteration. In this case, visual content and style preservation are very important. The classic approach [8] used semantic labeling to reconstruct images from semantic maps while preserving boundaries between classes. Qin et al. [19] introduce an attentional guidance fusion module to obtain effective fused features for prediction. Zhu et al. [18] introduce region-wise style encoding and allow users to select input images with different styles for each semantic region. Gkitsas et al. [2] applied the above method to panoramic images of indoor scenes, according to the normalization texture matrix, the Manhattan structure of indoor panorama is filled and completed the reconstructed of empty room background.

In this paper, we single out important contributions of conditional information for boundary inpainting and semantic information normalization for texture preservation in image-to-image translation based on a 2D inpainting model, propose a hybrid prior-based diminished reality method for indoor panoramic images, generates background textures that are realistic (not just visually realistic, but strictly respect for context) while preserving the structure of the scene.

3 Method

We devise a hybrid prior-based diminished reality method to remove objects from indoor panoramic images without visual inconsistency. The whole pipeline of our proposed method is depicted in Fig. 2, consisting of structure restoration module (SRM), structured region texture extraction module (SRTE-M) and fast Fourier convolution fusion module (FFCF).

3.1 Structure Restoration

In indoor (re-) planning applications, structural preservation of the scene is crucial to ensure spatial realism. Due to the distortion problem caused by the Equi-Rectangular Projection and high resolution of panoramic images, although recent

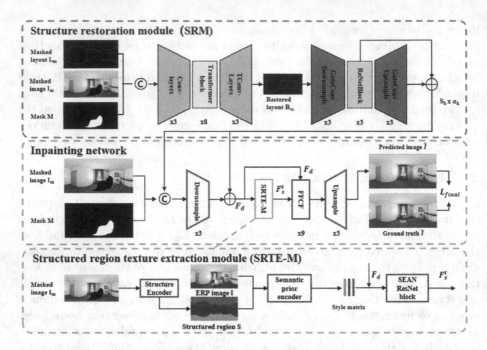

Fig. 2. Overview of our proposed model. First, the SRM module is used to recover the layout boundary and extract the structure features, then added to the FFCF module to restore the indoor structure. Subsequently, the SRFE-M module is used to encode the structured region of an indoor panoramic image and generate a structured region style matrix. Then a SEAN ResNet block is used to extract the structured region texture feature which can help the inpainting network restore the local texture information by using the FFCF module.

data-driven image inpainting methods based on 2D images have made significant progress in generating visually realistic images, there are still structural loss, boundary artifacts and other issues, and can only guarantee to generate plausible images, lacking background authenticity. Thus, we propose a structure restoration module (SRM) [6] for restoring the layout of the masked indoor scene. We chose Manhattan layout boundary priors as a structural guidance, which is more suitable for structure restoration and object removal of indoor panoramic images. We also extract layout boundary features to assist the restoration module to restore the indoor panoramic Manhattan boundary. For the same scene, it can be guided to reconstruct the empty background after removing the target object, thus ensuring the generation of realistic indoor scene structures.

To address this issue, we employ the transformer [6] as a backbone to restore the global layout boundaries at lower resolutions. In order to obtain a layout boundary prior L for an indoor panoramic image, the LayoutNet [14] is utilized to reconstruct 3D room layout boundary P from an ERP image I. Subsequently, we concatenate the masked layout boundary image L_m, the mask M and the masked panoramic image I_m. To reduce the computational burden of attention learning, the concatenated map is fed into three convolutions to produce the downsampled feature F_l. Afterwards, the feature F_l is fed into a Transformer block [6] to restore layout structure feature at low resolution, and generate a complete layout boundary map R_m. The formula is as follows,

$$R_m = Trans(M, I_m, L_m). \tag{1}$$

Afterwards, we use a fully convolutional network to extract the complete layout boundary feature from R_m, which consists of three downsampled gated-convolution layers (encoder), three residual blocks with dilated convolutions, and three upsampled gated-convolution layers (decoder). The gated convolution can selectively transfer useful features. We select four coarse-to-fine feature maps of the last intermediate layer and three decoder layers to obtain the structure feature S_k. And zero initialization α_k is used to fuse the individual relevant feature maps S_k of SRM.

3.2 Structured Region Texture Extraction

The image-to-image translation method can transfer the input image to the target domain, and output different styles. Inspired by this, we developed a structured region texture extraction module (SRTE-M) in order to use contextual texture information to fill the target area during the restoration process to assist the real background recovery after the removal of the target object. In our approach, following the framework of PanoDR's [2] structure coding and style coding, we aim to generate images that meet the texture characteristics of the domain by giving panoramic images and corresponding domains.

In particular, we first take the masked panoramic image $I_m = I \times \overline{M} + 1 \times M$ as the input. A structure encoder [15] is employed to segment the masked panoramic image I_m into three structured regions (wall, ceiling and floor) and produce the structured region map S. The structure encoder consists of four downsampling and upsampling convolution layers connected by four skip connections. The batch normalization and ReLU are used to perform activation operations.

Afterwards, we feed the segmented structured regions $S = \{wall, ceiling, floor\}$ and the original image I into a semantic prior encoder to produce a set of style matrices of dimension 512×3 for each structured region by means of average pooling of the output features, where 3 indicates the number of structured regions. The semantic prior encoder includes four convolutions, four transposed convolutions, and a region-wise average pooling. The bottleneck structure and average pooling layer can exclude irrelevant texture information from the image. We then feed the style matrix into a SEAN ResNet [18] to extract local features, and adjust the local texture of the repair area while respecting the global structure. Finally, the textural feature F_s^t of structured regions is obtained.

3.3 Fast Fourier Convolution Fusion

Because the Fast Fourier Convolution [11] can help to produce high-quality inpainting results at high resolution. Therefore, we use the Fast Fourier Convolution in our designed inpainting network for frequency domain learning. In addition, we introduce a structure restoration module and a structured region texture extraction module for improving the inpainting capability of the proposed method. On the one hand, the global structural features provided by the structure restoration module are used to restore the panoramic Manhattan structure of the indoor image. On the one hand, the local texture features provided by the structured region texture extraction module are consistent with the context of the structured region to fill the structured mask, so that the local texture features are consistent with the context. Finally, the results of the two branches are fused to achieve the best result on the global structure and texture.

Concretely, to effectively combine the textural feature F_s^t and layout feature F_d, we introduce a fast Fourier convolution fusion module (FFCF) to aggregate the features in the frequency domain. Specifically, the layout feature F_d is first fed into a convolution layer and a spectral transform block, respectively. The output features are added together, and activated by a Batch Normalization and ReLU layers to generate the layout feature $\hat{F}_d$ in the frequency domain. Subsequently, to exploit the relation among the textural feature F_s^t and layout feature F_d, we feed the layout feature F_d into a convolution layer, and then add the textural feature F_s^t. The output feature is then activated by a Batch Normalization and ReLU layers to produce the combined feature $\hat{F}_{st}^d$. Finally, the feature $\hat{F}_{st}^d$ and $\hat{F}_d$ are fed into a fusion module that includes a concatenation layer and three convolution layers. After upsampling, the restored image $\hat{I}$ is produced for the masked panoramic image.

3.4 Loss Function

To better optimize our proposed method, we design a hybrid loss that includes L1 loss $\mathcal{L}_{L1}$ [6], adversarial loss $\mathcal{L}_{adv}$ [16], high-level synthesis loss $\mathcal{L}_{high}$ [2] and perception loss $\mathcal{L}_{prec}$ [11].

We utilize the pixel-based L1 loss $\mathcal{L}_{L1}$ to calculate the differences of unmasked regions between the restored panoramic image $\hat{I}$ and the ground truth $\tilde{I}$.

$$\mathcal{L}_{L1} = (1 - \mathcal{M}) \odot |\hat{I} - \tilde{I}|_1, \tag{2}$$

where $\mathcal{M}$ denotes the $0 - 1$ mask and 1 for the occluded region. $\odot$ represents the element-wise multiplication.

The high-level synthesis loss $\mathcal{L}_{high}$ is comprised of the perception loss and style loss, which enforces the similar feature aggregation between $\hat{I}$ and $\tilde{I}$.

$$\mathcal{L}_{perc} = \mathbb{E} \left(\sum_j^{P_j} \frac{1}{N_j} \sum_\rho^{\Omega_j} |\Phi_j(\hat{I}) - \Phi_j(\tilde{I})| \right), \tag{3}$$

$$\mathcal{L}_{style} = \mathbb{E} \left(\sum_j^{S_j} \frac{1}{N_j} \sum_\rho^{\Omega_j} \frac{1}{N_j} |\mathcal{G}(\Phi_j(\hat{I})) - \mathcal{G}(\Phi_j(\tilde{I}))| \right), \tag{4}$$

$$\mathcal{L}_{high} = \lambda_{perc}\mathcal{L}_{perc} + \lambda_{style}\mathcal{L}_{style}, \tag{5}$$

where $\mathbb{E}$ is the mean operation, Φ denotes the activation layer of the network, Ω indicates the structure feature region, and N is the total number of feature elements in the feature map. $\mathcal{G}(M) = MMT$ denotes the Gram matrix function. P_j and S_j are the feature sets for perception and style loss [10]. And the λ_{prep} and λ_{style} are empirically set to 0.12, 40.0.

Additionally, to adaptively improve the quality of the restored panoramic image, we construct an adversarial loss in the FFCM module, which includes a discriminator loss $\mathcal{L}_D$, a generator loss $\mathcal{L}_G$, and a feature match loss $\mathcal{L}_{FM}$. The adversarial loss is provided as follows,

$$\mathcal{L}_D = -\mathbb{E}_{\hat{\mathcal{I}}}\left[\log D(\tilde{\mathcal{I}})\right] - \mathbb{E}_{\tilde{\mathcal{I}},\mathcal{M}}\left[\log D(\tilde{\mathcal{I}}) \odot (1 - \mathcal{M})\right] \\ -\mathbb{E}_{\tilde{\mathcal{I}},\mathcal{M}}\left[\log(1 - D(\tilde{\mathcal{I}})) \odot \mathcal{M}\right], \tag{6}$$

$$\mathcal{L}_G = -\mathbb{E}_{\hat{\mathcal{I}}}\left[\log G(\tilde{\mathcal{I}})\right], \tag{7}$$

$$\mathcal{L}_{adv} = \mathcal{L}_D + \mathcal{L}_G + \lambda_{FM}\mathcal{L}_{FM}, \tag{8}$$

where $\mathcal{L}_{FM}$ is based on $\mathcal{L}_{L1}$ which is usually used for stable GAN training and has a marginally positive impact on performance.

In addition, the high receptive field perceived loss $\mathcal{L}_{prec}$ proposed in [11]. The basic pre-training network of the high receptive field (using Fourier convolution), more attention to the understanding of the global structure, which can help the model achieve better results at higher resolution. Finally, the whole loss function of our proposed method is as follows,

$$\mathcal{L}_{final} = \lambda_{L1}\mathcal{L}_{L1} + \lambda_{adv}\mathcal{L}_{adv} + \lambda_{high}\mathcal{L}_{high} + \lambda_{perc}\mathcal{L}_{perc}, \tag{9}$$

where the λ_{L1}, λ_{adv}, and λ_{perc} are empirically set to 10.0, 10.0 and 30.0.

4   Experiments

4.1   Experimental Setup and Implementation Details

Dataset. Based on the existing Structured3D dataset, we construct a new challenging data set named SD dataset like PanoDR [2]. This dataset includes 14,527 groups of indoor panoramic images, masked images, and object-removed panoramic images with a resolution of 1024×512. We use about 10527 images from various scenes as the training set, 2000 images as the validation, and 2000 images as the test set.

Evaluation Metrics. To evaluate the performance of our proposed method, we employ four widely used metrics, including mean absolute error (MAE), peak signal-to-noise ratio (PSNR), structural similarity (SSIM), and learned perceptual similarity (LPIPS).

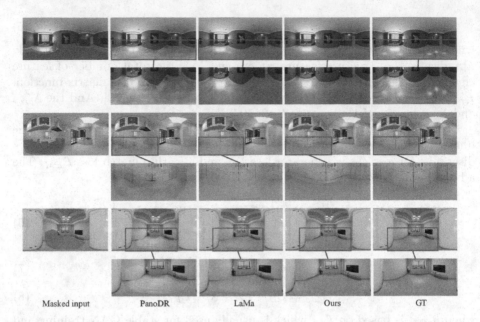

Masked input   PanoDR   LaMa   Ours   GT

Fig. 3. Qualitative results for diminished reality from scenes in our test set. From left to right: Input image with the diminished area masked with transparent purple, compared among PanoDR, LaMa, and Ours

Implementation Details. We implement our proposed model by using Pytorch, and all experiments were conducted on a GeForce RTX 3090 GPU. For the training procedure of the SRM module, we utilize the Adam optimizer with a learning rate of $6e-4$, a warmup step of 1000 and a cosine decay. The structure encoder used in the SRTE-M module is optimized by using the default parameters of the Adam, with a learning rate of 0.0001 and a batch size of 4. The FFCF module is trained using the Adam optimizer with learning rates of $1e-3$ and $1e-4$ for generators and discriminators, respectively. In addition, the resolution of the input panoramic image is 512×256. The weight of the structure encoder is initialized by the weight in [9], and the weights of other submodels are initialized with zero and normal distributions of $\sigma = 0.02$.

4.2 Quantitative and Qualitative Comparisons

We retrained the compared model on the SD data set until convergence using the same ground-truth image. The comparison results are shown in Table 1. The 2D LaMa [11] method obtains better performance than PanoDR [2]. This may be caused by the fact that the PanoDR [2] method does not smooth the boundary of the filled region. The CTSDG [12] method generates several paradoxical results. The texture of the filled part is inconsistent with the context, and it is difficult to restore the structure of the panoramic image. Although ZITS [6] method can recover part of the results, the generated filling part will produce fish scale arti-

Table 1. Quantitative comparison results of our proposed method and state-of-the-art methods on the SD dataset.

Method	Params ↓	PSNR ↑	SSIM ↑	MAE ↓	LPIPS ↓	User Study ↑
CTSDG [12]	52M	14.807	0.593	0.133	0.534	1.69%
ZITS [6]	68M	28.027	0.929	0.020	0.338	4.23%
LDMs [13]	387M	29.064	0.983	0.007	0.073	2.54%
LaMa [11]	27M	**38.787**	0.983	0.006	0.030	36.44%
PanoDR [2]	20M	32.049	0.968	0.012	0.028	9.74%
Ours	76M	35.358	**0.988**	**0.004**	**0.026**	**45.33%**
Ours-SRM	–	35.074	0.973	0.004	0.028	–
Ours-SRTE-M	–	35.245	0.973	0.004	0.027	–

facts, so the PSNR results are not good. The recently popular diffusion method LDMs [13] is still inferior to LaMa [11] method. This could be caused by the fact that it ignores the structural information in panoramic images. Our proposed method achieves a high LPIPS metrics than other methods, which illustrates that the panoramic images restored by our proposed method are closer to the ground truths. Moreover, the proposed method achieves better performance on SSIM and MAE metrics.

To further demonstrate the effectiveness of our approach, we conducted a subjective user study. Twenty volunteers with relevant knowledge in computer vision research participated in the evaluation, who were invited to select the most realistic image from images inpainted by our proposed method and representative state-of-the-art methods. Specifically, each participant evaluated a total of 10 sets of images randomly selected from the SD dataset. The results of our statistical vote are shown in the Table 1. Compared with other methods, our method has better performance.

Furthermore, to better indicate the advantages of the proposed model, we provide qualitative comparisons among the proposed method and the other methods in Fig. 3. We can observe that the proposed method restores the Manhattan structure of indoor panoramic images more precisely than other image inpainting methods, and the generated texture is more consistent with the ground truth. Although there are obvious traces of texture splicing in the PanoDR [2] method, it can better restore the structure information of the panoramic image. In addition, the panoramic image texture recovered by the LaMa [11] method is smoother, but there is still a certain deviation in the recovery of indoor structures. In contrast, the proposed method combines the layout boundary information of indoor images and extracts structured region information, thus benefiting more realistic and accurate image restoration than other methods.

4.3 Ablation Study

We perform several ablation studies to evaluate the effectiveness of each component in our proposed method, including only the structure restoration component termed as Ours-SRM, only the structured region texture extraction component termed as Ours-SRTE-M, and the full version of our proposed method termed as Ours. The comparison results are reported in Table 1. From this table, we can discover that the performance of Ours-SRTE-M is better than Ours-SRM. This is due to the fact that Ours-SRTE-M uses structured region as input, which not only provides the local textural information but also the local structure information to restore the local information of the masked region in the panoramic image. The Ours-SRM only provides the layout boundary information for the masked region. By comparing the method Ours-SRM, Ours-SRTE-M, and Ours, we can see that our proposed full-version method achieves better performance than Ours-SRM and Ours-SRTE-M. This indicates that structure layout and the structured region texture information have an interaction that affects the realism of the final indoor panoramic image.

5 Conclusion

In this paper, we develop a hybrid prior-based diminished reality method for indoor panoramic images, which leverages the structure layout and texture priors of the indoor structured region to restore the masked panoramic image. Although the data set we created can meet the task requirements, the generated ground truth has the problem of removing the target object together with other objects partially occluded by the target object. In the future, we will use a blender to re-render the virtual scene before and after the object removal, producing a realistic and accurate data set that can be used to diminished reality of indoor panoramic images. In addition, we will further explore a faster and more effective indoor panoramic image diminished reality algorithm, and explore the use of text-guided methods to generate masks in real time to facilitate user interaction.

References

1. Takeuchi, Y., Perlin, K.: ClayVision: the (elastic) image of the city. In: Proceedings of the SIGCHI Conference on Human Factors in Computing Systems, pp. 2411–2420 (2012)
2. Gkitsas, V., Sterzentsenko, V., Zioulis, N., Albanis, G., Zarpalas, D.: PanoDR: spherical panorama diminished reality for indoor scenes. In: Proceedings of the IEEE/CVF Conference on Computer Vision and Pattern Recognition, pp. 3716–3726 (2021)
3. Kawai, N., Sato, T., Yokoya, N.: Diminished reality based on image inpainting considering background geometry. IEEE Trans. Visual Comput. Graph. **22**(3), 1236–1247 (2015)
4. Bertel, T., Campbell, N.D.F., Richardt, C.: MegaParallax: casual 360 panoramas with motion parallax. IEEE Trans. Visual Comput. Graph. **25**(5), 1828–1835 (2019)

5. Nazeri, K., Ng, E., Joseph, T., Qureshi, F., Ebrahimi, M.: EdgeConnect: structure guided image inpainting using edge prediction. In: Proceedings of the IEEE/CVF International Conference on Computer Vision Workshops (2019)
6. Dong, Q., Cao, C., Fu, Y.: Incremental transformer structure enhanced image inpainting with masking positional encoding. In: Proceedings of the IEEE/CVF Conference on Computer Vision and Pattern Recognition, pp. 11358–11368 (2022)
7. Pintore, G., Agus, M., Almansa, E., Gobbetti, E.: Instant automatic emptying of panoramic indoor scenes. IEEE Trans. Visual Comput. Graph. **28**(11), 3629–3639 (2022)
8. Chen, Q., Koltun, V.: Photographic image synthesis with cascaded refinement networks. In: Proceedings of the IEEE International Conference on Computer Vision, pp. 1511–1520 (2017)
9. He, K., Zhang, X., Ren, S., Sun, J.: Delving deep into rectifiers: surpassing human-level performance on ImageNet classification. In: Proceedings of the IEEE International Conference on Computer Vision, pp. 1026–1034 (2015)
10. Dong, H., Yu, S., Wu, C., Guo, Y.: Semantic image synthesis via adversarial learning. In: Proceedings of the IEEE International Conference on Computer Vision, pp. 5706–5714 (2017)
11. Suvorov, R., et al.: Resolution-robust large mask inpainting with Fourier convolutions. In: Proceedings of the IEEE/CVF Winter Conference on Applications of Computer Vision, pp. 2149–2159 (2022)
12. Guo, X., Yang, H., Huang, D.: Image inpainting via conditional texture and structure dual generation. In: Proceedings of the IEEE/CVF International Conference on Computer Vision, pp. 14134–14143 (2021)
13. Rombach, R., Blattmann, A., Lorenz, D., Esser, P., Ommer, B.: High-resolution image synthesis with latent diffusion models. In: Proceedings of the IEEE/CVF Conference on Computer Vision and Pattern Recognition, pp. 10684–10695 (2022)
14. Zou, C., Colburn, A., Shan, Q., Hoiem, D.: LayoutNet: reconstructing the 3D room layout from a single RGB image. In: Proceedings of the IEEE Conference on Computer Vision and Pattern Recognition, pp. 2051–2059 (2018)
15. Ronneberger, O., Fischer, P., Brox, T.: U-Net: convolutional networks for biomedical image segmentation. In: Navab, N., Hornegger, J., Wells, W.M., Frangi, A.F. (eds.) MICCAI 2015. LNCS, vol. 9351, pp. 234–241. Springer, Cham (2015). https://doi.org/10.1007/978-3-319-24574-4_28
16. Lim, J.H., Ye, J.C.: Geometric GAN. arXiv preprint arXiv:1705.02894 (2017)
17. Barnes, C., Shechtman, E., Finkelstein, A., Goldman, D.B.: PatchMatch: a randomized correspondence algorithm for structural image editing. ACM Trans. Graph. **28**(3), 24 (2009)
18. Zhu, P., Abdal, R., Qin, Y., Wonka, P.: Sean: image synthesis with semantic region-adaptive normalization. In: Proceedings of the IEEE/CVF Conference on Computer Vision and Pattern Recognition, pp. 5104–5113 (2020)
19. Qin, Y., Chi, X., Sheng, B., Lau, R.W.: GuideRender: large-scale scene navigation based on multi-modal view frustum movement prediction. Visual Comput. 1–11 (2023)
20. Rudolph, C., Brunnett, G., Bretschneider, M., Meyer, B., Asbrock, F.: TechnoSapiens: merging humans with technology in augmented reality. Visual Comput. 1–16 (2023)
21. Kim, T., Kim, G.J.: Real-time and on-line removal of moving human figures in hand-held mobile augmented reality. Vis. Comput. **39**(7), 2571–2582 (2023)
22. Chung, S.J., Lee, T.H., Jeong, B.R., et al.: VRCAT: VR collision alarming technique for user safety. Vis. Comput. **39**(7), 3145–3159 (2023)

Virtual Reality for the Preservation and Promotion of Historical Real Tennis

Ronan Gaugne[1]([🖂]) [iD], Sony Saint-Auret[2], Pierre Duc-Martin[3], and Valérie Gouranton[3] [iD]

[1] Univ Rennes, Inria, CNRS, IRISA, Rennes, France
ronan.gaugne@irisa.fr
[2] Inria, CNRS, IRISA, Rennes, France
[3] Univ Rennes, INSA Rennes, Inria, CNRS, IRISA, Rennes, France

Abstract. Real tennis or "courte paume" in its original naming in French, is a racket sport that has been played for centuries and is considered the ancestor of tennis. It was a very popular sport in Europe during the Renaissance period, practiced in every layer of the society. It is still practiced today in few courts in the world, especially in United Kingdom, France, Australia, and USA. It has been listed in the Inventory of Intangible Cultural Heritage in France since 2012. The goal of our project is to elicit interest in this historical sport and for the new and future generations to experience it. We developed a virtual environment that enables its users to experience real tennis game. This environment was then tested to assess its acceptability and usability in different context of use. We found that such use of virtual reality enabled our participants to discover the history and rules of this sport, in a didactic and pleasant manner. We hope that our VR application will encourage younger and future generations to play real tennis.

Keywords: Digital Cultural Heritage · Virtual reality · Intangible Heritage · Sport Heritage

1 Introduction

Traditional sports are considered intangible cultural heritage (ICH) because they represent the cultural expressions and practices of a particular community. Intangible cultural heritage is defined by UNESCO as "the practices, representations, expressions, knowledge, skills - as well as the instruments, objects, artifacts and cultural spaces associated therewith - that communities, groups and, in some cases, individuals recognize as part of their cultural heritage" [24].

Traditional sports are deeply rooted in the culture and history of a particular community or region. These sports are an essential part of intangible cultural heritage and have been often passed down through generations as oral traditions, with many of the rules and techniques of these sports being learned through practice and experience rather than through written instruction [6].

Supported by EUR Digisport ANR-18-EURE-0022 and Equipex+ Continuum ANR-21-ESRE-0030.

The preservation of traditional sports as intangible heritage is essential because it helps to maintain cultural diversity and promote understanding between different communities. Traditional sports can also have economic benefits, with many communities using them as a means of attracting tourism and generating revenue. By preserving traditional sports, we can ensure that these cultural expressions are passed down to future generations and continue to contribute to the cultural heritage of the world.

However, preserving traditional sports can be challenging, especially when they are not widely practiced or are in danger of being lost due to social or economic changes. Lim *et al.* [11], emphasise the importance of preserving traditional human activities and point out that advances in the production and 3D animation of virtual humans support the growth of interactive simulations and experiences of these activities.

In this work, we present the design and an evaluation of a Virtual Reality (VR) application dedicated to the preservation and promotion of a European traditional sport, real tennis.

2   Related Works

2.1   Real Tennis

Real tennis, considered as the ancestor of racket sports such as tennis, squash or Basque pelota, has an important historical interest in European culture [3,14].

Real tennis was played since the 15th c. in dedicated buildings, either in aristocratic estates or in city centers. After the decline of real tennis in 18th c., these buildings were destroyed or modified and reallocated to other uses. It is not uncommon to find foundations of real tennis buildings during archaeological excavations in the cities, and their characteristic dimensions, 10 m wide and 30 m long, facilitate their identification.

It was practiced in every layer of the society, by women as well as by men, and it was not uncommon to attend mixed matches. It is particularly studied in France [7], as it has left important traces in French culture, many linguistic expressions still used today are coming from this sport. Real tennis is still played, mainly in UK, the USA, France, and Australia, with international competitions, but the number of players is small because of the limited number of courts. There is a will to develop this sport, with the construction of several new courts in the world, as in Sidney and Amsterdam, and the restoration of old courts that were no longer used to play, as the court of Chinon in France. The game is played inside a covered court separated into two parts by a net, the Service side and the Hazard side. The court is surrounded by two (*Quarre* court) or three penthouses (*Dedans* court), covered by a sloping roof (Fig. 1). The openings in the penthouses can vary a little from one court to another.

2.2   The Use of Virtual Reality for Cultural Heritage Preservation

Virtual reality (VR) and more generally extended realities (XR), are now widely used in the domain of cultural heritage as they provide the means of documenting, recovering and presenting historical contexts [2]. Beyond historical material

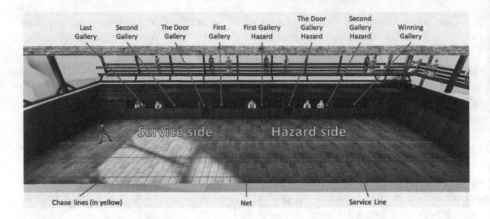

Fig. 1. Overview of a real tennis court (Quarre court).

such as artefacts, buildings, monuments, or cities, XR also allows to represent intangible cultural heritage with many different human activities such as crafting [16], artistic expression, [1,4,20], or traditional sports [23].

Skublewska-Paszkowska et al. [21] conducted a systematic review of the literature to identify relevant studies related to 3D technologies and intangible cultural heritage preservation. They specifically review two studies related to sport, [10,12]. Both focus on the extraction and reproduction of 3D sports movements, from 2D images. The 3D animations provided in these two works can be used to animate human characters in immersive simulations. This approach is developped further in the work of Tisserand *et al.*, [23], which proposes a framework for the preservation of traditional sports through gamification, applied to traditional Gaelic sport and Basque pelota, based on low cost motion capture to train users to perform correct movements. In the same idea, Lo et al., [13] used VR to create a virtual exhibition showcasing traditional Chinese martial arts. The exhibition allowed visitors to engage with the martial arts through interactive simulations, such as practicing martial arts moves with a virtual instructor. This kind of approach is also widely used for the preservation of traditional and folkloric dances [1,15,17].

Beyond movement, traditional sports activities also rely on other features, such as cultural contexts and game rules. These aspects are important to preserve, and virtual reality offers an interesting medium for both. As an example, Selmanović *et al.*, [18] explored the use of VR to propose experiencing traditional bridge diving at Stari Most, the old bridge in the historic city of Mostar in Bosnia and Herzegovina, a UNESCO World Heritage Site. The experience is enhanced by narrative elements that present the cultural context, with the associated festival, as well as the history of the bridge. In the same vein, the article by [26] proposes a visit to the archaeological site of Olympia in augmented reality during which visitors can observe reconstitutions of sporting events from Antiquity. While the two previous studies did not take into account sports rules, the work of Setiawan *et al.*, [19], in contrast, focuses on the implementation of the rules of the traditional Indonesian game Benthik in VR, but without representation of the cultural context. The virtual environment is completely abstract, the objective being to propose a motivating and fun environment for an initiation to Benthik.

With different but complementary approaches, these works aim to propose solutions to preserve traditional sports. These different approaches thus highlight the complexity of traditional sports preservation as intangible cultural heritage. In this work, we want to address the human activity involved in a traditional sports, its cultural context, the associated rules, and the specific movements.

3   Method

The work presented in this paper is an extension of the methodological paper [9] that studies the representation of sport heritage in VR, with a focus on Real Tennis. In this previous paper, we propose a model to identify the main elements to consider in order to propose a virtual environment (VE) through different perspectives.

We can identify three different and complementary goals for a traditional sport reconstruction.

- Propose a realistic practice of the sport, with a focus on faithful reproduction of the movements.
- Preserve the traditional and popular culture associated with the sport. In this perspective, the sport must be considered in a more general and cultural context. VR applications can support such aim, through a sensory representation (graphic, sound...), associated to narrative scenarios.
- Disseminate and promote traditional sports. The aim, here, is to give the possibility to a large public to discover and be initiated to traditional sports.

In this new work, we address the second and third objectives through an immersive experience comprising a presentation of real tennis' cultural context based on a structured scenario, with a playful tutorial to introduce the basics and rules of the game. Furthermore, we present the results of a user study we conducted to evaluate the presence, acceptability and usability of the VE.

3.1   Design and Implementation

The VE presented in [9] proposes (i) a representation of the cultural and historical heritage associated to this traditional sport, (ii) an implementation of the rules and flows of the sport, and (iii) natural interactions for realistic sensations of real tennis.

In order to implement a didactic interactive scenario to guide the user in the discovery of real tennis, we integrated the scenario engine Xareus for Unity (based on [8]), available under licence at https://xareus.insa-rennes.fr/. It is a scripting engine, based on Petri nets constituted of places, transitions and arcs. Tokens can be found in the places, and evolve from place to place through transitions. A transition can host a sensor and/or an effector that carry the relationship between a scenario and the VE. A sensor allows to observe elements of the scene, and blocks the transition as long as its condition is not validated. An effector allows to act on the scene when the transition is crossed by a token. A graphical representation is presented in Fig. 2, Left. Xareus integrates a graphical window in the Unity editor that allows to create, edit and follow the scenario.

The advantage of using such a scenario engine is to establish a clear framework to design and implement a didactic tutorial in VR that can evolve easily according to users feedback without coding effort. The complete didactic scenario is structured in two parts. First, a technical tutorial presents the basic concepts of the sport, and invites the user to practice two different actions in the game, a serve and a chase (Fig. 2, Right). The second part gives the user the possibility to visit the building with a presentation of the different parts of the court and the cultural aspects of the sport, to practice a full match against the virtual player, or to leave the experience.

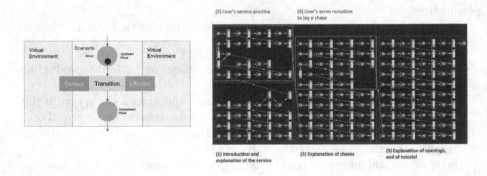

Fig. 2. Left : Petri net extended with event model. Right: Tutorial scenario.

User Perspective of the Didactic Scenario. From the user's point of view, he or she is first orally introduced to the terrain and the service rule, using visual metaphors that highlight the targets (Fig. 3). The user is then invited to practice. The scenario enters the loop described above, which exits only after one successful serve, or after 10 failed attempts. In order to perform the service, the user has one raquette in one hand and the ball in the other hand. He or she must grasp the ball by pulling the trigger of the controller, and throws it by launching the ball and releasing the trigger in a synchronised gesture, as in a real service. Then, the basic of chase rule is explained and the player changes side. He has to receive a serve from the virtual opponent, and return it on the other side, to mark a chase. This phase is also in a 10 tries loop and exit at the first success. The chase area to win is highlighted on the court. At the end of this

Fig. 3. Top, Left: Service training, Right: Chase Training, Bottom, Left: Guided visit, Right: Score display.

tutorial phase, a visit of the site is proposed, with teleportation to explanation panels, and the visitor has also the possibility to play a complete match.

3.2 Experimental Protocol

We conducted a user study focusing on the evaluations of presence, acceptance and usability of the didactic scenario. We based the presence evaluation on the standard Slater-Usoh-Steed (SUS) questionnaire [22] consisting of 6 questions evaluated with a 7-point Likert scale, 1 meaning "Not at all", 7 meaning "Completely" (Fig. 4, top, left). For the acceptance and usability evaluation, we used the extension of the standard unified theory of acceptance and use of technology UTAUT2 questionnaire proposed by Venkatesh *et al.* in [25]. It contains 9 questions, with at least one question per category of the model: performance expectation, effort expectation, social influence, facilitating conditions, hedonic motivation, perceived pleasure and habits (Fig. 4, top right). These questions are inspired and adapted from those proposed by [5]. Finally, the questionnaire also integrates more general questions about the user and his/her experience, listed in Fig. 4, bottom, as well as a free response section. For this study, we used an Oculus Quest 2, in stand-alone mode, in a large room to define a physical space of 10 m × 10 m to allow real movement.

Id	Question	Id	Question	Id	Question
P1	Please rate your sense of being in the virtual environment.	U1	I think this virtual environment allows me to learn faster than traditional methods.	G1	I think this virtual environment is useful for heritage conservation.
P2	To what extent were there times during the experience when the virtual environment was the reality for you?	U2	I think this virtual environment is easy to use.	G2	I think this virtual environment is useful for sport promotion.
P3	When you think back to the experience, do you think of virtual environment more as images that you saw or more as somewhere that you visited	U3	I think people around me would like to use this virtual environment to discover a new sport.	G3	I think this virtual environment is useful for sport training.
P4	During the time of the experience, which was the strongest on the whole, your sense of being in the real room or of being in the virtual room?	U4	I think people around me would like to use this virtual environment to practice a sport regularly.	G4	I learnt new things (rules, history. . .) on real tennis.
P5	Consider your memory of being in the virtual room. How similar in terms of the structure of the memory is this to the structure of the memory of other places you have been today? By 'structure of the memory' consider things like the extent to which you have a visual memory of the virtual environment, whether that memory is in colour, the extent to which the memory seems vivid or realistic, its size, location in your imagination, the extent to which it is panoramic in your imagination, and other such structural elements.	U5	This virtual environment seems to me to be complementary with traditional learning methods.	G5	I would like to discover more about the real tennis.
		U6	The use of this virtual environment is fun.	G6	I felt discomfort during the experiment. (7= no discomfort).
		U7	I enjoyed learning in this virtual environment.	G7	Overall evaluation of your experience.
		U8	I am ready to use this virtual environment again for a new session.		
P6	During the time of your experience, did you often think to yourself that you were actually in the real room?	U9	If I have the opportunity, I will recommend the use of this virtual environment to my friends and family.		

Fig. 4. Top, Left: Presence questionnaire, Right: Acceptability and Usability questionnaire, Bottom: General questionnaire.

The experimentations were conducted in two phases. In the first phase, XP1, the experiments involved a panel of 10 participants (4 men, 6 women) and took place in the historical Court building represented in the VR application (Fig. 5, left). In the second phase, XP2, the experiments involved a panel of 18 participants (14 men, 4 women) and took place in a gymnasium (Fig. 5, right).

One of the objectives of this two-phase study was to determine whether the location used for the VR experience had an impact on the usability and acceptability reported by the users. Indeed, it is questionable whether the VR application can be used as effectively in a real-world environment unrelated to the cultural heritage context being promoted.

It is important to note that the participant populations were very different between the two phases. In the XP1 phase, the population was mainly made up of inhabitants of the city centre district, with a fairly high average age ($m = 55.4$, $\sigma = 14.9$). The XP2 phase was conducted in a gymnasium located on the campus of the University of Science of the city. The population was made up of students with a younger average age ($m = 22.1$, $\sigma = 3.5$).

For the XP1 phase, the VR room was co-located with the real room. The participants therefore had the initial striking effect when they put on the headset of having a change of atmosphere without a change of physical location, and they could physically touch the boundaries of the court in VR, in the 10 m × 10 m space. The user experience started with the tutorial presented in Sect. 3.1. Once the scenario was completed, participants were able to visit the historical site or play a match. After the experience, they were invited to fill the questionnaire.

4 Results

4.1 Presence, Usability and Acceptability Analysis

The mean results of the questionnaires are presented in Fig. 6. From these questionnaires, three main score variables were computed, Presence, Acceptability and two arbitrary constructs named PROM and TRAIN:

Fig. 5. User study in (left) the original building, and (right) a modern gymnasium.

Question	XP1 (m,σ)	XP2 (m,σ)	Total (m,σ)	Question	XP1 (m,σ)	XP2 (m,σ)	Total (m,σ)	Question	XP1 (m,σ)	XP2 (m,σ)	Total (m,σ)
P1	6.56 , 0.73	6.11 , 0.76	6.26 , 0.76	U1	4.89 , 2.09	4.5 , 1.65	4.63 , 1.78	G1	6.78 , 0.67	6.33 , 0.97	6.48 , 0.89
P2	5.44 , 1.51	5.06 , 1.35	5.19 , 1.39	U2	3.22 , 2.33	4.72 , 1.78	4.22 , 2.06	G2	6.44 , 1.13	5.67 , 1.28	5.93 , 1.27
P3	4.78 , 2.17	5.28 , 1.27	5.11 , 1.6	U3	6 , 1.22	5.94 , 1.11	5.96 , 1.13	G3	5.22 , 1.99	3.61 , 1.58	4.15 , 1.85
P4	5.11 , 2.03	5.17 , 1.04	5.15 , 1.41	U4	4.44 , 2.19	2.83 , 1.34	3.37 , 1.8	G4	6.44 , 1.13	6.33 , 0.84	6.37 , 0.93
P5	4.44 , 1.51	5.11 , 1.32	4.89 , 1.4	U5	6 , 1.12	5.67 , 1.33	5.78 , 1.25	G5	6.44 , 0.73	5.72 , 1.07	5.96 , 1.02
P6	4.44 , 2.3	4.06 , 1.66	4.19 , 1.86	U6	6.56 , 0.53	6.5 , 0.71	6.52 , 0.64	G6	5.67 , 2.06	5.28 , 1.49	5.41 , 1.67
				U7	6.22 , 1.3	6.33 , 0.77	6.3 , 0.95	G7	6.33 , 1	6 , 0.97	6.11 , 0.97
				U8	6.11 , 1.36	6.33 , 1.03	6.26 , 1.13				
				U9	6.11 , 1.96	6.44 , 0.86	6.33 , 1.3				

Fig. 6. Left: SUS results, Center: UTAUT2 results, Right: General results.

Firstly, based on the SUS questionnaire's items, participants reported a mean score of Presence of 5.07 ± 0.75 for the whole population, 5.11 ± 0.55 for the XP2's group and 4.98 ± 1.08 for the XP1's group.

Then, based on the UTAUT2 questionnaire's items, participants reported a mean score of Acceptance of 5.49 ± 0.82 for the whole population, 5.48 ± 0.55 for the XP2's group and 5.51 ± 1.23 for the XP1's groups.

In order to assess the impact of our system on real tennis preservation and promotion, we consider the construct, PROM, based on the questions (U3, U5, U6, U7, U8, U9, G1, G2, G4, G5). In addition, in order to get feedback on sport training aspect from users, we consider a second construct, TRAIN, based on questions (U4, G3). The PROM construct presents a mean score of 6.19 ± 0.64 for the whole population, a mean score of 6.13 ± 0.51 for XP2's participants, and 6.31 ± 0.88 for XP1's participants. The TRAIN construct shows a total mean score of 3.76 ± 1.63, XP2 is 3.22 ± 1.19, and XP1 is 4.83 ± 1.92.

4.2 Impact of the Experiment Location on Questionnaire Answers

We then compared the results obtained in our two groups. Most of our data didn't follow a normal distribution. Thus, Wilcoxon signed rank test was used to compare answers between XP2's participants and XP1's participants. Answers tend to be high with no statistically significant difference between the two groups, except for questions **U4** ($p = 0.041$) and **G3** ($p = 0.033$) where participants from XP2 provided lower scores in general compared to XP1's participants.

4.3   Impact of Location on Presence, Acceptance and PROM Scores

To measure the impact of the experimentation location on the different scores, we ran a statistical analysis with location as a factor, and the presence, acceptance and PROM scores as dependent variables.

Homoscedasticity was rejected for presence ($p = 0.011$), and normality was rejected for PROM ($p = 0.003$). As such, Kruskal-Wallis was used for these constructs. No significant result was found (presence: $\chi^2 = 0.003$, $p = 0.959$, $df = 1$, $p_{wilcox} = 0.979$; PROM: $\chi^2 = 2.57$, $p = 0.109$, $df = 1$, $p_{wilcox} = 0.115$). As for acceptance, normality and homoscedasticity assumptions were not rejected ($p = 0.0686$ and $p = 0.116$ respectively), so an ANOVA was performed instead. But similarly to presence and PROM, results for acceptance weren't significant ($F(1, 25) = 0.008$, $p = 0.928$, $p_{adj,tukey} = 0.979$).

5   Discussion

5.1   Questionnaires Discussion

On average, questionnaires' scores are high, meaning that overall the participants felt engaged in the simulation, and showed interest and acceptance for the use of this technology to learn more about the traditional sport that is real tennis. The level of presence is high in both contexts of the experiment and we note that participants' feedback show no discomfort (**G6**: $m = 5.41$, $\sigma = 1.67$). This gives a good indication that the VR application is working properly and that the participants had an enjoyable experience. Particularly, the high mean score for the construct PROM supports the value of using VR technology for the preservation and promotion of real tennis. It is particularly important to note that the questions on pleasure (U6 and U7) have particularly high averages with a fairly low response gap, showing a fairly unanimous feeling among the participants. The questions on usefulness for heritage preservation (**G1**) and the impression of having learned new things (**G4**) also scored highly (>6). As a result of these observations, the level of confidence in the usefulness of our VR application for the preservation and promotion of real tennis is high.

However, based on the low scores in both groups for the TRAIN construct, this simulation appears to be not yet convincing enough for the training and practice of the sport. Although this objective was not a target for this work, the user feedback on the subject raises legitimate questions about the use of our simulator for sports practice. The information gathered during these initial user studies does not allow us to identify any particular causes to explain the results obtained on this aspect of the VR application. However, we can put forward a few hypotheses which constitute research avenues for improving the simulator. An important aspect of sports training applications is bio-fidelity, which concerns the credibility of the behaviour and movements of the virtual opponent, the physical behaviour of the ball during collisions with the racket and obstacles on the court, as well as the user's perception of the interactions, particularly the weight of the racket. It is thus important to consider these different aspects to improve the experience proposed to the users.

We also observed a positive correlation between question U4 and the number of attempts during the chase tutorial ($r = 0.50, p = 0.047$). Perhaps the level of challenge felt by the subjects made them more likely to think that this VR simulation was worth using for real tennis training. It can be interesting to propose training sessions on certain aspects of real tennis, or certain phases of the game, by proposing progressive challenges to the players in order to build on their motivation and competitive spirit. Furthermore, a statistically significant difference was observed between the participants in the gym and those in the historical court, with the former giving lower scores on the TRAIN construct. Two main differences between the two populations may have played a role in this difference: The first being location, it is possible that being physically on the real court represented in the virtual environment had a positive impact on the feeling of playing real tennis in a real situation. The second is age, which was higher in the XP1 population than in the XP2 one. This could be related to the relationship between age and sport, but it is difficult to conclude without further experimentation.

5.2   Historical Court Presence Ambiguity

Looking at the standard deviations of the participants' answers, it is interesting to notice that variability is higher in the XP1 dataset compared to the XP2 dataset, especially for the presence questionnaire. The reason may be attributed to age differences between the two groups. Additionally, some questions from the presence questionnaire, such as P4 and P6, may have been confusing in the Court condition, as the VR environment simulates this setting so the notions of real and virtual environment overlap.

5.3   Impact of Location on Presence, Acceptance and Cultural Heritage and Sport Promotion

The results were not conclusive enough to be able to say whether or not location had an impact on the different mean scores. The main assumption, although not testable, would be that the different constructs are independent of location as the VR simulation isolates the user from their real environment, in particular vision, so that what may vary visually in reality should not have an impact on the constructs studied. On the other hand, it is important to nuance these results as it should be noted that the discrepancy in average age between the XP1 and XP2 participants may have included a bias.

6   Conclusions

We presented the design and implementation of a VR environment dedicated to the preservation and promotion of real tennis. The environment offers a discovery of real tennis through a tutorial implemented with a scenario engine, and a free visit of the reconstructed historical building and the practice of the sport.

We conducted an experiment with users to assess the quality of experience and usability of a VR environment for the preservation and promotion of real tennis. The results revealed positive user feedback and corroborate the interest of the approach for the objective set at the beginning.

The user feedback encourages us to investigate new aspects and objectives for real tennis in virtual reality, particularly with regard to its use in sports practice. For this, we will rely on a collaboration with a national real tennis federation which will allow us to work directly with high level players.

VR has the potential to play a significant role in the preservation of traditional sports in ICH. The technology allows for the creation of engaging and immersive simulations that can bring intangible cultural heritage to life and increase accessibility to preservation efforts. As VR technology continues to evolve and become more accessible, it is likely that we will see more innovative uses of VR in traditional sports preservation and ICH more broadly.

References

1. Aristidou, A., et al.: Safeguarding our dance cultural heritage. In: Eurographics 2022 (2022)
2. Bekele, M.K., Pierdicca, R., Frontoni, E., Malinverni, E.S., Gain, J.: A survey of augmented, virtual, and mixed reality for cultural heritage. J. Comput. Cult. Heritage (JOCCH) **11**(2), 1–36 (2018)
3. Bondt, C.: Royal Tennis in Renaissance Italy. Brepols, Turnhout (2006)
4. Bouville, R., Gouranton, V., Arnaldi, B.: Virtual reality rehearsals for acting with visual effects. In: International Conference on Computer Graphics & Interactive Techniques, pp. 1–8. GI, Victoria-BC, Canada (2016). https://inria.hal.science/hal-01314839
5. Bracq, M.S., et al.: Learning procedural skills with a virtual reality simulator an acceptability study. Nurse Educ. Today **79**, 153–160 (2019)
6. Bronikowska, M., Groll, M.: Definition, classification, preservation and dissemination of traditional sports & games in Europe. Tafisa Recall, Games of the Past, Sports for Today, pp. 1–10 (2015)
7. Carlier, Y., Bernard-Tambour, T.: Jeu des rois, roi des jeux. le jeu de paume en France, 2001. Dix-Huitième Siècle **34**(1), 605–605 (2002)
8. Claude, G., Gouranton, V., Bouville Berthelot, R., Arnaldi, B.: #SEVEN, a sensor effector based scenarios model for driving collaborative virtual environment. In: ICAT-EGVE, pp. 1–4. Bremen, Germany (2014)
9. Gaugne, R., Barreau, J.B., Duc-Martin, P., Esnault, E., Gouranton, V.: Sport heritage in VR: real tennis case study. Front. Virtual Reality **3**, 922415 (2022)
10. Goenetxea, J., Unzueta, L., Linaza, M.T., Rodriguez, M., O'Connor, N., Moran, K.: Capturing the sporting heroes of our past by extracting 3D Movements from legacy

video content. In: Ioannides, M., Magnenat-Thalmann, N., Fink, E., Žarnić, R., Yen, A.-Y., Quak, E. (eds.) EuroMed 2014. LNCS, vol. 8740, pp. 48–58. Springer, Cham (2014). https://doi.org/10.1007/978-3-319-13695-0_5

11. Lim, C.K., Cani, M.P., Galvane, Q., Pettre, J., Talib, A.Z.: Simulation of past life: controlling agent behaviors from the interactions between ethnic groups. In: Digital Heritage International Congress, vol. 1, pp. 589–596. IEEE (2013)

12. Linaza, M., Moran, K., O'Connor, N.: Traditional sports and games: a new opportunity for personalized access to cultural heritage. In: CEUR Workshop Proceedings, p. 997 (2013)

13. Lo, P., et al.: Visualising and revitalising traditional Chinese martial arts: visitors' engagement and learning experience at the 300 years of Hakka Kungfu. Libr. Hi Tech **37**(2), 269–288 (2019)

14. Lyndhurst, B., Aberdare, M.: The Willis Faber Book of Tennis and Rackets. Quiller Press Limited, Seattle (1998)

15. Rallis, I., Voulodimos, A., Bakalos, N., Protopapadakis, E., Doulamis, N., Doulamis, A.: Machine learning for intangible cultural heritage: a review of techniques on dance analysis. In: Liarokapis, F., Voulodimos, A., Doulamis, N., Doulamis, A. (eds.) Visual Computing for Cultural Heritage. SSCC, pp. 103–119. Springer, Cham (2020). https://doi.org/10.1007/978-3-030-37191-3_6

16. Rossau, I.G., Skovfoged, M.M., Czapla, J.J., Sokolov, M.K., Rodil, K.: Dovetailing: safeguarding traditional craftsmanship using virtual, reality. Int. J. Intang. Heritage **14**, 103–120 (2019)

17. Sarupuri, B., Kulpa, R., Aristidou, A., Multon, F.: Dancing in virtual reality as an inclusive platform for social and physical fitness activities: a survey. Visual Comput. 1432–2315 (2023). https://doi.org/10.1007/s00371-023-03068-6

18. Selmanović, E., et al.: Improving accessibility to intangible cultural heritage preservation using virtual reality. J. Comput. Cult. Herit. **13**(2), 1–19 (2020)

19. Setiawan, A., Nugraha, A.S., Haryanto, H., Gamayanto, I.: Benthix VR: a virtual reality simulation application to preserve traditional Benthik game. ComTech: Comput. Math. Eng. Appl. **8**(4), 183–189 (2017)

20. Shi, Y., Ying, F., Chen, X., Pan, Z., Yu, J.: Restoration of traditional Chinese shadow play-Piying art from tangible interaction. Comput. Animation Virtual Worlds **25**(1), 33–43 (2014)

21. Skublewska-Paszkowska, M., Milosz, M., Powroznik, P., Lukasik, E.: 3D technologies for intangible cultural heritage preservation-literature review for selected databases. Heritage Sci. **10**(1), 1–24 (2022)

22. Slater, M., Usoh, M., Steed, A.: Depth of presence in virtual environments. Presence: Teleoperators Virtual Environ. **3**(2), 130–144 (1994)

23. Tisserand, Y., et al.: Preservation and gamification of traditional sports. In: Mixed Reality and Gamification for Cultural Heritage, pp. 421–446. Springer, Cham (2017). https://doi.org/10.1007/978-3-319-49607-8_17

24. UNESCO: Traditional sports and games (2020). https://en.unesco.org/themes/sport-and-anti-doping/traditional-sports-and-games. Accessed 22 May 2020

25. Venkatesh, V., Thong, J., Xu, X.: Consumer acceptance and use of information technology: extending the unified theory of acceptance and use of technology. MIS Q. **36**, 157–178 (2012). https://doi.org/10.2307/41410412

26. Vlahakis, V., et al.: Archeoguide: an augmented reality guide for archaeological sites. IEEE Comput. Graph. Appl. **22**, 52–60 (2002)

Medical Imaging and Robotics

SLf-UNet: Improved UNet for Brain MRI Segmentation by Combining Spatial and Low-Frequency Domain Features

Hui Ding[1,2]([📧]) [iD], Jiacheng Lu[1] [iD], Junwei Cai[1], Yawei Zhang[1], and Yuanyuan Shang[1,2]

[1] College of Information Engineering, Capital Normal University, Beijing, China
dhui@cnu.edu.cn
[2] Beijing Advanced Innovation Center for Imaging Technology, Beijing, China

Abstract. Deep learning-based methods have shown remarkable performance in brain tumor image segmentation. However, there is a lack of research on segmenting brain tumor lesions using frequency domain features of images. To address this gap, an improved network SLf-UNet has been proposed in this paper, which is a two-dimensional encoder-decoder architecture combining spatial and low-frequency domain features based on U-Net. The proposed model effectively learns information from spatial and frequency domains. Herein, we present a novel upsample approach by using zero padding in the high-frequency region and replacing the part of the convolution operation with a convolution block combining spatial frequency domain features. Our experimental results demonstrate that our method outperforms current mainstream approaches on BraTS 2019 and BraTS 2020 datasets. Code is available soon at https://github.com/noseDewdrop/SLf-UNet.

Keywords: Frequency Analysis · BraTS · Image Segmentation

1 Introduction

Medical image segmentation is a crucial tool for disease diagnosis, treatment planning, and follow-up services. In particular, brain MRI analysis often uses image segmentation to measure and visualize the regions and volumes of brain tumors. Since 2012, the Brain Tumor Segmentation (BraTS) Challenge has been held annually at MICCAI (Medical Image Computing and Computer Assisted Intervention). Has become a leading benchmark in the field of medical image segmentation [1,2]. Gliomas are malignant brain tumors that vary in aggressiveness. Therefore, automated and accurate segmentation of these malignancies on magnetic resonance imaging (MRI) is essential for clinical diagnosis [3].

Automated medical image segmentation techniques have proven effective for accurately delineating brain tumors [4]. Recently, deep learning approaches [5–8]

Supported by the National Natural Science Foundation of China (61876112).

have achieved state-of-the-art performance for brain tumor segmentation on various benchmarks, owing to the powerful feature extraction of CNNs [9]. The U-Net architecture [10], using an encoder-decoder structure with skip connections for detail retention, has become mainstream. UNet3+ [11] and UCTransnet [12] further improved UNet-like models by enhancing skip connections. The former employs full-scale connections for multi-scale feature fusion, while the latter adopts channel-wise attention for a more effective combination.

Chen et al. proposed CTUNet based on a Transformer and achieved high performance on the segmentation tasksn [13]. Additionally, the researchers combined GAN with convolutions for the Liver Major Vessels task and achieved good results [14]. Usually, three-dimensional (3D) deep learning frameworks would achieve higher accuracy in brain tumor segmentation tasks but encounter obstacles like a high computational burden. Facing these challenges, how to further optimize brain tumor segmentation models to improve segmentation accuracy remains an important issue [15–17].

Frequency analysis decomposes images into components, providing rich representations for more effective image understanding over spatial-only approaches [18]. In brain tumor images, tissue edges exhibit high-frequency changes, while lesions show gentle, low-frequency variations. Incorporating frequency domain analysis enhances lesion features and improves model feature extraction.

Based on frequency analysis, this paper proposed an improved network SLf-UNet, the following are the contributions of this work:

1) The proposed network, SLf-UNet, incorporates both spatial domain and low-frequency domain characteristics. And the impact of high and low-frequency components on segmentation was discussed and analyzed through experiments.
2) SF-block is proposed for effective fusion in the space-frequency domain. It utilizes both spatial and frequency information from feature maps to achieve information fusion.
3) For upsampling, we present a novel module zFUP, which solved the different scale matching between spatial and frequency domains in deep convolution layers by using zero-padding in the spectrum.
4) The proposed network structure achieves excellent performance on BraTS 2019 and BraTS 2020 datasets.

2   Related Works

While most research concentrates on model architectures, some recent work leverages frequency domain information to address medical imaging challenges using frequency transforms.

Stuchi et al. [19] enhanced image classification via frequency analysis. Luan et al. [20] used high-frequency filtering to enhance the edge and fine structure of breast images. Hu et al. [21] used high and low-pass filters for ultrasound thyroid segmentation. Li et al. [22] utilized wavelet transform in medical multispectral image fusion to exploit the frequency domain information of the images, which helps highlight features of the target area. Azad et al. [23] pointed out that vanilla CNNs tend to be biased towards textures while overlooking shape information for medical image segmentation. They proposed an adaptive frequency recalibration to reduce this bias and improve feature discrimination.

For brain tumor segmentation, Tang et al. proposed a novel model called tKFC-Net [24], which integrates spatial and frequency domain features via the Fast Fourier Transform (FFT). However, it is worth noting that t-KFC incurs a high computational cost, and its adoption of high-frequency components renders it not necessary for brain tumor image segmentation. This limitation arises from the concentration of valuable information in the low-frequency region of brain tumor images, as will be verified in Sect. 4.5. Therefore, while the proposed tKFC-Net model demonstrates an innovative approach to incorporating frequency representations within CNNs, its limitations regarding computational efficiency and compatibility with brain tumor segmentation tasks warrant further investigation and optimization.

3   Method

In this paper, we proposed an improved frequency network, which combing the spatial and low-frequency convolution, and using the zero-padding to enhancement the up-sampling.

3.1   SLf-UNet

Figure 1 illustrates the architecture of SLf-UNet, a 2D model for BraTS. This model is based on a U-Net encoder-decoder architecture that utilizes skip connections to combine high-level and low-level features. The key components of this model are the Spatial Frequency domain combining block (SF-block) and Zero-padding Upsampling Pyramid in Frequency Domain (zFUP).

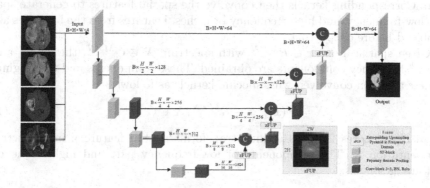

Fig. 1. The overall architecture of SLf-UNet. The architecture primarily comprises zFUP, SF-block, frequency domain pooling, while retaining the classical U-Net skeleton.

The model input consists of 4-channel brain tumor slices. To enhance performance, we incorporated SF-Blocks in the first two encoder layers and last two decoder layers to introduce low-frequencies and enable effective learning. Applying SF-Blocks to all layers would significantly increase computational cost. Moreover, the impact of low-frequencies diminishes as layer depth increases. Hence, we opted to use SF-Blocks only in the first half of the encoder and corresponding decoder layers, balancing low-frequency introduction and complexity. Additionally, we replaced all pooling methods with frequency domain pooling blocks and utilized zFUP for upsampling to align multi-scale features.

3.2   Spatial Frequency Domain Combining Block (SF-Block)

SF-block, which integrates both spatial and frequency domain features for CNNs in brain tumor segmentation. The module utilizes frequency domain information while preserving spatial cues. To analyze the influence of the two domains, we designed several optional branches in the structure (Fig. 2).

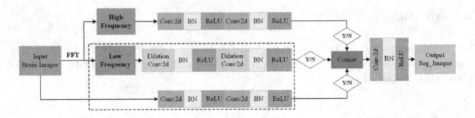

Fig. 2. Spatial and frequency domain Fourier convolution (SF-block). Three optional branches are given in the figure, namely the spatial branch, the low-frequency branch and the high-frequency branch. The influence of different components on the segmentation results is tested through different choices.

It first obtains high and low frequencies via a 2D discrete Fourier transform. Corresponding kernels then convolve the spatial features to generate spatial, low-frequency, and high-frequency branches. Features from the branches are combined before outputting.

Given spatial input $x \in R^{M \times N}$ with spectrum $X \in C^{M \times N}$, the low x^l and high x^h frequency components are obtained. These components and the original input x are then convolved with specific kernels as follows:

$$X = F(x) \quad x \in R^{M \times N}, X \in C^{M \times N} \tag{1}$$

where $F(\bullet)$ denotes 2D-DFT, which transforms spatial feature x into spectral representation X. The components of low-frequency part and high-frequency part are as follows:

$$X_{mn}^l = \begin{cases} X_{mn} & \frac{M}{4} < m \leq \frac{3 \times M}{4}, \frac{N}{4} < n \leq \frac{3 \times N}{4} \\ 0 & \text{others} \end{cases} \tag{2}$$

$$X^h_{mn} = \begin{cases} 0 & \frac{M}{4} < m \leq \frac{3 \times M}{4}, \frac{N}{4} < n \leq \frac{3 \times N}{4} \\ X_{mn} & others \end{cases} \tag{3}$$

where X^l_{mn} denote low frequency part, X^h_{mn} denote high frequency part, and M and N denote the width and height of the feature map. Then transform the frequency parts back to spatial domain:

$$x^l = F^{-1}(X^l) \quad x^l \in R^{M \times N} \tag{4}$$

$$x^h = F^{-1}(X^h) \quad x^h \in R^{M \times N} \tag{5}$$

where x^l denotes spatial features of low frequency partes, and x^h denotes spatial features of high frequency partes, $F^{-1}(\bullet)$ denotes 2D-IDFT.

Figure 3 demonstrates branching in the SF-block. As frequency components increase computation, the high-frequency section here contains less lesion information. Thus, removing this branch to eliminate irrelevant interference can facilitate lesion segmentation.

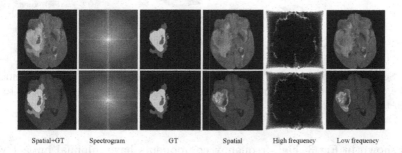

Spatial+GT   Spectrogram   GT   Spatial   High frequency   Low frequency

Fig. 3. Component examples in SF-block. The top and bottom rows present flair and t1ce modalities. Columns 4–6 are outputs of the spatial, high-frequency (binarized), and low-frequency branches respectively, with columns 1 and 3 displaying the corresponding ground truths and column 2 showing the spatial spectral image.

For the three branches, the original spatial feature branch and the high frequency branch adopts normal 3×3 kernel while the low frequency feature employs a dilated kernel with rate of 2, which benefits the smooth low frequency components and yields a broader sight vision. Then different branch combinations are selected, and lastly they are combined in series and input into the subsequent network structure:

$$x^{out} = concat(ax, bx^l, cx^h) \quad x^{out} \in R^{M \times N} \tag{6}$$

Here, a, b, and c are binary variables (1 being selected, 0 not selected) indicating the selection of three branches. This improved frequency domain convolution structure utilizes both spatial and frequency information, where the two complementary image cues produce refined features with rich semantics and details.

3.3   Zero-Padding Upsampling Pyramid (zFUP)

UNet adopts an encoder-decoder framework to learn image features via convolutions. As the extracted feature maps are downsized, the decoder upsamples them to regain the original image sizes for final predictions. Common upsampling methods like deconvolution and bilinear interpolation directly enlarge feature maps. Although restoring the size and most information, they may introduce noise. Here, we recommend using zFUP - zero-padding for frequency-domain upsampling (Fig. 4, and Fig. 1 bottom right).

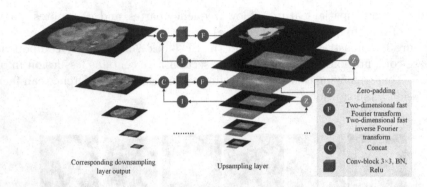

Fig. 4. Schematic diagram of zFUP. During the zFUP, each layer of input is combined with the output of the corresponding downsampling layer after zero-/padding to pass through the convolutional layer.

As shown in Fig. 3, high-frequency components have minimal impact while low-frequency ones greatly affect segmentation. Unlike zFUP, tKFC-Net's [24] upsampling divides the previous output into low and high-frequency regions, generating padded results through a weighted approach. This enables propagating high-frequency information from the preceding layer to the low-frequency region of the subsequent layer. In contrast, the zFUP module directly takes the previous output as the central frequency domain for the next layer, applies zero-padding, then concatenates with the inverse-transformed spatial image. This strategy focuses learning on low-frequency features and optimizes computation by avoiding other padding techniques.

The proposed approach begins by subjecting the input feature map to a Fourier transform, converting it into the frequency domain. Subsequently, the spectrum is padded, doubling the size of each frequency dimension to simulate conventional pooling with a dilation rate of 2. We introduce adjustable padding with the same rate for frequency upsampling. Finally, the inverse transformation reconverts the data back to the spatial domain, resulting in an upsampled map of twice the original size.

3.4 Loss Function

In training, a hybrid loss function combining cross-entropy loss and Dice loss is adopted. The cross-entropy loss is defined as:

$$L_{bce} = -\sum_{i=1}^{W}\sum_{j=1}^{H}[T_{ij}\ \log(P_{ij}\ ) + (1 - T_{ij}\ )\ \log(1 - P_{ij}\ )\ ] \tag{7}$$

where W and H denote the width and height of the predicted image P_{ij} and the ground-truth image T_{ij}. And (i, j) are the coordinates of the pixels in the predicted image P_{ij} and the ground truth image T_{ij}.

And the Dice loss is defined as:

$$L_{dice}(P, T) = 1 - 2 \times \frac{\sum_{i=1}^{N} p_i g_i + \tau}{\sum_{i=1}^{N} p_i + \sum_{i=1}^{N} g_i + \tau} \tag{8}$$

where summation is carried over the N voxels of the ground truth volume $t_i \in T$ and the predicted volume $p_i \in P$, and τ is a minimal constant to prevent division by zero.

Based on the above two loss functions, we propose a joint loss function composed of BCE and Dice:

$$L_{joint} = \sum_{i=1}^{3}(\lambda L_{dice_i} + (1 - \lambda)L_{bce_i}) \tag{9}$$

where λ is the weight to balance different losses, the value range is $0 < \lambda < 1$, and set to 1 in the experiment. In order to reduce the complexity of the task, we divide the task of segmenting the three-category lesion area into a single-category segmentation task with 3 channels, and calculate the loss separately. Where L_{dice_i} and L_{bce_i} represent the Dice loss and BCE loss of the i-th channel, respectively.

4 Experiments

4.1 Datasets

This paper utilizes BraTS 2019 and 2020 datasets, providing 3D MRI with voxel-wise ground truth labels annotated by physicians for evaluating state-of-the-art brain tumor segmentation methods [25–27]. BraTS 2019 contains 259 HGG and 76 LGG cases, while BraTS 2020 has 369 scans with more HGG cases. Each patient has four modalities: T1, T2, T1ce, and FLAIR MRI. Experts labeled the images into background, non-enhanced region, edema, and enhancing tumor based on unified standards. All scans have $240 \times 240 \times 155$ voxel sizes. We focus on segmenting three regions: enhancing tumor for ET; whole tumor with ET + NET + ED; and tumor core containing ET + NET.

4.2   Pre-processing

The image contrast of the four modalities of the glioma image dataset is different, so the z-score method is used to normalize the images of each modality separately. The 1% highest and lowest intensities are removed, and subtracting the mean and dividing by the standard deviation of the intensities within the body. And after, cropping the size of images into $160 \times 160 \times 155$ to eliminate the unnecessary background. Then, obtained the slices of 3D brain tumor MRI images. In order to address the class imbalance problem, the slices without label pixels are excluded from trainset. Finally, the slices of the four modalities of the data are combined into multi-channel, and finally saved in npy for subsequent experiments.

4.3   Implementation Details

The experimental environment is: Ubuntu 18.04, NVIDIA GeForce GTX 2080Ti x1, Intel Core i7-4790k @ 4.00 GHz quad-core CPU. And the experiment is based on the deep learning framework of Python 3.6 and Pytorch 1.6.0. We employed the Adam optimizer with an initial learning rate of 3e−4. Model regularization was conducted using L2 norm with a weight decay rate of 1e−4. For all models, we set the maximum number of training epochs to 500 and implemented early stopping after 50 epochs. Most models were terminated around 300 epochs during training. All models were implemented in Pytorch.

4.4   Evaluation Metrics

In this paper, we evaluate brain tumor segmentation using two widely used medical imaging metrics - Dice similarity coefficient (DSC) and Hausdorff distance (HD). DSC measures overlap and similarity between segmentation and ground truth. It weights recall and false positives equally. DSC is defined as:

$$DSC(P,T) = \frac{2|P_1 \cap T_1|}{|P_1| + |T_1|} \tag{10}$$

where P_1 is the predicted tumor region, T_1 is the true tumor region. DSC ranges from 0 to 1, higher values signify better segmentation.

Hausdorff distance (HD) evaluates structural differences between segmentation and truth. It is defined as:

$$Haus(T,P) = max\{sup_{t \in T} inf_{p \in P}, sup_{p \in P} inf_{t \in T} d(t,p)\} \tag{11}$$

where the inf and sup denote the lowest and highest distances, t and p are surfaces of the true and predicted regions, and $d(t,p)$ calculates distance between points t and p.

4.5   Ablation Study

To analyze the impacts of spatial and frequency domains, we conducted SLf-UNet with different channel settings (Table 1): solely spatial, solely low-frequency, solely high-frequency, and jointly spatial-low. Results in Table 1 show adding high-frequency channels decreased segmentation performance. Hence, we focused on exploring the synergistic effects of low-frequency and spatial channels.

Table 1. Ablation study on BraTS 2019 dataset.

Model	Dice_score (%)			Haussdorff95		
	ET↑	WT↑	TC↑	ET↓	WT↓	TC↓
SLf-UNet (spatial only)	86.23	**83.37**	84.74	1.6124	**2.6319**	1.6599
SLf-UNet (low frequency only)	86.14	83.35	85.35	1.6153	2.7217	1.6783
SLf-UNet (high frequency only)	54.25	61.30	58.99	2.5454	3.5946	2.6147
SLf-UNet (spatial and lowfrq, ours)	**87.61**	83.31	**86.86**	**1.5695**	2.7135	**1.6244**

Table 1 presents ablation results on BraTS 2019. Combining low-frequency and spatial channels yielded Dice scores of 87.61, 83.31, and 86.86 for ET, WT, and TC, outperforming other settings except WT. As Sect. 3.2 and Fig. 3 explain, low-frequencies contain most lesion information but lack whole tumor edge details, possibly contributing to the slight WT decrease. These results demonstrate incorporating spatial and low-frequency cues enhances SLf-UNet's effectiveness in segmenting medical images like BraTS.

4.6   Multi-method Comparison

Table 2 and 3 show the comparison of the brain tumor segmentation performance of our proposed Network SLf-UNet and the performance of other representative segmentation networks, included U-Net, UNet3+, UCTansNet, tKFC-Net, and transUNet. For BraTS'19, 285 subjects were used for training and 50 for testing. After preprocessing, the dataset had 15,138 images for training, 3,785 for validation and 3,219 for testing. Table 2 evaluates segmentation of WT, TC and ET using the mentioned metrics. In the BraTS'20 experiment, the 369 subjects in the dataset were divided into training and test sets at a 8:2 ratio. The preprocessed slices were evaluated, including ground-truths.

Table 3 compares SLf-UNet with other networks. The experimental results in Tables 2-3 demonstrate that the improved SLf-UNet achieves comparable WT segmentation performance to other networks, while attaining higher accuracy on ET and TC. On BraTS 2019, SLf-UNet obtained Dice scores of 87.61, 83.31, 86.86 for ET, WT, TC respectively; and HD95 values of 1.5695, 2.7135, 1.6244 respectively. On BraTS 2020, it achieved Dice scores of 91.83, 87.62, 88.94; and HD95 values of 0.6662, 1.3166, 0.8873 respectively. Figure 5 presents SLf-UNet segmentation outputs and multi-modal examples. As shown, the segmentation results exhibit improved effects on details and edges.

Table 2. Performance on BraTS 2019 dataset.

Model	Source	Dice_score(%)			Haussdorff95		
		ET↑	WT↑	TC↑	ET↓	WT↓	TC↓
U-Net	2015 MICCAI	77.10	84.06	84.50	–	–	–
UNet 3+	2020 ICASSP	87.04	83.48	86.06	1.5654	**2.6372**	1.6306
tKFC-Net	2021 CMPB	78.15	**84.57**	86.52	–	–	–
TransUNet	2021arxiv	80.69	80.74	77.23	1.7599	2.7598	1.8783
UCTransnet	2022 AAAI	84.99	84.32	83.43	1.5951	2.6471	1.7347
SLf-UNet(our)		**87.61**	83.31	**86.86**	**1.5695**	2.7135	**1.6244**

Table 3. Performance on BraTS 2020 dataset.

Model	Source	Dice_score (%)			Haussdorff95		
		ET↑	WT↑	TC↑	ET↓	WT↓	TC↓
U-Net	2015 MICCAI	90.87	86.3	87.76	0.6813	1.3916	0.9049
UNet3+	2020 ICASSP	91.53	87.35	88.61	0.6781	1.3207	0.8903
TransUNet	2021arxiv	89.75	84.01	86.81	0.7272	1.4253	0.9507
UCTransnet	2022 AAAI	90.37	**88.18**	88.56	0.6971	**1.2707**	0.9063
SLf-UNet (ours)		**91.83**	87.62	**88.94**	**0.6662**	1.3166	**0.8873**

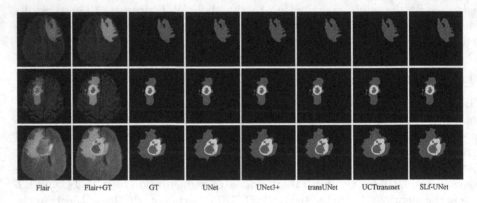

Flair   Flair+GT   GT   UNet   UNet3+   transUNet   UCTtransnet   SLf-UNet

Fig. 5. Examples of Multi-method segmentation results. For the segmentation result image, where Green: peritumoral edematous/invaded tissue, red: necrotic tumor core, yellow: GD-enhancing tumor. (Color figure online)

5   Conclusion

We propose a novel 2D multi-modal spatial-frequency segmentation algorithm for brain tumor MRI, validated on BraTS 2019 and 2020. Experiments show our network outperforms most cutting-edge methods. The core innovation is incorporating frequency domain information through adaptive Fourier transforms, learnable convolution kernels, and an efficient upsampling module zFUP. Future work will explore advanced frequency integration techniques to further improve tumor segmentation and broader medical image analysis.

References

1. Withey, D., Koles, Z.: Three generations of medical image segmentation: methods and available software. Int. J. Bioelectromagnetism **9**, 67–68 (2007)
2. Lai, M.: Deep learning for medical image segmentation. arXiv preprint arXiv:1505.02000 (2015)
3. Wang, W., Chen, C., Ding, M., Yu, H., Zha, S., Li, J.: TransBTS: multimodal brain tumor segmentation using transformer. In: de Bruijne, M., et al. (eds.) MICCAI 2021. LNCS, vol. 12901, pp. 109–119. Springer, Cham (2021). https://doi.org/10.1007/978-3-030-87193-2_11
4. Huo, Y., et al.: 3D whole brain segmentation using spatially localized atlas network tiles. Neuroimage **194**, 105–119 (2019)
5. Isensee, F., Jäger, P.F., Full, P.M., Vollmuth, P., Maier-Hein, K.H.: nnU-Net for brain tumor segmentation. In: Crimi, A., Bakas, S. (eds.) BrainLes 2020. LNCS, vol. 12659, pp. 118–132. Springer, Cham (2021). https://doi.org/10.1007/978-3-030-72087-2_11
6. Jiang, Z., Ding, C., Liu, M., Tao, D.: Two-stage cascaded U-Net: 1st place solution to BraTS challenge 2019 segmentation task. In: Crimi, A., Bakas, S. (eds.) BrainLes 2019. LNCS, vol. 11992, pp. 231–241. Springer, Cham (2020). https://doi.org/10.1007/978-3-030-46640-4_22
7. Milletari, F., Navab, N., Ahmadi, S.A.: V-Net: fully convolutional neural networks for volumetric medical image segmentation. In: Fourth International Conference on 3D Vision (3DV), pp. 565–571. IEEE (2016)
8. Bischke, B., Helber, P., Folz, J., Borth, D., Dengel, A.: Multi-task learning for segmentation of building footprints with deep neural networks. In: IEEE International Conference on Image Processing (ICIP), pp. 1480–1484. IEEE (2019)
9. Hatamizadeh, A., Nath, V., Tang, Y., Yang, D., Roth, H.R., Xu, D.: Swin UNETR: swin transformers for semantic segmentation of brain tumors in MRI images. In: Crimi, A., Bakas, S. (eds.) BrainLes 2021. LNCS, vol. 12962, pp. 272–284. Springer, Cham (2021). https://doi.org/10.1007/978-3-031-08999-2_22
10. Ronneberger, O., Fischer, P., Brox, T.: U-Net: convolutional networks for biomedical image segmentation. In: Navab, N., Hornegger, J., Wells, W.M., Frangi, A.F. (eds.) MICCAI 2015. LNCS, vol. 9351, pp. 234–241. Springer, Cham (2015). https://doi.org/10.1007/978-3-319-24574-4_28
11. Huang, H., et al.: UNet 3+: a full-scale connected UNet for medical image segmentation. In: IEEE International Conference on Acoustics, Speech and Signal Processing (ICASSP), pp. 1055–1059. IEEE (2020)
12. Wang, H., Cao, P., Wang, J., Zaiane, O.R.: UCTransNet: rethinking the skip connections in U-Net from a channel-wise perspective with transformer. In: Proceedings of the AAAI Conference on Artificial Intelligence, pp. 2441–2449. AAAI Press (2022)
13. Chen, L., Wan, L.: CTUNet: automatic pancreas segmentation using a channel-wise transformer and 3D U-Net. Vis. Comput. (2022). https://doi.org/10.1007/s00371-022-02656-2

14. Cheema, M.N., et al.: Modified GAN-CAED to minimize risk of unintentional liver major vessels cutting by controlled segmentation using CTA/SPET-CT. IEEE Trans. Ind. Inform. **17**(12), 7991–8002 (2021). https://doi.org/10.1109/TII.2021. 3064369

15. Liu, X., Song, L., Liu, S., Zhang, Y.: A review of deep-learning-based medical image segmentation methods. Sustainability **13**, 1224 (2021)

16. Hesamian, M.H., Jia, W., He, X., Kennedy, P.: Deep learning techniques for medical image segmentation: achievements and challenges. J. Digit. Imaging **32**, 582–596 (2019)

17. Nazir, A., Cheema, M.N., et al.: ECSU-Net: an embedded clustering sliced U-Net coupled with fusing strategy for efficient intervertebral disc segmentation and classification. IEEE Trans. Image Process. **31**, 880–893 (2021)

18. Brosch, T., Tam, R.: Efficient training of convolutional deep belief networks in the frequency domain for application to high-resolution 2D and 3D images. Neural Comput. **27**, 211–227 (2015)

19. Stuchi, J.A., et al.: Improving image classification with frequency domain layers for feature extraction. In: IEEE 27th International Workshop on Machine Learning for Signal Processing (MLSP), pp. 1–6. IEEE (2017)

20. Luan M, Cui G, S.W.: Mammogram image enhancement method based on power-law transformation and high frequency emphasis filtering. J. Bohai Univ. (Nat. Sci. Ed.) **40**(04), 378–384 (2019)

21. Hu, Y., Qin, P., Zeng, J., Chai, R., Wang, L.: Ultrasound thyroid segmentation based on segmented frequency domain and local attention. J. Image Graph. **25**, 2195–2205 (2020)

22. Li, J., Chen, C., Wang, L.: Fusion algorithm of multi-spectral images based on dual-tree complex wavelet transform and frequency-domain U-Net. J. Biomed. Eng. Res. **39**, 145–150 (2020)

23. Azad, R., Bozorgpour, A., Asadi-Aghbolaghi, M., Merhof, D., Escalera, S.: Deep frequency re-calibration u-net for medical image segmentation. In: Proceedings of the IEEE/CVF International Conference on Computer Vision, pp. 3274–3283. IEEE (2021)

24. Tang, X., Peng, J., Zhong, B., Li, J., Yan, Z.: Introducing frequency representation into convolution neural networks for medical image segmentation via twin-kernel Fourier convolution. Comput. Methods Programs Biomed. **205**, 106110 (2021)

25. Menze, B.H., et al.: The multimodal brain tumor image segmentation benchmark (BraTS). IEEE Trans. Med. Imaging **34**, 1993–2024 (2014)

26. Bakas, S., et al.: Advancing the cancer genome atlas glioma MRI collections with expert segmentation labels and radiomic features. Sci. Data **4**, 1–13 (2017)

27. Bakas, S., et al.: Identifying the best machine learning algorithms for brain tumor segmentation, progression assessment, and overall survival prediction in the BraTS challenge. arXiv preprint arXiv:1811.02629 (2018)

Exploring the Transferability of a Foundation Model for Fundus Images: Application to Hypertensive Retinopathy

Julio Silva-Rodriguez[1]([✉]), Jihed Chelbi[2], Waziha Kabir[2], Hadi Chakor[2], Jose Dolz[1], Ismail Ben Ayed[1], and Riadh Kobbi[2]

[1] ETS Montreal, Quebec, Canada
julio-jose.silva-rodriguez@etsmtl.ca
[2] DIAGNOS Inc., Quebec, Canada

Abstract. Using deep learning models pre-trained on Imagenet is the traditional solution for medical image classification to deal with data scarcity. Nevertheless, relevant literature supports that this strategy may offer limited gains due to the high dissimilarity between domains. Currently, the paradigm of adapting domain-specialized foundation models is proving to be a promising alternative. However, how to perform such knowledge transfer, and the benefits and limitations it presents, are under study. The CGI-HRDC challenge for Hypertensive Retinopathy diagnosis on fundus images introduces an appealing opportunity to evaluate the transferability of a recently released vision-language foundation model of the retina, FLAIR [42]. In this work, we explore the potential of using FLAIR features as starting point for fundus image classification, and we compare its performance with regard to Imagenet initialization on two popular transfer learning methods: Linear Probing (LP) and Fine-Tuning (FP). Our empirical observations suggest that, in any case, the use of the traditional strategy provides performance gains. In contrast, direct transferability from FLAIR model allows gains of ~2.5%. When fine-tuning the whole network, the performance gap increases up to ~4%. In this case, we show that avoiding feature deterioration via LP initialization of the classifier allows the best re-use of the rich pre-trained features. Although direct transferability using LP still offers limited performance, we believe that foundation models such as FLAIR will drive the evolution of deep-learning-based fundus image analysis.

Keywords: Foundation Models · Transfer Learning · Hypertensive Retinopathy

1 Introduction

A foundation model for image understanding is a generic pre-trained deep learning model on a large dataset, serving as a base for developing specialized vision models through fine-tuning on task-specific data. Recently, foundation models

B. Sheng et al. (Eds.): CGI 2023, LNCS 14497, pp. 427–437, 2024.
https://doi.org/10.1007/978-3-031-50075-6_33

trained on natural images have gained popularity by the impressive resource-efficient transferability capabilities they present. Successful examples include pre-trained models on ImageNet, vision-language pre-training as CLIP [39] or ALIGN [20], or models for image segmentation as SAM [23]. Despite its promising results in the natural image context, these models have shown limited performance for transferability to expert fields such as medical image analysis [8,10,47]. Although the limited benefit of using transfer learning from large pre-trained models when exists a large domain gap is not new [40], these observations have encouraged the recent development of foundation models specialized in concrete medical domains (see Fig. 1). As a result, a paradigm shift is occurring in this field. The use of specialized foundation models promises to improve the efficiency of the resources needed to create task-specific solutions, in both samples and computational power. Some successful models have been developed for radiology [47], histology [33], fundus images [42], volumetric segmentation [30,43], and 2D image segmentation [4]. However, the potential of the *pre-train and adapt* paradigm remains largely unexplored in many medical imaging domains. This motivates the realization of empirical studies to analyze the benefits of such models in comparison with the more traditional paradigms.

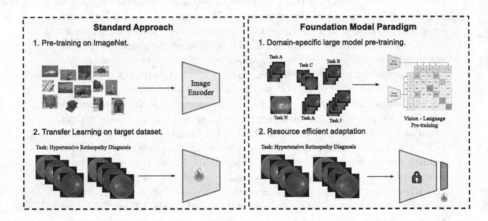

Fig. 1. Standard vs. Foundation Model Paradigms. Deep learning solutions on medical image analysis are traditionally built upon models pre-trained on ImageNet to alleviate the need for large datasets. Nevertheless, the benefits of transfer learning might be limited when a substantial domain gap from source to target exists [40]. Foundation models on specific domains, such as FLAIR [42] for fundus image analysis, which is pre-trained on heterogeneous data sources and tasks, offer better resource-efficient transferability to new tasks.

The CGI-HRDC Challenge for Hypertensive Retinopathy diagnosis through fundus images constitutes an ideal setting to study the potential of foundation models. The analysis of hypertensive retinopathy is burdened by the necessary manual inspection of fundus images from experienced ophthalmologists. Therefore, it is paramount to provide ophthalmologists with an accurate computer system that facilitates the analysis of the course of the disease. Moreover, the scarcity of available data sources with hypertensive cases further challenges the development of task-specific deep learning models. Thus, the objective of this work is to study the limitations and potential of a recently released foundation model for fundus image analysis, FLAIR [42], and compare its transferability capabilities for Hypertensive Retinopathy detection, in comparison with standard solutions using models pre-trained on Imagenet.

2   Related Works

2.1   Transfer Learning on Fundus Images

Deep learning has achieved remarkable performance on a wide variety of fundus image analysis tasks, and offers a potential solution for large-scale screening and early detection of ophthalmologic conditions [2,3]. Among others, outstanding applications include diabetic retinopathy grading [7,32], cataract diagnosis [19], lupus detection [31], or multi-disease classification [21,41]. Nevertheless, training such models from scratch demands substantial datasets and extensive computational resources [11]. In the medical domain, specifically in fundus image analysis, achieving the prerequisite of large datasets is often unattainable, and the norm involves working with small, task-specific datasets. Consequently, transfer learning from natural images has emerged as the primary approach for medical image classification [40]. However, empirical studies have revealed that transfer learning may yield limited performance improvements in specific medical image classification scenarios [35,40], in which a large inter-domain gap exists [1]. These limitations have motivated the use of pre-trained models for further transferability to downstream tasks. For example, self-supervised [44] or task-specific pre-training [32] using public datasets have shown promising improvements for diabetic retinopathy grading. However, it is important to note that task-specific models are prone to produce too specific inductive biases on specific features, resulting in poor generalization when transferred to other less-related tasks [42]. In this context, vision-language pre-training has raised as a promising solution to group heterogeneous data sources and tasks for pre-training, aligned through text supervision, and thus capturing generic features and representations in large foundation models. This strategy has shown promising transferability performance in the medical context for radiology [47], histology [33], and recently in fundus images [42].

2.2   FLAIR

The foundation model FLAIR[1] [42] (A Foundation LAnguage Image model of the Retina) is a recently released pre-trained model for universal disease detection on fundus images through text supervision, which has shown remarkable transferability to downstream tasks even on unseen diseases.

---

[1] Available at https://github.com/jusiro/FLAIR.

FLAIR Pre-training Datasets. The foundation model was built using an assembly dataset from 37 publicly available sources, which include up to 286,916 fundus images from heterogeneous tasks, consisting of 96 different categories. These tasks include *diabetic retinopathy grading*: EYEPACS[2], IDRID [38], JICHI [45], PARAGUAY [5], SYSU [29], OIA-DDR [28] and BRSET [34]; *Glaucoma detection*: LAG [27], PAPILA [24], CHAKSU [26] and AIROGS ([46]); *lesion segmentation*: DR1-2 [37], SYSU [29], OIA-DDR [28] and HEI-MED [12]; *image description*: EYENET [18], ODIR-5K[3], and STARE [16,17]; and the detection of *other diseases*: RFMid [36], 1000×39 [6], BRSET [34] and FUND-OCT1 [13,14]. From the last group, it is worth mentioning that nearly 400 samples from two different datasets contained hypertensive retinopathy findings, which constitutes less than 0.2% of the entire assembly dataset.

Model Architecture. FLAIR model consists of a vision encoder, ResNet-50 [15], and a text encoder, with the architecture of BioClinicalBert[4], which takes as input a fundus image and a text prompt describing its content, respectively. The produced individual modality embeddings are projected into an l2-normalized multimodal space.

Optimization Criteria. The foundation model is pre-trained using a contrastive vision-language alignment approach, aiming to create a multimodal feature representation in which images and expert knowledge descriptors of the same category are similar while maximizing differences between unrelated samples. This three-dimensional alignment, encompassing image, text, and categories, results in a more comprehensive and richer representation through text semantics, able to inter-correlate different conditions (e.g. diabetic retinopathy and microaneurysms) by efficiently leveraging expert domain knowledge.

2.3   Transferability

In the context of foundation models, transferability refers to the process of using or adapting the features learned in large pre-trained models to downstream tasks and related domains. In this work, we focus on the transferability in the medium data regime, where a few hundred training examples are available, and we explore only adaptation through the vision encoder. Two popular transfer learning methods are Linear Probing (LP) and Fine-Tuning (FT). The former involves direct transferability of the features by adjusting only the linear classifier. For the latter, all the parameters of the model are re-trained to the target dataset. Fine-tuning all layers of a network can modify the pre-trained features by adapting/improving them to the downstream task, while linear probing, on the other hand, only relies on the frozen features without any further adjustments.

---

[2] https://www.kaggle.com/c/diabetic-retinopathy-detection.
[3] https://odir2019.grand-challenge.org/.
[4] https://huggingface.co/emilyalsentzer/Bio_ClinicalBERT.

3 Method: Transfer Learning from FLAIR Model

In this work, we aim to explore the potential and limitations of transferring a general-purpose foundation model of the retina for the challenging task of Hypertensive Retinopathy. In particular, we focus on adapting the image encoder from the recently published FLAIR [42] model.

Pre-processing. The fundus images are processed accordingly to the foundation model pre-training. Concretely, the samples are resized to 800×800 pixels, and the intensity is scaled between $[0, 1]$.

Linear Probe (LP) Adaptation. For LP adaptation, a classification head is trained over the features extracted from the pre-trained FLAIR model. Two feature representations are considered for LP adaptation: the vision encoder representation (LP (vision)), and the multimodal vision-language projection (LP (proj)).

Fine-Tuning (FT). In this setting, a classification head is initialized with random weights, which uses as input the vision encoder features, and the whole network is retrained on the target task. Concretely, the encoder and classifier are trained to minimize the binary cross-entropy between reference and predicted sigmoid scores via stochastic gradient descent.

Linear Probe and Fine-Tuning (LP+FT). Last, we follow a recently popularized two-step strategy. First, the classifier is trained with the backbone frozen as in LP, and then the whole network is regularly fine-tuned to the objective task [22,25].

4 Experiments

4.1 Dataset

The CGI-HRDC dataset comprises two different tasks: Task 1 involves hypertension classification, determining whether the patient has hypertension, while Task 2 focuses on Hypertensive Retinopathy detection, aiming to identify signs of Hypertensive Retinopathy in the target fundus image. For each task, the development dataset includes 712 samples for training. In addition, the Challenge includes 288 cases for testing for each task, which remain unavailable during the development stage. The samples consist of macula-centered fundus images, each with dimensions of 800×800 pixels.

4.2 Implementation Details

The pre-trained FLAIR vision encoder is transferred to the different tasks related to hypertensive retinopathy diagnosis using the strategies indicated in Sect. 3. For LP adaptation, We follow the same solver as in CLIP [39], and we applied class weights to account for class imbalances. For full backbone fine-tuning,

ADAM is used as an optimizer with an initial learning rate of $1e-4$, and training is carried out using mini-batches of 4 images, during 20 epochs. To account for class imbalance, a re-sampling strategy of the minority class is carried out. Data augmentation is applied for each iteration using random horizontal flips, rotations of $[-5, 5]$ degrees, zoom scaling in the range $[0.9, 1.1]$, and color jitter. Also, the convergence is tracked on the internal validation set, and the best model in this subset is saved as the final solution for evaluation. For each stage of LP+FT method, we follow the same aforementioned implementation details. The adaptation code was part of the official FLAIR repository, publicly accessible at: https://github.com/jusiro/FLAIR.

4.3   Baselines

To evaluate the benefits of using a domain-specific foundation model for transferring feature representations, we use the ResNet-50 [15] (the same vision backbone used in FLAIR) with weights pre-trained on ImageNet [9], for natural image classification. In particular, the different transfer learning strategies set for FLAIR are applied to this model for adaptation to the challenge tasks. The hyperparameters and implementation details of these baselines were the same as the foundation model adaptation. Hereafter, we refer to this weights initialization as *Imagenet*.

4.4   Evaluation Protocol and Metrics

During the method development stage, a 5 fold cross-validation partition is performed on the CGI-HRDC development dataset to evaluate the different proposed methods. In each fold iteration, 20% of training samples for each class are randomly retrieved for evaluation, while 70%, is used for training and 10% for internal validation. The evaluation metrics used are the Kappa, F1 score, and specificity, which are averaged into a global score. All metrics are averaged fold-wise during the cross-validation stage.

5   Results

5.1   Development Dataset Results

The cross-validation results obtained in the training subset using the different strategies for adapting FLAIR model and the corresponding baselines for hypertensive classification (Task 1) and Hypertensive Retinopathy detection (Task 2) are presented in Table 1 and Table 2, respectively.

The obtained results unveil the benefit of using foundation models pre-trained on medical domains. ***Linear Probe (LP) adaptation.*** Direct transferability (i.e. LP) - of FLAIR features improves in $\sim+2.5\%$ the score compared to *Imagenet* features on both Tasks. It is worth mentioning that, in the case of FLAIR,

Table 1. Cross-Validation results for Task 1: Hypertensive classification LP: Linear Probe; FT: Fine-Tuning; proj: projection. Gray indicates the method submitted for the testing phase.

Method	Metric			
	Kappa	F1	Specificity	Avg.
Imagenet - LP	0.324(0.039)	0.666(0.019)	0.651(0.035)	0.547
Imagenet - FT	0.335(0.112)	0.659(0.078)	0.682(0.019)	0.558
Imagenet - LP+FT	0.389(0.074)	**0.711**(0.023)	0.637(0.113)	0.579
FLAIR - LP (proj)	0.240(0.037)	0.593(0.017)	0.685(0.051)	0.506
FLAIR - LP (vision)	0.358(0.066)	0.680(0.033)	0.676(0.035)	0.571
FLAIR - FT	0.366(0.110)	0.697(0.039)	0.640(0.121)	0.567
FLAIR - LP+FT	**0.420**(0.043)	0.703(0.026)	**0.730**(0.058)	**0.617**

Table 2. Cross-Validation results for Task 2: Hypertensive Retinopathy classification LP: Linear Probe; FT: Fine-Tuning; proj: projection. Gray indicates the method submitted for the testing phase.

Method	Metric			
	Kappa	F1	Specificity	Avg.
Imagenet - LP	0.404(0.068)	0.652(0.040)	0.740(0.040)	0.598
Imagenet - FT	0.623(0.049)	0.770(0.030)	0.874(0.049)	0.755
Imagenet - LP+FT	0.636(0.103)	0.781(0.061)	0.869(0.049)	0.762
FLAIR - LP (proj)	0.258(0.089)	0.533(0.068)	0.759(0.045)	0.516
FLAIR - LP (vision)	0.439(0.052)	0.670(0.033)	0.764(0.034)	0.624
FLAIR - FT	0.622(0.027)	0.772(0.017)	0.862(0.062)	0.752
FLAIR - LP+FT	**0.695**(0.060)	**0.816**(0.034)	**0.893**(0.062)	**0.801**

using the features of the multimodal projection results in a significant performance drop. Despite this feature representation is commonly used for the transferability of vision-language pre-trained models on other works (e.g. CLIP [39], MedCLIP [47]), our empirical results evidence that they might produce suboptimal solutions. This may be caused by the specific patterns of Hypertensive Retinopathy, and the low prevalence of this condition in the FLAIR pre-training dataset (<0.2%). Thus, tuning the vision encoder for this task seems necessary in this case. *Fine-Tuning (FT)*. After fine-tuning, the obtained performance increases notably for Task 2, while modest improvements are observed for Task 1. In this case, minor differences between *Imagenet* and FLAIR initialization can be observed. Interestingly, in the case of Task 1, just LP outperforms FT for the whole network. As it is widely known, full FT is an aggressive adaptation strategy, which might distort pre-trained features [25]. *Linear Probe and Fine-Tuning (LP+FT)*. When using the classifier initialized via LP, then the use of a domain-specific Foundation model highlights its benefits. This solution prevents the distortion of pre-trained features, and the performance consistently improves in $\sim+4\%$ compared to using *Imagenet* representations. Although the benefits of LP+FT observations have been previously reported for regular fine-tuning [22] and out-of-distribution inference [25], our empirical results suggest that the quality of the initialization features and classifier for the target domain also plays an important role in this setting. ***Performance discrepancies between tasks.*** The results obtained in Task 1 are consistently worse compared to the performance of the models observed in Task 2. This might be produced by the hardness of the target case. While Hypertension might be a global condition of the patient, with scarce feature representation on the particular eye of the sample, Hypertensive Retinopathy ensures the presence of a disease in the retina of the target fundus image.

5.2   CGI-HRDC Hidden Test Results

After the development stage, we decided to use the Linear Probe adaptation with the FLAIR vision encoder features (i.e. FLAIR - LP (vision) in Tables 1 and 2) as our solution for the CGI-HRDC challenge. Although this was not the best method in the cross-validation set, the motivation behind this decision was to test the direct transferability of the foundation model in a real use case. Thus, a classifier for each task was trained on top of the frozen vision encoder of FLAIR using the whole challenge development dataset. Under this setting, a global average score of 0.500 (#3rd on the official test Leaderboard) and 0.545 (#2nd on the official test Leaderboard) was obtained for Task 1 and Task 2, respectively. It is worth mentioning that the proposed method experiences a consistent drop of $\sim-8\%$ with respect to the cross-validation stage which might be caused by disparities in class balance or the presence of harder samples on the hidden test subset.

6   Conclusions

In this work, we have explored the transferability of a foundation model for fundus images, FLAIR [42], to tasks related to Hypertensive Retinopathy detection, in the context of the CGI-HRDC challenge. FLAIR model, although pre-trained through contrastive vision-language alignment in a wide variety of Fundus conditions, contains less than 0.2% of training samples with pathologies related to hypertension. Still, the learned feature representations show promising capability for direct transferability on such a challenging task, with gains of $\sim+4\%$ compared to pre-training on *Imagenet*. Nevertheless, the modest results obtained using Linear Probing in comparison with other methods participating in the challenge highlight the current limitations of direct transferability for reaching state-of-the-art performance in medium-sized datasets. Thus, we have explored fine-tuning the whole model for adaptation. In any case, using the model pre-trained on *Imagenet* - which is the *de-facto* solution on transfer learning for medical image analysis - has shown any advantage compared to using FLAIR.

In particular, preventing feature distortion of the Foundation model through Linear Probing initialization showed promising benefits for both tasks. We believe that developing foundation models on medical domains and enhancing the adaptation of their rich feature representations to downstream tasks is an appealing future direction for medical image analysis and, more specifically, for the characterization of fundus images.

Acknowledgments. The work of J. Silva-Rodríguez was partially funded by the *Fonds de recherche du Québec (FRQ)* under the Postdoctoral Merit Scholarship for Foreign Students (PBEEE).

References

1. Azizpour, H., Razavian, A.S., Sullivan, J., Maki, A., Carlsson, S.: Factors of transferability for a generic convnet representation. In: CVPR Workshop: DeepVision, June 2014
2. Balyen, L., Peto, T.: Promising artificial intelligence-machine learning-deep learning algorithms in ophthalmology. Asia-Pac. J. Ophthalmol. **8**, 264–272 (2019)
3. Bellemo, V., et al.: Artificial intelligence using deep learning to screen for referable and vision-threatening diabetic retinopathy in Africa: a clinical validation study. Lancet Digit. Health **1**, e35–e44 (2019)
4. Butoi, V.I., Ortiz, J.J.G., Ma, T., Sabuncu, M.R., Guttag, J., Dalca, A.V.: Universeg: universal medical image segmentation. In: ArXiv Preprint, April 2023. http://arxiv.org/abs/2304.06131
5. Castillo Benítez, V.E., et al.: Dataset from fundus images for the study of diabetic retinopathy. Data Brief **36**, 107068 (2021)
6. Cen, L.P., et al.: Automatic detection of 39 fundus diseases and conditions in retinal photographs using deep neural networks. Nat. Commun. **12**, 4828 (2021)
7. Chandrasekaran, R., Loganathan, B.: Retinopathy grading with deep learning and wavelet hyper-analytic activations. Vis. Comput. 2741–2756 (2023)
8. Cheng, D., Qin, Z., Jiang, Z., Zhang, S., Lao, Q., Li, K.: Sam on medical images: a comprehensive study on three prompt modes. In: ArXiv Preprint (2023)
9. Deng, J., Dong, W., Socher, R., Li, L.J., Li, K., Fei-Fei, L.: Imagenet: a large-scale hierarchical image database. In: Proceedings of the IEEE Computer Society Conference on Computer Vision and Pattern Recognition (CVPR), pp. 1–8 (2009)
10. Deng, R., et al.: Segment anything model (SAM) for digital pathology: assess zero-shot segmentation on whole slide imaging. In: ArXiv Preprint (2023)
11. Erhan, D., Manzagol, P.A., Bengio, Y., Bengio, S., Vincent, P.: The difficulty of training deep architectures and the effect of unsupervised pre-training. In: Proceedings of the International Conference on Artificial Intelligence and Statistics (PMLR), pp. 153–160 (2009)
12. Giancardo, L., et al.: Exudate-based diabetic macular edema detection in fundus images using publicly available datasets. Med. Image Anal. **16**, 216–226 (2012)
13. Hassan, T., Akram, M.U., Masood, M.F., Yasin, U.: Deep structure tensor graph search framework for automated extraction and characterization of retinal layers and fluid pathology in retinal SD-OCT scans. Comput. Biol. Med. **105**, 112–124 (2019)

14. Hassan, T., Akram, M.U., Werghi, N., Nazir, M.N.: RAG-FW: a hybrid convolutional framework for the automated extraction of retinal lesions and lesion-influenced grading of human retinal pathology. IEEE J. Biomed. Health Inform. **25**(1), 108–120 (2021)

15. He, K., Zhang, X., Ren, S., Sun, J.: Deep residual learning for image recognition. In: Proceedings of the Conference on Computer Vision and Pattern Recognition (CVPR), pp. 1–12, December 2016

16. Hoover, A.: Locating blood vessels in retinal images by piecewise threshold probing of a matched filter response. IEEE Trans. Med. Imaging **19**, 203–210 (2000)

17. Hoover, A., Goldbaum, M.: Locating the optic nerve in a retinal image using the fuzzy convergence of the blood vessels. IEEE Trans. Med. Imaging **22**, 951–958 (2003)

18. Huang, J.H., et al.: Deepopht: medical report generation for retinal images via deep models and visual explanation. In: Proceedings of the Winter Conference on Applications of Computer Vision (WACV), pp. 2442–2452 (2021)

19. Imran, A., Li, J., Pei, Y., Akhtar, F., Mahmood, T., Zhang, L.: Fundus image-based cataract classification using a hybrid convolutional and recurrent neural network. Vis. Comput. (2020)

20. Jia, C., et al.: Scaling up visual and vision-language representation learning with noisy text supervision. In: International Conference on Machine Learning, pp. 4904–4916 (2021)

21. Jin, K., et al.: FIVES: a fundus image dataset for artificial intelligence based vessel segmentation. Sci. Data **9**, 475 (2022)

22. Kanavati, F., Tsuneki, M.: Partial transfusion: on the expressive influence of trainable batch norm parameters for transfer learning. In: MIDL (2021)

23. Kirillov, A., et al.: Segment anything. In: ArXiv Preprint (2023)

24. Kovalyk, O., et al.: PAPILA: dataset with fundus images and clinical data of both eyes of the same patient for glaucoma assessment. Sci. Data **9**, 291 (2022)

25. Kumar, A., Raghunathan, A., Jones, R.M., Ma, T., Liang, P.: Fine-tuning can distort pretrained features and underperform out-of-distribution. In: International Conference on Learning Representations (ICLR) (2022)

26. Kumar, J.R., et al.: Chaksu: a glaucoma specific fundus image database. Sci. Data **10** (2023)

27. Li, L., Xu, M., Wang, X., Jiang, L., Liu, H.: Attention based glaucoma detection: a large-scale database and CNN model. In: Proceedings of the IEEE Computer Society Conference on Computer Vision and Pattern Recognition (CVPR), pp. 1–10 (2019)

28. Li, T., Gao, Y., Wang, K., Guo, S., Liu, H., Kang, H.: Diagnostic assessment of deep learning algorithms for diabetic retinopathy screening. Inf. Sci. **501**, 511–522 (2019)

29. Lin, L., et al.: The SUSTech-SYSU dataset for automated exudate detection and diabetic retinopathy grading. Sci. Data **7** (2020)

30. Liu, J., et al.: Clip-driven universal model for organ segmentation and tumor detection. In: ArXiv Preprint, January 2023. http://arxiv.org/abs/2301.00785

31. Liu, R., et al.: TMM-Nets: transferred multi- to mono-modal generation for lupus retinopathy diagnosis. IEEE Trans. Med. Imaging **42**, 1083–1094 (2023)

32. Liu, R., et al.: Deepdrid: diabetic retinopathy-grading and image quality estimation challenge. Patterns **3** (2022)

33. Lu, M.Y., et al.: Visual language pretrained multiple instance zero-shot transfer for histopathology images. In: Proceedings of the IEEE Computer Society Conference on Computer Vision and Pattern Recognition (CVPR), October 2023

34. Nakayama, L.F., et al.: A Brazilian multilabel ophthalmological dataset (BRSET). In: PhysioNet (2023)
35. Neyshabur, B., Sedghi, H., Zhang, C.: What is being transferred in transfer learning? In: Advances in Neural Information Processing Systems (NeurIPS), August 2020
36. Pachade, S., et al.: Retinal fundus multi-disease image dataset (RFMiD): a dataset for multi-disease detection research. Data **6**, 1–14 (2021)
37. Pires, R., Jelinek, H.F., Wainer, J., Valle, E., Rocha, A.: Advancing bag-of-visual-words representations for lesion classification in retinal images. PLoS ONE **9** (2014)
38. Porwal, P., et al.: IDRiD: diabetic retinopathy – segmentation and grading challenge. Med. Image Anal. **59**, 101561 (2020)
39. Radford, A., et al.: Learning transferable visual models from natural language supervision. In: ArXiv Preprint (2021)
40. Raghu, M., Zhang, C., Kleinberg, J., Bengio, S.: Transfusion: understanding transfer learning for medical imaging. In: Advances in Neural Information Processing Systems (NeurIPS) (2019)
41. Salam, A.A., Mahadevappa, M., Das, A., Nair, M.S.: RDD-Net: retinal disease diagnosis network: a computer-aided diagnosis technique using graph learning and feature descriptors. Vis. Comput. (2022)
42. Silva-Rodriguez, J., Chakor, H., Riadh, K., Dolz, J., Ayed, I.B.: A foundation language-image model of the retina (FLAIR): encoding expert knowledge in text supervision. ArXiv Preprint (2023)
43. Silva-Rodriguez, J., Dolz, J., Ayed, I.B.: Transductive few-shot adapters for medical image segmentation. arXiv Preprint (2023)
44. Srinivasan, V., Strodthoff, N., Ma, J., Binder, A., Müller, K.R., Samek, W.: To pretrain or not? A systematic analysis of the benefits of pretraining in diabetic retinopathy. PLoS ONE **17** (2022)
45. Takahashi, H., Tampo, H., Arai, Y., Inoue, Y., Kawashima, H.: Applying artificial intelligence to disease staging: deep learning for improved staging of diabetic retinopathy. PLoS ONE **12** (2017)
46. de Vente, C., et al.: AIROGS: artificial intelligence for robust glaucoma screening challenge. ArXiv preprint (2023)
47. Wang, Z., Wu, Z., Agarwal, D., Sun, J.: Medclip: contrastive learning from unpaired medical images and text. In: Empirical Methods in Natural Language Processing (EMNLP), October 2022

Research on Deep Learning-Based Lightweight Object Grasping Algorithm for Robots

Yancheng Zhao, Tianxu Wei, Baoshuai Du, and Jingbo Zhao[✉]

School of Information and Control Engineering, Qingdao University of Technology, Qingdao, Shandong, China
zhaoyancheng2021@163.com

Abstract. In order to enhance the efficiency and accuracy of robots in automated production lines and address issues such as inaccurate positioning and limited real-time capabilities in robot-controlled grasping, a deep learning-based lightweight algorithm for robot object grasping is proposed. This algorithm optimizes the lightweight network GG-CNN2 as the base model. Firstly, the depth of the backbone network is increased, and transpose convolutions are replaced with dilated convolutions to enhance the network's feature extraction for grasping detection. Secondly, the ASPP module is introduced to obtain a wider receptive field and multi-scale feature information. Furthermore, the shallow feature maps are merged with the deep feature maps to incorporate more semantic and detailed information from the images. Experimental results demonstrate that the algorithm achieves an accuracy of 81.27% on the Cornell dataset. Compared to the original GG-CNN2 network, the accuracy has improved by 11.68%, achieving a balance between speed and accuracy. Finally, grasping verification is conducted on the Panda robot arm, with an average success rate of 89.62%, which validates the superiority of the algorithm and showcases the theoretical and practical value of this research.

Keywords: robot · computer vision · lightweight network · object grasping

1 Introduction

With the remarkable advancement in deep learning technology and computer processing power, researchers and technologists have applied deep learning to robot grasping detection to extract target features [1]. Compared to manually designed features, utilizing convolutional neural networks in deep learning to train existing or self-made datasets enables the acquisition of target feature information that is more generalizable. By utilizing these features, robots can improve the accuracy and speed of grasping. Lenz et al. [2] proposed a cascaded network that combines the widely popular support vector machine (SVM) in machine learning with deep learning. However, due to the sliding window traversal of the entire image to extract a large number of candidate boxes, the cascaded network is time-consuming and challenging to achieve real-time grasping detection. Ma et al. [3] introduced a lightweight network-based grasping algorithm. This algorithm utilizes SqueezeNet as the base network and incorporates the idea of multiple bypass connections from the DenseNet to enhance feature utilization. The algorithm can extract multimodal feature vectors from color images and enable the gripper actuator to predict the optimal grasping position and orientation.

To achieve a balance between speed and accuracy in robotic grasping and enable the deployment of the network model on resource-constrained or computationally limited devices, The main innovations of this paper can be summarized as follows:

(1) Improvement using the lightweight grasping network GG-CNN2 by deepening the network and adding batch normalization (BN) layers after the convolutional layers and before the activation function, which facilitates fast network training and prediction. The ASPP module is introduced in the backbone network to expand the receptive field, and multi-scale feature fusion is employed to enhance the feature extraction capability.
(2) To enhance the network's performance, the paper augments the multi-object samples in the Cornell dataset to address the limitations of the dataset in terms of lacking multi-object scenarios. Data augmentation techniques are applied to expand the dataset. To overcome the issues of discrete grasp labels and incomplete grasp possibilities, the paper adopts a pixel-level annotation method and generates annotation files for pixel-level grasp poses for network training. Finally, experiments are conducted to validate the network on a simulated robotic arm.

2   GG-CNN Network

The Generate Grasping Convolutional Neural Network (GG-CNN) is a pixel-level, real-time closed-loop grasping algorithm that provides the grasping quality and poses for each pixel of the target object [4]. Compared to other grasping algorithms, this approach effectively addresses the limitations of convolutional neural networks in terms of long computation time and the inability to continuously sample grasp samples. Importantly, this algorithm has a smaller parameter size, making it suitable for real-time grasping implementation on devices [5, 6]. The backbone network structure of GG-CNN consists of a classic encoder-decoder architecture. The encoder consists of three convolutional layers with different convolutional kernels, while the decoder consists of three transpose convolutions. As a fully convolutional neural network, this network eliminates pooling layers that reduce the size of feature maps and adopts 1x1 convolutions for dimensionality reduction. This resolves the issue of pooling layers introducing invariant features that hinder the sensitivity of certain grasping parameters in the algorithm [7]. The network structure of GG-CNN is illustrated in Fig. 1.

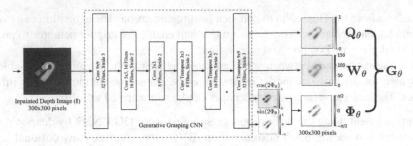

Fig. 1. GG-CNN network structure diagram

GG-CNN2 is a real-time grasping detection network that has been improved based on GG-CNN. Both networks have the same input and output dimensions and are fully convolutional neural networks. The specific network structure is illustrated in Fig. 2. A depth image of size 300×300 undergoes an 11×11 convolution, three 5×5 standard convolutions, and two 2×2 max-pooling layers. Two additional dilated convolution layers with dilation rates of 2 and 4 are added, followed by transpose convolutions to obtain the grasp feature map. Compared to GG-CNN, GG-CNN2 only increases the parameter count by 4000 but possesses a more complex network, resulting in more precise results. Therefore, GG-CNN2 is selected as the baseline network for optimization in this study.

3 Improvement of GG-CNN Network

3.1 Deepening of Backbone Based Networks

The performance of lightweight networks is poor in detection accuracy due to the fewer layers in the backbone network, making it difficult to extract effective features from the input images. To improve the detection accuracy, we added two 5×5 convolutional layers and a max pooling layer based on the original network of GG-CNN2. We replaced the transpose convolution with dilated convolution layers and added a transpose convolution layer to maintain the same input and output dimensions of the network. This way, the network can obtain more feature maps with different dimensions and extract more favorable features for grasp detection.

To simplify and expedite the training process of the network, a Batch Normalization layer was introduced after the convolutional layer and before the activation function. The inclusion of the BN layer facilitates network convergence and helps avoid issues such as gradient explosion and vanishing. The max pooling layer is set to 2×2, and to ensure effective scale transformation, the input size is adjusted to 360×360. The modified network architecture is shown in Table 1.

Table 1. Improved GGCNN2 backbone network

Layer Name	Output Size	Layers
Input	360×360	-
Conv1	360×360	$11 \times 11 \times 1 \times 16$
Conv2	360×360	$5 \times 5 \times 1 \times 16$
Max Pool1	180×180	2×2
Conv3	180×180	$5 \times 5 \times 1 \times 16$
Conv4	180×180	$5 \times 5 \times 1 \times 16$
Max Pool2	90×90	2×2
Conv5	90×90	$5 \times 5 \times 1 \times 16$
Conv6	90×90	$5 \times 5 \times 1 \times 16$
Max Pool3	45×45	2×2
Dilation Conv1	45×45	$5 \times 5 \times 1 \times 16$
Dilation Conv2	45×45	$5 \times 5 \times 1 \times 16$
TransConv1	90×90	$3 \times 3 \times 2 \times 16$
TransConv2	180×180	$3 \times 3 \times 2 \times 16$
TransConv3	360×360	$3 \times 3 \times 2 \times 16$

3.2 ASPP-Based Adaptive Feature Fusion

The GG-CNN2 network differs from GG-CNN not only in the increased number of convolutional layers but also in the introduction of dilated convolutions, which effectively expands the network's receptive field. Unlike pooling layers, which reduce spatial resolution while expanding the receptive field and negatively impact the network, dilated convolutions have the advantage of extracting features at different scales by using different dilation rates without introducing additional parameters [8]. In this study, the atrous spatial pyramid pooling module is introduced, which not only brings a small number of parameters but also further enhances the network's receptive field and captures features at different scales. The ASPP module is an improvement based on the spatial pyramid pooling structure [9]. It processes the feature maps by varying the dilation rates of the atrous convolution kernels, as shown in Fig. 2.

The feature maps are separately processed through a 1×1 convolutional kernel, a 3×3 convolutional kernel with a dilation rate of 6, a 3×3 convolutional kernel with a dilation rate of 12, and a 3×3 convolutional kernel with a dilation rate of 18. The resulting feature maps at four different scales are concatenated along the channel dimension and then passed through a 1×1 convolutional kernel to obtain the output feature map. To avoid introducing excessive parameters, the 3×3 convolutions are replaced with a 1×3 convolution and a 3×1 convolution. The ASPP structure is placed before the two dilated convolutional layers in the backbone network. The improved architecture of the backbone network is illustrated in Fig. 3.

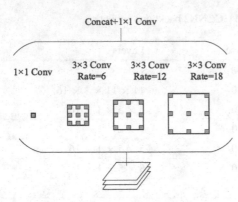

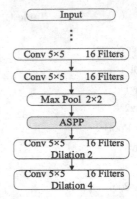

Fig. 2. ASPP structure diagram   **Fig. 3.** New backbone network

3.3 Based on Multi-scale Feature Fusion

The information contained in the feature maps extracted by each layer of a convolutional neural network differs. The feature maps produced by shallow networks are more suitable for detecting small target objects due to their smaller receptive field and clear resolution. On the other hand, feature maps output by deep networks, with their larger receptive field and lower resolution, are more suitable for detecting medium to large-sized target objects. As the number of layers in the CNN increases, the feature information transitions from detailed information to semantic information. By combining the feature maps from shallow and deep networks, the output feature maps not only capture fine-grained features but also possess rich semantic features. Through feature fusion, the detection accuracy can be significantly improved [10].

The network structure of GG-CNN2 incorporates transpose convolution to ensure the preservation of input and output dimensions. In this paper, we combine the feature maps extracted from both shallow and deep networks, ensuring the effective utilization of both semantic and detailed information. This integration enables the network to extract a greater number of features, thereby facilitating grasping detection. The network structure is illustrated in Fig. 4.

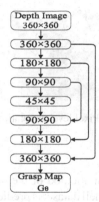

Fig. 4. Backbone network diagram with feature fusion

4 Algorithm Crawl Experiment

4.1 Dataset Production

The Cornell dataset is a commonly used dataset for object grasping and is widely used to validate grasping algorithms in the field. For each type of grasping sample, there are multiple images with different poses and corresponding label data, as shown in Fig. 5. Each sample on the detection image has multiple valid and invalid grasp box labels, and the optimal grasp box can be obtained through algorithmic detection [11, 12].

Fig. 5. Partial image of Corenell with grabbing frame

The GG-CNN algorithm is a pixel-based grasping detection algorithm, by analyzing the grasping labels of Cornell image labeling in Fig. 5, the grasping frame labeling is more discrete and cannot reflect all the grasping possibilities that may exist for the whole grasping sample, the GGCNN series algorithm to obtain a new grasping method by transforming the grasping frame will also have corresponding disadvantages, this paper adopts a new labeling method from the AFFGA-Net algorithm, which is achieved by labeling each The pixel points are labeled [13] with multiple grasping angles and grasping widths, and in order to make the approach applicable to GG-CNN2, only one grasping angle and grasping width are retained for each pixel point, and the annotation files of the grasping position, grasping angle, and grasping width of the pixel points are generated for the training of the network, and the annotated images are shown in Fig. 6.

Fig. 6. Pixel level annotation map

4.2 Evaluation Indicators

Due to the change in the annotation method of the dataset, the evaluation method for whether the grasping box in the Cornell dataset is predicted correctly is no longer applicable. Therefore, in order to verify the improved algorithm, the following three conditions are considered accurate and effective predictions, and accuracy and the time is taken per image are selected as the evaluation indicators for the detection algorithm.

(1) When the difference between the predicted grasping angle and the actual labeled grasping angle is less than 30°;
(2) When the difference between the predicted grasping point distance and the actual labeled grasping point distance is less than 5 pixels;
(3) When the ratio between the predicted grasping width and the actual labeled grasping width is less than 0.8.

4.3 Analysis of Experimental Results

The labeled dataset was used to train the network, and the input size was adjusted from 300 × 300 to 360 × 360 to accommodate the change in input size due to the increase in convolutional layers in the backbone network. The original GG-CNN2 algorithm was designated as Algorithm A, the network with deepened layers in the backbone network was set as Algorithm B, the backbone network with an added ASPP module was set as Algorithm C, and the backbone network with feature fusion and ASPP improvement was set as Algorithm D. A 20% subset of the dataset was used to validate the algorithms, and the experimental results are presented in Table 2.

Table 2. Effect of improved algorithm on GG-CNN2 network performance

	convolutional layers	ASPP	Feature Fusion	Accuracy /%	TPP/s
A				69.59	0.0078
B	√			74.85	0.0084
C	√	√		77.78	0.0097
D	√	√	√	**81.27**	**0.0104**

From the data analysis in Table 2, it can be observed that this network significantly improves the detection accuracy by optimizing the backbone network. By adding convolutional layers and BN regularization layers, the number of extracted features is substantially increased, resulting in a 5.26% increase in detection precision while adding only 0.0006 s per image for detection time. Moreover, the inclusion of ASPP adaptive feature fusion module in the backbone network expands the receptive field of the network, further enhancing the detection accuracy. With these improvements, the detection accuracy of the network reaches 81.27%, with only a 0.0026s increase in detection time per image. Figure 7 shows the output images of the grasp network, and it can be observed that the improved network accurately identifies the optimal grasping positions.

Fig. 7. Cascade network detection result diagram

5   Robot Grasping Experiment

In order to validate the feasibility and effectiveness of the improved GG-CNN2 algorithm, this section conducted grasping validation using a Panda-simulated robotic arm. The experiment followed the actual procedure of robotic arm grasping and adjusted the appearance, shape, and size of the grasped objects to match real-world proportions. The advantage of this experiment is that it is not constrained by time and space, allowing for algorithm verification and validation of the improved model [14].

5.1   Robot Grasping System

The deep learning-based lightweight target grasping control system mainly consists of three major components: the image acquisition module, the target grasping pose detection module, and the grasping execution module, as shown in Fig. 8.

(1) The image acquisition module captures images and depth information of the target objects to be detected using a depth camera.
(2) The target grasp pose detection module obtains the optimal grasp parameters for the target by processing the collected information through a grasp network, The improved GG-CNN2 model serves as the target grasping network in the module.

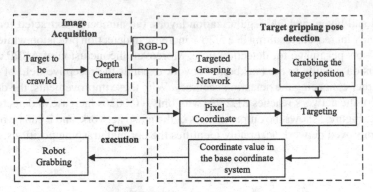

Fig. 8. Robot grasping system process

(3) The grasping execution module achieves the final goal by using the robotic arm to grasp the target.

The experiments in this study utilized a seven-degree-of-freedom Panda robot arm, consisting of multiple joints and links, as the executing mechanism to validate the grasping algorithm. The structure of the Panda robot arm, as shown in Fig. 9, exhibits good humanoid characteristics. The figure illustrates the seven degrees of freedom from the base to the gripper, labeled as A1, A2, A3, A4, A5, A6, and A7. Following the division based on the human arm, the shoulder joint includes three degrees of freedom (A1, A2, A3), the elbow joint includes one degree of freedom (A4), and the wrist joint includes three degrees of freedom (A5, A6, A7) [15].

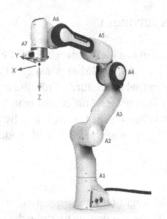

Fig. 9. Panda 7-DOF mechanical arm

5.2 Analysis of Experimental Results

In this experiment, we selected five objects (light bulb, toy, shoe, irregular object, rectangular paper box) for the grasping experiments. These objects were chosen to represent different categories, shapes, and sizes. We recorded the success rate of each grasp and to obtain more accurate results, we conducted 50 grasp experiments. Each experiment involved placing the target object in a different position. The obtained results are shown in Fig. 10.

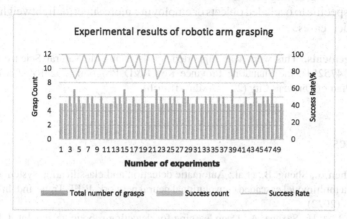

Fig. 10. Results of grasping experiment of Panda manipulator

By analyzing Fig. 10, where the horizontal axis represents the number of experiments (a total of 50 trials), the left vertical axis represents the success rate of the nth grasping experiment, and the right vertical axis represents the number of grasping attempts performed by the robotic arm. The success rate is calculated as the ratio of successful attempts to the total number of attempts. The experimental results demonstrate that the average success rate of the robotic arm in grasping objects is 89.62%. Due to the random generation of target positions in each grasping attempt, some instances with overlapping occlusion or difficult-to-predict grasping positions may result in failed attempts, requiring multiple attempts to achieve successful grasps. However, the overall average success rate aligns well with the performance of the lightweight network's recognition accuracy. The experimental results in this section validate the effectiveness of the proposed algorithm.

6   Conclusion

In order to improve the efficiency and accuracy of robots in automated production lines, and to enable easy deployment of the network model on resource-limited devices while addressing the issues in the grasping process, this paper adopts a lightweight GG-CNN2 pixel-level, real-time closed-loop grasping network and makes improvements on it. Experimental results demonstrate that the accuracy of our algorithm on the Cornell dataset reaches 81.27%, with a detection time of 0.0104s per image. Compared to the original GG-CNN2 network, the accuracy has been improved by 11.68%, with only a 0.0026s increase in detection time per image, which is still much faster than the current mainstream lightweight networks' detection speed. Finally, we conducted grasping experiments on the Panda robotic arm, and the results show an average success rate of 89.62% for grasping. These experimental results demonstrate the excellent performance of our algorithm in target grasping, with a high grasping success rate and meeting the real-time requirements during the robot grasping process. In the future, we will address the issue of poor grasping performance for targets that are occluded or stacked by using algorithms specific to occluded objects or employing more superior lightweight networks to handle such cases.

Acknowledgements. This work was supported by the National Natural Science Foundation of China (51475251), the Shandong Province Key R&D Program (2023RZA02017) and the Livelihood Plan of Qingdao City (22-3-7-xdny-18-nsh).

References

1. Li, J., Chen, J., Sheng, B., et al.: Automatic detection and classification system of domestic waste via multimodel cascaded convolutional neural network. IEEE Trans. Ind. Inform. **18**(1), 163–173 (2022)
2. Lenz, I., Lee, H., Saxena, A.: Deep learning for detecting robotic grasps. Int. J. Robot. Res. **34**(4–5), 705–724 (2015)
3. Ma, Q., Li, X., Shi, Z.: Lightweight convolutional neural networks for robot grasping detection. Comput. Eng. Appl. **56**(10), 141–148 (2020)
4. Li, C.: Deep learning-based pose estimation for unknown targets. Southwest University of Science and Technology (2022)
5. Morrison, D., Corke, P., Leitner, J.: Learning robust, real-time, reactive robotic grasping. Int. J. Robot. Res. **39**(2/3), 183–201 (2020)
6. Zhang, X., Xi, Y., Huang, Z., et al.: Active hand-eye calibration via online accuracy-driven next-best-view selection. Vis. Comput. **4–5**, 1–11 (2022)
7. Wang, C.H.: Grabbing Configuration Prediction Based on RGB-D Images and Deep Learning. Shandong University (2020)
8. Zhang, X., Gao, H., Wan, L.: Classification of fine-grained crop disease by dilated convolution and improved channel attention module. Agriculture **12**(10), 1727 (2022)
9. Chen, L.C., Papandreou, G., Kokkinos, I., et al.: DeepLab: semantic image segmentation with deep convolutional nets, atrous convolution, and fully connected CRFs. IEEE Trans. Pattern Anal. Mach. Intell. **40**(4), 834–848 (2016)
10. Zhao, J., Du, B.: Development of small target detection technology based on deep learning [J/OL]. Electro-Optics Control 1–10 (2022)
11. Chu, H., Leng, Q., Zhang, X.Q.: Multimode feature robotic arm grasping pose detection incorporating attention mechanism[J/OL]. Control Decis. 1–9 (2022)
12. Du, S.Z.K.: Vision-based robotic grasping from object localization, object pose estimation to grasp estimation for parallel grippers: a review. Artif. Intell. Rev.: Int. Sci. Eng. J. **54**(3) (2021)
13. Wang, D.: Research on robot grasping detection algorithm in stacked scenes based on deep learning. Shandong University (2022)
14. Hsiao, K., Lozano-Pérez, T.: Imitation Learning of Whole. In: IEEE/RSJ International Conference on Intelligent Robots & Systems (2006)
15. Chen, Z., Qiu, J., Sheng, B., et al.: GPSD: generative parking spot detection using multi-clue recovery model. Vis. Comput. **37**(6), 2657–2669 (2021)

The ST-GRNN Cooperative Training Model Based on Complex Network for Air Quality Prediction

Shijie Chen, Song Wang(✉), Yipan Liu, and Dongliang Ma

School of Computer Science and Technology, Southwest University of Science and Technology, Mianyang 621010, Sichuan, China
wangsong@swust.edu.cn

Abstract. In recent years, air pollution forecasting has become an important reference for governments when formulating environmental policies. However, accurate prediction of regional air quality has become a challenge due to the sparse spatial distribution of atmospheric monitoring stations. To address this problem, this paper proposes a neural network cooperative training and prediction model called "ST-GRNN". The model incorporates complex network, Extreme Learning Machine (ELM), Long Short-Term Memory Network (LSTM), and Generalized Regression Neural Network (GRNN) to identify spatio-temporal features and accurately predict regional air quality. Comparative experiments using real datasets to predict PM2.5 concentrations show that the accuracy of the ST-GRNN model outperforms other methods.

Keywords: Air pollution · Neural network · Complex network · Prediction model · PM2.5

1 Introduction

Air quality prediction has become a popular topic of scientific research. Ground-level air quality monitoring stations near pollutant emission points are an important source of data for studying air quality changes. However, there are still areas without air quality monitoring systems, resulting in sparse and infrequent data samples. In addition, the formation of air pollutants involves chemical processes that vary over time and space.

Currently, conventional air quality prediction methods can be categorized into two types: traditional prediction methods and machine learning algorithms. Traditional forecasting methods mainly comprise of numerical model forecasting techniques [1] and statistical methods [2]. While these approaches effectively combine multi-domain knowledge, they have limitations like the absence of a flexible multi-scale framework and computational errors. As a result, researchers have started to employ nonlinear machine learning methods, including support vector regression (SVR) [3] and random forest regression (RFR) [4]. However,

B. Sheng et al. (Eds.): CGI 2023, LNCS 14497, pp. 449–461, 2024.
https://doi.org/10.1007/978-3-031-50075-6_35

many struggle with capturing time-series patterns of air quality and fail to learn the effects of long-term air pollution, resulting in decreased prediction accuracy to some extent.

Deep learning methods, such as RNN [5], GRU [6], LSTM [7], and TCN [8], are extensively used in air quality prediction due to their powerful modeling and nonlinear processing capabilities. However, while these methods demonstrate good prediction accuracy, they have limitations in capturing spatial transmission effects and considering time and space dependence. GNNs, including GCN [9], GAT [10], and GraphSAGE [11], exhibit high accuracy and robustness in air quality prediction but do not consider time and space dependence.

In summary, the accuracy of air quality prediction can be compromised if only one temporal or spatial dimension is considered. In this paper, we propose a neural network co-training prediction model based on a complex network (Fig. 1). The complex network of air quality in Shandong Province is constructed by studying the interaction effects between air pollution monitoring stations. Spatio-temporal features in the complex network are extracted using EML and LSTM networks. These features are then trained using GRNN to develop a model capable of accurately predicting air quality in the region. The main contributions of this paper are as follows.

- We construct an air quality complex network to reflect the internal structure of air quality distribution scientifically and to reveal the dynamic evolution of air pollution.
- By combining ELM and LSTM, the proposed model learns data features in both time and space dimensions, enhancing prediction accuracy.
- The proposed ST-GRNN simultaneously processes spatio-temporal features and integrates temporal and spatial information to better understand the data relationship, thereby improving prediction accuracy.

2   Related Work

2.1   Air Quality Complex Network

In recent years, complex network theory has emerged as a powerful tool for modeling and analyzing air pollution spread.

The Hybrid Single Particle Lagrangian Integrated Trajectory model (HYS-PLIT) [12] was widely used for analyzing pollution sources. However, it had limitations as it only considered residence time and ignored differences in pollutant transport between various pollutants during air pollution transport. Several studies tackled these concerns by examining how wind speed affected the dispersion of pollutant particles through the use of a Lagrangian Dispersion Model (LDM) [13,14]. The LDM simulates the diffusion process of air pollutants. Deng et al. [15] created a pattern mining framework that models pollutant transport and extracts propagation patterns from atmospheric data. Ren et al. [16] simplified transmission relationships between regions into a dynamic network and

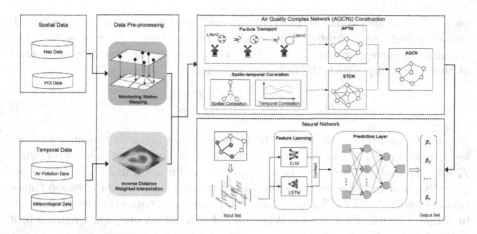

Fig. 1. The workflow of ST-GRNN prediction model, which consists of data preprocessing, air quality complex network construction, prediction model construction.

presented visual analysis methods to investigate spatio-temporal patterns of air pollution transmission. Further research using complex networks in this area would mitigate the harmful effects of air pollution in urban areas.

2.2 Air Quality Forecast

With the development of neural network technology, researchers have explored air quality prediction based on a recursive neural network (RNN) [17], using particle swarm optimisation (PSO) to determine the optimal structure. Zhou et al. [18] integrated PM2.5 dispersion and deep learning utilizing the DPGN model. Zhao et al. [19] proposed a comprehensive prediction method combining the AQSTN with the GCN. Neural network-based air quality prediction methods have been widely studied and applied, with different models and algorithms selected and optimized according to datasets and objectives for better results. In addition, the researchers used other methods to predict air quality [22–25].

3 Methods

3.1 Air Quality Complex Network Characterisation

Air pollution transmission is influenced by geography, meteorology, and the pollutants themselves. Particle tracking methods [16] quantify the transfer of pollutants among stations using collected heterogeneous data.

Transport Simulating. In the transmission simulation, we use the concept of air parcels from environmental science literature [21] to simulate the movement of air pollutants based on a quantitative sampling method. The coordinates and lifetime of the air parcels at any time are updated by meteorological factors. If the air parcels pass through the neighborhood (a circle with radius r) of one station, the current station is recorded. We update the lifetime of an air parcel at the time stamp t with the following equation:

$$life_i = life_{i-1}(1 - \lambda \frac{v_i * T_i * m_i}{H_i * P_i} * \Delta t) \tag{1}$$

where $life_i$ and $life_{i-1}$ represent the lifetime of air parcels at timestamps i and $i-1$, respectively. v_i denotes the velocity of an air parcel at timestamp i, while T_i, m_i, H_i, and P_i represent the temperature, pollutant particle concentration, humidity, and pressure at timestamp i. Δt is the time interval between timestamps i and $i-1$. To enhance calculation accuracy, a correction coefficient λ is introduced to minimize errors. When the lifetime of an air parcel reaches 0, it ceases to move (Fig. 2).

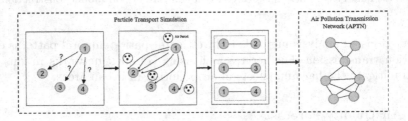

Fig. 2. Transport Simulating of pollutant particles, which generates air quality transmission network.

Space-Temporal Complex Network Definition. The STCN is a weighted, undirected network that represents the spatial and temporal correlation of air quality in the region. It is defined as follows:

$$STCN(t_n) = \{V, E | SR \cap TR\} \tag{2}$$

In STCN, node set $V = \{v_1, v_2, ..., v_m\}$ represents nodes for a region. Each node v_i is defined as a tuple containing information about the node's location and air quality data at a specific time t. Specifically, $v_i = \{t, Lng, Lat, wd_t, p_t\}$, where m is the total number of nodes, Lng and Lat are the longitude and latitude of node i, wd_t denotes the wind direction of node i at timestamp t, and p_t is the pollutant concentration of node i at time t. The edge set $E = \{e_{ij} | i, j = 1, 2, ..., m\}$ represents the edges connecting different air quality monitoring stations. Each edge e_{ij} is defined as an unordered pair of nodes $\langle v_i, v_j \rangle$. Spatio-temporal air quality factors influence a constraint condition represented by the matrix $SR \cap TR$. This condition constrains the network topology by considering both spatial and temporal correlations of air pollution data.

To calculate the temporal correlation (TR), we establish the pollutant concentration time series C_i. For a given time period $t = T_0$, the temporal sequence C_i is generated by selecting consecutive hourly data and recorded as $C_i = \{c_1, c_2, ..., c_{t-1}, c_t\}$. These pollutant concentration time series from all monitoring stations form the set $C = \{C_1, C_2, ..., C_n\}$. where n is the total number of air quality monitoring stations. We then compute the temporal correlation matrix TR based on the established pollutant time series C. The calculation involves using the First-Order Temporal Correlation Coefficient, which measures the correlation between two consecutive sequences.

$$r_{ij} = \frac{\sum_{t=1}^{T_0-1} (c_{i,t} - \overline{c_i})(c_{j,t+1} - \overline{c_j})}{\sqrt{\sum_{t=1}^{T_0-1} (c_{i,t} - \overline{c_i})^2 \sum_{t=1}^{T_0-1} (c_{j,t+1} - \overline{c_j})^2}} \tag{3}$$

where $\overline{c_i}$ and $\overline{c_j}$ denote the means of C_i and C_j, respectively. Finally, TR is obtained by arranging the calculated correlation coefficients into a square matrix.

The spatial correlation (SR) measures the degree of interaction between nodes based on the distance matrix $(Dist)$ and wind angle matrix (Θ). In this paper, the Haversine spherical distance calculation method is used to form the distance matrix, which is formulated as follows:

$$hav(\frac{d_{ij}}{r}) = hav(Lat_j - lat_i) + \cos(Lat_i)\cos(Lat_j)hav(Lng_j - Lng_i) \tag{4}$$

where $hav(\theta) = \sin^2(\frac{\theta}{2}) = \frac{1-\cos(\theta)}{2}$, d_{ij} is the spherical distance between two points, r is the radius of the sphere. The wind angle $\theta_{ij} = |wd_t - \overrightarrow{v_i v_j}|$, where the wd_t represents the wind direction of node i, and $\overrightarrow{v_i v_j}$ is the edge direction from node v_i to node v_j. After obtaining the SR and the TR, the STCN is established. To filter stations based on distance and wind direction, thresholds are set. A wind angle threshold of 45 degrees is used to exclude stations with excessively large wind angles. The average distance is used as the distance threshold to filter out stations that are too far away. Additionally, a temporal correlation threshold ρ is set to exclude neighboring sites that exhibit negative correlations.

Air Quality Complex Network Construction. The APTN and STCN are mapped into two separate graphs. The air quality complex network (AQCN) is calculated as follows:

$$AQCN = APTN \cap STCN \tag{5}$$

The weights of edges in a complex network are calculated to represent the strength of interaction between monitoring stations. The weight calculation is defined as follows:

$$W_{ab}(t) = \begin{cases} \dfrac{f_{ab}(t) + |\Delta p_{ab}(t)|}{Dist_{ab}}; \overrightarrow{E_{ab}} = 1, \Delta p_{ab}(t) \geqslant 0 \\[3mm] \dfrac{f_{ab}(t) - |\Delta p_{ab}(t)|}{Dist_{ab}}; \overrightarrow{E_{ab}} = 1, \Delta p_{ab}(t) < 0 \\[3mm] 0 \qquad\qquad ; \overrightarrow{E_{ab}} = 0, \end{cases} \qquad (6)$$

where $f_{ab}(t) = S_a(t) * \cos\theta_{ab}$ represents the wind coefficient from station a to station b at timestamp t. Here, the $S_a(t)$ denotes the wind speed at timestamp t, the θ_{ab} represents the wind angle. The $\Delta p_{ab}(t)$ represents the pollutant concentration difference between station a and station b at timestamp t. The direction of the edge pointing from monitoring station a towards monitoring station b is denoted by the vector $\overrightarrow{E_{ab}}$.

3.2 Deep Collaborative Forecasting Model Based on Complex Network

Construction of an ELM-Based Spatial Prediction Model. The ELM model is commonly used for solving complex air quality prediction problems in the spatial dimension. The input feature samples $K_s = [k_1, k_i, ..., k_n]^T$ represent the input feature dataset of monitoring stations. In our study, $k_i = (p_i * W_i, t_i)$, where p_i represents the concentration of air pollutants in the i-th station. The W_i indicates the interaction strength of the i-th monitoring station with others. The t_i denotes the corresponding meteorological variables, such as temperature, humidity, and pressure.

In the neural network, the input weights W_i and biases b_i are randomly assigned. The number of hidden nodes $\tilde{n}$ is determined, where $\tilde{n} \leqslant n$. The input data is then non-linearly mapped into a feature space using a specified activation function $g(x)$. This mapping produces the hidden output matrix H. Each i-th hidden neuron is connected to the input neurons through the weight vector $W_i = [w_{i1}, w_{i2}, ..., w_{in}]$. Additionally, it is connected to the output neuron via the weight vector $\beta = [\beta_1, \beta_2, ..., \beta_n]$. The threshold value of the i-th hidden neuron is represented by b_i.

$$E = \sum_{j=1}^{n} \left(\sum_{i=1}^{\tilde{n}} \beta_i g(W_i t_i + b_i) - p_j \right)^2 \qquad (7)$$

In the ELM training process, the only parameter that requires adjustment is the weight between the hidden layer and the output layer. There exist weight vectors β_i, W_i, and threshold b_i in theory that satisfy the following equation:

$$\sum_{i=1}^{\tilde{n}} \beta_i g(w_i t_i + b_i) = p_j, j = 1, 2, ..., n. \qquad (8)$$

This equation can be abbreviated as $H\beta = P$.

In the second stage of ELM training, the weights connecting the hidden layer and output layer are obtained by solving the following equation:

$$\beta^* = H^+ P \tag{9}$$

where H^+ denotes the Moore-Penrose generalized inverse of matrix H, and P is the target matrix for the training data.

Construction of the Temporal Prediction Model based on LSTM. To consider the influence of past moments on current air quality at a monitoring station, a sliding window-based value smoothing approach [20] is employed. It selects five sequences of air quality index with six consecutive moments represented as $K_T = [p_i(t-1), p_i(t-2), p_i(t), p_i(t+1), p_i(t+2)]$. The training set is then fed into the LSTM network, and the sigmoid function is chosen as the activation function:

$$f(x) = \frac{1}{1 + e^{-x}} \tag{10}$$

The predicted value is obtained and compared with the true value using a loss function. A logarithmic loss function is selected, as shown in Eq. 11:

$$L(Y, P(Y|X)) = -\log_2 P(Y|X) \tag{11}$$

If the loss function converges within a certain range, the training process terminates. Otherwise, back-propagation is employed to continue the training. Ultimately, the actual values can be substituted with the input index set K_T to make predictions.

Construction of Collaborative Training Model based on GRNN. The ELM model is trained using the spatial feature set K_S, while the LSTM model is trained using the temporal feature set K_T. This study uses the generalized regression neural network (GRNN) to conduct collaborative training using spatial and temporal features, due to the strong non-linearity exhibited by both models. GRNN's advantage of removing weight connections between hidden and output layers results in more efficient training times.

The GRNN comprises four layers: input layer, pattern layer, summation layer, and output layer. The spatio-temporal features from the ELM and LSTM models are combined and used as the input set for the GRNN. The input layer receives and stores the input data as $X_i = [x_1, x_2, ..., x_n]$. The pattern layer, which is non-linear, captures the interaction between the input neurons and itself. A pattern based on the Gaussian function P_i can be represented as follows:

$$P_i = \exp[-\frac{(X - X_i)^T (X - X_i)}{2\sigma^2}] \ (i = 1, 2, ..., n) \tag{12}$$

where, σ is the smoothing or diffusion parameter. X represents the input variable, and x_i represents a more precise training sample from neuron i. The summation layer calculates the numerator and denominator.

$$S_s = \sum_{i=1} P_i, (i = 1, 2, ..., n) \qquad (13)$$

$$S_\omega = \sum_{i=1} \omega_i P_i, (i = 1, 2, ..., n) \qquad (14)$$

S_s represents the denominator, S_ω represents the numerator, and ω_i represents the weight of the mode neuron i connected to the summation layer. The output layer performs the final calculations, resulting in the air quality index predictions obtained through training.

$$y = \frac{S_s}{S_\omega} \qquad (15)$$

4   Experiment and Results

4.1   Dataset and Data-Processing

To evaluate the performance of the proposed model, two real atmospheric datasets are collected from air quality monitoring stations in Shandong: an air quality dataset and a meteorological factor dataset (Table 1). To handle the issue of missing values in the raw data, the Inverse Distance Weighted (IDW) interpolation method is applied to fill in these gaps.

Table 1. Details of the data set.

Data Type	Time Scale	Properties
Air quality	From 00:00 on January 1st, 2016 to 00:00 on February 1st, 2016	PM2.5, PM10, SO2, NO2, CO, O3
Meteorological factor	From 00:00 on January 1st, 2016 to 00:00 on February 1st, 2016	Zonal wind speed (u), Meridional wind speed (v), Temperature (T), Humidity (H), and Pressure (P)

4.2   Air Quality Complex Network

Figure 3a shows the air quality network generated from the simulation of the air pollution transmission network (APTN). Figure 3b depicts the space-temporal complex network (STCN) obtained from the simulation. Figure 3c presents the complex air quality network formed by merging the APTN and STCN. By comparing with the topographic map of Shandong Province (Fig. 3d), it can be observed that hilly-dominated areas hinder the dispersion of air pollutants,

Fig. 3. Air quality complex network results: (a) The presentation of air pollution transmission network (APTN). (b) The presentation of spatio-temporal complex network (STCN). (c) The presentation of air quality complex network (AQCN). (d) Topographic presentation of Shandong province.

Table 2. Air quality Complex network assessment.

	Nodes (n)	Edges (m)	l	c
AQCN	52	90	0.243902	3.8358901
ER (AQCN)	52	90	0.065278	3.361111

which aligns with existing empirical evidence in the region. To evaluate the performance of AQCN, the clustering coefficient (c), the average path length (l), and the modularity (Q) are calculated respectively.

Table 2 shows AQCN and its ER random graph. The ER random graph is a commonly used model where nodes are randomly connected to achieve a specific number of edges. The columns represent the number of nodes, number of edges, average clustering coefficient, and average path length. AQCN has a comparable average path length to the random graph but a much larger average clustering coefficient, indicating a "small-world" property. This property facilitates faster information spread within the network. Adjusting the information dissemination method, such as cutting off multiple pollutant transmission paths, can significantly improve the overall air quality status in the network. Three community mining algorithms (Louvain, Spectral Clustering, and GN) are used to calculate AQCN modularity, resulting in values of 0.567086, 0.502429, and 0.575274 respectively. The modularity of AQCN exceeds 0.5, indicating a significant community structure. A modularity greater than 0.3 is considered indicative of a substantial community structure.

4.3   Air Quality Prediction Assessment and Dispaly

The air quality prediction in the local network "1656A" is conducted using the monitoring stations depicted in Fig. 4.

We compare four prediction models, EML, LSTM, ST-GRNN (proposed), and CNN-LSTM, based on the "1656A" local air quality complex network. Table 3 presents the prediction errors of these models for the monitoring station "1656A". The ST-GRNN model outperforms the other models in all three indicators. The RMSE, MAE, and MAPE values for EML and LSTM are (13.74, 13.04), (1063.10.29), (20.29%, 18.92%) respectively. Since these models only

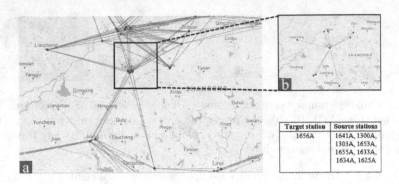

Target station	Source stations
1656A	1641A, 1300A, 1303A, 1653A, 1655A, 1633A, 1634A, 1625A

Fig. 4. Air quality complex network results: (a) Location of the monitoring station "1656A" on the network. (b) Connection between the monitoring station and its neighboring stations.

focus on a single dimension (either space or time), the accuracy of their predictions is more affected. The ST-GRNN model, which considers both spatiotemporal factors, significantly improves accuracy with RMSE, MAE, and MAPE of 4.93, 4.18, and 8.49% respectively. Additionally, we compare the ST-GRNN prediction model with the CNN-LSTM model, which combines the strengths of convolutional neural networks (CNN) and long and short-term memory networks (LSTM) to handle time series data and spatial information. However, even in this comparison, the ST-GRNN model demonstrates better prediction results than CNN-LSTM.

Table 3. Errors in forecast results of different models.

	EML	LSTM	ST-GRNN	CNN-LSTM
RMSE	13.74	13.04	4.93	18.24
MAE	10.63	10.29	4.18	16.29
MAPE	20.29%	18.92%	8.49%	28.79%

We use the air quality prediction model, ST-GRNN, proposed in this article to predict PM2.5 for all air stations in the local air quality complex network of "1656A". As shown in Fig. 5, the trend of the model's prediction is consistent with the actual values, which reflects the effectiveness of the model in predicting PM2.5 after extracting spatio-temporal information.

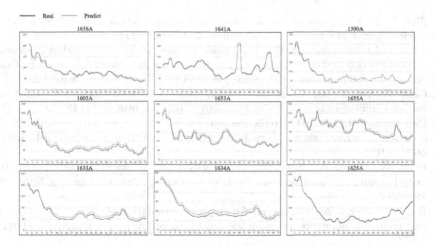

Fig. 5. The results of ST-GRNN prediction model.

5   Conclusions and Discussion

In this paper, we propose the ST-GRNN model, a multi-neural network cooperative training model based on a complex network. We build the Air Quality Complex Network (AQCN) by combining relevant knowledge in air quality research.
Nodes and edges are extracted from the complex network to form the input set
for neural networks. Extreme Learning Machine (EML) and Long Short-Term
Memory (LSTM) are used for spatial and temporal feature training respectively.
Generalized Regression Neural Network (GRNN) is employed to predict PM2.5
content in the air. Experimental results demonstrate the superior prediction performance of our proposed model compared to EML, LSTM, and CNN-LSTM, as
indicated by RMSE, MAE, and MAPE. In conclusion, our cooperative training
method based on a complex network significantly improves air quality prediction.

Acknowledgements. This study was supported by the Natural Science Foundation of
Sichuan Province (Grant No. 2022NSFSC0961), the Doctoral Foundation of Southwest
University of Science and Technology (Grant No. 19zx7144), and the Special Research
Fund of the Research Centre for Network Emergency Management in China (Mianyang)
Science and Technology City (Grant No. WLYJGL2023ZD04).

References

1. An, J., Huang, M., Wang, Z., et al.: Numerical regional air quality forecast tests
   over the Mainland of China. In: Satake, K., et al. (eds.) Acid rain 2000, pp. 1781–
   1786. Springer, Dordrecht (2001). https://doi.org/10.1007/978-94-007-0810-5_144
2. Taheri Shahraiyni, H., Sodoudi, S.: Statistical modeling approaches for PM10 prediction in urban areas; a review of 21st-century studies. Atmosphere **7**(2), 15 (2016)

460   S. Chen et al.

3. Zhu, S., Lian, X., Liu, H., et al.: Daily air quality index forecasting with hybrid models: a case in China. Environ. Pollut. **231**, 1232–1244 (2017)
4. Jaiswal, J.K., Samikannu, R.: Application of random forest algorithm on feature subset selection and classification and regression. In: 2017 World Congress on Computing and Communication Technologies (WCCCT), pp. 65–68. IEEE (2017)
5. Geng, X., He, X., Xu, L., et al.: Graph correlated attention recurrent neural network for multivariate time series forecasting. Inf. Sci. **606**, 126–142 (2022)
6. Pan, C., Tan, J., Feng, D.: Prediction intervals estimation of solar generation based on gated recurrent unit and kernel density estimation. Neurocomputing **453**, 552–562 (2021)
7. Fang, W., Zhuo, W., Song, Y., et al.: Δfree-LSTM: an error distribution free deep learning for short-term traffic flow forecasting. Neurocomputing **526**, 180–190 (2023)
8. Bai, S., Kolter, J.Z., Koltun, V.: An empirical evaluation of generic convolutional and recurrent networks for sequence modeling. arXiv preprint arXiv:1803.01271 (2018)
9. Bruna, J., Zaremba, W., Szlam, A., et al.: Spectral networks and locally connected networks on graphs. arXiv preprint arXiv:1312.6203 (2013)
10. Jiang, N., Jie, W., Li, J., et al.: GATrust: a multi-aspect graph attention network model for trust assessment in OSNs. IEEE Trans. Knowl. Data Eng. (2022)
11. Chen, Z., Deng, Q., Zhao, Z., et al.: Energy consumption prediction of cold source system based on GraphSAGE. IFAC-PapersOnLine **54**(11), 37–42 (2021)
12. Stein, A.F., Draxler, R.R., Rolph, G.D., et al.: NOAA's HYSPLIT atmospheric transport and dispersion modeling system. Bull. Am. Meteorol. Soc. **96**(12), 2059–2077 (2015)
13. Bahiraei, M., Hosseinalipour, S.M.: Thermal dispersion model compared with Euler-Lagrange approach in simulation of convective heat transfer for nanoparticle suspensions. J. Dispers. Sci. Technol. **34**(12), 1778–1789 (2013)
14. Carvalho, J.C., De Vilhena, M.T.M.B.: Pollutant dispersion simulation for low wind speed condition by the ILS method. Atmos. Environ. **39**(34), 6282–6288 (2005)
15. Deng, Z., Weng, D., Chen, J., et al.: AirVis: visual analytics of air pollution propagation. IEEE Trans. Vis. Comput. Graph. **26**(1), 800–810 (2019)
16. Ren, K., Wu, Y., Zhang, H., et al.: Visual analytics of air pollution propagation through dynamic network analysis. IEEE Access **8**, 205289–205306 (2020)
17. Siwek, K., Osowski, S.: Data mining methods for prediction of air pollution. Int. J. Appl. Math. Comput. Sci. **26**(2), 467–478 (2016)
18. Zhou, H., Zhang, F., Du, Z., et al.: A theory-guided graph networks based PM2. 5 forecasting method. Environ. Pollut. **293**, 118569 (2022)
19. Zhao, G., He, H., Huang, Y., et al.: Near-surface PM2. 5 prediction combining the complex network characterization and graph convolution neural network. Neural Comput. Appl. **33**, 17081–17101 (2021)
20. Chen, C., Zhang, Q., Kashani, M.H., et al.: Forecast of rainfall distribution based on fixed sliding window long short-term memory. Eng. Appl. Comput. Fluid Mech. **16**(1), 248–261 (2022)
21. Seinfeld, J.H.: Urban air pollution: state of the science. Science **243**(4892), 745–752 (1989)

22. Qin, Y., Chi, X., Sheng, B., et al.: GuideRender: large-scale scene navigation based on multi-modal view frustum movement prediction. Vis. Comput. 1–11 (2023)
23. Xie, Z., Zhang, W., Sheng, B., et al.: BaGFN: broad attentive graph fusion network for high-order feature interactions. IEEE Trans. Neural Netw. Learn. Syst. (2021)
24. An, H., Zheng, L.: RETRACTED ARTICLE: ambient air quality prediction and unbounded variational continuous function based on big data. Arab. J. Geosci. 14(17), 1737 (2021)
25. Wang, J., Li, J., Wang, X., et al.: An quality prediction model based on CNN-BiNLSTM-attention. Environ. Dev. Sustain. 1–16 (2022)

Multi-sensory Consistency Experience: A 6-DOF Simulation System Based on Video Automatically Generated Motion Effects

Hongqiu Luan, Yu Wang, Li Huang, Lutong Wang, Gaorong Lv, Wei Gai[✉],
Xiaona Luan[✉], and Chenglei Yang

Shandong University, Ji'nan, China
gw@sdu.edu.cn, xiaona0412@126.com

Abstract. In this paper, we present a multi-sensory perception consistent 6-DOF motion system. The system automatically extracts the motion trajectory of the virtual camera as motion data from video and maps the motion data to the 6-DOF Stewart motion platform through a human perception-based wash-out algorithm and incorporates multi-sensory simulations of visual, auditory, tactile, and proprioceptive sensory perceptual consistency of the motion effect. The results of the user study showed that the system effectively enhanced the participants' sense of realism and reduced the subjective perception of simulator discomfort. In addition, the system well supported users to self-create motion virtual environment through video, so that the public became the designer of motion experience content in the metaverse.

Keywords: Multi-sensory consistency · Virtual reality · Motion platform · Simulation experience

1 Introduction

With the advancements in virtual reality (VR) and interactive technology, the use of motion seats in 3D cinema [27], digital cultural tourism [22], and driving simulation [31] is becoming increasingly widespread. The motion platform with seats integrates multiple sensory modalities, such as vestibular motion, tactile vibration, olfactory senses, and wind to enhance the immersion and realism of the simulation experience.

The motion seat system is a key element to achieve the "immersive" effect [14], which allows the audience to be more deeply integrated into the movie plot. Many studies have constructed dynamic simulation experience systems [1,13] using computer-generated virtual scenes on the Stewart [25] six-degree-of-freedom (6-DOF) dynamic seat. However, CG virtual scenes require professional modelers to build and design the scene, set specific driving routes, and simulate motion data. It leads to a lack of realism in CG virtual scenes, and they do not support ordinary users to create, resulting in limited experience content and slow scene updates. With the development of multimedia technology, video has become a popular form of visual presentation. Traditional video-based dynamic data generation methods mainly include manual or rocker methods [5]. As the lens changes, the expert manually makes the motion parameters corresponding to the dynamic seat in a single frame according to their own inner experiences and feelings. In the rocker method, the expert holds a joystick and shakes it while viewing, using a measuring device to track its movement and generate dynamic data. However, the above methods require professional experts to operate, which is labor-intensive, inefficient, and costly. Additionally, there are subjective factors in obtaining motion data.

To reduce the difficulty of creating motion virtual environment and improve user experience, this paper proposed a multisensory consistent simulation experience system based on the 6-DOF motion platform. The system supports users to import self-captured videos as virtual scenes. Then, with the video frame image and camera parameter data as input, the ORB-SLAM3 system is used to obtain the global motion pose of the virtual camera in the video to automatically generate motion data. The system is based on 6-DOF dynamic seats, three-screen parallel display devices, audio and fan, and other immersion enhancement devices, providing users with a multi-sensory perceptual consistency of visual, auditory, skin, proprioceptive and other immersive experience. Based on this method, we constructed simulated scenes in the form of video and CG-virtual scenes for comparative experiments. The results show that our system has better usability and brings a more realistic experience to users.

In summary, the contributions are as follows:

(1) Universal motion data extraction and virtual scene production. Users can easily create motion simulation experiences by uploading videos, empowering everyone to become a creator of virtual environments.
(2) Integrated multi-sensory perceptual consistency for immersive experience. The system provided users with a multi-sensory perceptual consistency of visual, auditory, skin, proprioceptive and other immersive experiences based on a 6-DOF motion platform.
(3) Constructed 6-DOF motion platform simulation scene according to video automatic generating motion data and CG-virtual scene with manual making motion data for the user study.

2 Related Work

2.1 Simulation Experience System on Motion Platform

Dynamic cinema integrates visual, auditory, olfactory, tactile, and motion senses perfectly [21]. However, the development of dynamic movies is limited due to slow content updates and low repeat visit rates [11]. Therefore, Shi et al. [24] proposed a video-based motion effect automatic generation framework, which estimated the 3D trajectory of the camera. Then, the angular velocity and linear acceleration were sent to the classic washout filter to create motion commands for the motion seat. Lee et al. [14] used optical flow to find corresponding points between two consecutive frames and used epipolar constraints to estimate the relative camera motion between adjacent frames. In addition, Sheng et al. [23] proposed temporally broad learning system to enforce temporal consistency between frames. It provides a good basis for estimating the motion of the camera, which enables the dynamic experience of the motion platform. Zhu et al. [30] proposed a stable and efficient 3D CIP scheme to animating turbulent fluid. In general, simulation experience in VR has become more and more common, which also makes how to provide users with a multi-sensory consistent simulation experience has become a hot topic [29].

2.2   Motion Simulation of 6-DOF Stewart Platform

The 6-DOF Stewart platform is a motion simulation technology mainly used to achieve a sense of motion in a limited range of motion to simulate a real environment. The most common approach currently used is to use a washout filter to transform the actual motion of the virtual camera into a signal that can be perceived similarly by humans and can be implemented by the simulator [3].

Many studies on adjusting washout filters [3,17] have been successfully applied to motion simulators such as flight simulators and car simulators, greatly improving the sense of reality. The classical washout algorithm [16] uses high-pass and low-pass filters to solve the problem of the limited motion range of the simulation platform. However, the structure and parameters of this algorithm are fixed and cannot be automatically adjusted according to changing input signals. Mohammad et al. [18] proposed the optimal washout algorithm, which uses mathematical optimal control theory to select the form of the filter and introduces the human vestibular model to reduce the distortion of the user's perception. Based on the optimal washout algorithm, Houshyar et al. [2] proposed an improved adaptive washout algorithm that uses optimized fuzzy control systems to solve the drawbacks associated with the existing optimal MCAs of the motion simulators.

2.3   Multi-sensory Consistent Design

Objective and subjective measures of performance in VR environments increase as more sensory cues are delivered and as simulation fidelity increases [7]. The multisensory experience [8,9] combines various stimuli such as visual, auditory, olfactory, and proprioceptive senses to integrate the information received from each sense, allowing users to perceive product or system information in a comprehensive and multi-layered way. Nimesha et al. [19] presented Season Traveller, which extends the traditional audio-visual VR technology to achieve multi-sensory interactive experience by adding olfactive and tactile stimuli. Mi et al. [10] proposed that multisensory feedback in virtual environments can improve user experience and performance when studying the tactile experience in a walking immersive virtual environment. Kaliuzhna et al. [12] studied the simultaneous interaction between visual, tactile, and vestibular senses and proposed a layered multisensory interaction method that supports proprioceptive modulation. These studies demonstrate that human centered interaction design, considering multi-sensory interaction, is crucial in various fields.

3 Multi-sensory 6-DOF Motion Platform Simulation System Design and Implementation

The system consists of a motion data generation module, motion simulation module, and multi-sensory perception consistency design, as shown in Fig. 1. The following subsection describes in detail the functionality of each module and the specific implementation process:

Fig. 1. Multi-sensory 6-DOF motion platform simulation system.

3.1 Motion Data Generation Module

The system processes the video uploaded by the user and automatically generates motion data, providing seat-driving data for the motion simulation module. To ensure the consistency and smoothness of video playback and seat motion, we uniformly adjust the video frame rate to 30fps and generate a timestamp file corresponding to video frames. Then, the system takes the video frame and camera parameters as input, and extracts the global 6-DOF motion pose of the camera in videos based on the ORB-SLAM3 framework [6], as shown in Fig. 2.

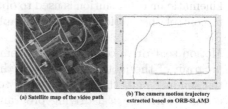

(a) Satellite map of the video path   (b) The camera motion trajectory extracted based on ORB-SLAM3

Fig. 2. Camera motion trajectory diagram (green line). (Color figure online)

Fig. 3. Comparison of satellite map and camera position.

Each frame in the video corresponds to the global pose data of the camera motion[timestamp, t_x, t_y, t_z, q_1, q_2, q_3, q_w]. The t_x, t_y, t_z represent the position of the current frame. The q_1, q_2, q_3, q_w are Quaternions of rotation, so the Q $= q_1{}^*$i $+ q_2{}^*$j $+ q_3{}^*$k $+ q_w$ is representing the camera rotation posture of the current frame. Figure 3 shows a comparison between the satellite map of the panoramic video path we captured and the camera pose trajectory extracted based on ORB-SLAM3.

3.2   Motion Simulation Module

The motion simulation of this system is achieved by using a 6-DOF Stewart motion platform and a three-screen parallel vision system, as shown in Fig. 4.

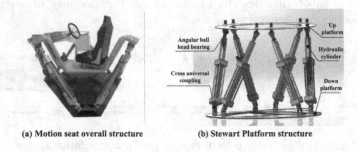

(a) Motion seat overall structure   (b) Stewart Platform structure

Fig. 4. Motion seat structure in our system.

In this system, the proprioception simulation mainly performs the global motion of the virtual camera in the video. The motion platform can apply acceleration and force to the user, matching the visual content, thereby achieving the function of dynamic simulation.

The main functions of the motion simulation module are as follows:

(1) Camera motion simulation. Firstly, the interpolated and smoothed camera pose data (virtual camera pose data) is converted into linear acceleration and angular velocity. And a human perception-based washout algorithm [26] is used to generate the 6-DOF motion platform pose command. Then, the kinematic inverse solution is used to obtain the driving signals of each branch to control the motion of each hydraulic cylinder. The process is shown in Fig. 5.
(2) Motion seat drive control. The system communicates with the seat control program of the motion platform to drive the seat motion in real-time. As the sending end, the system needs to establish a request data packet to connect with the seat-driving program. After the connection is successful, message transmission can be performed. On the seat driving program side, the Receiver Class is created to receive various commands and drive the seat motion. The functional class is shown in Fig. 6.

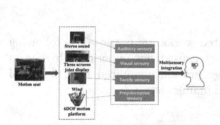

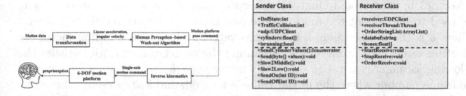

Fig. 5. Motion simulation process.   **Fig. 6.** Functional class diagram.

3.3 Consistent Design for Multi-sensory Perception

Multisensory perceptual consistency refers to the spatial, temporal and motor consistency of multiple senses, which is an effective guarantee of natural and comfortable human-computer interaction [15]. In this system, users can obtain multi-sensory perceptual consistency of visual, auditory, tactile, and proprioception senses during motion experience. The analysis of multi-sensory perception is shown in Fig. 7.

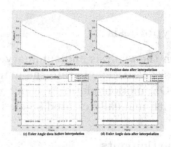

Fig. 7. Multisensory integration.   **Fig. 8.** Posture and euler angles.

The system ensures audio-visual consistency by addressing synchronization and parallelism issues during video pre-processing. Synchronization maintains a natural relationship between sound and image, while parallelism aligns the audio closely with the video content, enhancing emotional expression.

Additionally, the system ensures that motion data processing aligns with video playback frames. Developed using Unity 3D with FixedUpdate(), the system processes motion data per fixed frame update, ensuring a consistent correspondence between video frames and motion data rows. This is achieved by equating the camera pose data, denoted as N_1, with the number of video frames, denoted as N_2, resulting in the equation $N_1 - N_2$. Assuming the duration of video playback and seat movement is t, the mathematical model for visual and proprioception consistency can be represented as $N_1 = N_2 = t * fps$.

As the system is implemented based on the Unity engine to map camera motion to various branch control signals, the interpolation of camera pose data needs to follow the data smoothing characteristics of Unity. Vector3Lerp(Vector3 a, Vector3 b, float t) and QuaternionLerp(Quaternion a, Quaternion b, float t) are used to implement the motion pose and attitude quaternion of the camera. Where a is the initial value, b is the end value, and t is the deciding factor for inserting values between a and b. Assuming the target value is r, it satisfies the following formula: $r = a + (b - a) * t$, where $t = 1/(b_n - a_n + 1)$, a_n represents the frame number where the initial value is located, and b_n represents the frame number where the end value is located. Taking the "Pacific Coastal Highway" video under the "City Car Travel" type in the system as an example, the camera pose data obtained is interpolated based on this model, and the data of 8–100 frames is shown in Fig. 8. Additionally, we synchronized fan speed with camera movement to match blowing sensation.

4 Evaluations

The experiment aims to investigate whether a 6-DOF motion platform generated with video-based content and automated motion data offers a superior multisensory consistency experience compared to one based on 3D modeling and manual motion data generating.

4.1 Hypothesis

Based on the analysis and summary of related works, we propose the following hypothesis: Participants rate the multisensory consistency experience higher on the 6-DOF motion platform using video generation compared to CG-virtual scenes with manually created single frame dynamic data.

4.2 Participants

Our participants were 30 adults, 14 females and 16 males (M = 24.73 years, SD = 2.94 years). They were undergraduate and graduate students recruited on campus who were interested in the study. None of the participants had known audiovisual behavior or sensory disturbances. They received a gift of appreciation after the experiment.

4.3 Experimental Design

The user study employed a single-factor within-subject experimental design. The within-subject factor was two types of dynamic sensory experience scenes: a multi-sensory consistency simulation experience motion system generated based on video (called Video-auto) and a CG-virtual scene with a manual making data motion system (called CG-manual). Other factors, except for the presentation content and the method of generating dynamic data, were kept consistent between the two conditions. The dependent variables included realism, immersion, fatigue, motion sickness, consistency, comprehensibility, misdirection, and personal preference, as shown in Table 1.

4.4 Experimental Environment and Task

The Video-auto system presents low-cost videos as the presentation content and automatically generates driving paths for users by extracting camera movements from the videos, providing corresponding dynamic sensory experiences. The CG-manual system built using 3D modeling presents technical expert virtual scenes as the presentation content and provides users with corresponding dynamic sensory experiences by pre-setting paths manually. This user study aims to validate the usability of our proposed method and its ability to provide users with more realistic multi-sensory consistency experiences.

To reduce the impact of novelty bias caused by inconsistent content, the two systems' experience scenes were both "mountain road" driving types, as shown in Fig. 9. Participants experience each scene in a balanced sequence and they were required to rest for at least 5 min after experiencing one scene. The questionnaires were completed after their experience.

The hardware used in the experiment is a 6-DOF motion seat with a Stewart platform, as shown in Fig. 10. The multisensory consistency experience system on the 6-DOF motion platform based on video generation is developed using Unity 2018.4.15f1 and runs on a 64-bit Windows 10 Professional Edition.

Fig. 9. (a) CG-manual scene and (b) Video-auto scene.

Fig. 10. 6-DOF dynamic platform multisensory consistent experience.

4.5 Measurement

(1) Evaluation of system usability. We employed the PSSUQ V3.0 (Post-Study System Usability Questionnaire) to assess the availability of our system. The reliability of the scale (Cronbach's $\alpha = 0.8642$) in this study is good.

(2) Evaluation of user experience. Questions Q1-Q4 evaluate the user's overall dynamic sensory experience, while questions Q5-Q8 evaluate the quality of the dynamic sensory effects. The questionnaire design was based on the study by Yun et al. [28], and questions were designed to assess aspects such as realism, immersion, motion sickness, fatigue, consistency, comprehensibility, misdirection, and personal preference. The answer options were designed using a 7-point Likert scale, and the reliability (Cronbach's $\alpha = 0.8201$) in this study is good.

470   H. Luan et al.

Table 1. Evaluation of user experience.

Evaluation Metrics	Item Description
Degree of vertigo	Refer to Simulator Sickness Questionnaire [4]
Fatigue	After the experience, I felt very tired
Realism	I felt as if I was actually in a driving car
Immersion	Refer to Flow experience [20]
Consistency	Audio-visual information as well as haptic feedback (wind) are matched to the motion effect
Comprehensibility	I can understand the relationship between audio-visual information and motion effects
Misdirection	There are motion effects that I don't understand why should be provided
Preference	I like motion simulation that automatically generates motion data based on video

4.6 Results

(1) System usability analysis. The average scores for system satisfaction are shown in Fig. 11. The analysis results indicate that the system scored higher than the reference scores in terms of usability, information quality, and user interface quality, indicating that the system has good usability.

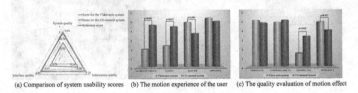

(a) Comparison of system usability scores   (b) The motion experience of the user   (c) The quality evaluation of motion effect

Fig. 11. Score comparison of users' evaluation.

(2) User Experience analysis. The results of the Shapiro-Wilk test indicated that all data in this study were normally distributed. Further, we conducted a paired-sample t-test on the questionnaire data, and the descriptive statistics and testing results are shown in Fig. 11. The analysis results indicate that there are significant differences between the two systems in terms of SSQ, fatigue, and realism scores in the evaluation of immersive experiences (Q1–Q4) ($t = 0.462$, $p = 0.006$; $t = 2.943$, $p = 0.031$; $t = 4.951$, $p = 0.004$). Our Video-auto system provides users with a more realistic experience and reduces the occurrence of motion sickness and fatigue compared to the CG-manual system. However, there is no significant difference between the two systems in terms of immersion scores ($t = 1.649$, $p = 0.513$). In terms of the quality evaluation of immersive effects (Q5–Q8), there is no significant difference between the two systems in terms of consistency and comprehensibility scores ($t = 2.461$, $p = 0.183$; $t = 1.607$, $p = 0.116$). However, there are significant differences in terms of misleadingness and personal preferences ($t = 2.455$, $p = 0.016$; $t = 1.449$, $p = 0.027$).

5   Discussion

In this study, we present a system that enhances multi-sensory perception consistency using a video-generated 6-DOF motion platform. The system simulates the user's perspective by extracting motion data from the global 6-DOF motion pose of the virtual camera in the video. This data is then optimized and mapped to the motion platform's axes using a perception-based algorithm. Users can import their own videos and experience multi-sensory immersion, including visual, auditory, tactile (wind), and proprioceptive feedback through the 6-DOF Stewart platform seat. To evaluate our system, we conducted a user study comparing it to a computer-generated virtual scene with manually created motion data. The results demonstrate that our system provides users with a more realistic and consistent multi-sensory perception experience.

In terms of motion experience, our system and the CG-Virtual Scene with manual making-based system both provide good immersive feedback. However, based on the SSQ and fatigue scores, the motion experience system based on CG-Virtual Scene with manual making seems to be more likely to bring unpleasant experiences to users. In contrast, the video-generated 6-DOF motion platform largely ensures multi-sensory perception consistency experience, reducing SSQ and fatigue to some extent. It is worth noting that although there is no significant difference in the average consistency scores between our system and the CG-Virtual Scene with the manual making-based system, our system still has a slightly higher average score. In terms of personal preferences, most participants prefer our system, largely because the video-based motion experience can provide them with a stronger sense of reality.

In addition, our work also has some limitations. The video-generated 6-DOF motion platform multi-sensory perception consistency experience system has not yet integrated olfactory and gustatory perceptions. In future work, we will continue to explore multi-sensory perception consistency experience and design participatory user research from capturing to motion experience.

6   Conclusion

We proposed a system that combines video-generated 6-DOF motion platform technology with multi-sensory perception consistency. The system captures motion footage using a motion camera, extracts motion trajectory data from the virtual camera, and maps it to the 6-DOF Stewart motion platform using a perception-based washing algorithm. An experimental study was conducted to evaluate the usability and user experience of the system. The results demonstrate that our proposed system offers users a more realistic motion experience while incorporating multiple senses such as visual, auditory, tactile (wind), and proprioceptive feedback. Additionally, it reduces the likelihood of motion sickness and fatigue in VR. The system provides a convenient and efficient approach for designing 6-DOF motion experience content, enabling ordinary users to contribute to motion experience content creation through video shooting.

Acknowledgements. We would like to thank all reviewers for their valuable comments. This work is supported by the National Natural Science Foundation of China under Grant (61972233, 62007021, 62277035).

References

1. Adel, A., et al.: Design of a 6-DOF hydraulic vehicle driving simulator. In: 2020 International Conference on Innovative Trends in Communication and Computer Engineering (ITCE), pp. 170–175. IEEE (2020)
2. Asadi, H., Bellmann, T., Mohamed, S., Lim, C.P., Khosravi, A., Nahavandi, S.: Adaptive motion cueing algorithm using optimized fuzzy control system for motion simulators. IEEE Trans. Intell. Veh. **8**, 390–403 (2022)
3. Asadi, H., Lim, C.P., Mohamed, S., Nahavandi, D., Nahavandi, S.: Increasing motion fidelity in driving simulators using a fuzzy-based washout filter. IEEE Trans. Intell. Veh. **4**(2), 298–308 (2019)
4. Bimberg, P., Weissker, T., Kulik, A.: On the usage of the simulator sickness questionnaire for virtual reality research. In: 2020 IEEE Conference on Virtual Reality and 3D User Interfaces Abstracts and Workshops (VRW), pp. 464–467. IEEE (2020)
5. Buzan, D., Sclaroff, S., Kollios, G.: Extraction and clustering of motion trajectories in video. In: Proceedings of the 17th International Conference on Pattern Recognition, 2004. ICPR 2004, vol. 2, pp. 521–524. IEEE (2004)
6. Campos, C., Elvira, R., Rodríguez, J.J.G., Montiel, J.M., Tardós, J.D.: ORB-SLAM3: an accurate open-source library for visual, visual-inertial, and multimap slam. IEEE Trans. Robot. **37**(6), 1874–1890 (2021)
7. Clifton, J., Palmisano, S.: Effects of steering locomotion and teleporting on cybersickness and presence in HMD-based virtual reality. Virtual Reality **24**(3), 453–468 (2020)
8. Dinh, H.Q., Walker, N., Hodges, L.F., Song, C., Kobayashi, A.: Evaluating the importance of multi-sensory input on memory and the sense of presence in virtual environments. In: Proceedings of the IEEE Virtual Reality (Cat. No. 99CB36316), pp. 222–228. IEEE (1999)
9. Feng, M., Dey, A., Lindeman, R.W.: The effect of multi-sensory cues on performance and experience during walking in immersive virtual environments. In: 2016 IEEE Virtual Reality (VR), pp. 173–174. IEEE (2016)
10. Feng, M., Dey, A., Lindeman, R.W.: An initial exploration of a multi-sensory design space: tactile support for walking in immersive virtual environments. In: 2016 IEEE Symposium on 3D User Interfaces (3DUI), pp. 95–104. IEEE (2016)
11. Hawkins, D.G.: Virtual reality and passive simulators: the future of fun. Commun. Age Virtual Reality **1**, 159–89 (1995)
12. Kaliuzhna, M., Ferrè, E.R., Herbelin, B., Blanke, O., Haggard, P.: Multisensory effects on somatosensation: a trimodal visuo-vestibular-tactile interaction. Sci. Rep. **6**(1), 26301 (2016)
13. Khusro, Y.R., Zheng, Y., Grottoli, M., Shyrokau, B.: MPC-based motion-cueing algorithm for a 6-DOF driving simulator with actuator constraints. Vehicles **2**(4), 625–647 (2020)
14. Lee, J., Han, B., Choi, S.: Motion effects synthesis for 4d films. IEEE Trans. Vis. Comput. Graph. **22**(10), 2300–2314 (2015)

15. Melo, M., Gonçalves, G., Monteiro, P., Coelho, H., Vasconcelos-Raposo, J., Bessa, M.: Do multisensory stimuli benefit the virtual reality experience? A systematic review. IEEE Trans. Vis. Comput. Graph. **28**(2), 1428–1442 (2020)
16. Nehaoua, L., Mohellebi, H., Amouri, A., Arioui, H., Espié, S., Kheddar, A.: Design and control of a small-clearance driving simulator. IEEE Trans. Veh. Technol. **57**(2), 736–746 (2008)
17. Qazani, M.R.C., Asadi, H., Bellmann, T., Mohamed, S., Lim, C.P., Nahavandi, S.: Adaptive washout filter based on fuzzy logic for a motion simulation platform with consideration of joints' limitations. IEEE Trans. Veh. Technol. **69**(11), 12547–12558 (2020)
18. Qazani, M.R.C., Asadi, H., Nahavandi, S.: An optimal motion cueing algorithm using the inverse kinematic solution of the hexapod simulation platform. IEEE Trans. Intell. Veh. **7**(1), 73–82 (2021)
19. Ranasinghe, N., et al.: Season traveller: multisensory narration for enhancing the virtual reality experience. In: Proceedings of the 2018 CHI Conference on Human Factors in Computing Systems, pp. 1–13 (2018)
20. Rheinberg, F., Engeser, S., Vollmeyer, R.: Measuring components of flow: the flow-short-scale. In: Proceedings of the 1st International Positive Psychology Summit (2002)
21. Seo, S.M., Kimm, M.J.: Analysis of Virtual Reality Movies: Focusing on the Effect of Virtual Reality Movie's Distinction on User Experience, pp. 308–312, July 2023. https://doi.org/10.1007/978-3-031-36004-6_42
22. Sharma, A., Sharma, S., Chaudhary, M.: Are small travel agencies ready for digital marketing? Views of travel agency managers. Tour. Manag. **79**, 104078 (2020)
23. Sheng, B., Li, P., Ali, R., Chen, C.L.P.: Improving video temporal consistency via broad learning system. IEEE Trans. Cybern. **52**(7), 6662–6675 (2022). https://doi.org/10.1109/TCYB.2021.3079311
24. Shin, S., Yoo, B., Han, S.: A framework for automatic creation of motion effects from theatrical motion pictures. Multimedia Syst. **20**, 327–346 (2014)
25. Stewart, D.: A platform with six degrees of freedom. Proc. Inst. Mech. Eng. **180**(1), 371–386 (1965)
26. Wang, Y., Sun, X., Shen, H., Yin, Y.: Research on improvement and optimization of washout algorithm for moving platform navigation simulator. In: 2021 IEEE 7th International Conference on Virtual Reality (ICVR), pp. 400–406. IEEE (2021)
27. Yang, T., Lai, I.K.W., Fan, Z.B., Mo, Q.M.: The impact of a 360 virtual tour on the reduction of psychological stress caused by COVID-19. Technol. Soc. **64**, 101514 (2021)
28. Yun, G., Lee, H., Han, S., Choi, S.: Improving viewing experiences of first-person shooter gameplays with automatically-generated motion effects. In: Proceedings of the 2021 CHI Conference on Human Factors in Computing Systems, pp. 1–14 (2021)
29. Zachmann, G., Alcañiz Raya, M., Bourdot, P., Marchal, M., Stefanucci, J., Yang, X.: Correction to: virtual reality and mixed reality. In: Zachmann, G., Alcaniz Raya, M., Bourdot, P., Marchal, M., Stefanucci, J., Yang, X. (eds.) Virtual Reality and Mixed Reality. EuroXR 2022. LNCS, vol. 13484, p. C1. Springer, Cham (2023). https://doi.org/10.1007/978-3-031-16234-3_14
30. Zhu, J., et al.: Animating turbulent fluid with a robust and efficient high-order advection method. Comput. Animat. Virtual Worlds **31**(4–5), e1951 (2020)
31. Zou, X., et al.: On-road virtual reality autonomous vehicle (VRAV) simulator: an empirical study on user experience. Transp. Res. Part C Emerg. Technol. **126**, 103090 (2021)

3DP Code-Based Compression and AR Visualization for Cardiovascular Palpation Training

Zhendong Chen[1], Bo Peng[2,3(✉)], Kaifeng Gong[1], Yinan Hao[2], and Xiaohua Xie[1]

[1] School of Computer Science and Engineering, Sun Yat-sen University, Guangzhou 510006, China

[2] Department of Musical Instrument Engineering, Xinghai Conservatory of Music, Guangzhou 510006, China
pengbo@xhcom.edu.cn

[3] Sniow Research and Development Laboratory, Foshan 528000, China

Abstract. This paper introduces an augmented reality (AR) visualisation based on the three-dimensional palpation code (3DP code) to enhance palpation training in cardiovascular examination. Traditional palpation training methods, such as textbook descriptions and subjective evaluations, may fail to adequately differentiate between tactile image patterns under varying vascular conditions. Moreover, the large amount of data involved in creating dynamic 3D tactile images for palpation complicates their storage, transmission, and display. Our method, demonstrated using a typical artery palpation example, provides interactive 3D visualisations and interactions, accompanied by efficient encoding, decoding, and compression techniques for large tactile data sets. Assessment results show a data compression ratio of 1/360, preserving over 95% of physiological information. The proposed webAR program is also highly adaptable, performing smoothly on most mobile platforms, providing potential benefits for medical and academic communities in improving teaching experience.

Keywords: Palpation training · Augmented reality (AR) · Tactile imaging · Data compression · Cardiovascular examination

1 Introduction

Palpation techniques play an essential role in cardiovascular research and practice. As a non-invasive and gentle technique, it can be employed in a variety of clinical settings [4]. As a diagnostic method in the cardiovascular examination, palpation can be used to check the condition of a patient's heart and blood vessels with the advantage of being fast, easy, and non-invasive [7, 16, 25]. It is also imperative to master the techniques and methods of palpation in medical education [6, 7]. Thus, a more effective method of palpation training is needed. As technology develops, augmented reality (AR) seems to be gaining traction in a wide variety of fields, including medicine, entertainment, and education [1, 8, 11, 21, 23].

However, three urgent issues must be addressed before advanced AR technology can be considered for palpation training. Firstly, due to the difficulties in modelling and visualising physicians' tactile perceptions during palpation, there are currently few feasible and standardised AR tactile visualisation techniques or workflows available.

B. Sheng et al. (Eds.): CGI 2023, LNCS 14497, pp. 474–486, 2024.
https://doi.org/10.1007/978-3-031-50075-6_37

Second, tactile data visualisation involves modelling data over time. In recent years, a series of three-dimensional pulse diagnostic instruments were developed [14, 15, 18] for the acquisition of three-dimensional pulse waves. Large amounts of data complicate AR model development, as well as affecting the speed of data transmission and visualisation [1, 10]. Finally, given the sensitive information involved in the medical field, data privacy protection must be ensured. In order to address the three problems mentioned above, an innovative approach is presented here. Our solution is based on 3DP codes (three-dimensional palpation codes) and augmented reality to promote accessibility and quality of palpation training. The 3DPI fitting equation was used in combination with a mixed integer nonlinear programming method [5] and information embedding techniques to make 3DP code an informative data carrier with high compression ratios. With web-based AR, any device with an internet browser can display interactive 3D tactile models, making palpation training more accessible to both researchers and practitioners. In summary, the major contributions of our framework are five-fold:

(1) **Off-line accessibility**: Our framework allows researchers, physicians, patients, and other users to access information using 3DP codes attached to displays, textbooks, case reports, and other carriers.
(2) **Accurate replication**: The use of 3DP codes enables our framework to accurately replicate the main information from tactile data, with a reduction degree of 95%.
(3) **Universality**: Through the use of open-source software such as Three.js and QR codes, our framework realises cross-browser, cross-platform, and cross-device compatibility.
(4) **Privacy protection**: The proposed framework in this paper ensures the privacy of medical data while generating 3DP codes. Only clients with the decoding tool can access sensitive patient information, thereby reducing the risk of patient privacy breaches.
(5) **Extensibility**: As a demonstration, tactile imaging of radial artery pulse is presented in this paper. Furthermore, our framework may also be used for other palpation tasks, such as venous vessels and tumours.

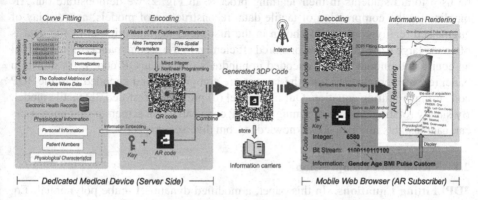

Fig. 1. The System Architecture of the Proposed 3DP Code-based AR Application.

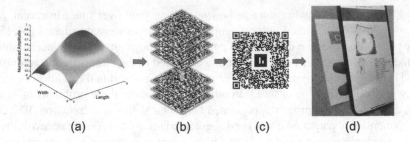

(a)   (b)   (c)   (d)

Fig. 2. A demonstration of the use of our web-based AR pipeline for tactile data compression, model reconstruction, and AR display. From left to right: (a) Preprocessed three-dimensional tactile data; (b) An equivalent amount of data encoded in hundreds of regular QR codes; (c) The data is then compressed and encoded into a 3DP code; (d) The mobile AR application allows users to view the restored 3D tactile model.

2   System Design and Implementation

The following section provides details on our web-based AR pipeline. According to Fig. 1, the architecture comprises five modules: Data Acquisition and Preprocessing, Curve Fitting, Encoding, Decoding, and Information Rendering. The process involves obtaining tactile data using a multi-channel sensor and performing preprocessing steps, such as noise removal and data normalization [24]. The proposed 3DPI fitting equations compress the tactile images into spatiotemporal parameters. Information embedding and mixed integer programming are used for encoding, generating 3DP codes that store a large amount of de-identified medical data. A set of code scripts for the decoding and rendering information are distributed over the Internet. During the Rendering step, a dynamic AR tactile model is simulated and rendered for display. The AR markers calculate the 3D position and Euler angles of the model, making it appear that it is attached to the 3DP code from a 3D perspective. In addition to 3D models, the AR program provides supplemental information. The additional information provided can be used to aid students in their learning process. In Fig. 2, we demonstrate our AR pipeline for the compression of tactile data, reconstruction of models, and display of augmented reality content. As shown in the first panel (a), the original tactile data is often too large to be transmitted or stored efficiently. In the second panel (b), we present an equivalent amount of data encoded in hundreds of regular QR codes. As shown in panel (c), we demonstrate how the images are compressed and encoded into the 3DP code using the fitting equation. Our final panel (d) presents a restored 3D tactile model. By simply rotating and repositioning the 3DP code carrier on screen or on paper, users can gain insights into palpation knowledge from diverse perspectives.

2.1   Tactile Data Compression

3DPI Fitting Equations. In this paper, a modified dynamic L-cube polynomial (Eq. (1)) is used as a fitting equation for 3D palpation images [15]. By using the equation, a tactile data matrix can be compressed into fourteen parameters, which include nine temporal parameters and five spatial parameters.

$$P(t,x,y) = C(t)e^{\frac{-\sigma}{r^2+1}\left\{r^2[(x-x_c)\cos\theta+(y-y_c)\sin\theta]^2+[-(x-x_c)\sin\theta+(y-y_c)\cos\theta]^2\right\}} \tag{1}$$

where parameters r, σ, θ, x_c, and y_c are used to describe the shape, slope, rotation, and peak position characteristics of a three-dimensional pulse image. The variables x and y represent the width and length of a vessel, respectively.

A time-varying amplitude parameter $C(t)$ in Eq. (2) can be represented as follows to illustrate the dynamic characteristics of a tactile image:

$$C(t) = \sum_{i=1}^{3} A_i \times e^{-[(t-\tau_i)/u_i]^2} \tag{2}$$

where A_i is the maximum amplitude of the $i-th$ Gaussian function, τ_i is the centre position of the $i-th$ Gaussian function, and u_i is the width of the $i-th$ Gaussian function.

An equation for fitting a three-dimensional pulse image consists of two parts: a time curve equation that describes the pulse wave amplitude function over time. Accordingly, a one-dimensional pulse wave can be viewed as a time curve equation. Another type of equation describes how pulse wave amplitudes are distributed within a specific area, which is known as a spatial surface equation [22]. Time curve equations are often constructed using a combination of three Gaussian functions. Following is a three-term Gaussian equation that is used to fit the pulse amplitude vs time curve [6, 26, 27].

$$f(x) = A_1 \times e^{-c_1 \times \frac{(x-\tau_1)^2}{\mu_1^2 \times x}} + A_2 \times e^{-\frac{1}{2}c_2 \times \frac{(x-\tau_2)^2}{\mu_2 \times x}} + A_3 \times e^{-\left(\frac{x-\tau_3}{\mu_3}\right)^2} \tag{3}$$

where parameters A_1, A_2, A_3, τ_1, τ_2, τ_3, μ_1, μ_2, and μ_3 are nine temporal parameters. The second-order polynomial tactile surface equation (Eq. (4)) used in this study is as follows.

$$f(x,y) = e^{\frac{-\sigma}{r^2+1}r^2\left\{[(x-x_c)\cos\theta+(y-y_c)\sin\theta]^2+[-(x-x_c)\sin\theta+(y-y_c)\cos\theta]^2\right\}} \tag{4}$$

where parameters σ, r, x_c, y_c, and θ are five spatial parameters. Subsequently, the pulse wave data is fed into the predefined temporal curve equation and tactile surface equation to determine the precise values of the fourteen parameters. These equations allow for the compression of extensive tactile data into a limited number of parameters, enabling efficient storage and transmission of tactile information. This data compression methodology helps to address the challenge of handling the abundant data involved in high-fidelity tactile rendering and interaction.

Information Embedding for Physiological Indicators. In order to further reduce the complexity of QR codes, some information can also be embedded into the parameters of the fitting function. A demonstration is provided by integrating two physiological indicators into the parameters of the time-fitting equation. The embedded physiological indicators include heart rate and the key point value h_2. Key physiological points P_1, P_2, P_3, and P_4 represent four specific moments in the pulse wave. In this case, P_2 is the peak of the reflected wave, with h_2 reflecting its amplitude. By embedding h_2, we are able to improve the accuracy of our fitting procedure since h_2 may be altered during encoding [17]. By using this technique, we are able to obtain more accurate and reliable results.

Fig. 3. An example of the proposed 3DP code.

Mixed Integer Nonlinear Programming. The curve-fitting problem in this paper is formulated as a Mixed Integer Nonlinear Programming (MINLP) problem to facilitate information embedding [5]. There are two physiological indicators in parameters that are integer variables, while the others are continuous variables. Considering the tactile image time equation in this study, the following objective function is used:

$$min.\ D(t) = C(t) - P(t) = \sum_{i=1}^{3} A_i e^{-\left(\frac{t-\tau_i}{\mu_i}\right)^2} - P(t). \tag{5}$$

where t represents the time, $C(t)$ denotes the fitted curve, $P(t)$ denotes the original curve, and $D(t)$ denotes the difference between the fitted curve and the original curve. The constraint condition is the range of values of the nine temporal parameters in $C(t)$. The remaining parameters are continuous, except for parameters τ_2, μ_2, and μ_3, which are integer variables that encode physiological information. One digit of μ_2, μ_3 is locked, as well as the value of τ_2. In this study, we will solve this mixed integer nonlinear programming problem using the Python package pymoo, which is a multi-objective optimisation framework that provides a wide variety of optimisation algorithms.

2.2   Encoding and Decoding Methods Design

The Encoding of the Proposed 3DP Code. In today's society, QR codes (abbreviation for Quick Response Codes) are becoming increasingly prevalent as a powerful and reliable tool for delivering information [8]. In this paper, we have proposed a modified QR code called 3DP code, which enhances the storage efficiency and privacy of codes, making them suitable for medical applications. Additionally, the proposed 3DP code is designed to integrate with the AR application in order to enhance user experience.

As illustrated in Fig. 3, the 3DP code is a combination of a QR code (represented by the orange, green, and black regions) and an AR code (represented by the purple region). The orange and green patterns assist in locating and aligning the QR code during recognition. In the QR code, a data region encoded in UTF-8 encoding format contains compressed tactile measurements, the website URL, and error correction codewords to ensure reliable and accurate data collection. AR codes utilise redundant positions within QR codes to increase storage capacity and separate highly sensitive patient data from tactile measurements. The AR code is designed as a binary 4×4

matrix with 13 bits of storage after removing the three bits used for position detection. Using the proposed encoding method, the AR code encodes physiological information, such as age, gender, body mass index, etc.

Table 1. AR Code Information Encoding Methods and Associated Research Studies.

Information	Abbreviation	Illustration	Related researches
Gender	GNDR	Male or female	Gender differences [13]
Age	AGE	Underage(0-17 years old), Youth(18-65), Middle-aged(66-79), and Elderly(80+).	Vascular rigidity and vessel elasticity [9]
Body Mass Index	BMI	Underweight (under 18.5 kg/m^2), Normal weight (18.5 to 24.9 kg/m^2), Overweight (25 to 29.9 kg/m^2), and Obese (30 kg/m^2 or more).	BMI as an indicator of adult cardiometabolic risk factors [2]
Pulse	PLS	Normal pulse, Alternating pulse (pulsus alternans), Pulsus bisferiens, Bigeminal pulse (dicrotic pulse), Large bounding pulse (hyperkinetic pulse), Paradoxic pulse (pulsus paradoxus), Pulsus parvus et tardus, and Water-hammer pulse (corrigan pulse/ collapsing pulse).	2DL and 2DT arterial stiffness [9], pulse wave velocity [25], and heart rate variability [19]
Custom	CUS	A 5-bit binary storage space has been reserved. Customized content can be provided to meet the needs of researchers.	Augmentation index [18], as well as systolic and diastolic blood pressure [12]

Using the example in Fig. 3, the integer information stored in the AR code is "6580", which corresponds to the bit stream "1100110110100". There are red boxes and arrows in the figure indicating the encoded information for each bit. For instance, the "10" at the age position indicates that the patient falls within the Middle-aged category. A detailed explanation of the AR code encoding method can be found in Table 1. In addition to the physiological indicators mentioned above, the 3DP code in this paper provides reserved storage spaces for researchers to customise the content.

The AR code also serves as the ARTag, which can be used as the AR anchor, a fiducial marker system, used to detect the relative position of a camera with respect to an object in augmented reality. The figure also indicates the complexity of the AR code, denoted by **W**, and the border width of the ARTag, denoted by **B**. As **W** increases in bit count, more information can be stored. As the number of bits in **W** increases, the boarder width **B** decreases, resulting in a lower recognition rate. As part of the clinical record, the 3DP codes must remain confidential in addition to being informative. The AR code stores highly sensitive patient information (e.g., personal information, patient numbers, physiological characteristics, etc.) only accessible with a particular mapping program during the encode and decode process.

3DP Code Detection and Decoding. Using the above procedure, 3D palpation information is compressed into plaintext code that can be stored and transmitted. At the receiving and display ends, a ready-to-use detection and decoding algorithm can be used to extract 3DP codes. As described in Algorithm 1, the approach extracts 3DP codes and derives three-dimensional dynamic model matrices and patient information

---

Algorithm 1. 3DP Code Detection and Decoding.

Input: A captured image frame: $F^{M \times N}(width : M, height : N)$; The quantity of models: q;
Output: Dynamic model matrices: $D^{R \times C \times T} = D_1, D_2, ..., D_n$; Spatial coordinates: (X_0, Y_0, Z_0);
    Euler angles: $(Pitch, Yaw, Roll)$; An array of physiological data: $m = m_1, m_2, ..., m_k$;
1: Initialize q matrices $D^{R \times C \times T}$;
2: Initialze q arrays of model faces with the size of $2R \times C \times T$;
3: Convert the captured image $F^{M \times N}$ from RGB to greyscale.
4: **for** $i = 1$ to q **do**
5:     Perform QR code detection.
6:     **if** result $= null$ **OR** result $=$ irrelevant QR Code **OR** result is already in the database **then**
    break
7:     **end if**
8:     Perform code positioning.
9: **end for**
10: Generating the dynamic model matrix $D^{R \times C \times T}$. Apply perspective transformation.
11: Detect the AR code and get the string $s = S_1, S_2, ..., S_n$ in the code.
12: Compute the number of blocks $k = floor(n / b)$.
13: **for each** block i **do**
14:     Initialize the message $m_i = 0$.
15:     **for each** j in the block **do**
16:         Get the position in s: $pos = (i-1) \times b + j$. The value is $\theta = s[pos]$.
17:         Compute the weight factor: $\omega = 2^{(b-j)}$. Update the message $m_i = m_i + \theta \times \omega$.
18:     **end for**
19:     Append the decrypted message to the list: $m.append(m_i)$.
20: **end for**
21: Obtain the corresponding k physiological information $m = m_1, m_2, ..., m_k$.
22: Compute spatial coordinates (X_0, Y_0, Z_0) and Euler angles $(Pitch, Yaw, Roll)$.

---

from captured image frames. The algorithm requires basic image processing techniques and utilises code detection and decryption to achieve its objectives. The input to the algorithm is a captured image frame, represented as an $M \times N$ matrix. The algorithm commences with the initialization of q matrices $D^{R \times C \times T}$ with zero values in the client-side memory. The QR code detection is executed within the main loop (Steps 4–9), where the algorithm iterates through each detected QR code and verifies that it is in the correct format and not already present in the database. A dynamic model matrix is generated by utilising the fourteen parameters in the QR code as inputs to the spatial and temporal equations. Next, the algorithm applies a perspective transformation to retrieve the internal AR code of the detected 3DP code (Step 10). In the AR code decryption phase, the algorithm detects the AR code and computes the number of message blocks. It initialises the message for each block and updates it using the calculated value of θ and ω. Finally, the current AR code is set as the marker and AR anchor, and the distance and angle between the marker and the camera are determined by analysing the AR code transformation.

2.3 Information Rendering

As shown in Fig. 4(a), the orientation of a virtual object over a fixed physical marker is determined by the relationship between the camera coordinates and the marker

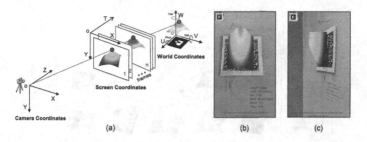

Fig. 4. 3D tactile model rendering and AR marker coordinate mapping. (a): Relationship between AR marker coordinates and user camera coordinates. (b): A sample 3D tactile model rendered on top of the 3DP code. (c): The sample 3D tactile model view form a different angle.

coordinates. Three different coordinate systems are involved in the pinhole camera model or pose estimation in computer vision: camera coordinates, camera screen coordinates, and marker coordinates in reality. A static camera observing a 3D object can observe only two types of motion: translation and rotation. It corresponds to a camera moving from one point (X, Y, Z) to another (X', Y', Z') in 3D space and has three degrees of freedom, which can be shown in Fig. 4(a). The rotation occurs when the camera is rotated about the X, Y, or Z axes and can be represented using Euler angles (roll, pitch, and yaw). Translation describes the movement of the camera along vectors in 3D space, while rotation is the rotation of the camera around the X, Y and Z axes. Once the camera position is calculated relative to the marker, the virtual information can be merged into the real-world environment. The rendered AR image is displayed on a screen, creating the illusion of a tactile model present in a three-dimensional world. The continuous switching of frames on the screen simulates continuous sensation changes in fingers during an actual tactile examination. Figure 4(b) provides an example of AR rendering, while Fig. 4(c) shows the effect from a different perspective.

3   Results and Validation

3.1   Experimental Design

For the purpose of demonstrating the advantages of the architecture presented in this paper, vascular palpation was chosen as a more challenging case. The radial artery vascular palpation dataset was collected by a pulse diagnosis instrument (PDI) [18]. The dataset comprises measurements from 24 healthy subjects, including 14 males and 10 females, with a mean age of 22.2 ± 3.7 (mean $\pm$ SD) years. All participants were randomly selected healthy students, with systolic/diastolic blood pressure values of $112.1 \pm 4.7/74.0 \pm 3.4$ mmHg. Normal pulse data were obtained from these subjects in a normal state. Taut pulse images were induced by the cold pressor test (CPT) [19]. After CPT, the stiffness of the subject's blood vessels increases, enabling the simulation of a scenario similar to hypertension.

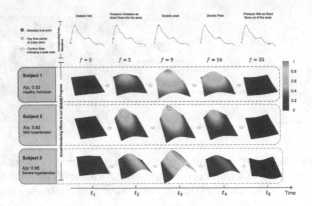

Fig. 5. Three examples of compression and AR rendering effects in the dataset. These cases illustrate the increasing severity of hypertension: (a) Subject 1, a healthy individual; (b) Subject 2, mild hypertension; (c) Subject 3, severe hypertension.

3.2   Application Implementation

In this section, we describe the implementation of our AR program using AR.js, a cross-platform application framework that supports WebGL and WebRTC [20,21]. To ensure compatibility with most devices (stationary or mobile), we developed a browser-based client interface, which eliminates the need for maintaining different repositories for different versions (Windows, Mac OS, Linux, iOS, Android, etc.) of our AR web program. In this scenario, the AR model is generated, rendered, and presented on the mobile device of the user. Once the web page has been refreshed, communication with the server ceases [1]. This eliminates the need for the user to maintain a connection to the server, making the process more efficient and cost-effective. The AR model is generated on the device in real time, so the user does not have to wait for the server to update it. Additionally, this allows for a more secure experience since the data does not need to be sent to the server.

Figure 5 illustrates the effectiveness of the proposed method using actual cases in the dataset. Three cases are included, including the palpation data of Subject 1, a healthy individual, as well as Subject 2 and Subject 3, who underwent a relatively short and long CPT respectively, and can be considered to have mild and severe hypertension. Five key time points of the pulse waveform are selected to illustrate the crucial nodes of the cardiac cycle. On frame $f = 9$, the region delineated by a red dashed line corresponds to the contour area of the tactile model at the systolic peak.

3.3   Compression and Performance Analysis

In the experiment, the size of a 3D tactile image for one cycle is 4×6 (height:4, width:6), with approximately 80 frames per cycle in accordance with the heart rate of a normal person. A single data point in the image occupies six bytes when encoded using UTF-8. In this regard, the proposed method achieves approximately a compression ratio of 1/360 to 1/240, i.e., $(16 \times 2)/(4 \times 6 \times 80 \times 6)$ to $(16 \times 3)/(4 \times 6 \times 80 \times 6)$. In

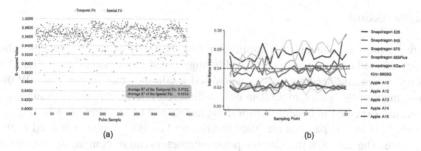

Fig. 6. Results of compression and performance analysis. (a): Time and space fitting results obtained using the 3DPI fitting equation on the dataset used in this study. (b): Performance comparison of our application. An inter-frame interval of less than or equal to 0.04 indicates a more pleasing visual experience.

addition, we use the coefficient of determination (R^2) to determine the degree of reduction. A higher reduction degree can serve as evidence that the framework described in this article is more capable of resembling the actual palpation sensation. The R-squared test is defined by the following equation:

$$R^2 = \frac{\sum_{i=1}^{n} (\hat{y}_i - \bar{y})^2}{\sum_{i=1}^{n} (y_i - \bar{y})^2} = 1 - \frac{\sum_{i=1}^{n} (\hat{y}_i - y_i)^2}{\sum_{i=1}^{n} (y_i - \bar{y})^2} \qquad (6)$$

where y_i represents the $i-th$ value of the original data, $\hat{y}_i$ represents the $i-th$ fitted data value, and $\bar{y}$ represents the mean value of the original data. The value of R^2 ranges from 0 to 1, and higher values indicate a better fit. As can be seen in Fig. 6(a), the temporal fit is evaluated by comparing the R-square of the fitted one-dimensional pulse wave with the original one-dimensional pulse wave. The spatial fit is assessed by comparing the R-square of the fitted map at its peak amplitude with that of the original tactile image at its peak amplitude. The average fit percentage in this study was over 95%, ensuring the accuracy of tactile images presented by the proposed AR program.

In addition, AR application performance has a direct bearing on the user experience and usability of the application [3]. Several major mobile phones launched in the past six years were tested in this article for their AR capabilities (see Fig. 6(b)). All tested phones scanned the same 3DP code and rendered the tactile model, and average frame intervals of every ten frames were recorded to determine their computing performance. In this experiment, 30 samples were tested, with 300 frame intervals recorded separately for each processor. The horizontal axis represents sampling points, each representing a ten-frame interval between samples, and the vertical axis represents the average inter-frame interval (IFI) between samples. A longer interframe interval (orange line) was observed due to an increase in the temperature of the Snapdragon 8Gen1 processor during the testing process. Additionally, this webAR program generates and renders models locally by the client and does not occupy the computing resources of the cloud server. In current AR applications, a substantial amount of time is spent downloading resources from the cloud. Accordingly, the program proposed in this paper has the potential to support an unlimited number of concurrent users, which provides a strong guarantee for the promotion of our framework.

4 Discussion

This paper presents a mobile AR application based on 3DP codes. The results indicate that this method can produce a high-quality augmented reality experience. The idea of "precision medicine training" or "personalised medicine" can be achieved. With the advancement of this study, more than one million relevant researchers, physicians, and patients are expected to benefit from it. Several aspects of this study can be improved, including: (1) In this paper, a modified three-term Gaussian function is used to fit the pulse wave. The values of the nine temporal parameters can be compressed into an arbitrary number of discrete numbers using a mapping relationship. In this manner, additional storage space may be saved. (2) The dynamic 3D pulse wave display showcased in this study extends to other palpation scenarios like observing venous haemangiomas and tumors.

5 Conclusion

This paper introduces a 3DP code-based mobile AR application for supporting the visualisation process of palpation training. This framework combines QR codes with AR codes in an innovative way that is offline, accurate, universal, and extensible, striking the right balance between computational efficiency and presentation quality. By improving the spatial and temporal equations, dynamic 3D tactile data could be effectively fitted to reduce their parameters to a manageable size. As a result, our framework can offer universal compatibility across web browsers, platforms, and devices. Performance tests indicated that all the major mobile phones launched over the past six years could run the AR program smoothly. In our view, this could be a helpful tool for the medical and academic communities to produce and display content, and to use it not only for dissemination purposes, but also for their automated workflow.

Acknowledgements. This research was funded by the National Natural Science Foundation of China, grant number 62071497.

References

1. Al-Zoube, A.M.: Efficient vision-based multi-target augmented reality in the browser. Multimed. Tools Appl. **81**, 14303–14320 (2022)
2. Ashwell, M., Gunn, P., Gibson, S.: Waist-to-height ratio is a better screening tool than waist circumference and BMI for adult cardiometabolic risk factors: systematic review and meta-analysis. Obes. Rev. **13**(3), 275–286 (2012)
3. Baker, L., Ventura, J., Langlotz, T., et al.: Localization and tracking of stationary users for augmented reality. Vis. Comput. **2**, 1–18 (2023)
4. Ball, J.W., Dains, J.E., Flynn, J.A.: Seidel's guide to physical examination: an interprofessional approach. Elsevier Health Sciences, St. Louis, Missouri (2014)

5. Bussieck, M.R., Drud, A.S., Meeraus, A.: MINLPLib–a collection of test models for mixed-integer nonlinear programming. INFORMS J. Comput. **15**(1), 114–119 (2003)
6. Chen, Y., Zhang, L., Zhang, D., Zhang, D.: Wrist pulse signal diagnosis using modified gaussian models and fuzzy C-Means classification. Med. Eng. Phys. **31**(10), 1283–1289 (2009)
7. Chen, Y., Zhang, L., Zhang, D., Zhang, D.: Computerized wrist pulse signal diagnosis using modified auto-regressive models. J. Med. Syst. **35**(3), 321–328 (2011)
8. Ertugrul, E., Zhang, H., Zhu, F., Lu, P., Li, P., Sheng, B., et al.: Embedding 3D models in offline physical environments. Comput. Animat. Virtual Worlds **31**(4–5), 1–15 (2020)
9. Gauthier, C.J., Lefort, M., Mekary, S., Desjardins-Crépeau, L., Skimminge, A., Iversen, P., et al.: Hearts and minds: linking vascular rigidity and aerobic fitness with cognitive aging. Neurobiol. Aging **36**(1), 304–314 (2015)
10. Hanna, M.G., Ahmed, I., Nine, J., Prajapati, S., Pantanowitz, L.: Augmented reality technology using Microsoft HoloLens in anatomic pathology. Arch. Pathol. Lab. Med. **142**(5), 638–644 (2018)
11. Hussain, R., Lalande, A., Guigou, C., Bozorg-Grayeli, A.: Contribution of augmented reality to minimally invasive computer-assisted cranial base surgery. IEEE J. Biomed. Health Inform. **24**(7), 2093–2106 (2020)
12. Jeon, Y.J., Kim, J.U., Lee, H.J., Lee, J., Ryu, H.H., Lee, Y.J., et al.: A clinical study of the pulse wave characteristics at the three pulse diagnosis positions of Chon, Gwan and Cheok. Evid. Based. Complement. Alternat. Med. **2011**, 904056 (2011)
13. Lee, B.J., Jeon, Y.J., Bae, J.H., Yim, M.H., Kim, J.Y.: Gender differences in arterial pulse wave and anatomical properties in healthy Korean adults. Eur. J. Integr. Med. **25**, 41–48 (2019)
14. Luo, C.H., Su, C.J., Huang, T.Y., Chung, C.Y.: Non-invasive holistic health measurements using pulse diagnosis: i. validation by three-dimensional pulse mapping. Eur. J. Integr. Med. **8**(6), 921–925 (2016)
15. Luo, C.H., Zhang, Z., Peng, B., Xie, X., Lee, T.L., Tsai, L.M.: The novel three-dimensional pulse images analyzed by dynamic l-cube polynomial model. Med. Biol. Eng. Comput. **59**(2), 315–326 (2021)
16. McGee, S.: Evidence-based Physical Diagnosis, 5th edn. Elsevier - Health Sciences Division, Philadelphia, PA (2021)
17. Peng, B., et al.: Cross-channel dynamic weighting RPCA: a de-noising algorithm for multi-channel arterial pulse signal. Appl. Sci. **2022**(6), 2931 (2022)
18. Peng, B., Luo, C.H., Chan, W.Y., Shieh, M.D., Su, C.J., Tai, C.C.: Development and testing of a prototype for 3D radial pulse image measurement and compatible with 1D pulse wave analysis. IEEE Access **7**, 182846–182859 (2019)
19. Peng, B., Luo, C.H., Sinha, N., Tai, C.C., Xie, X., Xie, H.: Fourier series analysis for novel spatiotemporal pulse waves: normal, taut, and slippery pulse images. Evid. Based Complement. Altern. Med. **2019**, 5734018 (2019)
20. Potenziani, M., Callieri, M., Dellepiane, M., Corsini, M., Ponchio, F., Scopigno, R.: 3DHOP: 3d heritage online presenter. Comput. Graph. **52**, 129–141 (2015)
21. Roy, S.G., Kanjilal, U.: Web-based augmented reality for information delivery services: a performance study. DESIDOC J. Libr. Inf. Technol. **41**(3), 167–174 (2021)
22. Sandwell, D.T.: Biharmonic spline interpolation of GEOS-3 and SEASAT altimeter data. Geophys. Res. Lett. **14**(2), 139–142 (1987)
23. Shi, Y., Yu, C.: Intelligent interaction in mixed reality. Virtual Real. Intell. Hardw. **4**(2), ii–iii (2022)
24. Upadhyay, K., Agrawal, M., Vashist, P.: Learning multi-scale deep fusion for retinal blood vessel extraction in fundus images. Vis. Comput. **7**, 1–13 (2022)
25. Vlachopoulos, C., O'rourke, M., Nichols, W.W.: McDonald's Blood Flow in Arteries: Theoretical, Experimental and Clinical Principles. CRC Press, London (2011)

26. Wang, D., Zhang, D., Lu, G.: Generalized feature extraction for wrist pulse analysis: from 1D time series to 2D matrix. IEEE J. Biomed. Health Inform. **21**(4), 978–985 (2017)
27. Wang, L., Xu, L., Feng, S., Meng, M.Q.H., Kuanquan, W.: Multi-Gaussian fitting for pulse waveform using weighted least squares and multi-criteria decision making method. Comput. Biol. Med. **43**(11), 1661–1672 (2013)

Determine the Camera Eigenmatrix from Large Parallax Images

Zhenlong Du[1]([✉]), Yu Feng[1], Xiaoli Li[1], Dong Chen[1], and Xiangjun Zhao[2]

[1] College of Computer and Information Engineering, Nanjing Tech University, Nanjing, China
duzhl-cad@163.com
[2] College of Information Engineering, Nanjing Xiaozhuang University, Nanjing, China

Abstract. Recovering camera parameters from a group of image pairs is an important problem in computer vision. The traditional 4-point solution is vulnerable to insufficient or too concentrated number of corresponding point pairs when the viewpoint changes greatly, which leads to the failure of camera parameter recovery. This paper presents a method to quickly determine the corresponding point pairs from a group of image pairs with parallax by calculating the polar geometry. By using: for the pixel p in camera (viewpoint) A, all pixels corresponding to p in camera (viewpoint) B are located at the same epipolar line. Similarly, the line passing through the center of A and p on B is located at a epipolar line. Therefore, when A and B are synchronized, the instantaneous point of two objects projecting to the same pixel p at time t_1 and t_2 of A is located on a epipolar line of B. The camera eigenmatrix is calculated by using epipolar line pairs instead of points, and the search space for polar line matching is greatly reduced by using pixels recording multiple depths to accelerate the calculation of camera eigenmatrix, so as to achieve camera parameters quickly and accurately.

Keywords: Epipolar geometry · camera eigenmatrix · large parallax · point match

1 Introduction

An important part of computer vision is to calculate the epipolar geometry corresponding to a given set of assumed image points. Matching points of two images with parallax are more prone to errors, so before finding a good solution, we need to sample the point subset to perform robust estimation. For example, the commonly used method is random sample consistency (RANSAC) [1]. Based on the computation of camera intrinsic matrix, a set of minimum assumed points are sampled iteratively. The number of iterations varies from 1 to 3 according to the number of solutions. It also has a disadvantage. If there exist a large number of mismatched points, a large number of assumptions need to be evaluated for obtaining a reliable model.

In this paper, we present an approach of robust estimation of camera eigenmatrix from line correspondence in dynamic scenes. The eigenmatrix of the camera is the matrix with 3×3, rank 2 and 8 unknowns. The traditional algorithm for solving the camera eigenmatrix is an eight-point (four pairs of corresponding points) algorithm [2, 4, 5]. However, when the shooting angle between cameras changes sharply, the corresponding point pairs are difficult to detect, sometimes even do not exist, which might cause the camera eigenmatrix to have no solution. It is hard to assure to find corresponding point pairs from large view image sequences or videos. Even if dense sampling is adopted, it is not guaranteed to obtain enough point pairs to calculate the eigenmatrix.

In the paper the epipolar line pairs instead of point pairs is used to calculate the camera eigenmatrix, which has the following advantages: the exponent in the execution time of RANSAC depends on the minimum sample set size required for the calculation model (algorithm). The camera eigenmatrix of epipolar geometry calculation needs at least 3 pairs of corresponding epipolar lines, and the camera eigenmatrix of corresponding point pairs needs at least 4 pairs. In actual calculation, we usually use ≥ 3 pairs of corresponding epipolar lines or ≥ 4 pairs of corresponding point pairs to calculate the camera eigenmatrix.

Similar to previous methods, we assume that moving objects and static cameras have been extracted by background subtraction. The contributions of this paper are as follows: 1) Compared with other motion-based methods [6–8], we use epipolar lines instead of corresponding point matching, and use pixels recording multiple depths to significantly reduce the search space of epipolar lines to accelerate the calculation of camera eigen-matrix. 2) Based on the moving barcode [3] technology, a pair of synchronous cameras are calibrated, which has less complexity, higher accuracy and robustness.

2 Related Works

This section introduces the relevant technology of camera parameter recovery based on epipolar geometry. The camera eigenmatrix is usually calculated using the 7-point or 8-point algorithm [9–11]. In order to reduce the number of corresponding points, the five-point algorithm [12] can also be used if the camera parameters are known. Compared with points, epipolar lines can bring higher accuracy and lower computational complexity.

2.1 Motion Barcode

The moving barcode [3] represents the moving object in the image sequence or video by whether the frame image line intersects with the moving object. The moving object in the video is extracted by background subtraction. If the line in the frame intersects with the moving object, it is represented by 1, otherwise it is represented by 0. That is, after background subtraction, we get a binary video, where 0 represents a static background and 1 represents a moving object. The moving barcode technology is used to represent moving objects in moving barcode video.

For a given video, $b_l(i) = 1$ indicates that the motion barcode of line l in the frame i is a binary vector b_l in $\{0,1\}^N$. As shown in Fig. 1, when the moving object intersects the line l in frame i, the value of $b_l(i)$ is "1" (black item), otherwise it is "0" (white item). Assuming that the moving object intersects with l at frame i and does not intersect with l at frame j, the moving barcode of epipolar l is 1 and 0 at frame i and j respectively. Therefore, the moving barcode indicates whether there is a point of intersection between the line and the moving object in the frame, and indirectly indicates the moving object. When l is an epipolar line, the corresponding motion barcode indicates whether the epipolar line and the moving object have intersections.

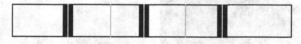

Fig. 1. Motion barcode

When two frames are captured simultaneously from different camera viewpoints, the corresponding two pixels are projected by a single 3D point. However, in a dynamic scene, the pixels in one view must correspond to different pixels in another view at different times, and it is located on the corresponding epipolar line. As shown in Fig. 2, a single pixel in the right view corresponds to a pixel in the left view at time t_1. In time t_2, the same pixel corresponds to different pixels in another view because of the motion of objects in the scene. For a video sequence captured by a fixed camera, the corresponding pixel will always keep on the corresponding epipolar line.

It can be seen that if a epipolar line contains at least one contour pixel at time t, its corresponding epipolar line should also contain such a contour pixel. As shown in Fig. 3 illustration, for time t_2 and t_3, there are some points from the object projected onto the corresponding epipolar line. If a point on the line l is part of the contour, then this point or another contour point blocking it will be seen on the line l'.

As shown in Fig. 3 demostration, when t_2 and t_3, the two corresponding epipolar lines contain a contour point, which can also be a different 3D point due to parallax. For example, the motion bar code of the two epipolar lines l, l' is [0, 1, 1].

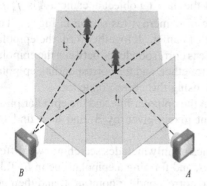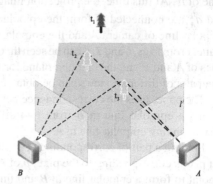

Fig. 2. Pixel correspondence in dynamic scene

Fig. 3. Corresponding contour pixel map of corresponding epipolar line

Based on the Intel Real Sense depth camera, we shot the classroom scene for half an hour continuously. We applied background subtraction to extract the object outline in the scene, as shown in Fig. 4. Then the moving bar code is applied to represent the moving object information, as shown in Fig. 5.

The moving bar code of the epipolar line l indicates whether there is a point of intersection between l and the moving object, and the moving barcode of the epipolar

Fig. 4. Background subtraction for achieving the contour map

Fig. 5. Moving barcode represents moving object

line l' indicates the point of intersection between l' and the moving object, so the similarity measure of the moving barcode of l and l' can be used to find the epipolar line.

2.2   Epiolar Line and Epipolar Plane

Let p, q and r be different pixels, and p_A^t represents the projection imaging of the moving object at time t at camera A. $\overleftrightarrow{q_B r_B}$ is the image of moving object pixel p at camera A which at camera B at time t and connected by a epipolar line.

As shown by Fig. 6, A and B are the two different cameras with relevance to the image sequence or video, let the projection imaging p_A of the moving object at the camera A at the time t_i, and the projection imaging $q_B^{t_i}$ at the camera B. The projective imaging $q_B^{t_j}$ of the moving object at the camera B at t_j. $q_B^{t_i}$ and $q_B^{t_j}$ are connected to form a epipolar line. The point $q_B^{t_k}$ on the epipolar line of camera B is the projection of the moving object at the time of t_k. At this time, the projection image of the moving object at camera A is $q_A^{t_k} \cdot p_A$ and $q_A^{t_k}$ are connected to form the epipolar line of camera A (as shown in Fig. 7). The epipolar line of camera A and the epipolar line of camera B together form the epipolar plane. From Figs. 6 and 7, it can be seen that there is correspondence between the epipolar lines of A and B and the epipolar plane formed together, and the corresponding epipolar line pairs of different views can be obtained by using this correspondence.

The paper uses the correspondence between the epipolar line and the epipolar plane to find a epipolar line in B from two different pixels given by A, and then find the corresponding epipolar line in A.

Finding a pair of corresponding epipolar lines mainly includes searching two different pixels corresponding to the pixel p of A in B, and forming a epipolar line in B. Take a point to form a epipolar line in B and find the corresponding point in A, and then get the epipolar line in A.

3   Determine the Camera Eigenmatrix from Large Parallax Images

The given method includes the background subtraction, the candidate corresponding epipolar lines sets construction, together with the camera eigenmatrix determination. The background subtraction [13–15] is used to extract the mask sequence or mask

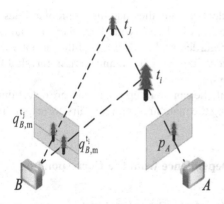 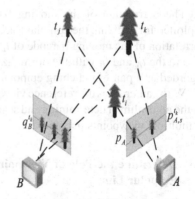

Fig. 6. Corresponding pixel on the determined epipolar line

Fig. 7. Candidate epipolar line searching for matching epipolar line at viewpoint

video of moving objects from a group of content-related image sequences or videos. The candidate corresponding epipolar lines sets of viewpoint (camera) A and viewpoint (camera) B are determined. Determine the corresponding epipolar lines pairs of A and B. Determine the epipolar lines on which the viewpoint depends from the corresponding pole. Then, the camera eigenmatrix is calculated from the epipolar lines and poles.

3.1 Determination of Viewpoint Corresponding to Epipolar Line

Assume that camera (viewpoint) A contains pixels in both frames at time t_i and t_j. To search for corresponding pixels $\{q_{B,1}^{t_i}, q_{B,2}^{t_i}...\}$ and $\{q_{B,1}^{t_j}, q_{B,2}^{t_j}...\}$ from all pixels in camera (viewpoint) B. The ordered pixels in the two frames determine a candidate epipolar line for $\{q_{B,m}^{t_i}, q_{B,n}^{t_j}\}$, and set $\Lambda_B = \{\overleftrightarrow{q_{B,m}^{t_i} q_{B,n}^{t_j}}\}$ be the set of all epipolar lines. As shown in Fig. 6 description, the two pixels corresponding to pixel p_A are located on the epipolar line determined by $q_{B,m}^{t_i}$ and $q_{B,n}^{t_j}$.

Each epipolar line in Λ_B searches for the matching epipolar line at A. For $\forall l_B \in \Lambda_B$, search all $p_A^{t_k}$ that meet the conditions at the frame of $t_k (t_k \neq t_i, t_k \neq t_j)$ to achieve $\Lambda_A = \{p_{A,1}^{t_k}, p_{A,2}^{t_k}, \cdots\}$. $p_{A,s}^{t_k}$ at any point in p_A and Λ_A gets the epipolar line $\Lambda_A = \{\overleftrightarrow{p_A, p_{A,s}^{t_k}}\}$ corresponding to l_B, as shown in Fig. 7 demonstration.

3.2 Search for Matching Epipolar Pairs

Let the motion barcodes of epipolar lines l_A as well as l_B, l_A and l_B corresponding to cameras A and B be B_{l_A} and B_{l_B} with length N, and the normalized correlation definition of l_A and l_B is shown in Eq. 1.

$$corr(l_A, l_B) = \sum_{i=1}^{N} \frac{(b_{l_A}(i) - mean(B_{l_A})) \bullet (b_{l_B}(i) - mean(B_{l_B}))}{\|B_{l_A} - mean(B_{l_A})\|_2 \|B_{l_B} - mean(B_{l_B})\|_2} \qquad (1)$$

Where $b_{l_A}(i) \in B_{l_A}$, $b_{l_B}(i) \in B_{l_B}$, operator $mean(\cdot)$ calculate the mean value.

The correlation of the moving barcode between the matching epipolar lines is exploited for deciding the epipolar line. The epipolar line l_A with the highest normalized correlation of the moving barcode of l_B is regarded as the candidate of the epipolar line l_B, and the l_A and l_B with the normalized correlation greater than a certain threshold is regarded as a pair of matching epipolar pairs.

With camera B as the reference viewpoint, the candidate epipolar pairs are determined by the algorithm of determining and searching the matching epipolar pairs corresponding to multiple viewpoints in camera A.

3.3 Determine the Pole of Viewpoint Dependence from the Corresponding Epipolar Line

Two pairs of corresponding epipolar lines $l_{A,1}$, $l_{B,1}$ and $l_{A,2}$, $l_{B,2}$ are obtained by searching the matching epipolar pairs. The random sampling consistency algorithm RANSAC is used to sample and determine the pole position. The sampling probability is proportional to the normalized correlation of the matched moving barcode. As shown in Fig. 8 illustration, the intersection points of two epipolar lines of camera A and camera B are e_A and e_B, respectively.

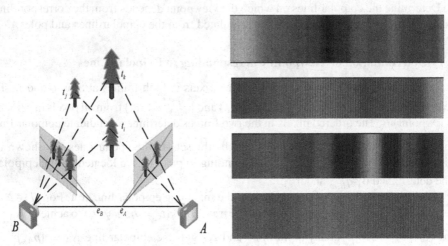

Fig. 8. Poles corresponding to epipolar line   **Fig. 9.** Moving barcode representing moving to determine viewpoint dependence   objects

Randomly select the frame at the time t_s, assuming that $T_A = \{p_A^{t_s}\overleftrightarrow{e_A}\}$ and $T_B = \{q_B^{t_s}\overleftrightarrow{e_B}\}$ connect all the most significant pixels to the poles, calculate the normalized correlation and match the moving barcodes of T_A and T_B, and take the best candidate barcode as the third pair of matching poles.

The determined three pairs of epipolar lines provide a definite solution condition for calculating the camera eigenmatrix.

Evenly sample 20 lines around the pole e_A on which the camera A depends, search for the matching epipolar pair, and find for the corresponding epipolar line passing through the e_B on the camera (viewpoint) B, calculate the normalized cross correlation of the moving barcode between the 20 pairs of epipolar lines, and select the matching epipolar pair with the highest normalized cross correlation to calculate the eigenmatrix.

3.4 Calculation of Eigenmatrix from Epipolar Lines and Poles

Let the camera eigenmatrix be F, $l_B = F[e_A]_\times l_A$ and $l_A = F^T[e_B]_\times l_B$ hold. When the scene contains plane objects, $l_B = Hl_A$, where H is the homography matrix. H is calculated from multiple sets of epipolar pairs, then the camera eigenmatrix $F = [e_A]_\times H$ is calculated.

4 Experiments

(1) Dataset
We conducted experiments on the Tanks and Temples [16] real dataset, which includes the wide-baseline camera pose and the images taken by handheld cameras in the urban courtyard scene.

For this dataset, we sampled 1500 pairs of images, at least 20 of which matched, and the distance between the symmetrical poles is less than or equal to 1 pixel relative to the ground truth, then the dataset is used for evaluation. We show that our method can successfully calculate the eigenmatrix of these different sets of image pairs in the real world, achieve an efficient estimation process.

We applied Intel Real Sense depth camera to shoot classroom scenes for half an hour continuously. Based on this video set, we showed the following groups of results, as shown by Fig. 9.

(2) The Matching Process from Point to Line
The Fig. 10 shows an example of our method to restore the point corresponding line of a pair of parallax pictures. Take the first act as an example, the inline ratio is 0.75. There are 640 inline lines in 719 hypothetical correspondences, with an error of 0.65. Meanwhile, we performed an eight-point matching based on the random sampling consensus algorithm. Among 719 hypothetical correspondences, there are 615 inline lines with an error of 0.68. Compared with the eight-point matching based on RANSAC, our method shows more inline lines and smaller errors.

In general, we want to match lines with a large number of inline lines and low homography error. In 100 sets of matching for Tanks and Temples dataset, the average number of points on the matching line is 7.21. When the single threshold is set to 0.9, the average number of inline lines on the corresponding line is 5.95. Fig. 11 shows the probability of having a given number of inline lines in the matching line for this homography error. Figure 12 shows the probability of a given uniaxial error on the matching line. 97% of the inline single response error is less than 0.4, and 99% of the inline single response error is less than 0.5, which is our default threshold.

(3) Evaluation
On the Tanks and Temples dataset, we compared the accuracy of the eight-point algorithm

Image1   **Image2**

Fig. 10. Result of match lines and corresponding points

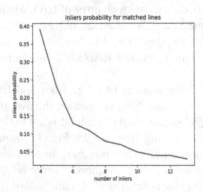

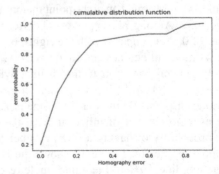

Fig. 11. Probability distribution of inline lines in matching lines

Fig. 12. Probability of a given homography error on the matching line

Image1   Image2   Image1   Image2

Fig. 13. Comparison with the eight-point algorithm based on RANSAC and LEMDS

Fig. 14. Results of larger parallax angle

Table 1. Quality evaluation of comparison results

	inliers(%)	F-score	Mean
RANSAC	45.6	0.73 ± 0.06	0.69
LEMDS	44.9	0.72 ± 0.04	0.68
Ours	47.2	0.74 ± 0.06	0.63

based on RANSAC and the eight-point algorithm based on LEMDS [17]. The results are shown in Table 1.

Figure 13 shows the process of comparing the method in this paper with the eight-point algorithm based on RANSAC and LEMDS. The first and second rows are the methods of this paper. The third and fourth lines are the results of the eight-point algorithm based on RANSAC. The third and fourth rows are based on the LEMDS method. The homography thresholds of the three methods are set to be 0.5. The method in this paper has 895 inline lines in 916 hypothetical correspondences, with an error of 0.19. Similarly, we performed an eight-point matching based on RANSAC. Among the 916 hypothetical correspondences, there are 872 inline lines, with an error of 0.6. Based on the LEMDS-based method, there are 636 inline lines in 684 hypothetical correspondences, with an error of 0.64.

Figure 14 shows the results of several sets of larger parallax angles. Our method shows accurate results.

5   Conclusion

In the paper a method of determine the camera eigenmatrix from large parallax images is proposed. Firstly, this paper uses the background subtraction algorithm to extract the mask sequence or mask video of moving objects from a group of content-related image sequences or videos. Secondly, the candidate corresponding epipolar line sets of viewpoint (camera) A and viewpoint (camera) B are determined. Determine the corresponding epipolar line pairs of A and B. Determine the pole on which the viewpoint depends from the corresponding pole. Finally, the camera eigenmatrix can be calculated from the poles and epipolar lines. The experimental results show that results compared with the previous algorithm, this paper can achieve fast and accurate camera calibration, with low computational time complexity and small error.

References

1. Fischler, M.A., Bolles, R.C.: Random sample consensus: a paradigm for model fitting with applications to image analysis and automated cartography. Commun. ACM **24**(6), 381–395 (1981)
2. Kasten, Y., Ben-Artzi, G., Peleg, S., Werman, M.: Fundamental matrices from moving objects using line motion barcodes. In: Proceedings of European Conference on Computer Vision (ECCV'2016), pp. 220–228(2016)
3. Ben-Artzi, G., Kasten, Y., Peleg, S., Werman, M.: Camera calibration from dynamic silhouettes using motion barcodes. In: Proceedings of the IEEE Conference on Computer Vision and Pattern Recognition, pp. 4095–4103 (2016)
4. Hartley, R., Zisserman, A.: Multiple View Geometry in Computer Vision. Cambridge University Press (2003)
5. Faugeras, O., Luong, Q.-T., Papadopoulos, T.: The geometry of multiple images: the laws that govern the formation of multiple images of a scene and some of their applications. Comput. Sci. (2001)
6. Sinha, S., Pollefeys, M.: Camera network calibration and synchronization from silhouettes in archived video. Int. J. Comput. Vis. **87**(3), 266–283 (2010)
7. Ben-Artzi, G., Halperin, T., Werman, T., Peleg, S.: Epipolar geometry based on line similarity. In: Proceedings of International Conference on Pattern Recognition, pp. 1864–1869 (2016)
8. Izadi, S., Kim, D., Hilliges, O., et al.: Kinect fusion: real-time 3D reconstruction and interaction using a moving depth camera. In: Proceedings of the 24th annual ACM symposium on User interface software and technology, pp. 559–568 (2011)

9. Longuet-Higgins, H.C.: A computer algorithm for reconstructing a scene from two projections. Nature (1987) 61–62
10. Feng, S., Kan, J., Wu, Y.: An improved method to estimate the fundamental matrix based on 7-point algorithm. J. Theor. Appl. Inf. Technol. **46**(1), 212–217 (2012)
11. Hartley, R.I.: In defense of the eight-point algorithm. IEEE Trans., Pattern Anal. Mach. Intell. **19**(6), 580–593 (1997)
12. Nister, D.: An effificient solution to the five-point relative pose problem. IEEE Trans. Pattern Anal. Mac. Intell. **26**(6), 756–777 (2004)
13. Tsai, D., Lai, S.-C.: Independent component analysis-based background subtraction for indoor surveillance. IEEE Trans. Image Process. **18**(1), 158–160 (2009)
14. Benezeth, Y., Jodoin, P., Emile, B., Laurent, H., Rosenberger, C.: Review and evaluation of commonly implemented background subtraction algorithms. In: Proceedings of International Conference on Pattern Recognition, pp. 1–4 (2008)
15. Seki, M., Wada, T., Fujiwara, H., Sumi, K.: Background subtraction based on cooccurrence of image variations. In: Proceedings of IEEE Conference on Computer Vision and Pattern Recognition, pp. 65–72 (2003)
16. Knapitsch, A., Park, J., Zhou, Q.-Y., Koltun, V.: Tanks and temples: benchmarking large-scale scene reconstruction. ACM Trans. Graphics **36**(4), 1–13 (2017)
17. Peter, J.R.: Least median of squares regression. J. Am. Stat. Assoc. **79**(388), 871–880 (1984)

Action Recognition via Fine-Tuned CLIP Model and Temporal Transformer

Xiaoyu Yang$^{(\boxtimes)}$, Yuzhuo Fu, and Ting Liu

Shanghai Jiao Tong University, Shanghai, China
freeze_yangxy@163.com

Abstract. Contrastive image-text pre-trained model, *i.e.* CLIP, has been proved successful transferring to the video domain. It shows remarkable "zero-shot" generalization ability for various large-scale datasets. However, most researches are based on the datasets like Kinetics and UCF-101. These datasets focus more on appearance rather than temporal order information. In other words, training on these datasets may not reward good temporal understanding in videos. We want to capture the long-range dependencies of frames along the temporal dimension.

In this paper, we deal with this problem by applying a temporal transformer module and the backbone fine-tuning strategy. Fine-tuning the backbone model helps the image based model fits the video environment, and the temporal transformer module captures detailed spatiotemporal information We mainly focus the performance on the action-centered dataset Something V2 because it contains a large proportion of temporal classes. We adopt the language-image pretrained models like CLIP to further study the zero-shot ability.

Keywords: Vision-language model · Spatiotemporal Fusion · Video Recognition · Contrasive Language-Image Pre-training

1 Introduction

Pre-trained visual-language models such as CLIP [36], ALIGN [14] and Florence [50] have shown strong generalization and transfer capabilities. These models are trained using millions of image-text pairs sourced from the Internet. Recently these image-text based multi-modal methods are proved successful in video domain and make impressive performance for various downstream tasks, *e.g.* classification, detection, segmentation and classification.

However, most CLIP based model in video domain mainly discuss the performance on datasets like Kinetics [17]. These datasets contains fewer temporal classes and is comprised of a large amount of static classes [7,13,22,38]. For example, [7] reports that changing temporal order of kinetic videos does not drop the recognition performance, and [51] represents 2 famous Video Transformers Timesformer [3] and Motionformer [33] have almost the same accuracy even their input video frames are randomly shuffled. These observations reveal that

B. Sheng et al. (Eds.): CGI 2023, LNCS 14497, pp. 498–513, 2024.
https://doi.org/10.1007/978-3-031-50075-6_39

although these recent Video Transformer based methods are designed to learn more temporal information, they are still likely to be biased to learn the spatial information rather than temporal ones. Whether these architectural advances can fully capture the temporal dynamics in a video is a problem.

Unlike Kinetics, Something-Something v2 dataset (SSv2) [10] is specifically designed to be action-centered and independent of the objects appearing in the scene, which makes it particularly relevant to our study. It contains a large proportion of temporal classes than other video datasets. TIME [51] show recent Video Transformer fail to capture the temporal order of video frames and are likely to be biased to learn spatial dynamics. However, studying few-shot and zero-shot tasks using CLIP based model on dataset like SSv2 is challenging due to the following reason: 1). CLIP based method rarely consider the complex temporal information in the video and 2). The format of label in SSv2 and the importance of temporal information is different from the ImageNet pre-trained CLIP text encoder.

For the first problem, we consider to apply extra temporal information strengthen module to deal more temporal information. To this end, we propose an Temporal Video Fine-tuning framework based on CLIP backbone and a lightweight Temporal Transformer decoder.

For the second problem, we fine-tune the full CLIP backbone as [37] did. Such fine-tuning helps the model to focus on current dataset, especially moving-objects and inter-object relationships, which is important for SSv2. It also helps the model to adjust the text information to adapt it to SSv2 dataset

The major contribution of this paper are summarized as follows:

1. We apply different temporal information module Temporal Convolution, Temporal Positional Embedding and Temporal Cross-Attention in CLIP based model to increase the performance.
2. We fine-tune the image and text encoder in the CLIP backbone to study the performance on Something-Something V2 dataset.
3. We conduct experiments on different settings including zero-shot and few-shot tasks. We show better or competitive performance as compared to the state-of art approaches.

2   Related Work

In this section, we review the related work in Vision Language Models and Video Action Recognition.

2.1   Vision Language Models

Vision-Language (VL) pre-training are proved efficient for various downstream tasks. Models like CLIP [36] and ALIGN [14] pre-train vision-language models with a contrastive loss on a large-scale image-caption pairs. These models are effectively used as the pre-trained model in many follow-up works including few-shot and zero-shot recognition [52,55,56], object detection [2,11,57], and image segmentation [6,19,54]. VideoCLIP [48] extends the image-level pre-training to the video by substituting the image-text data with video-text ones. However, such video-text pre-training is computationally expensive and requires a large scale of video-text dataset for example HowTo100M [29].

Recently, many efforts are made to introduce image-text based VL pertrained model like CLIP for video related downstream tasks [15,28,44]. Action-Clip [44] propose the "pre-train, prompt and fine-tune" framework for action recognition. Ju *et al.* [15] propose to optimize a few random vectors for adapting CLIP to various video understanding tasks and transfer the zero-shot generalization capability of CLIP to videos. X-CLIP [32] and Vita-CLIP [46] further study the temporal message and the video-specific text prompting scheme in video clips. ViFi-CLIP [37] introduce the process of fine-tuning the image and text encoder of the CLIP backbone.

In our work, based on CLIP backbone fine-tuning method, we further learn the method of capturing more spatiotemporal information in the video.

2.2 Video Action Recognition

In many traditional approaches, 3D convolution is widely used [35,41,43,47] because it can exploit the spatiotemporal information from the RGB video data. For example, Slowfast [8] captures short- and long-range of time dependencies by using two different speed of pathways for video. However, 3D-CNN suffers from high computational cost. Some studies insert the temporal modules into 2D CNNs [21,23,27] to avoid the high computation cost.

Recent proposed video transformer based architectures [1,26,49] proposes to effectively deal with the spatial-temporal information and have shown great improvements over CNNs. For example, ViViT [1], AVT [9], VTN [31] use a frame-level encoder followed by a temporal encoder and Swin-transformer [26] utilizes 3D attention while having high computational cost.

Besides these uni-model solutions, multimodal methods like ActionCLIP [44], XCLIP [32] and Ju *et al.* [15] adopt CLIP to video recognition. These methods utilize the rich generalized vision-language representations of CLIP with some additional temporal components to deal with video temporal information.

In our work, we pretrained multimodal Transformer to keep the zero-shot transfer ability, and propose to apply some additional temporal modules to enhance the temporal performance of a CLIP based model.

2.3 Video Datasets

Progress in video understanding is closely related to the growth of video datasets in data scale and richness of taxonomy. The first two datasets were UCF-101 [39] containing 101 classes and HMDB-51 [18] containing 51 classes of single label videos of human action. The first large-scale dataset Sports-1M [16] provides 1M videos of sports actions. In the last few years, researches collect human annotations to create more challenging datasets. Kinetics [17] includes 400/600/700 classes of human actions in different environments and is popular in recent classification tasks. Moments-In-Time [30] dataset contains 1M short videos corresponding to over 300 event classes. In this paper, we mainly discuss the Something-Something [10] dataset, which contains categories of actions independent to objects, trying to study the physical movements regardless of the object it self.

3   Our Method

In this section, we present our proposed framework in detail. First, we briefly overview our framework in Sect. 3.1. Then the Temporal Transformer Decoder is introduced in Sect. 3.2. Finally. we depict the backbone fine-tuning strategy in Sect. 3.3.

3.1   Overall Structure

In our model, we use a CLIP based model as the baseline. The model works to adapt pre-trained image-based vision-language models for videos. The overall structure is illustrated in Fig. 1. The image encoder extracts features from each frame independently and the text encoder extracts the label information. A multi-layer spatiotemporal transformer module follows the visual encoder to get the temporal information from the spatial features.

Given a video clip $V \in \mathbb{R}^{T \times H \times W \times C}$ of spatial size $H \times W$ with T frames, a ViT based video encoder f_{θ_v} is used to extract features from each frame independently and produce the frame-level representations $\mathbf{x} \in \mathbb{R}^{T \times D}$.

$$\mathbf{x} = f_{\theta_v}(V), \tag{1}$$

In this paper, we further send the frame-level feature into a spatiotemporal transformer decoder module and get the new representation $\hat{\mathbf{x}} \in \mathbb{R}^{T \times D}$. The decoder performs global aggregation of multi-layer features: a video-level classification token [CLS] is learned to act as a query, and multiple feature volumes from different backbone blocks are fed as key and value. The operation of the spatiotemporal transformer decoder can be expressed as follows:

$$\begin{aligned}
\mathbf{Y}_i &= f_{temp}([x_{N-M+i,1}, x_{N-M+i,2}, \ldots, x_{N-M+i,T}]), \\
\hat{\mathbf{q}}_i &= \mathbf{q}_{i-1} + \mathtt{MHA}_i(\mathbf{q}_{i-1}, \hat{\mathbf{Y}}_i, \hat{\mathbf{Y}}_i), \\
\mathbf{q}_i &= \hat{\mathbf{q}}_i + \mathtt{MLP}_i(\hat{\mathbf{q}}_i), \\
\hat{\mathbf{x}} &= \mathbf{q}_M.
\end{aligned} \tag{2}$$

where f_{temp} denotes the frame-level feature enhance method introduced in Sect. 3.2. $x_{n,t}$ denotes the frame features of the t-th frame extracted from the n-th layer of the CLIP backbone, N is the number of blocks in the backbone image encoder layer, and M is the number of blocks in the spatiotemporal transformer decoder layer. $\mathbf{Y}_i$ denotes the temporal modulated feature calculated from the i-th layer of the decoder layer. $\mathbf{q}_i$ is the progressively refined query token with $\mathbf{q}_0$ as learnable parameters. The output of the last decoder layer $\mathbf{q}_M$ is regarded as the adjusted frame level feature $\hat{\mathbf{x}}$. The last final MLP layer enhances the frame representations globally by encoding the temporal context from different frames in the video and outputs spatio-temporally enriched frame-level representations according to [40].

Then, these adjusted frame-level embedding are then average-pooled to obtain a video-level representation $\mathbf{v} \in \mathbb{R}^D$ since we need to calculate the similarity between visual and text features.

$$\mathbf{v} = \texttt{AvgPool}(\hat{\mathbf{x}}). \tag{3}$$

For the corresponding textual representation $C \in \mathcal{C}$, we follow the previous works using a manually defined textual prompts such as "A photo of a {label}" as the text description C and the text feature $\mathbf{c}$ is calculated by a text encoder f_{θ_c}

$$\mathbf{c} = f_{\theta_c}(C). \tag{4}$$

Finally, a cosine similarity function $\texttt{sim}(\mathbf{v}, \mathbf{c})$ is utilized to compute the similarity between the visual and textual representations:

$$\texttt{sim}(\mathbf{v}, \mathbf{c}) = \frac{\langle \mathbf{v}, \mathbf{c} \rangle}{\|\mathbf{v}\|\,\|\mathbf{c}\|} \tag{5}$$

3.2   Temporal Information Enrichment

The Temporal Transformer Decoder can capture the global temporal information. To further enhance the performance on SSv2 dataset, the local temporal information may also be important. We try 3 different methods: Temporal Convolution, Temporal Positional Embedding and Temporal Cross Attention, to enhance temporal information

Temporal Convolution. Temporal convolutions are proved to be efficient and effective capturing local feature variations along temporal dimension [8,42]. The temporal convolutions are usually written as

$$\mathbf{Y}_{\text{conv}}(t, c) = \sum_{\Delta t \in \{-1, 0, 1\}} \mathbf{W}_{\text{conv}}(\Delta t, c)\mathbf{x}(t + \Delta t, c) + \mathbf{b}_{conv}(c). \tag{6}$$

where $\mathbf{Y}_{\text{conv}}$ is the feature encoded by the temporal convolution.

Temporal Positional Embeddings. Similar to the spatial positional embedding, a temporal positional embedding can be used to enable the temporal differentiation of features and is already used in other video related tasks, *e.g.* re-id [12], 3d human pose estimation [20]. In this paper, we use a set of T vectors of dimension C, denoted as $\mathbf{P} \in \mathbb{R}^{T \times C}$ as the temporal positional embedding to keep the temporal position information of the video.

$$\mathbf{Y}_{\text{pos}}(t, c) = \mathbf{P}(t, c). \tag{7}$$

Compared to other temporal information enrichment methods, temporal positional embeddings are more likely to capture long-range temporal information. It can also make similar features at different time distinguishable.

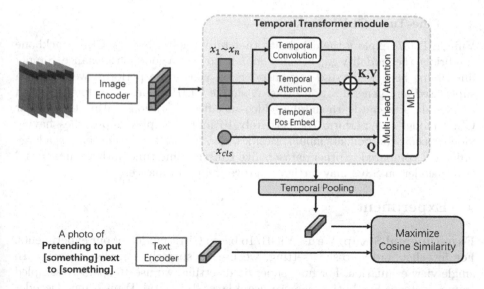

Fig. 1. Model Structure Overview. (a) Temporal Transformer Decoder block: temporal modeling is added to the raw frame features $\mathbf{x}_i$. **(b)** Overview of the architecture. For the Text encoder, a textual prompt "A photo of a {label}" is used to generate text feature. For the frame feature, 4 layers of Temporal Transformer Module is applied to get the temporal enhanced video feature. To calculate the similarity between frame and text features, a temporal pooling module is used to combine the frame features into a video feature.

Temporal Cross Attention. The attention structure is another method usually used to enhance temporal information in recent researches, *e.g.* [25,40]. We follow the cross attention mentioned in EVL [24], As attention maps reflect feature correspondence, using the attention maps between adjacent frames can represent object movement information. The attention maps $\mathbf{A}_{\text{prev}}$ and $\mathbf{A}_{\text{next}}$ can be written as

$$
\begin{aligned}
\mathbf{A}_{\text{prev}}(t) &= \texttt{Softmax}((\mathbf{Q}\mathbf{x}(t))^T(\mathbf{K}\mathbf{x}(t-1))) \\
\mathbf{A}_{\text{next}}(t) &= \texttt{Softmax}((\mathbf{Q}\mathbf{x}(t))^T(\mathbf{K}\mathbf{x}(t+1)))
\end{aligned}
\tag{8}
$$

We average across all heads in the implementation and linearly project it into feature dimension.

$$
\begin{aligned}
\mathbf{Y}_{\texttt{attn}}(t,h,w,c) = \\
\sum_{h'=1}^{H}\sum_{w'=1}^{W}\mathbf{W}_{\text{prev}}(h-h',w-w',c)\mathbf{A}_{\text{prev}}(t,h',w') \\
+ \mathbf{W}_{\text{next}}(h-h',w-w',c)\mathbf{A}_{\text{next}}(t,h',w')
\end{aligned}
\tag{9}
$$

Finally, we can get the frame-level feature enrichment function f_{temp} as

$$
f_{temp}(\mathbf{x}) = \mathbf{x} + \mathbf{Y}_{\text{conv}} + \mathbf{Y}_{\text{pos}} + \mathbf{Y}_{\text{attn}}
\tag{10}
$$

3.3   Fine-Tune CLIP Backbone

Vifi-CLIP [37] explore the capability that fully fine-tuning the CLIP backbone can bridge the modality gap in video domain and get a good performance. Simply fine-tuning both vision and text encoders on video data performs well on both supervised and generalization tasks. A simple CLIP model when fine-tuned on a video dataset can learn suitable video-specific adaptations within the regular CLIP model and perform competitively to more complex approaches having video-specific components inbuilt. Besides, the class label information has a large difference compared to other datasets like Kinetics, fine-tune both the image and text encoder on SSv2 may further improve the performance.

4   Experiment

Experimental Setup: We use Vit-B/16 based CLIP model for our experiments. For few-shot and zero-shot setting, we use 32 sparsely sampled frames with single view evaluation. For fully-supervised setting, we use 16 sparsely sampled frames instead. For both tasks, we use 4-layer Temporal Transformer Decoder modules in our model. We conduct our analysis mainly on Something Something v2 (SSv2) benchmark in fully-supervised setting.

4.1   Fully Supervised Setting

In Fully supervised setting, the result on SSv2 is shown in Table 1. Due to lack of comparison in CLIP based method, we compare the performance of our model trained on SSv2 with some pre-trained image Visual-Language models together with some uni-model architectures. We can see our method outperforms the best Vision-Language based model.

However, compared to the uni-model architectures, which use cross-entropy-based methods, it is still difficult to catch up with these ones. The most possible reason fine-grained nature of the SSv2 class descriptions. The class description of SSv2 is more difficult to differentiate compared to other datasets like Kinetics classes. The CLIP pre-training relies more on object information for action recognition. Since there is no specific object description in SSv2 class description (use "something" instead), it is much harder for the model to recognize the fine-grained motions.

4.2   Few-Shot Setting

We use this setting to test the learning ability of the model under limited supervision. For a dataset D_S with label $Y_S = \{y_i\}_{i=0}^{k}$, a general K-shot data is created, where K-samples are randomly selected from each category $y_i \in Y_S$ for training.

In Table 2, we show the effect of out model in the few-shot setting along the methods that adapt CLIP for videos. We find that for in most shots ($K = 2, 4, 8$), it provides better results than other CLIP based methods. In $K = 16$ shot, it outperforms most results and is competitive with the ViFi-CLIP result.

Table 1. Comparison with CLIP-based methods on SSv2 in fully-supervised setting: We compare the modified model with approaches that explicitly adapt CLIP for video action recognition on SSv2. The uni-model architectures only studies vision information and using cross entropy loss to calculate similarity. The CLIP based models study the relationship between vision information and text information, which is much harder than methods only consider the vision ones.

Fully-supervised setting		
Method	Zero-shot	Top-1
Adapting uni-model architectures.		
Methods with Vision training.		
TRN [53]	✗	48.8
Slowfast [8]	✗	61.7
TSM [23]	✗	63.4
ViViT [1]	✗	65.9
Swin-B [26]	✗	69.6
Adapting CLIP based architectures.		
Methods with Vision-Language training.		
B2 [15]	✔	38.1
Vita-CLIP [46]	✔	48.7
Our method	✔	56.7

Table 2. Comparison with CLIP-based methods on SSv2 in few-shot setting: We compare the modified model with approaches that explicitly adapt CLIP for video action recognition on SSv2. The best result is underlined.

Few-shot setting				
	$K=2$	$K=4$	$K=8$	$K=16$
Adapting pre-trained image VL models				
Vanilla CLIP [36]	2.7	2.7	2.7	2.7
Action CLIP [44]	4.1	5.8	8.4	11.1
XCLIP [32]	3.9	4.5	6.8	10.0
A5 [15]	4.4	5.1	6.1	9.7
Tuning pre-trained image VL models				
ViFi-CLIP [37]	6.2	7.4	8.5	<u>12.4</u>
Our method	<u>11.90</u>	<u>11.51</u>	<u>11.87</u>	11.93

4.3 Zero-Shot Setting

Since our goal is to strengthen the ability of capturing temporal information, we still need to maintain the transfer ability of VL model. We test the cross-dataset generalization ability in a zero-shot setting. We train the model on the

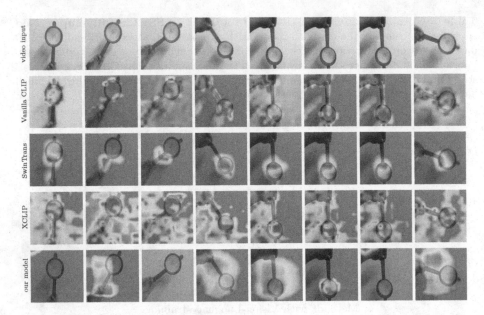

Fig. 2. Attention map visualization: The attention map visualization of our model in comparison with other models (vanilla CLIP, Swin Transformer, XCLIP) on example from SSv2 dataset. As we can see, vanilla CLIP and Swin Transformer focuses on the object and the hand all the time, which is not important in video of SSv2 dataset. The XCLIP model also fails to capture the temporal difference between adjacent frames. Compared to these methods, our model clearly classify the movement of the object along temporal dimension, showing the movement of the object in the video between different frames.

large video action recognition dataset, Kinetics-400 and evaluate across different datasets, HMDB-51 and UCF-101 in order to compare the result with other models. In Table 3, we compare out results with other uni-model or multi-model VL methods. Our model show impressive generalization ability when capturing more temporal information. Our model reaches the highest accuracy on UCF-101 dataset, and it provides competitive performance when compared with other methods on HMDB-51 dataset.

Table 3. Comparison with CLIP-based methods on SSv2 in zero-shot setting: We compare the modified model with other methods. Models are trained on Kinetics-400 and evaluated directly on HMDB-51, UCF-101.

Zero-shot setting		
Method	HMDB51	UCF101
uni-model zero-shot action recognition models		
ASR [45]	21.8	24.4
ZSECOC [34]	22.6	15.1
UR [58]	24.4	17.5
E2E [4]	32.7	48
ER-ZSAR [5]	35.3	51.8
Adapting pre-trained image VL models		
Vanilla CLIP [36]	40.8	63.2
Action CLIP [44]	40.8	58.3
XCLIP [32]	44.6	72.0
A5 [15]	44.3	69.3
ViFi-CLIP [37]	51.3	76.8
Our method	50.15	77.46

4.4 Ablation and Analysis

We fine-tune image and text encoders and compare it with the fully fine-tuned model. Due to the time consumption, we use fully supervised setting on SSv2 to test the performance. The result is shown in Table 4. We can see the performance of fine-tuning both image and text encoder can get a higher performance. Compared to the visual fine-tuning process, the text fine-tuning process performs better. This shows that fine-tuning the label information helps to deal with the difference between SSv2 and other datasets. This also helps explain the result in Sect. 4.1 that the fine-grained nature of the SSv2 class descriptions are more difficult to differentiate compared to, for example, Kinetics-400 classes.

We also test the ability of the temporal attention module. The temporal attention module works very well on SSv2 dataset. As shown in Table 5, using the whole 3 temporal methods: the temporal convolution, temporal positional embedding and temporal cross attention can reach the highest performance.

Table 4. Effects of fine-tuning pre-trained VL backbone: Local temporal information for SSv2 dataset under fully supervised setting. Fine-tune the CLIP backbone provides the highest performance, showing the simple fine-tune process helps the result in SSv2 dataset. Moreover, the performance of text-only fine-tune is higher than the performance of visual-only fine-tune.

Tuning pre-trained image VL models	
Frozen CLIP	26.55
Visual Fine-tune	52.16
Text Fine-tune	27.67
Full Fine-tune	56.70

Table 5. Comparison experiment results using fine-tuned CLIP backbone-with temporal Transformer decoder module.

Conv	Pos	Attn	Acc.
✔	✗	✗	53.43
✗	✔	✗	53.06
✗	✗	✔	44.51
✔	✔	✔	56.70

4.5   Model Complexity

We further study the compute complexity of our model in comparison to other models in Table 6. Due to the extra temporal decoder, the FLOPs is much higher than ViFi-CLIP and XCLIP because the CLIP backbone fine-tuning process is still computationally expensive. We still need to find a method to reduce the FLOPs.

Table 6. Model Complexity: Compute comparison of our model with methods that adapt CLIP with additional components. Our model has advantage in parameter count, but is still heavy in-terms of GFLOPs.

Method	GFLOPs	Params(M)
Action CLIP [44]	563	168.5
XCLIP [32]	287	131.5
ViFi-CLIP [37]	281	124.7
Our method	523	110.8

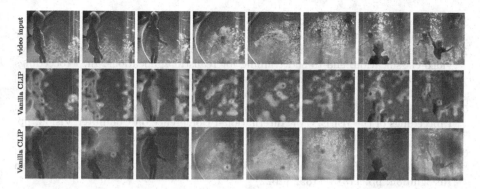

Fig. 3. Attention map visualization: The attention map visualization of our model from Kinetics 400 dataset. As we can see, our model can still classify the important movement of the object along temporal dimension.

4.6 Visualization

To better understand what temporal relations are captured, by our model on SSv2 dataset, we present attention map visualizations between our model and other models like XCLIP [32] in Fig. 2. We can see our model mainly focuses on scene dynamics and moving objects, while other models attends to the object itself. The observation indicate that the temporal transformer decoder module works well on capturing the temporal relation in the video. We also present attention map for Kinetics in Fig. 3. This represents our model can still be applied to other datasets that cares more about appearance information.

5 Conclusion

In this paper, we propose a spatiotemporal method which can be used in zero-shot and few-shot video action recognition. We also apply a simple fine-tuning method on CLIP backbone to improve the performance for action-centered dataset. We achieve a remarkable performance on zero-shot and few-shot task on SSv2 dataset. However, fine-tining the CLIP backbone is still heavy in calculation. Moreover, the number of temporal transform decoder module is also a question worth discussing.

References

1. Arnab, A., Dehghani, M., Heigold, G., Sun, C., Lučić, M., Schmid, C.: ViViT: a video vision transformer. In: Proceedings of the IEEE/CVF International Conference on Computer Vision, pp. 6836–6846 (2021)
2. Bangalath, H., Maaz, M., Khattak, M.U., Khan, S.H., Shahbaz Khan, F.: Bridging the gap between object and image-level representations for open-vocabulary detection. In: Advances in Neural Information Processing Systems, vol. 35, pp. 33781–33794 (2022)

3. Bertasius, G., Wang, H., Torresani, L.: Is space-time attention all you need for video understanding? In: ICML, vol. 2, p. 4 (2021)

4. Brattoli, B., Tighe, J., Zhdanov, F., Perona, P., Chalupka, K.: Rethinking zero-shot video classification: end-to-end training for realistic applications. In: Proceedings of the IEEE/CVF Conference on Computer Vision and Pattern Recognition, pp. 4613–4623 (2020)

5. Chen, S., Huang, D.: Elaborative rehearsal for zero-shot action recognition. In: Proceedings of the IEEE/CVF International Conference on Computer Vision, pp. 13638–13647 (2021)

6. Ding, J., Xue, N., Xia, G.S., Dai, D.: Decoupling zero-shot semantic segmentation. In: Proceedings of the IEEE/CVF Conference on Computer Vision and Pattern Recognition, pp. 11583–11592 (2022)

7. Fan, Q., et al.: An image classifier can suffice for video understanding. arXiv preprint: arXiv:2106.14104 (2021)

8. Feichtenhofer, C.: X3D: expanding architectures for efficient video recognition. In: Proceedings of the IEEE/CVF Conference on Computer Vision and Pattern Recognition, pp. 203–213 (2020)

9. Girdhar, R., Grauman, K.: Anticipative video transformer. In: Proceedings of the IEEE/CVF International Conference on Computer Vision, pp. 13505–13515 (2021)

10. Goyal, R., et al.: The "something something" video database for learning and evaluating visual common sense. In: Proceedings of the IEEE International Conference on Computer Vision, pp. 5842–5850 (2017)

11. Gu, X., Lin, T.Y., Kuo, W., Cui, Y.: Open-vocabulary object detection via vision and language knowledge distillation. arXiv preprint: arXiv:2104.13921 (2021)

12. He, T., Jin, X., Shen, X., Huang, J., Chen, Z., Hua, X.S.: Dense interaction learning for video-based person re-identification. In: Proceedings of the IEEE/CVF International Conference on Computer Vision, pp. 1490–1501 (2021)

13. Huang, D.A., et al.: What makes a video a video: analyzing temporal information in video understanding models and datasets. In: Proceedings of the IEEE Conference on Computer Vision and Pattern Recognition, pp. 7366–7375 (2018)

14. Jia, C., et al.: Scaling up visual and vision-language representation learning with noisy text supervision. In: International Conference on Machine Learning, pp. 4904–4916. PMLR (2021)

15. Ju, C., Han, T., Zheng, K., Zhang, Y., Xie, W.: Prompting visual-language models for efficient video understanding. In: Avidan, S., Brostow, G., Cisse, M., Farinella, G.M., Hassner, T. (eds.) Computer Vision-ECCV 2022. Lecture Notes in Computer Science, vol. 13695, pp. 105–124. Springer, Cham (2022). https://doi.org/10.1007/978-3-031-19833-5_7

16. Karpathy, A., Toderici, G., Shetty, S., Leung, T., Sukthankar, R., Fei-Fei, L.: Large-scale video classification with convolutional neural networks. In: Proceedings of the IEEE Conference on Computer Vision and Pattern Recognition, pp. 1725–1732 (2014)

17. Kay, W., et al.: The kinetics human action video dataset. arXiv preprint: arXiv:1705.06950 (2017)

18. Kuehne, H., Jhuang, H., Garrote, E., Poggio, T., Serre, T.: HMDB: a large video database for human motion recognition. In: 2011 International Conference on Computer Vision, pp. 2556–2563. IEEE (2011)

19. Li, B., Weinberger, K.Q., Belongie, S., Koltun, V., Ranftl, R.: Language-driven semantic segmentation. arXiv preprint: arXiv:2201.03546 (2022)

20. Li, W., Liu, H., Tang, H., Wang, P., Van Gool, L.: MHFormer: multi-hypothesis transformer for 3D human pose estimation. In: Proceedings of the IEEE/CVF Conference on Computer Vision and Pattern Recognition, pp. 13147–13156 (2022)
21. Li, Y., Ji, B., Shi, X., Zhang, J., Kang, B., Wang, L.: Tea: temporal excitation and aggregation for action recognition. In: Proceedings of the IEEE/CVF Conference on Computer Vision and Pattern Recognition, pp. 909–918 (2020)
22. Li, Y., Vasconcelos, N.: REPAIR: removing representation bias by dataset resampling. In: Proceedings of the IEEE/CVF Conference on Computer Vision and Pattern Recognition, pp. 9572–9581 (2019)
23. Lin, J., Gan, C., Han, S.: TSM: temporal shift module for efficient video understanding. In: Proceedings of the IEEE/CVF International Conference on Computer Vision, pp. 7083–7093 (2019)
24. Lin, Z., et al.: Frozen clip models are efficient video learners. In: Avidan, S., Brostow, G., Cisse, M., Farinella, G.M., Hassner, T. (eds.) Computer Vision - ECCV 2022. Lecture Notes in Computer Science, vol. 13695, pp. 388–404. Springer, Cham (2022). https://doi.org/10.1007/978-3-031-19833-5_23
25. Liu, X., Zhang, H., Pirsiavash, H.: MASTAF: a model-agnostic spatio-temporal attention fusion network for few-shot video classification. In: Proceedings of the IEEE/CVF Winter Conference on Applications of Computer Vision, pp. 2508–2517 (2023)
26. Liu, Z., et al.: Video swin transformer. In: Proceedings of the IEEE/CVF Conference on Computer Vision and Pattern Recognition, pp. 3202–3211 (2022)
27. Liu, Z., Wang, L., Wu, W., Qian, C., Lu, T.: TAM: temporal adaptive module for video recognition. In: Proceedings of the IEEE/CVF International Conference on Computer Vision, pp. 13708–13718 (2021)
28. Luo, H., et al.: Clip4clip: an empirical study of clip for end to end video clip retrieval and captioning. Neurocomputing **508**, 293–304 (2022)
29. Miech, A., Zhukov, D., Alayrac, J.B., Tapaswi, M., Laptev, I., Sivic, J.: HowTo100M: learning a text-video embedding by watching hundred million narrated video clips. In: Proceedings of the IEEE/CVF International Conference on Computer Vision, pp. 2630–2640 (2019)
30. Monfort, M., et al.: Moments in time dataset: one million videos for event understanding. IEEE Trans. Pattern Anal. Mach. Intell. **42**(2), 502–508 (2019)
31. Neimark, D., Bar, O., Zohar, M., Asselmann, D.: Video transformer network. In: Proceedings of the IEEE/CVF International Conference on Computer Vision, pp. 3163–3172 (2021)
32. Ni, B., et al.: Expanding language-image pretrained models for general video recognition. In: Avidan, S., Brostow, G., Cisse, M., Farinella, G.M., Hassner, T. (eds.) Computer Vision - ECCV 2022. Lecture Notes in Computer Science, vol. 13664, pp. 1–18. Springer, Cham (2022). https://doi.org/10.1007/978-3-031-19772-7_1
33. Patrick, M., et al.: Keeping your eye on the ball: trajectory attention in video transformers. In: Advances in Neural Information Processing Systems, vol. 34, pp. 12493–12506 (2021)
34. Qin, J., et al.: Zero-shot action recognition with error-correcting output codes. In: Proceedings of the IEEE Conference on Computer Vision and Pattern Recognition, pp. 2833–2842 (2017)
35. Qiu, Z., Yao, T., Mei, T.: Learning spatio-temporal representation with pseudo-3D residual networks. In: proceedings of the IEEE International Conference on Computer Vision, pp. 5533–5541 (2017)

36. Radford, A., et al.: Learning transferable visual models from natural language supervision. In: International Conference on Machine Learning, pp. 8748–8763. PMLR (2021)

37. Rasheed, H., Khattak, M.U., Maaz, M., Khan, S., Khan, F.S.: Fine-tuned clip models are efficient video learners. arXiv preprint: arXiv:2212.03640 (2022)

38. Sevilla-Lara, L., Zha, S., Yan, Z., Goswami, V., Feiszli, M., Torresani, L.: Only time can tell: Discovering temporal data for temporal modeling. In: Proceedings of the IEEE/CVF Winter Conference on Applications of Computer Vision, pp. 535–544 (2021)

39. Soomro, K., Zamir, A.R., Shah, M.: UCF101: a dataset of 101 human actions classes from videos in the wild. arXiv preprint: arXiv:1212.0402 (2012)

40. Thatipelli, A., Narayan, S., Khan, S., Anwer, R.M., Khan, F.S., Ghanem, B.: Spatio-temporal relation modeling for few-shot action recognition. In: Proceedings of the IEEE/CVF Conference on Computer Vision and Pattern Recognition, pp. 19958–19967 (2022)

41. Tran, D., Bourdev, L., Fergus, R., Torresani, L., Paluri, M.: Learning spatiotemporal features with 3D convolutional networks. In: Proceedings of the IEEE International Conference on Computer Vision, pp. 4489–4497 (2015)

42. Tran, D., Wang, H., Torresani, L., Feiszli, M.: Video classification with channel-separated convolutional networks. In: Proceedings of the IEEE/CVF International Conference on Computer Vision, pp. 5552–5561 (2019)

43. Tran, D., Wang, H., Torresani, L., Ray, J., LeCun, Y., Paluri, M.: A closer look at spatiotemporal convolutions for action recognition. In: Proceedings of the IEEE Conference on Computer Vision and Pattern Recognition, pp. 6450–6459 (2018)

44. Wang, M., Xing, J., Liu, Y.: ActionCLIP: a new paradigm for video action recognition. arXiv preprint: arXiv:2109.08472 (2021)

45. Wang, Q., Chen, K.: Alternative semantic representations for zero-shot human action recognition. In: Ceci, M., Hollmén, J., Todorovski, L., Vens, C., Džeroski, S. (eds.) ECML PKDD 2017. LNCS (LNAI), vol. 10534, pp. 87–102. Springer, Cham (2017). https://doi.org/10.1007/978-3-319-71249-9_6

46. Wasim, S.T., Naseer, M., Khan, S., Khan, F.S., Shah, M.: Vita-clip: video and text adaptive clip via multimodal prompting. arXiv preprint: arXiv:2304.03307 (2023)

47. Xie, S., Sun, C., Huang, J., Tu, Z., Murphy, K.: Rethinking spatiotemporal feature learning: speed-accuracy trade-offs in video classification. In: Ferrari, V., Hebert, M., Sminchisescu, C., Weiss, Y. (eds.) ECCV 2018. LNCS, vol. 11219, pp. 318–335. Springer, Cham (2018). https://doi.org/10.1007/978-3-030-01267-0_19

48. Xu, H., et al.: Videoclip: contrastive pre-training for zero-shot video-text understanding. arXiv preprint: arXiv:2109.14084 (2021)

49. Yan, S., et al.: Multiview transformers for video recognition. In: Proceedings of the IEEE/CVF Conference on Computer Vision and Pattern Recognition, pp. 3333–3343 (2022)

50. Yuan, L., et al.: Florence: A new foundation model for computer vision. arXiv preprint: arXiv:2111.11432 (2021)

51. Yun, S., Kim, J., Han, D., Song, H., Ha, J.W., Shin, J.: Time is matter: temporal self-supervision for video transformers. arXiv preprint: arXiv:2207.09067 (2022)

52. Zhang, R., et al.: Tip-adapter: training-free clip-adapter for better vision-language modeling. arXiv preprint: arXiv:2111.03930 (2021)

53. Zhou, B., Andonian, A., Oliva, A., Torralba, A.: Temporal relational reasoning in videos. In: Proceedings of the European Conference on Computer Vision (ECCV), pp. 803–818 (2018)

54. Zhou, C., Loy, C.C., Dai, B.: DenseCLIP: extract free dense labels from clip. arXiv preprint: arXiv:2112.01071 (2021)
55. Zhou, K., Yang, J., Loy, C.C., Liu, Z.: Conditional prompt learning for vision-language models. In: Proceedings of the IEEE/CVF Conference on Computer Vision and Pattern Recognition, pp. 16816–16825 (2022)
56. Zhou, K., Yang, J., Loy, C.C., Liu, Z.: Learning to prompt for vision-language models. Int. J. Comput. Vision **130**(9), 2337–2348 (2022)
57. Zhou, X., Girdhar, R., Joulin, A., Krähenbühl, P., Misra, I.: Detecting twenty-thousand classes using image-level supervision. In: Avidan, S., Brostow, G., Cisse, M., Farinella, G.M., Hassner, T. (eds.) Computer Vision - ECCV 2022. Lecture Notes in Computer Science, vol. 13669, pp. 350–368. Springer, Cham (2022). https://doi.org/10.1007/978-3-031-20077-9_21
58. Zhu, Y., Long, Y., Guan, Y., Newsam, S., Shao, L.: Towards universal representation for unseen action recognition. In: Proceedings of the IEEE Conference on Computer Vision and Pattern Recognition, pp. 9436–9445 (2018)

Author Index

Printed in the United States
by Baker & Taylor Publisher Services